Creating Dynamic Space in Higher Education:

Modern Shifts in Policy, Competencies, and Governance

George Ngwacho Areba
Kisii University, Kenya

Billiah Nyamoita Gisore
Kisii University, Kenya

Evelyn Wanjiru Njurai
Kisii University, Kenya

IGI Global
Publishing Tomorrow's Research Today

Vice President of Editorial Melissa Wagner
Managing Editor of Acquisitions Mikaela Felty
Managing Editor of Book Development Jocelynn Hessler
Production Manager Mike Brehm
Cover Design Phillip Shickler

Published in the United States of America by
IGI Global Scientific Publishing
701 East Chocolate Avenue
Hershey, PA, 17033, USA
Tel: 717-533-8845
Fax: 717-533-8661
E-mail: cust@igi-global.com
Website: https://www.igi-global.com

Library of Congress Cataloging-in-Publication Data

Names: Areba, George, 1978- editor. | Gisore, Billiah, 1972- editor. | Njurai, Evelyn Wanjiru, editor.
Title: Creating dynamic space in higher education : modern shifts in policy, competencies, and governance / Edited by George Areba, Billiah Gisore, Evelyn Njurai.
Description: Hershey, PA : IGI Global, [2025] | Includes bibliographical references and index. | Summary: "This handbook will ignite further research on higher education policies, competencies, and governance on the ongoing education transformations"-- Provided by publisher.
Identifiers: LCCN 2024048764 (print) | LCCN 2024048765 (ebook) | ISBN 9798369369302 (hardcover) | ISBN 9798369369340 (paperback) | ISBN 9798369369319 (ebook)
Subjects: LCSH: Higher education and state. | Educational change. | Education, Higher--Effect of technological innovations on. | Education, Higher--Aims and objectives.
Classification: LCC LC171 .C74 2025 (print) | LCC LC171 (ebook) | DDC 371.829/68073--dc23/eng/2024
LC record available at https://lccn.loc.gov/2024048764
LC ebook record available at https://lccn.loc.gov/2024048765

British Cataloguing in Publication Data
A Cataloguing in Publication record for this book is available from the British Library.

Table of Contents

Preface xiii

Chapter 1
Restructuring Education Policy and Practices: Pre- and Post-Pandemic Interventions 1
George Ngwacho Areba, Kisii University, Kenya
Eliud Nyakundi, Kisii University, Kenya

Chapter 2
Establishment of Open Universities and Policy Implications: Towards Enhancing Equity, Access, and Inclusivity - The Case of Open University of Kenya 25
Daniel Karanja, State Department for Higher Education and Research, Kenya
George Ngwacho Areba, Kisii University, Kenya

Chapter 3
Emergent or Planned? Crafting Employability Strategies in Higher Education Institutions 57
Francesca Sgobbi, University of Brescia, Italy & DINÂMIA'CET-Iscte, Portugal

Chapter 4
Benefits and Challenges of Internationalization of Higher Education 89
Josephine Oranga, Kisii University, Kenya

Chapter 5
Nexus Between Experiential and Academic Learning for Employability Skills in Higher Education Institutions: Students and Faculty Perspectives 113
Caroline Sabina Wekullo, MMUST, Kenya
James Bill Ouda, MMUST, Kenya
Rose Atione Opiyo, MMUST, Kenya

Chapter 6
Innovative Learning Spaces and Blended Learning: Quest for 21st Century Competency Teaching and Learning Approaches 139
Norah Adera, Aga Khan University, Tanzania

Chapter 7
Advancements and Challenges of Problem-Based Learning: A Case Study of Daystar University 175
Anne Anjao Eboi, Daystar University, Kenya
Levi Obonyo, Daystar University, Kenya
Rosemary Nyaole Kowuor, Daystar University, Kenya
Daniel Robert Aswani, Daystar University, Kenya
Lydia Ouma Radoli, Daystar University, Kenya

Chapter 8
Leveraging Statistical Simulation for Enhancing Academic Rigor and Practical Skills 215
Fred Nyamitago Monari, Kisii University, Kenya

Chapter 9
The Evolving Roles of Faculty in Modern Classrooms: A Shift From Lecturer to Facilitator 253
Lorna Wafula, Moi University, Kenya

Chapter 10
A Model for Developing Multi-Competence in Graduates for a Supercomplex World 283
Charles Mottanya Nyandusi, Moi University, Kenya

Chapter 11
Sustainability Competency Framework: A Practical Guide for Re-Orienting Higher Education Curricula 313
Peter Ngwa, The University of Yaounde I, Cameroon
Awono Mengada Gisèle Xaverie, The University of Yaounde II, Cameroon

Chapter 12
The Role of Institutional Research (IR) in Informing Higher Education Governance Practices in East Africa 347
Charles Eryenyu, Busitema University, Uganda
Dennis Zami Atibuni, Busitema University, Uganda

Chapter 13
Climate Change: Opportunities for Strengthening Research Capacity and Knowledge Dissemination 383
Billiah Nyamoita Gisore, Kisii University, Kenya

Compilation of References 411

About the Contributors 475

Index 481

Detailed Table of Contents

Preface...xiii

Chapter 1
Restructuring Education Policy and Practices: Pre- and Post-Pandemic Interventions 1
George Ngwacho Areba, Kisii University, Kenya
Eliud Nyakundi, Kisii University, Kenya

Implications of pandemics such as COVID-19 have had varied impacts on the core fundamentals of humanity. In specific, the effect has laid bare the inadequacies of both practices and policy in education. Many of the world's education policies' frameworks particularly the sub-Saharan Africa have been disparaged as insufficient to mitigate the novel escalating crises. Thus, extensive education policy review is crucial to give impetus to efforts made in recent policy initiatives such as the hundred percent student transition policy in almost all levels of education. This being a theoretical review, largely secondary data was utilized. Current methodical and meta-analysis of literature assessments were utilized for cross-validating the reviewed outcomes. This study established that there is a need to supplement efforts and synergies geared towards restructuring education policy frameworks to mitigate the 21st-century education challenges. Significantly, the findings will strengthen higher education capacity in handling new unique 21st-century crises and pandemics.

Chapter 2
Establishment of Open Universities and Policy Implications: Towards Enhancing Equity, Access, and Inclusivity - The Case of Open University of Kenya 25
Daniel Karanja, State Department for Higher Education and Research, Kenya
George Ngwacho Areba, Kisii University, Kenya

Issues of access, equity, and inclusivity in higher education have been of concern. This has been coupled with the emergence of innovative and interruptive technologies. The motivation behind the establishment of open higher institutions of learning is chiefly the provision of accessible higher education to a wider populace. The global shift has been heralded by the establishment of the Open University of the United Kingdom (OU-UK). The OU-UK slogan of being "open to people, open to places; open to methods; and open to ideas" has revolutionized the role of a university in society. In this context, many countries have followed the OU-UK philosophy of university education being open and established their own open universities. It is on this premise that the Open University of Kenya (OUK) is anchored. Given that this is a novel venture there is need to interrogate the policy implications with a view to enhance its functionality.

Chapter 3
Emergent or Planned? Crafting Employability Strategies in Higher Education Institutions.. 57
Francesca Sgobbi, University of Brescia, Italy & DINÂMIA'CET-Iscte, Portugal

The employability of graduates has become a key issue for higher education institutions (HEIs) worldwide. Students, families, businesses, and institutions are increasingly focused on the career prospects of young graduates, as employability reflects educational quality and influences rankings and funding. Developing effective employability strategies is crucial for HEIs to fulfil their educational mission and remain competitive. However, there is often confusion between employability and employment, and the global discourse on employability strategies is uneven, with most research concentrated in Anglo-Saxon countries and assuming an intentional approach to strategy planning. This research examines four case HEIs in Italy and Portugal, finding that employability strategies are emerging from a mix of top-down and bottom-up initiatives, heavily influenced by national norms and available resources. The study underscores the importance of managing the dynamic process of strategy formation, highlighting the emergent nature of employability strategies in higher education.

Chapter 4
Benefits and Challenges of Internationalization of Higher Education 89
Josephine Oranga, Kisii University, Kenya

Universities the world over are increasingly being measured by how internationalized and global they are, yet not many studies have explored the benefits and challenges of internationalizing higher education. This article, thus, highlights the benefits of internationalization of higher education, while dwelling more on the challenges faced. From the analysis the benefits include: cultural exchanges, research collaboration, income generation, increased access to higher education, production/exchange of new knowledge, mobility of professionals, human resource capacity-building, foreign language acquisition/proficiency and harmonization of higher education systems. The challenges on the other hand include: commercialization of programs, rise of rogue education providers, low-quality education, over-use of English language, brain drain, domestic employers reluctance to recognize foreign qualifications, financial constraints, divergent ethical, religious and political beliefs of host countries, lack of institutional preparedness and the challenge of attaining an international curriculum.

Chapter 5
Nexus Between Experiential and Academic Learning for Employability Skills in Higher Education Institutions: Students and Faculty Perspectives................ 113
Caroline Sabina Wekullo, MMUST, Kenya
James Bill Ouda, MMUST, Kenya
Rose Atione Opiyo, MMUST, Kenya

A skilled workforce is crucial to countries' economic transformation. Higher education institutions have been under pressure to promote employability by ensuring learners acquire the 21st century skills needed to succeed in the real world. However, there are still gaps in balancing academic and experiential learning approaches. Using data from selected higher education institutions in Kenya, the chapter examines the perspectives of students and faculty on the nexus between experiential and academic learning for employability skills in higher education institutions. Specifically, the chapter seeks to determine whether the current curriculum incorporates experiential skills alongside academic learning and assess whether students are provided with opportunities to apply academic knowledge in real-world contexts through experiential learning. The findings have significant implications for policy makers, education officers, key stakeholders including trainers, employers and students in ensuring a match between experiential and academic training for employability skills

Chapter 6
Innovative Learning Spaces and Blended Learning: Quest for 21st Century Competency Teaching and Learning Approaches 139
Norah Adera, Aga Khan University, Tanzania

Adopting teaching and learning approaches focused on 21st-century competencies necessitates creative solutions that span traditional classroom settings and the internet world in the quickly changing educational landscape. To cultivate these competencies, this chapter explores the transformative potential of novel learning spaces and blended learning approaches. This theoretical review uses secondary data as its main source and incorporates the most recent methodological and meta-analytical literature evaluations to cross-validate its conclusions. By merging flexible and adaptable physical and virtual environments with advanced technological tools, this chapter offers practical strategies for educators and policymakers to enhance student engagement and promote critical thinking, creativity, collaboration, and digital literacy. It aims to empower educational institutions to embrace and sustain these innovative approaches, ensuring all students acquire the skills necessary to thrive in a digital and interconnected world.

Chapter 7
Advancements and Challenges of Problem-Based Learning: A Case Study of Daystar University.. 175
Anne Anjao Eboi, Daystar University, Kenya
Levi Obonyo, Daystar University, Kenya
Rosemary Nyaole Kowuor, Daystar University, Kenya
Daniel Robert Aswani, Daystar University, Kenya
Lydia Ouma Radoli, Daystar University, Kenya

The global higher education landscape is fast evolving, demanding that universities equip students with critical knowledge and 21st-century skills. Daystar University (DU) 's switch from teacher-centered models to Problem-Based Learning (PBL) reflects this shift. PBL stresses critical thinking and real-world problem-solving, essential for today's interconnected world. The chapter examined the challenges and advancements of PBL implementation at DU using qualitative methods involving interviews with 30 selected informants and document analysis. Findings show that while PBL has been integrated across various programs, challenges like resistance to change, insufficient faculty training, and resource limitations persist. However, significant progress has been made, including adopting technology-enhanced tools, increased faculty collaboration, and a growing culture of innovation among students. The study recommends targeted faculty development, improved infrastructure, and stronger support systems to enhance PBL's effectiveness in fostering more profound learning experiences.

Chapter 8
Leveraging Statistical Simulation for Enhancing Academic Rigor and Practical Skills 215
Fred Nyamitago Monari, Kisii University, Kenya

This chapter explores how integrating statistical simulation in higher education enhances learning, highlighting benefits, challenges, and best practices. It starts with an overview of simulation techniques and their applications across disciplines. It then focuses on student-centered methods like problem-based and project-based learning, along with flipped classrooms, supported by successful case studies. Examples show how simulation-based courses boost engagement and outcomes. The chapter addresses challenges like technology needs, faculty training, and assessment, offering solutions. It concludes with strategies to overcome institutional resistance and financial constraints, showcasing the transformative potential of simulation-based learning.

Chapter 9
The Evolving Roles of Faculty in Modern Classrooms: A Shift From Lecturer to Facilitator 253
Lorna Wafula, Moi University, Kenya

The role of faculty in modern classrooms has evolved from traditional lecturing to dynamic facilitation of learning This chapter examined this paradigm shift in higher education. It investigated how faculty facilitate active student centered learning. The study was anchored on Piaget and Vygotsky's constructivist learning theory and Siemens and Downes' connectivism theory. A descriptive research design was embraced. Lecturers in public universities in Kenya formed the population of the study. Convenient and simple random sampling were used to select the participants. Data was collected using document analysis and questionnaires and was analyzed descriptively. The study established that a significant number of faculty used facilitative teaching methods. The study recommended that universities should promote facilitative teaching among faculty and educate students on benefits of interactive learning. Further studies should be carried out on sustainable models of professional development that support the ongoing evolution of teaching practices.

Chapter 10
A Model for Developing Multi-Competence in Graduates for a Supercomplex World 283
Charles Mottanya Nyandusi, Moi University, Kenya

The world today is characterized not only by fluidity in the creation, dissemination and decay of knowledge and meaning, but also by the proliferation of variegated frames of reference and understanding. It is a supercomplex world. It is this world that the 21st century university has to serve. To remain relevant in such supercomplexity necessitates that the university needs to sustain its traditional intrinsic function -- the advancement of knowledge and the search for truth, while at the same time espousing a newer, extrinsic function – the preparation of students for the world of work; that is, enhancing the employability of graduates. This Chapter posits that the two functions can and should be integrated, so that the university can develop a multicompetent graduate through the Holistic Graduate Identity Curriculum (HoGIC) model proposed here.

Chapter 11
Sustainability Competency Framework: A Practical Guide for Re-Orienting Higher Education Curricula 313
Peter Ngwa, The University of Yaounde I, Cameroon
Awono Mengada Gisèle Xaverie, The University of Yaounde II, Cameroon

It has become increasingly important worldwide, especially in the context of higher education, to support these skills in order to prepare students for employment in the 21st-century labor market that is focused on sustainability and alternative industries.A conceptual framework that describes the sustainability competencies that should be emphasized in higher education curricula to provide graduates with employability skills. Findings demonstrated take into account the needs of the labor market

Chapter 12
The Role of Institutional Research (IR) in Informing Higher Education Governance Practices in East Africa 347
Charles Eryenyu, Busitema University, Uganda
Dennis Zami Atibuni, Busitema University, Uganda

This chapter examines the role of institutional research (IR) in higher education governance in East Africa (EA). It aims to provide insights into data-driven practices for informed decision-making within academic institutions and national higher education systems. The chapter serves three distinct purposes: (a) to offer perspectives on the future paths and prospects for research-driven policies and practices in East African higher education space; (b) to suggest methods for reinforcing IR roles and improving governance practices within the EA higher education sector; and (c) to serve as a wakeup call to East African higher education institutions (HEIs) to embrace the concept of IR, adapt its practices, recognise it as a management strategy for good governance, and make provisions for practicing it. The discussions in the chapter comprehensively examine how institutional research can contribute to evidence-based policy and governance practices in higher education in the East African context and recommend a framework for implementing IR in the East African region.

Chapter 13
Climate Change: Opportunities for Strengthening Research Capacity and Knowledge Dissemination 383
Billiah Nyamoita Gisore, Kisii University, Kenya

The IPCC Report indicates that by 2100, global temperatures will be 1.8-4 ° C higher than the current ones, causing many regions to experience severe and frequent droughts. This affects food security and causes health problems. The understanding climate change seems to be at a low levels in the community. This can be improved by strengthening research capacity to address the causes, impacts, mitigation and adaptation needs. It seems that the communication that has been occurring has not been effective, resulting in information deficit. More delay will cause the future impact be large and costly. From research, practical guidance on how to access, interpret and apply climate data and information should be availed to targeted users. There should be a strong research base with clear dissemination channels. Climate change adaptation and mitigation strategies should be context specific. Opportunities are available for strengthening research capacity and knowledge dissemination.

Compilation of References 411

About the Contributors 475

Index 481

Preface

In today's fast-paced and ever-changing world, the role of research in higher education is not just important; it is absolutely essential. *Creating Dynamic Space in Higher Education: Modern Shifts in Policy, Competencies, and Governance* boldly addresses this necessity, showcasing how rigorous research can be the catalyst for transformative change.

As educators, policymakers, and stakeholders, we face an array of pressing challenges—from maintaining academic quality amid dwindling state funding to adapting our teaching methods to fit the needs of diverse and evolving student populations. This book makes a compelling case that only through dedicated research can we effectively confront these issues and shape a brighter future for our institutions and learners alike.

Research serves as the backbone of innovation, providing us with the insights and data needed to navigate the complexities of 21st-century education in terms of policies, competencies and governance. Each chapter of this volume offers not just theoretical insights but practical, evidence-based solutions that can be implemented in real-world settings. The book delves into emergent areas of concern, such as the shift towards student-centered learning, the integration of cutting-edge technologies, and the urgent need for equitable access in education—all underpinned by robust research findings.

Imagine the possibilities when research informs policy and practice: a classroom where teaching methods are not only effective but also engaging, where students thrive in an inclusive environment, and where educational leaders are equipped to make decisions grounded in empirical evidence. This is not a distant dream; it is within our reach, and this book lays out a roadmap to achieve it.

The reader is urged to embrace the wealth of knowledge contained in the chapters that have been crafted to empower, innovate and inspire change within educational contexts. By applying the findings, the reader can directly contribute to solving educational challenges in higher education that lie ahead, ultimately enhancing the quality of education.

Through the power of research, the book tackles complexities of higher education, ensuring that students are equipped with the skills, knowledge, and competencies necessary for success in an unpredictable world.

Join us on this transformative journey as we harness the potential of research to create a higher education landscape that is not only resilient but also vibrant and forward-thinking. Together, we can shape a future that truly reflects the needs and aspirations of our diverse global community.

In *Creating Dynamic Space in Higher Education: Modern Shifts in Policy, Competencies, and Governance*, each chapter serves as a vital contribution to understanding and addressing the complexities of contemporary higher education. As editors, we invite you to explore these carefully curated insights that tackle pressing issues and propose actionable solutions.

Chapter 1: Restructuring Education Policy and Practices: Pre- and Post-Pandemic Interventions

This chapter critically examines the impact of the COVID-19 pandemic on education policies and practices, particularly in sub-Saharan Africa. It argues for a comprehensive review and restructuring of existing frameworks to better address emerging crises. By analyzing secondary data and conducting a meta-analysis of current literature, the authors highlight the urgent need for policy initiatives, such as the commitment to ensuring a hundred percent student transition across educational levels. The findings emphasize the importance of fortifying higher education systems to better withstand future challenges.

Chapter 2: Establishment of Open Universities and Policy Implications: Towards Enhancing Equity, Access, and Inclusivity - The Case of Open University of Kenya

Focusing on the Open University of Kenya, this chapter explores the necessity of open universities in enhancing access and inclusivity in higher education. Drawing inspiration from the Open University of the United Kingdom, the authors investigate the policy implications of such institutions in broadening educational horizons for diverse populations. The chapter urges a careful examination of the operational policies that will enable open universities to fulfill their mission of providing equitable education.

Chapter 3: Emergent or Planned? Crafting Employment Strategies in Higher Education Institutions

This chapter delves into the critical issue of graduate employability, dissecting the strategies employed by higher education institutions (HEIs) across different countries. By analyzing case studies from Italy and Portugal, the authors reveal that employability strategies often emerge from a combination of top-down and grassroots initiatives, influenced by national contexts. The chapter calls for a nuanced understanding of employability and its distinction from mere employment, urging institutions to develop robust strategies that align with global standards while being adaptable to local needs.

Chapter 4: Benefits and Challenges of Internationalization of Higher Education

In an increasingly interconnected world, this chapter assesses the multifaceted benefits and challenges of internationalizing higher education. While acknowledging the potential for cultural exchange, research collaboration, and increased access, the authors also highlight significant obstacles, including financial constraints and varying recognition of foreign qualifications. By providing a comprehensive analysis, this chapter serves as a critical resource for institutions looking to navigate the complexities of global engagement effectively.

Chapter 5: Nexus Between Experiential and Academic Learning for Employability Skills in Higher Education Institutions: Students and Faculty Perspectives

This chapter examines the vital link between experiential learning and academic curricula in preparing students for employability. By gathering perspectives from both students and faculty in Kenyan institutions, the authors reveal gaps in current educational practices that hinder the development of practical skills. The findings underscore the importance of integrating experiential learning opportunities to enhance student preparedness for the workforce, thereby informing policy and practice across the educational spectrum.

Chapter 6: Innovative Learning Spaces and Blended Learning: Quest for 21st Century Competency Teaching and Learning Approaches

Exploring the transformative potential of blended learning environments, this chapter advocates for teaching strategies that foster 21st-century competencies. Utilizing a theoretical framework supported by extensive literature reviews, the authors present practical solutions for educators and policymakers to create flexible, engaging learning spaces that cultivate critical thinking, creativity, and digital literacy among students.

Chapter 7: Advancements and Challenges of Problem-Based Learning: A Case Study of Daystar University

Through a case study approach, this chapter evaluates the implementation of Problem-Based Learning (PBL) at Daystar University. It highlights the advancements made in fostering critical thinking and real-world problem-solving while addressing challenges such as faculty resistance and resource constraints. The authors offer recommendations for enhancing PBL effectiveness, thereby contributing to the broader discourse on innovative pedagogical approaches in higher education.

Chapter 8: Leveraging Statistical Simulation for Enhancing Academic Rigor and Practical Skills

This chapter discusses the integration of statistical simulation techniques into higher education, showcasing their benefits in enhancing academic rigor and practical skills. By examining student-centered learning methods such as problem-based and project-based learning, the authors illustrate how simulation can engage students and improve educational outcomes, while also addressing implementation challenges and offering solutions to overcome institutional barriers.

Chapter 9: The Evolving Roles of Faculty in Modern Classrooms: A shift from Lecturer to Facilitator

Investigating the evolving role of faculty, this chapter highlights the transition from traditional lecturing to facilitative teaching methods that promote active learning. Anchored in constructivist and connectivist theories, the study reveals that many faculty members have adopted facilitative practices. The authors advocate for ongoing professional development and student education to ensure the effective implementation of these teaching methods.

Chapter 10: A Model for Developing Multi-Competence in Graduates for a Supercomplex World

This chapter introduces the Holistic Graduate Identity Curriculum (HoGIC) model, positing that universities must blend their traditional mission of knowledge advancement with the need to prepare students for the workforce. The authors argue that integrating these functions can produce multicompetent graduates capable of thriving in a complex, rapidly changing world, thus enhancing their employability and relevance in the job market.

Chapter 11: Sustainability Competency Framework: A Practical Guide for Re-Orienting Higher Education Curricula

Highlighting the growing importance of sustainability in higher education, this chapter presents a conceptual framework for integrating sustainability competencies into curricula. By aligning educational outcomes with labor market needs, the authors provide a roadmap for institutions aiming to prepare graduates for careers in sustainability-focused industries.

Chapter 12: The Role of Institutional Research (IR) in Informing Higher Education Governance Practices in East Africa

This chapter emphasizes the pivotal role of institutional research in shaping effective governance practices within East African higher education. By advocating for data-driven decision-making, the authors outline strategies for enhancing the role of IR in policy formulation and governance, urging institutions to adopt a proactive stance towards evidence-based management.

Chapter 13: Climate Change: Opportunities for Strengthening Research Capacity and Knowledge Dissemination

Addressing the urgent need for climate action, this chapter explores how strengthening research capacity can enhance knowledge dissemination on climate change issues. The authors argue for targeted research initiatives and clear communication channels to improve community understanding of climate impacts and mitigation strategies, highlighting the role of higher education in fostering informed responses.

Together, these chapters form a comprehensive tapestry of ideas and solutions that reflect the dynamic space of higher education in the 21st century. We invite you to engage with the rich discussions and insights presented, which we hope will inspire transformative actions in your own educational contexts.

As we look ahead, it is essential to recognize that the journey toward transformative change in higher education is ongoing. The insights and strategies presented in this volume are not merely a blueprint; they are invitations to engage in dialogue, experimentation, and reflection. Each chapter challenges us to reconsider our practices and assumptions, urging us to innovate while remaining rooted in robust research and evidence.

This book encourages you to adopt a forward-thinking mindset—one that embraces agility and resilience in the face of evolving educational landscapes. It calls upon us to interrogate existing paradigms and to foster environments where creativity and critical thinking are not just encouraged but expected. By prioritizing a research-driven approach, we can ensure that our educational systems are not only effective but also dynamic and capable of adapting to unforeseen challenges.

Moreover, as we confront global issues such as climate change, social inequality, and technological disruption, the role of higher education as a catalyst for positive change becomes ever more critical. The chapters underscore that our institutions have the power to contribute to society's well-being by producing graduates who are not only knowledgeable but also equipped with the skills to enact meaningful change. This responsibility extends beyond the classroom; it encompasses our roles as community leaders, researchers, and advocates for social justice.

In this light, we invite you to reflect on how you can leverage the ideas and research presented in this book within your own context. Whether you are a faculty member seeking to enhance your teaching practices, an administrator aiming to implement strategic policies, or a student aspiring to become an agent of change, the potential for impact is immense. Embrace the challenges and opportunities before you, and consider how you can contribute to the ongoing evolution of higher education.

Finally, we would like to express our gratitude to all contributors, whose expertise and dedication have made this volume possible. Your insights are invaluable, and together, we have crafted a resource that not only informs but also inspires action. As we move forward, let us remain committed to the ideals of collaboration, inclusivity, and rigorous inquiry that are so crucial to the success of higher education.

In the spirit of innovation and progress, we encourage you to engage deeply with this book, to share its findings with your colleagues and communities, and to become active participants in the transformative journey ahead. Let us work together to create dynamic spaces in higher education that empower all learners and foster a brighter, more equitable future for generations to come.

Chapter 1
Restructuring Education Policy and Practices:
Pre- and Post-Pandemic Interventions

George Ngwacho Areba
https://orcid.org/0000-0001-5661-3090
Kisii University, Kenya

Eliud Nyakundi
Kisii University, Kenya

ABSTRACT

Implications of pandemics such as COVID-19 have had varied impacts on the core fundamentals of humanity. In specific, the effect has laid bare the inadequacies of both practices and policy in education. Many of the world's education policies' frameworks particularly the sub-Saharan Africa have been disparaged as insufficient to mitigate the novel escalating crises. Thus, extensive education policy review is crucial to give impetus to efforts made in recent policy initiatives such as the hundred percent student transition policy in almost all levels of education. This being a theoretical review, largely secondary data was utilized. Current methodical and meta-analysis of literature assessments were utilized for cross-validating the reviewed outcomes. This study established that there is a need to supplement efforts and synergies geared towards restructuring education policy frameworks to mitigate the 21st-century education challenges. Significantly, the findings will strengthen higher education capacity in handling new unique 21st-century crises and pandemics.

DOI: 10.4018/979-8-3693-6930-2.ch001

INTRODUCTION

Areba (2020) postulates that for African Sub-Saharan's already feeble education base, the interruption by COVID-19 has heightened the existing unique challenges for the states, educators, students, and parents. The emerging pandemics have laid bare knuckle some policy gaps in the education sector (Areba, 2020). These challenges have impelled rushed temporal solutions like virtual classes. Depending solely on virtual strategies as a panacea implies that students from vulnerable families are plummeting behind under education system that already discriminates against them (UWEZO, 2020). As the affected states begin to wrestle with these challenges, a fundamental question lingers: How can education policy be re-conceptualized to adapt to global changing trends to give all learners equal education opportunities regardless of the background they come from?

Before the COVID-19 pandemic struck in late 2019, many countries in the world were already tackling daunting tasks meant to honor access to schooling which is one of the basic rights of everyone. In spite of the widespread enrolments at the initial levels in several states, millions of learners – over 250 million globally – have dropped out of schools, and another almost 800 million grown-ups are functionally illiterate (World Bank, 2020a). Furthermore, even those enrolled in schools are not sure of continued participation. About 387 million which is 56% of school-age learners globally were projected to lack basic literacy skills (World Bank, 2020b). From the funding perspective, there existed a formidable challenge prior to the emergence of Corona Virus Disease-19. The initial year's (2020) approximation of the financing deficit to achieve the Sustainable Development Goals (UNESCO, 2020d), particularly for the purpose of provision of education of high quality in developing nations is a stunning $148 billion yearly. Experts project that the unprecedented pandemics might aggravate these funding deficits by up to a third (UNESCO, 2020d).

Corona Virus Disease-19 was identified first in Wuhan Province of China in December 2019 and spread swiftly to Europe, Asia, and the rest of the globe. As of 22nd September 2020, there were 31,174,627 reported COVID-19 incidents, with 962,613 deaths worldwide (COVID-19 WHO African Region External Situation Report 30, 2020, henceforth, COVID-19 WHO, ARESR, 2020). Both the worldwide number of established Corona Virus cases and deaths constantly increased ominously. As of that period, 215 states and a single global conveyance had confirmed Corona virus incidents. Ten nations had the highest number of incidents: The USA with 6, 740, 464 cases; India with 5, 562, 663; Brazil with 4, 544, 629 cases; Russian Federation with 1,115, 810 cases; Peru with 768, 895 cases; Colombia with 765, 076 cases; Mexico with 697, 663 cases; South Africa with 663,282 cases; Spain with 640,040 cases; and Argentina with 631, 365 cases (COVID-19 WHO, ARESR, 2020).

In the same period, it was reported that a collective 1,149,940 Corona-Virus cases were in the African continent, with a single case in the Democratic Republic of Congo (DRC). To date, South Africa has more than half, 58% (663,282) of incidents in the continent. Others with a significant number of cases are Ethiopia with 70,422; Nigeria with 57,613; Algeria with 50,214; Ghana with 46, 062; the Republic of Kenya with 37,218; Cameroon with 20,690; Côte d'Ivoire with 19,327, Madagascar with 16,136; and Senegal with 14,759. The ten countries account for 995,723 of all reported cases which is 87% (COVID-19 WHO, ARESR, 2020).

The aggregate number of fatalities reported in the African continent in the same period was 25 008, involving forty-five countries, giving a general case casualty ratio (CFR) of 2.2%. From its inception in Africa, the majority of causalities have been in South Africa with 64% which is 16,118 persons; Algeria with 6.8% which is 1,689 persons; Ethiopia with 4.5% which is 1,127; Nigeria with 4.4% which is 1,100 persons; Kenya with 2.6% which is 659 persons among others. Countries including Ethiopia, Nigeria, Kenya, South Africa, and Algeria, bear 83% of confirmed deaths which translates to 20,693 deaths confirmed in the continent. The itemized figures in the continent denote 3.7% of established Corona-Virus incidents and 2.6% of casualties reported globally (COVID-19 WHO, ARESR, 2020). Many of the casualties in these death rates are educators, learners, and providers of education necessities. This implies a big setback to the education sector.

LITERATURE REVIEW

Globally almost all African states had executed measures to reinforce social distancing, concentrating on border and travel restraints, institutional cessations, sanctions on large assemblies, full lockdown restrictions, and partial lockdowns. Subsequently, the Corona Virus Disease-19 epidemic caused the greatest interruption of the education sector; something that has never happened, depriving about 1.6 billion learners in over 190 nations of education rights. Cessations of institutions and other educational avenues affected 94% of the global learner population and up to about 99% in lower-middle- and low-income countries (Olingo, 2020).

In March 2020, Kenya just like other states issued directives on the cessation of all schools, colleges, and higher institutions to avert any further spread of the pandemic due to discovery the of the region's first positive victim. The cessation affected about 18 million students in all levels of education as well as one hundred and fifty thousand refugees (State Department of Early Learning & Basic Education, Kenya (SDELBEK, 2020). Individual states began their own strategy initiatives to mitigate the effects. For Kenya, the MoE SDELBEK issued the Kenya Basic Education Corona Virus Disease-19 Response Strategy to provide guidance for the continuity of learning during school closures and the transition back to school after the pandemic had subsided (SDELBEK, 2020). The plan aimed to:

- Provide access to equitable, inclusive, and quality, equitable schooling to learners during and after the pandemic to make sure there is uninterrupted learning.
- To facilitate the production of virtual teaching and learning resources, and to further develop existing open/distance learning programs.
- Train facilitators to effectively support open/distance learning, which includes monitoring, and assessing progress.
- Develop, and implement intervention programs targeting the sidelined and vulnerable learners; specifically, girls and special needs learners.
- Provide psychosocial support to education officers, educators, learners, and other shareholders in the education sector.

Despite these hasty efforts, minimal learning or no learning took place. As per UWEZO Kenya (2020), 2 out of 10 parents were not prepared and informed that leaners were supposed to continue learning through online platform, or by other means, while at home and didn't have the necessary infrastructure. It is generally acknowledged that there is no policy on institutions and educators' preparedness. Educators are not yet equipped with the skills needed to effectively execute distance learning.

COVID-19 aggravated educational imbalances that existed before it existed by sinking the chances of education attainment for the majority of the mostly susceptible learners, young people, and adults–especially those from among the poor from informal settlements, girl children, refugees, persons with incapacities and compulsorily expatriated persons from continuing with their learning (Mbovane, 2020). Losses due to this pandemic threaten to spread across coming generations and expunge years of development, negatively affecting assistance of girl children and women's education with regard to access and retention. About 23.8 million other learners and young people (up to the tertiary level) were feared to drop learning or not enroll at all in the coming years due to the epidemic's economic effect alone. Likewise, the education distraction might spill over to other critical aspects of human existence. Cessations of learning organizations prevent the unhindered delivery of important services to students and populations, which includes accessing enough food, access to work (by parents), and an increase in the risk of violence against girls and women (Mbovane, 2020).

As financial pressures upsurge and growth aid is drained, educational funding might be confronted with significant bottlenecks, aggravating enormous pre- and post-pandemic financing gaps in education. For developing countries Kenya inclusive, that gap is at an astounding $148 billion yearly and it might go up by up to 33.3% (International Monetary Fund, 2020).

Further to that, this catastrophe has inspired a spirit of innovativeness within the education sector as evidenced in the approaches espoused during the pandemic including the use of television, radio, and take-home assignments as a way of continuing with education and training (UWEZO, 2020). Online learning solutions were established; appreciation for fast responses by states and stakeholders all over the globe in assisting education continuity was noticeable, including the Global Education Coalition convened by UNESCO (SDELBEK, 2020). The crucial function of educators, states, and other main stakeholders is underscored too. It is observed that these transformations have underscored the promising future of learning. In particular, the fast-tracked reforms in methods of ensuring educational quality might not be disconnected from the urgency of ensuring all learners are enrolled and learning without exception. This applies to learners who are affected by meager resources to access learning (Black, 2020a).

The situation is similar for the facilitators and the urgency for improved training in fresh approaches to delivering education. This scenario calls for the restructuring of Education Policy and Practice following incidences of COVID-19 globally. The Corona Virus Disease-19 catastrophe plus the unmatched distraction in the education sector are not over yet, world-wide states, parents, unions, and learners are contending with the aftermaths and the way to approach the subsequent phases and related pandemics likely to emerge (Global Education Cluster, 2020). The policy interventions to be put in place bear huge socio-economic repercussions and might portend lifelong consequences on educators, learners, parents, and other concerned stakeholders (Global Education Cluster,2020). Averting the access to learning catastrophe from deteriorating to a disaster across generations is an urgent issue that needs to be addressed by global leadership and all stakeholders in education through policy re-evaluation. This is one of the surest ways to protect the welfare of millions of learners and educators.

The ramifications of the Covid-19 pandemic have been differently experienced globally in all sectors of the economy. Specifically, the pandemic has raised questions on the efficacy of both policy and practice in education. In most African states, education policy frameworks have been criticized as being inadequate to address such challenges as the ones posed by the Covid-19 pandemic (Areba, 2020). Notwithstanding improvement in increasing access, retention, quality, and completion rates, most African states' education systems continue to face major legal and regulatory policy challenges. Most remarkably, there are several laws pertaining to education which are weak, disjointed, and often inconsistent (UWEZO, 2020). Conversely, ineffective facilities and inadequate funding have hindered the setting up of ICT structures in most of Africa's learning institutions. Consequently, substantial education policy review is essential to consolidate the gains that have so far been made in this sector such as the 100% learner transition policy at the basic level of learning geared towards increasing enrollment in tertiary institutions.

IMPACT OF THE COVID-19 PANDEMIC ON EDUCATION

School Closures and Learning Disruptions

The COVID-19 pandemic led to unprecedented school closures, affecting over 1.6 billion learners in more than 190 countries (UNESCO, 2020). These closures resulted in significant learning disruptions, particularly for vulnerable and marginalized students. The sudden shift to remote learning exposed the weaknesses in existing education systems, particularly the lack of preparedness for such a large-scale transition (Anderson, 2020).

Rapid Transition to Remote Learning

In response to school closures, educational institutions worldwide rapidly transitioned to remote learning. This shift highlighted the critical role of technology in education, as digital platforms became the primary means of delivering instruction. However, this transition was far from smooth. Many schools and educators were unprepared for the demands of online teaching, leading to a range of challenges, including issues with student engagement, assessment, and the digital divide (Dhawan, 2020).

The Digital Divide

The pandemic exacerbated existing inequities in education, particularly regarding access to technology. The digital divide—referring to the gap between those with access to digital technologies and those without—became more pronounced during the pandemic. Students from low-income families, rural areas, and developing countries were disproportionately affected, with limited access to the internet, devices, and other necessary resources (Di Pietro et al., 2020). This divide further widened educational disparities, as many students struggled to participate in remote learning.

Mental Health and Well-being

The pandemic also had a significant impact on the mental health and well-being of students, teachers, and parents. The abrupt transition to remote learning, combined with social isolation, economic uncertainty, and health concerns, contributed to increased levels of stress, anxiety, and depression (O'Reilly et al., 2020). The lack of face-to-face interaction and support from peers and teachers further exacerbated these issues, leading to concerns about the long-term effects on students' mental health and academic performance.

THEORETICAL ORIENTATION FOR THE STUDY

This study is based on the justice and fairness theory whose proponent is John Rawls (1971) who believes in justice as a principle in the contemporary social order. The framework offers a context that clarifies the significance of a society that is assumed to comprise of equal and free people of political and personal liberty, cooperative arrangement, and equal opportunity that benefit the more and less advantaged members of societies. It supports the idea of justice from the viewpoint that people are equal and free (Rawls, 1971). Educational system frameworks must do away with hurdles that prevent able children from poor backgrounds from exploiting their talents in order to achieve their best (Rawls, 1971).

The theory emphasizes that society's most important goods that is wealth and income; opportunity and liberty; and the bases of self-respect are supposed to be shared equally so that all in society are able to realize their potential (Rawls,1999). Any uneven distribution is, unavoidably, to the detriment of the pursuit of the interests of the less fortunate. Any disparities are to be organized in a manner that to the greatest extent, is beneficial to the less fortunate under conditions of fairness and parity. The theory emphasizes that each citizen should be accorded, through schooling, an opportunity to exercise freedom and improve their status. Restructuring the education policy following the interruptions caused by pandemics it is a panacea for making education accessible to learners from all classes (Rawls, 1971).

With respect to policy in education, the issue is essentially seen as one of providing access to poor but bright learners (Republic of Kenya, 2005). The theory maintains that children need to have equal opportunities at all levels of education irrespective of their social and economic backgrounds. Through relevant education policy reform, this will guarantee appropriate conditions to implement the pillars of equal opportunity, where all have access to an education that suits them (Rawls, 1971).

The nature of pandemics experienced from the past to the present has challenged the efficacy of both policy and practice in the sector of education. As already underscored, most of Africa's states' policies on education framework have been criticized as being inadequate to address such challenges hence exposing learners and teachers to all sorts of injustices leading to inequalities in offering education as a common good.

METHODOLOGY

A systematic review of empirical literature and meta-analysis was utilized in this study. The reviews were done under the following sub-themes:

- Policy initiatives to enhance education financing and coordination for long-lasting impact.
- Policy initiatives to enhance robust and flexible systems of education for equitable and sustainable development.
- Education policy initiatives to encourage innovations to hasten change in teaching and learning.

This study utilized discourse analysis which interprets documents in order for the investigator to give meaning and voice to a topic under assessment (Bowen, 2009).

RESULTS AND DISCUSSION

The study sought to review education policy and practices following the occurrence of the Corona Virus Disease-19 in Kenya under the following sub-titles:

- Policy initiatives to enhance education financing and coordination for long-lasting impact.
- Policy initiatives to enhance robust and flexible systems of education for equitable and sustainable development.
- Education policy initiatives to encourage innovations to hasten change in teaching and learning.

Policy Choices to Mitigate the COVID-19 Catastrophe in Sub-Saharan Africa

As forementioned, the COVID-19 pandemic has precipitated significant upheavals in educational systems worldwide, necessitating immediate and innovative responses from policymakers and educators. The pandemic exposed pre-existing vulnerabilities in education systems, leading to calls for restructuring policies and practices to enhance resilience and adaptability (UNESCO, 2020). To be able to lessen the potentially upsetting effects of the Corona Virus Disease-19, states and other shareholders need to consider the following policy options:

Policy Initiatives to Enhance Education Financing and Coordination for Long-Lasting Impact

The COVID-19 pandemic highlighted the need for increased investment in education, especially in low-income countries where educational infrastructure is underfunded. Pre-pandemic, many education systems already faced challenges in securing adequate financing. However, the pandemic exacerbated these issues, necessitating a restructuring of financing policies. The World Bank has advocated for more strategic investment in education, suggesting that financing should focus not only on immediate needs but also on building long-term resilience in education systems (World Bank, 2020). Moreover, coordinated efforts between governments, international organizations, and private sectors have been emphasized as critical to creating sustainable and impactful educational outcomes (OECD, 2021).

According to the International Monetary Fund's (IMF) Outlook (2020) on the global economy, the epidemic has taken the globe into the worst worldwide recession in history. This result might have an enduring impact on economic growth and public financing. The ramifications have been particularly severe in developing countries. The national governments need to craft policies to alleviate long-range effects on school-age children in spite of limitations on public spending, with educational mediations being part of the national Corona Virus Disease-19 inducement programs along with public health, and social protection initiatives. The global community might need to intervene to protect financing of education. Increasing monetary space, something that is already prominent in the international agenda, especially with regard to education, is already an obvious issue (IMF, 2020). There are several conjointly reinforcing entry avenues to get there:

Reinforce Domestic Resource Mobilization Policies, Give Education First Importance and Deal with Ineptitude.

Since broadening the tax framework in nations with big informal sectors takes long, alternative measures such as being strict on tax evasion and avoidance, revising tax inducements and agreements, among others, need to be explored urgently (Archer,2016). Undeniably, education institutions share a responsibility to raise the economic base by making better education service delivery and cost-effectiveness. Priority should be given to reforms and innovations that are going on at the moment. The relevant state ministries like Education and Finance should systematically and sustainably work out an allocation formula that should increase allocation to the education sector to reduce the negative effects occasioned by the Corona Virus Disease-19. Locally and internationally, stakeholders should argue for investments in education and in other sectors in order to give fresh urgency to, and to progress in reforms to do with monetary support for related development and reform in public fiscal administration as a whole (World Bank,2020a)

Reinforce Global Coordination Policies to Address the Debt Crunch

A number of low-income nations categorized as heavily indebted poor countries (HIPCs) have unrelentingly experienced snags in servicing their huge external debts. Many of these nations comprising of Kenya are in Sub-Saharan Africa. The comparatively escalating level of external debts and mounting debt liability carries with it severe repercussions on the countries' progress and liability sustainability responsibility (IMF 2001a and IMF 2001b). Similarly, in many low-income Sub-Saharan African states, a bigger percentage of external debt comprises of official debts. A breakdown of official debt indicates that in the 1970s, debt was largely from bilateral base. As from1980s multilateral debt adds up to the main percentage of overall debt stock. The portion of the multilateral debt was augmented temperately in the 1980s chiefly as a consequence of huge payouts of modified loaning by the World Bank (O'Brien and Ryan 1999).

As of 1990s, the percentage of concessional debt has been increasing. Kenya's debt is estimated to hit sixty-nine percent of GDP by 2023. An upsurge of over 10% points over pre-crisis levels. Public debt service is estimated to rise from 9 to 12% of GDP between 2020 and 2025. In the absence of access to supplementary aid in the form of debt relief and concessional financing, the nation will find it difficult to fulfill creditor dues in the near future (World Bank.2020a). The G20 nations recently granted a "debt service cessation" for the developing nations for a brief period of time (OECD, 2020). The cessation might allow a brief financial elasticity, but it falls short of addressing the plight of many susceptible nations in Africa; it also does not apply itself to the long-range question which is the sustainability of debt. To relieve, postpone, and restructure debt for developing nations that request patience needs to be one of the approaches to lay an economic base for nations to spend on education, and this needs all stakeholders to act.

Develop a Policy to Safeguard Formal Development Aid for Education

Because of the magnitude of the worldwide emergency in education, sponsors are required to make sure that assistance pledges to the sector are, constant, augmented, and focused especially on risk, and especially for children in emergencies. The pandemic has made worse the result of connecting inequalities in educational opportunities; leveraging educational activities to communicate essential alterations to public health behavior is important (Global Education Monitoring Report, 2020).

Increased Public and Private Investment

Governments should prioritize education in their national budgets, ensuring that education receives sufficient funding to meet the demands of both current and future crises. This involves not only direct investment in schools and educational infrastructure but also in digital technologies and teacher training.

Public-Private Partnerships (PPPs)

Encouraging partnerships between governments, private sector players, and non-governmental organizations (NGOs) can mobilize additional resources and expertise. These collaborations can be particularly effective in areas like technology integration, infrastructure development, and the provision of learning materials.

Strengthening Coordination Mechanisms to Streamline Resources

Establishing or reinforcing inter-agency and inter-ministerial coordination mechanisms can help streamline efforts and avoid duplication of resources. Effective coordination between various stakeholders—local and international—will ensure a more coherent response to educational challenges.

Transparent and Accountable Financing

Implementing strict financial governance and accountability measures is essential to ensure that allocated funds are used efficiently and effectively. Regular audits and transparent reporting can help maintain public trust and ensure that funds reach the intended beneficiaries.

Policy to Reinforce the Flexibility of Systems of Education for Equitable and Sustainable Growth

Education, as an indisputable right of everyone, is the foundation of equal, just, and inclusive civilizations and also a major factor of sustainable growth. Reinforcing the flexibility of education systems allows nations to react to the instantaneous difficulties of re-opening institutions safely and helps them to cope in a better way with future catastrophes.

To create an equitable and sustainable education system, policies must support the development of robust and flexible systems. The pandemic has shown that rigid education systems are vulnerable to disruption, which disproportionately affects marginalized groups. The UNESCO report on education in emergencies suggests that post-pandemic recovery should prioritize inclusive education systems that can adapt to various crises, ensuring that all students, regardless of background, have access to quality education (UNESCO, 2020). Flexibility in curriculum delivery, including the integration of digital tools and blended learning models, has been identified as a key strategy for maintaining educational continuity and supporting equitable access (UNICEF, 2021). This is possible through:

Policies Focusing on Equity and Inclusion

Over one million Kenyan learners are perpetually out of learning institutions regularly on the grounds that they are too poor, too far from schools, or incapacitated (The UNESCO Institute for Statistics (UIS), *2009*). Approaches to build robust education systems to cater for all students and the necessity to know and supply group needs that are marginalized and make sure that they access quality and full-term education as a key. Students in areas that are marginalized need to be given first priority so that their learning is not further put in danger. School feeding programs are also of significance to vulnerable children, as are incentives to encourage participation rates, increasing school re-enrollment and attendance, and more so, girl children from poor homes who might not afford food (Mundy & Proulx, 2019). The government and donors have to guarantee that the education system addresses the susceptibilities and necessities specific to children, adults, and gender dynamics in catastrophes. Out-dated gender customs, with monetary pressures on families, must not stand in the way of girls and less privileged students from going back to school and completing their schooling.

Development of Hybrid Learning Models

The pandemic necessitated a rapid shift to online learning, revealing the need for systems that can seamlessly switch between in-person and remote education. Policies should support the development of hybrid models that are flexible, resilient, and capable of reaching all students, regardless of their geographical location.

Inclusive Education Policies

To address the inequities exacerbated by the pandemic, education policies must focus on inclusivity. This includes supporting students with disabilities, those from marginalized communities, and those in rural or underserved areas. Policies should also address the gender disparities in access to education.

Curriculum Reform

The curriculum should be reformed to be more adaptable and relevant to the rapidly changing global landscape. This includes integrating digital literacy, critical thinking, and socio-emotional learning into the curriculum. There should also be a focus on lifelong learning, preparing students for a world where continuous skill development is necessary.

Teacher Training and Professional Development

Investing in continuous professional development for teachers is crucial for the successful implementation of any education reform. Policies should support regular training programs that equip teachers with the skills to use new technologies, manage hybrid classrooms, and address the diverse needs of their students.

Strengthen Policies on Capacities to Manage Risks at All Levels of Education

To survive disasters, capacity development is needed at the individual and institutional levels. It is the capability to make and implement emergency strategies, including alternate education pathways to alleviate impacts. The capabilities of stakeholders in education, in many cases, need reinforcement to assess and review prevailing sector strategies and policies–to add to adaptive reactions to the Corona Virus Disease-19 disaster. To achieve this, incorporating data about risks and effects on information systems and educational management helps to facilitate the planning and implementation of educational policies that are crisis-sensitive and programs, which include plans on disaster preparedness. Education players at the grassroots require capacity building to analyze risks to the health of students, educators, and parents, and to detect students on the verge of leaving school. The grassroots shareholders require the ability to evaluate the scope and efficiency of alternate frameworks for the continuity of quality education provision (Jacklin, 2020).

Guarantee Robust Leadership and Organization Policies

The many relevant stakeholders required to address and mitigate the impact of disasters can result in replication, ineptitude, and misperception when there is no vigorous leadership and organization. The leadership for disaster planning and management at the Ministry of Education is important for flexibility in the education sector. National education leadership warrants that human-centered approaches are supportable, are affiliated with country-wide priorities and are able to alleviate the effect of calamities on students and education communities. Vigorous organization approaches are also required in order to optimize the inputs of all shareholders, building on complementarities, including civil society groups, to address the needs of those most sidelined (Mundy & Hares, 2020).

Policy on Enhancing Consultation and Communication Strategies

Education officers, educators, parents, guardians, and those who give care to children play essential roles in the responses to the Corona Virus Disease-19 catastrophe and take on supplementary tasks in unfamiliar times. Engaging these shareholders in education might, therefore, boost the education sector's elasticity. Consulting and communicating with all education stakeholders including educators, students, and those most sidelined are significant to the actual implementation of strategies and reactions, supplying the prerequisites of students, and enriching their flexibility as well as that of the education sector (Jacklin, 2020).

Encourage Education Policies on Innovation to Speed Up Positive Revolution in Learning and Teaching

The pandemic has also accelerated the need for innovation in education. With the sudden shift to online learning, educators and policymakers have had to rethink traditional teaching methods. Policy initiatives that encourage innovation in educational technology and pedagogical approaches are crucial for adapting to the new realities of teaching and learning. For instance, the Global Education Coalition, launched by UNESCO, promotes collaborative efforts to harness technology and innovative teaching practices to address educational disruptions caused by the pandemic (UNESCO, 2021). Additionally, policies that support teacher training and professional development in using digital tools are essential for fostering an environment conducive to innovation and effective learning (Anderson & Hira, 2020).

Innovation with regard to reactions to aid schooling and instruction in the wake of the worldwide closing of schools and slowing down of non-formal training is also key. However, reactions have revealed important divisions, starting with the digital divide. Losses with regard to learning as a result of long school closures indicate that a number of educational outcomes are in danger. UNESCO (2020) states that it is not possible to have the world as it was before the onset of the Corona Virus Disease and so we seek to "build back resilience", there is a need to warrant that the education sector is inclusive, flexible, and equitable. The extensive efforts put in the present to react to the effects on the education system remind all that any variations formerly considered hard or incredible to execute are possible. Society has to utilize the chance to discover novel approaches to mitigate the difficulties in learning and generate solutions that are workable. The suggested strategies include:

Promoting Educational Technology (EdTech) Innovations

Governments should encourage the development and adoption of innovative EdTech solutions that can enhance teaching and learning. This includes supporting startups and research initiatives focused on developing tools that make learning more engaging, personalized, and accessible.

Incentivizing Creative Pedagogical Approaches

Educational policies should create an environment where teachers are encouraged to experiment with and implement creative teaching methods. This could include project-based learning, flipped classrooms, and other student-centered approaches that have been shown to improve engagement and learning outcomes.

Research and Development in Education

Allocating funds for research and development in the education sector can drive innovation. This includes funding studies on effective teaching practices, learning outcomes, and the impact of various educational interventions. Research can also inform the scaling of successful pilot programs.

Building Collaborative Learning Communities

Policies should support the establishment of collaborative learning communities where educators, students, parents, and other stakeholders can share best practices and learn from one another. This can be facilitated through online platforms, professional networks, and regular conferences or workshops.

Crafting Policies to Address Learning Losses and Averting Dropouts, Particularly of Relegated Students

As the country reflects on post-COVID-19 aftershocks, it should be underscored that what has been learned from the pandemic hinges on three priorities: (i) making up for losses to learning (ii) returning students at risk of dropping out of institutions, and (iii) concentrating on socio-emotional welfare of learner population, educators and non-teaching staff. Any meaningful policy enhancements should revolve around these three priorities.

Policies to Aid Educators' Readiness

If inclusive and equitable learning is to be assured in the midst of the Corona Virus pandemic, it is important that all stakeholders; teachers, tutors, lecturers, support staff, managers among others are prepared and assisted in their mandate. Use of technology, on its own, might not guarantee improved learning outcomes. A greater consideration than empowering educators with ICT knowledge is guaranteeing them assessment and skills on pedagogy to address learner deficits and to put to work the fast-tracked curriculum and differentiated learning approaches which might surface on resumption of learning. Digital systems require appropriate content, suitable instructional models, operative teaching practices, and a reassuring learning environment (Jacklin, 2020). Trainers' capacity building and professionalization are significant to make sure they are adequately qualified, rewarded, and equipped. The government has to reinforce support systems for educators, organizers, and guardians in the successful and safe utilization of technologies for learning (Jacklin, 2020)

Re-Conceptualizing Definition of The Right to Education to Encompass Internet Access as Right

There has been substantial responsiveness with regard to the utilization of technologies to guarantee continuity of learning as COVID-19 escalates in numbers. In countries like Kenya, the Ministry of Education launched several initiatives premeditated to enhance continuity in learning, which encompassed education programs that were aired through TV, radio, and YouTube. In collaboration with the Kenya Publishers Association, the MoE made electronic copies of textbooks accessible at no cost on the Kenya Education Cloud for all schoolchildren. The MoE, through the Kenya Civil Aviation Authority and in collaboration with Telkom Kenya deployed Google's Loon Balloons carrying 4G base stations over Kenyan airspace (UWEZO,2020). Nevertheless, while these are sound measures premeditated to ensure that no learner is disadvantaged, it is a reality that access to these services is erratic and several learners have not benefited from these initiatives, in both rural and urban areas (UWEZO,2020).

The digital remedies to enhance leaning which were in place on the eve of the pandemic need to make central inclusion and equity, to ensure that all students are beneficiaries. There is a need for an open and free source of technologies for instruction and learning since it is not possible to provide quality education with content built external to the instructional context and foreign to the human relations between instructors and learners (UNESCO, 2020). It is also not possible that education can depend on digital contexts whose control is by private entities alone (UNESCO, 2020). The government should support open educational provisions and open digital access from all sectors.

Reform Policy to Eliminate Obstacles to Connectivity

The catastrophe revealed the reality of the deep digital divide and associated equity gaps, which need critical attention (World Bank, 2020a). To eliminate technological obstacles, the government and development partners need to work harmoniously by spending on digital resources and bringing down the costs on connectivity. Narrowing the digital divide needs investment in digital literacy for the marginalized. Equally, depending on technology might not result in actual learning, especially the ones sidelined. It is essential to make sure that, as students get access to the internet, guardian support and accessibility of learning materials are assured which will permit optimum benefit from digital solutions (Karen & Susannah, 2020). Low-technology and no-technology methods must not be disregarded for people who have poor access to technology. Generally, governments are required to come up with a policy to ensure that learners from the humblest families will not continue to lag behind (Republic of Kenya, 2005).

Reinforce Policies on Monitoring Records of Learning

Dealing with the global pandemic requires incessant monitoring of data to do with students, educators, and that regarding institutions. Monitoring should be based on a combination of prevailing data and assessment structures and feasible new methodologies customized to this specific setting (UNDP, 2020). To strengthen flexibility, data collected should aid in monitoring the learning-teaching environment, and assist in evaluating school accountability. The timeliness and quality of data are important, and suggest a matching approach that brings down the digital divide and increases educators' skills in teaching practices for distance education. The importance of a system of education monitoring is as important as the data underlying it, and commitments should be made through thorough policies to assist institutions generate quality data that they utilize and forward upstream to permit the continuous monitoring of the learning outcomes (UNDP, 2020).

Reinforce Policies on Articulation and Flexibility Across All Levels of Education

A significant component of a robust system of education is its flexibility, which generally depends on a robust articulation between types and levels of education and also the capacity to put together alternate approaches to delivering education. For instance, hybrid/mixed learning which offers quasi-personalized learning paths for earners demands an amalgamation of teaching approaches, and mobilizing alternative pedagogical resources from country-level and global avenues. However, mixed learning brings up the question of recognition. Looking at preserving combined systems, robust connections should be established between formal and non-formal structures, which include recognizing, validating, and accrediting skills and knowledge attained through all types of learning. These robust connections will permit the education system in the respective countries to become more equitable and inclusive, as well as more operative in fulfilling its mission, more effective in its operations and prudent use of resources, and better prepared to serve the wants of its clients and society at large (UNESCO, 2020b).

FUTURE RESEARCH DIRECTIONS

The current findings on restructuring education policy and practices will strengthen higher education capacity in handling new unique 21st-century crises and pandemics. There is however a need for researchers to explore current novel strategies on how to capacity-build managers and other education stakeholders on best practices for handling crises as opposed to the usual primordial safety routines which have been overtaken by time.

CONCLUSION

The tremor caused in education by the COVID-19 pandemic has been extraordinary. It brings to the spotlight efforts to achieve global education goals but also the marginalized poor. This far, education stakeholders have remained robust and this lays the ground for a re-bounce. However, there is a risk of a spiral to exclusion and learning loss. Yet, each negative spiral of aggravating socio-economic circumstances indicates its reverse image of a positive spiral, one which might lead to the future of the education we want: one of the inclusive changes in education delivery, of releasing the potential of individuals and of collective fulfillment in all aspects of life, through education policy reform. There is a limitless drive and untapped resources on which we can count for the restoration, not only of education's essential services but of its essential targets through the reform of policy. It is the responsibility of governments globally to live true to principle and institute reforms through comprehensive policies, so that not only will learners regain their promised future but that all education stakeholders find their role in making it happen. In a nutshell, the restructuring of education policy and practices in the post-pandemic era requires a multifaceted approach that addresses financing, system robustness, and innovation. By focusing on these areas, education systems can become more resilient, equitable, and capable of preparing students for the challenges of the 21st century.

REFERENCES

Allan, O. (2020). *Economy hit hard as services slow down; Daily Nation April 29th 2020*. Nation Media Group.

Anderson, T., & Hira, A. (2020). The Impact of COVID-19 on Teaching and Learning: A Critical Perspective. *Journal of Educational Technology*, 51(4), 678–689.

Archer, D. (2016). Domestic tax and education. Background Paper for the Education Commission, available at: http://report. Education commission. org/resources/ (accessed November 1, 2019).

Areba, G. N. (2020). COVID-19 pandemic impact on Kenyan education sector: Learner challenges and mitigations. *Journal of Research Innovation and Implications in Education*, 4(2), 128–139.

Black, S. (2020a).The problem with Stephen Grootes' views about online learning. Daily Maverick [online]. Available at https://www.dailymaverick.co.za/opinionista/2020-05-11-the-problem-with-stephen-grootes-views-ab out-online-learning/ [accessed 5th November 2020].

Black, S. (2020b). Conceptualizing school overcrowding: Exploring relations between (mal)distribution and (inadequate) provision at different scales. Unpublished working paper.

Bowen, G. A. (2009). Document Analysis as a Qualitative Research Method. *Qualitative Research Journal*, 9(2), 27–40. DOI: 10.3316/QRJ0902027

Dhawan, S. (2020). Online Learning: A Panacea in the Time of COVID-19 Crisis. *Journal of Educational Technology Systems*, 49(1), 5–22. DOI: 10.1177/0047239520934018

Di Pietro et al. (2020). *The Likely Impact of COVID-19 on Education Reflections Based on the Existing Literature and Recent International Datasets*. Publications Office of the European Union.

Global Education Cluster. (2020). "Safe back to school: a practitioner's guide", 2020, *available at*https://educationcluster.app.box.com/v/Safeback2schoolGuide

Global Education Monitoring Report, "Policy Paper 41", available at https://unesdoc .unesco.org/ark:/48223/pf0000373844/PDF/373844eng.pdf.multi.

IMF (International Monetary Fund). (2001a). *'Debt Relief under the Heavily Indebted Poor Countries (HIPC) Initiative'. A factsheet, April*. IMF.

IMF (International Monetary Fund). (2001b). *'100 Percent Debt Cancellation? A Response from the IMF and the World Bank'. A factsheet, July*. IMF.

International Monetary Fund (IMF). (2020). "World Economic Outlook: A Crisis Like No

Jacklin, H. (2020). Re-opening schools is an ill-considered move. *Daily Maverick [online]. Available at*https://www.dailymaverick.co.za/opinionista/2020-06-05-reopening-schools-is-an-ill-considered-move-ask-the-teachers-not-the-economists/ *[accessed 10 June 2020].*

Karen Mundy & Susannah Hares. (2020). "Equity-Focused Approaches to Learning Loss during COVID-19", *Center for Global Development Blog, 16 April 2020, available at*https://www.cgdev.org/blog/equity-focused-approaches-learning-loss-during-covid-19

Mbovane, T. (2020). Covid-19: SASSA runs out of food parcels in Uitenhage. GroundUp [online].*Available athttps://www.groundup.org.za/article/covid-19-sassa-runs-out-food-parcels-uitenhage/[accessed 20 October 2020].*

O'Brien, F. S., & Ryan, T. C. I. (1999). *'Aid and Reform in Africa: Kenya Case Study'. Aid and Reform in Africa Papers*. The World Bank Group.

O'Reilly, M. (2020). Social media and adolescent mental health: The good, the bad and the ugly. *Journal of Mental Health*, 29(2), 200–206.Organization for Economic Cooperation and Development (OECD).(2020). "A 'debt standstill' for the poorest countries: How much is at stake?", 27 May 2020, available at http://www.oecd.org/coronavirus/policy-responses/a-debt-standstill-for-the-poorest-countries-how-much-is-at-stake-462eabd8/#endnotea0z2

OECD. (2021). *Education Policy Outlook 2021: Shaping Responsive and Resilient Education in a Changing World*. OECD Publishing.

Rawls, J. (1971). *A Theory of Justice*. Harvard University Press.

Region: External situation report 30 / 2020. *World Health Organization. Regional Office for Africa*.https://apps.who.int/iris/handle/

Republic of Kenya. (2005). Sessional Paper No.1 of 2005 on a policy framework for Education Training and Research. Nairobi: MoEST.

State Department of Early Learning and Basic Education, Kenya (SDELBEK). (2020). *Kenya BasicEducation COVID-19 Emergency Response Plan* .

UNESCO. (2020). *Education in Emergencies: A Focus on Equity and Inclusion*. UNESCO Publishing.

UNESCO. (2020c): "The impact of Covid-19 on the cost of achieving SDG 4", GEM Report Policy Paper 42. 6 Ibid.

UNESCO. (2020d). International Commission on the Futures of Education, "*Education in a post COVID-19 world: Nine ideas for action", 2020, available at*https:// unesdoc.unesco.org/ark:/48223/pf0000373717/PDF/373717eng.pdf.multi

UNESCO Institute for Statistics (UIS). (2017). "Out-of-School Children and Youth", *available at*http://uis.unesco.org/en/ topic/out-school-children-and-youth

UNESCO, UNICEF, WFP, World Bank. (2020a). Framework for reopening schools", available at https://unesdoc.unesco.org/ark:/48223/ pf0000373348 and "Reopening schools. UNESCO. (2020b).How to get education back on track after. https://www .iiep.unesco.org/en/reopening-schools-how-get-education-back-track-after-covid -19-13424

UNICEF. (2021). *Building Resilient Education Systems: Lessons from the COVID-19 Pandemic*. UNICEF Publications.

United Nations Development Programme. (2020). COVID-19 and human development: *Assessing the crisis, envisioning the recovery. 2020 Human Development Perspectives, 2020, New York: UNDP, available at*https://hdr.undp.org/en/hdp-covid

UWEZO. (2020). *Are Our Children Learning? The Status of Remote-learning among School-going Children in Kenya during the COVID-19 crisis.*https://palnetwork.org/ wp- content/uploads/2020/05/Usawa-Agenda-2020-Report.pdf

World Bank. (2020). *Investing in Education for Long-Term Resilience. World Bank Publications World Bank. (2020a). The COVID-19 Pandemic: Shocks to Education and Policy responses.* World Bank.

World Bank. (2020b). Literacy rate, adult total (% of people ages 15 and above). https://data.worldbank.org/indicator/SE.ADT.LITR

ADDITIONAL READING

Angote, J. (2020). *Learners to Begin Squeezed School Calendar in January 2021; Daily Nation November 17th 2020.* Nation Media Group.

Wango, G. (2002). *The legal Framework for Kenya's Education System. Nairobi, Kenya Edu Staff institute*

KEY TERMS AND DEFINITIONS

Higher Education: Alludes to various types of education offered in postsecondary institutions of learning. It essentially leads to a degree, diploma, or certificate upon finishing a given course of study.

Policy: Refers to a set of concepts, laws, or strategies that serve as a rationale for decision-making in the education context and other sectors.

Practices: Denotes routine undertakings, or mannerisms that institutional staff engage in. Practices can extensively influence outcomes, particularly in education.

Pre- and Post-Pandemic Interventions: These are remedies taken prior and after a pandemic ensues. The aim is to avert or mitigate the effect of a pandemic. This is purposed towards rebuilding, recovery, and mitigating long-term side-effects.

Restructuring: Reinvent, Reevaluate, and rethink the role of higher education in Africa aiming at new perspectives.

Chapter 2
Establishment of Open Universities and Policy Implications:
Towards Enhancing Equity, Access, and Inclusivity – The Case of Open University of Kenya

Daniel Karanja
https://orcid.org/0000-0001-6849-149X
State Department for Higher Education and Research, Kenya

George Ngwacho Areba
https://orcid.org/0000-0001-5661-3090
Kisii University, Kenya

ABSTRACT

Issues of access, equity, and inclusivity in higher education have been of concern. This has been coupled with the emergence of innovative and interruptive technologies. The motivation behind the establishment of open higher institutions of learning is chiefly the provision of accessible higher education to a wider populace. The global shift has been heralded by the establishment of the Open University of the United Kingdom (OU-UK). The OU-UK slogan of being "open to people, open to places; open to methods; and open to ideas" has revolutionized the role of a university in society. In this context, many countries have followed the OU-UK philosophy of university education being open and established their own open universities. It is on this premise that the Open University of Kenya (OUK) is anchored. Given that this is a novel venture there is need to interrogate the policy implications with a

DOI: 10.4018/979-8-3693-6930-2.ch002

view to enhance its functionality.

INTRODUCTION

In the contemporary educational landscape, the concept of open universities has emerged as a transformative force, reshaping how higher education is delivered and accessed. The rise of these institutions reflects a broader global movement towards greater educational equity, accessibility, and inclusivity. This chapter delves into the establishment of open universities, examining their impact on education systems worldwide with a particular focus on Africa. Open universities, characterized by their flexible, distance-based learning models, have been pivotal in expanding educational opportunities and addressing systemic barriers that have long hindered equitable access to higher education.

The Emergence of Open Universities Globally

Open universities represent a paradigm shift from traditional, brick-and-mortar institutions to flexible, accessible platforms for learning. This shift is driven by the need to accommodate diverse learner needs and contexts, particularly in regions where conventional educational infrastructures are insufficient. A seminal example of this global trend is the Open University in the United Kingdom, established in 1969. This institution was founded on the principle that education should be available to all, regardless of geographical or socio-economic constraints (Open University, 2022). The Open University's model of distance learning, characterized by its use of radio, television, and online resources, has served as a blueprint for similar institutions worldwide.

In the United States, the concept of open education is embodied by institutions such as the University of Phoenix and Western Governors University. These institutions have capitalized on online learning technologies to provide flexible and accessible educational opportunities for non-traditional students, including working adults and those with family commitments (University of Phoenix, 2023; Western Governors University, 2023). Their success illustrates how open universities can bridge gaps in higher education accessibility, catering to diverse learner profiles and life circumstances.

Open Universities in Other Regions of the World

Beyond the United States and the UK, open universities have made significant strides in various regions. For instance, in India, the Indira Gandhi National Open University (IGNOU) has been instrumental in democratizing higher education. Established in 1985, IGNOU offers a range of undergraduate, postgraduate, and diploma programs through distance education, reaching millions of learners across the country's vast and diverse population (IGNOU, 2022). This model has been particularly effective in addressing educational disparities in rural and remote areas, where traditional universities are often inaccessible.

In Australia, the Open Universities Australia (OUA) platform provides a similar service, offering courses from multiple universities through a single online portal. This approach not only enhances accessibility but also allows for greater flexibility in course selection and scheduling, thus accommodating the needs of a wide range of learners (Open Universities Australia, 2023). The OUA model illustrates how open universities can leverage technological advancements to provide a more inclusive and adaptable educational experience.

Open Universities in Africa

Turning to Africa, the need for open universities is particularly acute given the continent's unique educational challenges. The African continent is marked by a diverse array of educational needs, including high rates of illiteracy, inadequate infrastructure, and socio-economic disparities. In this context, open universities offer a promising solution to these challenges by providing flexible, accessible education that can reach underserved populations.

A notable example is the University of South Africa (UNISA), one of the largest open universities in Africa. Established in 1873 and transitioning to an open university model in the 1940s, UNISA has played a crucial role in expanding higher education access in South Africa and beyond. The university offers a wide range of programs through distance learning, catering to students who might otherwise be excluded from the higher education system due to geographic or economic barriers (University of South Africa, 2023). UNISA's model has demonstrated how open universities can address systemic inequalities and provide opportunities for lifelong learning.

In Nigeria, the National Open University of Nigeria (NOUN) serves a similar function. Established in 1983, NOUN was created to address the need for accessible higher education in a country with significant regional disparities in educational infrastructure. NOUN employs a combination of print materials, online resources, and face-to-face tutorials to deliver education across Nigeria's vast and varied landscape

(National Open University of Nigeria, 2023). This approach has been particularly effective in reaching learners in remote and underserved areas.

The Quest Towards Open University in Kenya

In preparation for a policy on distance learning, the Ministry of Education, Science and Technology in collaboration with the Commonwealth of Learning (CoL) organised a '***National Consultative Forum on the Policy for Open Learning and Distance Education in Kenya'*** Conference in Windsor Hotel, Kiambu in 2004. This Conference conceived the idea of an open university in Kenya. The communique issued after the Conference recommended "working out-out modalities for the establishment of a National Open University". Prior to Windsor Conference, previous government reports including the *Sessional Paper No.6 of 1988* and the *Second University in Kenya (1981)* only made reference only to the need to adopt open distance and e-learning learning or continuing education in existing conventional institutions as a means of expanding access in higher education sector.

The interest of the government in establishing an open university heightened between 2005 and 2014. This interest is reflected in Sessional Paper No 1 of 2005; the recommendation by PUIB of 2006; the commissioning of a consultant to work out a road map for the establishment of a distance-teaching National University in Kenya in 2008; Sessional Paper No. 14 of 2012; and the setting up of a Planning and Implementation Committee in 2014.

The Sessional Paper No 1 of 2005 identified three directions for future university development in Kenya: rationalization of academic programmes among universities with the aim of creating centres of excellence and making each university have a comparative advantage (p. 55); promoting open universities, and distance education to increase learning opportunities (p. 56); and with respect to financing university education, the Government will "work out a programme for reduced support to university education and training" (p. 94). The Technical Working Committee noted from this Sessional Paper that there are implications with respect to NOUK. These implications include: a) that given the diversity of expected profile of learners, OUK needs to work towards being a comprehensive university rather than having a specific niche; b) that tuition fees and scalability of numbers/enrollment will be the only sustainable route for OUK.

The Public Universities Inspection Board (PUIB) (2006) came out clearly on two aspects of enhancing access in higher education, namely: that Open University be established by 2008; and that prior learning be recognised as part of the admission criteria for applicants who have acquired knowledge, skills and competences in non-formal settings. Though the Open University was not established by 2008, the Technical Working Committee noted that the adoption of the concept of prior learning by OUK is still valid.

The Commissioning of Prof Greville Rumble in 2008 to come up with a road map for establishing a distance-teaching National University in Kenya became the prime mover of more aggressive attempts to establish an open university. Subsequently, the government proposed in Sessional Paper No. 14 of 2012 (p.123) to expand open and distance education in existing universities and establish the Open University of Kenya by 2014 and as part of implementing Rumble Report, the government set up in 2014 the Planning and Implementation Committee that developed the first Blue Print, the Proposal, and the Charter for the establishment of a National Open University of Kenya. In developing these documents, the Committee reviewed past reports on education reforms and policy documents, gathered views from stakeholders, and visited distance learning institutions in India, the United Kingdom, South Africa, and Tanzania. The institutions visited in these countries included Indra Gandhi National Open University, the Open University of the United Kingdom, the University of South Africa, and the Open University of Tanzania.

Though the details of the Technical Working Committee's review on past technical reports and the recommendations are fully integrated into the blueprint, the Proposal, and the Charter briefly described in Chapter 4 and a full dossier submitted to the Commission for University Education, the major changes introduced in relation to 2014 documentations are with respect to the name of the institution, vision, mission, philosophy, core values, programs, the choice of technology for course delivery, justification and the uniqueness of the University. One major departure from the past recommendation is on the name of the institution. The Technical Working Committee recommended that the institution be named the Open University of Kenya instead of the National Open University of Kenya. The rationale behind this change is on the likelihood of misconception. The Open University of Kenya being a transnational University, the connotation of "National" may be misunderstood to mean a university operating only within the territory of Kenya.

Borrowing from Best Practices

In addressing part of the second terms of reference on the best practices, the Technical Working Committee solicited and received presentations from regional and global institutions that are offering distance learning or supporting distance learning institutions and individual experts on their experiences and practices. It was the view of the Technical Working Committee that the practices and the lessons learned from these institutions and experts are beneficial to OUK in setting its foundation at this infancy stage of development.

Commonwealth of Learning Experience

The experience of Commonwealth of Learning which was presented by Dr Sanjaya Mishra, Director Education Sector highlighted the following: First, different ODL institutions have adopted different ways of handling learner support services including using existing institutions during the weekends or establishment of learning or study centres. Second, assessment rubrics being made available to the learners prior to the learners' engagement with the module. Third, that the decision to establish learning centres for the provision of learner support services depends on the level of technology that is available. There are two scenarios, namely: where there is high technology use, there is low use of learning centres; and where the use of technology is low the education provider resorts to high use of study centres or what CoL calls high touch.

Leaders of Africa Institute Experiences

Prof Peter Penar, the CEO of the Leaders of Africa Institute (LoAI), made a presentation on the mandate of LoAI, the activities and programs, and possible areas of collaboration with OUK. The LoAI offers the following opportunities to OUK:

a) LoAI is prepared to partner with OUK to support training and capacity-building, data science, curriculum design, the administration of programs, development of technology resources, institutional strategy, research, and sourcing funding.
b) LoAI has also proposed the joint administration of programs and the exchange of faculty to execute quality instruction. LoAI serves as a resource for collaborative programming and retaining subject matter experts.
c) LoAI is prepared to partner with OUK to build communities of practice that enhance knowledge and experience sharing without borders. Given that programs at OUK cover areas of international relevance and importance, OUK can draw on the network of experts and collaborators within the LoAI network.
d) One of the key pillars of OUK is to build a financially sustainable model that will thrive in the higher education space. LoAI is a ready partner in the pursuit of sourcing funding from diverse sources to ensure that OUK's programming is fully supported alongside the structures that are required to support professional development, student support, quality assurance, technological development and maintenance, and ongoing research.

GLOBAL OPEN UNIVERSITIES EXPERIENCES

Open University Malaysia Experiences

The physical presentation by the Vice-Chancellor, Open University Malaysia highlighted the following lessons: First, prior to Covid 19, the Open University Malaysia had 35 learning centres. During Covid 19, the University moved to online learning and after Covid 19, the learners became more interested in learning through the online mode. Hence online learning has become a new norm and the learning centres are now underutilized and are being let out to other institutions. Several open distance universities in developing countries use learning centres for the provision of learners support services such as tutorials or physical face-to-face sessions, reading space, counselling, computer laboratory, consultation and academic advising, and examinations. The cost of running learning centres can be high and if they cannot be financed by the government through subsidy this cost burden has to be passed to learner in terms of tuition fees. Second, the Open University Malaysia offers micro-credentials, that is, when learners complete a certain numbers of courses, they can be awarded a certificate. The courses need to be junked for purposes of micro-credential/certification. The micro-credentials are accumulated for the final conferment of a degree. Third, the admission criterion recognises prior learning or experiential learning. Fourth, in accommodating flexibility, the University has three intakes per academic year. Fifth, assessment is provided through smart proctoring system. Sixth, collaborations are useful when developing new programs as experts from collaborative universities come together (Dhanarajan,1992).

African Council for Distance Education Experiences

The Technical Working Committee received a presentation from the Africa Council for Distance Education (ACDE). The Committee noted that ACDE has developed a robust Quality Assurance Tool Kit that borrowed heavily from UNESCO and that ACDE is a good forum for sharing ODL experiences and practices.

Kenya National Qualifications Authority Experiences

The Technical Working Committee's interaction with KNQA highlighted three critical aspects: assessment for learning irrespective of the learning settings-formal or informal; the element of inclusivity; the recognition of prior learning; and that prior learning can be recognised through appropriate forms of assessment which may include: interviews, and/or challenge examinations, and/or assignments or projects, and/or demonstrations of skills; and/or validation of previous qualifications, and/

or a combination of the all these forms. These provisions are clear indications that the admission criteria based on prior learning is anchored in law.

The Zambian Open University Experiences

The Zambian Open University offers undergraduate and postgraduate degrees in Agriculture, Business, Education, and Law (Kapaale,1993). The presentation on the experiences of the Zambian Open University (ZAOU) was made by Prof Richard Siaciwena, the former Vice-Chancellor. Prof Siaciwena was requested to address the experiences of the Zambia Open University with respect to costing and financing. ZAOU is one of the few private open universities in Africa and hence its sustainability practices are useful lessons for an upcoming Open University of Kenya. The following are ZAOU experiences that the presentation highlighted:

a) That a new open university needs to give priority to capacity building. This is to ensure that members of staff in different units have ODL teaching and technology skills; understand and accept their roles and responsibilities.
b) That in view of the competition from traditional universities, public relations, marketing and marketing strategy is critical. At the beginning, marketing may be outsourced. Though this may appear to be costly, this will enable the University to get professionals and engaging permanent staff will cost more to the institutions with respect to monthly salaries and other benefits.
c) That provision of short courses for various professionals/working class is a good source of income generation. This can be done in collaboration with other institutions.
d) That collaboration with other universities and industry at infancy stage of development is essential and builds credibility.
e) That Quality Assurance Policy and Unit be put in place to monitor and report on the performance of various units of the university.
f) That in order to save on staffing costs, cost-effective student-staff ratios; academic-nonacademic staff, and full-time to part-time staff ratios create room for reducing costs significantly. The ratio of full-time staff to part-time staff varies from program to program. In some cases, it is 1:10; 1:5; 1:3
g) That part-time tutors at times create challenges of not providing support to learners such as not responding to the learners at times of need. This challenge can be addressed through:
    i. University's frequent interaction with part-timers. This encourages them to feel that they are part of the University.

ii. Providing students with a facility where they send the information on the challenges they are facing and the same information is automatically rerouted to the tutor and a university official in charge of learner support services such as the Dean of Students.

h) That in view of the importance of learners' support services, the university should provide strong ICT support services that include but are not limited to: emails the students can access; WhatsApp; among others.

Open University of United Kingdom Experiences

The Technical Working Committee held a virtual meeting with the Open University of United Kingdom technical team. What emerged from the discussions included the need for a new university to pay attention to: ICT operation systems such as Learning Management Systems; and capacity building. OU-UK has grown to a level that it has its own custom-designed LMS, and generates substantial revenue through consultancy in such areas as: program development; learning design; module/content development; and LMS development.

Common Practices

The presentations from these regional and global ODL institutions shared the following practices: in addition to the normal admission criteria, prior learning or experiential learning is an acceptable admission criteria; where prior learning applies challenge test may form part of assessing the applicant's skills and maturity to cope successfully with the university's challenging academic work; the use of learning centres for learner support services depends on the level of technology support available-where the technology is low, the use of learner centres becomes high; institutional collaboration provides an opportunity for the collaborating institutions to pool together their experts and other resources in the development of new curriculum/program and training; that the capacity the institution has built is an asset that can generate revenue to the institution through consultancy.

STRUCTURE OF THE OPEN UNIVERSITY OF KENYA

Though OUK was established under the Universities Act 2012 as a specialised University, its governance structure adheres to a great extent to that of any university in any country and globe. This is in light of the universal functions and mandate of any university. The only difference between OUK and the other universities is its mode of program/course delivery and being single mode open distance learning-teaching University.

Rationale for Establishment of the Open University of Kenya

The rationale for the establishment of OUK has been built around the following issues:

ODL Historical Trend

Throughout human history, education as a process of knowledge and skills acquisition has neither been confined to one mode of learning, or delivery nor to one type of setting. Indeed, its delivery mode has always been dependent on the level of technological advancement. Invariably, face-to-face or in-person encounter has been the predominant mode of delivery of instructions. This mode will continue being in place despite the emergence of other modes. Print-based mode of delivery of learning emerged as a result of the availability of print technology. The shift from print was propelled by the ubiquitous nature of e-learning and today most institutions are embracing open, distance, and e-learning in lieu of print-based mode. Indeed, the growth of the global shift to distance learning was heralded by the establishment of the Open University of the United Kingdom (OU-UK) in 1969. OU-UK became a catalyst for change in its admission criteria, production of learning materials that have received international acceptance, and delivery of instructions. Today OU-UK course materials are widely used by traditional universities in a multitude of different countries. The OU-UK slogan of being "open to people, open to places; open to methods; and open to ideas" has revolutionized the conception of the place and the role of a university in society. In this respect, many countries have followed the OU-UK philosophy of university education being open and hence established their own open universities. Table 1.1 shows a sample of distance learning institutions that have been established since 1969 and their enrollments.

Table 1. Some Post OU-UK Distance Learning Institutions

Institution	Country	Year Founded	Enrollment*
University of South Africa	South Africa	1873	420,000
National Centre for Distance Education	France	1939	350,000
Open University of United Kingdom	Britain	1969	250,000
Athabasca University	Canada	1970	43,000
National University of Distance Education	Spain	1972	260,000

continued on following page

Table 1. Continued

Institution	Country	Year Founded	Enrollment*
Sukhothai Thammathirat Open University	Thailand	1978	217,000
China TV University	China	1979	1,000,000
Korea National Open University	South Korea	1982	142,000
Anadolu University	Turkey	1982	1,900,000
University of Terbuka	Indonesia	1984	646,000
Indira Gandhi National Open University	India	1985	4,000,000
Payame Noor University	Iran	1988	940,000
The Open University of Tanzania	Tanzania	1992	92,000
Zimbabwe Open University	Zimbabwe	1999	30,000
Virtual University of Pakistan	Pakistan	2002	100,000
National Open University of Nigeria	Nigeria	2002	515,000

These distance learning institutions and many others not listed in table 1.1 offer all programs that are being offered in conventional universities. The popular programs on offer are in order of business and economics; followed by social sciences and applied sciences; third in order are life sciences, medicine and health, engineering and technology, and humanities and arts. The smallest numbers of distance education programs are recorded in environmental science, law, and natural sciences. Within the African continent, open universities enroll between 25% and 37% of total enrollment of university students. The leading universities are The Open University of Tanzania with 41%; the University of South Africa with 37%; Zimbabwe Open University with 33%; and the Open University of Nigeria with 26%.

The global and regional trends show that any programme can be offered through distance learning and that open universities provide an additional pathway to higher education. OUK's growth in programmes and student numbers is expected to be progressive. OUK was expected to be operational by 2008 (Public Universities Inspection Board, 2006), and hence its operationalisation after 14 years of dormancy is a strong indication of the goodwill for support from the government.

Impact of COVID-19 and Open Universities

Globally, university affordability has been strained by COVID-19. Many parents and adults lost their jobs or business. In the USA, about 7% of university students left the university to find full-time employment or alternative education options. To save on costs, those who attended private universities before COVID-19 have shifted to state universities. One important aspect that makes open universities affordable is the opportunity that is given to the learners to pay according to the modules they take and the flexible part-time study. Since open universities structure and deliver their courses in a modular approach, tuition fees are lower by between 30 and 39% of the fees paid by students attending conventional universities. COVID-19 and its variants may not go away on this planet earth and hence mitigation measures are required in order to minimise its disruption of learning and narrowing of access to education. As a result of COVID-19 African countries faced unprecedented challenges as learning institutions were closed and the few that did not close faced the challenges of how to deal with teaching and learning.

A Communique of the African Union STC-EST 3 noted on April 9th 2020 that the effects of COVID-19 were "worsening existing weaknesses in Africa's Education systems". The Communique further acknowledged "that unless we collectively act now to protect Education systems by providing alternative learning platforms and complementary programmes, societies and economies will feel the burden long after COVID-19". As a result of the unprecedented lockdowns of 2020 due to the COVID-19 epidemic, education providers shifted to virtual delivery of learning and training of teachers through e-platforms, social media, radio, and TV. The pandemic has shifted the mode of learning in higher education from reliance on traditional face-to-face to increasingly use of online learning management systems. The use of both asynchronised and synchronised learning platforms has become a common practice. However, not all learners accessed the learning platforms due to poor access to the internet, electricity, location, and socioeconomic barriers. The establishment of OUK is intended to adopt open distance and eLearning in order to build resilience through the provision of alternative learning platforms and be the national training hub in technology-enhanced teaching and learning.

Previous Education Commissions and Policy Frameworks in Kenya

The conception of distance learning as a viable vehicle for increasing access to education at all levels in Kenya has gradually evolved as evidenced in the various national education commissions that have looked into education reforms since independence and the government policy documents that have recognised the need for it being mainstreamed. These include:

- Kenya Education Commission Report (1964)
- The Presidential Working Party on the Establishment of the Second University (1981)
- Sessional Paper No.6 of 1988 on Education and Manpower Training for the Next Decade and Beyond

- Sessional Paper No.1 of 2005 on a Policy Framework for Education, Training, and Research
- Kenya Vision 2030
- Public Universities Inspection Board on Transformation of Higher Education and Training in Kenya (2006)
- Rumble Report: Establishing A Distance-Teaching National University in Kenya (2008)
- National Strategy for University Education (2007-2015)
- Universities Act of 2012
- Sessional Paper No.14 of 2012 on Reforming Education and Training Sectors in Kenya
- Sessional Paper No. 1 of 2019 on a Policy Framework for Reforming Education, Training, and Research for Sustainable Development
- National Education Sector Strategic Plan (2018-2022).

All these twelve reports and policy documents recognised three key aspects of distance learning in enhancing access to higher education, namely: opening up opportunities for lifelong learning; increasing flexibility of programmes being offered; and its cost-effectiveness. The recommendations of the Public University Inspection Board moved the idea of distance learning from the periphery to centre stage in education discourse by recommending the mainstreaming of distance learning through the formulation of appropriate policies and establishment of an Open University of Kenya by 2008. This is the first time in Kenya that strong emphasis was placed on distance learning in a government report. The PUIB report observed that the high cost of attending a conventional public university as a full fee-paying student and the non-flexible admission criteria limit access to higher education. Other key observations of PUIB include the need for the country to explore alternative methods of expanding opportunities to a diverse range of Kenyan learners and learning from experiences from other countries where ODeL programmes have been implemented.

One other challenge that emerged is that public universities in Kenya have to some extent lost some of their strong regional and international makeup in terms of the proportion of foreign students enrolled. The establishment of OUK is envisaged to: fill the gaps that the various commissions on education reforms have identified; become a vehicle for enhancing EAC regional integration through the provision of education through distance learning mode in Member States; and export of education. Open universities attract foreign students. In the Open University of the United Kingdom the proportion of foreign students is 1%; Open University of Tanzania with 1% the majority are from Rwanda, Namibia and Kenya; UNISA with 10%; and the National Open University of Nigeria with 15%. (Shikulo, Lukas & Mapheleba Lekhetho, 2020).

Open Universities Complementary Role in Kenya's 100% Transition Policy

Under the government policy of 100% transition from primary to secondary, the 1.2 million children who sat for the Kenya Primary School Education Assessment (KPSEA) in 2022 will be seeking university admission in 2030. Assuming a dropout rate of 5% per annum (Sessional, 2008c) a large number of over 1.03 million will still complete Grade 12. Even though others will join other training institutions, the balance will still be large. This is still a tsunami of applicants. The conventional universities may not be able to accommodate this number of applicants. A university that requires minimal physical infrastructure lends itself to benefiting from economies of scale. The Open University of Kenya will in this situation supplement and complement the conventional universities. Further, the new school curriculum is expected to produce job creators and hence there will be a sizable number of school leavers who may want to continue with flexible part-time learning while developing or building their business. Flexibility in the provision of the needed education and training that will be in-built in OUK makes it more attractive and convenient as those engaged in other activities are able to learn at the time and place of their choice all year round, unless required for occasional practical lessons in a different location.

Regional and Continental Development Forces Factor on Open Universities

As a result of the globalisation of the world economy and rapidly developing cooperation and integration of processes, the internationalisation of education has also become an important requirement. The revitalisation and strengthening of the East African Community, the development of the African Continental Free Trade Area and the resulting enlarged markets and opportunities for labour mobility have brought with them new possibilities for those who will have the right knowledge and skills to access cross border employment and trade. As Africa opens up, it is increasingly essential to harmonise education qualifications, enhance skills portability and facilitate credit transfer for more Africans to access education and training as well as work across the continent. This is necessary for Africa to reap demographic dividends and claim the 21st century. Additionally, the Science, Technology and Innovation Strategy for Africa's Agenda 63 (STISA) envisions an Africa whose transformation is led by innovation and which will create a knowledge-based economy. OUK will recognise this trend as it crafts its identity into the future as a transcontinental higher education provider.

Impact of ICT Revolution on Open Universities

The Information and Communication Technology (ICT) revolution has profoundly transformed various sectors, with higher education being one of the most impacted areas. Open universities, which have historically focused on providing flexible and accessible education, have experienced significant changes due to advancements in ICT. This section explores the impact of the ICT revolution on open universities globally, with a particular focus on the African and Kenyan context.

GLOBAL PERSPECTIVES ON ICT AND OPEN UNIVERSITIES

Globally, the integration of ICT into open universities has enhanced educational delivery and accessibility. In the United States, institutions like the University of Phoenix and Western Governors University have leveraged online platforms to offer flexible learning options (Seaman & Allen, 2018). These universities use Learning Management Systems (LMS) such as Blackboard and Canvas to facilitate online courses, manage student interactions, and deliver content effectively. The use of multimedia tools and interactive platforms has made learning more engaging and accessible to a diverse student body (Allen & Seaman, 2017).

In Europe, open universities such as the Open University in the UK have utilized ICT to reach students across the continent. The university's use of online forums, video lectures, and digital resources has supported a more personalized learning experience (Perraton, 2016). Similarly, the European Distance and E-Learning Network (EDEN) promotes best practices and innovation in distance education through ICT, contributing to the growth and development of open universities in the region (Bates, 2015).

Asia has also seen substantial advancements due to ICT. The Indira Gandhi National Open University (IGNOU) in India has implemented various ICT tools, including MOOCs (Massive Open Online Courses), to provide educational opportunities to millions of students across the country (Raj & Sulaiman, 2018).

ICT and Open Universities in Africa

In Africa, the impact of the ICT revolution on open universities is increasingly significant, though challenges remain. The African Virtual University (AVU), a notable example, has utilized ICT to provide quality education across the continent. The AVU uses online platforms and digital resources to offer courses in fields such as information technology and business management. This approach helps address the scarcity of physical educational infrastructure and qualified instructors (AVU, 2020).

However, the implementation of ICT in African open universities faces several challenges. Limited internet connectivity, inadequate infrastructure, and socio-economic barriers can hinder the effectiveness of ICT-based education. For instance, in rural areas of sub-Saharan Africa, students may struggle with unreliable internet access, which can affect their ability to participate in online learning effectively (Mtebe & Raisamo, 2014).

Despite these challenges, some African open universities are making strides. The University of South Africa (UNISA) has adopted various ICT tools to enhance its distance education programs. UNISA's use of online resources, virtual classrooms, and digital libraries has expanded educational opportunities for students across the continent (Mavurah, 2020). The university's initiatives demonstrate the potential of ICT to overcome geographical and infrastructural barriers in African higher education.

In Kenya, the realization that conventional methods of teaching are no longer sufficient to meet the 21st-century education requirements, has made the nation to embrace significant changes in its higher education offering, which are geared to make education more accessible, open, flexible, professional, and responsive to change. By leveraging technology, the Open University of Kenya (OUK) promises to provide opportunities for lifelong learning and help to meet the skill requirements of the 21st century, making it a valuable addition to the country's educational landscape. Technology has the potential to support OUK achieve its mandate in a number of ways including:

- Provision of opportunities to individually engage learners in deep, authentic learning experiences, at their pace and regardless of time and place;
- Fueling many innovations that have had tremendous influence on societies and economies across the world;
- Facilitating the development of highly skilled human resource to support a knowledge-based economy.
- Facilitating OUK to provide continuous staff professional development.
- Stimulation of a learner-centered learning culture.
- Creation of a research and innovation culture: where those involve in country and across the country constantly review, share, and apply research and evidence-based practices to advance innovative teaching and learning.

The Uniqueness Factor

The Open University of Kenya was established to support and strengthen the provision and access to higher education in-country and across borders. OUK seeks to make a difference in the delivery of learning by making education accessible to a wide range of learners who have been constrained by lack of flexibility in learning and lack of openness in the traditional mode of education delivery. OUK is therefore envisaged to be a unique university in the country in a number of ways including building on the following strategies:

Openness Strategy

The United Nations (UN) convention and the Kenyan Constitution recognize education as a fundamental human right and a common good to the community. This noble position of education has remained elusive as a result of constraints imposed by admission requirements. OUK will unlock these constraints through the adoption of the principle of openness in admission. OUK sees openness as a way of fostering access and equity in education by providing a second chance to continue learning at any point or age. Without compromising on the quality, national, and international credibility of OUK's qualifications upon graduation, OUK will put in place the best ODL practices. The openness as practice in OUK implies three things, namely: putting fewer restrictions on admission; provision of more control to learners in terms of when and where they can access their learning materials; and ensuring that learning materials developed by OUK for use by learners are open to public scrutiny.

Flexibility Strategy

The border between flexibility and openness in distance learning is porous. OUK will be a learner-centered environment underpinned by flexibility in learning. This is a principle of access. The facets of this flexibility will be the time and place of study. The time of learners' study will accommodate the exigencies of their work as they can engage with their studies at any time that is convenient to them. The only time learners will be required to adhere to a specific time is when there is a scheduled discussion or chat or assessment. With respect to place, learners are not required to be at OUK and hence can choose a place where they can concentrate and at their convenience. In this respect the location of a learner is not a problem. To access the online course the learner needs only be able to access the internet and pay for the bundles. With this flexibility, OUK will be able to offer programmes to those who work in high-mobility jobs such as the armed forces. The other ingredients of OUK learning practices will be allowing self-pacing, by creating a situation whereby learners are not confined in terms of course completion to the rigid semester system prevailing in traditional universities and hence can move through their course at their own pace. When a candidate is satisfied that he/she has mastered the course requirement he/she can apply to be given an examination. OUK will allow non-government-sponsored students to register for examinations when they are ready or next offered.

Affordability Strategy

Affordability has been a major deterrent to access to higher education. This is linked to how courses are structured and delivered. While in a conventional university, an on-campus student can take up to seven courses in a semester, distance learners who share their time with other responsibilities cannot take a load of seven courses and hence subject to the limit of courses to be taken, OUK will allow a distance learner to have a choice on the number of courses they can take and pay for.

Online Learning Mode Factor

Offering online learning to supplement traditional modes of teaching and learning is not equivalent to or a miniature of an open university. Online learning will be the engine of course delivery at NOUK. Though learning will incorporate the blended mode that takes into account limited face-to-face and hands-on learning, the primary mode of instruction will be through e-learning mode. While AVU as an intergovernmental organization has been delivering e-learning courses since 1997 it has had little or no impact in increasing access to higher education in Kenya, partly because it had no programmes that Kenyans could register for. OUK will therefore be the only single-mode ODeL institution in the country. In this respect OUK will be the hub of distance learning in Kenya in terms of training and innovations in e-learning.

Single Mode Factor

Two types of institutions have been involved in the provision of distance learning, namely; the dual mode institutions and the single mode institutions. Dual-mode institutions are those learning institutions that offer their programmes through both conventional and distance learning modes. All public universities were legally established to teach solely on-campus students whether while on campus or off campus. Since early 2000 Kenyan conventional universities moved to a dual-mode system. Though they claim to offer distance learning, their practices are conventional in nature. The challenges of the dual mode institutions with respect to services and learning offered to the learners include lecturers' duality of assignments; treatment of teaching distance learning stream as a part-time activity; commercialization of distance learning stream; and the treatment of distance learning units as peripheral units with temporary staff on deployment basis from others departments. In dual-mode institutions, lecturers teach both on-campus and distance learners. Besides conventional teaching, in these institutions, there are two types of online learners-those who take part of their courses online and the working class. The duality of assignments to lecturers prevents them from giving adequate time to working-class learners (Paul & Alan, 2019).

The second challenge faced by dual-mode institutions in service provision is the treatment of distance learning activities as part-time activities. This means that distance learning is not a mainstream activity of the university. In this context, lecturers' perception is that their preoccupation is on on-campus learners rather than online learners. The growth of dual-mode institutions was driven by the need to create an alternative revenue source rather than increase access among the vulnerable groups in society. The admission to Module II/self-sponsored was on the basis of the ability to pay. Single-mode universities have been established solely to teach at a distance and are more efficient and advantageous in distance learning provision. The World Bank (1992) described single-mode universities as "top-of-the-line" in distance learning. In single-mode institutions, all financial and human resources are dedicated to serving distance learners. The establishment of OUK as a single mode University will therefore consolidate the human and financial resources for the maximum delivery of learning.

Prior Learning Recognition Factor

The concept of prior learning has not been well-interrogated and embraced in our higher education system. The Public Universities Inspection Board (2006) articulated well the essence of prior learning by stating in its recommendation that: "access to tertiary institutions should be opened to those who have acquired knowledge, skills, and competencies in non-formal settings in addition to the current practice of admitting students who have gone through the formal school system and attained the required academic admission criteria" (p.38).

This position has not been built into the admission criteria. In the 1970s individuals were being admitted to public universities through the Mature Age entry route. The approach recognizes knowledge, skills, and competencies acquired from workplace training; work experience in a relevant field, and short courses. In the early 1990s universities introduced bridging or foundation courses for those who were seeking admission but had low grades in compulsory courses that were required for a degree programme. This access route is no longer in place. Currently, conventional universities require formal qualifications for admission. Those who missed to acquire formal qualifications or certifications are denied further learning. Fortunately, technology has opened many avenues of self-development. Today MOOCS provides self-development and in many cases, learners do not receive certificates upon completion of the modules. Self-development cannot be discarded on grounds of any earlier or past poor academic records at KCSE. As an ODL institution, OUK will incorporate upon approval by CUE prior learning in its admission policy.

The incorporation of prior learning in OUK admission criteria will be a cure for the "diploma/certificate disease" the country has suffered from since independence. The skills demand in the 21st century is downgrading the fixation of anchoring every employment opportunity to academic certification. Though most of those in *Jua Kali* and building construction have secondary education qualifications, their hands-on skills or experiential learning have not been recognized. The failure to recognize hands-on skills has denied many Kenyans an opportunity to access employment opportunities abroad or secure local contracts. A Kenya Certificate of Secondary Education (KCSE) graduate who has had five years of supervised experience in a special aspect of construction work cannot be dismissed as unqualified. Further studies at the university level should be enhanced by experiential learning acquired through work experiences.

Progressive Certification as Factor

In many instances, society has been on the side of blaming the victims of socio-economic circumstances or locational barriers for their failure to acquire the pre-requisite requirements for formal admission. For these victims, the acquisition of qualifications has been a road of turns and twists. For example, the Teachers Service Commission requires that those who aspire to join the teaching profession and do not have a C Plus grade in KCSE can undertake a diploma programme. However, upon the completion of their diploma, they cannot be registered as teachers; this cadre of graduates is required to proceed to degree-level qualification. The challenge built in this policy is that the diploma graduates have to apply to join a degree programme and start afresh. OUK plans to remove this barrier and time-wasting system through the segmentation of a programme into modules that when a learner completes, he/she is awarded a certificate or diploma. The advantages of this approach to a learner, include flexibility, affordability, time-saving, and provision of opportunity to use the acquired qualifications for employment or promotion at any stage of study. The proposed approach also gives the learner an opportunity to re-enter the programme at ease at a later date.

Exporting Education Factor

E-learning is borderless and hence the establishment of OUK as an e-learning University in Kenya will serve the educational needs of those in the diaspora and attract international students. Through the provision of borderless higher education, OUK will put Kenya in the leagues of nations that provide and export higher education across the borders. In this respect, Kenyan citizens in the diaspora will have an opportunity for their children to take such courses as Kiswahili when developed as either a short course or long-term programme. With respect to the recent development in the African Union with regard to the recognition of Kiswahili as one of AU official languages, Kiswahili is poised to be a continental language and OUK will take advantage by coming up with programmes for this new market. Kiswahili will open the way for other OUK programmes to enter the continental market.

High Impact Community Service Factor

One of the mandates of the University is community service. The era of a university being an ivory tower has passed. Alternative ways of widening access to learning have been opened up mainly by Western universities through the provision of free tailor-made courses being delivered through such platforms as MOOCS. OUK-community nexus will be through the provision of free short courses of high impact in transforming lives in communities such as agriculture and Small and Medium and Entrepreneurship (SME). In the spirit of contributing to food security in the community, OUK plans to offer free in its first year of operation such short-time courses as poultry keeping and environmental conservation.

IMPACT OF OPEN UNIVERSITIES ON EDUCATIONAL AND INSTITUTIONAL POLICIES

The advent of open universities has substantially influenced educational and institutional policies, shaping areas such as admission criteria, bed capacities, university cut-off points, and employer job requirements. By offering flexible learning opportunities and broad access, open universities have initiated significant changes within higher education systems globally and, more specifically, in Africa.

Global Policy Impacts of Open Universities

Admission Policies and Cut-Off Points

Open universities have pioneered inclusive admission policies that challenge traditional entry requirements. The Open University in the UK, for instance, has set a precedent with its open admissions policy, allowing students to enroll without traditional academic qualifications. This model has encouraged other universities to rethink rigid admission standards and adopt more flexible criteria (Bates, 2015). As a result, traditional universities in the UK and beyond have adjusted their cut-off points to accommodate a broader range of students (Daniel, 2012).

In Australia, the Open University of Australia offers courses without stringent prerequisites, significantly impacting national higher education policies. This approach has influenced conventional universities to reconsider their admission practices and adopt more inclusive policies to align with the growing demand for higher education (Brown & McCormack, 2013). The flexibility in admission criteria has become a standard practice, promoting broader access to education and accommodating non-traditional students.

Impact on Bed Capacities

The rise of open universities has alleviated some of the pressures on physical campus infrastructures. Open universities primarily rely on online and distance learning platforms, reducing the need for large physical spaces. This shift has had a profound impact on traditional universities, which often face challenges related to limited bed capacities and overcrowded facilities (Simonson et al., 2015). By providing alternative learning modalities, open universities have helped mitigate these issues and allowed traditional institutions to focus on enhancing their physical infrastructures to meet increasing demands.

Employer Job Requirements

The proliferation of open universities has also influenced employer expectations and job requirements. With a growing number of graduates from open universities entering the job market, employers have had to adapt their hiring criteria. Open university graduates are often required to demonstrate practical skills and competencies beyond traditional academic achievements, reflecting the emphasis these institutions place on skill development and lifelong learning (Tait, 2013). As a result, employers are increasingly valuing practical experience and competencies over formal educational qualifications, which has led to a shift in job requirements and expectations.

Policy Impacts of Open Universities in Africa

Admission Policies and Cut-Off Points

In Africa, the impact of open universities is particularly notable in countries with limited access to higher education. The University of South Africa (UNISA), a major open university established in 1946, has been instrumental in reshaping educational policies across the continent. UNISA's open admissions policy has prompted traditional universities in South Africa to reassess their entry requirements and embrace more inclusive practices (Msimang, 2017). This shift has led to a reduction in university cut-off points and an increase in the number of students admitted to higher education institutions.

Similarly, in Nigeria, the National Open University of Nigeria (NOUN) has had a significant impact on higher education policies. NOUN's model of distance learning and open admissions has challenged conventional universities to address issues related to admission policies and bed capacities (Ogunyemi, 2020). The need to accommodate a growing and diverse student body has led to policy changes that aim to improve access to education and enhance institutional infrastructure.

Impact on Bed Capacities

The introduction of open universities in Africa has also addressed challenges related to bed capacities. Traditional universities in the region often struggle with overcrowded facilities and limited space. By offering distance and online learning options, open universities have alleviated some of these pressures, allowing conventional institutions to better manage their physical resources and expand their capacity (Mojapelo & Mhlanga, 2020). This shift has enabled a more balanced distribution of educational resources and improved access to higher education.

Employer Job Requirements

In Africa, the influence of open universities on job requirements is becoming increasingly evident. As open university graduates enter the workforce, employers are adjusting their expectations to align with the skills and competencies acquired through these institutions. For example, in countries like Kenya and Ghana, employers are recognizing the value of practical skills and experience gained through open university programs, which has led to a shift in job requirements away from strict academic qualifications (Karanja, 2021). This trend reflects the broader impact of open universities on labor market dynamics and educational expectations.

THE OPEN UNIVERSITY OF KENYA ESTABLISHMENT IMPLICATION ON POLICIES IN KENYA

The Open University of Kenya (OUK) was finally established following its award of Charter on 3rd August 2023. This followed several failed attempts with the notable ones being in years 2010 and 2014. The university is going to operate in an Open Distance and Electronic Learning (ODeL) model and is expected to expand and increase access to higher education opportunities in the country and beyond. This is in line with the current Kenya Kwanza government's desires as enshrined in its policy of Bottom-Up Economic Transformation Agenda (BETA) as well as the country's Vision 2030. It is also consistent with Africa's Agenda 2063 on the establishment of e-universities that will use ICTs to increase access to tertiary and continuing education.

The establishment of OUK will help advance the universal Sustainable Development Goals (SDGs) specifically, SDG 4 on ensuring inclusive and equitable quality education and promoting lifelong learning opportunities for all. OUK operations in the country are likely to cause a shift in the policy environment. For instance, its admission requirement that recognizes prior learning is set to change the use of cut-off points for university admission. This will ensure that all those interested in university education will have a chance of being considered after showing requisite ability. In the same vein, employers and practitioners who have been using secondary school grades to determine who join their professions may have to reconsider this requirement. This will enable all university graduates to have equal chances of competing in the labour market (Betts, 2017).

The policy of pegging university admissions to bed capacity may have to permanently be done away with. This is because OUK as well as universities who adopt the ODeL model will serve learners who will likely not be physically present onsite. The policies on class attendance and assessment, particularly for the ODeL students will need to be redefined to accommodate the flexibilities envisioned by the model. This should also take into account the aspect of self-paced learning. On human resource, the current requirements by the Commission for University Education (CUE) that universities operate largely with full-time faculties will have to be relooked at since open universities rely on adjunct tutors to be sustainable through the use of economies of scale (Betts, 2017).

Lastly, there has to be established a university funding policy that will incorporate the unique needs of ODeL students. The current funding model may not be adequate to cater to the technological and extraneous requirements that is associated with ODeL learning. This is because such students require advanced computing devices and reliable Internet connectivity to participate in the learning process. They are also expected to create time within their other schedules to access education. By critically looking through the highlighted policies, the existence of OUK in Kenya will help break barriers to access to university education that have been associated with the rigid conditions of conventional universities, locations, and socio-economic backgrounds (Aduol & Associates 2009).

FUTURE RESEARCH DIRECTIONS

Future research on open universities in higher education needs to focus on technology transfer with the view of investigating how open innovation strategies can facilitate technology transfer between universities and industries. Understanding this process can lead to valuable insights for both sectors. Further research on collaborative avenues for open universities and industry to explore factors influencing successful collaboration between industry and open universities for wider employment opportunities for graduates and assist in identifying effective practices that can enhance knowledge exchange and co-creation for wider education transformation. These research directions can benefit the education sector, students, graduates, and the broader community in a wider margin.

CONCLUSION

Open universities offer a unique approach to higher education. Unlike traditional universities with strict entry requirements, open universities provide accessible learning opportunities for anyone. Whether you're working full-time, seeking flexibility, or aiming for international recognition, open universities can be an excellent choice. Their commitment to widening access and flexible entrance requirements make them an attractive option for diverse learners.

The establishment of open universities has profoundly impacted educational and institutional policies worldwide and in Africa. By promoting flexible admission criteria, influencing university cut-off points, and addressing issues related to bed capacities, open universities have reshaped the higher education landscape. Additionally, the evolving expectations of employers reflect the broader influence of open universities on job requirements and labor market dynamics. As open universities continue to grow, their impact on educational policies and institutional practices is likely to expand further.

REFERENCES

Aduol, F and Associates (2009). Financing University Education in Kenya: A Report to the Ministry of Higher Education, Science and Technology.

Allen, I. E., & Seaman, J. (2017). *Digital learning compass: Distance education enrollment report 2017*. Babson Survey Research Group.

AVU. (2020). *Annual report*. African Virtual University.

Bates, A. W. (2015). *Teaching in a digital age: Guidelines for designing teaching and learning*. Tony Bates Associates Ltd.

Betts, K. (2017). *The growth of online learning: How universities must adjust to the new norm*. Education Dive.

Brown, M., & McCormack, C. (2013). The Future of Open Universities in Australia. *Australian Educational Researcher*, 40(3), 263–279. DOI: 10.1007/s13384-013-0107-4

Daniel, J. (2012). Making Sense of Distance Education: A Critical Review. *Distance Education*, 33(1), 105–117. DOI: 10.1080/01587919.2012.667020

Dhanarajan, G. (1992). 'Dual Mode Institutions: The Off-Campus Centre of Universiti Sains Malaysia'. In Mudridge I. (ed), Distance Education in Single and Dual Mode Institutions, Vancouver, Commonwealth of Learning.

Greville, R. (2008). Road Mapping: A Design of Implementation Plan for a Distance Teaching National University of Kenya.

IGNOU. (2022). *Indira Gandhi National Open University*. Retrieved from_https://www.ignou.ac.in

Kabiru and Kinyanjui. (2006). *Public Universities Inspection Board, Peter Kinyanjui Report: Transformation of Higher Education and Training in Kenya*. Cited on.

Kapaale, R.S (1993). The Distance Education Programmes at the University of Zambia –Mimeograph.

Karanja, M. (2021). Employer Perceptions of Open University Graduates in Kenya. *Journal of Higher Education Policy and Management*, 43(2), 179–194. DOI: 10.1080/1360080X.2021.1924052

Kinyanjui, P. (2007). *Public Universities Inspection Board, Peter Kinyanjui Report: Transformation of Higher education and Training in Kenya*. Government Press.

Kinyanjui, P. B. (2010). *The Republic of Kenya, A Proposal for the Establishment of the Open University of Kenya*. Government Press.

Mavurah, R. (2020). The role of ICT in distance education at the University of South Africa. *Journal of Distance Education*, 35(1), 35–50.

Mimang, D. (2017). The Role of Open Universities in South African Higher Education. *South African Journal of Higher Education*, 31(2), 56–71. DOI: 10.20853/31-2-860

Ministry of Education. (2005). *Sessional Paper No. 1 of 2005, A Policy Framework for Education, Training and Research*. Government Press.

Ministry of Education. (2018). National Education Sector Strategic Plan for the Period 2018 –2022 Government Press: Nairobi.

MoEST. (2012). *Sessional Paper No 2 of 2015*. Reforming the Education and Training Sector in Kenya Government Press.

Mojapelo, N., & Mhlanga, M. (2020). Distance Learning and Its Impact on Traditional Universities in South Africa. *South African Journal of Education*, 40(1), 1–15. DOI: 10.15700/saje.v40n1a1864

Mtebe, J. S., & Raisamo, R. (2014). Challenges and strategies in implementing e-learning in developing countries: A case of Tanzania. *International Review of Research in Open and Distributed Learning*, 15(2), 44–68.

National Open University of Nigeria. (2023). *National Open University of Nigeria*. Retrieved from https://www.nou.edu.ng

Ogunyemi, A. (2020). Impact of Open Universities on Nigerian Higher Education Policies. *Journal of African Higher Education*, 10(1), 22–34. DOI: 10.1080/23323256.2020.1750293

Open Universities Australia. (2023). *Open Universities Australia*. Retrieved from https://www.open.edu.au

Open University. (2022). *The Open University*. Retrieved from https://www.open.ac.uk

Paul, R., & Tait, A. (2019). Special Issue: Open Universities: Past, Present and Future. *International Review of Research in Open and Distributed Learning*, 20(4), i–viii. DOI: 10.19173/irrodl.v20i4.4575

Perraton, H. (2016). *Open and distance learning in the developing world*. Routledge.

Raj, R., & Sulaiman, T. (2018). The impact of MOOCs on open universities: A case study of IGNOU. *Journal of Educational Technology*, 21(4), 29–40.

Republic of Kenya. (1981). *Second University in Kenya: Report of the Presidential Working Party Republic of Kenya. (1964). Kenya Education Commission Report.* Government Printer. Nairobi.

Republic of Kenya. (1988). *Sessional Paper No. 06 of 1988 on Education and Manpower Training for the Next Decade and Beyond.* Government Press.

Republic of Kenya. (2005). *Sessional Paper No. 1 of 2005 A Policy Framework for Education, Training and Research Republic of Kenya. (2007). Report of the task force for the development of the National Strategy for University Education (The Wandiga Report).* Government Printer.

Republic of Kenya. (2007). *Government of Kenya, Vision 2030.* Nairobi: Government Press Public Universities Inspection Board (PUIB) Report (2006) Transformation of Higher Education and Training in Kenya Government Press: Nairobi.

Republic of Kenya. (2008). *Sessional Paper No. 1 of 2008 A Policy Framework for Education, Training and Research.* Government Press.

Republic of Kenya. (2008). *Sessional Paper No. 14 of 2012 A Policy Framework for Reforming Education and Training Sectors in Kenya.* Government Press.

Republic of Kenya. (2009). *Sessional paper No 1 of 2019 on Reforming Education, Training and Research for Sustainable Development.* Government Press.

Republic of Kenya. (2009). *Kenya Education Sector Support Programme (2005 - 2010).* Government Press.

Republic of Kenya. (2010). The Constitution of Kenya. Nairobi: Government Press: Nairobi.

Republic of Kenya. (2012). *Universities Act, 2012.* Government Press.

Republic of Kenya. (2012). *Session Paper No. 14 (2012). Reforming Education and Training in Kenya.* Government Press.

Rumble, R. (2008). *Republic of Kenya, Road Map for Open University.* Government Press.

Seaman, J., & Allen, I. E. (2018). *Grade level: Tracking online education in the United States.* Babson Survey Research Group.

Shikulo, Lukas and Mapheleba Lekhetho (2020). Exploring student support services of a distance learning centre at a Namibian university, Cogent Social Sciences. International Review of Research in Open and Distributed Learning.

Simonson, M., Smaldino, S. E., Albright, M., & Zvacek, S. (2015). *Teaching and Learning at a Distance: Foundations of Distance Education*. Pearson.

Tait, A. (2013). Open Education and the Development of Open Universities. *Open Learning*, 28(2), 102–115. DOI: 10.1080/02680513.2013.793829

University of Phoenix. (2023). *University of Phoenix*. Retrieved from https://www.phoenix.edu

University of South Africa. (2023). *University of South Africa*. Retrieved from https://www.unisa.ac.za

Western Governors University. (2023). *Western Governors University*. Retrieved from https://www.wgu.edu

ADDITIONAL READING

Republic of Kenya. (2006). *Transformation of higher education and training in Kenya to secure Kenya's development in the knowledge economy: report of the Public Universities Inspection Board*. Government Printer.

Republic of Kenya. (2010). *Session Paper No. 10 (2010). Kenya Vision 2030 Nairobi*. Government Press.

Republic of Kenya. (2010). *Task force report on the re-alignment of the education sector to the Constitution of Kenya 2010: towards a globally competitive quality education for sustainable development Nairobi*. Government Press.

UNESCO. (2015). World Education Forum 2015: Incheon declaration, Education 2030: Towards inclusive and equitable quality Education and lifelong learning for all. Geneva: UNESCO

UNESCO. (2015). *Repositioning and reconceptualizing the curriculum for the effective realization of sustainable development goal four, for holistic development and sustainable ways of living. IBE: repositioning curriculum in education quality and development, relevance*. UNESCO.

KEY TERMS AND DEFINITIONS

Access: Unlimited entry to open courses.

Equity: Devoid of biases or favoritism and tending towards impartiality and fairness in connection to university education access.

Implications: An unspecified inference that can be drawn from open universities, though not explicit.

Inclusivity: Equal access to higher education opportunities and resources for learners who might otherwise be excluded or marginalized.

Kenya: A country situated in the East Africa region along the Indian Ocean

Open University: The OU focuses on distance learning and online courses, making education accessible to a wide range of learners.

Policy: This is a statement of intent that outlines a course of action or a plan. It serves as a basis for making decisions, especially in areas such as education.

Chapter 3
Emergent or Planned?
Crafting Employability Strategies in Higher Education Institutions

Francesca Sgobbi
University of Brescia, Italy & DINÂMIA'CET-Iscte, Portugal

ABSTRACT

The employability of graduates has become a key issue for higher education institutions (HEIs) worldwide. Students, families, businesses, and institutions are increasingly focused on the career prospects of young graduates, as employability reflects educational quality and influences rankings and funding. Developing effective employability strategies is crucial for HEIs to fulfil their educational mission and remain competitive. However, there is often confusion between employability and employment, and the global discourse on employability strategies is uneven, with most research concentrated in Anglo-Saxon countries and assuming an intentional approach to strategy planning. This research examines four case HEIs in Italy and Portugal, finding that employability strategies are emerging from a mix of top-down and bottom-up initiatives, heavily influenced by national norms and available resources. The study underscores the importance of managing the dynamic process of strategy formation, highlighting the emergent nature of employability strategies in higher education.

INTRODUCTION

Recent years have witnessed an increasing attention to the career outcomes of young graduates from higher education (Tomlison, 2012; Burke *et al.*, 2017; Green & Henseke, 2021). If students and their families are interested in the expected return of their tangible and intangible efforts in education, businesses want to forecast the

DOI: 10.4018/979-8-3693-6930-2.ch003

professional skills and competences of potential new recruits, while institutional players need to assess the collective benefits from public investments in higher education (HE) and identify the targets of new initiatives.

Not surprisingly, employability has turned into a key indicator of the educational quality of higher education institutions (HEIs) and its measures significantly affect HEI national and international rankings, impacting the allocation of public resources and the choices of future students (Jackson & Bridgstock, 2018; Capano & Pritoni, 2020). Consequently, developing effective employability strategies is becoming more and more crucial for HEIs to fulfil their educational missions, compete in attracting students, and secure public and private funding (Farenga & Quinlan, 2016; Bridgstock & Jackson, 2019).

However, recognising the increasing importance of employability is often decoupled from designing and implementing clear employability strategies. This occurs due to the frequent confusion between graduates' employability and employment outcomes. While employment outcomes concern the attainment of post-diploma positions in line with HE studies, employability indicates the capability of developing a coherent career path across subsequent positions and experiences (Holmes 2013; Burke *et al.*, 2017). Accordingly, if the employment outcomes of a HE graduate cohort can be measured by indicators such as the average time to attain the first post-degree position, the average employment rates and wages at fixed intervals after graduation (e.g., one, three, or five years), or the alignment between education and occupation contents, employability measures should include long-term assessment of professional achievements and per-sonal growth (Jackson & Bridgstock, 2018), To this end, for instance, in 2012 the European Commission adopted a list of five indicators that benchmark graduate employ-ability and has been monitoring their use by HEIs in member states of the European Union (EU) and other European countries ever since (Table 1).

The importance attached to the employability strategies of HEIs is still uneven across the globe, as awareness and understanding of this concept vary according to institutional and social contexts. While graduate employability is now a recognised issue in many countries (Fakunle & Higson, 2021; Saito & Pham, 2021), most research and empirical evidence still focus on Western countries, particularly Anglo-Saxon nations where public institutions first mandated formal employability strategies (Holmes, 2013; Blackmore *et al.*, 2016; Bridgstock & Jackson, 2019).

In line with the increasing interest of stakeholders, recent years have seen a growing number of academic papers on the topic of HEI employment strategies. Theoretical contributions have developed frameworks to classify employability strategies available to HEIs (Holmes, 2013; Hooley *et al.*, 2023). Empirical analyses have confirmed how the approaches adopted to improve graduates' employability vary with the overall strategy of an HEI (Farenga & Quinlan, 2016; Bennet *et al.*,

2017; Okay-Somerville & Scholarios, 2017; Hooley *et al.*, 2023). However, newer studies suggest that HEIs may also display non-linear and not always planned behaviours when it comes to their employability strategies (Sgobbi, 2023). Tensions often build up between official employment strategies and their understanding by HEI academic and administrative staff (Divan *et al.*, 2019; Sin *et al.*, 2019). These insights have led to more explorative analyses that move away from normative assumptions that all HEIs have an intended employability strategy and that official and implemented strategies always align.

Table 1. Implementation of HE graduates' employability indicators by European countries, 2018/2019

	Systematic use of regular labour market forecasting	Employers involved in external quality assurance	Requirements or incentives for work placements for all students	Career guidance for all students in HEIs	Systematic use of regular graduate surveys
Austria		X		X	X
Belgium (Flemish)		X		X	X
Belgium (Franch)	X	X		X	X
Belgium (German)		X	X		
Bosnia Herzegovina	X	X			
Bulgaria	X	X	X	X	X
Croatia		X			X
Cyprus				X	
Czechia		X		X	
Denmark		X		X	X
Estonia	X	X	X	X	X
Finland	X			X	
France	X	X	X	X	X
Germany		X		X	X
Greece	X	X		X	
Hungary		X		X	X
Iceland				X	
Ireland	X			X	X
Italy	X	X	X	X	X
Latvia	X	X			
Liechtenstein		X		X	X
Lithuania	X	X	X	X	

continued on following page

Table 1. Continued

	Systematic use of regular labour market forecasting	Employers involved in external quality assurance	Requirements or incentives for work placements for all students	Career guidance for all students in HEIs	Systematic use of regular graduate surveys
Luxembourg				X	
Malta		X	X	X	
Montenegro	X	X	X	X	X
Netherlands	X	X		X	X
North Macedonia	X	X	X	X	X
Norway	X			X	X
Poland	X	X		X	X
Portugal		X		X	
Romania		X	X	X	X
Serbia					
Slovakia				X	X
Slovenia		X		X	
Spain		X	X	X	
Sweden	X	X		X	X
Turkey				X	
United Kingdom	X			X	X

Source: European Commission/EACEA/Eurydice (2019)

HEIs that are still figuring out how to improve graduate employability may find helpful assistance from a better understanding of the processes that underpin the creation of an employability strategy. To this end, this chapter explores the development of employability strategies by examining two contrasting hypotheses of strategy formation: the planned strategy, which presents strategy as a clear and intentional plan fully devised before implementation, is opposed to the emergent strategy, where the strategy gradually unfolds due to circumstances and interactions among involved players (Mintzberg, 1978; Mintzberg & Waters, 1985). Based on a past study (Sgobbi, 2023), this research tests these hypotheses based on four case HEIs in Italy and Portugal, drawing on interviews with academic staff responsible for employability programs and officers from employability and careers services. Official HEI documents and plans further supplement the collected interviews.

By shifting attention from strategy classification to strategy formation, this study highlights the emergent nature of HEI employability strategies and supports the hypothesis of strategy-as-pattern (Mintzberg, 1978): strategy is not just a deliberate, for-mal plan but also a consistent pattern of actions and behaviours that emerges over time, even if not explicitly intended. In all four examined HEIs, employability strategies are emerging from the ex-post rationalisation of a mix of top-down and bottom-up initiatives. The external environment, particularly national norms and available resources, plays a significant role in raising awareness and guiding HEIs towards formulating an explicit employability strategy. In addition, findings from the case HEIs show that the success of the emerging strategies heavily dependent on voluntarism and individual ef-fort and that managing the tensions that arise during the rationalisation and socialisation process is critical for establishing a successful employability strategy.

The rest of the chapter is organized as follows. The next section reviews the literature on employability strategies in HEIs, emphasising the need to bridge the gap be-tween intended and realised approaches to employability. Section 3 describes data collection and the methodology used in the empirical analysis. Section 4 presents evidence from the four case studies and Section 5 discusses the findings. Eventually, the final sections point out future research directions and offer some concluding remarks.

PAST RESEARCH ON HEI EMPLOYABILITY STRATEGIES

In the recent years the concept of employability has significantly evolved. If until the end of the last century it focused on the ideal attributes of labour suppliers, nowadays employability involves a comprehensive notion that includes lifelong employment and career success (Burke *et al.*, 2017). In the case of graduates from tertiary education employability concerns "the likelihood that [a graduate] will gain what may be deemed as appropriate employment" (Holmes 2013, p. 541), that is, "one where most of the skills used are usually acquired in the course of tertiary education. [...] Those skills include, inter alia, cognitive skills, knowledge creation, management and planning skills, information-processing, and interpersonal skills" (Green & Henseke, 2021, pp. 4-5). In this broader view, employability is a context-specific construct that emerges from the interplay between the traits and identities of students and graduates, HEIs, and prospective employers (Kinash *et al.*, 2016).

Tomlison (2012), Humburg *et al.* (2017), Okay-Somerville & Scholarios (2017), Altmann *et al.* (2018), Deming & Noray (2020), Anderson & Tomlison (2021), Jackson & Bridgstock (2021), and Okay-Somerville & Scholarios (2022) are just some of the authors who have contributed to the body of literature concerning graduates' and employers' understanding of employability. This literature has often underlined the impact of social and cognitive background on students' and recent graduates' perceptions about their employability, as well as employers' tendency to associate HE graduates' employability with the availability of ready-to-use skills and competences.

In contrast, the role of HEIs in the discourse on employability is still receiving insufficient attention (Farenga & Quinlan, 2016), despite the central role of tertiary education institutions in providing graduates with the skills and knowledge they need, as well as in acting as mediators between the interests of public institutions on the one hand and those of citizens and employers on the other (Holmes, 2013).

An HEI's approach to employability deserves attention because three interconnected factors have recently contributed to amplifying HEIs' potential impact on graduates' employability. Firstly, the rapid advancement of skills-displacing technological change increases the demand for high-skilled work (Green & Henseke, 2021). This trend underscores the dynamic and relational dimension of professional skills, particularly in the case of graduate occupations (McGuinness *et al.*, 2021), and requires not only change but also frequent updating of the content and didactic approach of HE learning programmes.

Secondly, the expansion and consequent massification of higher education has led to greater diversity in graduates' skill sets (Tomlison, 2007; Bridgstock & Jackson, 2019; Okay-Somerville & Scholarios, 2022), resulting in a higher risk of underemployment or unemployment for individuals with lower employability. This risk becomes more acute when the supply of graduates in the labour market exceeds the availability of graduate-level jobs, such as during economic slowdowns or when the substitute effects of technological change prevail over the complementary ones, even in higher-end occupations (Green & Henseke, 2021).

Thirdly, since the 1980s, governments have increasingly adopted target-driven management strategies within tertiary education. This shift, which marked a departure from the previously centralised and bureaucratic structures, aims to streamline operations, improve the efficiency of resource allocation, and focus HEIs on their core missions of education and research Capano, 2014; Capano & Pritoni, 2020). As a consequence, especially in North America and in Europe, there has been a significant expansion in the assessment of institutional performance, now incorporating indicators that measure graduate employability (Jackson & Bridgstock, 2018). Emphasis on outcome measurement via quantitative indicators has conferred a dual meaning on employability for HEIs. On one hand, when employability is used as a proxy for HEI performance, employability rankings drive access to public funding distributed on a meritocratic basis. On the other hand, employability becomes a strategic tool for enhancing the reputation of HEIs and gaining a competitive advantage in attracting both students and further funding opportunities. As a result, the formulation and implementation of an employability strategy have become indispensable for HEIs. Such a strategy provides a structured framework for improving graduates' employability skills and positioning HEIs effectively within the competitive landscape of higher education.

Most empirical studies on HEI employability strategies aim to classify the approaches adopted based on Holmes' influential paper (2013), which outlines three main approaches: possessional, positional, and processual. The possessional approach, long the dominant perspective on graduate employability (Burke *et al.*, 2017), suggests that employability emerges from specific personal skills and attributes that support career development. Strategies derived from this view detail codified employability requirements and design formal learning activities that signal the acquisition of desired skills to potential employers, often through formal credentials that supplement a HE diploma. Conversely, the positional approach frames employability as an understanding of the labour market that results from social and relational capital (Tomlinson, 2012). Strategies based on this approach focus on attracting and selecting elite candidates to activate a mutually reinforcing cycle between students' social networks and skills and HEI reputation, thereby reinforcing existing social hierarchies and perpetuating student population segmentation. Lastly, the processual approach conceptualises employability as a dynamic result of career self-management practices (Burke *et al.*, 2017; Okay-Somerville & Scholarios, 2017). This perspective emphasises the role of individual experiences in shaping a graduate identity, where graduates "act in ways that lead others to ascribe to them the identity of being a person worthy of being employed" (Holmes, 2013, p. 549). According to the processual approach HEIs can enhance graduate employability through both curricular and extracurricular activities aimed at developing self-awareness of individual capabilities, individual values, and their composition along a career path. This approach highlights the need for continuous development and adaptability and encourages HEIs to design programmes that assist students in actively managing their careers and developing a professional identity over time. By cultivating an environment that supports self-management and adaptability, HEIs can better equip graduates for the modern labour market, ensuring they possess not only the required skills but also the social and professional intelligence needed for success.

Empirical research into the HEI employability strategies identified by Holmes (2013) not only validates theoretical expectations but also reveals important correlations among strategy choices, student demographics, and institute reputation (Farenga and Quinlan, 2016). However, archetypal strategies are not evenly distributed: Okay-Somerville & Scholarios (2017) observe a prevalent adoption of strategies aligned with a processual approach. In addition, Bennet *et al.* (2017) report the presence of hybrid solutions alongside "pure" models.

In a more recent development, Hooley *et al.* (2023) explore Sultana's (2018) typology, which categorises career education into technocratic, humanistic, and emancipatory rationalities. They propose a novel tripartite classification of the perspectives that guide the development of HEI employability strategies. Technocratic rationalities reflect the possessional approach by focusing on refining graduates' skills to meet specific employer demands within the labour market. Humanistic rationalities recall Holmes' processual approach in their attention to developing an awareness of professional identity. However, humanistic rationalities extend beyond professional identity development to include the exploration of students' personal interests and abilities beyond work-related issues. Emancipatory rationalities adopt an even broader perspective, viewing students and graduates not merely as job seekers but as active agents of societal change. The objective of emancipatory rationalities is to equip individuals with the knowledge and skills to comprehend and potentially reform the labour market, in pursue of sustainable and dignified employment opportunities. Thus, employability emerges not only as preparation for economic participation but also as "a process of developing active citizens rather than just efficient labour market actors" (Hooley *et al.*, 2023, p. 15). This diversified perspective underlines the dynamic nature of HEI strategies, which reflect a spectrum of educational philosophies and societal aspirations that shape future workforce readiness and societal progress.

The empirical analysis by Hooley *et al.* (2023) concerns HEI attitude towards employability rather than the design and deployment of actual strategies. However, they also provided a preliminary empirical test based on repeated runs of interviews with careers service and academic staff in a sample of 18 HEIs from eight countries Hooley *et al.* (2023) classified the emerging rationalities as either technocratic or humanistic. Only one HEI seemed closer to an emancipatory rationality. In line with Bennet *et al.* (2017) the authors recognise that the boundaries between alternative approaches often tend to get blurred and acknowledge the existence of mixed solutions in a significant number of cases.

Current literature examining HEI employability strategies demonstrates a nuanced understanding of the diverse needs of students and graduates, as well as the complex dynamics of the graduate labour market. However, by assuming that a strategy exists classification studies often oversimplify the difficulties and uncertainties that HEIs face in designing their own path towards graduates' employability. More recent contributions challenge this notion by highlighting the fluidity of strategies and the non-linear relationship between strategy formulation and execution. Some scholars underscore discrepancies in perceptions of employability goals among HEI faculty (Sin *et al.*, 2019; Sin & Amaral, 2021), which lead to tensions between institutional policies and actual practices (Divan *et al.*, 2019). The adaptability of operational tools[1] (Bridgstock & Jackson, 2019) and the inherent trade-offs in implementing employability initiatives[2] (Jackson & Tomlison, 2022) further deepen these ambiguities.

Moreover, the prevalent use of short-term indicators of labour market outcomes to gauge employability goals perpetuates confusion between employability and employment, *i.e.* immediate job placement, both within HEIs and among the regulatory bodies in charge of evaluating HEI performance (Jackson & Bridgstock, 2018). This confusion undermines clarity regarding the true aims and content of strategic employability plans.

Exploring strategy formation can complement the existing classifications of employability strategies and offer additional insights into the conditions that support agreement on a cohesive and potentially effective approach to employability. Business literature has long highlighted the gap between management's plans and actual organisational practices. Mintzberg (1978) first introduced the concept of emergent strategies, describing coherent patterns of decisions and actions that arise, either partially or entirely, without explicit planning based on predefined goals.

In principle, in stable and favourable environments organisations adopt intended strategies that stem from clearly articulated intentions and are communicated to all members via structured plans (Mintzberg & Waters, 1985). However, the inherent imperfect rationality of decision-makers and the unpredictability of both internal dynamics and external factors require adaptation to accommodate imperfectly defined goals, communication challenges, opportunistic behaviours by organisation members, and unforeseen circumstances. Accordingly, real-world strategies distribute along a spectrum between purely intended strategies and entirely emergent ones, where consistent patterns of action emerge over time without deliberate planning. This continuum underlines the dynamic nature of strategy formation within organisations and highlights the need for flexibility and adaptive responses to achieve strategic objectives in complex environments.

Empirical research on strategy formation in business confirms the existence of a spectrum of hybrid approaches, ranging from planned to emergent strategies, shaped by both internal and external conditions (Idenburg, 1993; Slevin & Covin, 1997; Neugebauer *et al.*, 2016). Efrat *et al.* (2022) show that adopting an emergent strategy can alleviate tensions among stakeholders, provided the new strategy becomes fully embedded within the organisational framework. The importance of legitimising emergent strategies to achieve prospective targets is further stressed by Mirabeau & Maguire (2014), who suggest engaging organisation members and adapting structures through the creation of new teams, procedures, routines, and organisational goals.

The literature on HEI strategy has also contrasted planned and emergent approaches to uncover strategy formation processes in these organisations. A significant number of studies has identified the concurrent use of planned and emergent strategies (Meyer *et al.*, 2012; Frølich *et al.*, 2017; Zabotto & Alves Filho, 2019), especially in unpredictable settings (Mallon, 2019). Compared to business organisations or to more centralised public administrations, strong identity values, significant autonomy for academic staff, and diverse objectives across teaching, research, and community engagement increase the likelihood that changes in HEIs will trigger tensions among organisation members or units (Frølich et al., 2017). For this reason, an emergent approach to strategy formation is particularly appropriate for HEIs when new strategies challenge the institution's established identity (MacDonald, 2013) or when competing strategies present conflicting narratives (Holstein *et al.*, 2018).

Despite these insights on overall strategic approach, the exploration of emergent strategies within specific HEI domains remains limited. In the context of internationalisation, Soliman *et al.* (2019) demonstrate that emergent approaches can gain legitimacy by aligning with broader HEI strategies. In this view, formal planning complements strategy emergence by introducing new organisational languages that contribute to evolving organisational culture and embed new goals and procedures (Mallon, 2019). However, there is still a lack of studies focusing on the formation of employability strategies within HEIs. As employability becomes increasingly significant in higher education, it is important to understand how HEIs can effectively develop and implement strategies to improve graduate career and personal life outcomes.

DATA AND EMPIRICAL APPROACH

To study strategy formation processes by HEIs this chapter adopts a case study approach based on a multi-case method (Lijphart, 1975) of four public HEIs from Italy and Portugal. By linking observed phenomena with their environments and offering insights into how variables interact in specific contexts, case studies provide depth and context that quantitative methods may overlook (Yin, 2018). A case study approach is therefore particularly appropriate to appreciate strategy formation, which is intimately connected with the context and the people it originates from (Branicki *et al.*, 2019).

Several reasons justify a focus on Italy and Portugal. First, the case studies examined provide additional insight on HEI employability strategies outside the more explored experience of Anglo-Saxon countries. Second, the membership of both countries in the European Union (EU) ensures that all four case HEIs face a similar institutional framework, as the Bologna Process, agreed upon in 1999 and implemented by most EU states since 2006, has been creating a more cohesive and comparable system of higher education across Europe, promoting student mobility and ensuring quality and comparability of qualifications.

In both countries, the impact of the EU Bologna Process on the HE system has stimulated the debate on graduates' employability (European Commission, 2014; Sin *et al.*, 2019; Kroher *et al.*, 2021) due to the contrast between a growth rate of the tertiary-educated working-age population among the fastest in Europe and a notable decline in the wage premium of higher education (Green & Henseke, 2021). In addition, in both countries HEI employability strategies are influenced by the monitoring measures implemented by state agencies as part of the overall quality assurance of the HE system (European Commission, 2019). However, significant differences also exist. On one hand, while both countries' governments aimed to enhance the effectiveness and efficiency of their HE systems by implementing governance changes in HEIs, Capano & Pritoni (2020) argue that Italian HEIs face greater evaluation pressures that limit their autonomy, whereas Portuguese governments have placed stronger emphasis on granting autonomy to HEIs. On the other hand, the more stringent compliance requirements imposed on Italian HEIs contribute to the availability of systematic data that informs discussions on employability. This includes national-level regular labour market forecasts, regular graduate surveys, and work placement programs for all students (European Commission, 2019).

The original data was gathered from nine semi-structured interviews conducted in 2022. Interviews were held with academic and careers service staff in charge of providing employability services (Table 2) and concerned the meaning attributed to the concept of employability by the respondents' institution, changes in the importance of this concept, the actions undertaken to promote graduates' employability, the role played by the HEI and its stakeholders in employability development, and the indicators and tools used to gauge the achievement of employability goals. To maintain interviewees' anonymity, the subsequent sections of the paper will refer to each case HEI using an abbreviation of the originating country followed by a sequential number (*i.e.*, It1, It2, Pt1, and Pt2). In each HEI interviewees are identified by a letter that specifies their role within the organisation (P for members of the academic staff and A for members of the administrative staff) and a sequential number to discriminate between multiple participants in similar positions (Table 2).

The members of the research team, including the author of this paper, agreed on a three-step procedure to analyse the collected interviews. In the first step, each recorded interview was transcribed. In the second step, each researcher independently identified references to the primary drivers for engaging with employability, the institutional strategy, the actions taken to support graduate employability, and the challenges noted by the interviewees. The written grids created by each researcher were subsequently reviewed and integrated by the other members of the research team. Following Eisenhardt's (1989) method, the team then jointly discussed the findings to highlight key facts and resolve any differing perceptions.

Table 2. Case HEIs and interview participants

HEI	Academic staff	Career service staff
It1	P1 – Professor, Vice president for placement and internships	--
It2	P1 – Professor, Vice president for placement and internships P2 – Professor, Department delegate for recruitment and placement	A1 – Director
Pt1	P1 – Professor, Vice president for entrepreneurship and employability P2 – Professor, Faculty Dean	--
Pt2	P1 – Professor, Vice president for social engagement P2 – Professor, Faculty Dean for placement and internships	A1 – Director, Faculty level

In the context of this paper, interview transcripts and report grids were carefully reviewed to identify and outline the three key elements of the employability strategies that distinguish between planned and emergent strategies (Mintzberg, 1978; Mintzberg & Waters, 1985). These elements include intended objectives, communication plans and solutions aimed at establishing shared understanding of employability targets, and the actions related to the employability strategy.

The interviews were supplemented by additional information retrieved from the websites of each HEIs concerning HEI strategic plans and, when available, employability reports and data on academic and administrative organisational structures to deliver employability services. In line with past research (Farenga & Quinlan, 2016; Divan *et al.*, 2019), the adoption of a mixed method that integrates interviews and institutional documents allows to overcome the shortcomings of purely website-based analyses (*e.g.*, Bennet *et al.*, 2017), which risk overlooking the gap between intended and realised strategies by emphasising official narratives (Divan *et al.*, 2019).

The four case HEIs were selected to display similarities in the characteristics of the organisational environment and the organisational culture. All case HEIs are located in industrialised areas characterised by comparatively low unemployment rates and a high demand for HE-graduate skills. Despite those favourable conditions, all case HEIs compete with more reputed universities located in the main city of their respective regions.

In all cases the HEI mission focuses on serving the needs of local stakeholders, as local businesses compete with the more attractive careers and the higher wages offered to HE graduates in closer larger cities. The HEI mission is pursued by means of intense co-operation with businesses, public administrations, and students and their families, and is supported by an organisational culture that emphasises local networks and local resources. Interviewees reported intense external partnerships not only in research activities, but also in student recruitment, teaching, and placement.

However, the case HEIs still differ in structural dimensions, including size, impact as measured by international rankings, and specialisation (Table 3), allowing for the emergence of relationships among those dimensions and nature of the employability strategy (Eisenhardt, 1989). In addition, the two Portuguese HEIs reflect the duality of the Portuguese HE system, which includes research-oriented universities, such as Pt2, and polytechnics, which have a vocational mission and are more responsive to local economic needs, such as Pt1 (Tavares & Amaral, 2019).

Table 3. The case HEIs; Main features

HEI		It1	It2	Pt1	Pt2
Enrolled students (2022)		~21,000	~15,000	~6,000	~20,000
Decile of 2022 Scimago ranking [(a)]		5th	2nd	9th	2nd
Teaching and research domains	Humanities	X	X		X
	Economics	X	X		X
	Management	X	X	X	X
	Medicine and Health		X		X
	Science	X	X		X
	Engineering and Technology	X	X	X	X

[(a)] Scimago overall university ranking, https://www.scimagoir.com/

EMERGENT EMPLOYABILITY STRATEGIES: FINDINGS FROM MULTIPLE CASE STUDIES

The presentation of the outcomes from the four case studies is structured into three sections, each dedicated to one of the distinguishing factors between planned and emergent strategies (Mintzberg, 1978; Mintzberg & Waters, 1985). Accordingly, the following sections critically examine the strategic objectives, the communication plans and solutions, and the implementation approaches that characterise the employability strategies adopted by the case HEIs.

Strategic Employability Objectives

To gain insight into the employability goals pursued by the case HEIs the interviews preliminarily explored the understanding of this construct and its practical implementation in day-to-day practices. When asked to provide the meaning of employability according to their HEI, interviewees' definitions remind a mix of process and possessional perspectives (Holmes, 2013) that sometimes also evoke an emancipatory approach (Hooley et al., 2023).

The general meaning we attribute to the term 'employability' relates to the theme of helping or supporting students approaching graduation and graduates to understand the essential skills required to enter the job market [...], what is the most suitable path for one's profile and career, and also the characteristics specific to one's passions, as well as providing some more pragmatic support in preparing for the world of work, such as simulating job interviews or writing resumes (It1, P1).

Our mission is in that sense. To address immediate needs on one hand, but not to be subservient to immediate needs, rather to prepare [the students] for what is an industry of the future and with a future (Pt2, P1).

We don't just want to train individuals focused on meeting specific market needs, but we also want to educate citizens (Pt1, P2).

However, in several instances after the initial definition interviewees show a tendency to equate employability with employment, while in other cases an awareness emerges of a discrepancy between the understanding of staff involved in employability initiatives and that of the HEI top management.

First and foremost, we need to prepare graduates who are ready to meet the demands of the market (Pt2, A1).

Based on my experience, this university gives a very pragmatic meaning to the term employability, namely the number of students who find employment after graduation. I have not yet noticed, except among a few colleagues with whom I have worked on these issues, but certainly not within the governance, the meaning of 'we give our students the opportunity to start off on the right foot when they seek employment, we give them the opportunity to be happy in their work' (It2, P1).

A similar contrast between broader definitions and narrower operationalisations arises from official documents. Employability never features among the main concerns of the strategic plans published on the HEI websites, even if existing references suggest a 360-degree approach to the technical and human training of the future graduates. However, the declaration of operative targets tends to conflate employability with employment rates. For instance, the strategic plan of HEI Pt1 declares a willingness to promote employability by means of "a clear focus on fostering critical and independent thinking [and] active citizenship [...] through education", while all indicators chosen to gauge employability improvements concern graduates' short-term employment rate. In a similar way, the "Employability reports" periodically provided by HEI Pt2 rather concern employment and unemployment rates by graduates' discipline areas.

In summary, while the intended targets of HEIs emphasise graduate employment, interviewed staff tends to perceive employability objectives in a broader sense, closely aligned with the socio-educational mission of their institution.

The standards set by national agencies for HE evaluation may play a role in the identification of employability official targets with indicators of graduates' employment rates. Both ANVUR, the Italian agency, and A3ES, the Portuguese one, include employment rates after graduation among the indicators used for the periodical assessment of study programs, thus focusing the attention of HEIs on those measures.

Communication of Employability Objectives

The interviews did not highlight specific initiatives aimed at communicating employability targets to internal and external stakeholders.

The university should be a bit more aware of the need to promote [employability] initiatives not only among students but also among faculty members. There should be a more significant communication plan to let everyone know about these initiatives, and perhaps there should be more collaboration with the faculty (It2, A1).

The HEI strategic plans and, above all, the structure and the resources allocated to the units that coordinate and deliver employability actions therefore seem to be the main tools to share employability intended and unintended objectives.

In all case HEIs the organisation of employability actions is based on three pillars: career services to manage structured and repetitive activities such as internships or career days; academic staff in charge of managing employability projects at the HEI or at the faculty/department level; and all the remining members of the academic staff variously engaged in deploying either co-ordinated or individually planned employability actions.

The current organisation of formal employability actions reflects the legacy of a traditional focus on graduates' placement, as apparent from the job titles of academic staff in Table 2. Faculty and department delegates are expected to co-ordinate with HEI vice-presidents and with centralised career services but in the case of HEI Pt2, whose strategic plan acknowledges "a natural tension between a common mission and the specialised projects" pursued by discipline-specific faculties. Accordingly, faculty delegates enjoy higher autonomy and co-ordinate with faculty-level education and career services.

In all case HEIs, institution-wide procedures often emerge from the post-hoc rationalisation of solutions and procedures that initially originated at a decentralised level.

Until some time ago, the departments themselves were the ones who, in some way, promoted [employability] initiatives. Not so much my office, not so much the vice-presidency for entrepreneurship and employability (Pt1, P1).

A lot of bottom-up work is also being done, I would say, to begin socialising the cultural change associated with employability (It1, P1).

The procedures governing career services appear to be leaner and more consolidated in Italian HEIs, also due to their membership in AlmaLaurea. AlmaLaurea is a consortium of 80 Italian universities that offers a shared platform for managing student internships and post-graduation placements. In addition, the consortium conducts regular surveys on graduates' labour market outcomes one, three, and five years after graduation. Interviews with staff from the two Portuguese HEIs consistently emphasise the challenges resulting from the absence of such services or their fragmented distribution across faculties and departments.

What I intend to do is an observatory on employability [...] At the moment, we don't have indicators. That is the big problem (Pt1, P1).

We have some planned projects that we believe will be of great help, such as a database and new programs that allow us to directly post offers, reducing our dependence on the dean's office. These are always things that need to be negotiated... (Pt2, A1).

All interviewees are aware that formal delegates for employability manage and oversee only a minority of the existing initiatives, which are autonomously developed also by members of the academic staff and by career service officers. This is recognised as a valuable source of creativity, which, if supported by well-structured communication plans, could become a systematic resource for fostering innovation in employability initiatives and facilitating the selection and dissemination of best practices.

I feel that within the university there are many interesting initiatives related to career guidance, so we should work together more as a group, building a stronger network (It2, A1).

Certainly, there are many department-level initiatives that may not necessarily be specifically designed under the umbrella of outgoing guidance, but they connect students with local organisations and companies (It1, P1).

In my opinion, what is lacking in our university is more storytelling among one another (It2, P2).

What I want to do is make businesses and the academic community aware that there are protocols here that can be used in support of the initiatives we want to undertake. If we don't know those protocols exist, it's hard for us to take advantage of them (Pt1, P1).

Another common point arising from the interviews concerns the complaints about the limited resources allocated to employability actions in terms of budget and personnel, and the lack of recognition associated with the management of employability projects. These remarks confirm that the case HEIs still demonstrate a formal commitment to graduates' employability rather than integrating it into their strategic plans. They also reflect the mixed emotions of the personnel involved, torn between the passion of being part of employability projects and the stress and fatigue of working with limited resources and vague incentives.

Every year [the career day] brings in a significant amount of profit for the University, and every year it's a battle to allocate part of that money to further placement activities (It2, P1).

We need more people. We cannot monitor a graduate's journey (Pt2, P1).

There is a severe understaffing issue because the office is called 'placement', but in reality, it also supports internships (It2, P1).

We are just creating more work. With each event we are just creating more work for ourselves (Pt2, A1).

What happens with professors and researchers is that we do not earn more based on the number of projects with companies [...] We all do this out of mission and passion (Pt2, P1).

Alongside with additional work overloads the interviewees at the smaller and younger case HEI, Pt1, openly report the importance of personnel engagement and self-involvement as essential tools to support employability projects.

The institutions are the people [...]. People need to fall in love with the project, feel it, get involved, because this requires much more than just regular working hours (Pt1, P2).

Interviewees also acknowledge that a loose definition of employability targets and a lack of a formal commitment as defined by official communication plans can lead to a reduction in employability efforts in case new targets compete for limited available resources.

At the moment, this area [of employability] is somewhat sidelined. This area was part of a unit in charge of communication. What happened is that we undertook an ambitious project with other European universities, which somehow directed all resources towards internationalisation actions. As a result, employability ended up being somewhat neglected (Pt1, P1).

Overall, the lack of a communication plan on HEI employability targets, the limited resources allocated to employability initiatives, and the large use of ex-post rationalisation instead of preliminary planning in employability practices communicate the secondary role attached to employability by case HEIs. Communication gaps involve both top-down and bottom-up information flows, with the risk of balkanising actions and perceptions, besides demotivating staff and missing potential synergies.

Employability-related Actions

Collected interviews and official records document a large number of actions, projects, and events aimed at fostering graduates' employability. Alongside with more consolidated initiatives repeated in time, such as career days or job interview simulations, reported actions include also more innovative and creative projects such as the development of a library of on-demand videos on entrepreneurship and employability (It2), inter-departmental soft-skill training experiences (It2 and Pt2), or mentoring by alumni (It1, It2, Pt1, and Pt2).

Compared to other Italian and Portuguese institutes of tertiary education the case HEIs place a much larger emphasis on their engagement with business companies and public administrations also in non-technical degree programmes. With the exclusion of embedded learning, students and graduates' participation in employability initiatives is always voluntary.

In each case HEI the range of embedded, co-curricular, and extra-curricular employability actions spans across all the typologies identified in the literature[3] (Kinash et al., 2016; Bridgstock & Jackson, 2019). Intra-institution variety and inter-institution similarity reflect a rational approach to the design of employability interventions already noted by Hooley et al. (2023), who question whether "different [underlying perspectives] actually result in qualitatively different provision, or whether such debates actually serve as ideological cover for similar practices" (p. 16).

If the analysis of the type and nature of implemented employability initiatives provides no insight into the peculiarities of the case HEI employability strategies, understanding may come from searching for a pattern in decisions and actions concerning employability. A common characteristics of the case HEIs is the trust demonstrated by top management towards the unwavering commitment of both academic and administrative staff members in aligning employability initiatives with the institution's core values and mission. This approach can be observed in the development of new lines of action. Participants in the interviews are highly confident in putting forward new ideas and prospecting their implementation.

We are free to choose the initiatives we want (Pt2, A1).

Certainly, companies need an additional support, so we help them not only to understand how to manage our job market platform but also to identify profiles that could be more aligned with their job offers [...] It is an initiative of our office because I believe it is essential that we have a good understanding not only of our degree programmes but also of the employment prospects for our graduates when interacting with companies (It2, A1).

We want to explore initiatives that can facilitate, in a way, the customisation and personalisation of the student's path, incorporating skills that may also come from other parts of the university and other degree programmes (It1, P1).

At the same time, large delegation and autonomy rule also the expansion and continuous improvement of existing initiatives.

We have been the first service to enter the university's quality system, so for many years now, all activities have been recorded from start to finish, capturing satisfaction levels, participation rates, and more [...] We have all the data we need, among other things, to understand how to redesign the activity for the following year, if any modifications are necessary (It2, A1).

We are considering the initiatives and processes that have been implemented [...], and therefore, an incremental re-evaluation of the actions that are already in place. For example, rethinking career days, re-evaluating internships, re-considering the entire network of relationships with local organisations, and beyond, to understand if there is anything missing [...], in order to expand and strengthen this network or seek synergies (It1, P1).

We have an innovative competition in which we evaluate students' entrepreneurial projects [...] We haven't been doing a follow-up afterwards, and I intend for it to happen. What I aim for is that, in some way, if the students wish to progress with this idea into something more structured, we can also provide support to these students (Pt2, P2).

Nevertheless, autonomy can prove challenging for decision-makers, especially under high uncertainty or when, as in the case of academic staff, delegates may miss field-specific competences. Underlining the need for more information and training on employability practices and approaches, two academic interviewees manifested a need to compare their own perspectives and choices with those of colleagues from other HEIs.

I would also be curious, if I may ask, to understand the situation of other universities both in Italy and abroad, as I have noticed that the interview project also involves Portugal. (It1, P1).

I am also interested in being involved in these types of interviews to better understand what is being done (Pt1, P1).

The analysis of the employability-enhancing actions implemented across the case HEIs show a diverse array of initiatives which reflect an alignment with the institutions' core values and mission. The trust placed by top management in both academic and administrative staff fosters an environment where new ideas are actively pursued and implemented with confidence. However, the recognised need for more field-specific expertise signals the complexity of shaping effective employability strategies.

DISCUSSION

The exam of the case HEIs in this study contributes to the debate on HEI employability strategies in two ways. Firstly, it shows that despite the decades elapsed since its initial introduction, the discourse on employability is still evolving and its integration in the strategic plans of HEIs cannot be taken for granted. Secondly, the analysis proposed suggests that when employability strategies are still under development, shifting from strategy classification to strategy formation can provide valuable insights to uncover emerging perspectives and address potential contrasts more effectively.

As demonstrated by the exam of the case HEI strategy plans, Employability still represents a secondary issue in the agenda of the case HEIs, irrespective of the national background and the nature of the institution (research university, as It1, It2, and Pt2, or teaching university, as Pt1). Employability has a limited space in the HEIs strategic plans, which rather indulge in the brilliant employment rates achieved by graduates. When employability is explicitly addressed, there is a notable contrast between the declared perspective, which aligns closely with a process/emancipatory approach, and the operational targets that tend to conflate employability with employment. Moreover, the strategic plans of the case HEIs never specify the actions and plans that are supposed to result in the intended employability targets.

The limited importance attributed to employability by official documents is reflected in the insufficient allocation of resources to achieve the intended targets. Contrary to recommendations in the literature (Mirabeau & McGuire, 2014), the adoption of employability goals did not entail the creation of new organisation units or the development of new procedures. Academic and administrative staff members already in charge of internship and placement duties are now responsible of employability actions. An exception to this pattern is observed in the case of HEI Pt1, where a dedicated organisational unit for entrepreneurship and employability was established a few months prior to our interview to centralise previously scattered responsibilities. Furthermore, the interviews revealed a lack of proactive planning in developing procedures to govern employability-related processes. The case HEIs primarily rely on adapting procedures that were initially developed at decentralised levels or responding to the demands of external stakeholders, such as national evaluation agencies or AlmaLaurea in the case of the two Italian HEIs.

The interviews revealed concern on the low budget assigned to employability actions, primarily limited to administrative services' wages[4], which were unanimously declared as understaffed. In addition, all the case HEIs invest limited resources to communicate top-down employability targets and initiatives, as well as to collect bottom-up information on the numerous projects and actions carried out by academic staff and career services alongside their regular responsibilities. Inadequate communication plans and channels negatively affect participation rates, thereby diminishing the effectiveness of planned actions. They also lead to duplicate efforts, loss of synergies, and risk of demotivating the initiators by limiting recognition of their efforts.

Nevertheless, the employability actions mentioned in interviews and official documents go well beyond the intended targets of graduates' employment levels. Despite limited resources, inadequate communication, and poor training in employability scope and tools, both high-level academic delegates, career service officers, and members of the academic staff actively participate in designing and delivering clusters of actions that coherently target employability from a process perspective (Holmes, 2013). Besides operative tools to bridge the gap between education and work such as career days, assistance with curriculum writing and job interview preparation, or placement services, students are provided with various opportunities that target the development of a more mature approach to work and career. These opportunities include internships, immersive courses that foster the development of both soft and technical skills, talks and seminars with entrepreneurs, managers, and public officers, problem-solving on real-world cases, participation in national or international contests, and the chance to collaborate with students from different degree programmes to explore technical or societal challenges. Furthermore, all the case HEIs are either planning or already offering mentoring services to students and graduates, facilitated by alumni.

The internalisation of the HEI mission by organisation members, which centres on serving the needs of the local stakeholders, provides an explanation for the coherence of decentralised efforts even under weak central guidance and control. Graduates' employability in the broader sense of lifelong employment and career success emerges as an unintended yet aligned objective that is consistent with the overall goals of the HEIs. Soliman *et al.* (2019) propose the integration of an area-specific strategy within the broader HEI strategy to facilitate communication and acceptance. However, strategy formation at the case HEIs appears to proceed in the opposite way. By grounding non-budgeted actions into the values and norms of their institution the members of the organisation establish the foundation for the future design of an intended employability strategy that aligns with the comprehensive strategy of the HEI. It can be argued that emergent strategies are developing at all the case HEIs, although there remains a lack of clarity regarding this awareness among both top management and staff members.

The four case studies demonstrate that an employability strategy can develop even without explicit planning. At the same time, they also shed light on critical factors that impact the long-term viability of this approach. The continuity of academic and administrative staff's engagement with the employability discourse and the sustainability of undertaken initiatives may be questioned by the persisting lack of financial, organisational, and institutional support. While widespread organisational values centred on students and businesses' needs have so far driven the proliferation of essentially coherent initiatives, strong leadership is required to transform emerging processes into a deliberate strategy (Mirabeau & Maguire, 2014). Additionally, strong leadership is necessary to embed consistent employability practices throughout the institution (Blackmore *et al.*, 2016) and manage the tensions that naturally arise when choices must be made between competing approaches or procedures developed in different parts of the same organisation (Holstein *et al.*, 2018). A clear articulation of organisational strategy is important, (Mirabeau & Maguire, 2014) because the socialisation of strategic plans not only makes goals and actions explicit but also revitalises organisational values and rituals, guiding organisations in new directions (Mallon, 2019).

The four case studies confirm the impact of the external environment in driving the path of an emergent strategy (Mintzberg, 1978; Mintzberg & Waters, 1985). In all cases the high demand for graduates by the local labour market conceals potential issues regarding the long-term labour market outcomes of graduates from the examined HEIs and redirects HEI top management's focus away from employability. The shared emphasis on meeting the needs of the territory facilitates employability initiatives that capitalise on interactions with local stakeholders and reinforces the existing culture of mutual collaboration. It has to be noted that the autonomy of decentralised decision-makers and loosely structured budget and plans provide flexibility in response to unexpected events that may require operative changes or engaging in a new round of negotiation with external and internal partners.

Accountability to national agencies responsible for evaluating the HE system plays an important role in prioritising graduates' employment rates within the intended targets of HEI strategic plans. The Italian ANVUR includes the percentage of graduates in employment one and three years after completing their studies among the indicators for the periodical assessment of degree programmes, while the Portuguese A3ES requires the reporting of the unemployment rate[5].

A difference between Italian and Portuguese case HEIs surfaces in relation to national information systems, whose availability conditions the prioritisation of employability initiatives. In the interviews, all Portuguese participants expressed frustration over the absence of national data on graduates' careers, leading each HEI to invest in developing their own dataset and collection system and hindering benchmarking with other institutions. They also reported investing in HEI-specific platforms to facilitate the matching between the demand and supply of student internships and graduate jobs. In contrast, membership in the AlmaLaurea consortium grants the two Italian HEIs access to periodic and highly informative surveys on the professional paths and satisfaction levels reported by graduates from all partner institutions. Additionally, AlmaLaurea provides the software infrastructure for managing internships and job placements. Consequently, these HEIs can direct their resources and efforts towards providing additional services and enhancing existing ones.

FUTURE RESEARCH DIRECTIONS

This chapter provides an exploratory analysis based on a limited number of case studies. Future research could gain more insights into HEI employability strategies and the internal and external factors that enable or hinder their development by examining more and more diverse case studies across a wider range of countries.

Two important dimensions of employability strategy were not addressed in the interviews, indicating further areas for future research. First, integrating employability initiatives into regular curricula and recognising the significant role of lecturers in imparting employability skills highlights the need to connect employability strategies with pedagogical approaches (Cook, 2022). Further efforts are needed to develop training initiatives that support active and self-aware engagement in employability actions by lecturers. Second, considering the diverse backgrounds of students and alumni, a one-size-fits-all employability strategy is unlikely to be effective (Okay-Somerville & Scholarios, 2022). Employability strategies should explicitly account for student diversity to ensure their effectiveness.

CONCLUSION

This study analysed the employability strategies of four HEIs in Italy and Portugal, identifying whether their approaches were planned or emergent. Based on interviews with academic and administrative staff, and supported by official documents and reports, the case studies revealed that the case institutions predominantly manifest an emergent approach. Employability strategies are arising via the ex-post rationalisation of initially fragmented ideas and initiatives. Despite displaying a partial divergence between intended and realised targets, those emergent strategies often surpass the modest goals initially set by the institutions.

The development process of the observed emergent employability strategies is uneven, influenced by both internal and external factors. Frequent stops and starts occur, driven by the need to manage ongoing tensions between official declarations and individual understandings, and between centralised and decentralised management of initiatives and resources. So far, voluntarism and alignment with institutional vision and values have helped navigate these tensions. However, resource scarcity and inadequate planning and leadership pose risks to the long-term sustainability of these employability initiatives.

This study adds to the existing literature on HEI employability strategies, particularly by offering detailed case studies from Italy and Portugal, regions where this area is still under-researched. It also contributes to the broader discourse on organisational strategy by shifting the focus from classification to the formation of strategies. Specifically, this chapter extends the analysis of strategy formation in HEIs beyond overall and internationalisation strategies to include employability strategies.

By showing that issues such as poor coordination, heavy reliance on voluntarism, and resource scarcity could jeopardise the success of current employability approaches, this study provides useful insights to help HEI managers design better-grounded employability strategies aligned with the overall institutional strategy. Developing more formal and explicit plans could enhance HEI employability performance. However, caution is necessary before implementing external mandates for intended employability strategies, as lessons from other countries suggest that these can lead to discrepancies between intended and realised strategies, creating tensions between HEI management and staff (Kinash *et al.*, 2016; Bridgstock & Jackson, 2019; Divan *et al.*, 2019). Rather than external mandates, public investment is essential to increase awareness of the importance and the contents of graduate employability among all stakeholders. Public investment is also important to address the resource shortages currently faced by HEIs, thus supporting the rationalisation and socialisation of emergent strategies and fostering a transformative change that may lead to better outcomes.

This chapter provides an exploratory analysis based on a limited number of case studies. Future research could gain more insights into HEI employability strategies and the internal and external factors that enable or hinder their development by examining more and more diverse case studies across a wider range of countries.

Two important dimensions of employability strategy were not addressed in the interviews, indicating further areas for future research. First, integrating employability initiatives into regular curricula and recognising the significant role of lecturers in imparting employability skills highlights the need to connect employability strategies with pedagogical approaches (Cook, 2022). Further efforts are needed to develop training initiatives that support active and self-aware engagement in employability actions by lecturers. Second, considering the diverse backgrounds of students and alumni, a one-size-fits-all employability strategy is unlikely to be effective (Okay-Somerville & Scholarios, 2022). Employability strategies should explicitly account for student diversity to ensure their effectiveness.

ACKNOWLEDGMENT

This research was supported by the Portuguese Foundation for Science and Technology (Fundação para a Ciência e a Tecnologia) under the project BRIGHET [grant PTDC/SOC-SOC/30016/2017]. The author wishes to thank the anonymous participants at the four case institutions. I also appreciate valuable help and collaboration from the team members of the BRIGHET project, and particularly from Emília Araújo, Fátima Suleman, and Pedro Videira.

This chapter is a revised version of an earlier research paper: Sgobbi F. (2023), "How intentional are the employability strategies of Higher Education Institutions?", DINÂMIA'CET Working Papers 2023-02, Lisbon: DINÂMIA'CET-Iscte, DOI: 10.15847/dinamiacet-iul.wp.2023.02.

REFERENCES

A3ES (2018). *Guião para a autoavaliação. Ciclo de estudos em funcionamento (Ensino Universitário e Politécnico)*. https://a3es.pt/sites/default/files/Gui%C3%A3o%20ACEF-PERA%202018-2023_PT_V1.0.pdf

Altmann, S., Falk, A., Jäger, S., & Zimmermann, F. (2018). Learning about job search: A field experiment with job seekers in Germany. *Journal of Public Economics*, 164(C), 33–49. DOI: 10.1016/j.jpubeco.2018.05.003

Anderson, V., & Tomlinson, M. (2021). Signaling standout graduate employability: The employer perspective. *Human Resource Management Journal*, 31(3), 675–693. DOI: 10.1111/1748-8583.12334

ANVUR. (2017). *Linee Guida AVA per l'accreditamento periodico delle Sedi e dei corsi di studio universitari*. https://www.anvur.it/attivita/ava/accreditamento-periodico/linee-guida-per-laccreditamento-periodico

Bennet, D., Knight, E., Divan, A., Kuchel, L., Horn, J., van Reyk, D., & Burke da Silva, K. (2017). How do research-intensive universities portray employability strategies? A review of their websites. *Australian Journal of Career Development*, 26(2), 52–61. DOI: 10.1177/1038416217714475

Blackmore, P., Bulaitis, Z. H., Jackman, A. H., & Tan, E. (2016). *Employability in Higher Education: A review of practice and strategies around the world*. Pearson Efficacy & Research. Pearson Education.

Bridgstock, R., & Jackson, D. (2019). Strategic institutional approaches to graduate employability: Navigating meanings, measurements and what really matters. *Journal of Higher Education Policy and Management*, 41(5), 468–484. DOI: 10.1080/1360080X.2019.1646378

Burke, C., Scurry, T., Blenkinsopp, J., & Graley, K. (2017). Critical perspectives on graduate employability. In Tomlinson, M., & Holmes, L. (Eds.), *Graduate employability in context* (pp. 87–107). Palgrave Macmillan. DOI: 10.1057/978-1-137-57168-7_4

Capano, G. (2014). The re-regulation of the Italian university system through quality assurance. A mechanistic perspective. *Policy and Society*. 33, 199-213. DOI: . 001DOI: 10.1016/j.polsoc.2014.08

Capano, G., & Pritoni, A. (2020). What really happens in higher education governance? Trajectories of adopted policy instruments in higher education over time in 16 European countries. *Higher Education*, 80(5), 989–1010. DOI: 10.1007/s10734-020-00529-y

Cook, E. J. (2022). A narrative review of graduate employability models: Their paradigms, and relationships to teaching and curricula. *Journal of Teaching and Learning for Graduate Employability*, 13(1), 37–64. DOI: 10.21153/jtlge2022vol13no1art1483

Deming, D. J., & Noray, K. L. (2020). Earnings Dynamics, Changing job Skills and STEM Careers. *The Quarterly Journal of Economics*, 135(4), 1965–2005. DOI: 10.1093/qje/qjaa021

Divan, A., Knight, E., Bennett, D., & Bell, K. (2019). Marketing graduate employability: Understanding the tensions between institutional practice and external messaging. *Journal of Higher Education Policy and Management*, 41(5), 485–499. DOI: 10.1080/1360080X.2019.1652427

Efrat, K., Souchon, A. L., Wald, A., Hughes, P., & Cai, J. (2022). Mitigating coopetition tensions: The forgotten formation stage. *European Management Review*, 19(4), 527–548. DOI: 10.1111/emre.12498

Eisenhardt, K.M. (1989). Building Theories from Case Study Research. *Academy of Management Review*. 14(4), 532-550. DOI: . 4308385DOI: 10.5465/amr.1989

European Commission/EACEA/Eurydice (2014). *Modernisation of Higher Education in Europe: Access, Retention and Employability 2014*. Eurydice Report. Publications Office of the European Union. DOI: DOI: 10.2797/72146

European Commission/EACEA/Eurydice (2019). *Structural Indicators for Monitoring Education and Training Systems in Europe – 2019: Overview of major reforms since 2015*. Eurydice Report. Publications Office of the European Union. DOI:DOI: 10.2797/256641

Fakunle, O., & Higson, H. (2021). Interrogating theoretical and empirical approaches to em+ployability in different global regions. *Higher Education Quarterly*, 75(4), 525–534. DOI: 10.1111/hequ.12345

Farenga, S. A., & Quinlan, K. M. (2016). Classifying university employability strategies: Three case studies and implications for practice and research. *Journal of Education and Work*, 29(7), 767–787. DOI: 10.1080/13639080.2015.1064517

Frølich, N., Huisman, J., & Stensaker, B. (2017). Understanding strategy practices in universi-ties. In Bleiklie, I., Enders, J., & Lepori, B. (Eds.), *Managing universities: Policy and organizational change from a Western European comparative perspective* (pp. 167–188). Palgrave Macmillan. DOI: 10.1007/978-3-319-53865-5_7

Green, F., & Henseke, G. (2021). Europe's evolving graduate labour markets: Supply, demand, underemployment and pay. *Journal for Labour Market Research*, 55(2), 2. Advance online publication. DOI: 10.1186/s12651-021-00288-y

Holmes, L. (2013). Competing perspectives on graduate employability: possession, position or process?. *Studies in Higher Education*. 38(4), 538-554. DOI: .587140DOI: 10.1080/03075079.2011

Holstein, J., Starkey, K., & Wright, M. (2018). Strategy and narrative in higher education. *Strategic Organization*, 16(1), 61–91. DOI: 10.1177/1476127016674877

Hooley, T. J., Bennett, D., & Knight, E. B. (2023). Rationalities that underpin employability provision in higher education across eight countries. *Higher Education*, 86(5), 1003–1023. Advance online publication. DOI: 10.1007/s10734-022-00957-y

Humburg, M., de Grip, A., & van der Velden, R. (2017). Which skills protect graduates against a slack labour market? *International Labour Review*, 156(1), 25–43. DOI: 10.1111/j.1564-913X.2015.00046.x

Idenburg, P. J. (1993). Four styles of strategy development. *Long Range Planning*, 26(6), 132–137. DOI: 10.1016/0024-6301(93)90215-2

Jackson, D., & Bridgstock, R. (2018). Evidencing student success in the contemporary world-of-work: Renewing our thinking. *Higher Education Research & Development*, 37(5), 984–998. DOI: 10.1080/07294360.2018.1469603

Jackson, D., & Bridgstock, R. (2021). What actually works to enhance graduate employabil-ity? The relative value of curricular, co-curricular, and extra-curricular learning and paid work. *Higher Education*, 81(4), 723–739. DOI: 10.1007/s10734-020-00570-x

Jackson, D., & Tomlinson, M. (2022). The relative importance of work experience, extra-curricular and university-based activities on student employability. *Higher Education Research & Development*, 41(4), 1119–1135. DOI: 10.1080/07294360.2021.1901663

Kinash, S., Crane, L., Judd, M., & Knight, C. (2016). Discrepant stakeholder perspectives on graduate employability strategies. *Higher Education Research & Development*, 35(5), 951–967. DOI: 10.1080/07294360.2016.1139555

Kroher, M., Leuze, K., Thomsen, S. L., & Trunzer, J. (2021). Did the 'Bologna Process' Achieve Its Goals? 20 Years of Empirical Evidence on Student Enrolment, Study Success and Labour Market Outcomes. *IZA Discussion Paper*, No. 14757. IZA.

Lijphart, A. (1975). The Comparable-cases Strategy in Comparative Research. *Comparative Political Studies*, 8(2), 158–177. DOI: 10.1177/001041407500800203

MacDonald, G.P. (2013). Theorizing university identity development: multiple perspectives and common goals. *High Education*. 65, 153.166. DOI: DOI: 10.1007/s10734-012-9526-3

Mallon, W. T. (2019). Does Strategic Planning Matter? *Academic Medicine*, 94(10), 1408–1411. DOI: 10.1097/ACM.0000000000002848 PMID: 31219813

McGuinness, S., Pouliakas, K., & Redmond, P. (2021). Skills displacing technological change and its impact on jobs: Challenging technological alarmism? *Economics of Innovation and New Technology*. Advance online publication. DOI: 10.1080/10438599.2021.1919517

Meyer, V.Jr, Pascucci, L., & Mangolin, L. (2012). Gestão estratégica: Um exame de práticas em universidades privadas. *Revista de Administração Pública*, 46(1), 49–70. DOI: 10.1590/S0034-76122012000100004

Mintzberg, H. (1978). Patterns in Strategy Formation. *Management Science*, 24(9), 934–948. DOI: 10.1287/mnsc.24.9.934

Mintzberg, H., & Waters, J. A. (1985). Of Strategies, Deliberate and Emergent. *Strategic Management Journal*, 6(3), 257–272. DOI: 10.1002/smj.4250060306

Mirabeau, L., & Maguire, S. (2014). From Autonomous Strategic Behavior to Emergent Strategy. *Strategic Management Journal*, 35(8), 1202–1229. DOI: 10.1002/smj.2149

Neugebauer, F., Figge, F., & Hahn, T. (2016). Planned or Emergent Strategy Making? Exploring the Formation of Corporate Sustainability Strategies. *Business Strategy and the Environment*, 25(5), 323–336. DOI: 10.1002/bse.1875

Okay-Somerville, B., & Scholarios, D. (2017). Position, possession or process? Understanding objective and subjective employability during university-to-work transitions. *Studies in Higher Education*, 42(7), 1275–1291. DOI: 10.1080/03075079.2015.1091813

Okay-Somerville, B., & Scholarios, D. (2022). Focused for Some, Exploratory for Others: Job Search Strategies and Successful University-to-Work Transitions in the Context of Labor Market Ambiguity. *Journal of Career Development*, 49(1), 126–143. DOI: 10.1177/08948453211016058

Saito, E., & Pham, T. (2021). A comparative institutional analysis on strategies deployed by Australian and Japanese universities to prepare students for employment. *Higher Education Research & Development*, 40(5), 1085–1099. DOI: 10.1080/07294360.2020.1800596

Sgobbi, F. (2023), How intentional are the employability strategies of Higher Education Institutions? *DINÂMIA'CET Working Papers*, 2023-02. Lisbon: DINÂMIA'CET-Iscte, DOI: DOI: 10.15847/dinamiacet-iul.wp.2023.02

Sin, C., & Amaral, A. (2021). Academics' and employers' perceptions about responsibilities for employability and their initiatives towards its development. *Higher Education*, 73(1), 97–111. DOI: 10.1007/s10734-016-0007-y

Sin, C., Tavares, O., & Amaral, A. (2019). Accepting employability as a purpose of higher education? Academics' perceptions and practices. *Studies in Higher Education*, 44(6), 920–931. DOI: 10.1080/03075079.2017.1402174

Slevin, D. P., & Covin, J. G. (1997). Strategy Formation Patterns, Performance, and the Significance of Context. *Journal of Management*, 23(2), 189–209. DOI: 10.1177/014920639702300205

Soliman, S., Anchor, J., & Taylor, D. (2019). The international strategies of universities: deliberate or emergent?. *Studies in Higher Education*. 44(8), 1413-1424. DOI: . 2018.1445985DOI: 10.1080/03075079

Sultana, R. G. (2018). Precarity, austerity and the social contract in a liquid world: career guidance mediating the citizen and the state. In Hooley, T., Sultana, R. G., & Thomsen, R. (Eds.), *Career Guidance for Social Justice: Contesting Neoliberalism* (pp. 63–76). Routledge.

Tomlinson, M. (2007). Graduate employability and student attitudes and orientations to the la-bour market. *Journal of Education and Work*, 20(4), 285–304. DOI: 10.1080/13639080701650164

Tomlinson, M. (2012). Graduate Employability: A Review of Conceptual and Empirical Themes. *Higher Education Policy*, 25(4), 407–431. DOI: 10.1057/hep.2011.26

Yin, R. K. (2018). *Case Study Research and Applications: Design and Methods* (6th ed.). Sage.

Zabotto, M. A. C., & Alves Filho, A. G. (2019). Formulation and monitoring of strategic plans in a public university: An analysis based on strategy as practice. *Gestão & Produção*, 26(2), e2546. DOI: 10.1590/0104-530x2546-19

ADDITIONAL READING

Blackmore, P., Blackwell, R., & Edmondson, M. (2016). *Tackling wicked issues: Prestige and employment outcomes in the teaching excellence framework*. Higher Education Policy Institute.

Brennan, J., Edmunds, R., Houston, M., Jary, D., Lebeau, Y., Osborne, M., & Richardson, J. (2010). *Improving what is learned at university: An exploration of the social and organisational diversity of university education*. Routledge. DOI: 10.4324/9780203863237

Official Journal of the European Union (2009). *Council conclusions of 12 May 2009 on a strategic framework for European cooperation in education and training ('ET 2020')*. OJ 2009/C 119/02, 28.5.2009.

Official Journal of the European Union (2012). *Council conclusions of 11 May 2012 on the employability of graduates from education and training*. OJ 2012/C 169/04, 15.6.2012.

Teixeira, P. N., & Shin, J. C. (Eds.). (2020). *The international encyclopedia of higher education systems and institutions*. Springer Dordrecht., DOI: 10.1007/978-94-017-8905-9

KEY TERMS AND DEFINITIONS

Emergent strategy: A coherent pattern of decisions and actions that arise in an organisation, either partially or entirely, without explicit planning based on predefined goals.

Employability: The set of skills, knowledge, attributes, and personal qualities that enable an individual to find, maintain, and succeed in a job. Employability goes beyond the qualifications for a specific role, as it also includes the ability to adapt to changes in the workplace, continuously develop professional skills, and make meaningful contributions to organisations and communities.

Employment: A relationship between an individual (the employee) and an organisation or individual (the employer), in which the employee performs work or services in exchange for compensation, typically in the form of wages or a salary.

Intended strategy: The plans and goals that an organization consciously formulates and aims to implement.

Higher education: The stage of learning that occurs after secondary education, typically provided by universities, colleges, and similar institutions that offer academic degrees, diplomas, or certificates. According to the International Standard Classification of Education (ISCED), developed by UNESCO, higher education corresponds to levels 6, 7, and 8, which cover bachelor's, master's, and doctoral degrees, respectively.

Higher education institution: Any organisation that provides education beyond secondary schooling, typically offering courses or programs that lead to a qualification at the tertiary level. Higher education institutions include universities, colleges, polytechnics, and similar institutions. According to the International Standard Classification of Education (ISCED), developed by UNESCO, the qualifications provided by higher education institutions correspond to ISCED level 5 (Short-cycle tertiary education), 6 (Bachelor's or equivalent level), 7 (Master's or equivalent level), or 8 (Doctoral or equivalent level).

Strategy: A plan of action designed to achieve specific goals or objectives.

ENDNOTES

1 For instance, work-integrated learning may support a possessional approach to employability by awarding *ad hoc* certificates to participating students, as well as a processual approach by contributing to the development of graduates' identity.

2 For instance, integrating employability activities into classes directly impacts students' learning but demands pedagogical skills and commitment from academic staff. Conversely, the central provision of employability activities by career services allows for economies of scale and a transdisciplinary approach but generally has a lower impact on students' learning (Jackson & Tomlinson, 2022).

3 For instance, Bridgstock & Jackson (2019) identify six clusters of employability actions, namely capability development, curriculum composition, career development learning focus, career development learning initiatives, work integrated learning, and key stakeholder partnerships.

4 In all case HEIs academic staff receive no additional reward for adding the management of employability initiatives to their research and teaching duties.

5 See ANVUR (2017) and A3ES (2018).

Chapter 4
Benefits and Challenges of Internationalization of Higher Education

Josephine Oranga
https://orcid.org/0000-0002-1406-5839
Kisii University, Kenya

ABSTRACT

Universities the world over are increasingly being measured by how internationalized and global they are, yet not many studies have explored the benefits and challenges of internationalizing higher education. This article, thus, highlights the benefits of internationalization of higher education, while dwelling more on the challenges faced. From the analysis the benefits include: cultural exchanges, research collaboration, income generation, increased access to higher education, production/exchange of new knowledge, mobility of professionals, human resource capacity-building, foreign language acquisition/proficiency and harmonization of higher education systems. The challenges on the other hand include: commercialization of programs, rise of rogue education providers, low-quality education, over-use of English language, brain drain, domestic employers reluctance to recognize foreign qualifications, financial constraints, divergent ethical, religious and political beliefs of host countries, lack of institutional preparedness and the challenge of attaining an international curriculum.

DOI: 10.4018/979-8-3693-6930-2.ch004

INTRODUCTION

In past two decades, higher education internationalization has emerged as a significant factor shaping higher education development worldwide. As a result, internationalization of higher education has become a trend in the global educational landscape, transforming educational practices, fostering cross-cultural understanding and enhancing the academic prestige of institutions. This chapter, thus, explores the motivations behind this phenomenon and the benefits and challenges faced as institutions strive to internationalise their programmes. By exploring the complexities of internationalization, the phenomenon can be better understood and appreciated and strategies of intervening on the challenges invented, all aimed at shaping the future of higher education and the global society.

Several scholars have defined internationalization (Knight, 2003; Khorsandi, 2014; Babones, 2019; Bastrikin, 2020). Generally speaking, it is the process of incorporating and integrating international, intercultural and the global dimension into the functions and purpose of post-secondary education. In practice, internationalization of higher education is also viewed as the process and practice of commercializing post-secondary education and research through the recruitment of international students from wealthy countries with a view to generating revenue, building an international reputation and securing a national profile (Khorsandi 2014). Hence, the main tenets of internationalization of higher education are recruitment of foreign students, scholars/staff exchange, research collaboration and partnerships and internationalization of institutional curricula (De Wit & Altbach, 2022).

Notably, motivations for internationalization are multifaceted, including generation of revenue, pursuit of academic excellence and the promotion of global citizenship (Bastrikin, 2020; Babones 2019). Consequently, institutions are increasingly investing in student mobility programs, developing joint degrees, and forging partnerships with foreign universities to enrich their educational offerings and bolster their international standing. However, the path to successful internationalization is fraught with challenges, including issues related to quality assurance, cultural integration, and financial sustainability.

BACKGROUND

Internationalization, particularly through student recruitment and mobility, gained prominence during the Cold War, when education schemes, for instance, Fulbright, were used by rival powers to promote and uphold their respective political ideologies (Rizvi, 2011). Internationalization is, consequently, closely associated to the collapse of the Berlin Wall in 1989 and the subsequent rise of global capitalism, dominated by the US. After the Cold War, internationalization in higher education has grown exponentially and currently occupies a central place in the vast majority of institutions of higher education worldwide. Furthermore, internationalization has emerged as a key area of study/specialization within the field of Higher Education (De Wit, 2002; Tight, 2022; Bamberger et al., 2019)

Ideally, by recruiting international students, fostering collaboration, exchange programs and diverse curricula, institutions aim to enhance educational quality and prepare students for a globalized world (Schartner & Cho, 2017). While the benefits of this trend are substantial, it also presents several challenges that must be addressed to maximize its benefits and effectiveness. This is even more imperative considering that there is a growing body of knowledge attesting to the fact that higher education institutions in the developed world have grown dependent on high fee-paying international students (Marginson &Wende 2009, Bunoti 2011Bastrikin 2020).

For instance, the Australian Bureau of Statistics (2019) indicates that international students alone contributed $37.6 billion to the Australian economy in the 2018-2019 fiscal year, translating into a $5 billion rise from the past year, consequently making education the fourth highest export behind only iron, natural gas, coal and ahead of tourism, gold, meat and aluminum. Accordingly, education has gradually become Australia's top service-based export supporting over 250, 000 jobs, business opportunities and general economic growth. This reaffirms the fact that education as an export plays a leading role in the vast majority of developed economies.

Notably, pandemic-related border closures significantly impacted the ability of foreign learners to physically travel and study on campus, thereby bringing to light the limited nature of mobility-reliant internationalization strategies. As a result, De Wit and Altbach (2022) discuss the uncertainty of the future of mobility-based internationalization of higher education and recommends re-evaluation of the approaches and strategies.

Several studies highlight the benefits of internationalization of higher education (Bastrikin, 2020; Babones 2019 & Bevis 2011). In particular, Marangell (2020) explored students' experiences at internationalized Australian universities and the results indicated that the students appreciated international-minded courses and a culturally diverse students' body. Related to this is a study conducted by Schartner and Cho (2017) in Britain aimed at determining how students and staff pictured an 'international university'. The findings revealed that diversity and inward mobility of staff and students were the key elements of an internationalized university.

On a different note, Babones (2019) indicates that it is common practice for universities worldwide to compromise quality and standards in order to accommodate foreign students. Accordingly, the fact that foreign students pay more fees as compared to their domestic counterparts propels higher education institutions to water-down admission requirements and academic standards in an effort to recruit and accommodate them. Furthermore, Babones (2019) contends that alternative admission pathways that allow foreign students to navigate through the English language requirements and the use of commission-based brokerage agents have resulted in intentional academic negligence by a vast majority of Australian universities.

Consequently, studies (Brunner, 2023; Bunoti; 2011), indicate that internationalization is bound to beget low quality education that is driven only by the need to make profits. Accordingly, the market of low quality higher education is as a result of low funding from government, total commercialization of education and entry of unregulated private providers, made worse by the high demand for education in developing countries. Additionally, according to the author, low quality education is also driven by the perception that the possession of a higher education certificate is a gateway to success in life. Mpata (2010), on the other hand contends that rogue education providers emerge to fill a gap occasioned by the demand due to unplanned release of too many high schools graduates without pre-planned programs for their absorption. Jabeen (2015), on the other hand, recommends that higher institutions of learning should desist from competing in income generation and instead focus on their goals, visions and missions. On the other hand, Marginson and Wende (2009) observe that globalization and internationalization of education is both a benefit and a curse to institutions of higher learning. Daniels, Rodebaugh, and Sullivan (2015) indicate that internationalization as a business strategy or idea is unique and is dependent on myriad factors, the most significant being business objectives, administrative decisions and expected returns. As already mentioned, most universities internationalize with the aim of increasing the institutions' incomes.

Breaden, et al., (2023) contends that people seek higher education outside their borders for many reasons including; failing to get an opportunity in a course of interest in local institutions, joining relatives abroad, scholarship conditions, exploration, lower costs (in some cases), high quality education, to learn a new language, amongst others. Daniels (2015) also indicates that the vast majority of cross border seekers of higher education do so because of cost or lack of opportunity at home. Moreover, Marek (2019) indicates that students, who gained an outside-US-experience, on their return home, were more sensitive to multiculturalism, diversity and performed better than those without this experience. Moreover, students with an outside-US-experience have little conflict with peers and exhibit enhanced cross-cultural interactions (Bevis, 2011). Accordingly, these positive transformations are expected to trickle down to the students' choice of work and interactions at work.

Thus, internationalization of higher education has its pros and cons that need to be examined keenly by higher education institutions before embarking on it. As mentioned, universities and economies in the developed world have grown dependent on high fee-paying international students, especially those from Asia. As a result, the economic significance of these students in these universities and countries cannot be overemphasized. Furthermore, the extreme dependence on international students has seen some universities, for instance, the University of Illinois; begin to take insurance policies to cushion themselves against a decline in Chinese students' enrollment in their Campuses (Marek. 2019 and Bastrikin, 2020).

Theorizing Internationalization in Higher Education: World-Systems Theory

World-Systems theory as developed and postulated by sociologist Wallerstein (1974) provides a framework for understanding internationalisation of higher education with regard to global economic system and related social dynamics. The theory posits that the world is divided into core, semi-periphery, and periphery jurisdictions each with distinct roles and relationships in the global economy. This theory can be used to explain and comprehend internationalization of higher education practices globally by examining how different nations (core, semi-periphery and periphery) and institutions interact within the global educational landscape (Wallerstein, 2000; Wallerstein, 2004).

In line with world systems theory, core countries are economically developed nations (Wallerstein, 2004), with advanced educational institutions (for instance, the United States and the United Kingdom). Accordingly, these countries attract the vast majority of international students as they are home to various prestigious universities with robust research capabilities. Semi-peripheral countries are the higher middle income countries (for instance Brazil, Chile and Argentina) that play a transitional role and manifest characteristics of both core and peripheral countries. They commonly host international students as well and still establish partnerships with core countries. On the other hand, Peripheral countries are less economically developed countries, mostly domiciled in the global south. These countries often lack resources for higher education and commonly send students abroad in search of better educational opportunities but face challenges in attracting international students. Hence, in tandem with world systems theory, core institutions set the trend in research and education that ultimately trickle down to the semi-peripheral and peripheral regions. This eventually leads to a concentration of academic power and resources in core countries, perpetuating inequality in the educational landscape.

World systems theory also highlights how the global hierarchy shapes educational policies and practices. Accordingly, Institutions in core countries prioritize internationalization strategies that enhance their global competitiveness (such as establishing overseas campuses or engaging in high-profile research collaborations) while peripheral institutions focus on partnerships that allow their students access to international experiences, often with limited resources.

Hence, internationalization as a phenomenon in higher education is well explicated and explored from the point of view of world-systems theory. Application of world-systems theory to internationalization of higher education processes offers deep insights into the unequal power dynamics that shape global academic interactions and explains the motivations behind student mobility, the establishment of partnerships, and the disparities in access to quality education. By understanding these dynamics, policymakers and educators can better address the challenges and opportunities presented by internationalization of higher education, aiming for more equitable outcomes across different regions and fostering a more inclusive and effective international educational environment.

METHODOLOGY

A systematic review of relevant literature and thematic interpretations of various studies was undertaken with the aim of highlighting the benefits and challenges of internationalization of higher education. This chapter thus, presents the benefits and challenges that arise from internationalizing higher education. It is presumed that these challenges, if addressed, would result in improved standards and practices and enhanced sociocultural and economic benefits of internationalization of higher education to both the learners, staff and institutions.

RESULTS AND DISCUSSION

The results and discussion of this review are presented under the sub-sections, benefits of internationalization of higher education and challenges of internationalization of higher education as follows:

BENEFITS OF INTERNATIONALIZATION OF HIGHER EDUCATION

Internationalization of higher education has emerged as a crucial strategy for fostering global collaboration, enhancing educational quality, and preparing students for the complexities of a global workforce. This section, thus, explores the myriad benefits of internationalizing higher education, highlighting its impact on cultural awareness, skill development, globalization, academic quality, and economic growth.

Cultural Awareness

Students who study abroad or engage in international programs get exposed to diverse cultures, languages, and worldviews (Breaden, et al., 2023; Bevis, 2011; Knight 2008). Consequently, this exposure fosters a sense of global citizenship, encouraging them to respect and appreciate differences while understanding the interconnectedness of global issues. By navigating various cultural contexts, students develop empathy and adaptability, essential traits in today's multicultural societies. To exemplify this further, a study conducted by Egron-Polak and Hudson (2014) indicated that students who had an outside-US-experience, upon returning home were more sensitive to multiculturalism, diversity and performed better than those without. Additionally, they had less conflict and had higher cross-cultural interactions (Brandenburg, Jones, & Leask, 2019; Bevis, 2011). Subsequently, this is expected to trickle down to their places of work, choice of work and interactions at work.

Moreover, internationalization of higher education fosters international and National citizenship as a result of student- migrations. Notably, migration is, more often than not, one of the main reasons students choose to study overseas. Hence internationalization of higher education influences prepares and necessitates students' migration to new jurisdictions (Hunter, 2015; Inamdar, 2019). Moreover, the practice of internationalization of education also fosters an immersive and inclusive academic environment and goes beyond recognition of international student's culture. The varied cultures are integrated and embraced in diverse environments into a rich educational experience for both learners and faculty. Accordingly, multiple knowledges and perspectives may ultimately aid learners to face plurality, uncertainty and conflict in the current interconnected world.

Academic Quality and Innovation

Improved academic quality and standards is another significant aspect that results from internationalizing higher education as institutional standards vary from one jurisdiction to another. With internationalization, higher education institutions get exposed to different standards and practices and might adopt beneficial practices that may eventually help them improve their own local standards (Egron-Polak & Hudson, 2014). Furthermore, research has revealed that International collaborations and co-authorship has a positive impact on research productivity and is, thus, highly encouraged by research and higher learning Institutions as it enhances their reputation and credibility and improves international recognition of research output (Halevi, Moed & Bar-Ilan, 2016; Bhalla, 2015; Khaiat, 2020). Higher education institutions can forge and better explore these collaborations and linkages through strategic partnerships.

Similarly, Marek (2019) contends that international collaborations and partnerships in higher education institutions lead to the sharing of best practices, resources, and research opportunities. Accordingly, Collaborative programs and exchanges enhance academic quality, fostering innovation in teaching and learning (Marek. 2019 & Bastrikin, 2020). Hence, by engaging with international faculty and students, universities can diversify their curricula, integrating global perspectives that enrich students' educational experience. Conclusively, the collaborative environment not only benefits students but also promotes faculty development through exposure to new ideas and research initiatives.

Income Generation

Internationalization of higher education plays a significant role in resource-generation for the host institution and country. Research further indicates that rationales and determinants of internationalization of higher education have shifted from cooperative efforts anchored on cultural, political, and academic arguments to commercial and economic-motivated reasons (De Wit and Altbach et al 2020; Wihlborg and Robson, 2018). Evidently, international students contribute significantly to local economies through tuition fees, living expenses, and cultural expenditures.

Accordingly, in many countries, the influx of international students bolsters the region, creating jobs and stimulating local businesses (Hunter, 2015; Inamdar, 2019). Accordingly, countries that prioritize internationalization of higher education often see a return on their investment (Khaiat, 2020). As mentioned earlier, the Australian Bureau of Statistics (2019) reveals that foreign learners alone contributed $37.6 billion to the Australian economy in the 2018-2019 fiscal year, translating into a $5 billion rise from the past year, consequently making education the fourth highest export behind only iron, natural gas, coal and ahead of tourism, gold, meat and aluminum. Accordingly, education has gradually become Australia's top service-based export supporting over 250, 000 jobs, business opportunities and general economic growth. This reaffirms the fact that education as an export plays a leading role in the vast majority of developed economies.

Moreover foreign-student recruitment quite often targets high fee-paying students, ultimately enabling universities to invest in varied programs, courses and activities from revenues generated from the high fee-paying international students (Alemu, Qu & Sakhiya, 2022). Hence, the economic implications of internationalizing higher education are substantial.

Human Resource and Institutional Capacity Building

Staff mobility as a result of internationalizing higher education systems brings about new views, perspectives, knowledge and skills especially in the supervision and support of postgraduate students. Accordingly, holding different views and perspectives in academic matters exposes the learners to varied boarder world–views that would help mould them to interrogate and explore different perspectives in their bid to solve societal problems (Bista, 2019). Similarly Jibeen (2015) contends that internationally experienced staff bring added value to the classroom and this particularly benefits countries or institutions where recruitment of international academic staff is restricted. Faculty staff mobility also leads to the expansion and enrichment of courses and content offered by institutions (Hunter, 2015: Jibeen, 2015).Furthermore, internationally qualified staff and their publications count a lot in world university rankings as the quality of education depends upon the quality of stuff and educational programs offered (Halevi, 2016). However, in order for staff mobility to be impactful and beneficial to the institutions and participants, the collaborating institutions must be reliable and committed to the partnership and have in place

adequate and suitable funding together with a strong backing by faculty and departments.

On the whole, mobility of staff contributes to a more international outlook within the institution of higher learning and provides staff with the requisite, relevant experiences and skills while also creating opportunities for further international collaborations and cooperation for stuff and students (Khaiat, 2020). Essentially, the mobility of both academic and administrative staff contribute to 'internationalization at home'

Foreign Language Acquisition/Proficiency

Immersion in different cultures boosts language skills, which eventually enhance employability and personal growth. Engaging in study abroad programs, international collaborations, or multilingual classrooms allows students to practice foreign languages in real-world contexts. This immersion fosters fluency, improves pronunciation, and enhances overall communication skills. As students interact with native speakers, they also develop a better understanding of cultural nuances, idiomatic expressions, and local dialects, which are essential for effective communication (Zhou & Cole, 2017)

In this regard, internationalization of higher education plays a vital role in enhancing foreign language proficiency amongst students, which is increasingly crucial in today's globalized world. Foreign language proficiency not only enriches individual students' language skills but also contributes to broader educational and professional outcomes (Egron-Polak & Hudson, 2014). On the other hand, Learning a foreign language enables students and staff from different jurisdictions gain a more in-depth understanding of the cultures within their vicinity thereby boosting their capability to live and work with individuals from varied backgrounds, ultimately helping create a more welcoming and inclusive environment (Zhou & Cole, 2017)..

Global Citizenship

Internationalization enhances awareness amongst learners concerning cultural diversity and global issues, ultimately making students more global-oriented and open-minded (Denson, Loveday & Dalton, 2010). Similarly, Schartner and Cho (2017) indicate that by recruiting international students, fostering collaboration, exchange programs and diverse curricula, institutions aim to prepare students for a globalized world.

Global citizenship has various definition, but basically implies empowering individuals, both globally and locally to become tolerant, peaceful and inclusion-oriented. Furthermore, Goren and Yemini (2017) describe global citizenship as global consciousness, global mindedness and transnationalism, all of which are fostered by internationalization of education systems. On a different (but related) note, Cho and Mosselson (2018) contend that Global Citizenship Education is a 'transformative social-justice oriented education that seeks to address social, political, economic and cultural inequalities.

Hence, internationalization of education exposes and enables learners to have diverse socializations, broadened world-views and a stronger sense of global citizenship. Apparently, students who have emigrated to attain international education also become more concerned with global issues as compared to their counterparts who never emigrated or attained an international education (Halevi, Moed & Bar-Ilan, 2016; Inamdar, 2019). Consequently,, internationalizing of higher education helps students gain exposure to diverse cultures, subsequently fostering global citizenship and cross-cultural understanding. As a result, internationalization brings about life-changing benefits for higher education institutions, learners, staff and the entire school community, as it links them to the global system (Brandenburg, Jones, & Leask, 2019; Inamdar, 2019).

Conclusively, internationalization of higher education stands beneficial when viewed from these perspectives in spite of the numerous barriers and challenges faced by different players. According to Middlehurst and Woodfield (2007), the various challenges work against the full integration of the concept of internationalization in institutions of higher learning.

THE CHALLENGES OF INTERNATIONALIZATION OF HIGHER EDUCATION

Internationalization of higher education has become a pivotal focus for institutions seeking to enhance their global presence and academic quality. While the benefits of internationalization-such as increased cultural exchange, improved research collaboration, and enhanced employability for graduates-are well-documented (Hunter, 2015; Zhou & Cole, 2017) the journey towards effective internationalization is fraught with significant challenges (Babones, 2019; Brunner, 2023). These challenges impede the success of initiatives designed to foster global academic engagements and vary widely across different institutions and regions.

Key challenges include ensuring the quality and recognition of qualifications across diverse educational systems, the risk of commercialising education and political, cultural and linguistic barriers that come with student integration (Zhou & Cole, 2017). The subsequent section, thus, delves into the multifaceted challenges associated with internationalizing higher education and determines how these issues impact students, faculty, and institutions. By understanding these challenges/ barriers/ risks, stakeholders in the education sub-sector can develop more effective strategies to foster a truly inclusive and globally engaged educational environment. The challenges are presented, thus:

Commercialization of Higher Education

Research indicates that rationales and determinants of internationalizing higher education have shifted from co-operative efforts anchored on cultural, political, and academic benefits and exchanges to commercial and economic-motivated reasons (De Wit and Altbach et al 2020; Wihlborg and Robson, 2018). Accordingly, the issues associated with changing global priorities compounded with fierce global competition and political aspects also play a role in shaping the rationale behind the commercialization and provision of higher education. As a result, an increasing number of countries are viewing internationalization of higher education as a service export implying that the amount of income earned from international students including their fees and accommodation is slowly taking precedence over educational standards and quality assurance measures.

As earlier indicated, the Australian Bureau of Statistics (2019), reveals that education exports to Australia in 2018/19 amounted to $37.556 billion, taking into account amounts spent on fees and goods and services by foreign students onshore in Australia (Australian Bureau of Statistics, 2020). This is a pointer to the fact that international students serve significant commercial function in the host countries. Education is, thus, gradually being reduced and turned into an income generating venture with profitability at the apex of its mandate, ultimately leading to the loss of brilliant students who cannot afford the high fees charged by the vast majority of international higher education providers. Furthermore, Halevi, Moed and Bar-Ilan (2016), indicate that most universities internationalize with the aim of increasing the institutions' incomes and not attracting high achieving students. Herbert (2006) too contends that the whole process of internationalizing higher education leads to commercialization of education, which in turn results in institutionalization of a market-driven curriculum.

Ultimately, Mains (2010) and Daniels et al (2015) recommend that a window of opportunity be left for brilliant students who face financial constraints, by offering them scholarships, intergovernmental grants and exchanges. This would benefit and bring on board gifted yet economically disadvantaged learners. Consequently, student mobility should not be viewed as a preserve of learners from wealthy backgrounds only. Additionally, exporters of higher education should be aware of the dynamic market trends that could render them meaningless if they remain solely motivated by profit. Hence, reserving spots for brilliant yet financially constrained learners would go a long way in helping justify the need for internationalization and give these institutions a more philanthropic face (Daniels et al, 2015).

Quality Attainment and Maintenance as a Challenge

Closely linked to commercialization of higher education is the aspect of quality. Mains (2012) and Fielden (2014) explicate that programs are more costly and most institutions of higher education pursue economic gain at the expense of the quality of the programs or students admitted. Consequently, the whole process of internationalization locks out brilliant students who lack financial resources. Similarly, scholars (Brunner, 202; Herman, 2017) contend that the decline in learning outcomes and academic standards as institutions concentrate on economic gains from international students is a reality. Furthermore, Bevis (2014) explicates that even though the issue of quality is central in many universities, internationalization practices and policies have been executed without much concern for quality assurance. This is despite the fact that internationalization of higher education was envisaged to as an instrument of realizing and achieving enhanced academic values, goals and objectives.

Moreover, internationalization in education has seen a steady rise in low-quality or rogue 'education' providers (as exemplified by the situation in Britain and the US) keen on getting a slice of the fees paid by students seeking an international education(Oranga, 2020). Furthermore, according to Damme (2001) and Oranga (2020), ingrained in most internationalization initiatives are several risks and challenges, which, in one way or another, have a direct bearing on the quality of education provided. Studies (Brunner, 2023; Herman, 2017; Main 2012;) maintain that quality assurance in internationalization practices is a significant issue that should be given utmost attention as higher education institutions strive to internationalize. Accordingly, failure to assure quality in the education provided renders the programs irredeemably compromised, consequently impacting negatively on the recipients of such an education system.

Similarly, Bevis, (2012) indicates that the questionable quality of degrees offered by internationalized foreign universities has resulted in qualifications not being recognized by some home-country domestic employers. Furthermore, institutions and countries are increasingly filtering foreign qualifications and determining which qualifications they deem strong enough, in a bid to shield themselves from rogue international higher education providers (Bevis. 2012). Accordingly, rogue universities admit unqualified foreign students as long as they pay the much needed fees (Lillies et al 2010; Herman, 2017)).

Herman (2017) indicates that the problem of low quality education provision has been made worse by the fact that nations around the world have been decreasing university funding in the belief that universities are earning substantial incomes from high-fee-paying foreign students. This has a counter-effect of making universities even more aggressive in inventing new strategies of attracting and maintaining international students. This more often than not leads to watering–down of admission requirements in order to get the high fee-paying international students. Subsequently, several university programs are funded and maintained by the fees paid by the foreign students. This phenomenon in itself has been detrimental and played a significant role in killing academic standards in internationalized universities (Wihlborg & Robson, 2018).

Consequently, authors (De Wit & Altbach et al 2020; Knight & Altbach, 2007) indicate that efforts to monitor international initiatives and ensure high standards should be central and ingrained in all internationalization efforts and process in higher education. Additionally, Mpaata (2010) recommends the integration of internationalization practices and quality assurance policies at institutional level for quality to be restored and maintained. Quality assurance processes should, thus, play a pivotal role in all higher education's internationalization processes. Furthermore, institutions need to be well- focused and well-funded to curb the menace of declining academic standards as a result of internationalization.

Internationalization of Curricula- Ethical, Religious and Political Considerations

Internationalization calls for curricula adaptations and modifications that result in curricula and syllabi that are responsive and sensitive to the needs of both the host country and the international learners (Middlehurst, 2007: Bhalla. 2015).However, most academic institutions find curriculum internationalization quite a challenge. Accordingly, developing and arriving at a curriculum that satisfies the needs of both international and local educational needs requires a lot of expertise and input. Bastrikin (2020) contends that infusing religious, ethical and political elements and considerations of different international countries/learners into the host country's curriculum poses a challenge to internationalization efforts. Accordingly, the host country's curriculum always reflects its political, ethical and religious beliefs which oftentimes clash with the beliefs of other countries from where international students come (Hirai, Frazier, & Syed, 2015).

On the other hand, some local aspects of the curriculum might infringe on the beliefs and ideologies of students from different countries and cultures. Hence, host countries should strive to modify their curricula in order to give them a more inclusive outlook (Brista, 2019; Bastrkin, 2020). Care should also be taken during modification so that the resultant curriculum does not disadvantage local students to whom the removed/modified religious aspects were relevant. Furthermore care should be taken so that the resultant curriculum remains in tandem with the host country's higher education objectives. This, thus, calls for a careful approach in response to the needs of both the local and international students. Notably, a well internationalized curriculum might go a long way in addressing the issue of non-recognition of foreign certificates, diplomas and degrees. Consequently, a good moderated curriculum also leads to the acknowledgment of credits and credit transfers by home countries of international students. The development and integration of a comprehensive internationalization of higher education policy frameworks may also aid in addressing issues associated with curriculum internationalization (Hirai, Frazier, & Syed, 2015).

The Challenge of Brain Drain

Alemu, Qu & Sakhiya (2022) also contends that the most devastating, significant consequence of **internationalization** of higher education in Africa has been brain drain, which has had far-reaching repercussions in knowledge production, publication and has resulted in most African higher education institutions perpetually depending on Western systems, support, standards and even knowledge generation. Accordingly, staff mobility is both beneficial and disadvantageous, depending on the countries involved. It is of great benefit to more advanced countries that are able to lure well trained staff whom they never trained, in the first place to work in their jurisdictions.

Similarly, scholars (Marangell, 2020; Marginson & Wende, 2009; Knight, 2008), indicate that internationalization and globalization constitute a threat to some higher education institutions in that it acts as a global academic marketplace for university dons, professors and students . This consequently means that the best students and staff may be lured away by being offered lucrative scholarships and salaries respectively, by economically endowed countries. Hence, if care is not taken internationalization of higher education might lead to mobility of qualified staff (brain drain) to more advanced countries leaving developing countries in perpetual need of experts in certain essential academic areas (Halevi, Moed & Bar-Ilan, 2016). Qualified professors in less developed countries with fewer resources, would, more often than not, prefer to work in developed countries where substantial amounts of resources are allocated to staff salaries and research, consequently impacting negatively on developing countries efforts to maintain scholars in various crucial areas. Evidently, developing countries may not compete with advanced countries in remuneration and retention of qualified staff by virtue of their weak economies (Hirai, Frazier, & Syed, 2015)

To help curb this problem, countries and jurisdictions may have to invent ways to ensure that dons work in their local countries for a stipulated number of years before moving to other jurisdictions (Kein, 2013). Moreover, the role played by monetary compensation should never be underestimated by developing countries even as they devise strategies of curbing brain drain.

Over-dependence on International "core" Journals for Promotion and Research Criteria

Sholars (Mian, 2012; Bastrikin, 2020) contend that internationalization of higher education leads to over-reliance on "core" journals (that are selective in terms of what they publish and from where the authors come) for promotion and research, ultimately placing professors and other academics in peripheral research universities at a disadvantage, despite being just as gifted just as those in the much- acclaimed universities (Bastrikin, 2020). Accordingly, it is an open secret that these journals quite often turn down manuscripts from authors affiliated to low-cadre peripheral universities. This totally, demotivates hardworking professors in non-core universities. Similarly Kein (2013) indicates that the top-ranking English journals have become increasingly selective, accepting only 5 to 10% of paper submissions, as universities worldwide continue to demand that their scholars and scientists publish in these core journals (Lillis & Curry 2010; Kein, 2013; Daniels, 2015).

Evidently, getting quality articles authored by scholars from peripheral universities published in these journals of repute is more often than not impossible (Zhou & Cole, 2017; Bhalla. 2015; Lillis & Curry 2010) as the journals are keen to maintain their class and honor by publishing articles majorly from highly-acclaimed institutions. Furthermore, since this journals are in English, scholars whose first language is not

English, have more often than not had their manuscripts rejected by the influential high esteem journals.

To address this challenge, as many journals as possible, that maintain high standards, should receive the recognition they deserve regardless of whether or not they are affiliated to a widely acclaimed university or not. Furthermore, affiliation to a core university should not be criteria to determine a professor's work or standards and credibility. Furthermore, according to Basheka, et al, (2009), institutions should not rely or insist on publication in certain specific journals as a mark of quality for their academics and professors under for examination and promotion as this has proved unfair and unachievable.

Over-use of English as a Medium of Communication

Higher education internationalization and collaboration efforts (staff and student exchange programs, research partnerships) require a common language for better communication and understanding. This has resulted in English, without any effort at all being the unifying language and 'lingua franca' for academic exchange and research, leading to what is currently referred to as 'overuse of English' as the language for research (Zhou & Cole, 2017). Bastrikin (2020) indicates that scholars elsewhere have been coerced to learn and adopt English as the publishing language in order to publish in high-esteeem core journals, which in essence, egocentrically reflect the values of the editorial boards in the Unites States of America, the United Kingdom, Australia, Canada, New Zealand and other metropolitan English speaking countries (Lillis & Curry 2010). This is because English has become an overriding influence on research and scholarship world-wide, a reality that research institutions' and universities have to contend with (Jibeen, 2015; Knight, 2007).

However, according to Alemu, Qu & Sakhiya (2022) this situation is unavoidable and English rose to this position without any effort or manipulation (Jibeen, 2015; Hunter, 2015). Subsequently, varied reactions abound concerning the utilization of English as the 'lingua franca' in research, publishing and academic exchanges (Daniels, 2015). Notably, the most influential and esteemed academic journals and scientific websites also happen to be in English. This has resulted in higher education institutions worldwide requiring that their academics publish in these high-esteem English-medium journals as a mark of quality in research and scholarship. On the other hand, since the signing of the Bologna declaration in Europe in 1999 (that sought to make higher education systems across European jurisdictions more coherent) many European higher education institutions have adopted English as the "scientific lingua franca", and subsequently initiated courses and entire degree programs with English as the medium of instruction.

Subsequently, some scholars perceive the current trend of English in academia as neo-colonialism as scholars the world over are under extreme pressure to conform and align to the aims and values of the metropolitan academic practices and systems that use English (Elkins 2008 & Daniels et al, 2015). On the other hand, researchers (Jibeen, 2015; Hunter, 2015) contend that it is imperative to develop a common scientific language and understanding for policy, regulations, research, and data collection purposes for the sake of uniformity in understanding/synthesis of significant scientific research outputs. Acceptance of the status quo would automatically make English the unifying research language worldwide consequently, leading to uniformity in understanding of research outputs. Hence Depending on how one looks at it, this state of affairs might call for the growth and adoption of alternative languages, (ultimately exacerbating division in scientific understanding by academic institution) or retention of English as the unifying scientific research language

The Challenge of Communication and Social Interaction

Studying in a foreign country can be a great adventure and opportunity but may also come with its own challenges. Students on foreign campuses often report feelings of loneliness, difficulties adjusting to cultural differences or experiencing discrimination (Hirai, Frazier & Syed, 2015). Notably, social interaction and contact has been widely explored as a significant, contributing factor to foreign students' cross-cultural and social adaptation. A study conducted to evaluate socialization and interaction amongst students on international campuses in the Netherlands in revealed that local students from particular national backgrounds had low mastery of the common language and, thus felt more comfortable socializing amongst themselves than interacting with the rest of the students' body. Yet on the other hand, local students' language preference was the reason why there was limited social interaction between them and locals students.

Accordingly, foreign students contended that local students preferred to use Dutch in social contexts and not any other language that the foreign students understood well. Hence this pattern of language preferences enhances further limited interactions between local and foreign students (Halevi, Moed & Bar-Ilan, 2016; Kondakci, 2008). Studies further reveal that friendly and cordial relationship/interactions between host and foreign students leads to high satisfaction (Gareis, 2012). On the other hand research have also explained that the lack of social integration amongst foreign and local students begets negative feelings regarding the host country (Lee, 2010; Zhou & Cole, 2017), implying that there is need to ensure improved quality interactions between local and international students. Apparently, interactions and relationships between international and local students has now become one of the most significant topics in literature with regard to internationalization of higher education. Accordingly, supportive relationships can help students surmount negative feelings and experiences during the acculturation process (Smith & Khawaja, 2011; Zhang & Goodson, 2011).

CONCLUSION

Internationalization of higher education represents a dynamic and multifaceted phenomenon that has the potential to reshape the educational landscape. While it offers numerous benefits, it also poses significant challenges that institutions must address to ensure equitable access and quality education. By fostering collaboration, embracing technology, and prioritizing sustainability, the future of internationalization in higher education can lead to a more interconnected and informed global community. As institutions navigate this complex terrain, their ability to adapt and innovate will be crucial for realizing the full potential of internationalization. Consequently, Internationalization of higher education continues to draw attention outside the education sub-sector, as its impacts and operations are continuously aligning with economic, social, cultural and political functions and interests of the countries involved.

As already discussed, internationalization of higher education comes with its own challenges that are rarely brought to the fore as the tendency, unfortunately, has been to explore and focus on the benefits while rarely bringing the risks and challenges to the fore. Thus, in order to internationalize, universities ought to keenly consider their ability to address the challenges discussed here vis-a-vis acquiring an international face. In addition, they should examine their ability to maintain high academic standards in the face of a growing global competition for international students (some of whom did not merit admission in their home countries) and shrinking government funding for higher education.

FUTURE RESEARCH DIRECTIONS

Further research could focus on determinants and barriers to internationalization in developing countries as internationalization of higher education as a phenomenon has yet to take off in most developing countries, and more so, Africa.

ACKNOWLEDGMENT

This chapter is a revised version of an earlier published Journal publication: Oranga, J., Nyakundi E. & Obuba, E. (2020). Is internationalization of higher education the way to go? Journal of Research Innovation and Implications in Education, 4(3), 133-144

(PDF) Is Internationalization of Higher Education the Way to Go?. Available at: https://www.researchgate.net/publication/344489936_Is_Internationalization_of_Higher_Education_the_Way_to_Go

REFERENCES

Aguilar, P. (2008). *Barriers to internationalization: Attitudes, resources, policy. Rapporteur: Martin Pantoja – Director.* International Relations, Universidad de Guanajuato.

Alemu, S. K., Qu, M., & Sakhiya, Z. (2022). Voices of internationalization of higher education from Sub-Saharan Africa, China and Indonesia. *Learning and Teaching*, 15(3), 2–31. DOI: 10.3167/latiss.2022.150303

Altbach, P. G., & Jalote, P. (2020). When will India Build World-Class Research Universities. World University News. Retrieved from: https://www.universityworldnews.com/post.php?story=20200921112203767

Altbach. J & Knight (2007)-The Internationalization of Higher Education: Motivations and Realities: Journal of Studies in International Education Fall/Win 11 -3-4, 290-305.

Australian Bureau of Statistics (2019) 5368.0.55.003 – International Trade: Supplementary Information, Financial Year, 2018-19.

Australian Bureau of Statistics (2020) – International Trade: Supplementary Information, Financial Year, 2019-20.

Aydin, O. T. *(2020) Local and International Students' Experiences at a Turkish University Social Interaction Between Students.* Available from: https://www.researchgate.net/publication/337185724_Local_and_International_Students'_Experiences_at_a_Turkish_University_Social_Interaction_Between_Students [accessed Jul 27 2024].

Babones, S. (2019). *The China Student Boom and the Risks It Poses to Australian Universities; Analysis paper 5.* The Centre for Independent. Sydney.

Bamberger, A., Morris, P., & Yemini, M. (2019). Neoliberalism, internationalisation and higher education: Connections, contradictions and alternatives. *Discourse (Abingdon)*, 40(2), 203–216. DOI: 10.1080/01596306.2019.1569879

Basheka, B. C., Muhenda, M. B., & Kittobe, J. (2009). *Programme Delivery, Quality Benchmarks and 143 Outcomes Based Education at Uganda Management Institute: A correlational approach*. NCHE.

Bastrikin, A. (2020). International Student Enrolment Statistics: educationdata.org. MI Bevis, T. B. (2002). At a glance: International students in the United States'. *International Educator*, 11(3), 12–17.

Bhalla, V. (2015). International students in Indian universities. *Industry and Higher Education*, 79(41), 24–31. DOI: 10.6017/ihe.2005.41.7500

Bista, K. (2019). Exploring the field: Understanding the international student experience. In K. Bista, K. (ed.), Global perspectives on international student experiences in higher education: Tensions and issues (pp. 1-16). Morgan State University: Routledge.

Brandenburg, U., De Wit, H., Jones, E., & Leask, B. (2019). Internationalisation in higher education for society. *University World News*. Retrieved from https://www.universityworldnews.com/post.php?story=20190414195843914

Breaden, J., Do, T., dos Anjos-Santos, L. M., & Normand-Marconnet, N. (2023). Student empowerment for internationalisation at a distance: Enacting the students as partners approach in virtual mobility. *Higher Education Research & Development*, 42(5), 1182–1196. DOI: 10.1080/07294360.2023.2193728

Brunner, L. R. (2023). Settler nation-building through immigration as a rationale for higher education: A critical discourse analysis. *Higher Education Research & Development*, 42(5), 1086–1102. DOI: 10.1080/07294360.2023.2193732

Bunoti, S. (2011). The quality of higher education in developing countries needs professional support. Retrieved from http://www.intconfhighered.org/FINAL%20Sarah%20Bunoti.pdf on 6th August, 2020.

Caruana, V., & Spurling, N. (2007). *The internationalisation of UK higher education- a review of selected material*. Higher Education Academy.

Cho, H., & Mosselson, J. (2018). Neoliberal Practices Amidst Social Justice Orientations: Global Citizenship Education in South Korea. *Compare: A Journal of Comparative Education*, 48(6), 861–878. DOI: 10.1080/03057925.2017.1364154

Daniels, J. D., Rodebaugh, L. H., & Sullivan, D. P. (2015). International Business Environments and Operations: Global Edition. 15 Edn. Pearson Education Limited. Edinburgh.

De Wit, H., & Altbach, P. G. (2022). The impact of COVID-19 on the internationalisation of higher education, revolutionary or not? In Kumar, C. R., Mukherjee, M., Belousova, T., & Nair, N. (Eds.), *Global higher education during and beyond COVID-19: Perspectives and challenges*. DOI: 10.1007/978-981-16-9049-5_18

Denson, N., Loveday, T., & Dalton, H. (2010). Student evaluation of courses: What predicts satisfaction? *Higher Education Research & Development*, 29(4), 339–356. DOI: 10.1080/07294360903394466

Dwyer, M. M. (2004). More Is Better: The Impact of Study Abroad Program Duration. *Frontiers: The Interdisciplinary Journal of Study Abroad*, 10(1), 151–164. DOI: 10.36366/frontiers.v10i1.139

Egron-Polak, E., & Hudson, R. (2014). *Internationalization of higher education: Growing expectations, fundamental values. IAU 4th Global Survey*. International Association of Universities.

Elkin, G., Devjee, F., & Farnsworth, J. (2005). Visualising the "internationalisation of universities. *International Journal of Educational Development*, 19(4), 318–329.

Elkin, G., Farnsworth, J., & Templer, A. (2008). Strategy and the internationalisation of universities. *International Journal of Educational Management*, 22(3), 239–250. www.emeraldinsight.com. DOI: 10.1108/09513540810861874

European Union. (2015). Centre for Higher Education Internationalization (CHEI). Retrieved from https://www.europarl.europa.eu/studies/

Fielden, J. (2008). *The Practice of Internationalisation: Managing International Activities in UK Universities*. The UK HE International Unit. Available at http:// www. Universitiesuk .ac.uk

Gareis, E. (2012). Intercultural friendship: Effects of home and host region. *Journal of International and Intercultural Communication*, 5(4), 309–328. DOI: 10.1080/17513057.2012.691525

Gondwe, M.&Walenkamp, J. (2011). Alignment of higher professional education with the needs of the local labour market: the case of Ghana.

Goren, H., & Yemini, M. (2017b). The Global Citizenship Education Gap: Teacher Perceptions of the Relationship between Global Citizenship Education and Students' Socio-Economic Status. *Teaching and Teacher Education*, 67, 9–22. DOI: 10.1016/j.tate.2017.05.009

Halevi, G., Moed, H. F., & Bar-Ilan, J. (2016). Does research mobility have an effect on productivity and impact? *Industry and Higher Education*, 86(86), 5–6. DOI: 10.6017/ihe.2016.86.9360

Hudson, R. (2014). Why universities want to internationalise; what stops them? Hunter, F. (2015) What's in a name? Refocusing internationalisation of higher education. European Association for International Education. Retrieved from https://www.eaie.org/blog/whats-in-a-name-refocusing-internationalisation-of-higher-education.html

Inamdar, N. (2019). Transcending Boundaries in Higher Education: Are We Really Ready? In Bhat, H. V., & Inamdar, N. (Eds.), *Internationalization of Higher Education: The Dynamics of Educational Ecology* (pp. 9–32). Manipal Universal Press.

Jibeen, T. (2015) Internationalization of Higher Education: Potential Benefits and Costs. International Journal of Evaluation and Research in Education. Retrieved from https://files.eric.ed.gov/fulltext/EJ1091722.pdf

Jones, E. & Brown, S. (2007). Internationalizing higher education UK: Rutledge

Khaiat, B. (2020). Key figures: Internationally mobile students around the world. Campus, France: campusfrance.org

Khorsandi, T. A. (2014). *A Critical Policy Analysis of Internationalization in Post-secondary Education: An Ontario Case Study*. Western University.

Knight, J. (2003). Updating the Definition of Internationalisation', The Journal of International Higher Education, 33 (Fall). Available at: https://www.bc.edu/bc

Kondakci, . (2008). Challenges of Internationalization from Foreign and Local Students' Perspectives: The Case of Management SchoolAsia Pacific. *Education Review*, 9(4), 448–463.

Marangell, S. (2020). Investigating the student experience of internationalization at an Australian university [Doctoral dissertation, University of Melbourne]. http://hdl.handle.net/11343/242198

Marek, L. (2019). Why University of Illinois is insuring itself literally against a drop in Chinese students: Crain's Chicago Business. Chicago.

Marginson, S., & van der Wende, M. (2009a): "Europeanisation, International Rankings, and Faculty Mobility: Three Cases in Higher Education Globalisation" in Higher Education to 2030, Vol 2,Globalisation, (ed.), Organisation for Economic Cooperation and Development (Paris: OECD), 109-41. (2009b)

Maringe, S. (2000). Strategies and challenges of internationalization in HE: An exploratory study of universities.

Middlehurst, R., & Woodfield, S. (2007). Responding to the internationalisation agenda: Implications for institutional strategy. Higher Education Academy [Online]. Available at: http://www.escalate.ac.uk

Mpaata, A. K. (2010). *University Competiveness through Quality assurance*. The Challenging Battle for Intellectuals.

Oranga, J., Nyakundi E. & Obuba, E. (2020). Is internationalization of higher education the way to go? Journal of Research Innovation and Implications in Education, 4(3), 133-144.

Schartner, A., & Cho, Y. (2017). 'Empty signifiers' and 'dreamy ideals': Perceptions of the 'international university' among higher education students and staff at a British university. *Higher Education*, 74(3), 455–472. DOI: 10.1007/s10734-016-0057-1

Tight, M. (2022). Internationalisation of higher education beyond the West: Challenges and opportunities–the research evidence. *Educational Research and Evaluation*, 27(3–4), 239–259. DOI: 10.1080/13803611.2022.2041853

Universities, U. K. (2005). Universities UK's international strategy -London: Universities UK. Vernon, R. (1966). International Investment and International Trade in the Product Cycle -. *The Quarterly Journal of Economics*, 80(2), 190–207.

Wallerstein, I. (1974). *The modern World System I: Capitalist Agriculture and the Origins of the European World-Economy in the Sixteenth Century*. Academic Press.

Wallerstein, I. (2004). *World-Systems Analysis: An Introduction*. Duke University Press.

Wihlborg, M., & Robson, S. (2018). Internationalisation of Higher Education: Drivers, Rationales, Priorities, Values and Impacts. *European Journal of Higher Education*, 8(1), 8–18. DOI: 10.1080/21568235.2017.1376696

Zhou, J., & Cole, D. (2017). Comparing international and American students: Involvement in college life and overall satisfaction. *Higher Education*, 73(5), 655–672. DOI: 10.1007/s10734-016-9982-2

ADDITIONAL READING

Dwyer, M. M. (2004). More Is Better: The Impact of Study Abroad Program Duration. *Frontiers: The Interdisciplinary Journal of Study Abroad*, 10(1), 151–164. DOI: 10.36366/frontiers.v10i1.139

Wallerstein, I. (2000). *The Essential Wallerstein*. The New York Press.

Warner, G. (1992). *Internationalization Models and the Role of the University*. International Education Magazine.

KEY TERMS AND DEFINITIONS

Brain Mobility: Refers to the movement of skilled workers or academic amongst different countries and jurisdictions.

Brain Drain: Refers to the permanent emigration of skilled individuals and academics from one country or jurisdiction to another due to better terms of service or monetary compensations offered by the receiving country.

Brain Gain: These are the benefit to a country as a result of the immigration of a highly-qualified person.

Brain Waste: Refers to a state where academic qualifications or skills are not recognized for one reason or another.

Commercialization of Education: This occurs when education as a process or services is treated as a marketable good, meant to attract clients at the expense of quality. Often times materializes itself in mushrooming of private schools and public and private universities.

Globalization of Education: Refers to the integration of international educational contents, systems and methodologies to enhance cross-cultural understanding and collaboration in the academic sphere.

Internationalization of Higher Education: The process of globalizing and commercializing postsecondary education and research through periodic recruitment of high fee- paying foreign students from wealthy backgrounds, exchange programs and research collaboration.

Staff Mobility: Implies the movement and exchanges of staff between institutions and the recruitment of staff from abroad.

Chapter 5
Nexus Between Experiential and Academic Learning for Employability Skills in Higher Education Institutions:
Students and Faculty Perspectives

Caroline Sabina Wekullo
https://orcid.org/0000-0002-0148-9069
MMUST, Kenya

James Bill Ouda
https://orcid.org/0000-0002-0942-6169
MMUST, Kenya

Rose Atione Opiyo
https://orcid.org/0000-0001-6881-7859
MMUST, Kenya

ABSTRACT

A skilled workforce is crucial to countries' economic transformation. Higher education institutions have been under pressure to promote employability by ensuring learners acquire the 21st century skills needed to succeed in the real world. However, there are still gaps in balancing academic and experiential learning approaches. Using data from selected higher education institutions in Kenya, the chapter examines the

DOI: 10.4018/979-8-3693-6930-2.ch005

perspectives of students and faculty on the nexus between experiential and academic learning for employability skills in higher education institutions. Specifically, the chapter seeks to determine whether the current curriculum incorporates experiential skills alongside academic learning and assess whether students are provided with opportunities to apply academic knowledge in real-world contexts through experiential learning. The findings have significant implications for policy makers, education officers, key stakeholders including trainers, employers and students in ensuring a match between experiential and academic training for employability skills

INTRODUCTION

A skilled workforce is crucial to countries' economic transformation. It enables firms to move up the value chain, adapt to economic changes, and spur innovation, while allowing workers to move out of low-productivity activities and earn more in their jobs (Kapareliotis,et al.,2019;Korucu-Kış,2021). The demand for skilled workforce is rapidly changing. Digital technologies are leading to automation of routine tasks and transforming or destroying jobs focused on routine and manual tasks (Dwyer, 2022). To accelerate economic transformation, countries are now making smart investments in skills development aimed at three policy goals: productivity growth, inclusion, and adaptability of both individuals and economies (Bakhshi, et al 2017).There is increased pressure for higher education to promote employability by ensuring that learners acquire a base of experiential skills in addition to academic skills, which is critical in the production of graduates who are useful to the economic development of a given country, region and overall globe (Bakhshi et al.,2017; Dwyer,2022).

The higher education sphere involves various stakeholders, including students, companies, universities competitors, public policy, tax, multinational agencies who determine what and how of teaching and learning (Dwyer, 2022).The contribution of the World Bank towards the application of academic and experiential skills cannot be overstated. World Bank works with various governments to ensure that individuals have access to quality education and training opportunities for skills development, support employers in their efforts to locate and invest in the skills they need using the Skills Toward Employment and Productivity (STEP) framework which helps in analyzing and building approaches for skills development strategies in low- and middle-income countries(Zanville, 2023). Higher education institutions and training centers like never before are redesigning their curriculum and education practices for the benefit of all the players in the economy (Dwyer,2022;Hammond et al, 2020).The pace is however so slow that going by the high number of educated and unemployed graduates.

The rate of educated and unemployed graduates has been on the rise in the recent past. In 2010, it was estimated that while over 750,000 graduates who are also youths entered the Kenyan labor market each year, only 16 percent succeeded in acquiring formal employment (The UNDP, 2010). As of 2020, a report by Kenya National Bureau of Statistics noted that youth aged 20 to 29 years old, - the age bracket of fresh university graduates- had an unemployment rate of over 32.4 percent, with a long-time unemployment rate of 7.9 percent (Munene, 2021). According to the Kenya National Bureau of Statistics report, the era of guaranteed white-collar employment for university graduates had waned in the last two decades. Many graduates were going through years of unemployment and underemployment and even the high-demanded professional disciplines like medical sciences, engineering, technology, and business have not been spared the scourge of unemployment(Munene,2021). The concerns of many stakeholders are: is there a problem with the training approaches being used? Is there a mismatch between training competencies being offered and those needed by employers on the labor market? Are there transformations in labor markets that institutions of higher learning have not kept pace with?

From a review of previous studies, training in most institutions of higher learning has traditionally focused on measuring proficiency rather than experiential knowledge and does not support community-based learning and immediate employment(Ngure, 2015). This has created a significant imbalance or mismatch between learning experience the market demands. While experiential skills are crucial, the current emphasis on academic skills alone is likely to result in a gap between academic qualifications and the employability skills employers need(Kolb & Kolb, 2006;Vault,2023). Consequently, employers have reported a mismatch in the skills the graduates/job seekers gained through educational training and their hiring needs (Awiti et al, 2019). Specifically, the employers cited that either graduates often lacked key soft skills or their skill levels are too low and that they need to invest a further 6-12 months of training for new employees recruited (Bradberry & De Maio, 2019; Ngure, 2015). An indication that most graduates are not getting the best out of their investment in education. There is therefore a need to incorporate both academic and experiential knowledge for a well- rounded education.

Whereas striking a balance between academic and experiential skills for employability can be challenging, it is crucial for a holistic career development. As Vault (2023) noted, academic knowledge provides a framework for understanding concepts, whereas experiential skills allow for hands-on-learning and provides a deeper understanding through personal experience. Combining academic and experiential is crucial for a comprehensive understanding and ability to effectively apply knowledge to real world situations. On the same note, scholars have suggested strategies to help achieve this balance, including identifying key skills in high demand by employers, aligning academic knowledge and experiential skills for real world, gaining practical experience through internships and co-op programs, creating a professional network and a well-rounded resume to attract potential employers (Sisol Recruitment,2024).

There's no doubt that the future of education is undergoing transformation. Similarly, the higher education landscape in Kenya, like elsewhere, is evolving in response to the ever-changing workforce, globally (Hicks,2023). Further, Hicks (2023) stated that institutions of higher learning are working to improve the learn-and work ecosystem. Specifically, institutions are developing new teaching approaches that include real-world scenarios, such as, career advising, designing new programs, digital platforms to expand opportunities for learners to apply their theoretical knowledge, data standards to enable interoperability of information, and policies to guide systems (Zanville, 2023). Despite the effort, there are still gaps on how all these innovative approaches can be achieved at higher education level. Moreso, the so-called evolving curriculum neither reflects the changing needs of the society nor ensures that students are equipped with current relevant knowledge and skills.

There is a need to equip students with essential 21st century skills and knowledge they need to succeed in the real world. Specifically, this chapter seeks to determine whether the current curriculum incorporates experiential skills alongside academic learning in Kenyan Higher education learning institutions and assess whether students are provided with opportunities to apply the academic knowledge in real-world contexts through experiential learning.

Integrating academic and experiential learning in the curriculum is a vital aspect of the future of education. This chapter has several significant contributions: First, to the existing literature on approaches for engaging students in the 21st century skills development both from the perspectives of students and faculty. Secondly, the chapter highlights the extent higher education institutions are incorporating experiential and academic learning, including providing learners with a deeper understanding of concepts and equipping them with employability skills, such as, problem solving, critical thinking, decision making and collaboration skills for the real-world application. In so doing, the chapter highlights the benefits of integrating both academic and experiential skills to bridge the gap between academic learning and real-life challenges, while preparing learners for a dynamic workforce. Thirdly, the chapter suggests opportunities for engaging students in experiential learning as a way to cultivate a well-rounded skill set that goes beyond memorization to foster employability, personal growth and development.

The rest of the chapter is organized as follows: The chapter presents literature review, methodology section, results, discussion of findings and implications, limitation of the study, and conclusion.

BACKGROUND

Experiential learning pedagogies are becoming increasingly popular in higher education. The approaches demonstrate a shift in learning from a teacher-centered, knowledge-transfer approach to the learner as an active participant in the learning process (Kolb & Kolb, 2006). Experiential learning is linked to increased opportunities for hands-on experiences, enhanced understanding, better vocational development (Fuco, 1996) increased likelihood of attending graduate school, graduation rates, employment outcomes, and acquisition of skills that are relevant to career success, including communication skills, self-confidence, appreciation for community, and professional growth (Bradberry & De Maio, 2019). Experiential learning places curricular concepts in the context of real-life situations, allows students to go through the process of reflective education and to gain further understanding of course content and of the discipline, learn civic or social responsibility through a scholarship of community engagement (Astin, et al 2000) apply newly acquired skills and knowledge to address real-life needs in their own communities (Phelps, 2012).

Equally, experiential advances a well-designed reflection process whereby knowledge is created through the transformation of experience(Kolb & Kolb 2006) and learning opportunities that contribute to significant learning, including problem solving skills, higher order reason, integrative thinking, goal clarification, openness to new ideas, ability to adopt new perspectives, and systematic thinking (Stewart and Wubben, 2015). Additionally, Kolb and Kolb (2005) found that experiential learning methods led to higher levels of student engagement, intrinsic motivation, better long-term retention of knowledge, better practical skills, more prepared for their careers and increased higher problem-solving abilities. Similarly, Hmelo-Silver (2004) found that problem-based learning, a form of experiential learning, significantly improved students' problem-solving skills. In a different study, Deslauriers et al.(2011) found that students in experiential learning environments retained information better than those in traditional lecture-based classes.

Many previous studies have shown that a use of both academic and experiential learning approaches have a positive influence on students' academic outcomes. For instance, Meta-analysis by Burch et al. (2019) found that the use of experiential learning methods was associated with significantly higher academic achievement compared to traditional lecture-based methods. Equally, Coker and Porter (2015) found that students who participated in experiential learning programs demonstrated significant improvements in critical thinking compared to those who did not. Furthermore, a Meta-analysis by Hilarsk (2013) found that experiential learning practices, for instance, the addition of a service-learning component and internship in higher education practices translated into deepened understanding of academic content, increase in overall understanding and application of classroom knowledge to "real-life" situation. On the same note Caspers and Olaru (2017) found that experiential learning increased interpersonal skills and professional confidence especially independence, career interests, development of a skills set including workplace skills, written and oral communication skills specifically the ability to communicate with different populations, leadership skills, in the same vein, Novak, et al., (2007)in a study on the benefits of experiential learning found that these mode of learning improved learning outcomes by about 53%.

Academic Learning in Kenya has been focused on understanding and application of abstract ideas, models, and frameworks as well as transmission of knowledge, concepts, and principles through lectures, readings, and other didactic methods (Bligh, 2000; Prince & Felder, 2006) development of solid foundation of knowledge and complex or foundational subjects (Biggs, 2003;Kirschner et al., 2006; Ramsden, 2003) and lack opportunities for hands-on practice and contextual application of knowledge (Hmelo-Silver, 2004). Whereas, experiential emphasizes on learning by doing, problem-solving, and reflection on concrete experiences Involves active engagement, such as simulations, internships, field work, and project-based learning (Hmelo-Silver, 2004;Wurdinger & Carlson, 2010),allows learners to apply knowledge to real-world situations and develop practical skills, promotes deeper understanding through the integration of theory and practice(Hmelo-Silver, 2004;Kolb, 1984), enhance motivation, critical thinking, and problem-solving abilities (Hmelo-Silver, 2004).

In blended approaches, many educational programs aim to strike a balance between theoretical and experiential learning (Biggs, 2003; Prince & Felder, 2006), leverages on the strengths of each approach and provide a more holistic learning experience (Prince & Felder, 2006). Under this approach, sequencing theoretical and experiential components, or integrating them in parallel, can reinforce learning (Hmelo-Silver, 2004) . Also, effective blending requires careful instructional design and alignment of learning objectives, activities, and assessments (Biggs, 2003; Ramsden, 2003).

In either approach, it is crucial to consider contextual factors: namely, (a) the optimal balance between theoretical and experiential learning can vary based on the subject matter, learner characteristics, educational level, and cultural/institutional norms. (b) resource availability, class sizes, and teaching methods can also influence the feasibility of experiential approaches (Wurdinger & Carlson, 2010; Hmelo-Silver, 2004)., and (c) Careful consideration of these contextual factors is important when designing effective learning environments (Biggs, 2003; Ramsden, 2003).

METHODOLOGY

The chapter aims to establish how balancing experiential and academic learning can improve university students' experiences and create pathways for employment. The study examines the perspectives of students and faculty members in Kenyan Universities.

Study design: The study adopts a descriptive cross-sectional survey design.

Data collection instruments A modified national survey of student Engagement (NSSE) tool and Faculty survey of student engagement (FSSE) which complements NSSE tool to collect data. NSSE was developed by Indiana universities in 1998 through funding from The Pew Charitable Trusts funds. The survey is updated periodically, to develop new measures, refine existing measures, improve clarity and update terminologies. As a complement to NSSE, FSSE collects data on instructional staff perceptions and expectations regarding student learning and development. Both NSSE and FSSE survey tools seek to support evidence-based improvement in postsecondary institutions. NSSE and FSSE survey items were customized to fit this study. The survey tools are standardized self- administered questionnaires that were managed through emails and google forms.

The study population comprised all fourth- year students in all disciplines in the four (4) selected universities in Kenya. The goal was to recruit 3250 fourth year students to participate in the study. This decision was informed by the rule of thumb of selecting the sample size of 30% as the minimum required to perform statistical analysis (Aguinis & Harden, 2009). Emails were sent to intranets of 3500 fourth year students in the selected universities through their division of research and research assistants. A total of 2525 students entered the survey, while only 1967 completed it. Thus, the study's completion rate and response rate were 72.15% and 77.9%. Of the 1967 respondents that participated in the study, female students comprised 69% (1,352) while male were 31.3% (615) of the respondents. The participants were drawn from various disciplines categorized as Humanities, Social sciences and Arts (n=610), Medicine (n=94), Applied Sciences (n=1,120), Pure and Natural Sciences(n=142). The same process was done to collect information from faculty members.

Measure: The study used a modified National Survey for Student Engagement (NSSE) and Faculty survey of student engagement (FSSE) tool, which is a complement to NSSE to collect data. The NSSE survey collects information on five categories: (1) background and demographic information, (2) participation in educationally purposeful activities, (3) institutional requirements and the challenging nature of coursework, (4) perceptions of the college environment, and (5) estimates of educational and personal growth. For instance, Questions related to educational purposeful activities included: perception about the emphasis of their coursework and to rate the extent their instructors engaged them on various activities. Concerning Institutional requirement for challenging nature of coursework, students were asked to rate the extent their courses challenged them to do their best work; rate how much their institution has contributed to knowledge, skills, and personal development in various competencies. The FSSE measures faculty members' expectations of student engagement in educational practices that are empirically linked to high levels of learning and development. How faculty are well equipped and supported to equipped learners with needed competencies.

Descriptive and contingence analysis were conducted using STATA Version 17. Data was weighted to consider the sampling design. Contingency analysis was used specifically as a follow up to descriptive analysis to determine whether the percentages of estimations were statistically significant.

Ethical Approval and Consent to Participate

Before data collection, the researchers sought for relevant ethical approvals from the Institutional Ethical Research committee of Masinde Muliro University of Science and Technology- and National Commission for Science, Technology and Innovation [NACOSTI]. Then, the research team sought the consent of all participants. Explained the purpose of the study to the respondents before the data collection. The respondents were assured that their participation in the research was completely voluntary and that they may quit at any moment, as they wish. The participants were assured of their anonymity and confidentiality of the information they provided throughout the process.

RESULTS

Preliminary Findings

Table 1 presents a summary of the numerical and categorical variables observed without transformation. From Table 1, the percentage missing data was highest (2%) in the student's age variable. A test of skewness of all variables was within the acceptable range of -1 and +1 except for the Age of students which was -2. A check of Kurtosis showed that most variables in the study had Kurtosis within the acceptable range of -4 and 4 except for two variables: academic performance and Age of students.

In total, 255 faculty members and 1967 students participated in the study. Of the faculty who participated, 65%(165) of the participants were male and 35% (90) were female. Of the students who participated in the study male were 615 representing 31.3% of the participants whereas female students were 1352 comprising 68.7% of student participants. The other demographic information of the participants included the age of the students which ranged between 18 and 31 years old. The participating students and faculty were drawn from selected public and private universities, across academic disciplines categorized as Applied Sciences, Humanities social sciences and arts, medical, pure and natural sciences and sciences. Of the faculty who participated in the survey, 84% (213) had attained the terminal degree and 17%(42) of the faculty who participated had not attained the terminal degree. Also, a majority(56%) of faculty members had teaching experience of 11 years and above an indication that they were qualified. The majority of faculty members(77%) who participated in the study their terms of employment were full time.

Students' overall education experience was captured. Of the participating students, about 940(48%) reported having a good overall academic experience. This was followed by 769(39.2%) of the students who reported having an excellent overall academic experience. Those who had fair and poor overall academic experiences were 12.1% and .7% respectively.

Table 1. Descriptive Statistics of Observed Variables without Data Transformation

Variable		**%Mis**	**Mean**	**SD**	**Min**	**Max**	**Skew**	**Kur**
Age (students)		2%	22.3	2.83	18	31	-2.06	12.67
Categorical Variable	**Code**	**%Mis**	**Freq.**	**%**	**Cum**		**Skew**	**Kur**
Gender (Faculty)	Male (1)	0%	165	65	65		.642	1.427
	Female (2	0%	90	35	100			
Gender (Students)	Male (1)	0%	615	31.3	31.3		-.8	1.0
	Female (2)	0%	1,352	68.7	100			
Academic Rank	Professor (1)	0%	6	2.6	2.6		-.908	3.233
	Ass. Professor (2)	0%	21	9.2	12			
	S. Lecturer (3)	0%	33	14.5	26.3			
	Lecturer (4)	0%	93	41	67.1			
	Ass. Lecturer (5)	0%	75	33	100			
Institution Type	Private (1)	0%	657	31.27	31.27		-1.807	4.268
	Public (2)	0%	1562	68.73	100			
Terminal degree	Yes (1) No (2)	0%	213	83.5	83.5		-.971	4.583
		0%	42	16.5	100			
Teaching experience	0-5yrs (1)	1%	45	17.4	17.4		.353	2.214
	6-10yrs (2)	1%	70	27	44.4			
	11-15yrs (3)	1%	81	31.3	75.7			
	16-20yrs (4)	1%	25	9.7	85.3			
	Above 20yrs (5)	1%	38	14.7	100			
Terms of employment	Contract (1)	0%	33	12.9	12.9		.353	2.214
	Part-time (2)	0%	24	9.4	22.35			
	Full-time (3)	0%	198	77.7	100			

continued on following page

Table 1. Continued

Variable		%Mis	Mean	SD	Min	Max	Skew	Kur
Academic discipline(F)	Applied Sciences (1)	0%	51	20	20		1.134	4.745
	H.S S& Arts (2)	0%	159	62.4	82.4			
	Medical (3)	0%	24	9.4	91.8			
	P&N Sciences (4)	0%	18	7.1	98.8			
	Science (5)	0%	3	1.2	100			
Academic discipline(S)	Applied Sciences (1)	1%	1,120	57	57		1.459	4.406
	H.S S& Arts (2)	1%	610	31.	88			
	Medical (3)	1%	94	4.8	92.8			
	P&N Science (4)	1%	142	7.2	100			
Overall Education exp.	Excellent coded (1)	1%	769	39.23	39.23		-.1535	1.236
	Good (2)	1%	940	48	87.23			
	Fair (3)	1%	238	12.14	99.47			
	Poor (4)	1%	13	0.66	100			

Note: %Mis= Percentage of missing data in variables; SD= standard deviation; Freq= Frequency; Cum= Cumulative; Skew =Skewness; Ku =Kurtosis; S = students; F= Faculty

Students and Faculty Perspectives of How the Current Curriculum Incorporates Experiential Skills Alongside Academic Learning

To establish the perspectives of students and faculty on how the current curriculum incorporates experiential skills alongside academic learning, students were asked to rate their experiences on how the institution has contributed to acquisition of various competencies ranging from writing, critical thinking, problem solving, team working to being an informed citizen. The students were also asked of their perception concerning the emphasis of coursework information in relation to memorizing, evaluating a point of view, application of facts and theories, and forming new ideas. Similarly, faculty members were asked to rate the extent their course structure helped students learn and develop job- related competencies. The results are presented in the subsections below.

Students' Perspectives on how Institution has Contributed to their Competency Development

The respondents were asked to rate their experiences on how their institution had contributed to development of various competencies, such as, writing, speaking, critical thinking, problem solving, work-related skills, analytical skills, team working, diversity and inclusion, and being an informed citizen. The summary of the responses by type of institution are presented in Figure 1.

The results showed that to some extent both public and private institutions endeavor to help students develop various competencies ranging from writing and speaking clearly, critical thinking, problem-solving, job-related skills to becoming a well informed and active citizen. The results showed no difference between public and private institutions on how they helped students build their ability to write effectively, represented by percent mean of 10.2 and how they built their team spirit represented by a percent mean of 10.

On the one hand, the results showed that students who attended public universities had a bit better experience as they were well prepared to acquire knowledge, skills and personal development to communicate clearly and effectively (percent mean of 9.9), think critically and analytically(10.8), solve real-world problems(9.5); and become informed and active citizen(percent mean 10.4). On the other hand, students who attended private institutions were well prepared to analyze statistical information (percent mean 10.0), acquire work-related competencies(9.5); develop personal philosophy(10.5), and to embrace inclusiveness and diversity by acknowledging others' diverse backgrounds(10.8).

Figure 1. How institution has contributed to students' various competencies

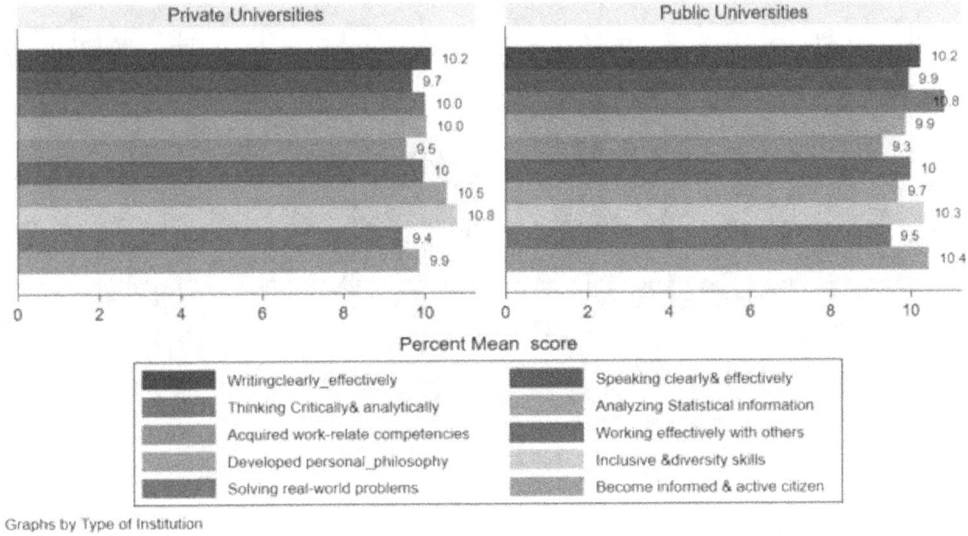

Students' Perception on Emphasis of their Coursework Information

The students were asked of their perception on how much their coursework emphasized memorizing, evaluating a point of view, application of facts and theories, and forming new ideas from various course information. The responses were compared across the programs and by type of institution and are presented in Figure 2.

The results showed that while coursework in both institutions contributed to memorizing course material, it was slightly higher among students in public universities by a point 4 percent compared to students in private universities. Course work in public institutions emphasized application of facts and theories, or methods to practical problems or new situations slightly more than the course work in private institutions represented by percent mean of 26.1 and 25.3 respectively.

Generally, coursework in private universities emphasized evaluating a point of view, decision, or information source, with medical programs taking the lead with a mean percent of 26,compared to public universities that had a percent mean of 24.3. Also, the results showed that coursework in both institutions emphasize creativity in coming up with new ideas from various information. However, the emphasis on this competency was slightly higher by percent of point 2 in private universities compared to public.

Figure 2. Students' views of Coursework Emphasis by program and Type of Institution

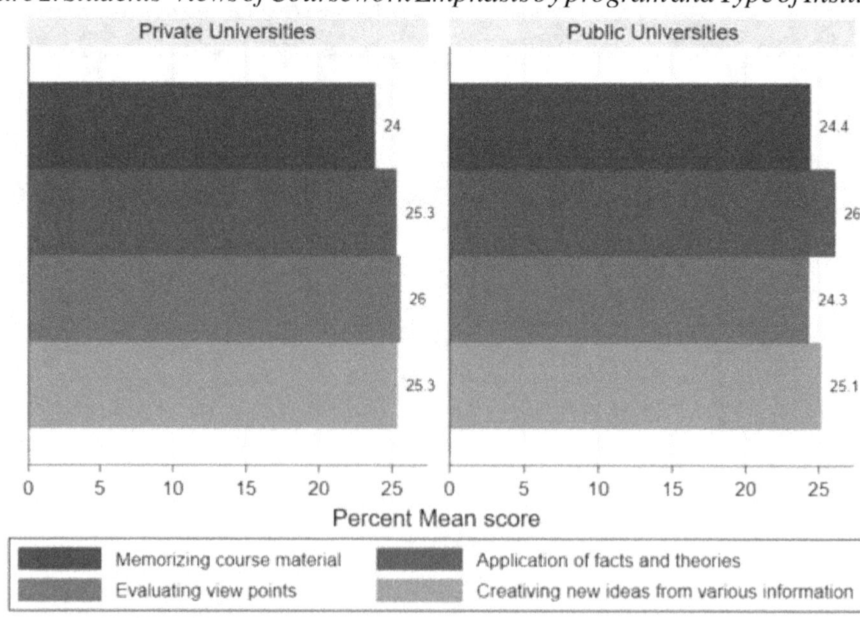

Faculty Perception on the Extent their Course Structure helped Students Learn and Develop job- Related Competencies

Faculty rated the extent the structure of their course helped students to learn and develop job related competencies. The responses were compared across course disciplines. Table 2 presents the results of contingence analysis.

The results showed that to some extent, the coursework was structured in a way that helped students learn and acquire job related competencies. Further, the results showed that except for five competencies, that is; acquiring job-related knowledge and skills; Working effectively with others; understanding people of other backgrounds; Solving complex real-world problems and becoming an informed and active citizen, the rest of the competencies positively and significantly helped students learn and develop job related competencies, though degree of extent varied across disciplines. For instance, writing clearly and effectively differed significantly at (p=.02); speaking clearly and effectively at (p=.03) Thinking critically and analytically at (p=.05); analyzing numerical and statistical information at (p=.001); developing or clarify a personal code of values & ethics at (p=.02).

Table 2. The extent Course work is structured to help student learn and develop Job-related competencies by course discipline

Work Related Competencies	M	SD	χ2	p-value
Write clearly and effectively	3.094	1.273	10.00	0.019**
Speak clearly and effectively	2.494	.793	7.20	0.027**
Think critically and analytically	3.353	1.207	7.70	0.05*
Analyze numerical and statistical information	2.953	1.267	16.89	0.001***
Acquire job- or work-related knowledge and skills	2.847	1.362	2.58	0.461
Work effectively with others	3.106	1.322	3.83	0.280
Develop or clarify a personal code of values & ethics	2.93	1.320	9.51	0.023**
Understand people of other backgrounds	2.93	1.329	4.56	0.207
Solve complex real-world problems	2.976	1.348	7.73	0.052
Become informed and active citizen	2.847	1.388	7.14	0.068

Note. N = 255; *p < .05, **p < .01, ***p< .001

Whether Students have Opportunities to Apply Academic Knowledge in Real-world Contexts Through Experiential Learning

To address the question on whether students are provided with opportunities to apply academic knowledge in real-world contexts through experiential learning, perspectives of students and faculty were sought differently concerning what undergraduate students should complete before graduating. The results are presented in the subsections below.

Students' Perspectives Concerning what they should Complete Before Graduating

Students were asked various statements to state what they plan to do, or do not plan to do, done/in progress or have not decided to do before they graduate. The responses by program are summarized in Table 3. The results showed that institutions at least have established programs to which students are required to complete before graduating ranging from internship, leadership responsibility, learning community to project work including comprehensive examination.

Further, the results of the analysis showed that the need to participate in an internship, field experience, student teaching, or clinical placement (p=0.187) and the need for students to Complete a culminating senior experience (project or thesis, portfolio, recital, comprehensive exam, etc.(p=0.07) were not statistically different across the course disciplines. This could indicate that various course disciplines have put in place structures that require students to participate in the two activities before graduating.

On the contrary, the results showed that there was a statistically difference among course disciplines in some statements including the need for students to hold a formal leadership role in a student organization or group (p=0.00); participate in a learning community or some other formal program where groups of students take two or more classes together (p=0.05) and work with a faculty member on a research project (p=0.00) before they graduate. This could indicate that various course disciplines varied in the level they required students to participate in some activities before graduating.

Table 3. Students' plan to complete Before Graduating

Statement	Responses	Applied Sciences F (%)	H. Social S &Arts F (%)	Medical F (%)	Pure & N Sciences F (%)	*P*-value
Participate in an internship, field experience, student teaching, or clinical placement	Do not plan to do Done /in progress Not Decided Plan to do	34(3) 309(27.6) 57(5.1) 720(64.3)	23(3.8) 244(9) 16(3) 389(64)	23(3.7) 3(40) 21(3.4) 322(56.4)	4(2.8) 31(21.8) 20(14.1) 87(61.3)	0.187
Hold a formal leadership role in a student organization or group	Do not plan to do Done /in progress Not Decided Plan to do	189(17) 368(32.9) 139(12.4) 424(38)	88(13.1) 272(44.6) 57(9.3) 193(31.6)	10(10.6) 42(44.7) 7(7.5) 35(37.2)	24(17) 52(37) 25(18) 41(29)	0.000***
Participate in a learning community or some other formal program where groups of students take two or more classes together	Do not plan to do Done /in progress Not Decided Plan to do	95(8.5) 508(45.4) 65(5.8) 452(40.4)	50(8) 312(51.2) 27(4.4) 221(36.2)	8(8.5) 55(58.5) 8(8.5) 23(24.5)	13(7.1) 65(45.8) 9(6.3) 55(38.7)	0.05*
Work with a faculty member on a research project	Do not plan to do Done /in progress Not Decided Plan to do	143(13) 321(28.7) 96(8.6) 560(50)	87(14.2) 224(36.8) 34(5.6) 265(43.4)	16(17) 38(49.4) 14(14.9) 26(31.7)	10(7) 61(43) 26(18.3) 45(31.7)	0.000***
Complete a culminating senior experience (project or thesis, portfolio, recital, comprehensive exam, etc.	Do not plan to do Done /in progress Not Decided Plan to do	152(13.6) 299(26.7) 104(9.3) 565(50.5)	56(9) 251(41.2) 47(8) 256(42)	21(22.3) 29(30.8) 8(8.5) 36(38.3)	14(10) 46(32.4) 27(19) 55(38)	0.07

Note: HSS&A= Humanities, Social Sciences & Arts; P&NS= Pure and Natural Sciences; S= Sciences; N = 1932; *p < .05, **p < .01, ***p< .001

Faculty Perspectives Concerning what Undergraduate Students Should Complete before Graduating

To assess faculty views of how they engaged students in experiential learning, faculty were asked of their perceptions concerning what undergraduate students should complete before graduating, faculty held differing views which also varied by area of discipline. Figure 3 presents a summary of the results.

The results presented in Figure 3 showed that at least all study disciplines engaged students in various activities ranging from practicum, formal leadership, participating in the learning community to engaging in community-based projects. However, the level of engagement in these activities varied by course discipline. For instance, whereas faculty in sciences were of the view that it was important for students to hold a formal leadership role and participate in learning community before graduating both represented by percent mean of 29, faculty in Pure and natural sciences held a view that it was important for undergraduate to participate in internship, learning community, and do a community -based project before graduating both represented by percent mean of 18.8. Faculty in the medical program were of the view that undergraduate students need to complete a community -based project before graduating represented by a percent mean of 21.1. Further, faculty in the programs of Applied Sciences and Humanities, social sciences and Arts were both of the view that undergraduate students need to participate in internship represented by average percent mean of 18.5 and 19.8 respectively. From Figure 3, it was evident that all departments find it important for undergraduate students to Participate in an internship, co-op, field experience, student teaching, or clinical placement before graduating.

Figure 3. Perception of faculty on what undergraduates should complete before graduating

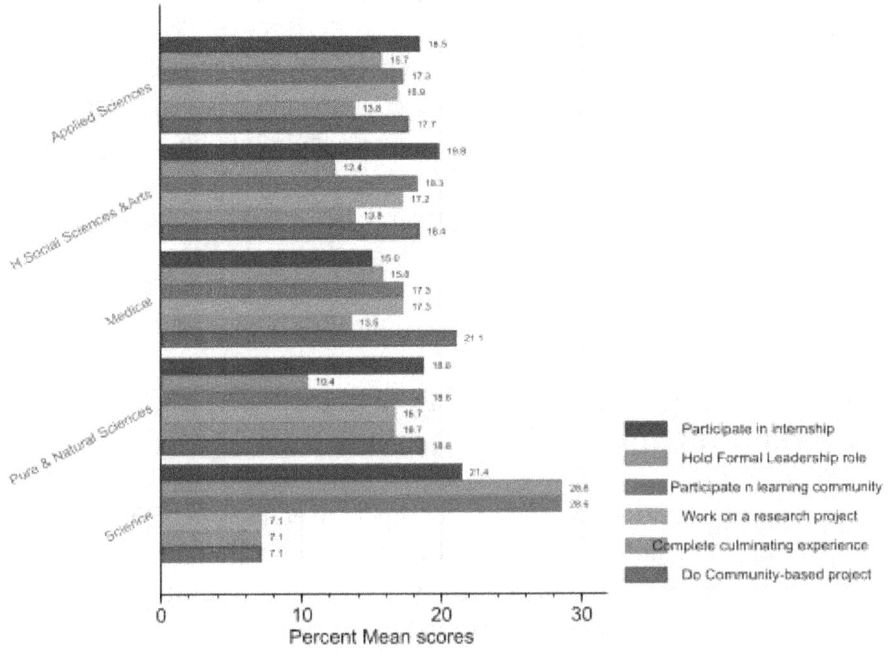

DISCUSSION AND IMPLICATIONS FOR PRACTICE

The finding according to students' views that institutions had contributed to their competency development, revealed important insights into how higher education institutions are incorporating experiential learning alongside academic learning. However, the high unemployment rates among graduates could indicate a significant mismatch between both experiential and academic skills acquired in higher education and what is required by employers (Kapareliotis,et al., 2019; Korucu-Kış, 2021; Munene, 2021). This finding aligns with the literature that highlights the need for a nexus between academic skills and experiential skills. Higher education institutions should not only focus on academic skills, but incorporate experiential skills needed for employability (Ngure, 2015). More importantly, this finding emphasizes the need for integrating experiential skills into curriculum design so as to better align educational outcomes with demands for the labor market. Moreover, it is consistent with the literature suggesting that institutions of higher education should strive to strike a balance between academic knowledge and experiential skills for holistic career development (Sisol Recruitment, 2024).

Based on the perspectives of students and faculty, the findings showed that both public and private institutions to some extent, though with variations in disciplines, contributed to the development of various competencies among their learners, such as, writing, critical thinking, problem-solving, and teamwork. The magnitude of variation in extent the disciplined helped learners acquire various competencies is an indication that there is still room for improvement in providing more experiential learning opportunities (Dwyer, 2022; Hammond et al., 2020). As Sisol Recruitment (2024) and Hicks (2023) suggested, providing more opportunities for experiential learning in addition to academic learning can be achieved through internships, co-op programs, and real-world scenarios in teaching.

Students' Perception on Emphasis of their Coursework Information

On the one hand, the findings that students perceived their coursework to focus more on memorization, indicates that very little to no experiential learning was happening. The increased emphasis on memorization in public universities indicates a traditional approach to education that prioritizes rote learning over critical thinking. Literature suggests that while memorization can help students retain information, it does not necessarily equip them with the skills needed to solve real-world problems (Ngure, 2015). While the practice of memorization was in public universities, there is a need for institutions of higher learning to balance between academic learning which emphasizes memorization and experiential learning that emphasizes practical application of the knowledge learned. On the other hand, students also stated that their institutions emphasized creativity, with a slightly higher emphasis in private universities. The finding highlights the importance of fostering innovative thinking among students. This is crucial for preparing students to adapt to and drive change in dynamic work environments (Hicks, 2023). Also, institutions of higher learning need to encourage creativity and formation of new ideas to equip students with the ability to think broadly and develop unique solutions to problems (Zanville, 2023).

The variation in emphasis on competencies across different programs, with medical programs in private universities leading in evaluating a point of view, suggests that certain disciplines may already be integrating experiential skills more effectively. This convergence between experiential learning and academic skills supports the idea that tailored approaches to curriculum design are necessary to meet the specific needs of different fields.

Faculty Perception on the Extent their Course Structure Helped Students Learn and Develop job/work- related Competencies

From the findings, faculty perceptions that their courses are somewhat structured to help students acquire job-related competencies aligns with the literature emphasizing the need for curriculum designers to create and include a nexus between academic and experiential skills (Dwyer, 2022). However, the fact that some competencies did not significantly help students indicates a gap in training, and in most cases a more focus on academic skills, which are mainly theoretical in nature and denies learners opportunity to practice the learned skills. The finding has significant implications for institutional leaders to work closely with potential employers to be at par with the changing skills demands and training needs in higher education spheres and to ensure convergence between academic and experiential skills in training for the labor market.

The variation in how different disciplines contribute to developing specific competencies suggests that tailored approaches are necessary for different fields of study. Literature supports the notion that discipline-specific needs must be considered to effectively prepare students for their respective job markets (Ngure, 2015). For instance, analytical skills might be more emphasized in STEM fields, while communication skills might be crucial in humanities and social sciences. Despite the nature of the institution, it is imperative that training upholds both experiential and academic skills. Institutions should ensure that all relevant competencies are integrated into each discipline's curriculum (Hicks, 2023).

The development of interpersonal skills, such as, working effectively with others and understanding people from different backgrounds, is critical for employability in a diverse and globalized job market (Awiti et al., 2019). The mixed results in these areas suggest that more emphasis is needed to ensure students are well-prepared for collaborative work environments. Additionally, developing a personal code of values and ethics is important for professional integrity and responsibility. The significant impact of coursework on this competency (p=.02) underlines the role of higher education in fostering ethical behavior (Zanville, 2023). While in most cases there is a need for an intersection and balance between academic and experiential skills, the soft skills required for teamwork and collaboration at the workplace are mainly learned theoretical but perfected through experiential learning. Moreso, the significant positive impact on writing clearly and effectively (p=.02) and speaking clearly and effectively (p=.03) reinforces the need for strong communication skills in the job market (Hicks, 2023). These skills are critical across all disciplines and should be continuously developed through coursework and experiential learning (Ngure, 2015).

Students and Faculty Perspectives Concerning What Undergraduate Students Should Complete Before Graduating

Based on the findings, students' and faculty views of what undergraduate should complete before graduating varied across disciplines. The lack of statistical significance on students' views concerning what they should complete before graduating provides huge insights into what is being taught and the need for incorporating experiential learning components into higher education programs. For instance, students overwhelmingly pointed out that internship and field experience before graduation was necessary. The lack of statistically significant suggests a widespread recognition of the importance of these experiential learning opportunities. Similarly, the consensus among faculty from all disciplines on the importance of internships, co-ops, field experiences, student teaching, or clinical placements aligns with the literature highlighting the critical role these experiences play in bridging the gap between academic learning and real-world application. Internships and similar experiences provide students with hands-on learning, exposure to professional environments, and the opportunity to apply academic knowledge in experiential settings. These experiences are essential for enhancing employability and preparing students for the job market (Dwyer,2022). The experiences also allow students to develop professional networks, understand workplace dynamics, and gain hands-on experience, which are all critical for their future careers (Vault, 2023).

Both students and faculty were of the views that undergraduates needed to have held a formal leadership role before graduating. From students and faculty views, there was a significant difference in the requirement for holding formal leadership roles across disciplines. This could suggest that some disciplines place more emphasis on leadership development than others. Nonetheless, leadership skills are essential for career advancement and effective teamwork in a professional setting (Awiti et al., 2019; Ngure, 2015). Since there are no known standard guides for exemplary leadership, this is a skill that can only be perfected through practice. It is therefore imperative that higher education institutions integrate leadership opportunities across all disciplines to develop well-rounded graduates.

From the findings, both students and faculty were of the view that undergraduate students were provided with opportunity to practice the academic and experiential skills learned before graduating, that is to complete a community-based project. Though there were variations in how various disciplines utilized collaborative learning environments, learning communities have potential to promote peer learning, critical thinking, and a sense of belonging, which are beneficial for academic and personal development (Hicks, 2023). For instance, the emphasis on community-based projects by faculty in medical programs and pure and natural sciences reflects the importance of the intersection between experiential learning and academic learning that involves real-world problem-solving and engaging with the community. Such projects help students develop a sense of social responsibility and apply their knowledge to address community needs (Zanville, 2023). Including community-based learning in higher education is supported by the literature as an effective way to enhance students' experiential skills, critical thinking, and ability to work collaboratively (Sisol Recruitment, 2024). These projects also foster a deeper understanding of societal issues and prepare students for roles that require public engagement and service (Ndiku et al., 2024). It is therefore imperative that institutions expand opportunities and avenues for experiential learning, to foster collaboration and citizenship among students.

Students reported that they were provided with opportunity for experiential learning through participating in learning communities, where students take classes together and engage in collaborative learning, promote peer support, critical thinking, and a sense of belonging. The literature supports the benefits of such communities in enhancing student engagement, academic performance, and personal development (Hicks, 2023). The overall findings suggest that both students and faculty support a holistic approach to education, which includes internships, leadership roles, community-based projects, and collaborative learning, as it is essential for preparing well-rounded graduates. Such an approach aligns with the literature advocating for balanced and integrative learning experiences that combine academic knowledge with experiential skills (Dwyer, 2022; Zanville, 2023).

FUTURE RESEARCH DIRECTIONS

The study has limitations that include: the sample of the participants was limited to only students in their fourth year of study in four higher education institutions whose perception of empirical evidence and its practical value could have been challenging. A future study may consider including students from other years of study. For instance, from first year to fourth year so as to gain a deeper insight into their experience with experiential learning. Further, the broad heterogeneity of the study population should be considered for the purpose of addressing diversity in location and size of the institutions. This study, therefore proposes a future study to increase the number of both public and private institutions selected into the study. This would help increase the generalizability of the study findings. Furthermore, this study proposes a future study to contact a tracer study of students from first year up to employment to capture a comprehensive perspective of an environment that fosters experiential learning alongside academic learning.

CONCLUSION

A balance between the theory and practice in education is crucial for excelling in the real- world situation. The results showed that while both public and private institutions endeavor to help students develop various competencies ranging from writing and speaking clearly, critical thinking, problem-solving, job-related skills to becoming a well informed and active citizen, the level of engagement varied by institution type except for how institutions helped students build their ability to write effectively and how they built their team spirit. Generally, coursework in both institutions emphasizes creativity in coming up with new ideas from various sources, though there are gaps of imbalance between academic and experiential learning that need to be addressed. To an extent, course work content was structured to help students learn and acquire job related competencies, though the degree of extent varied across disciplines and the effect was positive and significant except for five competencies, that is; acquiring job- or work-related knowledge and skills; Working effectively with others; understanding people of other backgrounds; Solving complex real-world problems and becoming an informed and active citizen, the rest of the competencies were not significant, an indication of imbalance between academic and experiential skills offered at institutions of higher learning. .Also, the results showed that at least all study disciplines engaged students in various activities ranging from practicum, formal leadership, participating in the learning community to engaging in community-based projects. The future of higher education lies in embracing both experiential and academic learning, creating a dynamic and relevant environment with opportunities for experiential learning. This requires concerted efforts of all higher education stakeholders in ensuring an education system that equips learners with both academic and experiential skills for their holistic growth and for success in real world challenges.

REFERENCES

Baker, G., & Henson, D. (2010). Promoting employability skills development in a research-intensive university. *Education + Training*, 52(1), 62–75. DOI: 10.1108/00400911011017681

Bakhshi, H., Downing, J., Osborne, M., & Schneider, P. (2017). The future of skills: Employment in 2030. Pearson and Nesta. https://futureskills.pearson.com/research/assets/pdfs/technical-report.pdf

Biggs, J. (2003). Aligning teaching and assessing to course objectives. *Teaching and Learning in Higher Education: New Trends and Innovations*, 2, 13–17.

Bligh, D. A. (2000). *What's theon*. Cambridge university press.

Dwyer, T. (2022). Conceptualizations of market orientation in the higher education literature. *Journal of Marketing for Higher Education*, •••, 1–23. DOI: 10.1080/08841241.2022.2089941

Hammond, K. L., Webster, R., & Hammond, N. (2020). Antecedents of market orientation in higher education: Empirical results from four key informant perspectives. *Global Journal of Management and Marketing*, 4(1), 113–134. https://www.igbr.org/wp-content/uploads/2020/04/GJMM_Vol_4_No_1_2020.pdF.113

Kapareliotis, I., Voutsina, K., & Patsiotis, A. (2019). Internship and employability prospects: Assessing student's work readiness, *Higher Education. Skills and Work-Based Learning*, 9(4), 538–549. DOI: 10.1108/HESWBL-08-2018-0086

Kirschner, P. A., Sweller, J., & Clark, R. E. (2006). Why minimal guidance during instruction does not work: An analysis of the failure of constructivist, discovery, problem-based, experiential, and inquiry-based teaching. *Educational Psychologist*, 41(2), 75–86. DOI: 10.1207/s15326985ep4102_1

Korucu-Kış, S. (2021). Preparing student teachers for *real* classrooms through *virtual vicarious* experiences of critical incidents during remote practicum: A meaningful-experiential learning perspective. *Education and Information Technologies*, 26(6), 6949–6971. DOI: 10.1007/s10639-021-10555-7 PMID: 33935573

Munene, I. I. (2021). *Universities and Labor Market Mismatch in Kenya. International*. Technology. Citizen Digital.

Ng, P. M. L., Chan, J. K. Y., Wut, T. M., Lo, M. F., & Szeto, I. (2021). What makes better career opportunities for young graduates? Examining acquired employability skills in higher education institutions. *Education + Training*, 63(6), 852–871. DOI: 10.1108/ET-08-2020-0231

Prince, M. J., & Felder, R. M. (2006). Inductive teaching and learning methods: Definitions, comparisons, and research bases. *Journal of Engineering Education*, 95(2), 123–138. DOI: 10.1002/j.2168-9830.2006.tb00884.x

Sisol Recruitment(March,1,2024).*Balancing academic knowledge with necessary skills for employment.* Sisol Recruitment (24) Balancing academic knowledge with necessary skills for employment. | LinkedIn.

Vault, T. (November 7,2023). Theory VS Practice(Knowledge and application). *Vivekanand Education Society*. Theoretical Knowledge Vs Practical Application (ves.ac.in)

World Bank. (2019). *Improving Higher Education Performance in Kenya: A Policy Report. Report No: AUS0001105*. The World Bank.

Wurdinger, S., & Carlson, J. (2010). *Teaching for experiential learning: Five approaches that work.* R&L Education.

FUTHER READINGS

Al Hinai, M. R., Bhuiyan, A. B., & Husin, N. A. (2021). The Active Learning Attributes and Employability Readiness Among Engineering Graduates in The High Education Institutes in Oman. *International Journal of Business and Management Future*, 6(1), 26–35. DOI: 10.46281/ijbmf.v6i1.1465

Bawica, I. M. (2021). The University Internship Program and its Effects on Students' Employability Readiness. *International Journal of Academe and Industry Research.*, 2(3), 86–101. Advance online publication. DOI: 10.53378/348731

Diery, A., Vogel, F., Knogler, M., & Seidel, T. (2020). *Evidence Based Practice in Higher Education: Teacher Educators'Attitude, Challenges, and Uses*. Front. Edu., 02June, 2020. Sec. *Teaching Education*. Advance online publication. DOI: 10.3389/feduc.2020.0006

Martínez Casanovas, M., Ruíz-Munzón, N., & Buil-Fabregá, M. (2022). Higher education: The best practices for fostering competences for sustainable development through the use of active learning methodologies. *International Journal of Sustainability in Higher Education*, 23(3), 703–727. DOI: 10.1108/IJSHE-03-2021-0082

Okolie, U. C., Nwali, A. C., Ogbaekirigwe, C. O., Ezemoyi, C. M., & Achilike, B. A. (2021). A closer look at how work placement learning influences student engagement in practical skills acquisition. *Higher Education Research & Development*, 41(7), 2278–2291. DOI: 10.1080/07294360.2021.1996338

KEY TERMS AND DEFINITIONS

Academic learning: refer to acquiring knowledge and skills theoretically in an educational setting.

Employability skills: asset of achievements- attitude, knowledge including soft and hard capabilities graduates require for the labor market.

Experiential learning: is a practical, hands-on approach to learning educators engage with students in direct and focused reflection in order to increase knowledge, develop skills, and clarify values

Faculty perspectives-: refers to instructors views and opinion about the experiential and academic aspects of teaching and learning.

Higher education institutions: refers to universities as the highest learning institutions

Students' perspectives,: refers to the views and opinion of learners concerning the experiential and academic approaches to learning and teaching

Chapter 6
Innovative Learning Spaces and Blended Learning:
Quest for 21st Century Competency Teaching and Learning Approaches

Norah Adera
Aga Khan University, Tanzania

ABSTRACT

Adopting teaching and learning approaches focused on 21st-century competencies necessitates creative solutions that span traditional classroom settings and the internet world in the quickly changing educational landscape. To cultivate these competencies, this chapter explores the transformative potential of novel learning spaces and blended learning approaches. This theoretical review uses secondary data as its main source and incorporates the most recent methodological and meta-analytical literature evaluations to cross-validate its conclusions. By merging flexible and adaptable physical and virtual environments with advanced technological tools, this chapter offers practical strategies for educators and policymakers to enhance student engagement and promote critical thinking, creativity, collaboration, and digital literacy. It aims to empower educational institutions to embrace and sustain these innovative approaches, ensuring all students acquire the skills necessary to thrive in a digital and interconnected world.

DOI: 10.4018/979-8-3693-6930-2.ch006

INTRODUCTION

The demands of the 21st century have necessitated a fundamental shift in how education is delivered, particularly in higher education. Traditional models of teaching, rooted in lecture-based instruction and passive learning, are increasingly seen as inadequate in preparing students for the complexities of a rapidly changing, interconnected, and digital world. (Okpara & Ezeador, 2024). Skills such as critical thinking, creativity, collaboration, and digital literacy are now essential competencies that students need to acquire to thrive both academically and professionally. (Lamb et al., 2017). Consequently, educators and policymakers are exploring more innovative teaching and learning approaches, including blended learning and the redesigning of physical and virtual learning environments.

The COVID-19 pandemic accelerated the adoption of these innovative learning methodologies across the globe. With physical classrooms closed, higher education institutions were forced to transition rapidly to online learning platforms, highlighting the importance of flexible, adaptable teaching strategies. (Turnbull et al., 2021). Additionally, rapid technological advancements, shifting workforce demands, globalization, and the increasing need for lifelong learning have all contributed to the quest for more effective teaching and learning strategies. (Lim et al., 2024). As higher education institutions move forward, there is a growing recognition that the combination of innovative learning spaces and blended learning is not just a temporary solution but a critical step toward fostering the competencies students need to succeed in the 21st century.

As a result, the academic environment is rapidly evolving, driven by the increasing demand for 21st-century skills such as critical thinking, creativity, collaboration, and digital literacy (Chu et al., 2017). Traditional classroom settings and teaching techniques are now inadequate for equipping students to navigate the complexities of today's world. Consequently, innovative learning spaces and blended learning models have emerged as crucial components in transforming education to meet these new demands (Castro, 2019). Transformations in higher education environments are necessary to reshape teaching and learning approaches. A strong emphasis is placed on creating adaptable, and student-centered experiences. This shift from traditional lecture-based instruction to a more interactive, technology-enhanced learning environment is driven by the need to actively engage students, foster collaboration, and develop critical thinking skills essential for today's digital world. (Holland & Holland, 2014). The interactive pedagogical strategies employed in higher institutions are crucial to engage students actively in their learning and foster a deeper understanding of concepts. They create an educational environment that is engaging, inclusive, and conducive to lifelong learning.

One of the most effective strategies is the flipped classroom model. In this approach, students engage with instructional material online before attending class sessions. This transforms the classroom into a space for interactive activities and in-depth discussions. It allows students to apply the knowledge they have acquired beforehand in a collaborative setting. By shifting the focus from passive listening to active participation, the flipped classroom promotes critical thinking and problem-solving skills. Additionally, this enables students to engage more deeply with the content (Zain & Sailin, 2020).

Project-based learning (PBL) involves students working on real-life projects to apply theory to solve problems. It is founded on critical thinking, teamwork, and creativity. Encouraging students to apply theoretical knowledge to practical problems, it fosters innovation and bridges the gap between abstract concepts and real-world applications. This hands-on approach enhances the understanding and development of essential skills such as collaboration, communication, and teamwork (Boss & Krauss, 2022).

Personalized learning paths are also integral to modern pedagogy. These paths allow students to progress through content at their own pace, ensuring they master each concept before moving on to more complex topics. Personalized learning caters to diverse learning styles and needs, ensuring each student receives support. This approach is particularly effective in promoting deeper and more personalized learning experiences, addressing the varied needs of students, and ensuring that no learner is left behind (Bernacki et al., 2021).

Technology-enhanced learning further complements these pedagogical strategies. The integration of digital tools and resources, such as Learning Management Systems (LMS) like Moodle and Canvas, along with interactive simulations and educational apps, provides students with engaging and interactive materials that cater to different learning styles. These tools enhance the learning experience by making complex concepts more accessible and easier to understand. Moreover, online collaboration tools such as Google Workspace and Microsoft Teams facilitate teamwork and communication, transforming learning into a more collaborative and dynamic process (Shurygin et al., 2021).

Therefore, this chapter examines the transformations in higher educational environments and the incorporation of technology into teaching methods. It offers educators and policymakers insights and practical strategies to create a more effective and inclusive educational experience for the students. Highlighting the essential competencies required for the 21st century, re-designing innovative learning spaces, and implementing blended learning approaches could enhance student engagement and competency development.

BACKGROUND

The shift toward Innovative Learning Spaces (ILS) and Blended Learning in higher education is the result of a convergence of both external and internal factors, with the COVID-19 pandemic acting as a major catalyst for these changes. However, the drivers behind this transformation extend far beyond the pandemic and are deeply rooted in broader societal, economic, and technological forces that necessitate new educational approaches. The COVID-19 pandemic brought to light the limitations of traditional education systems, prompting widespread closures of institutions and a rapid, and unplanned, transition to online learning environments. This abrupt shift exposed gaps in the conventional system and underscored the importance of digital literacy, adaptability, and flexible learning environments to accommodate diverse student needs (Lee et al., 2022).

As higher institutions adopted blended learning models, combining online and face-to-face components, innovative tools like virtual simulations, artificial intelligence-driven platforms, and interactive Learning Management Systems (LMS) such as Moodle and Canvas were employed to meet the varying needs of learners. According to Thahir et al. (2023), this period marked a significant acceleration in the use of digital tools in education. While the pandemic catalyzed these innovations, it also revealed longer-standing trends, particularly the need for personalized, student-centered learning environments. In an increasingly diverse world where students have different access to resources, learning preferences, and career aspirations, a one-size-fits-all approach is no longer viable. Educators and policymakers are now looking beyond the immediate impact of the pandemic to develop strategies that foster creativity, collaboration, critical thinking, and digital literacy.

Blended learning approaches have become popular to provide flexibility and cater to diverse students' learning styles. Integrating digital tools, these approaches enhance accessibility to up-to-date information and provide opportunities for personalized learning paths. Additionally, they allow students to progress at their own pace and individual needs (Boninger et al., 2019). Leveraging technological advancements, these approaches facilitate educators' utilization of a range of digital tools, including learning management systems (LMS), such as Moodle and Canvas to provide instructional materials, monitor students' progress, and facilitate communication and collaboration among students. Interactive simulations, artificial intelligence (AI), virtual reality, and adaptive learning platforms also create new opportunities for personalized and immersive learning experiences (Dai et al., 2024). Furthermore, Massive Open Online Courses (MOOCs), provide access to high-quality educational resources to students globally. They break down the geographical barriers and democratize education (Deng et al., 2020). Therefore, these tools enhance the flexibility and accessibility of higher education to improve students' educational outcomes.

The Digital revolution has also been a significant force in shaping teaching methodologies in higher education. Rapid technological advancements, particularly in artificial intelligence, virtual reality (VR), augmented reality (AR), and adaptive learning technologies, have provided educators with unprecedented tools to create immersive and interactive learning environments. According to Daniela (2020b), these technologies enable students to engage with content in a more dynamic and personalized way, which enhances both student engagement and learning outcomes. The integration of these technologies into Innovative Learning Spaces is critical to modern education. For instance, flexible classrooms equipped with digital tools such as interactive whiteboards and collaborative software encourage active learning and peer-to-peer interaction. Likewise, virtual learning environments accessible through LMS platforms enable students to engage with educational materials at their own pace, making education more accessible to a wide range of learners with diverse schedules and needs (Valtonen et al., 2021).

Due to globalization, industries have become increasingly interconnected, and the demand for professionals who possess both technical skills and global competencies such as cross-cultural communication, collaboration, and problem-solving abilities has intensified. This has placed pressure on higher education institutions to develop programs that are not only academically rigorous but also aligned with the demands of the global workforce. Blended learning models provide students with the opportunity to engage in Project-Based Learning (PBL), where they collaborate on real-world problems, integrating theoretical knowledge with practical application. These projects, as Boss & Krauss (2022) observed, help students develop critical thinking and teamwork skills, which are essential for navigating the complexities of modern work environments. Furthermore, platforms like Massive Open Online Courses (MOOCs) have democratized education by providing global access to high-quality educational resources, making education more inclusive and accessible (Cao, 2021).

In the face of rapid technological change, lifelong learning has gained increasing importance. The World Economic Forum (2020) highlighted the need for continuous upskilling and reskilling as automation and technological disruption reshape the workforce (Schwab & Zahidi, 2020). Higher education institutions, therefore, must design learning environments that support the ongoing development of skills relevant to an ever-evolving job market. Innovative learning spaces, designed to foster engagement, creativity, and adaptability, are essential in promoting lifelong learning. These environments not only provide students with foundational knowledge but also encourage critical thinking and the flexibility to adapt to new challenges. Rieckmann (2018) further emphasizes the role of sustainability and social responsibility in these learning spaces, which helps students to develop a global perspective and equips them to tackle the challenges of the 21st century.

Despite the clear benefits, there are significant internal challenges that institutions should address to fully embrace innovative teaching methodologies. For instance, institutional resistance to change, often driven by established traditions and organizational inertia, is one of the most prominent obstacles. Carbonell et al. (2013) reported that most universities are reluctant to abandon long-standing pedagogical models in favor of more flexible, technology-driven approaches. In addition, inadequate funding, and outdated infrastructure, particularly in developing regions, further hinder the adoption of innovative practices (Islam et al., 2015). Another key issue is the digital divide, which is the disparity in access to technology and digital resources. According to Sahni (2019), addressing this divide is crucial for ensuring that all students, regardless of socio-economic background, have equitable access to the educational opportunities offered by blended learning and innovative spaces.

The 21st Century competencies including critical thinking, creativity, collaboration, and digital literacy, are necessary to enable students to thrive in an increasingly digital and interconnected world. Critical thinking enables students to evaluate information and make better decisions (Evans, 2020). Creativity fosters innovation thus allowing students to develop innovative solutions to emerging challenges, while collaboration skills are vital for teamwork and communication across diverse cultures and disciplines (Gündoğdu & Merç, 2022). Additionally, digital literacy is crucial in this era where technology permeates every aspect of life and work (Spires et al., 2019). These competencies empower students to thrive in a digitally interconnected world.

THEORETICAL FRAMEWORK

This chapter argues that innovative learning spaces, blended learning models, and technology integration are essential frameworks for fostering student engagement and developing 21st-century competencies such as critical thinking, creativity, collaboration, and digital literacy. The frameworks that show the relationship among these variables include Constructivism, Experiential Learning Theory, and Self-Determination Theory. However, this chapter is underpinned by the theory of Social Constructivism by Vygotsky (1978). It explains the interconnection between these variables within the context of modern educational practices, emphasizing the active role of learners in constructing knowledge through social interaction and experiential learning. Social constructivism posits that learning is a social process and knowledge is constructed through interaction with others and the environment (Alanazi, 2016). This framework aligns with innovative learning spaces, which promote collaborative, experiential learning, and blended learning models, such as the flipped classroom, which allows students to engage with content both online and in-person. By fostering student engagement through collaborative group work and personalized learning paths, constructivism enables students to develop essential 21st-century competencies. The integration of technology through tools like Learning Management Systems (LMS), virtual simulations, and interactive platforms enhances these constructivist principles by providing dynamic, interactive, and flexible learning environments. This alignment of theory and practice ensures that students not only engage with content but also develop critical thinking and problem-solving skills in collaborative, real-world contexts.

INNOVATIVE LEARNING SPACES

Innovative learning spaces are environments specifically designed to facilitate novel methods of teaching and learning. These spaces can be physical, or virtual setups tailored to meet the diverse and evolving needs of modern students (Ossiannilsson, 2019). The physical spaces, including flexible classrooms, are equipped with movable furniture, interactive whiteboards, and collaborative zones such as break-out rooms that encourage teamwork and communication. This promotes a more interactive and student-centered learning experience while providing a break away from the traditional row-and-column seating arrangement. They foster educational environments where students can engage more dynamically with each other and with the learning materials. Besides, it enhances their understanding and retention of the course content.

The virtual learning environment encompasses online learning platforms and digital resources crucial to expanding educational accessibility and inclusivity. Also, they provide platforms where students can engage with digital resources, participate in online discussions, and access multimedia content These virtual spaces are particularly beneficial for students who face geographical, physical, or time constraints, thus ensuring that education is accessible to all (Valtonen et al., 2021). Learning Management Systems (LMS) like Canvas or Moodle, offer a virtual classroom where students can watch recorded lectures, participate in forums, access reading materials, complete and submit assignments, and receive feedback in real time. In addition, the adaptability of these spaces allows lecturers to integrate other digital tools, such as virtual reality (VR) simulations or interactive educational apps. These enhance students' learning experience by catering to students' different learning styles and needs, fostering their understanding and retention. Therefore, effective innovative learning spaces are flexible, adaptable, and incorporate technology to support student-focused learning encounters.

Flexibility and Adaptability in Physical Spaces

One of the defining features of Innovative Learning Spaces (ILS) is their inherent flexibility and adaptability. Traditional classrooms with fixed desks and rigid layouts are often not conducive to collaborative and interactive learning. In contrast, ILS is designed to be reconfigurable to support a variety of teaching approaches and learning activities. Movable furniture, such as tables and chairs on wheels, allows the space to be reorganized to suit different instructional needs, whether group work, individual study, or instructor-led discussions. According to Kariippanon et al. (2018), the ability to adapt the physical layout of a classroom contributes to a more dynamic learning environment that can cater to diverse learning preferences and instructional methods.

For example, at Stanford University, classrooms have been redesigned to include modular furniture and breakout zones that encourage students to collaborate in small groups. These flexible learning environments foster active learning, where students engage more deeply with the content through problem-solving, peer discussions, and hands-on activities. Similarly, the use of interactive whiteboards and digital displays allows students to engage visually with course material, promoting more interactive and participatory learning.

Technology Integration

The integration of digital technologies into innovative learning spaces is one of the key elements that distinguish these environments from traditional classrooms. The use of smartboards, touchscreens, tablets, and laptops in the classroom enables students to engage with digital content in real time, access online resources, and collaborate with their peers. This integration of technology not only enhances the learning experience but also mirrors the digital tools that students will encounter in their professional lives, fostering digital literacy and technological fluency (Valtonen et al., 2021).

Moreover, most innovative learning spaces now incorporate virtual reality (VR) and augmented reality (AR) to create immersive learning experiences. In fields such as medicine, architecture, and engineering, VR and AR simulations allow students to practice complex tasks in a safe, controlled environment. For instance, medical students at Harvard University have used VR to simulate surgeries and medical procedures, providing them with hands-on experience that would otherwise be difficult to replicate in a traditional classroom setting (Daniela, 2020). This type of experiential learning is invaluable in fostering critical thinking and problem-solving skills.

Collaborative Learning Environments

A key component of ILS is the emphasis on collaborative learning. Modern work environments often require individuals to work in teams, communicate effectively, and collaborate across different disciplines. Therefore, higher educational institutions are increasingly designing learning spaces that promote teamwork and peer-to-peer learning. Collaboration zones, which may include breakout rooms, lounge-style seating, or interactive digital hubs, allow students to work together on group projects, brainstorm solutions to problems, and share ideas.

Research by Ossiannilsson (2019) indicated that students who engage in collaborative learning environments tend to have higher levels of engagement and a deeper understanding of course material. Additionally, these spaces are often equipped with digital tools such as Google Workspace, Microsoft Teams, and Slack, which enable students to collaborate remotely, share documents, and communicate in real-time, even outside the classroom. This type of learning mirrors the collaborative technologies used in modern workplaces, thus preparing students for the demands of the global workforce.

Student-Centered and Personalized Learning

Innovative learning spaces are designed to put the student at the center of the learning process, moving away from the traditional instructor-centered model. These spaces allow for personalized learning experiences, where students can engage with the material in ways that suit their learning styles. Whether through self-paced online modules, interactive simulations, or collaborative group work, ILS provides opportunities for students to take ownership of their learning.

Personalized learning can be further enhanced by the integration of adaptive learning technologies, which adjust the difficulty of content based on a student's progress. For example, some innovative learning environments use AI-driven platforms that analyze a student's performance and suggest personalized learning paths to help them master specific concepts (Mondal et al., 2024). This approach ensures that each student is challenged at the appropriate level, reducing the risk of disengagement or frustration.

In addition, ILS often includes quiet zones or individual study areas where students can focus on independent work. This variety in learning spaces allows students to choose environments that best support their needs, whether they prefer collaborative group settings or quiet individual study time.

Inclusivity and Accessibility

Innovative learning spaces also emphasize inclusivity and accessibility. These spaces are designed to be accessible to all students, regardless of physical abilities or learning preferences. This may include features such as adjustable furniture, wide aisles, and assistive technologies to support students with disabilities (Narenthiran et al., 2022). For example, innovative classrooms at the University of Melbourne have been equipped with voice recognition software and braille displays to accommodate students with visual and hearing impairments.

Inclusivity in ILS also extends to culturally responsive design. Most institutions are now incorporating design elements that reflect the diversity of their student populations, creating environments that make all students feel welcome and represented. For instance, classrooms might include multicultural art or literature, offer bilingual learning materials, or provide space for group discussions that promote cross-cultural understanding. This not only fosters a sense of belonging but also supports the development of global competencies.

Sustainability in Innovative Learning Spaces

As global attention to environmental sustainability grows, educational institutions are incorporating sustainability principles into the design of their learning spaces. Green building materials, energy-efficient lighting, and natural ventilation systems are used to reduce the environmental impact of educational spaces. According to Rieckmann (2018), sustainable design in learning spaces not only helps reduce energy consumption but also creates healthier environments for students, with improved air quality and natural lighting.

Sustainable learning spaces can also serve as teaching tools, providing students with real-world examples of environmental stewardship. For example, green roofs, solar panels, and rainwater harvesting systems installed in learning spaces can be used to instruct students about sustainability and renewable energy. Additionally, sustainability-focused learning spaces encourage students to think critically about their environmental impact and develop the skills needed to address global environmental challenges.

Impact on Teaching Methods

Innovative learning spaces also transform the role of educators. In traditional classrooms, the instructor often serves as the "sage on the stage," delivering information to passive learners. However, in ILS, the instructor's role shifts to that of a facilitator or guide, helping students to navigate their learning journey. This shift is supported by active learning strategies, where students engage with the material through discussions, hands-on activities, and real-world applications. As educators adopt these new teaching methods, they become more responsive to the individual needs of their students, offering support and guidance tailored to each learner's progress. According to Serrano et al. (2019), instructors in innovative learning environments also benefit from greater flexibility in their teaching methods. They can incorporate digital tools, such as polling software and real-time feedback platforms, to assess student understanding during class and adjust their instruction accordingly. This real-time adaptation helps ensure that students are mastering the content and are not left behind.

DESIGN PRINCIPLES OF INNOVATIVE LEARNING SPACES

Effective innovative learning spaces are designed based on the principles of flexibility, adaptability, and student-centeredness. Flexibility is the ability of the space to be easily reconfigured to support different teaching and learning activities. This ensures a dynamic learning environment that can cater to diverse instructional methods and learning styles (Kariippanon et al., 2018). Adaptability involves incorporating technological infrastructure that can support various digital tools and resources. Moreover, the learning space can evolve with technological advancements and meet the needs of digital-native students (Pogue, 2019). A student-centered layout focuses on creating environments that facilitate collaboration, interaction, and active learning, which are essential in fostering engagement and deeper understanding among students. These principles ensure that learning spaces are not only functional but also conducive to the evolving needs of modern education.

Furthermore, innovative learning spaces prioritize inclusivity and accessibility. Inclusive design ensures that learning spaces are accessible and usable by all students, regardless of their physical abilities or learning preferences (Narenthiran et al., 2022). This involves incorporating adjustable furniture, clear signage, quiet areas for individual studies, collaborative zones for group work, and spaces equipped with assistive technologies to accommodate students with disabilities. Additionally, inclusivity involves creating culturally responsive environments that reflect the diverse backgrounds of the student body. This will enhance a sense of belonging and support academic success for all students (Museus et al., 2017). By prioritizing inclusivity, higher educational institutions will promote equity and diversity in learning, while complying with legal standards.

Integrating sustainability into the design of learning spaces aligns with the growing global emphasis on sustainability and prepares students to be responsible global citizens (Rieckmann, 2018). Sustainability minimizes the environmental impact of these spaces through energy-efficient systems, the use of renewable resources, and the incorporation of green building materials. These create healthier learning environments by improving air quality and natural lighting. Furthermore, sustainable designs can serve as a teaching tool, providing students with real-life examples of environmental stewardship and responsibility. By embedding sustainability into their core design principles, higher institutions can foster a culture of environmental awareness and accountability.

BLENDED LEARNING MODELS

Blended learning integrates conventional in-person teaching with online learning elements, leveraging the strengths of both modalities. This integration provides students with greater flexibility in how and when they engage with course content, while also allowing instructors to use a variety of pedagogical methods tailored to diverse learning needs. The versatility of blended learning has made it an increasingly popular approach in higher education, where institutions aim to foster 21st-century competencies such as critical thinking, digital literacy, collaboration, and creativity (Dakhi et al., 2020). Blended learning models offer various methodologies depending on the balance between in-person and online instruction. The commonly used blended learning approaches and their impacts on teaching and learning include.

Flipped Classroom Model

One of the most widely adopted blended learning approaches is the flipped classroom model, where students access instructional content such as recorded lectures, readings, or videos online before class and then engage in active learning activities during face-to-face sessions. This model inverts the traditional structure of teaching, where class time is typically devoted to lectures and homework is completed independently. Instead, students come to class prepared with foundational knowledge and use in-person time for collaborative problem-solving, discussions, and hands-on applications. The flipped classroom is particularly effective in fostering active learning, as students spend more time engaging with the material in meaningful ways rather than passively listening to lectures. According to Zain & Sailin (2020), this model promotes critical thinking and deep learning, as students are encouraged to apply concepts and analyze real-world problems during class sessions. For instance, in a physics course, students might watch video lectures on theoretical concepts at home and then use class time to conduct experiments and discuss their findings with peers. This model enhances both conceptual understanding and practical skills. Furthermore, the flipped classroom allows for greater differentiation in instruction.

Students can access online materials at their own pace, re-watching videos or reviewing readings as needed. This flexibility supports learners with diverse levels of prior knowledge and learning speeds, ensuring that all students can progress at a pace that suits them.

Hybrid Learning Model

The hybrid learning model blends online and face-to-face instruction throughout the course, with a more balanced distribution of both components. In this model, some course content is delivered entirely online, while other parts are taught in person. For example, students might complete online quizzes, watch lectures, and participate in discussion forums remotely, while in-person sessions are reserved for interactive workshops, lab sessions, or group activities. It offers significant flexibility, particularly for students who may have scheduling conflicts or who prefer self-paced learning. By allowing students to access lectures and materials online, institutions can accommodate learners who may be balancing education with work or other commitments. This model is particularly valuable in fields like health sciences and engineering, where lab work and hands-on activities are essential but can be supplemented with online learning to maximize flexibility. According to Raes (2022), students in hybrid learning environments often demonstrated improved academic performance due to the ability to revisit online content and seek help from instructors during in-person sessions. Hybrid learning models are also ideal for project-based learning (PBL), where students can research and collaborate on projects online and then come together in person to present and refine their work.

Enriched Virtual Model

In this model, students primarily learn online but attend occasional in-person sessions for specific activities, such as exams, workshops, or labs. This model is ideal for courses that require minimal face-to-face interaction but benefit from occasional hands-on experiences or collaborative work (Kayalar, 2021). For example, in a computer science course, students might complete most programming assignments and tutorials online but attend in-person workshops to collaborate on team-based coding projects or participate in final presentations. It provides maximum flexibility, as students can engage with the content remotely while still benefiting from periodic in-person interactions. This model has gained popularity in distance education programs, especially in regions where access to educational institutions is limited due to geographic or socio-economic barriers. Additionally, this approach is well-suited for adult learners and working professionals who may need to complete coursework at their own pace while managing other responsibilities.

Flex Blended Model

It offers students the most customizable learning experience, allowing students to choose how they want to engage with the course content. In this model, students have the option to attend in-person classes, participate in live online sessions, or access recorded lectures and learning materials at their own time. The flex model is particularly valuable for students with varying schedules or commitments, as it allows them to tailor their learning experience to fit their personal needs (Priya & Gowrishankar, 2022). For instance, in a business management course, students might choose to attend live online discussions during the week, watch recorded lectures over the weekend, or participate in in-person group meetings for collaborative projects. This model fosters self-directed learning, as students are responsible for managing their time and making decisions about how to engage with the material. The flex model is highly adaptable and has been shown to improve student engagement by giving learners autonomy over their educational experience. According to Boninger et al. (2019), students in flex model environments reported higher levels of satisfaction and academic performance, as they can choose the mode of learning that best suits their preferences.

Self-Blend Model

This is designed for students who wish to supplement their traditional face-to-face courses with additional online learning. In this model, students enroll in additional online courses to explore topics that are not covered in their regular curriculum or to gain extra credits(Bryan & Volchenkova, 2016). This model is often used by initiative-taking students who are seeking to enhance their knowledge in areas of personal or professional interest. For example, a psychology major might choose to take an online course in data science to develop research skills that are not offered in their core curriculum. The self-blend model provides students with the flexibility to customize their education, enabling them to pursue interdisciplinary studies and develop a broader skill set. One of the major advantages of the self-blend model is that it encourages lifelong learning. By allowing students to explore topics outside their main field of study, it fosters a culture of continuous education and curiosity. Additionally, this model promotes autonomous learning and helps students build the skills needed for independent research and inquiry.

Lab Rotation Model

This is commonly used in science and engineering courses, where students rotate between different learning stations, including online modules and hands-on laboratory work. In this model, students alternate between engaging in digital simulations, conducting experiments, and participating in collaborative activities (Kömür et al., 2023). For example, in a biology course, students might complete online modules on cellular processes, engage in virtual simulations of cell behavior, and then attend physical labs to observe real-life cellular structures under a microscope. It provides a blended learning experience that combines theoretical knowledge with practical application. By rotating between online and in-person learning, students gain a deeper understanding of scientific concepts and are better equipped to apply their knowledge in real-world scenarios. This model is particularly effective in promoting critical thinking and problem-solving skills, as students must integrate information from multiple sources and modalities.

Project-Based Model

Integrates online resources with in-person collaboration to work on real-world projects. Students are tasked with solving complex problems that require both online research and face-to-face teamwork. This model is particularly effective in developing critical thinking, collaboration, and practical application skills (Aliftika et al., 2021). For example, an engineering course might have students use online platforms to research sustainable building materials and then come together in a lab to design and construct a prototype building using those materials.

Competency-Based Blended Learning Model

This focuses on ensuring that students achieve specific competencies or skills at their own pace, often through a combination of online learning and in-person assessments (Ragg & Piers, 2017). Students progress as soon as they demonstrate mastery of the subject matter and skill, making it especially effective in skills-based vocational training programs. For instance, in a nursing program, students might complete online modules on patient care and safety, participate in virtual simulations, and then demonstrate their competencies in in-person clinical assessments. This model ensures that students acquire the practical skills necessary for their profession before moving on to more advanced topics Competency-based blended learning is ideal for programs that require a high level of skill proficiency, such as technical or medical training (Trujillo Maza et al., 2016). By allowing students to progress at their own pace, this model ensures that they achieve a thorough understanding of the material and are well-prepared for their future careers.

BLENDED LEARNING APPROACHES

Technological Integration

Successful blended learning models rely on the integration of various technologies to enhance student's educational experience and support their diverse learning needs. Learning Management Systems (LMS) like Canvas and Moodle provide a platform for organizing course materials, facilitating communication, and tracking students' progress (Shurygin et al., 2021). These systems enable the delivery of content efficiently and consistently, thus allowing students to access learning resources at their own pace and convenience. They promote personalized learning experiences. Digital tools and resources, such as interactive simulations and educational apps, enrich the learning journey by offering captivating and interactive materials. They provide students with hands-on learning experiences that simulate real-world scenarios, thus enhancing their understanding and retention of complex concepts (Mondal et al., 2024). These tools cater to students' different learning styles and foster critical thinking and problem-solving skills essential for today's digital age.

Moreover, online collaboration tools such as Google Workspace and Microsoft Teams facilitate students' collaboration on projects and tasks irrespective of their geographical distance (Sawant, 2021). These platforms promote real-time communication, file sharing, and collaborative document editing, which are crucial for group projects and discussions. They foster peer-to-peer interaction, collective knowledge construction, and the development of teamwork skills, preparing students for collaborative work environments in their future careers. Virtual and augmented reality tools, for example, can bring abstract concepts to life and create realistic scenarios for practical application (Daniela, 2020). Furthermore, technological integration supports differentiated instruction, identification of students' strengths and areas for improvement, and enhances the provision of targeted feedback and resources. Therefore, technology-enriched environments prepare students for the demands of the modern workforce and promote lifelong learning.

Pedagogical Strategies

Several pedagogical strategies are particularly effective in blended learning environments. The flipped classroom model promotes students' pre-class engagement with instructional materials online, thereby allowing class time for interactive activities and more profound discussions (Zain & Sailin, 2020). This approach provides students with foundational knowledge and frees up valuable class time for interactive activities and deeper discussions. This enhances overall engagement and understanding of concepts. Project-based learning entails students engaging in intricate, real-life projects that demand critical thinking, teamwork, and creativity (Boss & Krauss, 2022). It fosters the acquisition of problem-solving skills, collaboration, and innovation among students while they tackle complex problems. This firsthand approach reinforces theoretical concepts while preparing students for real-world challenges and professional environments.

Additionally, personalized learning paths allow students to progress through content at their own pace, ensuring that they master each concept before moving on to the next (Bernacki et al., 2021). It caters to individual student needs and learning styles. These pedagogical strategies are pivotal in higher education institutions to adapt learning to diverse student populations and evolving educational landscapes. By fostering active learning, collaboration, and self-directed inquiry, higher institutions can cultivate a learning environment that provides academic success and lifelong learning for career excellence.

CASE STUDIES AND BEST PRACTICES

Global Perspective

The global educational landscape is undergoing a significant transformation as institutions strive to equip students with 21st-century competencies. Innovative learning spaces and blended learning approaches are at the forefront of this shift. They offer flexible and technology-enhanced environments that foster critical thinking, creativity, collaboration, and digital literacy. Integrating physical and virtual environments, these approaches provide a more personalized and engaging learning experience using digital tools, as interactive and adaptive learning opportunities (Dimitriadou & Lanitis, 2023). This global trend highlights the potential of these approaches to create inclusive and accessible educational experiences that cater to a wide range of students' learning styles and preferences. Across different regions and institutions, the implementation of these approaches varies depending on cultural, economic, and technological contexts. Below are case studies and best practices from various parts of the world that demonstrate the efficacy of these models in enhancing student engagement, fostering critical thinking skills, and addressing unique educational challenges.

United States: Stanford University's Flexible Learning Spaces

Stanford University has been at the forefront of rethinking learning environments through its Learning Spaces Innovation Initiative. This project involves redesigning traditional classrooms into flexible, technology-enhanced spaces that allow for different modes of teaching, such as group collaboration, independent work, and instructor-led discussions. Movable furniture, interactive screens, and integrated technology like Zoom and virtual learning tools are key components of these redesigned spaces.

In their flipped classroom model, students access lectures and materials online before class, allowing in-person sessions to focus on interactive, hands-on learning. According to a study by Serrano et al. (2019), this model resulted in improved student engagement and higher retention of complex concepts compared to traditional lecture formats. The focus on flexibility, adaptability, and technology integration makes Stanford's approach a model of best practices in higher education, where innovation is aligned to foster critical thinking and creativity in students.

Australia: The University of Melbourne's Hybrid Learning Model

The University of Melbourne has successfully implemented a hybrid learning model, blending traditional in-person classes with online learning components. The university's "Flexible Academic Program (Flex AP)" framework was introduced to make education more accessible to both local and international students, providing them with a range of options to engage with their coursework. The online component of this model includes pre-recorded lectures, reading materials, quizzes, and interactive discussion boards, while face-to-face classes are used for labs, workshops, and in-depth discussions.

The Flex AP approach has been especially effective in addressing the diverse needs of students who may face time constraints, geographic limitations, or other barriers to traditional learning. In a post-implementation study by Raes (2022), student satisfaction increased significantly due to the flexibility and personalization that hybrid models provide, particularly in subjects like law and medical sciences, where practical application of theory is essential. This model serves as a best practice example for universities looking to adopt a more student-centered, adaptive approach to teaching.

Europe: The Open University, United Kingdom

The Open University (OU) in the UK has been a pioneer in distance and blended learning since its inception, offering higher education opportunities to students who might not otherwise have access due to geographic, economic, or time constraints. With the advent of digital technologies, OU has significantly expanded its reach, using a blended learning model that combines self-paced online learning with in-person tutorials and workshops.

OU's use of digital tools like AI-driven learning platforms and virtual reality simulations allows students to experience interactive learning environments from the comfort of their homes. For example, students in the engineering program use virtual labs to conduct experiments and simulations, which would otherwise be accessible only in physical laboratories. This not only makes the learning process more flexible but also ensures that students gain practical, hands-on experience in their fields of study (Dimitriadou & Lanitis, 2023). The success of OU's blended learning model lies in its commitment to continuous innovation. The institution regularly updates its platforms to incorporate the latest advancements in educational technology, ensuring that students receive the most current and relevant learning experiences.

India: Indian Institutes of Technology (IITs)

The institute has also embraced blended learning, particularly through its NPTEL (National Programme on Technology Enhanced Learning) initiative. This program allows students from across India to access recorded lectures, virtual labs, and online assessments while maintaining in-person tutoring and workshops at physical campuses. NPTEL's online resources are free to the public, making them accessible not just to IIT students but also to learners nationwide (Das, 2023). The initiative has been particularly effective in improving the quality of education in technical fields, such as computer science and engineering, where access to state-of-the-art resources is crucial for student success. As a result, IIT graduates are well-prepared to meet the demands of a rapidly evolving global job market, where technology skills are increasingly valued.

Africa

In Africa, the adoption of innovative learning methods and blended learning presents both opportunities and challenges. African higher educational institutions are increasingly recognizing the importance of preparing students for a digital and interconnected world. However, resource limitations, infrastructural challenges, and the digital divide remain significant barriers.

Sub-Saharan Africa: African Virtual University (AVU)

The African Virtual University (AVU) is a pan-African initiative that seeks to expand access to higher education across the continent through online and distance learning. Partnering with local universities, AVU provides a platform where students from remote or underserved areas can access high-quality education. The initiative focuses on using blended learning approaches, integrating online courses with in-person support provided by local universities. AVU has been particularly successful in the field of STEM (Science, Technology, Engineering, and Mathematics) and teacher training, where physical resources are limited (Barakabitze et al., 2019). The platform offers a mix of recorded lectures, real-time virtual classes, and online discussion forums. Students can engage with their peers and instructors across borders, promoting collaborative learning and cultural exchange. Despite challenges such as inconsistent internet access, AVU has demonstrated that blended learning can overcome geographical barriers and create more equitable access to education (Juma, 2004).

East Africa

In East Africa, higher educational institutions are exploring innovative learning spaces and blended learning to enhance student engagement and development of competencies. However, varying levels of technological infrastructure and access to resources pose challenges. Incorporating blended learning models will enhance flexibility in course delivery. It enables students to access course materials remotely thereby bridging geographical and economic barriers (Raes, 2022). In addition, the use of digital tools increases student engagement and fosters a dynamic learning experience (Thahir et al., 2023). Blended learning also improves academic performance and competency development, as personal engagement with course materials enhances better mastery of content and critical thinking skills (Zain & Sailin, 2020). Furthermore, the integration of digital tools will enhance digital literacy among students, preparing them for the global economy. The collaborative nature of blended learning environments will also strengthen teamwork and cross-cultural exchange, thus promoting a more inclusive and interactive educational experience. By leveraging digital tools and online platforms, East African institutions of higher learning can create more dynamic and interactive learning environments that prepare students for the demands of the digital age.

Aga Khan University Institute of Educational Development, Tanzania

The institute serves as a leading example of blended learning in East Africa. AKU-IED combines personalized online learning with in-person attendance, tailored to meet the needs of educators and professionals seeking to upgrade their qualifications while working full-time. This model has been instrumental in improving both student outcomes and faculty development. One of AKU-IED's most successful implementations is its scaffolded professional development program for teachers, where educators engage in a mix of online and face-to-face modules. Moodle is used to deliver coursework online, while face-to-face interactions focus on practical applications in the classroom. This program not only boosts teacher competency but also ensures that they are well-equipped to integrate innovative learning strategies into their classrooms, creating a ripple effect throughout the education system (Qasim Ali & Jafferani, 2024). AKU-IED's blended model has become a regional model for institutions across East Africa, offering a sustainable approach to professional development, particularly in areas with limited access to advanced educational facilities.

@iLab Africa in Strathmore University, Kenya, ICT innovation and e-learning strategies are developed. Additionally, Eneza Education, a Kenyan ed-tech company, delivers interactive learning content via mobile phones, offering quizzes, lessons, and live tutoring through SMS and web applications to students in remote areas (Adeniran et al., 2023). In Tanzania, the National ICT Policy for Higher Education focuses on integrating ICT into the curriculum by providing infrastructure, training, and digital content (Mahenge & Sanga, 2016). In partnership with Samsung, solar-powered digital classrooms also bring technology to off-grid areas. These initiatives highlight the innovative efforts to enhance educational access and quality through technology in the region.

IMPACT OF INNOVATIVE LEARNING SPACES AND BLENDED LEARNING APPROACHES ON TEACHING AND LEARNING

The adoption of Innovative Learning Spaces and Blended Learning Approaches has significantly reshaped the educational experience in higher education, transforming both teaching practices and student learning outcomes. These approaches, rooted in flexibility, adaptability, and the integration of technology, have made learning environments more dynamic and responsive to the diverse needs of students.

Enhancing Student Engagement

One of the most immediate and observable impacts of innovative learning spaces is the increase in student engagement. Traditional classrooms often foster passive learning, where students listen to lectures without much interaction. In contrast, innovative learning spaces, equipped with flexible seating arrangements, interactive digital tools, and collaborative zones, create opportunities for active learning. These environments encourage students to engage in discussions, work on group projects, and participate in hands-on activities, which research has shown to improve retention of material and deepen understanding (Serrano et al., 2019).

Similarly, blended learning models by incorporating both face-to-face and online learning components give students the flexibility to engage with materials at their own pace, leading to higher levels of involvement and motivation. According to Sahni (2019), the flexibility offered by blended learning significantly enhances student satisfaction, as learners can choose when and how to interact with the course material. Moreover, the use of interactive platforms such as Learning Management Systems (LMS) like Moodle or Canvas allows students to access learning resources from anywhere, fostering continuous learning even outside the classroom.

Personalized Learning and Differentiation

One of the key impacts of both innovative learning spaces and blended learning is the ability to personalize the learning experience. In traditional learning environments, it can be difficult to cater to the individual needs of each student, especially in large classes. However, blended learning approaches which often incorporate self-paced online modules allow students to progress through the material at their speed, spending more time on areas where they need additional support. This adaptability fosters a more inclusive learning environment, as students with different learning styles and needs can engage with content in ways that suit them best (Boninger et al., 2019).

Innovative learning spaces also support personalized learning by allowing for differentiated instruction. For example, flexible seating arrangements and the integration of technology enable instructors to create varied learning stations where students can engage in different types of activities, such as group work, individual research, or interactive digital simulations. This approach not only meets the diverse learning preferences of students but also fosters independence and self-directed learning, key skills for success in both academic and professional environments.

Fostering 21st-Century Competencies

The primary goal of innovative learning spaces and blended learning models is to develop 21st-century competencies such as critical thinking, creativity, collaboration, and digital literacy. These skills are essential for students to succeed in an increasingly globalized and technologically driven world. In a traditional classroom, the focus is often on rote memorization and passive absorption of knowledge. However, blended learning environments promote the development of critical thinking by encouraging students to engage with digital tools, conduct independent research, and collaborate with peers to solve real-world problems. (Castro, 2019).

Project-based learning (PBL), which is often a core component of blended learning models, enables students to apply theoretical knowledge to practical situations. Working in teams to solve complex problems fosters collaboration while requiring students to think creatively and critically about the solutions they develop. These skills are directly transferable to the workforce, where employers increasingly seek individuals who can work collaboratively across disciplines and think innovatively about the challenges they face.

Improving Learning Outcomes

The innovative learning spaces and blended learning approaches contribute to improved learning outcomes. A study by Asarta and Schmidt (2020) Found that students in blended learning environments demonstrated higher levels of mastery over course content compared to those in traditional settings. This improvement is largely attributed to the active learning and continuous feedback mechanisms built into these models. For instance, the use of formative assessments such as quizzes, reflective journals, and online discussion forums allows instructors to monitor student progress in real time and provide targeted feedback. This iterative process helps students identify areas for improvement early on, leading to better overall performance.

Furthermore, the use of adaptive learning technologies in blended learning environments has been shown to enhance learning retention. These technologies adjust the difficulty of tasks, and the pacing of content based on each student's progress, ensuring that they achieve mastery of concepts before moving on to more advanced material (Sajja et al., 2023). This personalized approach leads to a deeper understanding of the material and reduces the risk of students falling behind.

Preparing Students for the Digital Economy

As industries across the globe become increasingly reliant on technology, there is a growing demand for professionals who are proficient in digital literacy and technological fluency. The integration of digital tools into innovative learning spaces and blended learning environments ensures that students develop the necessary technological skills to thrive in the modern workforce. Learning Management Systems (LMS), collaborative tools like Google Workspace and Microsoft Teams, and virtual simulations provide students with hands-on experience in using the types of software and platforms that are prevalent in today's digital economy. (Koreneva et al., 2023).

Moreover, the use of artificial intelligence (AI) in educational platforms enhances students' ability to work with cutting-edge technology. For instance, AI-powered tools such as intelligent tutoring systems offer personalized guidance by adjusting the content to suit individual learners' needs. This exposure to AI and other emerging technologies ensures that students are not only consumers of digital content but also creators, capable of leveraging technology to solve complex problems (Owoc et al., 2019).

Promoting Lifelong Learning and Adaptability

In an era where the nature of work is constantly evolving, the ability to learn continuously and adapt to new challenges is crucial. Innovative learning spaces and blended learning models promote the development of these skills by fostering a learning culture that emphasizes flexibility, self-directed learning, and collaborative problem-solving (Uchkun, 2023). By engaging in environments that allow for constant interaction with peers, instructors, and digital tools, students are better prepared to adapt to the rapid changes that characterize today's professional landscape.

As the World Economic Forum (2020) emphasizes, the ability to upskill and reskill in response to changing market demands is now a critical competency (Schwab & Zahidi, 2020). Blended learning environments, which allow for self-paced and on-demand learning, are ideally suited for promoting lifelong learning. Students accustomed to navigating these environments are more likely to continue engaging in education throughout their careers, ensuring that they remain competitive in a rapidly changing workforce.

CHALLENGES AND CONSIDERATIONS

Barriers to Implementation

Despite the benefits of innovative learning spaces and blended learning models in higher educational systems, barriers to implementation include institutional resistance to change, often due to established traditions and practices (Carbonell et al., 2013). Higher education institutions may be reluctant to deviate from long-standing pedagogical approaches and organizational structures. This resistance could stem from a lack of understanding of the potential benefits of innovative methods, and discomfort with modern technologies. Resource and infrastructure limitations, such as inadequate funding and outdated technology, pose significant challenges. It prevents universities from acquiring the necessary tools and resources to support these modern educational approaches (Islam et al., 2015). Moreover, the digital divide among students can exacerbate inequalities and hinder the effectiveness of blended learning techniques.

Educators' Training and Support

Effective implementation also requires robust professional development and ongoing support for educators. Lecturers need training in new pedagogical strategies and technologies to effectively integrate them into their teaching practices (Sife et al., 2007). Yet, the training and professional development required to effectively implement and utilize these new strategies can be costly and time-consuming, further complicating the transition. Therefore, continuous collaboration and support networks, such as professional learning communities, are essential for sustaining these changes.

Equity and Access

Ensuring equity and access is critical in the shift to innovative learning spaces and blended learning. Efforts must be made to create inclusive learning environments that accommodate diverse learners' needs. Addressing physical accessibility and considering socio-economic factors may impact students' ability to fully participate in digital learning experiences. Providing equitable access to technology could empower students from all backgrounds to engage meaningfully in blended learning environments and benefit from educational opportunities afforded by innovative approaches (Sahni, 2019). This will address the digital divide, particularly in underserved communities, which is essential to guarantee that every student has access to the required technology and resources. Additionally, culturally responsive teaching practices and curriculum designs can further enhance equity by valuing students' diverse backgrounds and experiences. This fosters a more inclusive and supportive learning environment for all learners (Museus et al., 2017).

EMERGING TRENDS

Several emerging trends are poised to further transform education. Artificial intelligence (AI) in education offers the potential for personalized learning experiences and adaptive learning technologies (Rane et al., 2023). These technologies assess a student's understanding and progress, adjusting the difficulty level and type of content based on real-time performance assessment. They ensure a continuous response to individual student needs. Moreover, personalized learning enhances student engagement and outcomes by providing content tailored to each student's unique strengths and weaknesses. Adaptive learning technologies, which adjust content and pace based on student performance, are becoming increasingly sophisticated and effective (Sajja et al., 2023).

Furthermore, AI is driving innovation in educational content creation. AI algorithms can be used to generate customized quizzes, and interactive simulations, which cater to the specific needs and interests of students (Kaswan et al., 2024). This capability saves educators time and ensures that students receive engaging and relevant content that enhances their learning experience. Intelligent tutoring systems (ITS) offered by AI engage students in dialogue. They ask questions and provide hints, thus promoting the development of critical thinking and problem-solving skills. These systems can be adapted to the individual student's learning pace and style, thus providing personalized attention that is often a challenge in traditional classroom settings. Also, virtual and augmented reality (VR/AR) provide immersive learning experiences that can enhance understanding and engagement (Daniela, 2020a)

Social and Emotional Learning (SEL), which focuses on developing students' abilities to understand and manage their emotions, set, and achieve positive goals, feel and show empathy for others, establish and maintain positive relationships, and make responsible decisions is also emerging (Lawlor, 2016). It fosters reduced emotional distress, improved attitudes, academic success, and life skills.

Gamification is also becoming a key player in education to increase student motivation and engagement. This trend leverages the human inclination towards play and competition to make learning more enjoyable and interactive. Therefore, the increased focus on digital literacy and citizenship is also reshaping higher education. As technology becomes an ever more integral part of daily life, it equips students with the skills to navigate the digital world safely and responsibly (Buchholz et al., 2020). Higher institutions are increasingly incorporating digital literacy and citizenship into their curricula to prepare them for the challenges and opportunities of the digital age.

POLICY IMPLICATIONS

The shift towards innovative learning spaces and blended learning models has significant implications for educational policy. Policymakers must consider reforms that support the integration of technology and new pedagogical approaches in education (Willcox et al., 2016). Adequate funding and resource allocation are necessary to ensure higher institutions can implement these changes effectively. Policies that support professional development in digital pedagogy, ensure equitable access to technology, and foster a culture that values innovation and continuous improvement should be established. In addition, providing continuous professional development for educators, enhancing IT infrastructure, and implementing inclusive policies to bridge the digital divide are essential for fully leveraging technology in education and equipping students to face future challenges.

RESEARCH OPPORTUNITIES

Opportunities for research in the field of innovative learning spaces and blended learning include' longitudinal studies on blended learning outcomes to provide insights into the long-term effects on student achievement and competency development. Investigating innovations in learning space design can reveal best practices and design principles that could maximize student engagement and learning. In addition, examining the effectiveness of virtual reality (VR), augmented reality (AR), and artificial intelligence (AI) could show their impact on students' understanding and retention of complex concepts. Further research could address the challenges of integrating these technologies into curricula and physical spaces. The potential of blended learning in promoting work-life balance for students in higher education settings could also be explored.

CONCLUSION

The academic environment in higher institutions is rapidly evolving to meet the demands of the 21st century, which demands the development of critical thinking, creativity, collaboration, and digital literacy competencies. Traditional teaching methods are giving way to innovative learning spaces and blended learning models, which leverage technology to create flexible, personalized, and engaging educational experiences. These approaches enhance student engagement, support diverse learning styles, and promote equity and inclusion. Research opportunities in this field are vast, focusing on long-term outcomes, the impact of technological innovations in higher education, and the effectiveness of learning space designs. Policymakers must support these transformations through adequate funding, resource allocation, and professional development for educators to ensure all students are prepared for future challenges. Embracing these changes will create more effective, inclusive, and dynamic learning environments that equip students with essential 21st-century competencies.

REFERENCES

Alanazi, A. (2016). A critical review of constructivist theory and the emergence of constructionism. *American Research Journal of Humanities and Social Sciences*, 2(1), 1–8.

Aliftika, O., Astra, I., & Supriyati, Y. (2021). Project-based blended learning and independent learning on critical thinking skills. Journal of Physics: Conference Series, Asarta, C. J., & Schmidt, J. R. (2020). The effects of online and blended experience on outcomes in a blended learning environment. *The Internet and Higher Education*, 44, 100708.

Barakabitze, A. A., William-Andey Lazaro, A., Ainea, N., Mkwizu, M. H., Maziku, H., Matofali, A. X., Iddi, A., & Sanga, C. (2019). Transforming African education systems in science, technology, engineering, and mathematics (STEM) using ICTs: Challenges and opportunities. *Education Research International*, 2019(1), 6946809. DOI: 10.1155/2019/6946809

Bernacki, M. L., Greene, M. J., & Lobczowski, N. G. (2021). A systematic review of research on personalized learning: Personalized by whom, to what, how, and for what purpose (s)? *Educational Psychology Review*, 33(4), 1675–1715. DOI: 10.1007/s10648-021-09615-8

Boninger, F., Molnar, A., & Saldaña, C. M. (2019). *Personalized Learning and the Digital Privatization of Curriculum and Teaching*. National Education Policy Center.

Boss, S., & Krauss, J. (2022). *Reinventing project-based learning: Your field guide to real-world projects in the digital age*. International Society for Technology in Education.

Bryan, A., & Volchenkova, K. N. (2016). Blended learning: definition, models, implications for higher education. *Вестник Южно-Уральского государственного университета. Серия: Образование. Педагогические науки, 8*(2), 24-30.

Buchholz, B. A., DeHart, J., & Moorman, G. (2020). Digital citizenship during a global pandemic: Moving beyond digital literacy. *Journal of Adolescent & Adult Literacy*, 64(1), 11–17. DOI: 10.1002/jaal.1076 PMID: 32834710

Cao, H. (2021). *MOOCs and Education Access: Evidence from New Zealand*. Open Access Te Herenga Waka-Victoria University of Wellington.

Carbonell, K. B., Dailey-Hebert, A., & Gijselaers, W. (2013). Unleashing the creative potential of faculty to create blended learning. *The Internet and Higher Education*, 18, 29–37. DOI: 10.1016/j.iheduc.2012.10.004

Castro, R. (2019). Blended learning in higher education: Trends and capabilities. *Education and Information Technologies*, 24(4), 2523–2546. DOI: 10.1007/s10639-019-09886-3

Chu, S. K. W., Reynolds, R. B., Tavares, N. J., Notari, M., Lee, C. W. Y., Chu, S. K. W., Reynolds, R. B., Tavares, N. J., Notari, M., & Lee, C. W. Y. (2017). Twenty-first-century skills and global education roadmaps. *21st century skills development through inquiry-based learning: From theory to practice*, 17-32.

Dai, C.-P., Ke, F., Pan, Y., Moon, J., & Liu, Z. (2024). Effects of artificial intelligence-powered virtual agents on learning outcomes in computer-based simulations: A meta-analysis. *Educational Psychology Review*, 36(1), 31. DOI: 10.1007/s10648-024-09855-4

Dakhi, O., Jama, J., & Irfan, D. (2020). Blended learning: A 21st-century learning model at college. *International Journal Of Multi-Science*, 1(08), 50–65.

Daniela, L. (2020a). New perspectives on virtual and augmented reality. In *New Perspectives on Virtual and Augmented Reality*. Routledge. DOI: 10.4324/9781003001874

Daniela, L. (2020b). *Pedagogies of digital learning in higher education*. Routledge 2 Park Square, Milton Park, Abingdon, Oxon OX14 4RN.

Das, P. P. (2023). Perspective Chapter: MOOCs in India–Evolution, Innovation, Impact, and Roadmap. In *Massive Open Online Courses-Current Practice and Future Trends*. IntechOpen.

Dimitriadou, E., & Lanitis, A. (2023). A critical evaluation, challenges, and future perspectives of using artificial intelligence and emerging technologies in smart classrooms. *Smart Learning Environments*, 10(1), 12. DOI: 10.1186/s40561-023-00231-3

Evans, C. (2020). *Measuring student success skills: A review of the literature on critical thinking*. National Center for the Improvement of Educational Assessment.

Gündoğdu, B., & Merç, A. (2022). A systematic review of tech-supported collaborative creativity practices in the field of education. *Journal of Learning and Teaching in Digital Age*, 7(1), 76–89. DOI: 10.53850/joltida.953760

Holland, J., & Holland, J. (2014). Implications of shifting technology in education. *TechTrends*, 58(3), 16–25. DOI: 10.1007/s11528-014-0748-3

Islam, N., Beer, M., & Slack, F. (2015). E-learning challenges faced by academics in higher education. *Journal of Education and Training Studies*, 3(5), 102–112. DOI: 10.11114/jets.v3i5.947

Kariippanon, K. E., Cliff, D. P., Lancaster, S. L., Okely, A. D., & Parrish, A.-M. (2018). Perceived interplay between flexible learning spaces and teaching, learning, and student wellbeing. *Learning Environments Research*, 21(3), 301–320. DOI: 10.1007/s10984-017-9254-9

Kaswan, K. S., Dhatterwal, J. S., & Ojha, R. P. (2024). AI in personalized learning. In *Advances in Technological Innovations in Higher Education* (pp. 103–117). CRC Press. DOI: 10.1201/9781003376699-9

Kayalar, F. (2021). Importance of Enriched Virtual learning model in hybrid teaching application. *Proceedings of IAC in Budapest*, 23-27.

Kömür, İ. A., Kilinç, H., & Okur, M. R. (2023). The Rotation Model in Blended Learning. *Asian Journal of Distance Education*, 18(2), 63–74.

Koreneva, I., Myroshnychenko, N., Mykhailenko, L., Matiash, O., & Kuzmenko, H. (2023). The Use of Innovative Technologies in Education: Analysis of effectiveness and implementation at different levels of education. *Cadernos de Educação Tecnologia e Sociedade*, 16(3), 625–638. DOI: 10.14571/brajets.v16.n3.625-638

Lamb, S., Maire, Q., & Doecke, E. (2017). Key skills for the 21st century: An evidence-based review.

Lawlor, M. S. (2016). Mindfulness and social-emotional learning (SEL): A conceptual framework. *Handbook of mindfulness in education: Integrating theory and research into practice*, 65-80.

Lee, K., Fanguy, M., Bligh, B., & Lu, X. S. (2022). Adoption of online teaching during the COVID-19 Pandemic: A systematic analysis of changes in university teaching activity. *Educational Review*, 74(3), 460–483. DOI: 10.1080/00131911.2021.1978401

Lim, Z. Y., Yap, J. H., Lai, J. W., Mokhtar, I. A., Yeo, D. J., & Cheong, K. H. (2024). Advancing Lifelong Learning in the Digital Age: A Narrative Review of Singapore's SkillsFuture Programme. *Social Sciences (Basel, Switzerland)*, 13(2), 73. DOI: 10.3390/socsci13020073

Mondal, A. S., Zhu, Y., Bhagat, K. K., & Giacaman, N. (2024). Analyzing user reviews of interactive educational apps: A sentiment analysis approach. *Interactive Learning Environments*, 32(1), 355–372. DOI: 10.1080/10494820.2022.2086578

Museus, S. D., Yi, V., & Saelua, N. (2017). The impact of culturally engaging campus environments on the sense of belonging. *Review of Higher Education*, 40(2), 187–215. DOI: 10.1353/rhe.2017.0001

Narenthiran, O. P., Torero, J., & Woodrow, M. (2022). Inclusive design of workspaces: Mixed methods approach to understanding users. *Sustainability (Basel)*, 14(6), 3337. DOI: 10.3390/su14063337

Okpara, G. C., & Ezeador, C. N. (2024). Philosophy of Teaching: Exploring Various Teaching Methods for Improved Education in nigeria. *Nnadiebube Journal of Philosophy, 7*(3).

Ossiannilsson, E. (2019). Innovative Learning and Innovative Learning Spaces. *Asian Journal of Distance Education*, 14(1), 98–116.

Owoc, M. L., Sawicka, A., & Weichbroth, P. (2019). Artificial intelligence technologies in education: benefits, challenges, and strategies of implementation. *IFIP International Workshop on Artificial Intelligence for Knowledge Management.*

Pogue, M. (2019). *Computer self-efficacy as an inherent characteristic of digital natives in online learning environments*. Northcentral University.

Priya, J. J., & Gowrishankar, M. (2022). Blended Learning Approach: Significance of Flex and Self-Blend Models. *Constructivism in Teaching and Learning*, 178.

Raes, A. (2022). Exploring student and teacher experiences in hybrid learning environments: Does presence matter? *Postdigital Science and Education*, 4(1), 138–159. DOI: 10.1007/s42438-021-00274-0

Ragg, M., & Piers, J. (2017). Competency-Based Blended Learning: Flipping Professional Practice Classes to Enhance Competence Development. *IAFOR Journal of Education*, 5(SI), 47–66. DOI: 10.22492/ije.5.si.02

Rane, N., Choudhary, S., & Rane, J. (2023). Education 4.0 and 5.0: Integrating artificial intelligence (AI) for personalized and adaptive learning. *Available atSSRN* 4638365. DOI: 10.2139/ssrn.4638365

Rieckmann, M. (2018). Learning to transform the world: Key competencies in Education for Sustainable Development. *Issues and trends in education for sustainable development, 39*(1), 39-59.

Sahni, J. (2019). Does blended learning enhance student engagement? Evidence from higher education. *The Journal of Learning in Higher Education*, 2019, 1–14. DOI: 10.5171/2019.121518

Sajja, R., Sermet, Y., Cikmaz, M., Cwiertny, D., & Demir, I. (2023). Artificial Intelligence-Enabled Intelligent Assistant for Personalized and Adaptive Learning in Higher Education. *arXiv preprint arXiv:2309.10892.*

Sawant, S. (2021). Online collaborative learning tools and types: Their key role in managing classrooms without walls. In *Human-computer interaction and technology integration in modern society* (pp. 12–41). IGI Global. DOI: 10.4018/978-1-7998-5849-2.ch002

Schwab, K., & Zahidi, S. (2020). World Economic Forum.(2020). *The Global Competitiveness Report–How countries are performing on the road to recovery.*

Serrano, D. R., Dea-Ayuela, M. A., Gonzalez-Burgos, E., Serrano-Gil, A., & Lalatsa, A. (2019). Technology-enhanced learning in higher education: How to enhance student engagement through blended learning. *European Journal of Education*, 54(2), 273–286. DOI: 10.1111/ejed.12330

Shurygin, V., Saenko, N., Zekiy, A., Klochko, E., & Kulapov, M. (2021). Learning management systems in academic and corporate distance education. [iJET]. *International Journal of Emerging Technologies in Learning*, 16(11), 121–139. DOI: 10.3991/ijet.v16i11.20701

Sife, A., Lwoga, E., & Sanga, C. (2007). New technologies for teaching and learning: Challenges for higher learning institutions in developing countries. *International journal of education and development using ICT, 3*(2), 57-67.

Spires, H. A., Paul, C. M., & Kerkhoff, S. N. (2019). Digital literacy for the 21st century. In *Advanced methodologies and technologies in library science, information management, and scholarly inquiry* (pp. 12–21). IGI Global.

Thahir, M., Widiawati, W., & Baitillah, N. (2023). The post-pandemic education: A blended learning approach for teaching and learning in higher education in the new normal era. *International Journal of Ethno-Sciences and Education Research*, 3(3), 99–108. DOI: 10.46336/ijeer.v3i3.461

Trujillo Maza, E. M., Gómez Lozano, M. T., Cardozo Alarcón, A. C., Moreno Zuluaga, L., & Gamba Fadul, M. (2016). Blended learning supported by digital technology and competency-based medical education: A case study of the social medicine course at the Universidad de los Andes, Colombia. *International Journal of Educational Technology in Higher Education*, 13(1), 1–13. DOI: 10.1186/s41239-016-0027-9

Turnbull, D., Chugh, R., & Luck, J. (2021). Transitioning to E-Learning during the COVID-19 pandemic: How have Higher Education Institutions responded to the challenge? *Education and Information Technologies*, 26(5), 6401–6419. DOI: 10.1007/s10639-021-10633-w PMID: 34177349

Uchkun, E. (2023). Learning Strategies in Blended Learning. *Conferencea*, 18-23.

Willcox, K. E., Sarma, S., & Lippel, P. H. (2016). *Online education: A catalyst for higher education reforms*. Massachusetts Institute of Technology.

Zain, F. M., & Sailin, S. N. (2020). *Students' experience with flipped learning approach in higher education*. Universal Journal of Educational Research. DOI: 10.13189/ujer.2020.081067

ADDITIONAL READING

Acton, R. E. (2018). *Innovative learning spaces in higher education: Perception, pedagogic practice and place* (Doctoral dissertation, James Cook University).

Anthony, B., Kamaludin, A., Romli, A., & Raffei, A. F. M., Nincarean A/L Eh Phon, D., Abdullah, A., ... & Baba, S. (. (2019). Exploring the role of blended learning for teaching and learning effectiveness in institutions of higher learning: An empirical investigation. *Education and Information Technologies*, 24, 3433–3466. DOI: 10.1007/s10639-019-09941-z

Bizami, N. A., Tasir, Z., & Kew, S. N. (2023). Innovative pedagogical principles and technological tools capabilities for immersive blended learning: A systematic literature review. *Education and Information Technologies*, 28(2), 1373–1425. DOI: 10.1007/s10639-022-11243-w PMID: 35919874

Bligh, B. (2022). Physical learning spaces and teaching in the blended learning landscape. In *Encyclopedia of Teacher Education* (pp. 1285–1292). Springer Nature Singapore. DOI: 10.1007/978-981-16-8679-5_60

Darojat, O. (2016). Improving curriculum through blended learning pedagogy. *Turkish Online Journal of Distance Education*, 17(4).

Frelin, A., & Grannäs, J. (2021). Designing and building robust innovative learning environments. *Buildings*, 11(8), 345. DOI: 10.3390/buildings11080345

Hill, J., & Smith, K. (2023). Visions of blended learning: Identifying the challenges and opportunities in shaping institutional approaches to blended learning in higher education. *Technology, Pedagogy and Education*, 32(3), 289–303. DOI: 10.1080/1475939X.2023.2176916

Hughes, J. M., & Morrison, L. J. (2020, July). Innovative learning spaces in the making. [). Frontiers Media SA.]. *Frontiers in Education*, 5, 89. DOI: 10.3389/feduc.2020.00089

Jackson, A. K. (2023). *Closing the Digital Divide: Understanding Organizational Approaches to Digital Accessibility in Higher Education* (Doctoral dissertation, University of South Dakota).

Wood, P., Warwick, P., & Cox, D. (2012). Developing learning spaces in higher education: An evaluation of experimental spaces at the University of Leicester. *Learning and Teaching*, 5(2), 49–72. DOI: 10.3167/latiss.2012.050204

KEY TERMS AND DEFINITIONS

21st Century Competencies: A set of skills that are essential for an individual to thrive in today's rapidly evolving globe.

Blended Learning: This is a teaching strategy that combines face-to-face instruction with online learning components.

Critical thinking Skill: Is the skill of analyzing and evaluating information to solve complex problems, foster innovation, and apply theoretical knowledge in real-world situations within technology-enhanced learning environments.

Digital Literacy: It is the ability to effectively access, navigate, evaluate, and create information using digital technologies.

Innovative Learning Spaces: These are physical or virtual environments explicitly designed to enhance teaching and learning by ensuring flexibility, adaptability, and the integration of advanced technologies.

Student Engagement: This is the involvement of students in their learning process.

Technology Integration: This is the use of digital tools and online resources to enhance teaching and learning by creating interactive, flexible, and personalized learning experiences.

Chapter 7
Advancements and Challenges of Problem-Based Learning:
A Case Study of Daystar University

Anne Anjao Eboi
https://orcid.org/0000-0002-4026-3687
Daystar University, Kenya

Levi Obonyo
https://orcid.org/0000-0003-2124-6854
Daystar University, Kenya

Rosemary Nyaole Kowuor
Daystar University, Kenya

Daniel Robert Aswani
Daystar University, Kenya

Lydia Ouma Radoli
https://orcid.org/0000-0002-0853-6569
Daystar University, Kenya

ABSTRACT

The global higher education landscape is fast evolving, demanding that universities equip students with critical knowledge and 21st-century skills. Daystar University (DU) 's switch from teacher-centered models to Problem-Based Learning (PBL) reflects this shift. PBL stresses critical thinking and real-world problem-solving, essential for today's interconnected world. The chapter examined the challenges and

DOI: 10.4018/979-8-3693-6930-2.ch007

advancements of PBL implementation at DU using qualitative methods involving interviews with 30 selected informants and document analysis. Findings show that while PBL has been integrated across various programs, challenges like resistance to change, insufficient faculty training, and resource limitations persist. However, significant progress has been made, including adopting technology-enhanced tools, increased faculty collaboration, and a growing culture of innovation among students. The study recommends targeted faculty development, improved infrastructure, and stronger support systems to enhance PBL's effectiveness in fostering more profound learning experiences.

INTRODUCTION

Problem-Based Learning (PBL) is a pedagogical approach that places students at the center of the learning process, utilizing complex, real-world problems as the primary vehicle for promoting the acquisition of knowledge, concepts, and principles, rather than relying on the direct transmission of facts and concepts (Duch et al., 2001). Duch and colleagues argue that PBL fosters the development of critical thinking skills, enhances problem-solving abilities, improves communication skills, and deepens understanding of course content. In this approach, students collaborate in groups, critically assess research materials, and engage in continuous, lifelong learning. Furthermore, the Center for Innovation in Teaching and Learning (n.d.) characterizes PBL as a learning method wherein students explore a subject by collaboratively addressing an open-ended problem, with the problem itself catalyzing both motivation and learning.

There is an urgent need to implement Problem-Based Learning (PBL) in Kenyan universities today, given the technological advancements, especially in areas like Artificial Intelligence (AI), Machine Learning, and the Internet of Things (IoT). PBL has been proposed as the best method that Kenyan universities should adopt in the 21st Century (Jabu, 2022) because the country introduced the Competency-Based Curriculum (CBC) in 2016 with selected pilot schools, before being officially rolled out in 2017 (Kenya Institute of Curriculum Development, 2024). The first CBC batch is expected to enter the university in 2029, but there is a high likelihood that they will find the universities unprepared (Jabu, 2022). PBL and CBC focus on developing fundamental soft skills like problem-solving, critical thinking, communication, teamwork, digital literacy, and creativity, among others. Most universities in Kenya still teach rote learning, corresponding to the previous 8-4-4 education system that focused on content/syllabus coverage at the expense of skills development. Thus, PBL emerges as a transformative pedagogical approach for the 21st century. It challenges students to solve real-world problems through collaborative inquiry. The approach fosters a shift from passive learning to active engagement, equipping students with the essential skills to navigate the complexities of the contemporary world.

There are attempts to introduce PBL in higher learning institutions in East Africa. For instance, PBL East Africa was a joint initiative designed to develop best practices in problem-based education at the University of Nairobi, the University of Dar-es-Salaam, Makerere University, and Aalto University. It brought together multidisciplinary student teams from these four universities to develop sustainable solutions to community challenges in 2017-2022. Daystar University (DU), one of the oldest private Universities in Kenya, is among the few institutions in Kenya that have implemented PBL. Others, such as Moi University, have adopted PBL in select premier schools like the School of Medicine but allowed other schools and institutes to practice rote learning models.

Daystar University has seven Schools: The School of Communication; School of Law; School of Business and Economics; School of Science, Engineering and Health; School of Arts and Social Sciences; School of Applied Human Sciences; and School of Nursing. PBL was introduced to DU in January 2022 to first and second-year students (Hussein, 2021), but it has now been implemented at all levels and in all schools. Daystar University's vision is to revolutionize education in Africa through PBL. Its mission is to nurture a culture of excellence through innovative teaching and learning, research, scholarship and practical world-class solutions (DU, 2024).

BACKGROUND

Problem-based learning traces its roots to the philosophies of rationalism and American functionalism and emerged in conjunction with the cognitive revolution in psychology (Dewey, 1938). According to Boud and Feletti (1997), PBL (the term coined by Howard Burrows in 1974) evolved from innovative health sciences curricula in North America when Canadian McMaster University's medical faculty introduced the tutorial process in the 1960s as a specific instructional and student-centered method. The PBL approach was adopted in other medical schools in the 80s and 90s and accepted across North America and Europe. Plato initially proposed that a problem should come first before Dewey picked it up to establish an experimental school at the University of Chicago. Thus, PBL's history hinges on three ideas: Dewey's, Jerome Bruner's learning by discovery with the problem as the starting point for learning, and the Case Study Method pioneered at Harvard University in the 1930s. PBL expanded to primary, secondary and higher education institutions (HEIs) worldwide (Torp & Sage, 2002). PBL implementation principles include prior knowledge activation and elaboration through small-group problem analysis, problem-oriented semantic networks' construction, contextual cues resulting from professionally relevant problems, and promoting epistemic inquisitiveness (Schmidt, 1993).

Globally, scholars have demonstrated the advantages or advancements of PBL. Strobel and van Barneveld (2009) found PBL more effective than traditional approaches concerning long-term knowledge retention, performance-based assessment, and mixed knowledge and skills. Meanwhile, in Saudi Arabia, Alshaye et al. (2023) found that online PBL improved secondary students' problem-solving ability and higher-order thinking skills. Indonesian teachers showed a dominant preference for PBL and observed a significant improvement in students' learning outcomes (Gumartifa et al., 2023). In a systematic literature review of PBL in English teaching, Mutammimah and Padli (2023) revealed a noticeable increase in publications from 2020, most of which employed the quantitative approach with research subjects predominantly comprising college and undergraduate students.

The history of university education and training in Africa has diverse roots and development stages, and we will be committing academic injustice to collapse it into a single publication. Generally, the primary purpose of university education is knowledge and skills creation, intended to promote development. However, the prominence of rote learning in HEIs precludes realizing the envisaged development. Pon and Schendel (2020) establish the overreliance on older teaching methods in Kenya, Ghana, and Botswana, which hinders the development of new ways of teaching, such as fostering critical thinking among students.

Sub-Saharan African universities rely on a lecture-based approach leading to surface learning, hence the need to adjust the curricula to include the PBL approach to improve student's learning outcomes, especially within highly complex topics like soil and climate studies (Mulonda et al., 2022). However, the authors note the challenges in implementing PBL, such as large student numbers (particularly in standard introductory courses), lack of organizational skills, resources (e.g. field trips), time, and motivating the learner and the teacher. PBL has been implemented in an Ethiopian university's medical school, and results indicate that students preferred PBL to LBL. Thus, the authors recommended the incorporation of PBL across all HEIs as a formal instructional method (Tadesse et al., 2022). The following table compares PBL implementation across three universities (Ethiopia (2) and Uganda (1) in their medical schools:

Table 1. PBL Implementation in Selected East African Universities

Article Title/University	Implementation strategies	Successes	Challenges
Barriers to implementing problem-based learning at the School of Medicine of Debre Berhan University, Ethiopia	None discussed	None discussed	1.Student-related 2. Tutor-related 3. Case scenario-related 4. Assessment-related barriers
Implementation of problem-based learning in undergraduate medical education in Ethiopia: An exploratory qualitative study Addis Ababa University, Ethiopia	1.Establish a comprehensive curriculum document specifying the type of PBL curriculum 2. Resource allocation e.g. tutorial rooms 3.Faculty development 4. Robust program governance and monitoring system	PBL has the potential to improve students' problem-solving skills in a clinical setting	PBL implementation is haphazard and currently only in the pilot stage in respective departments.
Problem based learning: Tutors' views 5 years after implementation at a sub-Saharan University Makerere University, Uganda, School of Medicine	None	1.70-80% teachers judged that PBL had achieved the general intended aims of students attaining problem solving skills and teamwork 2. Community-based Education and Service (COBES) was effectively implemented (70% of respondents)	1. 50% teachers provided feedback to students 2. Assessment not in line with teaching method 3. 39% teachers were involved in COBES 4.Poor resource allocation
Problem Based Learning, curriculum development and change process at Faculty of Medicine, Makerere University, Uganda	Steps 1.Analysis of Uganda's health status 2. Analysis of old curriculum 3. Needs Assessment 4. Student-centered learning, a Problem-based approach, Integrated learning, Community-based education, Elective elements, and a Systematic approach (SPICES), a new model, was adopted	Successfully embarked on curriculum change through a participatory approach where all stakeholders have been involved	1.Fear among tutors 2.Some tutors not understood PBL 3.Some feel it is unrewarding and time-consuming 4.Too much emphasis on self-directed learning overriding useful methods like practicals 5.Student overloaded 6.Requires more resources 7.Hurriedly introduced 8. Limited departmental involvement

Source: Tefera et al. (2024); Mohammed, et al. (2024); Galukande et al. (2015); and Kiguli-Malwadde et al. (2006)

Chege (2015) criticizes the "graduate-mill" architecture of the Kenyan university and proposes a shift to a problem-solving education approach that aligns with Kenya's development needs and gives due attention to innovation, critical thinking and quality education. His views support Ondigi's (2011) perspective that the industry is less satisfied with the quality of university graduates because some lack information technology skills necessary for the socio-economic and political development of the country. Thus, Kitainge (2022) recommends training lecturers in HEIs to effectively use constructivist instructional methods, which promote active learning with learners' needs and interests in mind.

Recognizing the need for improving pedagogical approaches, scholars have presented findings on the most suitable teaching and learning methods given the changing global education trends. Suggestions include embracing various approaches such as PBL, work-based, project-based, workshop training, and tutorials in technical colleges to successfully impart practical skills and stir creativity (Migiro, 2022). Kiptoo (2015) proposes the adoption of a hybrid of four techniques, namely, skills training, problem-based, online learning, and lecture techniques. On their part, Munezero and Bekuta (2016) suggest a blended project-based approach combining PBL and participatory design to solve real-life forestry problems among Forestry and Information Communication Technology (ICT) undergraduate students.

Some universities in Kenya have implemented new teaching and learning approaches to improve outcomes. For example, Gitonga et al. (2017) explores Haiku, a problem-based online networking application that students and teachers use for learning, sharing and staying connected. The authors observe that Haiku presents an appropriate environment that empowers students to nurture, foster and enable PBL. The University of Eldoret introduced a blended approach (PBL and participatory design) to Forestry and ICT undergraduates as an extracurricular activity. Egerton University has developed a PBL teacher manual for AgriScale, a collaborative endeavor involving nine HEIs (from Africa and Europe).

Scholars have also examined the effects of competency-based learning in higher learning institutions. For instance, Simba and Kising'u (2024) found that problem-based and project-based learning positively and significantly affected entrepreneurial intention in university technical and vocational education and training institutions in Kenya. The authors recommend the adoption of competency-based learning in HEIs and policy review to encourage its adoption. On his part, Masinde (2023) decried the focus on classroom and institutional-centered training and recommended competency-based training in horticulture, particularly PBL. Kangethe and Mutema (n.d) report on the implementation of innovative training strategies, including competence-based learning and SPICES at Moi University.

Further, Moi University explored community-based education in its health programs, and students agreed that it helped them address real-life problems (Katwa, Ayiro et al., 2018). The authors, however, noted the method's limitation in terms of resources. Katwa, Obwoga et al. (2018) examined the SPICES model at Moi University's medical school's curriculum implementation and identified challenges which included students finding it confusing, too demanding, enabling laziness among lecturers and having overcrowded tutorials while the lecturers thought it is ineffective in student outcomes. While some lecturers suggested retraining, others wanted it abolished. Meanwhile, Ondieki et al. (2018) advocate for competency-based education and training (CBET) in Kenya's HEIs because it is rapidly being implemented in global academic circles and suggest the creation of a CBET policy at the university to improve graduates' employability and prepare HEIs to receive CBC graduates.

Indeed, the Ministry of Education (2024), through Sessional Paper No. X of 2024 has demonstrated awareness of the challenges CBC graduates are likely to encounter at the university level. The Government of Kenya (GoK) recognizes the need for CBC graduates' seamless transition into HEIs. However, it admits the lack of a standardized framework for university competency-based education (CBE) to guide its implementation in the university. Besides, most university programs lack alignment with CBE. Thus, the government is considering developing the University Competency-Based Curriculum and Assessment Framework and reviewing university programs to align with CBE (Ministry of Education, 2024).

Kenya has witnessed higher education evolution and transformation, with demands for quality and relevant university programs that will result in social, economic, and political development. The GoK has created or amended policies to facilitate these transformations. For example, the Universities Act (No. 42 of 2012) recognizes the need for quality and relevance of university education, research and innovation. Universities are also governed and regulated by other policies such as the STI Act (2013), HELB Act (1995) and State Corporations Act (2015). As a result, Kenya performs fairly well globally in innovation. For example, it ranked 86th of 132 countries in the global innovation index by the World Intellectual Property Organization in 2020, 62nd globally in the Global Start-up Ecosystem Index, as well as ranked relatively well on the education outcomes in Sub-Saharan Africa (Ministry of Education, 2024).

PBL promotes the acquisition of ICT skills. Oluoch and Osida (2014) view ICTs as key to a nation's sustainability, hence advocate for its integration in the teaching and learning process to increase productivity. Cunningham (2015) argues that HEIs need to adopt Technology-Enhanced Learning (TEL) but must first address the challenges that limit its uptake, such as infrastructure, training of faculty and institutional policies, among others. Odhiambo's (2018) view is that policy reforms and investment in ICT innovation in Kenya are critical because of the current situation in university ICT education. There is potential for a successful transition to PBL in HEIs in Sub-Saharan Africa because the students (largely Gen Z who are adept at technology) perceive it positively (Oladele et al., 2024).

However, the literature also indicates that PBL has encountered challenges in certain instances. McGraw Hill (2023) opines that the most significant challenges PBL faces include the lack of time, resources and student motivation. A study in a Bahraini primary school found that teachers could not successfully implement PBL as they faced challenges in selecting significant content, monitoring and assessment, time management, and lacking facilities (Aldabbus, 2018). Liu and Liu's (2021) study unearthed weaknesses in PBL implementation mainly caused by a reticent culture where teachers were still stuck in conventional methods and a resource-constraint environment. Kirui (2020) studied PBL at Moi University's School of Medicine and compiled the following challenges at the implementation stage: the shortage of qualified teachers, inadequate infrastructure like tutorial rooms, ill-equipped tutorial rooms, internet access challenges, ill-equipped computer labs, the lack of a basic science library, scarce finances, and a lack of PBL guidelines especially for the orientation of new faculty. Other challenges the author noted included the time-consuming nature of PBL and limited training opportunities.

The following table highlights the major PBL implementation cases in Kenya:

Table 2. PBL Implementation in Kenyan Universities

PBL/PBL Project	University- School	Purpose	Successes
PBL Bio-Africa (AgriScale) (2020-2024)	Egerton University and Jomo Kenyatta University of Agriculture and Technology (JKUAT) from Kenya; The University of Zambia and Mulungushi University from Zambia; Gulu University and Bishop Stuart University from Uganda; Häme University of Applied Sciences and Aalto University from Finland; and Italy's University of Pavia.	Create new network-based learning ecosystem by partnering with HEIs, the industrial sector, and societal partners for the continuous development of education even after AgriScales' lifetime.	1.Egerton University launched teacher manual 2. The 3 universities have initiated a Student Challenge Program to improve the productivity of crops and livestock of the Matungu Youth Group, Kakamega County 3. AgriScale triggered the accreditation of 3 curricula and revision of 8 in JKUAT and Egerton universities
PBL East Africa- spans 4 universities (2017-2020)	University of Nairobi's C4DLab; University of Dar-es Salaam's Innovation and Entrepreneurship Centre; Makerere University's College of Engineering, Design, Art and Technology; and Aalto University's (Finland) four programs	Pilot that can inform full implementation across East Africa	Initiated a student challenge program eg in Kenya, problem-solving was demonstrated in public safety transportation.
PBL as a teaching and learning approach (2022-date)	Daystar University across all seven schools	To align the university's pedagogy to 21st century skills	Currently ongoing and yet to be formally assessed

Source: UON (n.d); PBL East Africa (n.d); & DU (2024)

This study was anchored in the constructivism paradigm, hence, finds support in constructivism learning theory which emphasizes that learners play an active rather than a passive role in building their own understanding (McLeod, 2024). PBL's foundational underpinnings can be traced back to John Dewey's constructivism theory. Dewey believed that learning was active and that students needed to explore, think and reflect, as well as interact with their environment (Dewey, 1938). Elliott et al. (2000, p. 256) as cited in McLeod (2024) define constructivism as, 'an approach to learning that holds that people actively construct or make their own knowledge and that reality is determined by the experiences of the learner.'

Under constructivism learning theory, learning is a social activity because people work together and interact with each other (Dewey, 1938). Thus, all teaching and learning takes place when socially constructed knowledge is shared and negotiated among the people. Further, in constructivism, students' questions and interests are valued; learning materials include primary sources and manipulative materials; learning builds on what students already know; teachers dialogue with students who construct their own knowledge; the teacher's role is interactive, anchored in negotiation; the assessment process (students' work, observations, and point of view) is as important as the product; knowledge is dynamic and susceptible to change with experiences; and students work primarily in groups (University at Buffalo, 2024).

Moshman (1982) delineates three types of constructivism, i.e. exogenous constructivism (knowledge is formed from reconstructing an external reality), endogenous/cognitive constructivism (the individual constructs knowledge internally), and dialectical/social constructivism (individuals generate knowledge through social interactions). Constructivism principles are embodied in knowledge construction which takes different forms: people learn to learn as they learn, learning is an active process, learning is a social activity, learning is contextual, knowledge is personal, learning exists in the mind, and motivation is key to learning (Western Governor's University, 2020).

Constructive learning theory comprises five stages which build on top of each other, eventually building upon a student's learning. The stages include the engagement stage/ inviting ideas where the student is presented with a problem or situation to ponder about, exploration where students build new knowledge actively, proposition where students discuss what they've learned or observed; explanation/ elaboration and solution stage where students discuss their thought processes with the teacher, and taking action/evaluation phase, where the teacher asks students to sum up their cognitive process and discuss how their thoughts may have changed since the initial inviting ideas phase (National University, n.d.). However, critics of constructivism claim that it lacks a structure, which is beneficial to students who thrive in highly structured and organized learning environments (Western Governor's University, 2020).

Method

The chapter was shaped by the social constructivism paradigm, a philosophy, theoretical framework, or worldview that guided the research questions and method. Constructivists believe in the relativity of truth since there are various ways to interpret and understand truth (Creswell, 2014). The qualitative design, using in-depth interviews, was selected to understand the phenomenon under study deeply. The answers could only be found if the experts gave one-on-one interviews (Creswell, 2014). The in-depth interviews utilized semi-structured open-ended questions designed to gain from the depth of the informant's unfiltered opinions and views

(Creswell, 2014). Thus, eight PBL champions, ten faculty members, ten students, and two administrators from DU responded to in-depth interviews.

Additionally, a document analysis of PBL documents at Daystar University was undertaken, and the PBL write-ups and websites (Daystar University's PBL-related) were examined. The information from the interviews and documents was analyzed thematically. The interview data was audio-recorded and transcribed, and the texts were re-read several times to enable better understanding and accuracy. Open, axial and selective coding were employed, as Strauss and Corbin (1990) suggested. In open coding, the researchers broke down data into categories to help reduce bias before looking for relationships in those categories in axial coding. In selective coding, the researchers examined the core concepts that emerged from the previously identified coded data's central themes (Strauss & Corbin, 1990).

The study observed qualitative reliability (consistency) to ensure the approach is consistent across dissimilar researchers and tasks (Gibbs, 2007). Reliability was achieved by checking the raw data (transcripts) to ensure it was free from obvious mistakes made while transcribing and that the codes remained consistent. Qualitative validity (accuracy) was observed when the researchers checked for accuracy or trustworthiness in the findings by using some procedures (Creswell & Miller, 2000). These procedures were triangulation (using different data sources to justify the themes) and member checking (the transcripts given to informants to verify data accuracy). Ethical considerations included informed consent forms, which the participants signed and returned. The participants were assured of anonymity and that the findings of this study were only for academic purposes.

Thus, the study was guided by the following objectives: Examine the process of implementing PBL, document the advancements and challenges in implementing PBL, and determine the resources required for implementing of PBL at DU.

THE MAIN FOCUS OF THE CHAPTER

A thematic analysis revealed five themes and seven sub-themes. The themes are PBL process implementation, PBL advancements, Resources for successful implementation, Challenges of PBL implementation, and Faculty and student perspectives. The sub-themes include University policy, Preparation phase, Implementation phase, Monitoring and evaluation phase, Faculty/staff/student-related challenges, Resource-related challenges, and Implementation-related challenges. A rich, thick description was used to represent the participants' views. Quotations drawn from the interviewees are cited as KI-1 through to KI-8 for the PBL champions, KI-9-KI-18 for the students, KI-19-KI-28 for the faculty, and KI-29-KI-30 for the administrators.

Sources used in document analysis are represented as D-1 (DU-related websites) and D-2 (PBL literature developed within DU).

PBL Process Implementation

University Policy

Findings from the interviews show that DU's adoption of PBL is anchored in university policy. The university readily adopted PBL because it was in close alignment with its mission: "To nurture a culture of excellence through quality innovative teaching and learning, research, scholarship and practical world-class solutions" (D-1). Moreover, the university desires to produce graduates who are knowledgeable and capable of critical thinking and problem-solving in real-world contexts. Daystar University's vision is to revolutionize education in Africa through PBL (D-1).

According to D-2, Daystar University decided on a hybrid model where the curriculum ensures that all programs address theory and real-world problems. The PBL model agrees with DU's Academic Division Strategic Plan (2020-2023), which rests on four main pillars: education, research and scholarship, innovation, and student satisfaction and excellence, all aimed at learner transformation. Further, the strategic plan outlines several activities to ensure effective PBL implementation. These are:

1. Designing courses that challenge existing knowledge and attitude and that use interactive learning, practical assignments and projects
2. Including the experts and practitioners in the teaching team
3. Equipping the staff and faculty with the right practical skills
4. Establishing state-of-the-art research facilities, including high-speed internet connectivity and the latest research software
5. Promoting innovation through an entrepreneurial hub (incubation). (D-2)

DU has already established the Directorate of Enterprise and Planning, and one of its objectives is to oversee the realization of the Hub. Students, through boot camps, are expected to develop, test, and incubate promising ideas and nurture actual products. (D-2)

Thus, there is a need to align institutional policy to accommodate PBL. It has been established that Kenya has transitioned to CBC at the primary and secondary school levels. Still, the universities have been left to decide on the best methodology for content delivery. DU has the advantage of a policy that aligns with the CBC and PBL teaching methods, facilitating PBL's quick absorption into the system. DU's decision to adopt PBL agrees with Celinšek and Markič (n.d.), who conclude that PBL training should be planned according to the organization's principles. Further,

DU's PBL implementation aligns with Jabu's (2022) observation that PBL is the best method for Kenyan Universities as they wait to receive the first CBC graduates in 2029.

Preparation Phase

According to informants, DU decided to implement PBL following extensive research. Since CBC is not teacher-centered, there was a need to adopt a student-centered learning approach that thrives on collaboration, problem-solving skills, and the application of knowledge to practical scenarios; encourages knowledge discovery and expertise among students; patterns teaching and learning after the 21st-century skills; and employs an interdisciplinary pedagogy laced with technology enhancement to enable a holistic transformation of the learners.

We were seeking ways to shift toward a student-centered classroom, adopt a needs-based curriculum, produce skilled workers for the market and prepare for the future through mentorship and coaching compared to conventional hands-off lecturing. (KI-4)

The informants said that PBL is functioning at DU because of the immense support offered by the management. The leaders have been consistent not only in advocating for the method but also in monitoring it to ensure its success. From the very beginning, the Vice Chancellor (VC) led by the front, as evident in the following responses:

The VC held several meetings and training sessions for lecturers, deans, heads of departments, student leaders and the directors of various institutions to discuss the implementation. The Deputy VCs were also actively involved. (KI-2)

"This is an ideal Ayiro is prepared to die for," said the VC. "It must happen. If there's something I'm going to leave behind in Daystar, it's that we are going to produce students who are problem solvers." (D-1)

As part of his articulation and implementation of new strategies to improve the quality of teaching and learning at Daystar University, the new VC (then), tasked the academic affairs office to benchmark with leading universities on their learning models. The report they shared highlighted PBL as one of the most effective models of teaching and learning that went beyond regurgitating new knowledge to knowledge creation and problem-solving techniques. (KI-4)

The informants stated that there were extensive internal and external consultations on curriculum design. Faculty members provided insights on curriculum integration while curriculum developers worked on aligning PBL with academic standards. KI-3 revealed that the guidelines on case or problem identification were derived from the following: course objectives and content, the facilitator's practical or personal experience, web searches, and class textbooks, especially the beginning and end of chapters.

> *The major change was a total makeover of the course design. The curriculum included the learning outcomes and learning activities for each lesson. Cases were included in the course outlines, which also listed the specific knowledge desired and expected skills. (KI-3)*

According to informants, the current PBL curriculum at DU was designed through collaborative workshops involving faculty, industry experts and instructional designers. The focus was on designing interdisciplinary modules that reflect real-world problems. Further, problems were selected based on their relevance to the curriculum, alignment with learning objectives and potential to stimulate critical thinking. Since the intention was to encourage students to engage deeply and collaboratively, the problems chosen had to be challenging but achievable.

> *Using the PBL approach, existing structures of course outlines were revised extensively. The course syllabi were lengthened with details of problem cases forming weekly activities for learners to engage with. These cases were discipline-specific, and others were multidisciplinary. (KI-4)*

According to the informants, all the stakeholders were trained extensively before PBL was implemented. The training involved five modules: Module 1 (PBL and the philosophy behind it); Module 2 (The seven steps in the PBL approach); Module 3 (Problem design); Module 4 (Formative and summative assessment); and Module 5 (Problem construction and theory). DU has made provisions for strategic, continuous training in workshops involving students, faculty and staff. "Student representatives were part of the PBL training ahead of implementation. They also participated in PBL champions' training seminars with lecturers, heads of departments and deans" (KI-2).

> *Training was critical to successful implementation, so first was the appointment of faculty champions from each school. Additionally, student representatives (scribes) were appointed per school. This was followed by a training retreat for the faculty champions, student representatives, heads of departments, deans and directors. The champions then collaboratively developed a PBL handbook. Next was the training of all faculty members. Champions have continuously mainstreamed PBL to all faculty through regular training (KI-3).*

According to D-2, the preparation phase involved forming a team to oversee the design and implementation of the PBL model; developing implementation timelines; developing and seeking approval for the PBL training manual; redesigning the curriculum to reflect the new approach; training all faculty; implementing PBL in phases; and finally, fully adopting the PBL approach.

As evident in the DU case, PBL's successful implementation must follow a sound process, including extensive consultations, research and preparations. Research will involve benchmarking and looking for the best fit. Constructivism learning theory supports DU's shift from lecture-based learning to PBL because it recognizes that learners play an active rather than a passive role in building their own understanding (McLeod, 2024). Moreover, the study supports Suwastini et al. (2021), who find PBL appropriate for meeting 21st-century needs.

Implementation Phase

DU-1 reports that PBL was introduced to DU in phases beginning in January 2021, when it was offered to the first and second years. Today, the entire university is following the PBL approach. The PBL champion's task in implementation is 'to coordinate training and give input to PBL-compliant course outlines and teaching manual as well as report to the head of department and dean on matters concerning PBL in my department' (KI-6).

> *As a PBL champion, my role involves advocating for PBL, coordinating training sessions, supporting faculty in curriculum development and ensuring that best practices are shared across departments. I also liaise between faculty and administration to address any challenges and facilitate smooth implementation. (KI-8)*

Data from D-1 indicates that Daystar University has 10 PBL champions (also known as PBL board members) whose responsibility is to oversee the implementation of PBL in their respective schools or departments. These include the Director of Academic Programs, Senior Assistant Registrar, Ag. Director DLPDI, and seven representatives from the various schools.

> *The actual implementation of PBL in a typical class involved setting the curricular objectives, selecting a case suitable for the curricular objectives, compiling the necessary information, preparing an instructional guide, consulting colleagues for the improvement of case write-up, obtaining feedback from the lecturers and students, and revising where necessary before reusing the case. (KI-4)*

According to D-1, DU follows Maastricht's (2024) seven jump process for PBL implementation in the classroom: Identifying and clarifying terms in the scenario; Defining the problem; Brainstorming; Restructuring the problem; Formulating learning objectives/goals; Independent study; and Regrouping/Synthesis. Players in PBL (facilitators, learners, scribes and group leaders) each have a role to play. For instance, while the facilitator designs the curriculum, the learner communicates effectively in all sessions, while the group leader provides leadership and manages group dynamics.

As with DU, the implementation process is easier to handle when management has fully bought into it. Gustafson and Pollock (2015) advise that management support is crucial for successfully integrating PBL into the school system. The DU case suggests management support can come from direction, resource provision, training and monitoring. Further, sound management is instrumental in overseeing curriculum design and involves internal and external stakeholders. Kavanagh and Herrmann (2021) note that leaders can support PBL in four ways: establishing an ambitious yet specific vision, redefining what classrooms should look like, encouraging meaningful professional development, and setting priorities and re-evaluating policies. Another lesson that educators can glean from the DU case is the appointment of team leaders to oversee the implementation, assist with challenges, organize and facilitate training, and engage in monitoring and evaluation. To Celinšek and Markič (n.d.), successful PBL implementation requires good communication and an organizational culture that values cooperation and team learning. This chapter notes that PBL should be implemented in phases to realize success. Because it represents organizational change, PBL will be resisted as espoused by Kotter (1996), who introduced the 8-step model to counter resistance. Thus, DU introduced PBL in phases- the first and second years.

Monitoring and Evaluation Phase

Anonymous surveys designed by the office of Deputy Vice-Chancellor (DVC) Academics and administered to the stakeholders have been undertaken as stated by this informant: "The champions have administered surveys to faculty as well as written reports. Monitoring and evaluation also occurs during student assessments throughout the semester." (KI-3)

The School champions give periodic reports to the DVC Academic Affairs office. Besides, the end-of-trimester evaluation assessments capture the success and challenges of PBL to check if learning took place, and regular faculty workshops are conducted for continued capacity building. (KI-4)

The Directorate of Quality Assurance also monitors quality to assess PBL effectiveness and teaching standards.

From the quality assurance reports that reach us, there is a bit of improvement in the quality of teaching and learning, even though we have yet to arrive. Some improvement is desired on the learners' part, as well as more faculty training. (KI-7)

There has been positive feedback from the faculty who have been trained. The lecturers agreed the introduction of the PBL approach was timely, PBL is exciting and collaborative, and provides new knowledge. However, they decried the presence of joy riders among the students and the challenge of implementing PBL in a huge class setup. (D-2)

After PBL implementation, close, consistent monitoring and evaluation must follow to identify practical resolutions (Mohammed et al., 2024). This chapter notes that monitoring can be conducted by the existing quality assurance office and by team leaders. Evaluation can be done through surveys, in-depth interviews, observation, and student/faculty feedback (through the Learning Management System). Besides, student evaluations -both formative and summative -provide insight into PBL advances and limitations. The results will inform the solutions, such as more funding, training or benchmarking.

PBL Advancements at Daystar University

PBL has been running at DU for over two years, and several advancements/successes have been noted, such as: 'Some lecturers testify how the model has made teaching, learning and thinking easier among students' (KI-7). This informant also observed that recent industry reports indicate that DU students doing practicum and in employment are doing comparatively well. According to KI-3, 'more interaction among students has been noted, who are also more expressive and communicative than before.' On her part, KI-1 reveals that group discussions have made students proactive. Besides, students are prepared for the 21st Century marketplace since they can work in teams and have learned how to do proper PowerPoint presentations (KI-5).

Informants noted that the School of Communication, with some practical-oriented courses, has improved in how students handle their examinations. Student informants said their examination scores had improved since they no longer had to memorize content. They are intrigued by the problems to be solved, and because these students give the problems a lot of attention, they score well. KI-6 opined that DU is ahead of other universities in preparedness to receive CBC students, while K-23 noted: "The School of Law has made great strides with PBL, especially in the setting of exam questions. The questions enable critical thinking."

> *I have found that students can link education with real-life issues, which is a plus for our graduating students. Additionally, they have become more responsible and self-directed in their studies, as well as demonstrated application of problem-solving skills in the marketplace. (KI-3)*

Informants noted that despite little infrastructural progress in the last two years, the university still needs to increase physical space and an adequate number of computer labs, science labs and studios to handle PBL. Collaborative learning spaces, such as discussion rooms conducive to the PBL process, have been created. These spaces encourage group work and allow students to tackle problems in a setting that mirrors real-world professional environments. Nevertheless, the university is upgrading the physical learning environment to include more flexible classrooms and collaboration spaces.

Some progress has been realized on our Athi River campus. For example, a new complex with enough room for PBL was constructed which now houses the School of Nursing. Construction work is set to begin anytime on the David Musau Mumama Learning Complex which will host the School of Law's moot court and other PBL facilities. (KI-25)

The David Musau Mumama Learning Center is poised to be a game-changer for Daystar University and will provide top-notch facilities for its students and faculty, representing a significant leap forward in the University's infrastructure. This complex will house a 1000-seater lecture hall and four state-of-the-art 200-seater lecture halls. The School of Law will also benefit from a modern moot court, further enhancing the learning experience, alongside dedicated offices for the Dean and Faculty members. (D-1)

Feedback from the faculty shows that PBL has registered some level of success as shown in this perspective: "I find the model friendly to implement and it addresses a desirable shift in teaching, learning and thinking" (KI-27). On his part, KI-22 reports that PBL enabled the University to navigate the COVID-19 challenges for quality teaching and learning. According to faculty informants, their classroom experience has been transformed as lessons become more interesting with PBL, which has led to more interactive classes and students being able to solve societal problems. KI-20 has this to say: "I think for me, PBL has always been a part of the school of communication, so I wouldn't say it started recently. I think it helps better align theory and practice."

PBL has been a game changer and is a more practical approach to teaching and learning since it enables an experiential way that learners can create new concepts, discuss skills and carry out research as groups and sometimes individually. They are presented with a problem and left to develop creative solutions. For instance, one class that we teach is Psychology of Learning- we tell them to do a small research on if students on campus have learnt the code of conduct and are adhering to it. They go out and observe or interview their fellow students on the same. (K-26)

Guiding manuals for faculty have been developed, and faculty training is continuous. The training is focused on designing PBL activities, facilitating student discussions, and assessing student performance in a PBL context. Data from D-2 indicates that the University has held 20 trainings involving 107 staff trained on the five revised modules. Further, 107 PBL-compliant course outlines have been designed. Additionally, a problem bank has been created containing more than 30 scenarios.

Extensive training is a critical aspect of PBL implementation. Lim and Choy (2014) observe that successful PBL implementation requires a structured foundational training program that addresses its essential elements and the tutor's role, especially in the teaching beliefs of staff and their adaptation to the constructivist belief system found in PBL. The DU case provides lessons involving thorough, strategic, and continuous training of all concerned stakeholders, as well as significant financial support for these trainings, which can result in the collaborative creation of a PBL handbook. Borhan (2014) stresses the value of early training, where PBL should be introduced in teacher education to preservice students who acquire knowledge and develop skills for the future. Besides, Celinšek and Markič (n.d.) report of new knowledge and skills acquired by the teachers implementing PBL.

PBL at DU has led to the revision of course outlines and curricula and the development of case studies (D-2). Other achievements, according to D-2, include the development of an assessment rubric for each problem. The rubric covers scenario clarification, problem-identification comprehension, goals and objectives, class presentation, creativity, application or recommendations, individual student participation, and use of scripture.

Another advancement is curriculum integration since PBL is now embedded into the curriculum across several schools in DU. Further, the informants observed that students and lecturers are encouraged to share assignments and reading materials on the E-learning platform. There is also increased student engagement and participation as PBL encourages active learning. Students are more involved in learning, taking ownership of their projects and collaborating with peers to solve complex problems. The student community identifies active learning and critical thinking in PBL as a plus in their classroom experience, as exemplified by the following perspectives:

> *I've enjoyed the shift from passive learning to active, meaningful engagement. PBL has allowed me to apply theoretical knowledge to real-world problems, making the learning process more practical and relevant. I now think critically, think outside the box, and engage in significant brainstorming and teamwork. It helps me to begin looking at questions differently. (K-10)*
>
> *I love the method since open-ended questions have engaged my critical thinking and analytical skills to explore multiple solutions both in and out of school. PBL prepares me for the complexities I may encounter in future careers. (KI-15)*
>
> *We have had complex 'problems' to solve using the PBL, like in BIL 11X (Introduction to the Old Testament) where we had to solve an issue involving religion and their views on LGBTQI. Working through this one fostered a deeper understanding of the issue because it is a real-time problem and of human interest. (KI-11)*

Collaboration reduces the lecturer's load, resulting in adequate space and time for knowledge creation by both the student and lecturer. "Working in groups has been a highlight. It's pushed me to develop teamwork and communication skills, and I've learned a lot from the diverse perspectives of my peers (KI-9). Other advantages come with collaboration:

I've worked with a team of people of different ages. The PBL, being an interactive model of learning, gives room for group discussions, and this enhanced my ability to work with people I have not had time to meet physically. (KI-18)

I found the PBL model to be helpful at making someone a better communicator. Often times you will have to explain to fellow group members your thought process when dealing with certain scenarios. Over time, you become more and more comfortable and confident in explaining concepts to others. (KI-12)

PBL develops problem-solving and research skills, as highlighted by the students, who appreciate the model's ability to enable them to recognize certain details they would not have noticed. Students develop research skills (even things like referencing) since they are required to conduct research to solve problems, and they know they will need these skills in their careers. However, the students noted that it requires commitment from both students and faculty.

Some students see value for money in PBL because it brings out the best in them and makes them feel useful in society. Additionally, they experience better student-faculty interactions, which is important for developing social and leadership skills. Further, they learn useful skills which they can use in real time:

PBL is a good model because it makes it easier to understand how the world connects to what I'm learning in real time. An example is how in COM 243, we did an interview simulation after which we discussed the dos and don'ts of interviews. That approach was better than asking Google, watching on YouTube or asking people. (KI-13)

The model has brought the best out of introverted students. Having to work in groups to resolve problems in a number of classes over the long run improves our ability to communicate. I have seen many shy classmates evolve and become better at group communication. (KI-16)

Students also find PBL engaging and motivating, besides encouraging self-directed learning, communication and collaboration. "We were engaged intensely- this made communication and collaboration easier, which in turn led to finishing the work on time and diligently." (KI-14).

While doing an assignment on PBL, it brought us together. Some of us had the same ideas, while others came up with unique ones, which in turn made someone to think outside the box. This process motivated us to look forward to learning more. (KI-17)

The advancements/successes noted at DU find support in studies like Zakaria et al. (2024), who note that teachers perceived PBL positively and preferred it because there was a significant improvement in students' performance. This chapter's findings also support Mohamed et al. (2024), who found that students' problem-solving skills in analyzing real-world problems were enhanced when PBL was used. Additionally, Sebatana and Dudu (2021) hail PBL as a method that enhances communication and critical thinking skills and has the potential to enhance problem-solving and real-world application of knowledge. In constructivism learning theory, learning is a social activity as people work together and interact (Dewey, 1938 as cited in McLeod, 2024).

Required Resources for Successful PBL Implementation

As per the informants, human resources are key, and DU has invested heavily in faculty training. The university has ensured that academic staff have been effectively equipped and trained to guarantee effective learning through the PBL model, as noted here: "I am a PBL champion and have been adequately trained. My role is to ensure that there is successful and effective integration of PBL for online learning in Moodle." (KI-4)

The informants also opined that DU has committed significant resources to support PBL implementation. This includes funding for training programs, technology and access to a wide range of learning materials. However, the informants did not have any information regarding the amount of money DU spent implementing PBL.

> *According to KI-3, the university has facilitated PBL implementation by providing and strengthening an E-learning platform. PBL training is also held via videoconferencing applications like Class for Teams, Zoom, Google Meet, Teams, KENET, etc. Further, DU has equipped the library with learning resources that can be material sources as students engage with problem cases or scenarios (KI-1). For case studies, we use effective oral and written communication with the students. We also use observations, essays, performance tasks, interviews, portfolios, journals, student-created tests, peer evaluations, etc. For technological tools, we have Wikis, Classroom blogs, social networks, etc. (KI-19)*

Kirui (2020) notes the crucial need for infrastructural resources whose lack significantly impedes the successful realization of PBL at Moi University's medical school.

Stakeholder Perspectives on PBL at Daystar University

Despite the immense challenges experienced with PBL implementation, most of the faculty, champions, and administrators interviewed appreciated the model and believe the University is on the right path. Faculty members and champions agreed there is a need to shift pedagogy because the educational landscape now exists in a heavily technological environment. Technology, such as artificial intelligence, has created new jobs that require a new set of skills. They also noted that the job market has become very competitive, with employers seeking employees with multiple skills, particularly technical/technological skills. "Those who have not considered transformative pedagogy are burying their heads in the sand. With CBC graduates fast approaching, universities cannot afford to sit on their laurels!"

Daystar University is now well-placed in training students to handle the job market. AI is transforming the way many jobs are being handled. I can imagine a media and communications student who graduates without mobile journalism knowledge, including taking and editing videos. (KI-22)

Two participants did not have positive comments, as noted here. "Let me be the devil's advocate. PBL requires a lot of financing. Did I miss something? (KI-30) and "I am so mixed up about PBL. Many times, I wonder whether we are on the right path. I believe the implementation was poorly done- or it may have been rushed." (KI-29)

While administrators appreciate PBL, their main concern is resources, as exemplified below:

PBL is a very good system, but it needs adequate funding, which the university may not provide in the short-term. There is a need for purposeful and strategic resource mobilization initiatives. I can guarantee that once we complete implementation, complete with the required resources, DU will be a benchmarking site not only in Kenya but globally too. (KI-23)

Student informants (9/10) agreed that PBL is a worthwhile model which aids them in understanding the concepts faster: "Daystar is doing great, and I feel that it can be blended with the CBC model" (KI-22); "I'm content and very happy about it." (KI-28); "I initially was adamant because change can often be hard to accept but over time, I have come to appreciate PBL.' (KI-25)

PBL is a very good approach to learning since we cannot avoid pre-existing problems, current problems, as well as future problems. However, teachers must find ways to make students look forward to PBL assignments, rather than seeing it as a chore. (KI-21)

It's the university version of CBC and is very far reaching because it teaches how to bring theoretical issues to life rather than just reading and giving text-book answers. Second, it has given DU a unique branding identity that may have set it apart from other universities in the nation. (KI-28)

Most informants thought that DU incorporating PBL signified an innovative and positive step that corresponds to modern learning systems worldwide. The world today relies on skills like critical thinking, problem-solving, and the relevance of current knowledge. However, the informants felt that PBL can only work depending on its implementation.

The student community must be considered critically in the implementation process. Students may lack motivation, meaning that educators need to tailor the case study to the level of the students to avoid them getting overwhelmed or dispirited by the process and to offer ongoing support and guidance (McGraw Hill, 2023). The company suggests that with the right groundwork and tutor support, students will find PBL supportive and thought-provoking. In the DU case, the students identified the positive aspects of PBL, especially improving their examination outcomes and productive collaboration.

Challenges with PBL Implementation

Faculty/Staff/Student-related Challenges

According to student and faculty informants, one notable challenge is change management. Despite the intensive training offered to faculty members, some felt the lecture method is still effective. Faculty members felt unprepared or uncomfortable with the new approach, while students accustomed to lecture-based learning did not like the increased responsibility placed on them, leading to negative attitudes by both faculty and students. These perspectives are captured here. "Sometimes we lecturers don't understand PBL very well… thinking it's just group work that is an extension of the lessons. Some even call it CBC ya (of) University." (KI-24)

> *Most students don't want extra work and feel group work and assignments are excessive. Some faculty abandon students to total self-learning because they lack a good understanding of what PBL really is. Others have simply not understood the model or how to assess students under PBL. (KI-8)*
>
> *Some faculty members have completely missed the point of PBL as a learning mode. Some have unfortunately mistaken it for discussion groups, where students work on discussion questions by themselves, and then present in class. PBL is not an abandonment of learners to themselves, but a heavy supervision and guidance where the lecturer assumes the position of a facilitator. PBL requires more work on the faculty side and attention than traditional modes of learning. (KI-4)*
>
> *It should be noted that the university is circumventing the change management challenge through frequent training, while some faculty have quickly adopted and think highly of PBL, such as, "We are now teaching less and subjecting students to more thinking." (KI-3)*

Informants exposed the challenge of orienting new faculty. DU employs both full-time and part-time faculty. The turnover levels, particularly part-time faculty, may present the challenge of re-training and continuous training. KI-5 suggests that the training be done frequently, like once a trimester, for effectiveness. These many trainings have financial implications for the university. Usually, part-time staff join DU without PBL experience. However, DU mitigates this challenge through virtual training. Related to this challenge is the training of administrative staff, as revealed here:

Although the University set up an office under Academic Affairs to spearhead the implementation, this has run into challenges as the administrative assistants ought to have been part of the onboarding process at the beginning to check/audit the implementation but were not. (KI-6)

KI-4 opines that although faculty members were trained, the students were not included in the capacity-building sessions. Consequently, many do not know how to respond to PBL cases as tools for learning and assessment. KI-5 echoes this view with this perspective: "It is also necessary to have the students understand what PBL is since most complain of too much work from the lecturers. Besides, some students in the virtual mode may fail to participate" (KI-5).

Both faculty and students need help with managing time. PBL requires adequate time for both preparation and execution. Faculty members said they often need help balancing the demands of delivering PBL lessons with other academic responsibilities, such as research and administrative duties, which may lead to burnout. The students encounter challenges when balancing multiple projects and deadlines within PBL. The method usually encourages them to spend more time and energy searching for information and finding solutions to problems. Sometimes it can become stressful particularly when there is a deadline to meet on many projects.

PBL is time-consuming, as it is based on research, defining problems, restructuring, and finding solutions. I've been the scribe in almost all groups, and compressing the group members' contributions into one flowing document is a task. (KI-13)

Faculty experience challenges in assessment since traditional assessment methods are sometimes not well-suited to PBL. They encounter challenges in developing rubrics that accurately measure both the process and the outcome of PBL activities, especially when evaluating group work versus individual contributions. Further, lecturers teaching similar courses but with a different approach to project assessment create inconsistency, which can negatively impact grading.

Faculty felt that implementing PBL learning activities in large classes, especially the common units/courses, is challenging. The groups become too many, requiring extra time and attention from the faculty to monitor and assess the work. Additionally, PBL in online classes presents a challenge due to the limited student-faculty in-person interface, which limits student follow-up. Besides, even knowing how to approach the problem remains a challenge for faculty, as noted in this perspective:

The challenge is how to conceptualize the problem. I am still struggling to deliver content using the PBL model. It needs adequate time to conceptualize the problem, time we lack. Again, three days of training are insufficient to help us gain competence. We have not picked PBL properly and even the students are struggling to understand what PBL entails and their role in the process. The other challenge is that students are too familiar with their lecturers so may not take PBL seriously coming from a person struggling to use the mode. (KI-27)

Students experienced uneven participation in collaborations/teamwork because some group members deliberately absented themselves. They reported experiencing frustrations when the workload is unevenly distributed. Additionally, successful teamwork is hampered by over-dominance by some members and those who hardly speak. "Group work can promote laziness, as sometimes I rely on sources like ChatGPT to get quick information, rather than reading related books" (KI-16) and "It is tiresome when dealing with a large group, as some members are joyriders. Information gathered may be inaccurate, making us lose marks. Very overwhelming when you are lost." (KI-11)

On the downside, PBL group work is a challenge I've faced many times. When grouped with uncooperative members, it isn't easy to get work done. Some students don't care about their studies, hoping to joyride on others' work. I am aware that it is an option to tell lecturers, but that option doesn't help me grow interpersonal communication skills and keep my grades up at the same time. If there was a way to restructure how people are chosen for group work, that would work well in my favor. (KI-12)

Sometimes we call for virtual sessions for our meetings but only the serious ones attend. While some send in their work in time, others, especially the younger generation, can sometimes be very lazy and uncooperative. (KI-15)

Lack of participation pulls the group behind. Worse, some group members carry the load just to meet the goal of submitting the assignment. Other challenges include working with students you have not worked with before or newer students who are struggling to understand PBL, leading to loss of valuable time trying to bring them up to speed. (KI-13)

The students cited confusion and uncertainty in the implementation process and needed help to plug in. They feel a sound structure in delivering the content is lacking, with every lecturer doing their own thing. "The implementation, however well thought out, leaves the students to figure their way around" (KI-14); "Each lecturer seems to have their approach. Despite having the structured seven steps of the PBL, there's no predefined process or guidelines, and this causes confusion among us" (KI-16).

The problems in the assignments should be relatable and real-time and this can be difficult in some units. For example, we had a very complex PBL problem in BIL112X where we were tasked to analyze the Gospels of the New Testament. I was confused. (KI-10)

Thus, educators should note that PBL implementation has its challenges. Evenddy et al. (2023) found such difficulties as faculty resistance and readiness, complexities in curriculum design and assessment, time and resource constraints, and the need for effective project management strategies. Liu and Liu (2021) found that teachers still believed in the lecture method and were unwilling to change. However, Ishak et al. (2015) recorded different challenges that PBL implementation faced: designing a realistic problem, changing the students' and stakeholders' mindset, the inability of students to manage internal group conflicts, limited timeframe, and restricted ability of students to perform higher-order thinking.

Resource-related Challenges

Resource limitations include access to up-to-date technology, research materials, and adequate space for group work, which can hinder effective PBL implementation. Student informants reported that accessing materials was difficult, negatively impacting their ability to engage fully with the problem. KI-3 divulged concerns involving resources such as a handbook for the faculty and students and benchmarking opportunities.

> *For proper implementation of PBL, the learning environment must be transformed to adopt the 21st century classroom model. However, except for the university library on the Athi River campus, our learning spaces have not changed to fit the transition to PBL. (KI-4)*

> *The lecturers have been trained on using the PBL instructor's guide, but the challenge may be the lack of enough space for physical classes. Some classes are too huge to the extent that dividing the students into groups physically has been a challenge. (KI-5)*

According to KI-7, more financing is needed to expand the resource base. For instance, money would facilitate faculty taking students on class trips and allow learners to see contextually how some of the cases unfold.

> *Constant training is required to ensure that faculty members are up to date with the current methods of creating and articulating problem cases and management of a PBL classroom- and this requires adequate financing. (KI-2)*

The case of DU reveals that inadequate resources may interfere with successful PBL adoption. For instance, the lack of infrastructure and continuously orientating faculty, staff and students. The challenge of insufficient facilities is not new, as revealed by (Aldabbus, 2018). Liu and Liu (2021) also record the challenge of implementing PBL in a resource-constraint environment. The literature identifies several other resources required such as a problem bank or resource website which McGraw Hill (2023) created to support educators at the case study creation stage.

Implementation-related Challenges

Some informants opined that the implementation process could do with some improvements, as captured in these perspectives: "Classes and timetable scheduling were not adjusted to accommodate the PBL sessions, and this obstructed successful adoption of PBL" (KI-30).

> *I hope that the development of the 21st Century classrooms will facilitate a better understanding and implementation of PBL in the University. With this development, PBL will become the norm of teaching and learning at DU. (KI-4)*

> *So far, only the training of faculty and students has taken place. There has been very little done concerning implementation. However, the office of the Director Academic affairs does PBL training to onboard new faculty. (KI-6)*

There is also the challenge of sustaining the momentum with which DU started: "The students were very upbeat about the new learning method. The instructors were also receptive. Since there was no infrastructure to support the implementation, most of them lapsed back." (KI-6)

> *Student informants reported being initially confused about PBL and what it entails and provided rich data: "Initially, I found PBL confusing because it was so different from the lecture-based learning I was used to. It took some time to adjust to the self-directed nature of the work" (KI-12).*

> *The PBL study model increases the student's work and should not be used frequently in some courses like nursing, a practical course. The School of Nursing can consider other teaching methods than the PBL. (KI-14)*

> *This approach was introduced too hastily and forcefully to the students, and maybe even to the lecturers. The bad experiences while tackling an assignment, unfortunately, left a bad taste in my mouth, and, to date, I do not want to hear anything about PBL. (KI-10)*

> *From my observation, not every lecturer is well-equipped to handle PBL. We are exposed to different versions of PBL, which instead of advancing my learning as a student creates problems and confusion. That is the major shortcoming I see from my experience with exposure to PBL at DU. (KI-17)*

SOLUTIONS AND RECOMMENDATIONS

Solutions to the challenges identified above include enhanced faculty support that provides ongoing professional development, focuses on effective time management and advanced PBL techniques, and develops robust assessment tools. Periodic learning can also help cultivate a positive PBL culture. Mentorship programs where experienced PBL practitioners support newer faculty could be beneficial.

There is a need for a better orientation program, especially since DU admits new students every semester and preparatory programs for students before they engage with PBL. The University can use the orientation week for new students to orient all newcomers to PBL. Besides orientation, the University can host workshops and webinars on research skills, teamwork, time management, and PBL to help the students better adopt the model. More training on PBL is also required for continuing students and lecturers. Additionally, offering ongoing support throughout the semester, such as access to academic advisors and peer mentors, can help students adjust to the demands of PBL. Further, ongoing training for lecturers is required so that the PBL structure is uniform across all courses to avoid confusion.

Concerning feedback and assessments, lecturers can provide continuous and consistent feedback to allow necessary corrections and ensure effectiveness. Different evaluation sources can be included such as reflective journals, self-assessment, peer assessment, and project/process-based assessment to give a true picture of a learner's learning and mastery.

The university must make deliberate efforts to improve resources, such as e-resources, physical spaces and technology. Students should also be encouraged to use credible sources rather than random, unverified online social platforms, and lecturers should enforce this. DU needs to seek external partnerships and sponsorships to assist with inviting speakers, travelling with students to various organizations, buying equipment and all.

The university needs to effect change management strategies to help ease the transition to PBL. Kotter's 8-Step Change Model or Kurt Lewin's Change Model can help manage change. For example, clear communication about the benefits of PBL, success stories from within the university, and the creation of a culture that values innovation in teaching and learning. Faculty and student feedback should be continuously collected and used to refine the PBL process.

No class should have more than 30 students for large classes and effective PBL implementation. To enhance effectiveness, elements of variety should be incorporated into PBL. For instance, lecturers should use role-playing, case studies, group discussions, presentations, brainstorming sessions, etc., to define a problem about a given topic.

Solution Focused Learning (SFL) was proposed for collaborative meetings between faculty and students. DU requires a holistic approach where all staff and students undergo sufficient training. For instance, DU can schedule intensive training in segments, e.g. Year 1, Year 2 etc. or according to schools/departments. Additionally, experts need to be incorporated during these training sessions- the experts can visit classes and share their expertise. There is also a need for benchmarking to assist in the implementation process.

Faculty should offer organized assistance and clear guidance to avoid confusion and help students overcome complicated challenges. The lecturer could define expectations, provide resources for study and cooperation, and guide students on their research topics. Lecturers must also give guidance and examples on approaching the PBL assignments in the early stages. Further, lecturers should do regular check-ins to ensure all group members contribute equally and are on track. Moreover, creating a supportive environment where students feel comfortable seeking help from the lecturer and collaborating with other students enriches the learning experience.

Regarding uneven participation, lecturers can consider peer evaluations as part of the assessment process. Lecturers should also ask individual group members questions when presenting their assignments to ensure they understood and did the work. They should also aim for balanced group dynamics to confirm there are no dysfunctional groups. For example, they can assess the class and deliberately place the students into functional groups.

Because of the challenges some DU online students undergo, we propose that the university explore the integration of technology in PBL, such as online collaboration tools, virtual simulations, and digital resources, to facilitate problem-solving and group work. We further recommend that faculty and students be trained in using these technologies effectively.

Concerning policy, the chapter recommends that the government hastens the formulation and implementation of policy that will see the adoption of CBE in HEIs. Accordingly, it is this chapter's view that concerned stakeholders consider PBL in teacher training as a way to align with the CBC curriculum. This will present fewer challenges than training educators with already fixed mindsets, mainly if they have been in the field for many years.

Employers should begin taking pedagogical methods used in HEIs more seriously in their recruitment processes. This will spark conversations that will lead to more CBE implementation.

Thus, this chapter recommends that DU continues with PBL implementation and purpose to be a model university for other universities to emulate. Because of CBC, the university is well-placed for consultations with other institutions seeking to adopt PBL.

FUTURE RESEARCH DIRECTIONS

Future research may include a quantitative study to establish faculty/staff/students' attitudes towards PBL at DU. Specifically, we suggest a longitudinal study, perhaps five years after PBL implementation, to track the career paths and competencies of graduates who experienced PBL during their studies. We also suggest a study targeting Kenyan universities to determine their willingness to adopt PBL in line with CBC requirements.

CONCLUSION

The chapter examined the advances DU has registered in PBL and documented the challenges too. Additionally, it examined the implementation process as well as the required resources. The chapter records that DU has made several advancements since the introduction of PBL in January 2022. These include the development of materials such as PBL-compliant course outlines and teacher manuals, development of assessment tools, training, procurement of e-resources and other materials, construction of some classrooms, problem bank with more than 30 scenarios, PBL embraced by some faculty/staff, positive response from some students, and the industry's positive response about DU graduates/students.

Despite the advancements noted, the university has also experienced some challenges. These include faculty/staff/student-related challenges such as resistance, lack of PBL understanding, time constraints, large classrooms, confusion by faculty and students, and students' difficulties with collaboration. Additionally, orienting new staff is a continuous activity, which may present financial challenges. Moreover, most students have yet to undergo training, meaning they do not comprehend PBL. Further, financial challenges for field trips, infrastructure and purchasing resource materials were noted. There are also challenges with implementation, such as reduced momentum.

Daystar University adopted PBL through a deliberate process with solid backing from management. The first thing was to examine if the shift would align with university policy, and it did. Teams were appointed to oversee the process at the beginning, and the implementation was gradual. The implementation process was undertaken after adequate preparation involving extensive research and consultation. Additionally, monitoring and evaluation were and continue to be conducted. However, DU needs to engage with all the stakeholders for a buy-in.

Thus, it is imperative that universities in Kenya adopt PBL or CBE because these students are more proactive and better prepared for the 21st-century job market, which requires collaboration, creativity, communication skills, critical thinking, and problem-solving skills. CBC and CBE are in tandem with constructivism, a learner-centered theory that can assist with implementation.

ACKNOWLEDGEMENT

This research did not receive a grant from any agency in the public, commercial, or not-for-profit sectors. However, Daystar University provided the materials for this study.

REFERENCES

Aldabbus, S. (2018). Project-based learning: Implementation & challenges. *International Journal of Education, Learning and Development*, 6(3), 71–79.

Alshaye, I. A., Tasir, Z., & Jumaat, N. F. (2023). The effectiveness of online problem-based learning tasks on Riyadh's secondary school students' problem-solving ability and programming skills. *Open Education Studies*, 5(1), 20220208. DOI: 10.1515/edu-2022-0208

Barrows, H. S., & Neufeld, V. (1974). The "McMaster Philosophy": An approach to medical education. *Journal of Medical Education*, 49, 1040–1050. PMID: 4444006

Borhan, M. T. (2014). Problem-based learning (PBL) in teacher education: A review of the effect of PBL on pre-service teachers' knowledge and skills. *European Journal of Educational Sciences*, 1(1), 10. DOI: 10.19044/ejes.v1no1a9

Boud, D., & Feletti, G. (1997). *The challenge of problem-based learning* (1st ed.). Routledge., DOI: 10.4324/9781315042039

Celinšek, D., & Markič, M. (n.d.). Implementing a new approach in teaching and learning (problem-based learning) in a higher education learning organization. *In-Annual World International Congress for Effectiveness and Improvement,* Slovenia.

Centre for Innovation in Teaching and Learning. (n.d.). *Problem-based learning (PBL).*_https://citl.illinois.edu/citl-101/teaching-learning/resources/teaching-strategies/problem-based-learning-(pbl)

Chege, M. (2015). Re-inventing Kenya's university: From a "Graduate-mill" to a development-oriented paradigm. *International Journal of Educational Development*, 44, 21–27. DOI: 10.1016/j.ijedudev.2015.07.002

Creswell, J. W. (2014). *Research design: Qualitative, quantitative and mixed methods Approaches* (4th ed.). Sage.

Creswell, J. W., & Miller, D. L. (2000). Determining validity in qualitative inquiry: Theory into practice. *Theory into Practice*, 39(3), 124–130. DOI: 10.1207/s15430421tip3903_2

Cunningham, M. (2015). Factors impacting on adoption of technology-enhanced learning techniques by universities in Nairobi, Kenya. *2015 IEEE International Symposium on Technology and Society (ISTAS), 12*, 1–7. DOI: 10.1109/ISTAS.2015.7439446

Daystar University. (2024). What's PBL? *Daystar University*. https://www.daystar.ac.ke/academic-affairs/problem-based-learning

Dewey, J. (1938). *Experience and education*. Macmillan.

Duch, B. J., Groh, S. E., & Allen, D. E. (Eds.). (2001). *The power of problem-based learning*. Stylus Publishing.

East Africa, P. B. L. (n.d.). *PBL East Africa*. https://aaltoglobalimpact.org/pbl-east-africa/

Evenddy, S. S., Gailea, N., & Syafrizal, S. (2023). Exploring the benefits and challenges of project-based learning in higher education. *PPSDP International Journal of Education*, 2(2), 458–469. DOI: 10.59175/pijed.v2i2.148

Frida, S. W., & Kising'u, T. M. (2024). Competency-based learning and entrepreneurial intention in university technical and vocational education and training institutions in Kenya. *Journal of Education and Practice*, 1(5), 93–116.

Galukande, M., Katamba, A., Kiguli, S., Kiguli-Malwadde, E., Kijjambu, S., & Sewankambo, N. (2015). Problem based learning: Tutors' views 5 years after implementation at a sub-Saharan university. *African Health Sciences*, 15(1), 261. DOI: 10.4314/ahs.v15i1.34 PMID: 25834557

Gibbs, G. R. (2007). Analyzing qualitative data. *Sage (Atlanta, Ga.)*.

Gitonga, R., Onyango, G., & Rugar, T. (2017, November). Students' experiences in using Haiku learning platform to promote problem-based learning in a blended classroom in Kenya. In *Proceedings of the 2017 International Conference on Education and E-Learning* (pp. 30-33). DOI: 10.1145/3160908.3160919

Gufstafson, P., & Pollock, B. (2015). *District support strategies for a PBL launch*. https://www.edutopia.org/blog/district-support-strategies-pbl-launch-weyers-gustafson-pollock

Gumartifa, A., Syahri, I., Siroj, R. A., Nurrahmi, M., & Yusof, N. (2023). Perception of teachers regarding problem-based learning and traditional method in the classroom learning innovation process. [IJOLAE]. *Indonesian Journal on Learning and Advanced Education*, 5(2), 151–166. DOI: 10.23917/ijolae.v5i2.20714

Hussein, S. (5 January 2021). Daystar introduces problem-based learning. *Involvement.* https://involvement.co.ke/daystar-introduces-problem-based-learning/

Ishak, S., Che Omar, A. R., & Sum, MD, S. (2015). Implementation of problem-based learning: A review on the challenges. *International Journal of Education and Research*, 3(8), 381–394.

Jabu, K. (2022). *Why it's time for Kenyan universities to adopt the problem-based learning approach.* [PBL-BioAfrica]. https://ruforum.wordpress.com/2022/06/01/pbl-bioafrica-why-its-time-for-kenyan-universities-to-adopt-the-problem-based-learning-approach/

Kang'ethe, S., & Mutema, A. M. (n.d.). Innovative techniques in the training of health professionals: The case of Moi University, Faculty of Heath Sciences, Kenya.

Katwa, J. K., Ayiro, L., Kei, R., Obwoge, R. O., & Baliddawa, J. B. (2018). Successes and limitations of community-based education service at Moi University School of Medicine, Eldoret, Kenya. *World Journal of Medical Education and Research*, 16(1), 40–43.

Katwa, J. K., Obwoge, R. O., Baliddawa, J. B., Ayiro, L., & Kei, R. (2018). Knowledge and perception of lecturers regarding problem based learning as an educational approach in College of Health Sciences, Moi University. *IOSR Journal of Research & Method in Education (IOSR-JRME), 8(1),* 26-29.

Kavanagh, S. S., & Herrmann, Z. (2021). *How school leaders can support project-based learning.* https://www.gse.upenn.edu/news/how-school-leaders-can-support-project-based-learning

Kenya Institute of Curriculum Development. (n.d). *When did piloting of the new curriculum begin?* https://kicd.ac.ke/faqs/when-did-piloting-of-the-new-curriculum-begin/

Kiguli-Malwadde, E., Kijjambu, S., Kiguli, S., Galukande, M., Mwanika, A., Luboga, S., & Sewankambo, N. (2006). Problem based learning, curriculum development and change process at Faculty of Medicine, Makerere University, Uganda. *African Health Sciences*, 6(2), 127–130. PMID: 16916306

Kiptoo, A. K., Wambui, T. W., & David, G. (2015). Relevance of standardized class learning system on Y generation workforce, in Kenya. *International Journal of Academic Research in Business & Social Sciences*, 5(11). Advance online publication. DOI: 10.6007/IJARBSS/v5-i11/1901

Kirui, J. K. (2020). *Challenges in implementation of Problem-Based Learning (PBL) approach in Moi University School of Medicine Kenya: Perspectives of faculty members* [Unpublished doctoral dissertation], Moi University.

Kitainge, K. M. (2022). The status and challenges on the use of constructivist instructional methods in the implementation of in Higher Education in Kenya. *IOSR Journal of Research & Method in Education*, 12(2), 64–70.

Kotter, J. (1996). *The 8 steps for leading change.* https://www.kotterinc.com/methodology/8-steps/

Lim, L., & Choy, J. (2014). Preparing staff for problem-based learning: Outcomes of a comprehensive faculty development program. *International Journal of Research Studies in Education*, 4(3), 53–68. DOI: 10.5861/ijrse.2014.821

Liu, G., & Liu, Y. (2021, December). Problem-based learning: Its advantages, current situations and future development. In *2021 4th International Conference on Humanities Education and Social Sciences (ICHESS 2021)* (pp. 347-352). Atlantis Press.

Maastricht University. (2024). *Problem-based learning.* https://www.maastrichtuniversity.nl/education/why-um/problem-based-learning#sevensteps

Masinde, P., Arimi, J., Owiti, B., Maitethia, D., Nawiri, P., Wesonga, J., De Groote, B., Koomen, I., & Odhiambo, R. (2024). Innovative pedagogy of competence-based training in horticulture: Case study of TVET education in Kenya. *African Journal of Science. Technology and Social Sciences*, 2(2), 32–40.

Mburu, P. (8 March 2024). AgriScale project redefining agriculture education in universities. *Daily Nation.* https://nation.africa/kenya/news/education/agriscale-project-redefining-agriculture-education-in-universities-4550004

McGraw Hill. (2023). *The 3 biggest challenges of problem-based learning and how to overcome them.* https://www.mheducation.es/blog/biggest-challenges-of-problem-based-learning#:~:text=Problem%2Dbased%20learning%20challenges%3A%20lack%20of%20time&text=Students%20will%20also%20have%20to,to%20find%20their%20own%20way

McLeod, S. (2024). *Constructivism learning theory & philosophy of education.* https://www.simplypsychology.org/constructivism.html

Migiro, W. L. (2022). *The effect of selected teaching methods on acquisition of technical skills by mechanical engineering technician trainees: A case of national polytechnics in the western region of Kenya* [Unpublished doctoral dissertation]. University of Eldoret.

Ministry of Education. (2024). Sessional Paper No. X of 2024.

Mohammed, A. B., Zegeye, R. T., Dawed, H. A., & Tessema, Y. M. (2024). Implementation of problem-based learning in undergraduate medical education in Ethiopia: An exploratory qualitative study. *Advances in Medical Education and Practice*, 15, 105–119. DOI: 10.2147/AMEP.S443384 PMID: 38404356

Mosham, D. (1982). Exogenous, endogenous and dialectical constructivism. *Developmental Review*, 2(4), 371–384. DOI: 10.1016/0273-2297(82)90019-3

Mulonda, K., Indeche, A., Chabala, L. M., Kaluba, P., Simfukwe, P., Siatwiinda, S. M., & Laitinen, E. (2022). Application of problem-based learning in higher education in soil and climate change studies in Sub-Saharan Africa. *HAMK Unlimited Professional*, 16(6), 2022.

Munezero, M. D., & Bekuta, B. K. (2016). Benefits and challenges of introducing a blended project-based approach in higher education: Experiences from a Kenyan university. *International Journal of Education and Development Using Information and Communication Technology*, 12(2), 206–218.

Mutammimah, H., & Padli, P. (2023, June). Problem-based learning in English teaching: A systematic literature review. In *English Language and Literature International Conference (ELLiC). Proceedings*, 6, 487–503.

National University. (n.d). *Constructivism in education: What is constructivism?* https://www.nu.edu/blog/what-is-constructivism-in-education/#:~:text=Constructivism%20is%20an%20action%2Doriented,activities%20to%20help%20students%20learn

Neufeld, V. R., & Barrows, H. S. (1974). The "McMaster philosophy": An approach to medical education. *Academic Medicine*, 49(11), 1040–1050. DOI: 10.1097/00001888-197411000-00004 PMID: 4444006

Odhiambo, G. (2018). The role of Kenyan universities in national development. *FIRE: Forum for International Research in Education, 4*(3).

Oladele, J. I., Ndlovu, M., Spangenberg, E. D., Daramola, D. S., & Obimuyiwa, G. A. (2024). Transitioning to problem-based learning in higher education: Opportunities for producing 21st- century pre-service teachers in Sub-Saharan Africa. *Kurdish Studies*, 12(2), 609–626.

Oluoch, J., & Osida, J. (2014). Building strengths in information communication and technology in Kenyan universities: Way forward for the 21st century. *Wyno Academic Journal of Social Sciences*, 2(2), 10–16.

Ondieki, C., Kimani, G. N., & Tanui, E. K. (2018). Deficiencies of competency based education and training in higher education institutions in Kenya. *Scholars Journal of Arts. Humanities and Social Sciences*, 6(7), 1437–1447.

Ondigi, S. R. (2011). Globalization of university programs and community linkages: A case of two Kenyan universities. *International Journal of Humanities and Social Science*, 1(3), 96–105.

Pon, C., & Schendel, R. (2020). Exploring processes of teaching and learning in African university contexts: The case of education for critical thinking in Ghana, Kenya and Botswana. *International Journal of African Higher Education*, 7(1). Advance online publication. DOI: 10.6017/ijahe.v6i2.11355

Schmidt, H. G. (1993). Foundations of problem-based learning: Some explanatory notes. *Medical Education*, 27(5), 422–432. DOI: 10.1111/j.1365-2923.1993.tb00296.x PMID: 8208146

Sebatana, M. J., & Dudu, W. T. (2022). Reality or mirage: Enhancing 21st-century skills through problem-based learning while teaching particulate nature of matter. *International Journal of Science and Mathematics Education*, 20(5), 963–980. DOI: 10.1007/s10763-021-10206-w

Simba, F. W., & Kising'u, T. M. (2024). Competency-based learning and entrepreneurial intention in university technical and vocational education and training institutions in Kenya. *Journal of Education and Practice*, (5), 93–116.

Strauss, A., & Corbin, J. (1990). Basics of qualitative research: Grounded theory procedures and techniques. *Sage (Atlanta, Ga.)*.

Strobel, J., & Van Barneveld, A. (2009). When is PBL more effective? A meta-synthesis of meta-analyses comparing PBL to conventional classrooms. *The Interdisciplinary Journal of Problem-Based Learning*, 3(4). Advance online publication. DOI: 10.7771/1541-5015.1046

Suwastini, N. K. A., Puspawati, N. W. N., Adnyani, N. L. P. S., Dantes, G. R., & Rusnalasari, Z. D. (2021). Problem-based learning and 21st-century skills: Are they compatible? *EduLite: Journal of English Education. Literature and Culture*, 6(2), 326–340.

Tadesse, S. G., Tadesse, D. G., & Dagnaw, E. H. (2022). Problem based learning approach increases the academic satisfaction of health science students in Ethiopian universities: A comparative cross-sectional study. *BMC Medical Education*, 22(1), 334. DOI: 10.1186/s12909-022-03397-5 PMID: 35501812

Tefera, A. S., Melaku, E. E., Urgie, B. M., Hassen, E. M., Tamene, T. D., & Gebeyaw, E. D. (2024). Barriers to implementing problem-based learning at the School of Medicine of Debre Berhan University, Ethiopia. *BMC Medical Education*, 24(1), 501. DOI: 10.1186/s12909-024-05252-1 PMID: 38711080

Torp, L., & Sage, S. (2002). *Problems as possibilities: Problem-based learning for K-16 education* (2nd ed.). Association for Supervision and Curriculum Development.

University of Buffalo. (2024). Constructivism: Creating experiences that facilitate the construction of knowledge. *Center for Educational Innovation, University at Buffalo*. https://www.buffalo.edu/catt/teach/develop/theory/constructivism.html

University of Nairobi (UON). (n.d). *UON among varsities to roll out PBL-Bio Africa project in Africa*.https://sciencetechnology.uonbi.ac.ke/latest-news/uon-among-varsities-roll-out-pbl-bio-africa-project-africa

Western Governor's University. (2020). *What is constructivism?* https://www.wgu.edu/blog/what-constructivism2005.html

Zakaria, M. I., Noor Nasran, N. A., Ahmad Alhassora, N. S., & Pairan, R. (2024). Unleashing problem-based learning method among mathematics teachers. *International Journal of Academic Research in Progressive Education and Development*, 13(1). Advance online publication. DOI: 10.6007/IJARPED/v13-i1/20492

KEY TERMS AND DEFINITIONS

Advancements: Strides made over time/successes realized following PBL implementation

Challenges: Issues or problems encountered in the course of PBL implementation

Constructivism: A philosophical research paradigm in the qualitative field where people actively, individually and socially construct knowledge

Daystar University: A private, faith-based university based in Nairobi and Athi River, Kenya

PBL process implementation: The steps taken to establish and entrench PBL in a system

Problem-based learning: A teaching method that leverages groups and collaborations amongst students who learn through solving real-life problems

Resources: Materials and finances required for PBL implementation

Chapter 8
Leveraging Statistical Simulation for Enhancing Academic Rigor and Practical Skills

Fred Nyamitago Monari
https://orcid.org/0000-0002-3127-9310
Kisii University, Kenya

ABSTRACT

This chapter explores how integrating statistical simulation in higher education enhances learning, highlighting benefits, challenges, and best practices. It starts with an overview of simulation techniques and their applications across disciplines. It then focuses on student-centered methods like problem-based and project-based learning, along with flipped classrooms, supported by successful case studies. Examples show how simulation-based courses boost engagement and outcomes. The chapter addresses challenges like technology needs, faculty training, and assessment, offering solutions. It concludes with strategies to overcome institutional resistance and financial constraints, showcasing the transformative potential of simulation-based learning.

INTRODUCTION

In today's rapidly changing educational landscape, academic achievement alone is no longer sufficient to prepare students for the complexities of the modern world. As technology advances and the demands of the workplace evolve, there is a growing need to equip students with practical, real-world skills that extend beyond tradition-

DOI: 10.4018/979-8-3693-6930-2.ch008

al lecture-based instruction. This chapter explores the transformative potential of statistical simulation techniques in bridging the gap between theoretical knowledge and practical application, offering students a dynamic and engaging learning experience that fosters critical thinking, problem-solving, and decision-making skills.

Statistical simulation, at its core, is a powerful educational tool that allows students to explore and interact with real-world scenarios in a safe, controlled environment. By immersing themselves in these simulations, students gain a deeper understanding of complex concepts and learn how to apply them in practical settings. This hands-on approach not only enhances their comprehension of academic material but also prepares them to navigate the uncertainties and challenges they will encounter in their professional careers. In essence, statistical simulation transforms passive learning into an active, experiential process that equips students with the adaptability and innovation needed to thrive in a rapidly changing world.

The use of statistical simulation in education is not just about understanding abstract concepts; it is about preparing students for real-life situations. Through simulation, students can engage with scenarios that mirror the complexities of the workplace, allowing them to develop and refine their problem-solving abilities in a risk-free environment. This method fosters a growth mindset, encouraging students to learn from their mistakes and build resilience. As they navigate these simulated challenges, students become more adept at making informed decisions and solving problems creatively, skills that are highly valued in today's job market.

In the following sections, we will delve deeper into the ways statistical simulation can revolutionize education. We will examine various pedagogical approaches that leverage simulation techniques, share success stories from diverse academic fields, and discuss the challenges and opportunities associated with implementing simulation-based learning. Ultimately, this chapter aims to highlight the potential of statistical simulation to enhance academic rigor and equip students with the practical skills necessary for success beyond the classroom.

Background

The commercialization of teaching and learning in higher education has been a topic of much discussion and scrutiny in recent years. Universities increasingly rely on tuition fees and external funding sources to sustain their operations, raising concerns about potential trade-offs between maintaining academic excellence and ensuring financial stability (Marginson, 2016). This tension often creates a dilemma for institutions, as they strive to balance the pursuit of educational quality with the imperative to generate revenue and remain competitive in a market-driven environment.

The financial pressures faced by higher education institutions are further exacerbated by declining state funding, which forces many universities to seek alternative sources of revenue. This financial strain, combined with growing demands for accountability and measurable outcomes, places immense pressure on institutions to demonstrate their value proposition to students, parents, and society at large (Johnstone, 2016). As a result, there is a clear imperative for universities to innovate their pedagogical approaches to meet the evolving needs of their stakeholders and ensure their long-term sustainability.

Traditional lecture-based methods, while time-honored, may no longer be sufficient to engage students and foster deep learning experiences in today's fast-paced, technology-driven world. The abundance of information and rapid technological advancements require educators to find new ways to make learning more dynamic, interactive, and relevant to the real world (Garrison & Kanuka, 2004). This is where statistical simulation emerges as a compelling solution, offering a transformative approach to teaching and learning that transcends the limitations of conventional instructional methods.

Statistical simulation leverages the power of technology to create immersive, experiential learning environments that engage students in active, hands-on learning. By simulating real-world scenarios, educators can provide students with tangible examples and case studies that illustrate the practical applications of the theories they learn in class. Whether simulating market dynamics in economics, population trends in sociology, or chemical reactions in chemistry, these interactive experiences enable students to see the direct implications of their learning on real-world phenomena (Banks et al., 2014).

Moreover, statistical simulation offers a safe space for students to experiment, make mistakes, and learn from their failures—an essential aspect of the learning process that is often overlooked in traditional educational settings (Schmidt & Bjork, 1992). By encouraging exploration and discovery, simulation-based learning cultivates a growth mindset and resilience in students, preparing them to tackle complex challenges with confidence and adaptability. This approach not only enhances their academic achievement but also equips them with the practical skills needed to succeed in their future careers.

The integration of statistical simulation into higher education curricula also opens up new opportunities for collaboration between universities and industry partners. By developing simulation-based case studies and projects that mirror real-world challenges, institutions can create meaningful learning experiences that enhance students' readiness for the workforce (Aldrich, 2005). These collaborations not only enrich the educational experience but also strengthen the ties between academia and industry, ensuring that graduates are well-prepared to meet the demands of the job market.

Despite the numerous benefits of statistical simulation, its adoption in higher education is not without challenges. Implementing simulation techniques requires significant technological resources, faculty training, and curriculum development (Fowler, 2013). Additionally, assessing student learning outcomes in simulation-based courses can be complex, necessitating the development of new evaluation tools and metrics to measure the acquisition of practical skills and competencies.

In summary, statistical simulation represents a transformative pedagogical approach that addresses the dual imperatives of academic quality and financial sustainability in higher education. By engaging students in experiential learning and bridging the gap between theory and practice, simulation techniques empower educators to deliver dynamic, impactful educational experiences that prepare students for success in the 21st century and beyond.

Methodology

This chapter employs a qualitative research methodology, utilizing a comprehensive literature review to synthesize existing studies on the integration of statistical simulation in higher education. The analysis includes case studies from various disciplines to illustrate successful implementations of simulation-based learning. Data were collected from peer-reviewed journals, educational reports, and relevant academic publications to identify best practices, challenges, and pedagogical approaches. Additionally, expert opinions and theoretical frameworks were incorporated to provide a robust understanding of the impact of statistical simulation on academic rigor and practical skills development. This methodological approach ensures a thorough examination of the topic, highlighting both empirical evidence and theoretical insights.

A) INTRODUCTION TO STATISTICAL SIMULATION

Defining Statistical Simulation

Statistical simulation is a powerful educational tool that enables students to engage with and explore complex, real-world scenarios within a controlled, risk-free environment. This method involves creating models that imitate real-life processes and systems, allowing learners to observe and manipulate variables, conduct experiments, and analyze outcomes. The core idea behind statistical simulation is to replicate the behavior of a system or process using mathematical and computational techniques, thereby providing a tangible and interactive learning experience.

One of the primary techniques used in statistical simulation is the Monte Carlo method. Named after the famous casino in Monaco, the Monte Carlo method relies on repeated random sampling to compute results. This technique is particularly useful for understanding the impact of uncertainty and variability in complex systems. For example, in finance, Monte Carlo simulations are used to model the behavior of stock prices and assess the risk of investment portfolios (Glasserman, 2013). In healthcare, these simulations can predict patient outcomes and optimize treatment plans (Kroese et al., 2014).

Another popular technique is agent-based modeling (ABM), which involves simulating the interactions of autonomous agents within a given environment. These agents can represent individuals, groups, or entities that follow specific rules and behaviors. ABM is widely used in social sciences to study phenomena such as crowd behavior, disease spread, and market dynamics (Bonabeau, 2002). By observing the emergent patterns and outcomes resulting from these interactions, students can gain insights into the underlying mechanisms driving complex systems.

Applications in Higher Education

The versatility of statistical simulation makes it an invaluable tool across various disciplines in higher education. By integrating simulation techniques into the curriculum, educators can create immersive learning experiences that enhance students' understanding of theoretical concepts and their ability to apply this knowledge in practical settings.

In economics, for instance, statistical simulations can model market behavior and policy impacts. Students can explore how changes in supply and demand affect prices, or how fiscal policies influence economic growth and employment (Colander, 2017). By manipulating variables and observing outcomes, learners develop a deeper appreciation for the complexities of economic systems and the interplay of various factors.

In the field of public health, simulations can model the spread of infectious diseases and evaluate intervention strategies. During the COVID-19 pandemic, for example, epidemiological models were crucial in predicting the virus's trajectory and informing public health policies (Ferguson et al., 2020). By engaging with these simulations, students can understand the importance of timely interventions, the impact of different control measures, and the challenges of managing public health crises.

Engineering students can benefit from statistical simulations by modeling physical systems and optimizing designs. For example, in civil engineering, simulations can assess the structural integrity of buildings and bridges under different loads and stress conditions (Smith & Griffiths, 2014). In environmental engineering, simulations can evaluate the effectiveness of pollution control measures and the impact of environmental policies (Rubin & Davidson, 2001). These hands-on experiences enable students to apply theoretical knowledge to real-world problems, preparing them for the challenges of their profession.

In the social sciences, simulations can explore human behavior and social dynamics. For instance, agent-based models can simulate voting behavior, social networks, and migration patterns (Gilbert & Troitzsch, 2005). By analyzing the emergent outcomes of these interactions, students gain insights into the factors influencing individual and collective behavior, as well as the potential consequences of different policies and interventions.

Enhancing Learning Experiences

The integration of statistical simulation into higher education not only bridges the gap between theory and practice but also transforms the learning experience by making it more engaging and interactive. Traditional lecture-based methods often struggle to capture the complexity and dynamism of real-world systems, leading to passive learning and limited student engagement. In contrast, simulation-based learning encourages active participation, exploration, and experimentation, fostering a deeper understanding and retention of knowledge.

One of the key benefits of statistical simulation is its ability to provide immediate feedback. As students manipulate variables and observe outcomes in real-time, they can see the direct consequences of their actions and decisions. This feedback loop enhances their learning by reinforcing concepts and highlighting the connections between theory and practice. Moreover, the iterative nature of simulation allows students to learn from their mistakes and refine their approaches, cultivating critical thinking and problem-solving skills (Schmidt & Bjork, 1992).

Another advantage of simulation-based learning is its ability to accommodate different learning styles and paces. Students can engage with simulations individually or collaboratively, allowing them to work at their own speed and explore areas of interest in greater depth. This flexibility is particularly valuable in diverse classroom settings, where students may have varying levels of background knowledge and experience. By providing a personalized learning experience, simulations can enhance student engagement and motivation (Felder & Brent, 2005).

Furthermore, statistical simulations can facilitate interdisciplinary learning by highlighting the interconnectedness of different fields. For example, a simulation modeling the impact of climate change on agricultural productivity can integrate concepts from environmental science, economics, and public policy. By working on such multidisciplinary projects, students develop a holistic understanding of complex issues and appreciate the value of collaboration and cross-disciplinary thinking (National Research Council, 2012).

Case Studies and Examples

The effectiveness of statistical simulation in enhancing learning experiences is evident in various case studies and examples from diverse academic fields. In a study conducted at a major university, engineering students participated in a simulation-based course on structural analysis. The course incorporated simulations of building designs under different stress conditions, allowing students to test their theoretical knowledge and experiment with different design parameters. The results showed a significant improvement in students' understanding of structural concepts and their ability to apply this knowledge in practical scenarios (Smith & Griffiths, 2014).

In another example, a public health course used simulations to model the spread of infectious diseases and evaluate intervention strategies. Students engaged with these simulations to understand the dynamics of disease transmission, the impact of different control measures, and the importance of timely interventions. The hands-on experience not only enhanced their understanding of epidemiological concepts but also prepared them for real-world public health challenges (Ferguson et al., 2020).

A business course on market dynamics employed Monte Carlo simulations to model stock prices and assess investment risks. Students used these simulations to explore the effects of different market conditions and investment strategies, gaining insights into risk management and decision-making. The simulation-based approach not only improved their comprehension of financial concepts but also developed their analytical and critical thinking skills (Glasserman, 2013).

Challenges and Considerations

While the benefits of statistical simulation in education are substantial, implementing these techniques also presents several challenges and considerations. One of the primary challenges is the need for significant technological resources, including computer hardware, software, and technical support. Developing and maintaining simulation models can be resource-intensive, requiring expertise in both the subject matter and simulation techniques (Fowler, 2013).

Additionally, faculty training is crucial to the successful integration of simulation-based learning. Educators need to be proficient in using simulation tools and designing effective simulation-based activities. This requires ongoing professional development and support, as well as a willingness to adopt new pedagogical approaches (Felder & Brent, 2005).

Assessing student learning outcomes in simulation-based courses can also be complex. Traditional assessment methods, such as exams and quizzes, may not adequately capture the practical skills and competencies developed through simulation-based learning. Developing new evaluation tools and metrics, such as performance rubrics and reflective assessments, is essential to measure the full range of student learning (Schmidt & Bjork, 1992).

Future Directions

In summary, statistical simulation represents a transformative pedagogical approach that enhances academic rigor and equips students with practical skills essential for success in the 21st century. By providing an interactive and immersive learning experience, simulations bridge the gap between theory and practice, fostering critical thinking, problem-solving, and decision-making abilities. Despite the challenges associated with implementing simulation-based learning, the benefits far outweigh the costs, making it a valuable addition to higher education curricula. As technology continues to evolve and the demands of the workplace change, the integration of statistical simulation into education will become increasingly important in preparing students for the complexities of the modern world.

B) PEDAGOGICAL APPROACHES: HARNESSING STATISTICAL SIMULATION FOR STUDENT-CENTERED LEARNING

Introduction

In an era characterized by rapid technological advancements and an ever-evolving job market, the demand for innovative teaching methods that prepare students for real-world challenges has never been higher. Traditional lecture-based instruction, while foundational, often falls short in engaging students and fostering the practical skills needed in today's dynamic environment. To address this gap, educators are increasingly turning to student-centered teaching methods, such as problem-based learning (PBL), project-based learning (PjBL), and flipped classroom models. Integrating statistical simulation into these pedagogical approaches can significantly enhance their effectiveness, offering immersive, hands-on learning experiences that bridge the gap between theory and practice.

Problem-Based Learning (PBL)

Problem-based learning is an instructional method that places students at the center of the learning process, encouraging them to develop critical thinking and problem-solving skills by working through complex, real-world problems. In PBL, students are presented with a problem and, rather than being directly taught the material, they must research, collaborate, and apply their knowledge to find a solution.

Role of Statistical Simulation in PBL

Statistical simulation can be a powerful tool in PBL by providing a dynamic platform where students can test hypotheses, explore scenarios, and observe the outcomes of their decisions. For example, in a public health course, students might be tasked with managing an outbreak of an infectious disease. Using simulation software, they can model the spread of the disease under various conditions and evaluate the effectiveness of different intervention strategies. This hands-on approach not only reinforces theoretical knowledge but also allows students to understand the practical implications of their decisions (Albanese & Mitchell, 1993).

Case Study: Public Health Simulation

A study conducted at a major university integrated statistical simulation into a PBL curriculum for a public health course. Students were divided into groups and given the task of managing a simulated outbreak of a novel virus. They used statistical simulation tools to model the spread of the virus based on different public health interventions, such as social distancing, vaccination, and quarantine measures. The results showed that students not only developed a deeper understanding of epidemiological concepts but also enhanced their collaborative and decision-making skills (Barrows, 1996).

Project-Based Learning (PjBL)

Project-based learning is another student-centered approach that involves students in long-term, interdisciplinary projects. Unlike PBL, which typically focuses on solving a specific problem, PjBL engages students in comprehensive projects that require the application of knowledge and skills across various domains. This method promotes sustained inquiry, critical thinking, and practical application.

Role of Statistical Simulation in PjBL

Statistical simulation can enhance PjBL by providing a realistic and interactive environment where students can apply their knowledge to complex projects. For instance, in an environmental science course, students might work on a project to assess the impact of climate change on local ecosystems. By using simulation models, they can analyze data, predict future trends, and evaluate the effectiveness of different mitigation strategies. This approach not only makes learning more engaging but also helps students develop valuable skills in data analysis and scientific inquiry (Blumenfeld et al., 1991).

Case Study: Environmental Science Project

In a project-based learning initiative at a university, environmental science students undertook a semester-long project to study the effects of climate change on a local watershed. Using statistical simulation software, they modeled various climate scenarios and their potential impact on water quality and biodiversity. The project required students to collect and analyze data, collaborate with local environmental organizations, and present their findings to the community. The use of simulation tools provided a realistic and engaging way for students to apply their theoretical knowledge to real-world issues, fostering a deeper understanding and commitment to environmental stewardship (Krajcik & Blumenfeld, 2006).

Flipped Classroom Model

The flipped classroom model is an instructional strategy that inverts the traditional learning environment by delivering instructional content online outside of the classroom and moving activities, including those that would typically be considered homework, into the classroom. This model allows for more interactive and collaborative learning experiences during class time.

Role of Statistical Simulation in Flipped Classrooms

Statistical simulation can play a crucial role in flipped classrooms by providing interactive content that students can engage with outside of class, thereby freeing up classroom time for hands-on activities and discussions. For example, in a business analytics course, students might use simulation software to complete pre-class assignments, such as modeling business scenarios and analyzing data trends. In class, they can then work in groups to discuss their findings, share insights, and tackle more complex problems with the guidance of their instructor (Bishop & Verleger, 2013).

Case Study: Business Analytics Course

A business school implemented a flipped classroom model in a business analytics course, incorporating statistical simulation into both the pre-class and in-class activities. Students used simulation software to complete online modules that included video lectures and interactive exercises on topics such as market analysis and risk assessment. During class, they participated in group projects that involved developing business strategies based on their simulation results. The integration of simulation tools in the flipped classroom model led to increased student engagement, improved understanding of analytical concepts, and enhanced collaborative skills (Herreid & Schiller, 2013).

Challenges and Considerations

While the integration of statistical simulation into student-centered teaching methods offers numerous benefits, it also presents several challenges. One significant challenge is the need for adequate technological resources, including software, hardware, and technical support. Developing and maintaining simulation models can be resource-intensive, and not all institutions may have the necessary infrastructure (Fowler, 2013).

Faculty training is another critical consideration. Educators need to be proficient in using simulation tools and designing effective simulation-based activities. This requires ongoing professional development and support, as well as a willingness to adopt new pedagogical approaches (Felder & Brent, 2005).

Additionally, assessing student learning outcomes in simulation-based courses can be complex. Traditional assessment methods may not adequately capture the practical skills and competencies developed through simulation-based learning. Developing new evaluation tools and metrics, such as performance rubrics and reflective assessments, is essential to measure the full range of student learning (Schmidt & Bjork, 1992).

Summary of Findings

The integration of statistical simulation into student-centered teaching methods, such as problem-based learning, project-based learning, and flipped classroom models, holds significant potential for enhancing the educational experience. By providing interactive and immersive learning environments, simulations bridge the gap between theory and practice, fostering critical thinking, problem-solving, and decision-making abilities. Despite the challenges associated with implementing simulation-based learning, the benefits far outweigh the costs, making it a valuable addition to higher education curricula. As technology continues to evolve and the demands of the workplace change, the integration of statistical simulation into education will become increasingly important in preparing students for the complexities of the modern world.

C. CASE STUDIES AND BEST PRACTICES: SIMULATION-BASED COURSES IN DIVERSE ACADEMIC FIELDS

Introduction

The use of statistical simulation in higher education has gained significant traction across various disciplines. By providing students with interactive, hands-on learning experiences, simulation-based courses can bridge the gap between theoretical knowledge and real-world application. This section presents exemplary case studies from different academic fields, highlighting successful implementation strategies and outcomes. These case studies demonstrate the effectiveness of simulation in enhancing student engagement, promoting deeper learning, and equipping students with practical skills.

Case Study 1: Economics - Market Dynamics Simulation

Course Overview

In an undergraduate economics course, students explored market dynamics through simulation-based activities. The course aimed to teach concepts such as supply and demand, market equilibrium, and price elasticity using real-world data and scenarios.

Implementation Strategy

The instructor used R, a powerful statistical computing language, to create simulations that modeled different market conditions. Students worked in groups to manipulate variables such as consumer preferences, production costs, and government policies to observe their impact on market outcomes.

R Code Example: Market Simulation

Figure 1. Market Equilibrium under Different Scenarios

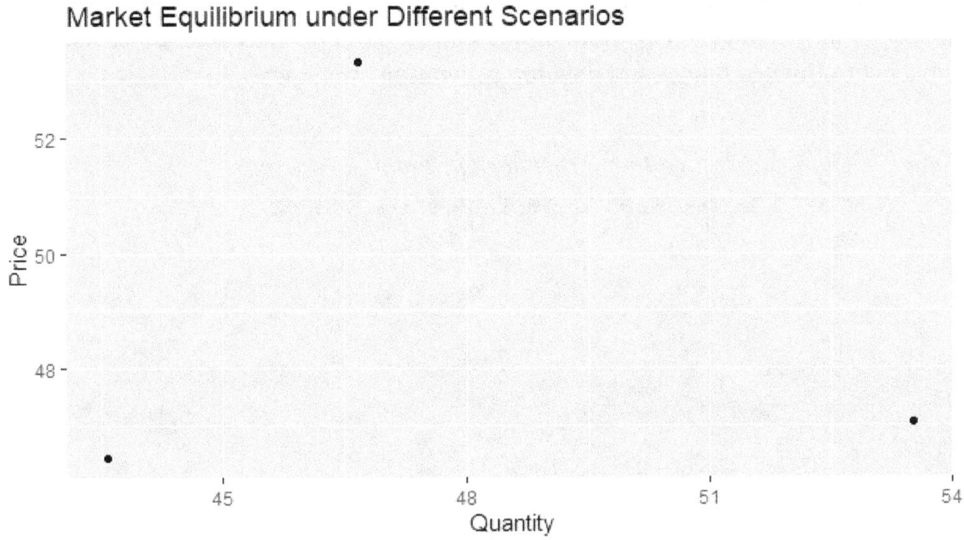

Outcomes

The simulation activities significantly enhanced students' understanding of economic principles. By experimenting with different variables, students developed a deeper appreciation for the complexities of market dynamics. They also improved their analytical and critical thinking skills by interpreting the simulation results and discussing their implications (Ghosh & Krishnan, 2015).

Case Study 2: Environmental Science - Climate Change Impact Simulation

Course Overview

In an environmental science course, students investigated the impact of climate change on local ecosystems. The course utilized simulation models to predict changes in temperature, precipitation, and biodiversity under various climate scenarios.

Implementation Strategy

Students used R to create and analyze climate models. They collected data from local weather stations and integrated it into their simulations to predict future environmental changes. The simulations helped students understand the potential impacts of climate change and develop mitigation strategies.

Figure 2. Climate Change Impact Under Different Scenarios

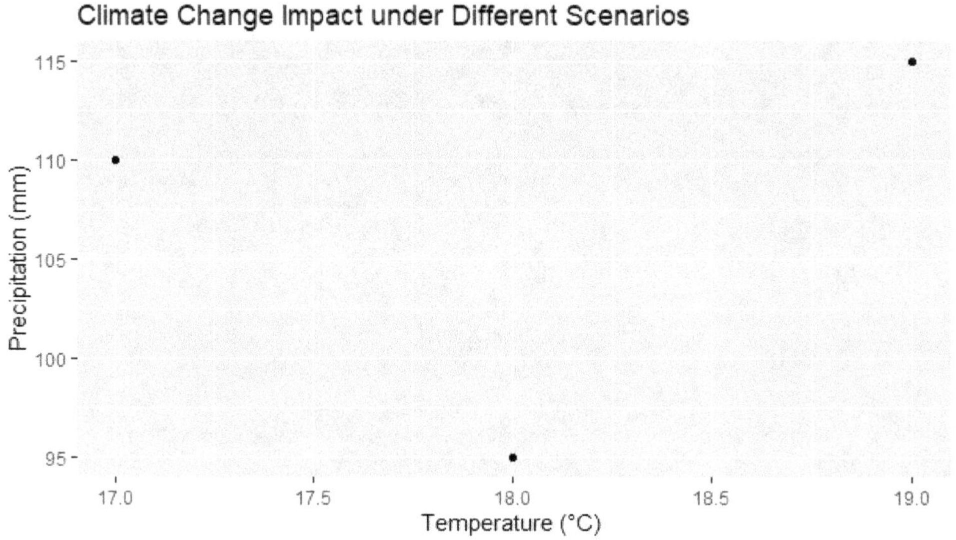

Outcomes

The climate change simulations enabled students to visualize the potential impacts of different climate scenarios on their local environment. This hands-on approach fostered a sense of urgency and responsibility among students, motivating them to engage in sustainability initiatives and advocate for environmental policies (Kolstø, 2010).

Case Study 3: Public Health - Disease Outbreak Simulation

Course Overview

A public health course focused on managing infectious disease outbreaks through simulation-based activities. The course aimed to teach students about epidemiology, disease transmission, and public health interventions.

Implementation Strategy

Using R, the instructor developed simulations to model the spread of infectious diseases under various intervention strategies. Students explored different scenarios, such as vaccination campaigns, quarantine measures, and social distancing, to assess their effectiveness in controlling outbreaks.

Figure 3. Disease Outbreak Simulation under Different Scenarios

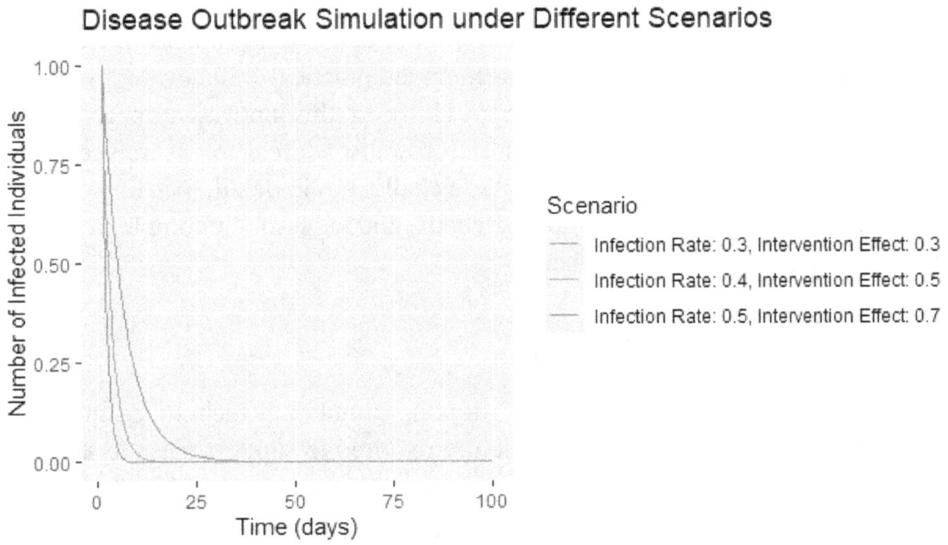

Outcomes

The disease outbreak simulations provided students with a realistic understanding of how infectious diseases spread and the impact of various public health interventions. By analyzing different scenarios, students learned to develop effective strategies for managing outbreaks and protecting public health. This experiential learning approach significantly enhanced their comprehension of epidemiological principles and preparedness for real-world public health challenges (Centers for Disease Control and Prevention, 2018).

Implications for Practise

These case studies demonstrate the transformative potential of statistical simulation in higher education across various disciplines. By integrating simulation-based activities into their curricula, educators can create immersive and interactive learning experiences that engage students, promote deeper understanding, and equip them with practical skills. Despite the challenges associated with implementing simulation-based learning, the benefits far outweigh the costs, making it a valuable addition to any academic program.

Challenges and Considerations in Adopting Simulation Techniques in Higher Education

Integrating simulation techniques into higher education promises a wealth of benefits, including enhanced student engagement, practical skill development, and deeper understanding of complex concepts. However, this innovative approach also comes with a set of challenges that institutions must address to ensure successful implementation. This section explores these challenges in detail, focusing on technological requirements, faculty training needs, and assessment complexities, and suggests strategies to overcome them.

Technological Requirements

One of the primary challenges in adopting simulation techniques in higher education is the technological infrastructure required to support these tools. Simulations often demand powerful computing resources, specialized software, and robust internet connectivity, which can be a significant barrier for many institutions, especially those with limited budgets.

Hardware and Software: Effective simulations often require high-performance computers and advanced software. For instance, running complex statistical simulations or 3D models may necessitate computers with substantial processing power and memory. Additionally, specialized software such as MATLAB, R, or proprietary simulation platforms can be costly and require regular updates and maintenance (McCulloch & Little, 2017).

Internet Connectivity: Reliable and high-speed internet is crucial for cloud-based simulations and for accessing online resources and collaborative tools. Unfortunately, not all institutions have the infrastructure to support such demands, particularly in rural or underfunded regions (Gomez, 2019).

Solution Strategies:

1. **Investment in Infrastructure:** Institutions need to prioritize investments in technological infrastructure. This may include seeking grants, forming partnerships with technology companies, or reallocating existing resources to upgrade hardware and software.
2. **Cloud Computing:** Leveraging cloud-based solutions can mitigate the need for high-end local hardware. Cloud services can provide scalable resources that institutions can use on-demand, making advanced simulations more accessible (Armbrust et al., 2010).
3. **Open-Source Software:** Utilizing open-source software like R and Python can reduce costs. These tools offer extensive libraries for statistical simulation and are continuously updated by a global community of developers (Peng, 2011).

Faculty Training Needs

Another significant challenge is the need for adequate faculty training. Many educators may not be familiar with simulation techniques or may lack the confidence to integrate them into their teaching. Effective use of simulations requires a solid understanding of both the subject matter and the technical aspects of the simulation tools.

Skill Gaps: Faculty members may have varying levels of familiarity with technology. Some may be comfortable using basic educational software, while others may find advanced simulation tools daunting (Herreid & Schiller, 2013).

Professional Development: Ongoing professional development is essential to help faculty stay updated with the latest technological advancements and pedagogical strategies. However, this requires time and financial investment, which can be scarce resources in academic settings (Brownell & Tanner, 2012).

Solution Strategies:

1. **Comprehensive Training Programs:** Institutions should implement comprehensive training programs that cover both the technical and pedagogical aspects of simulation. Workshops, online courses, and peer mentoring can help faculty build the necessary skills.

2. **Collaborative Learning:** Encouraging faculty collaboration can promote knowledge sharing and support. Creating a community of practice where educators can share experiences and resources can foster a supportive environment for adopting new technologies (Wenger, 1998).
3. **Technical Support:** Providing dedicated technical support can alleviate the burden on faculty. This includes hiring IT professionals who can assist with the setup and maintenance of simulation tools and offer on-demand help (Anderson & Anderson, 2010).

Assessment Complexities

Assessing student learning outcomes in simulation-based courses poses unique challenges. Traditional assessment methods, such as exams and quizzes, may not fully capture the skills and knowledge students gain through simulations. Therefore, developing effective assessment strategies is crucial to measure the impact of simulation-based learning.

Alignment with Learning Objectives: Assessments need to be closely aligned with the learning objectives of the simulation activities. This requires a clear understanding of what skills and knowledge the simulations are intended to develop (Biggs, 2003).

Diverse Assessment Methods: Simulations often foster higher-order thinking skills, such as critical thinking, problem-solving, and decision-making, which are not easily measured by traditional assessments. Therefore, alternative assessment methods, such as project-based assessments, reflective journals, and peer evaluations, may be more appropriate (Gikandi et al., 2011).

Solution Strategies:

1. **Rubrics and Performance Metrics:** Developing detailed rubrics and performance metrics can provide clear criteria for evaluating student performance in simulations. These tools can help ensure consistency and fairness in assessment (Reddy & Andrade, 2010).
2. **Formative Assessments:** Incorporating formative assessments throughout the simulation activities can provide ongoing feedback to students, helping them to improve their performance and understanding in real-time (Nicol & Macfarlane-Dick, 2006).
3. **Mixed-Methods Approach:** Using a mixed-methods approach to assessment can provide a more comprehensive picture of student learning. Combining quantitative assessments with qualitative evaluations, such as student re-

flections and case studies, can capture a broader range of learning outcomes (Johnson & Onwuegbuzie, 2004).

Overcoming Institutional Resistance

Adopting new teaching methodologies, such as simulation-based learning, often faces resistance at the institutional level. This resistance can stem from various factors, including a reluctance to change established teaching practices, concerns about the cost and effort required for implementation, and uncertainty about the effectiveness of new approaches.

Cultural Resistance: Faculty and administrators may be resistant to changing traditional teaching methods. This resistance can be rooted in a preference for familiar practices, skepticism about new methods, or fear of the unknown (Kezar, 2014).

Administrative Support: Gaining support from institutional leadership is crucial for the successful adoption of simulation techniques. Without administrative backing, efforts to implement new teaching methods can struggle to gain traction (Cuban, 2013).

Solution Strategies:

1. **Evidence-Based Advocacy:** Presenting evidence of the effectiveness of simulation-based learning can help overcome resistance. Sharing success stories, research findings, and case studies that demonstrate the benefits of simulations can persuade skeptics and garner support (Freeman et al., 2014).
2. **Pilot Programs:** Implementing pilot programs can provide a proof of concept. Starting with a small-scale implementation allows institutions to test and refine their approaches before scaling up, reducing perceived risks and building confidence in the new methods (Rogers, 2003).
3. **Inclusive Decision-Making:** Involving faculty, staff, and students in the decision-making process can foster a sense of ownership and buy-in. Collaborative planning and open communication can help address concerns and build a shared vision for the adoption of simulation techniques (Bryson, 2011).

Financial Constraints

Financial constraints are a common barrier to the adoption of new educational technologies. The cost of purchasing software, upgrading hardware, and providing training can be significant, particularly for institutions with limited budgets.

Budget Limitations: Many institutions operate under tight budgets, making it difficult to allocate funds for new initiatives. This can be especially challenging for public institutions that rely on state funding, which may be subject to budget cuts and fluctuations (Johnstone, 2005).

Cost-Benefit Analysis: Conducting a thorough cost-benefit analysis can help institutions make informed decisions about investing in simulation technologies. This analysis should consider not only the initial costs but also the long-term benefits and potential savings from improved learning outcomes and student retention (Drummond et al., 2005).

Solution Strategies:

1. **Grant Funding:** Seeking external funding through grants and partnerships can provide financial support for the adoption of simulation techniques. Many governmental and private organizations offer grants for educational innovation and technology integration (Kezar & Gehrke, 2017).
2. **Phased Implementation:** Implementing simulation techniques in phases can spread out the costs over time and allow institutions to gradually build the necessary infrastructure and expertise (Fullan, 2007).
3. **Cost-Sharing Models:** Exploring cost-sharing models, such as partnerships with other institutions or industry collaborations, can help reduce the financial burden. Joint investments in technology and training can create economies of scale and make simulation more affordable (Suri & Weiner, 2011).

Summary

While the adoption of simulation techniques in higher education presents several challenges, these can be effectively managed with careful planning and strategic implementation. By investing in technological infrastructure, providing comprehensive faculty training, developing robust assessment methods, overcoming institutional resistance, and addressing financial constraints, institutions can unlock the transformative potential of simulation-based learning. The benefits of enhanced student engagement, practical skill development, and improved learning outcomes far outweigh the challenges, making simulation an invaluable addition to contemporary higher education.

Future Directions

In the evolving landscape of higher education, the use of statistical simulation stands at the frontier of pedagogical innovation. This section delves into emerging trends and opportunities for further research and development in the application of statistical simulation for teaching and learning. By examining potential areas for growth, we can better understand how this transformative tool can be harnessed to meet the ever-changing demands of education in the 21st century.

The Rise of Big Data and Advanced Analytics

One of the most significant trends influencing the future of statistical simulation in education is the rise of big data and advanced analytics. The ability to collect, analyze, and interpret vast amounts of data opens new possibilities for creating more sophisticated and accurate simulations. Big data can enhance the realism and complexity of simulations, providing students with more authentic and challenging learning experiences (Manyika et al., 2011).

For instance, in medical education, simulations that incorporate real patient data can offer more precise and varied scenarios, better preparing students for clinical practice. Similarly, in business and economics, simulations using large datasets can model complex market dynamics, helping students develop a deeper understanding of economic theories and their applications (McAfee & Brynjolfsson, 2012).

Integration of Artificial Intelligence and Machine Learning

Artificial intelligence (AI) and machine learning (ML) are revolutionizing various fields, and their integration into statistical simulations holds immense promise for education. AI and ML can enhance the adaptability and personalization of simulations, allowing them to respond to individual student needs and learning styles (Baker & Inventado, 2014).

For example, adaptive learning systems powered by AI can adjust the difficulty level of simulations in real-time based on student performance. This personalized approach ensures that students remain challenged but not overwhelmed, promoting optimal learning outcomes. Additionally, AI can help educators analyze simulation data to identify patterns and trends, informing instructional strategies and curriculum design (Lynch et al., 2020).

Virtual and Augmented Reality

Virtual reality (VR) and augmented reality (AR) technologies are gaining traction in education, offering immersive and interactive learning experiences. When combined with statistical simulation, VR and AR can create highly engaging and realistic environments that enhance student understanding and retention (Pantelidis, 2010).

In engineering education, for example, VR simulations can allow students to explore complex structures and systems in a virtual space, providing hands-on experience without the need for physical resources. In environmental science, AR can overlay simulation data onto real-world landscapes, helping students visualize the impact of various environmental factors and interventions (Freina & Ott, 2015).

Interdisciplinary and Collaborative Approaches

As the boundaries between academic disciplines become increasingly fluid, there is a growing recognition of the value of interdisciplinary and collaborative approaches to education. Statistical simulations can facilitate these approaches by providing a common platform for integrating knowledge and skills from different fields (Borrego & Newswander, 2010).

For instance, a simulation-based project on sustainable urban planning can bring together students from architecture, engineering, environmental science, and social sciences. By working collaboratively on complex, real-world problems, students can develop a holistic understanding and appreciate the interconnectedness of different disciplines (National Academies of Sciences, Engineering, and Medicine, 2018).

Gamification and Engagement

Gamification, the application of game-design elements in non-game contexts, is another emerging trend with significant implications for statistical simulation in education. By incorporating elements such as points, badges, and leaderboards, simulations can become more engaging and motivating for students (Deterding et al., 2011).

In a gamified simulation, students might earn points for completing tasks or solving problems, with higher scores reflecting deeper understanding and skill mastery. Leaderboards can foster a sense of competition and camaraderie, encouraging students to strive for excellence. This approach not only makes learning more enjoyable but also helps students develop perseverance and resilience (Hamari et al., 2014).

Ethical and Social Considerations

As the use of statistical simulation in education grows, it is crucial to address the ethical and social implications. Issues such as data privacy, algorithmic bias, and accessibility must be carefully considered to ensure that simulations are fair and inclusive (O'Neil, 2016).

For example, simulations that rely on data must ensure that personal information is protected and used responsibly. Educators and developers must be vigilant about potential biases in algorithms that could disadvantage certain groups of students. Additionally, efforts should be made to ensure that all students, regardless of their background or abilities, have access to high-quality simulation-based learning experiences (West, 2019).

Future Research Directions

There are numerous avenues for future research in the use of statistical simulation for teaching and learning. Some potential areas include:

1. **Effectiveness and Impact**: Research is needed to evaluate the effectiveness of different types of simulations in various educational contexts. Studies should examine how simulations impact student learning outcomes, engagement, and skill development.
2. **Scalability and Implementation**: Investigating the scalability of simulation-based learning is crucial. Research should explore how simulations can be effectively implemented in different educational settings, from large universities to small community colleges.
3. **Faculty Development**: Effective use of simulations requires skilled and knowledgeable educators. Research should focus on identifying the best practices for faculty development and support, ensuring that educators are well-prepared to integrate simulations into their teaching (Darling-Hammond et al., 2017).
4. **Interdisciplinary Applications**: Further research is needed to explore how simulations can facilitate interdisciplinary learning and collaboration. Studies should investigate how simulations can be designed to integrate knowledge and skills from multiple disciplines and how they can be used to address complex, real-world problems.
5. **Technology Integration**: As new technologies emerge, research should examine how they can be integrated with statistical simulations to enhance learning. For example, studies could explore the use of AI, VR, and AR in simulations and their impact on student learning outcomes.

6. **Ethical and Inclusive Practices**: Research should focus on developing ethical guidelines and best practices for using simulations in education. This includes addressing issues related to data privacy, algorithmic bias, and accessibility to ensure that simulations are fair and inclusive for all students.

Recommendation for Educators

The future of statistical simulation in education is bright, with numerous opportunities for innovation and growth. By staying attuned to emerging trends and addressing the challenges that arise, educators can harness the power of simulation to create engaging, effective, and inclusive learning experiences. As we continue to explore and develop new applications for statistical simulation, we can look forward to a future where education is more dynamic, interactive, and responsive to the needs of students and society.

Through continued research, collaboration, and a commitment to ethical practices, we can unlock the full potential of statistical simulation in higher education. By doing so, we will not only enhance the quality of education but also prepare students to navigate the complexities of the modern world with confidence and competence.

Statistical simulation has rapidly emerged as a transformative tool in higher education, offering a dynamic and innovative approach to learning that enriches academic rigor and equips students with practical skills essential for success in the 21st century. This concluding section reflects on the impact of integrating simulation-based activities into the curriculum, emphasizing the benefits, challenges, and future directions of this approach.

Enhancing Academic Rigor Through Simulation

At its core, statistical simulation enhances academic rigor by providing students with a hands-on, experiential learning environment. Traditional teaching methods, while valuable, often fall short in bridging the gap between theoretical knowledge and real-world application. Statistical simulations address this gap by allowing students to explore and experiment with complex systems in a controlled, virtual setting (Anderson et al., 2012).

For instance, simulations can model intricate phenomena such as disease outbreaks, financial markets, or ecological systems, giving students a deeper understanding of how theoretical concepts apply to real-world scenarios. By engaging with simulations, students develop critical thinking and problem-solving skills, as they must analyze data, interpret results, and make decisions based on their findings (Gordon et al., 2016). This hands-on experience fosters a deeper grasp of the material, moving beyond rote memorization to cultivate a more nuanced and practical understanding of the subject matter.

Preparing Students for Complex Challenges

In an era characterized by rapid technological advancement and increasing complexity, the ability to confront and solve real-world problems is crucial. Statistical simulations offer a valuable tool for preparing students to navigate these challenges. Through simulations, students can tackle complex problems that reflect the uncertainties and dynamics of real-world situations (Wiggins & McTighe, 2005).

For example, in business education, simulations can replicate market dynamics, allowing students to experiment with different strategies and observe their outcomes. In engineering, simulations can model the behavior of structures under various conditions, helping students understand the implications of design decisions. This experiential learning not only enhances students' technical skills but also develops their ability to think critically and adapt to changing circumstances (Kolb, 1984).

Moreover, simulations can prepare students for interdisciplinary challenges by integrating knowledge from various fields. For instance, a simulation on sustainable urban development might combine elements of environmental science, engineering, and social policy, enabling students to appreciate the interconnectedness of different disciplines and develop holistic solutions (Borrego & Newswander, 2010).

Addressing the Challenges of Simulation-Based Learning

While the benefits of simulation-based learning are significant, several challenges must be addressed to fully realize its potential. These challenges include technological requirements, faculty training, and assessment complexities. By understanding and addressing these issues, higher education institutions can better integrate simulations into their curricula.

Technological Requirements

One of the primary challenges of implementing statistical simulations is the need for advanced technology. Simulations often require specialized software and hardware, which can be costly and may require significant investment from educational institutions (Becker & Park, 2011). Additionally, maintaining and updating these technologies can be resource-intensive.

To overcome these challenges, institutions can explore cost-effective solutions such as open-source simulation tools or cloud-based platforms that reduce the need for extensive hardware investments (Hershkovitz et al., 2016). Collaboration with technology providers and industry partners can also help institutions access the latest tools and resources.

Faculty Training

Effective use of simulations requires educators to be well-trained in both the technology and the pedagogical approaches associated with simulation-based learning. Faculty members must be familiar with simulation software, understand how to integrate simulations into their teaching, and be able to support students in navigating these tools (Lynch et al., 2020).

To address this need, institutions should invest in professional development programs that provide faculty with the necessary training and support. Workshops, seminars, and online courses can help educators develop the skills needed to effectively implement simulations in their teaching. Additionally, fostering a community of practice where educators can share experiences and best practices can enhance the overall effectiveness of simulation-based learning (Darling-Hammond et al., 2017).

Assessment Complexities

Assessing student learning in simulation-based courses can be more complex than traditional assessment methods. Evaluating the effectiveness of simulations requires careful consideration of both quantitative and qualitative data, including performance metrics, student feedback, and learning outcomes (Schraw, 2010).

Institutions can address these complexities by developing robust assessment frameworks that include clear rubrics and performance metrics. Incorporating formative assessments throughout the simulation process can provide ongoing feedback to students and help them improve their performance. Additionally, using a combination of self-assessments, peer assessments, and instructor evaluations can provide a comprehensive view of student learning (Biggs & Tang, 2011).

Future Directions and Opportunities

Looking ahead, there are several exciting opportunities for further research and innovation in the use of statistical simulation for teaching and learning. These future directions include the integration of emerging technologies, the exploration of interdisciplinary applications, and the development of ethical and inclusive practices.

Integration of Emerging Technologies

As technology continues to evolve, there is significant potential for integrating new tools and platforms into statistical simulations. For example, the incorporation of artificial intelligence (AI) and machine learning (ML) can enhance the adaptability and personalization of simulations, allowing them to better meet individual student needs (Baker & Inventado, 2014). Virtual reality (VR) and augmented reality (AR) technologies also offer opportunities for creating immersive and interactive learning experiences that can deepen student engagement and understanding (Freina & Ott, 2015).

Exploration of Interdisciplinary Applications

The interdisciplinary nature of many real-world problems makes it essential for educational simulations to integrate knowledge from multiple fields. Future research should explore how simulations can facilitate interdisciplinary learning and collaboration, helping students develop a holistic understanding of complex issues (National Academies of Sciences, Engineering, and Medicine, 2018). By bringing together insights from various disciplines, simulations can prepare students to tackle multifaceted challenges more effectively.

Development of Ethical and Inclusive Practices

As simulations become more prevalent in education, it is crucial to address ethical and social considerations. Ensuring data privacy, addressing algorithmic bias, and promoting accessibility are essential for creating fair and inclusive simulation-based learning environments (O'Neil, 2016). Research should focus on developing guidelines and best practices that ensure simulations are used responsibly and equitably.

Closing Remarks on Educational Innovation

Statistical simulation represents a powerful tool for enriching academic rigor and preparing students for the complexities of the 21st century. By integrating simulation-based activities into the curriculum, higher education institutions can create dynamic and engaging learning environments that foster practical skills and deep understanding. Despite the challenges associated with technology, faculty training, and assessment, the benefits of simulation-based learning are substantial. As institutions continue to innovate and adapt, the transformative potential of statistical simulation will undoubtedly play a central role in shaping the future of education.

Through ongoing research, collaboration, and a commitment to ethical practices, we can harness the full potential of statistical simulation to enhance teaching and learning. By doing so, we will not only improve educational outcomes but also equip students with the skills and knowledge they need to succeed in an increasingly complex and interconnected world.

REFERENCES

Albanese, M. A., & Mitchell, S. (1993). Problem-based learning: A review of literature on its outcomes and implementation issues. *Academic Medicine*, 68(1), 52–81. DOI: 10.1097/00001888-199301000-00012 PMID: 8447896

Aldrich, C. (2005). *Learning by doing: A comprehensive guide to simulations, computer games, and pedagogy in e-learning and other educational experiences*. John Wiley & Sons.

Anderson, J. R., Bothell, D., Byrne, M. D., Douglass, S., Lebiere, C., & Yang, Y. (2012). *An overview of the ACT-R 4.0 cognitive architecture*. Cambridge University Press.

Anderson, R. E., & Anderson, R. J. (2010). *Online professional development for teachers: Emerging models and methods*. Harvard Education Press.

Armbrust, M., Fox, A., Griffith, R., Joseph, A. D., Katz, R., Konwinski, A., Lee, G., Patterson, D., Rabkin, A., Stoica, I., & Zaharia, M. (2010). A view of cloud computing. *Communications of the ACM*, 53(4), 50–58. DOI: 10.1145/1721654.1721672

Baker, R. S., & Inventado, P. S. (2014). Educational data mining and learning analytics. In *Learning analytics* (pp. 61–75). Springer. DOI: 10.1007/978-1-4614-3305-7_4

Banks, J., Carson, J. S., Nelson, B. L., & Nicol, D. M. (2014). *Discrete-event system simulation*. Pearson.

Barrows, H. S. (1996). Problem-based learning in medicine and beyond: A brief overview. *New Directions for Teaching and Learning*, 1996(68), 3–12. DOI: 10.1002/tl.37219966804

Becker, K., & Park, K. (2011). Effects of technology on student achievement: A meta-analysis of studies from 1990 to 2010. *Journal of Research on Technology in Education*, 43(2), 159–184.

Biggs, J. (2003). *Aligning teaching and assessment to curriculum objectives*. LTSN Generic Centre.

Biggs, J., & Tang, C. (2011). *Teaching for quality learning at university: What the student does*. McGraw-Hill Education.

Bishop, J. L., & Verleger, M. A. (2013). The flipped classroom: A survey of the research. In *ASEE National Conference Proceedings,* Atlanta, GA (Vol. 30, No. 9, pp. 1-18). DOI: 10.18260/1-2--22585

Blumenfeld, P. C., Soloway, E., Marx, R. W., Krajcik, J. S., Guzdial, M., & Palincsar, A. (1991). Motivating project-based learning: Sustaining the doing, supporting the learning. *Educational Psychologist*, 26(3-4), 369–398. DOI: 10.1080/00461520.1991.9653139

Bonabeau, E. (2002). Agent-based modeling: Methods and techniques for simulating human systems. *Proceedings of the National Academy of Sciences of the United States of America*, 99(Suppl 3), 7280–7287. DOI: 10.1073/pnas.082080899 PMID: 12011407

Borrego, M., & Newswander, L. K. (2010). Definitions of interdisciplinary research: Toward graduate-level interdisciplinary learning outcomes. *Review of Higher Education*, 34(1), 61–84. DOI: 10.1353/rhe.2010.0006

Brownell, S. E., & Tanner, K. D. (2012). Barriers to faculty pedagogical change: Lack of training, time, incentives, and...tensions with professional identity? *CBE Life Sciences Education*, 11(4), 339–346. DOI: 10.1187/cbe.12-09-0163 PMID: 23222828

Bryson, J. M. (2011). *Strategic planning for public and nonprofit organizations: A guide to strengthening and sustaining organizational achievement*. John Wiley & Sons.

Centers for Disease Control and Prevention. (2018). Principles of epidemiology in public health practice. Retrieved from https://www.cdc.gov/csels/dsepd/ss1978/index.html

Colander, D. (2017). *Economics*. McGraw-Hill Education.

Cuban, L. (2013). *Inside the black box of classroom practice: Change without reform in American education*. Harvard Education Press.

Darling-Hammond, L., Hyler, M. E., & Gardner, M. (2017). *Effective teacher professional development*. Learning Policy Institute. DOI: 10.54300/122.311

Deterding, S., Dixon, D., Khaled, R., & Nacke, L. (2011). From game design elements to gamefulness: Defining" gamification". In Proceedings of the 15th international academic MindTrek conference: Envisioning future media environments (pp. 9-15).

Drummond, M. F., Sculpher, M. J., Torrance, G. W., O'Brien, B. J., & Stoddart, G. L. (2005). *Methods for the economic evaluation of health care programmes*. Oxford University Press. DOI: 10.1093/oso/9780198529446.001.0001

Felder, R. M., & Brent, R. (2005). Understanding student differences. *Journal of Engineering Education*, 94(1), 57–72. DOI: 10.1002/j.2168-9830.2005.tb00829.x

Ferguson, N. M., Laydon, D., Nedjati-Gilani, G., Imai, N., Ainslie, K., Baguelin, M., ... & Ghani, A. C. (2020). Impact of non-pharmaceutical interventions (NPIs) to reduce COVID-19 mortality and healthcare demand. *Imperial College COVID-19 Response Team.*

Fowler, C. (2013). Virtual reality and learning: Where is the pedagogy? *British Journal of Educational Technology*, 44(2), 174–185.

Freeman, S., Eddy, S. L., McDonough, M., Smith, M. K., Okoroafor, N., Jordt, H., & Wenderoth, M. P. (2014). Active learning increases student performance in science, engineering, and mathematics. *Proceedings of the National Academy of Sciences of the United States of America*, 111(23), 8410–8415. DOI: 10.1073/pnas.1319030111 PMID: 24821756

Freina, L., & Ott, M. (2015). A literature review on immersive virtual reality in education: State of the art and perspectives. In *The International Scientific Conference eLearning and Software for Education* (Vol. 1, p. 10). "Carol I" National Defence University. DOI: 10.12753/2066-026X-15-020

Fullan, M. (2007). *The new meaning of educational change*. Routledge.

Garrison, D. R., & Kanuka, H. (2004). Blended learning: Uncovering its transformative potential in higher education. *The Internet and Higher Education*, 7(2), 95–105. DOI: 10.1016/j.iheduc.2004.02.001

Ghosh, S., & Krishnan, R. (2015). Integrating problem-based learning with simulation: A case study in an undergraduate business course. *Journal of Education for Business*, 90(5), 242–248.

Gikandi, J. W., Morrow, D., & Davis, N. E. (2011). Online formative assessment in higher education: A review of the literature. *Computers & Education*, 57(4), 2333–2351. DOI: 10.1016/j.compedu.2011.06.004

Gilbert, N., & Troitzsch, K. G. (2005). *Simulation for the social scientist*. McGraw-Hill Education.

Glasserman, P. (2013). *Monte Carlo methods in financial engineering*. Springer Science & Business Media.

Gomez, M. (2019). Rural education in America: Challenges and solutions. *Rural Educator*, 40(2), 1–15.

Gordon, E., McGee, M., & Hicks, J. (2016). *Simulations and games for teaching and learning*. Routledge.

Hamari, J., Koivisto, J., & Sarsa, H. (2014). Does gamification work?--a literature review of empirical studies on gamification. In *2014 47th Hawaii international conference on system sciences* (pp. 3025-3034). IEEE.

Herreid, C. F., & Schiller, N. A. (2013). Case studies and the flipped classroom. *Journal of College Science Teaching*, 42(5), 62–66.

Hershkovitz, A., Margulies, A., & Dagan, Y. (2016). Cost-effective technology solutions for education: An exploration. *Journal of Educational Technology & Society*, 19(1), 77–89.

Hull, J. C. (2018). *Risk management and financial institutions*. Wiley.

Johnson, R. B., & Onwuegbuzie, A. J. (2004). Mixed methods research: A research paradigm whose time has come. *Educational Researcher*, 33(7), 14–26. DOI: 10.3102/0013189X033007014

Johnstone, D. B. (2005). Financing higher education: Who should pay? In *International handbook of educational policy* (pp. 637–655). Springer.

Johnstone, D. B. (2016). Financing higher education: Who pays and other issues. In Shin, J. C., & Teixeira, P. (Eds.), *Encyclopedia of international higher education systems and institutions* (pp. 1–4). Springer.

Kezar, A. (2014). *How colleges change: Understanding, leading, and enacting change*. Routledge.

Kezar, A., & Gehrke, S. (2017). Sustaining daily peace: The student voice and leadership in creating sustained change. In *Handbook of student affairs administration* (pp. 419–438). John Wiley & Sons.

Kolb, D. A. (1984). *Experiential learning: Experience as the source of learning and development*. Prentice Hall.

Kolstø, S. D. (2010). Scientific literacy for citizenship: Tools for dealing with the science dimension of controversial socioscientific issues. *Science Education*, 84(4), 291–310.

Krajcik, J. S., & Blumenfeld, P. C. (2006). Project-based learning. In *The Cambridge handbook of the learning sciences* (pp. 317–334). Cambridge University Press.

Kroese, D. P., Brereton, T., Taimre, T., & Botev, Z. I. (2014). Why the Monte Carlo method is so important today. *Wiley Interdisciplinary Reviews: Computational Statistics*, 6(6), 386–392. DOI: 10.1002/wics.1314

Lynch, G., Smyth, P., & Godfrey, A. (2020). AI and Machine Learning in Education. *EdTech Report.*

Manyika, J., Chui, M., Brown, B., Bughin, J., Dobbs, R., Roxburgh, C., & Byers, A. H. (2011). *Big data: The next frontier for innovation, competition, and productivity.* McKinsey Global Institute.

Marginson, S. (2016). *The dream is over: The crisis of Clark Kerr's California idea of higher education.* University of California Press.

McAfee, A., & Brynjolfsson, E. (2012). Big data: The management revolution. *Harvard Business Review*, 90(10), 60–68. PMID: 23074865

McAfee, A., & Brynjolfsson, E. (2012). Big data: The management revolution. *Harvard Business Review*, 90(10), 60–68. PMID: 23074865

McCulloch, A., & Little, S. (2017). Creating a comprehensive technology integration plan for higher education: A case study. *TechTrends*, 61(2), 149–158.

National Academies of Sciences, Engineering, and Medicine. (2018). *The integration of the humanities and arts with sciences, engineering, and medicine in higher education: Branches from the same tree.* National Academies Press.

National Research Council. (2012). *Discipline-based education research: Understanding and improving learning in undergraduate science and engineering.* National Academies Press.

Nicol, D. J., & Macfarlane-Dick, D. (2006). Formative assessment and self-regulated learning: A model and seven principles of good feedback practice. *Studies in Higher Education*, 31(2), 199–218. DOI: 10.1080/03075070600572090

O'Neil, C. (2016). *Weapons of math destruction: How big data increases inequality and threatens democracy.* Broadway Books.

Pantelidis, V. S. (2010). Reasons to use virtual reality in education and training courses and a model to determine when to use virtual reality. *Themes in Science and Technology Education*, 2(1-2), 59–70.

Peng, R. D. (2011). Reproducible research in computational science. *Science*, 334(6060), 1226–1227. DOI: 10.1126/science.1213847 PMID: 22144613

Reddy, Y. M., & Andrade, H. (2010). A review of rubric use in higher education. *Assessment & Evaluation in Higher Education*, 35(4), 435–448. DOI: 10.1080/02602930902862859

Rogers, E. M. (2003). *Diffusion of innovations* (5th ed.). Free Press.

Rubin, E. S., & Davidson, J. E. (2001). *Introduction to engineering and the environment*. McGraw-Hill Higher Education.

Schmidt, R. A., & Bjork, R. A. (1992). New conceptualizations of practice: Common principles in three paradigms suggest new concepts for training. *Psychological Science*, 3(4), 207–217. DOI: 10.1111/j.1467-9280.1992.tb00029.x

Schraw, G. (2010). Measuring self-regulation in computer-based learning environments. In *Handbook of research on educational communications and technology* (pp. 397–408). Routledge.

Smith, I. M., & Griffiths, D. V. (2014). *Programming the finite element method*. John Wiley & Sons.

Suri, H., & Weiner, L. (2011). The case for collaborative teaching in teacher education. In *Second international handbook of educational change* (pp. 579–598). Springer.

Wenger, E. (1998). Communities of practice: Learning, meaning, and identity. Cambridge University Press.Top of Form

West, S. M. (2019). Data capitalism: Redefining the logics of surveillance and privacy. *Business & Society*, 58(1), 20–41. DOI: 10.1177/0007650317718185

West, S. M. (2019). Data capitalism: Redefining the logics of surveillance and privacy. *Business & Society*, 58(1), 20–41. DOI: 10.1177/0007650317718185

Wiggins, G., & McTighe, J. (2005). *Understanding by design*. ASCD.

Additional Reading

Banks, J. (2005). *Discrete event system simulation*. Pearson Education India.

Freeman, S., Eddy, S. L., McDonough, M., Smith, M. K., Okoroafor, N., Jordt, H., & Wenderoth, M. P. (2014). Active learning increases student performance in science, engineering, and mathematics. *Proceedings of the National Academy of Sciences of the United States of America*, 111(23), 8410–8415. DOI: 10.1073/pnas.1319030111 PMID: 24821756

Garrison, D. R., & Kanuka, H. (2004). Blended learning: Uncovering its transformative potential in higher education. *The Internet and Higher Education*, 7(2), 95–105. DOI: 10.1016/j.iheduc.2004.02.001

Johnstone, D. B. (2016). The challenges of higher education funding. *Higher Education Policy*, 29(1), 1–20.

Nicol, D. J., & Macfarlane-Dick, D. (2006). Formative assessment and self-regulated learning: A model and seven principles of good feedback practice. *Studies in Higher Education*, 31(2), 199–218. DOI: 10.1080/03075070600572090

O'neil, C. (2017). *Weapons of math destruction: How big data increases inequality and threatens democracy*. Crown.

Pantelidis, V. S. (2010). Reasons to use virtual reality in education and training courses and a model to determine when to use virtual reality. *Themes in science and technology education, 2*(1-2), 59-70.

Wiggins, G. (2005). *Understanding by design*. Association for Supervision and Curriculum Development.

Key Words and Their Definitions

Flipped Classroom: An instructional strategy that reverses traditional teaching methods, delivering instructional content online outside of the classroom and engaging students in activities during class time.

Pedagogical Approaches: Strategies and methods employed by educators to facilitate learning and enhance student engagement.

Problem-Based Learning (PBL): An instructional method where students learn through the investigation of complex, real-world problems, fostering critical thinking and problem-solving skills.

Project-Based Learning (PjBL): A teaching method in which students gain knowledge and skills by working on a project over an extended period, culminating in a final product or presentation.

Statistical Simulation: A method that uses computational algorithms to model and analyze complex systems by generating random samples to understand their behavior under various conditions.

APPENDIX: R CODES

```
a) R Code Example: Market Simulation
# Load necessary libraries
library(ggplot2)
library(dplyr)
# Define market simulation function
market_simulation <- function(demand_intercept, supply_in-
tercept, demand_slope, supply_slope, external_shock) {
# Define demand and supply functions
demand <- function(price) demand_intercept - demand_slope
* price
supply <- function(price) supply_intercept + supply_slope
* price + external_shock
b) R Code Example: Climate Change Simulation
# Load necessary libraries
library(ggplot2)
library(dplyr)
# Define climate change simulation function
climate_simulation <- function(temp_increase, precip_change)
{
# Define baseline conditions
baseline_temp <- 15
baseline_precip <- 100
# Calculate future conditions
future_temp <- baseline_temp + temp_increase
future_precip <- baseline_precip * (1 + precip_change / 100)
return(data.frame(Temperature = future_temp, Precipitation
= future_precip))
}
# Simulate climate change impact with different scenarios
scenarios <- data.frame(
Temp_Increase = c(2, 3, 4),
Precip_Change = c(10, -5, 15)
)
results <- scenarios %>% rowwise() %>%
mutate(simulation = list(climate_simulation(Temp_Increase,
Precip_Change)))
# Extract and visualize results
climate_data <- bind_rows(results$simulation)
ggplot(climate_data, aes(x = Temperature, y = Precipita-
tion)) +
geom_point() +
labs(title = "Climate Change Impact under Different Scenar-
ios", x = "Temperature (°C)", y = "Precipitation (mm)")
# Find equilibrium price where demand equals supply
```

```
equilibrium_price <- uniroot(function(price) demand(price)
- supply(price), c(0, 100))$root
  equilibrium_quantity <- demand(equilibrium_price)
  return(data.frame(Price = equilibrium_price, Quantity =
equilibrium_quantity))
  }
  # Simulate market dynamics with different scenarios
  scenarios <- data.frame(
  Demand_Intercept = c(100, 110, 90),
  Supply_Intercept = c(20, 20, 30),
  Demand_Slope = c(1, 1.2, 1),
  Supply_Slope = c(0.5, 0.5, 0.4),
  External_Shock = c(0, 10, -5)
  )
  results <- scenarios %>% rowwise() %>%
  mutate(simulation = list(market_simulation(Demand_Intercept,
Supply_Intercept, Demand_Slope, Supply_Slope, External_Shock)))
  # Extract and visualize results
  equilibrium_data <- bind_rows(results$simulation)
  ggplot(equilibrium_data, aes(x = Quantity, y = Price)) +
  geom_point() +
  labs(title = "Market Equilibrium under Different Scenarios",
x = "Quantity", y = "Price")
```

c) Disease Outbreak Simulation Code

```
  # Load necessary libraries
  library(ggplot2)
  library(dplyr)
  # Define SIR model simulation function
  sir_simulation <- function(infection_rate, recovery_rate,
intervention_effect, days = 100) {
  # Initialize parameters
  S <- 999 # Initial number of susceptible individuals
  I <- 1 # Initial number of infected individuals
  R <- 0 # Initial number of recovered individuals
  N <- S + I + R # Total population
  # Create vectors to store results
  time <- 1:days
  susceptible <- numeric(days)
  infected <- numeric(days)
  recovered <- numeric(days)
  susceptible[1] <- S
  infected[1] <- I
  recovered[1] <- R
  # Simulation loop
  for (t in 2:days) {
  new_infected <- infection_rate * susceptible[t-1] * infect-
ed[t-1] / N
```

```
  new_recovered <- recovery_rate * infected[t-1]
  susceptible[t] <- susceptible[t-1] - new_infected
  infected[t] <- infected[t-1] + new_infected - new_recovered
  recovered[t] <- recovered[t-1] + new_recovered
  # Apply intervention effect
  infected[t] <- infected[t] * (1 - intervention_effect)
  }
  return(data.frame(Time = time, Susceptible = susceptible,
Infected = infected, Recovered = recovered))
  }
  # Simulate disease outbreak with different intervention sce-
narios
  scenarios <- data.frame(
  Infection_Rate = c(0.3, 0.4, 0.5),
  Recovery_Rate = c(0.1, 0.1, 0.1),
  Intervention_Effect = c(0.3, 0.5, 0.7)
  )
  results <- scenarios %>% rowwise() %>%
  mutate(simulation = list(sir_simulation(Infection_Rate,
Recovery_Rate, Intervention_Effect)))
  # Extract and visualize results
  outbreak_data <- bind_rows(lapply(1:nrow(scenarios), func-
tion(i) {
  data.frame(
  Time = results$simulation[[i]]$Time,
  Infected = results$simulation[[i]]$Infected,
  Scenario = paste0("Infection Rate: ", scenarios$Infec-
tion_Rate[i],
  ", Intervention Effect: ", scenarios$Intervention_Effect[i])
  )
  }))
  ggplot(outbreak_data, aes(x = Time, y = Infected, color =
Scenario)) +
  geom_line() +
  labs(title = "Disease Outbreak Simulation under Different
Scenarios", x = "Time (days)", y = "Number of Infected Indi-
viduals")
```

Chapter 9
The Evolving Roles of Faculty in Modern Classrooms:
A Shift From Lecturer to Facilitator

Lorna Wafula
Moi University, Kenya

ABSTRACT

The role of faculty in modern classrooms has evolved from traditional lecturing to dynamic facilitation of learning This chapter examined this paradigm shift in higher education. It investigated how faculty facilitate active student centered learning. The study was anchored on Piaget and Vygotsky's constructivist learning theory and Siemens and Downes' connectivism theory. A descriptive research design was embraced. Lecturers in public universities in Kenya formed the population of the study. Convenient and simple random sampling were used to select the participants. Data was collected using document analysis and questionnaires and was analyzed descriptively. The study established that a significant number of faculty used facilitative teaching methods. The study recommended that universities should promote facilitative teaching among faculty and educate students on benefits of interactive learning. Further studies should be carried out on sustainable models of professional development that support the ongoing evolution of teaching practices.

DOI: 10.4018/979-8-3693-6930-2.ch009

1.0 INTRODUCTION

The field of higher education is undergoing profound transformation. Historically, educators primarily assumed the role of lecturers, delivering information through one-way communication to passive recipients. However, as educational paradigms shift towards more interactive and student-centered approaches, the role of faculty is evolving into that of facilitators of learning. This chapter delves into this significant transition, exploring the factors driving the change, the methodologies being adopted, and the implications for both educators and students.

The impetus for this evolution stems from a growing recognition that active learning stategies enhance student engagement, retention, and critical thinking skills. Advances in technology, a better understanding of learning sciences, and changing workforce demands are all contributing to the shift. Faculty are now called upon to create dynamic learning environments where students participate actively in their education, collaborating with peers, and applying knowledge in practical contexts.

Various pedagogical strategies that exemplify this shift, such as flipped classrooms, project-based learning, and the integration of digital tools will be examined. These methods promote a more interactive and engaging classroom experience, encouraging students to take ownership of their learning journey. The chapter will also address the challenges faculty face in adapting to these new roles, including the need for professional development, support from educational institutions, and the balancing of traditional and innovative teaching methods.

Redefining their roles from lecturers to facilitators, faculty are better equipped to meet the diverse needs of modern students and prepare them for the complexities of the contemporary world. This chapter aims to provide a comprehensive overview of this transformation, offering insights and practical guidance to educators to navigate the dynamic educational landscape. Through an exploration of existing literature, theoretical frameworks, and practical applications, this chapter hopes to illuminate the pathways through which faculty can successfully transition to these evolving roles, ultimately enhancing the quality and impact of higher education.

1.1 Problem Statement

Driven by advancements in educational technology, changing student needs, and evolving pedagogical approaches, the traditional role of faculty as sole knowledge dispensers in classrooms has shifted significantly. Focus is on guiding students to actively engage in knowledge construction rather than passive participation. The integration of technology into education has played a pivotal role in altering classroom dynamics. With access to vast information resources online, students are no longer entirely dependent on teachers for knowledge acquisition. As a result, faculty members are expected to move from “sage on the stage” to “guide on the side” (King, 1993), emphasizing critical thinking, problem-solving, and collaboration. With these pedagogical shifts, educators are increasingly responsible for creating interactive, student-centered learning experiences that foster independent inquiry and the development of lifelong learning skills. Research shows that students retain information better when actively involved in the learning process, rather than being passive listeners (Freeman et al., 2014).

However, the transition from lecturer to facilitator has not been universally smooth. Faculty may struggle with balancing traditional expectations of their role with the new demands of facilitative teaching and student-centered learning. Therefore, there is need to explore how faculty members experience this shift and to understand the institutional structures that support or hinder their ability to fulfill these evolving roles.

1.2 Research Purpose

The purpose of the study was to investigate the evolving roles of faculty in modern classrooms: a shift from lecturer to facilitator

1.3 Objectives of the Study

The research objectives of this chapter were:

1. Explain the transformation of Facuty roles in contemporary lecturerooms
2. Analyze the drivers of the paradigm shift in contemporary lecture rooms
3. Explore the challenges faculty face in adopting the role of facilitator and the opportunities this shift presents.

2.0 BACKGROUND

The role of faculty in contemporary classrooms is undergoing significant transformation. Traditionally viewed as the primary source of knowledge, the role of educators is evolving towards being facilitators of learning. This shift is influenced by, historical contexts, various educational theories, technological advancements, and the changing needs of students.

2.1 Historical Contexts

The role of faculty in lecture rooms has undergone significant transformation over time, shaped by broader changes in educational philosophy, technology, and societal expectations. Historically, educators were viewed as the primary source of knowledge, responsible for imparting information through direct instruction. However, over time, this role has shifted towards facilitation, where the focus is on fostering active learning, critical thinking, and collaboration. This shift can be traced through several key periods.

2.1.1 Medieval Period

Historically, the traditional role of the faculty has been to deliver knowledge through lectures, a method rooted in the didactic approach of education. According to Barr & Tagg, (1995), faculty members are considered the central figures in the educational process, with students playing a largely passive role. However, evolution of educational methodologies from traditional lecturing to facilitation has been influenced by various educational views and educational theorists such as Piaget (1973) and Vygotsky (1978), societal needs, and technological advancements. In the medieval period University education was heavily influenced by philosophers like Socrates, Plato, and Aristotle. Socratic dialogue was a form of teaching through questioning, promoting critical thinking and deep understanding (Brickhouse & Smith, 2000). Teaching had a strong emphasis on memorization and recitation (Marrou, 1956). Lectures were the primary teaching method, where professors read authoritative texts aloud to students, a practice derived from monastic traditions (Haskins, in ancient Greece and medieval universities, teachers were considered the ultimate authority on knowledge. In this "teacher-centered" model, instructors were tasked with delivering lectures, a format rooted in the ancient practice of oral transmission of knowledge. Students were passive recipients, expected to memorize and reproduce the information conveyed by the lecturer (Harden & Crosby, 2000).

2.1.2 The Renaissance and Enlightenment Era

During the renaissance and enlightenment era education emphasized on humanism, which promoted the study of classical texts and the development of individual potential. Education began to include more diverse subjects, such as arts and sciences, fostering a more well-rounded development (Grendler, 1989). The Enlightenment period saw education shift towards reason, scientific inquiry, and empirical evidence (Porter, 2000).Thinkers like John Locke advocated for education that developed rational and independent thought, moving away from rote memorization (Axtell,

1968). In this era, the learners were given an opportunity to partially manage their own learning.

2.1.3 The 19th and Early 20th Century

The 19th and Early 20th Century which saw the industrial revolution brought about formalized schooling systems, designed to meet the needs of an industrial society. According to Tyack (1974) this era had emphasis on the "factory model" of education which emphasized on uniformity, discipline, and efficiency, with a strong focus on rote learning. This era was followed by the progressive education movement which saw a crop of scholars like John Dewey and other educational reformers who advocated for development of experiential learning, critical thinking and collaborative projects (Cremin, 1961).

2.1.4 The Mid and Late 20th Century

In the mid to late 20th century, the constructivist theory by Piaget and Vygotsky emerged. They posited that learners construct their own understanding through experiences (Piaget, 1973; Vygotsky, 1978). This led to the development of teaching methods that promoted active engagement and discovery, such as inquiry-based and project-based learning (Bruner, 1961).

2.1.5 The 21st Century

After the constructivists period, the 21st century emerged with technology in education. The introduction of computers and the internet has revolutionized education, providing new tools for interactive and self-paced learning (Papert, 1980). According to King (1993), the role of the lecturer has shifted from being a "sage on the stage" to a "guide on the side," facilitating student-led learning. Personalized, collaborative and social learning experiences tailored to individual needs have became common. Education now prioritizes skills like critical thinking, creativity, and problem-solving over rote memorization (Facione, 1990). There is also a recognition that learning continues throughout life. This has led to an increase in adult education, professional development, and continuing education programs (Schuller & Watson, 2009).

Technology has revolutionized education, providing tools that enable interactive and engaging learning experiences. Bonk & Graham, (2006) state that digital platforms facilitate collaboration and provide access to vast resources. Some prime examples of how technology is reshaping teaching roles include flipped Classroom models where students engage with new content at home through videos and use classroom time for deeper exploration. This model emphasizes faculty as facilitators rather than mere content deliverers (Bishop & Verleger, 2013). According to King (1993), The transition from the "sage on the stage" to the "guide on the side" underscores the shift in educational paradigms. Educators now focus more on facilitating learning experiences than on lecturing or direct instruction.

In their role as facilitators of learning, Freeman et al., (2014) explains that educators design and manage activities that promote active learning. They provide guidance and feedback, helping students engage with the material in a meaningful way. With this in mind, the roles of faculty are now expanding to include mentoring and coaching, supporting students in their academics, personal development and involvement in personalized interactions with them. As students take an active role in their education, they are more likely to retain information, develop a deeper understanding and prepare for the challenges and opportunities of the future.

2.1.6 Contemporary Trends

Today's classroom environments increasingly emphasize active learning, where faculty facilitate interactive activities that promote deeper engagement with content. Research has shown that active learning approaches, such as peer discussions and collaborative projects, lead to higher student performance compared to traditional lectures (Freeman et al., 2014). Faculty are now expected to design learning environments that support active, experiential learning, often leveraging technology to provide dynamic and interactive educational experiences.

2.2 Theoretical Underpinnings that Grounded this Research

This study was guided by Lev Vygotsky's social constructivism theory and Siemens and Downes' Connectivism Theory. Vygotsky is renowned for his contribution to the field of constructivist learning theory. Vygotsky (1978) posits that learners actively construct their own understanding and knowledge of the world through their experiences and their reflection on those experiences. He emphasized on the social and cultural context of learning. He believed that cognitive development is largely a socially mediated process and that interaction with more knowledgeable others (parents, teachers, peers) plays a crucial role in advancing a learner's understanding. For Vygotsky, learning is inherently a social process that occurs through participation in cultural activities and dialogues. One of Vygotsky's most influential ideas is the concept of the zone of proximal development (ZPD), which refers to the gap between what a learner can do independently and what they can do with the assistance of a more knowledgeable other. Learning is most effective when it occurs within the ZPD, with guidance and collaboration helping the learner reach higher levels of competence (Vygotsky, 1978). In this case, Vygotsky advocates for facilitative teaching which gives room to learners to explore and manage their knowledge.

Vygotsky also talks of scaffolding which refers to the temporary support provided by teachers or peers to help a learner master a new concept or skill. As the learner becomes more proficient, the support is gradually withdrawn, allowing for independent problem-solving (Wood, Bruner, & Ross, 1976). This calls for faculty to support their students and give them room for personal encounters that will enable them work independently to explore knowledge. The role of the lecturer in this case is clearly defined as a guide and facilitator in the learning process. Learners are not passive recipients of information, but rather active participants in the learning process. However, Vygotsky theory underplays the role of individual differences in cognitive development. It also does not fully account for how learners' intrinsic motivation and personal experiences influence learning (Miller, 2011).

Siemens and Downes' (2005) connectivism theory explains how learning occurs in a digital, networked age. It differs from traditional theories like behaviorism, cognitivism, and constructivism by emphasizing the role of technology, networks, and the flow of information in learning. Siemens and Downes argue that the rapidly evolving nature of knowledge and the proliferation of information networks require a new understanding of how individuals learn in an era defined by constant connectivity.

Siemens and Downes explain that learning is a networked process. According to Siemens (2005), knowledge exists not only within an individual but also within networks of people, organizations, technologies, and databases. Lecturers should encourage and support learners to develop the ability to navigate, evaluate, and create connections within these networks to effectively acquire and apply knowledge. In this sense, learning is not a solely individual cognitive process but an ongoing, dynamic activity shaped by interactions across a wide range of sources.

Siemens highlights the increasing importance of knowing where to find information rather than simply knowing facts. In a world overflowing with data, learners are better served by understanding how to connect with useful information sources and how to adapt to changing environments (Siemens, 2005). Universities and faculty can serve learners better by helping them connect with the right sources of information. Siemens and Downes argue that knowledge is distributed across networks and not confined to any single individual. This reflects the notion that the internet and modern technology have decentralized the authority of knowledge. Learners are now able to access vast amounts of information from multiple sources, and learning involves the ability to discern valuable knowledge within these networks (Downes, 2010). Learners should constantly integrate new information as the network evolves. Successful learners understand how to use technologies to access and engage with these networks, enabling them to stay informed and adaptable in rapidly changing environments.

2.3 The Drivers of the Paradigm Shift

The paradigm shift from traditional lecturing to a facilitator-based approach in lecture halls is driven by several interrelated factors, reflecting changes in educational philosophy, technology, and societal needs. The shift is significantly influenced by the adoption of constructivist and theories of learning, which emphasize that knowledge is actively constructed by learners rather than passively received. The constructivist theory emphasizes on the fact that learning is a process where learners build new understandings based on their own experiences and prior knowledge (Piaget, 1952; Vygotsky, 1978). This approach encourages facilitative teaching to guide students through this process, rather than merely deliver information.

Another driver of the paradigm shift is technological advancements. The advent of digital technology has transformed educational environments, providing tools that support interactive and personalized learning experiences.The availability of digital tools such as interactive whiteboards, online collaboration platforms, and educational software supports a more engaged and student-centered learning environment. These tools facilitate active learning, collaboration, and immediate feedback, aligning well with the facilitator role Redecker & Punie (2017).

Societal and Workforce Changes are yet another driver of the paradigm shift. Voogt & Roblin (2012) explain that the skills required in the modern workforce have shifted from rote memorization to critical thinking, problem-solving, and collaboration. This shift necessitates changes in educational practices. In the 21st century, employers increasingly value skills such as creativity, critical thinking, and the ability to work in teams. Facilitator-based teaching methods are better suited to developing these competencies, as they encourage students to engage deeply with content, work collaboratively, and apply their knowledge in practical contexts.

Student Engagement and Motivation are also a driver of the paradigm. Students are more engaged and motivated when they have a role in directing their own learning. Facilitator-based approaches promote active learning, where students participate in discussions, problem-solving, and hands-on activities. This active involvement enhances engagement and motivation, leading to better learning outcomes.

The need for inclusivity and differentiated instruction has also led to the paradigm shift. The facilitator approach allows for more personalized and differentiated instruction, catering to diverse learning styles and needs. Facilitators can better address the varying abilities, interests, and learning styles of students. This personalized approach can improve accessibility and inclusivity in the classroom, ensuring that all students have the opportunity to succeed (Heacox 2012).

2.4 Innovative Pedagogical Strategies

Innovative pedagogical strategies have emerged in response to evolving educational needs, advances in technology, and a deeper understanding of how students learn. These strategies aim to enhance student engagement, foster deeper understanding, and develop critical skills needed for the 21st century. key innovative pedagogical strategies include the following:

i. Flipped Classroom

The flipped classroom model reverses the traditional teaching approach by delivering instructional content, often online, outside of the classroom. In-class time is then devoted to exercises, projects, and discussions that deepen understanding. Research shows that the flipped classroom can increase student engagement and improve learning outcomes by allowing more time for active learning activities in the classroom (Bergmann & Sams, 2012; Bishop & Verleger, 2013).

ii. Project-Based Learning (PBL)

PBL is a student-centered pedagogy that involves students working on a project over a period of time. It engages them in solving a real-world problem or answering a complex question. PBL has been shown to increase student motivation and engagement by providing a sense of purpose and relevance to the learning process. It also helps develop critical thinking, collaboration, and communication skills (Blumenfeld et al., 1991; Krajcik & Blumenfeld, 2006).

iii. Inquiry-Based Learning

According to Savery (2015), Inquiry-based learning encourages students to ask questions, conduct research, and explore subjects in a way that mirrors the process of scientific inquiry.This method promotes critical thinking, fosters a deeper understanding of content, and stimulates students' natural curiosity.

iv. Gamification

Gamification involves incorporating game elements into the learning environment to motivate and engage students. Hamari et al., (2014) indicated that gamification can significantly enhance student motivation and engagement, leading to improved learning outcomes.

v. Blended Learning

Blended learning combines traditional face-to-face instruction with online learning, offering a flexible approach that can cater to different learning styles and needs. Graham (2006) explains that blended learning provides greater flexibility and accessibility, allowing students to learn at their own pace and access resources from anywhere. This approach has been found to improve student satisfaction and learning outcomes.

vi. Design Thinking

Design thinking is a solution-based approach to solving problems, emphasizing empathy, ideation, prototyping, and testing.This strategy encourages students to think creatively and approach problems from multiple perspectives. It has been shown to enhance innovation and collaborative skills (Razzouk & Shute, 2012; Carroll et al., 2010).

These innovative pedagogical strategies reflect a shift towards more student-centered, active, and engaging forms of learning. They are designed to develop critical 21st-century skills, enhance student motivation, and leverage technology to create more effective and personalized learning experiences.

2.5 Challenges and Opprtunities Faculty Face in Adopting the Role of Facilitator

In the contemporary higher education landscape, faculty roles are evolving beyond traditional didactic instruction to encompass a more dynamic and interactive approach. The shift towards a facilitator model reflects a broader educational trend that emphasizes student-centered learning, active engagement, and collaborative problem-solving (Biggs & Tang, 2011). This paradigm shift positions faculty as guides and mentors, rather than mere transmitters of knowledge, requiring them to navigate a complex array of challenges and opportunities. The challenges in adopting the role of a facilitator are considerable.The transition to a facilitator role necessitates new skills and strategies, which can be daunting without adequate professional development and support (Angelo & Cross, 1993).

Conversely, the shift towards facilitation presents opportunities for enhancing educational outcomes. By fostering a more engaging and collaborative learning environment, faculty can promote deeper learning and critical thinking (Freeman et al., 2014). The facilitator role allows for greater student autonomy and personalized learning experiences, which can improve student motivation and satisfaction (Hattie, 2009). Understanding the interplay between these challenges and opportunities is essential for institutions aiming to support faculty in their transition to facilitation roles. This section of the chapter will explore the barriers faced by educators, as well as the potential benefits of embracing this evolving pedagogical model, providing insights into how universities can foster an environment conducive to innovative and effective teaching practices.

One of the significant challenges is resistance to change from both faculty and institutions accustomed to traditional teaching methods. Prawat (1992) asserts that faculty who have spent years, or even decades, perfecting their lecture styles may find it challenging to adopt new, student-centered teaching strategies. They may find it time consuming, tedious and uncalled for since they believe in the ancient practices can still work. Resistance to change from both faculty and institutions can be a significant barrier to implementing new initiatives and innovations in higher education. Addressing this resistance effectively requires a multifaceted approach that involves understanding the underlying causes, fostering a supportive culture, and providing the necessary resources and support. Other strategies to address and overcome resistance to change include clearly articulating the benefits and rationale behind the proposed changes, demonstrating how the change aligns with the institution's mission and goals, Involving faculty, staff, and other stakeholders in the planning and decision-making process, seeking their input and addressing their concerns, fostering a sense of ownership and commitment to the change as stakeholders feel their opinions are valued and considered, offering targeted training and professional development opportunities to help faculty and staff acquire the skills and knowledge needed for the change, maintaining open and transparent communication throughout the change process. Providing regular updates and creating channels for feedback and questions.

Faculty are required to balance multiple roles, including being facilitators, mentors, and content experts. This balancing act can be difficult, as it requires a shift in mindset and the acquisition of new skills (Fink, 2013). Balancing these multiple roles requires one to clearly define and prioritize each role based on the context and needs of the course, effectively manage their time, ensures that each role receives adequate attention and helps in maintaining a balance between teaching, mentoring, and facilitation, use digital tools and platforms to streamline tasks and enhance efficiency, delegate and collaborate with colleagues to share responsibilities, set clear boundaries between different roles and communicate these to students to ensures that each role is addressed effectively without overlap or confusion, regularly reflect on the effectiveness of each role and adjust strategies as needed, gather feedback from students on how well the roles are being balanced and their impact on learning to allow for continuous improvement, monitor workload to prevent burnout, maintain a healthy work-life balance and seek support if needed. With these strategies, lecturers can more effectively balance the roles of facilitator, mentor, and content expert, providing a richer and more supportive learning experience for their students while maintaining their own well-being and effectiveness.

The integration of technology in classrooms can exacerbate the digital divide (Warschauer, 2004). Not all students have equal access to technological resources, which can create disparities in learning opportunities. Many students have challenges accessing technological devices. Due to this digital divide, there can be significant implications on educational outcomes and opportunities on individual students. Lecturers can adopt several strategies to handle digital disparities among students, ensuring that all learners have equal opportunities to succeed in a technology-enhanced educational environment. They can assess student needs through surveys to understand the digital access and proficiency levels of students, provide alternative access by offering printed materials, offline assignments, and other non-digital resources leverage campus resources by directing students to campus resources such as computer labs, loaner laptops, and internet access points, allow flexible deadlines and multiple methods for submitting assignments, choose digital tools and platforms that require minimal bandwidth and can function well on a variety of devices, provide training sessions or resources to help students develop essential digital skills, implement a mix of online and face-to-face instruction to accommodate students with varying levels of digital access, encourage group work and peer-to-peer support, where students can help each other with digital tasks, advocate for institutional support to create a more equitable learning environment by securing necessary resources for all students. These measures can help mitigate the impact of digital disparities, ensuring that all students have the opportunity to succeed in a technology-enhanced learning environment. This approach not only supports equitable access to education but also fosters a more inclusive and supportive classroom community.

Faculty members may also lack proficiency with new technologies, necessitating ongoing professional development and training. Ensuring that faculty are comfortable and competent with digital tools is essential for effective facilitation (Johnson et al., 2016). The lack of technological knowledge by educators can significantly impact learners in various ways, potentially hindering their educational experience and overall development. The teachers who are not proficient with technology may avoid using digital tools and resources that could enhance learning. This can result in a less engaging and interactive learning environment. Students might also find lessons less relevant and interesting if technology is not integrated, as they see the world around them becoming increasingly digital. Faculty members who lack proficiency with new technologies can be assisted through various targeted strategies to ensure they can effectively integrate digital tools into their teaching to make learning learner centered. Faculty should be offered professional development and training through workshops and seminars focused on different aspects of educational technology, online tutorials and courses, mentorship programs where less tech-savvy faculty are paired with tech-proficient colleagues who can provide one-on-one support and guidance, create physical or virtual resource centers where faculty can explore new technologies, receive training, and experiment with digital tools in a supportive environment, establish faculty learning communities or interest groups focused on exploring and implementing educational technologies. use collaboration platforms to facilitate the sharing of ideas, resources, and experiences among faculty, ensure that university leadership advocates for and supports the integration of technology in teaching, demonstrating its value and importance and collect regular feedback from faculty about their training needs and experiences with technology to continuously improve facilitator roles. By implementing these strategies, institutions can support faculty in developing the necessary skills and confidence to effectively use new technologies, ultimately enhancing the quality of education and the learning experiences for students.

There is a risk of overreliance on technology, where the human element of teaching is diminished. Effective facilitation requires a balance between using technology and maintaining meaningful interpersonal interactions (Selwyn, 2011). While overreliance on technology in education, may offer many benefits, it also carries several risks that can impact both teaching and learning. It may lead to diminished critical thinking and problem-solving skills, reduced interpersonal skills, digital divide since not all students have equal access to technology thus exacerbating existing educational inequalities, resource disparities, distractions by the internet and other digital devices leading to shorter attention spans and reduced ability to focus on tasks, health concerns, reduced creativity and security and privacy risks. By recognizing and addressing these risks of overreliance on technology, educators can create a more balanced and effective learning environment that leverages the benefits of technology without compromising essential skills and well-being. This can be done by educating students on the importance of digital well-being, managing screen time and understanding the impact of technology on mental health and promoting a healthy relationship with technology, preventing issues such as screen fatigue and digital addiction

Shifting from a lecturer to a facilitator role requires substantial professional development. Faculty need training in new pedagogical methods, technology use, and student engagement strategies (Guskey, 2002). Universities play a crucial role in shifting educators from traditional roles as primary information providers to facilitators of learning. This transition involves rethinking teaching methods, providing appropriate training and resources, and fostering an environment that supports active, student-centered learning. To fascilitate this, universities should offer workshops and courses on modern pedagogical techniques, such as active learning, flipped classrooms, and collaborative learning, Provide ongoing professional development opportunities to help lecturers stay updated on the latest teaching methods and technologies, equip classrooms with the necessary technology to facilitate interactive and collaborative learning, such as smart boards, clickers, and online collaboration platforms, implement robust LMS to support blended learning environments where lecturers can curate resources and manage student interactions, encourage and support the development of curricula that focus on student engagement, problem-solving, and critical thinking., promote interdisciplinary courses that require collaborative learning and diverse perspectives, fostering a facilitator approach, Support the implementation of flipped classrooms where students engage with lecture materials at home and use class time for interactive activities, Encourage lecturers to reflect on their teaching practices and seek ways to enhance their facilitation skills, Implement mentorship programs where experienced facilitators can guide and support their peers in adopting new teaching roles, llocate funding for initiatives that promote active learning and faculty development in facilitation skills, develop and communicate policies that support and encourage the shift from lecturer to facilitator, emphasizing the importance of student-centered learning and ensure that university leadership is committed to this shift and actively promotes a vision of collaborative and interactive learning. By taking these steps, universities can effectively support lecturers in transitioning to facilitators thus creating a more engaging, interactive, and effective learning environment for students.

Not all students are equally prepared for or comfortable with active learning and self-directed educational models. Therefore, facilitators must find ways to engage all students and accommodate diverse learning styles (Freeman et al., 2014). In most public Universities, students may lack technological gadgets that may enable them learn digitally. These may make them develop some phobia towards digital learning. These lot of students if not listened to may despair and eventually drop out. Educators can take several approaches to support these students by helping them build confidence and skills while ensuring that their learning experience is positive and productive. Facilitators should provide alternative ways to complete assignments that do not rely heavily on technology, ensuring that learning objectives are still met. A gradual introduction to technology will help, starting with simple tasks and progressively moving on to more complex ones. Facilitators should create a supportive learning environment showing understanding and patience towards these students who are struggling with technology.

Traditional assessment methods may not align with the goals of student-centered learning. Boud & Falchikov (2007) claim that developing effective assessment strategies that evaluate critical thinking, problem-solving, and collaboration skills can be complex. Developing student-centered assessment involves creating evaluation methods that prioritize the needs, interests, and growth of students. It focuses on making assessments meaningful and engaging for students, encouraging their active participation in the learning process. While this approach offers many benefits, such as increased student engagement and deeper learning, it also presents challenges especially for third world Universities which are still working on implementation modalities of assessment methods that are aligned to student centered learning. Student-centered assessments, while challenging, offer numerous opportunities to enhance learning and teaching at Universities such as: enhanced Student Engagement where Assessments can be aligned with students' interests and strengths, making learning more relevant and exciting, development of critical thinking and problem-solving skills, improved learning outcomes since ssessments is tailored to individual learning styles and paces Continuous feedback helps students identify areas for improvement and fosters a growth, empowerment and autonomy, where students take ownership of their learning, developing self-regulation and independent learning skills, collaboration and communication which allows for diverse perspectives and enhanced learning, inclusive education which results into flexibility in assessment methods that ensure all students have equal opportunities to demonstrate their knowledge and skills, real-world relevance since authentic assessments connect classroom learning to real-world situations, preparing students for future challenges where they can apply what they learn in meaningful contexts, enhancing the applicability of their education and an opportunity for continuous improvement for educators who gain insights into students' thought processes and learning progress, enabling more effective instructional strategies. By leveraging these opportunities, educators can create a more dynamic, responsive, and effective learning environment that supports the holistic development of students at Universities.

Kezar (2014) asserts that, institutions themselves may resist changes from traditional teaching models and policies to modern models and policies. Universities, despite being centers of knowledge and research, can sometimes contribute to the lagging behind of educational innovations due to several factors such as: institutional inertia where large institutions often have established traditions and practices that are resistant to change which can slow the adoption of new teaching methods and technologies, fixed or rigid curricula that do not easily accommodate new ideas or methods, resource constraints that hinder the adoption and scaling of new educational approaches, faculty resistance or hesitant to change their teaching practices due to a lack of training, perceived increased workload, or skepticism about the effectiveness of new methods, administrative and bureaucratic hurdles which delay the approval and implementation of new educational technologies and methodologies, lack of incentives for innovation, without recognition, rewards, or support for educational innovation, faculty members may be less motivated to experiment with new approaches, Technological Barriers that can limit the ability of faculty and students to engage with cutting-edge educational tools and resources and student resistance due to their believe in traditional teaching methods. Addressing these challenges requires a concerted effort from university leadership, faculty, and students to create a culture that values and supports educational innovation.

Universities can embrace educational innovations by creating a dynamic and responsive educational environment that embraces innovation and effectively prepares students for the future. This can effectively be done by: cultivating a culture of innovation where faculty and staff feel safe to experiment with new teaching methods without fear of being reprimanded, celebrate and reward successful implementations of innovative practices, provide professional development through regular training sessions, workshops on new educational technologies and methodologies, conferences and webinars, promote visionary leadership committed to fostering a culture of innovation, enhance collaboration and communication through innovation hubs, Establish dedicated centers or committees focused on educational innovation, promote student-led initiatives by supporting student-led projects and initiatives that foster innovation in learning, align innovations with institutional goals, leverage technology and infrastructure by upgrading technological infrastructure to support new teaching and learning tools, promote open-mindedness and adaptability that foster a mindset of continuous improvement and lifelong learning among faculty and students and engage in partnerships and networking with other universities and educational organizations to share resources and best practices to stay updated on the latest developments.

Cultural differences can impact the adoption of facilitator roles. In some cultures, the traditional lecture-based approach is deeply ingrained, and shifting to a more participatory model may face significant resistance (Hofstede, 2001). University culture plays a significant role in shaping how faculty members perceive and adopt facilitator roles in the educational process. To successfully adopt the facilitator roles the University and faculty should value teaching and learning by placing a high value on teaching excellence and student-centered learning, professional development and support, encourage collaboration and knowledge sharing among faculty to foster a community of practice that supports the adoption of facilitator roles, Adopt a culture that allows faculty autonomy and flexibility in their teaching approaches, Priovide strong leadership that articulates a clear vision for student-centered learning and allocate resources towards supporting innovative teaching practices. By fostering a culture that supports and values these elements, universities can create an environment where faculty are more willing and able to adopt facilitator roles, leading to more effective and engaging learning experiences for students.

3.0 RESEARCH METHODOLOGY

The study employed a qualitative research methodology and a descriptive research design to explore the evolving roles of faculty in modern classrooms, particularly the shift from lecturer to facilitator roles.The target population consisted of educators from two public universities in Kenya. Convenient sampling was used to select the two universities, while simple random sampling was applied to select the educators. Data was collected using two primary methods: detailed document analysis and questionnaires with both open and closed-ended questions. A total of 20 educators participated in the study, providing a diverse range of insights into faculty roles.

4.0 RESULTS AND DISCUSSIONS

4.1 Explain Faculty Roles in Contemporary Lecture Rooms

The first research objective was to explain the faculty roles in classrooms. The study found out that different age groups tended to engage learners in different ways. The study revealed that there was a prevalence of younger faculty in Universities who preferred engaging learners with new technologies unlike their older counterparts who engaged learners through ancient teaching approaches. The mid-career faculty who likely have substantial experience and possibly hold key administrative or leadership roles preferred blended methods, while the senior faculty who consisted of highly experienced professors and have been with the institutions for a long time and possibly hold senior or emeritus positions preferred the ancient methods. Diversity in age and experience suggests a mix of fresh perspectives and experienced guidance, which can enrich the educational environment. There is potential for mentorship since senior faculty can mentor younger colleagues, fostering professional development and continuity within the institution. Dynamic teaching approaches will be embraced since younger faculty might bring innovative teaching methods and technological proficiency, while older faculty can offer depth of knowledge and traditional pedagogical techniques. Understanding the age distribution among faculty members helps institutions tailor professional development programs, optimize mentorship structures, and enhance the overall educational experience for students.

The study also revealed that there is a nearly balanced representation of genders, with females slightly outnumbering males. This indicates progress towards gender diversity within faculty roles female faculty members are significantly represented in the academic workforce, potentially holding various roles from lecturers to senior professors. Men also continue to be well-represented in faculty roles, maintaining a strong presence in the academic environment. A balanced gender distribution brings diverse perspectives and approaches to teaching and academic management, enriching the educational experience.The presence of both male and female faculty provides a range of role models and mentors for students of all genders, promoting an inclusive academic culture that embraces facilitative teaching.This distribution suggests that efforts towards gender equality in academic hiring and promotion might be yielding positive results, offering equal opportunities for all genders. This balance supports a diverse and inclusive academic environment, contributing to a richer educational experience for students and fostering an equitable workplace for faculty.

The analysis of faculty members' opinions on whether the role of a faculty member should primarily be that of a facilitator rather than a lecturer revealed that a significant portion "Strongly agreed" with the statement. This indicates a strong belief among faculty members that their role should primarily focus on facilitating student learning rather than traditional lecturing. A minimal number "Strongly disagreed" with the statement. These Educators likely value traditional lecturing methods and may see the lecturer role as more central to their teaching philosophy. The overall trend towards agreeing with the facilitator role suggests a shift in teaching practices. Faculty members are increasingly adopting student-centered approaches, where they guide and support students in active learning rather than delivering content. The presence of neutral and disagreeing opinions among faculty indicates that a one-size-fits-all approach may not be ideal. Therefore, blended teaching strategies that incorporate both lecturing and facilitation can cater for diverse student needs and learning styles. Institutions can facilitate this change by offering resources, training and workshops on interactive teaching methods, classroom management, and student engagement to help faculty transition into facilitative roles more effectively.

4.2 Analyze the Drivers of Paradigm Shift in Contemporary Lecture Rooms.

The second objective was to analyze the the drivers of the paradigm shift in lecture rooms. According to the study, the shift from lecturer to facilitator in education has been driven by multiple factors. These factors can be broadly categorized into pedagogical advancements, technological innovations, and evolving societal needs. In terms of pedagogical advancements, social interaction plays a fundamental role in the development of cognition (Vygotsky, 1978). Therefore, facilitators should create environments where students can collaborate, discuss, and problem-solve together to enhance deeper learning. focus in learning has shifted from passive reception of information (lecture) to active engagement in the learning process (facilitation).

Focusing on technological innovations, the proliferation of digital learning tools, such as learning management systems (LMS), educational software, and online resources, has transformed the educational landscape. These tools enable personalized learning, immediate feedback, and access to a vast array of information beyond the classroom. According to Bates (2015), technology in education allows for more interactive and flexible learning experiences, aligning with the facilitator role.This trend has necessitated a shift from traditional lecturing to facilitation.

The study also revealed that the evolving societal needs in the 21st century are major drivers of the paradigm shift in classrooms. The skills required in the 21st century, such as critical thinking, creativity, collaboration, and communication, are best developed through active learning strategies. Facilitators should therefore assist students to develop these skills by creating interactive and collaborative learning environments. There is need for education systems to prioritize these competencies to prepare students for the modern workforce (The Partnership for 21st Century Skills, 2009).

4.3 Explore the Challenges and Opportunities Faculty Face

The third objective was to explore the challenges faculty face in adopting the role of facilitator and the opportunities this shift presents. The analysis of the challenges and opportunities faculty members face in implementing a facilitative teaching approach revealed the following challenges:

i. Large class sizes

Interactive and student-centered methods can be more challenging to execute effectively with many students, as they often require closer interaction and more personalized feedback. However, Universities could explore ways to reduce class sizes or provide additional support, such as teaching assistants, to help manage larger groups. Smaller class sizes can facilitate more effective use of interactive teaching methods

ii. Inadequate resources

A lack of necessary technology and materials hinders faculty members' ability to use interactive teaching methods. Adequate resources are crucial for creating an engaging and supportive learning environment that facilitates active learning. Ensuring that faculty members have access to the necessary technology and materials is crucial. Investments in classroom technology, digital resources, and other materials can support the implementation of facilitative teaching methods.

iii. Lack of time for preparation

Given that faculty engage in multiple roles, including being facilitators, mentors, and content experts. The balancing act of preparing for facilitative teaching can be difficult. Institutions can offer support in managing time, such as providing release time for faculty to develop interactive lessons or offering resources to streamline preparation.

iv. Insufficient institutional support (training/professional development)

A lack of training and professional development opportunities prevents faculty members from gaining the skills and knowledge needed to effectively use facilitative teaching methods. Providing ongoing training and professional development through workshops, seminars, and peer mentoring programs opportunities focused on facilitative teaching methods can be valuable in equiping faculty members with the skills they need.

v. Resistance from students

Some students may resist facilitative teaching approaches, preferring traditional lecture-based methods. This resistance can stem from unfamiliarity with interactive methods, a preference for passive learning or lack of technological ownership of gadgets. Addressing student resistance involves educating them about the benefits of interactive learning and providing support to help them adapt. Clear communication about the advantages of these methods and how they enhance learning outcomes can mitigate resistance.

5.0 CONCLUSION AND RECOMMENDATIONS

5.1 Conclusion

The study concluded that a significant number of faculty members are committed to using interactive teaching methods regularly. This trend towards active learning environments highlights the evolving roles of faculty in modern lecture halls, emphasizing engagement and student participation. By supporting and expanding these practices, educational institutions can enhance the overall quality of education and better prepare students for real-world challenges.

The study also concluded that the transition from lecturer to facilitator roles is driven by a combination of pedagogical advancements, technological innovations, and evolving societal needs. This shift reflects a broader understanding of how people learn best and the skills they need to succeed in the 21st century.

It further concluded that the challenges faculty members faced in implementing facilitative teaching approaches were mainly large class sizes, inadequate resources, lack of time for preparation, insufficient institutional support resistance from students. Addressing these challenges requires institutional support, including resource allocation, professional development, and strategies to manage class sizes and time effectively. By providing the necessary support and addressing student resistance, institutions can help faculty members successfully adopt and implement more facilitative and interactive teaching methods, ultimately enhancing student learning outcomes

5.2 Recommendations

Based on the study's findings, the following recommendations were made:

i. Universities should offer professional development programs that address the specific needs of faculty at different career stages
ii. Provide release time for faculty
iii. Develop structured mentorship programs where senior faculty mentor younger colleagues, iv. Foster professional development and continuity within the institution
iv. Encourage and support faculty to adopt blended teaching strategies that incorporate both traditional lecturing and facilitation methods
v. Ensure faculty members have access to necessary technology and materials by investing in classroom technology and digital resources and
vi. To educate students about the benefits of interactive learning and provide support to help them adapt.

5.3 Future Research Directions

As the educational landscape continues to evolve, several future research directions can be identified to further explore and optimize the shift of faculty roles from traditional lecturers to facilitators. A research can be conducted to explore sustainable models of professional development that support the ongoing evolution of teaching practices.

Conflict of Interest

The author declares no conflict of interest in this research.

Acknowledgment

The author acknowledges the support she got from the management of public universities in Kenya and faculty members who provided primary data for this chapter.

REFERENCES

Angelo, T. A., & Cross, K. P. (1993). *Classroom Assessment Techniques: A Handbook for College Teachers*. Jossey-Bass.

Axtell, J. (1968). *The Educational Writings of John Locke: A Critical Edition with Introduction and Notes*. Cambridge University Press.

Bates, A. W. (2015). *Teaching in a Digital Age: Guidelines for designing teaching and learning*. BCcampus.

Bergmann, J., & Sams, A. (2012). *Flip Your Classroom: Reach Every Student in Every Class Every Day*. International Society for Technology in Education.

Biggs, J., & Tang, C. (2011). *Teaching for Quality Learning at University: What the Student Does*. McGraw-Hill Education.

Bishop, J. L., & Verleger, M. A. (2013). The flipped classroom: A survey of the research. In *ASEE National Conference Proceedings,* Atlanta, GA (Vol. 30, No. 9, pp. 1-18). DOI: 10.18260/1-2--22585

Blumenfeld, P. C., Soloway, E., Marx, R. W., Krajcik, J. S., Guzdial, M., & Palincsar, A. (1991). Motivating project-based learning: Sustaining the doing, supporting the learning. *Educational Psychologist*, 26(3-4), 369–398. DOI: 10.1080/00461520.1991.9653139

Bonk, C. J., & Graham, C. R. (Eds.). (2006). *The Handbook of Blended Learning: Global Perspectives, Local Designs*. Pfeiffer.

Boud, D., & Falchikov, N. (Eds.). (2007). *Rethinking assessment in higher education: Learning for the longer term*. Routledge. DOI: 10.4324/9780203964309

Brickhouse, N. W., & Smith, J. P. (2000). The roles of ethnography and reflexivity in understanding teacher thinking, practice, and learning. *Educational Researcher*, 29(1), 4–13.

Bruner, J. S. (1961). *The act of discovery*. Harvard University Press.

Carroll, M., Goldman, S., Britos, L., Koh, J., Royalty, A., & Hornstein, M. (2010). Destination, imagination and the fires within: Design thinking in a middle school classroom. *International Journal of Art & Design Education*, 29(1), 37–53. DOI: 10.1111/j.1476-8070.2010.01632.x

Cremin, L. A. (1961). *The Transformation of the School: Progressivism in American Education, 1876-1957*. Knopf.

Downes, S. (2010). Learning networks and connective knowledge. In Yang, H., & Yuen, S. (Eds.), *Handbook of Research on Practices and Outcomes in E-Learning: Issues and Trends* (pp. 1–26). IGI Global.

Facione, P. A. (1990). *Critical Thinking: A Statement of Expert Consensus for Purposes of Educational Assessment and Instruction*. The Delphi Report. American Philosophical Association.

Fink, L. D. (2013). *Creating Significant Learning Experiences: An Integrated Approach to Designing College Courses*. Jossey-Bass.

Freeman, S., Eddy, S. L., McDonough, M., Smith, M. K., Okoroafor, N., Jordt, H., & Wenderoth, M. P. (2014). Active learning increases student performance in science, engineering, and mathematics. *Proceedings of the National Academy of Sciences of the United States of America*, 111(23), 8410–8415. DOI: 10.1073/pnas.1319030111 PMID: 24821756

Graham, C. R. (2006). Blended learning systems: Definition, current trends, and future directions. In Bonk, C. J., & Graham, C. R. (Eds.), *The Handbook of Blended Learning: Global Perspectives, Local Designs* (pp. 3–21). Pfeiffer.

Grendler, P. F. (1989). *Schooling in Renaissance Italy: Literacy and Learning, 1300-1600*. Johns Hopkins University Press. DOI: 10.56021/9780801837258

Guskey, T. R. (2002). Professional development and teacher change. *Teachers and Teaching*, 8(3), 381–391. DOI: 10.1080/135406002100000512

Hamari, J., Koivisto, J., & Sarsa, H. (2014). Does gamification work?--a literature review of empirical studies on gamification. In *2014 47th Hawaii International Conference on System Sciences* (pp. 3025-3034). IEEE.

Harden, R. M., & Crosby, J. R. (2000). The good teacher is more than a lecturer—The twelve roles of the teacher. *Medical Teacher*, 22(4), 334–347. DOI: 10.1080/014215900409429

Hattie, J. (2009). *Visible Learning: A Synthesis of Over 800 Meta-Analyses Relating to Achievement*. Routledge.

Heacox, D. (2012). *Differentiating Instruction in the Regular Classroom: How to Reach and Teach All Learners*. Free Spirit Publishing.

Hofstede, G. (2001). *Culture's Consequences: Comparing Values, Behaviors, Institutions and Organizations Across Nations*. SAGE Publications.

Johnson, L., Adams Becker, S., Estrada, V., & Freeman, A. (2016). *NMC Horizon Report: 2016 Higher Education Edition*. The New Media Consortium.

Kezar, A. (2014). *How Colleges Change: Understanding, Leading, and Enacting Change*. Routledge.

King, A. (1993). From sage on the stage to guide on the side. *College Teaching*, 41(1), 30–35. DOI: 10.1080/87567555.1993.9926781

King, R. (1993). Neurath, Otto (1882–1945). In Audi, R. (Ed.), *The Cambridge Dictionary of Philosophy* (pp. 542–543). Cambridge University Press.

Krajcik, J. S., & Blumenfeld, P. C. (2006). Project-based learning. In Sawyer, R. K. (Ed.), *The Cambridge Handbook of the Learning Sciences* (pp. 317–334). Cambridge University Press.

Marrou, H. I. (1956). *A History of Education in Antiquity* (Lamb, G., Trans.). Sheed and Ward.

Miller, P. H. (2011). *Theories of Developmental Psychology* (5th ed.). Worth Publishers.

Papert, S. (1980). *Mindstorms: Children, Computers, and Powerful Ideas*. Basic Books.

Partnership for 21st Century Skills. (2009). *Framework for 21st Century Learning*.

Piaget, J. (1952). *The Origins of Intelligence in Children*. International Universities Press. DOI: 10.1037/11494-000

Piaget, J. (1973). *To Understand Is to Invent: The Future of Education*. Grossman Publishers.

Porter, L. (2000). *Student behaviour: Theory and practice for teachers*. Allen & Unwin.

Prawat, R. S. (1992). Teachers' beliefs about teaching and learning: A constructivist perspective. *American Journal of Education*, 100(3), 354–395. DOI: 10.1086/444021

Razzouk, R., & Shute, V. (2012). What is design thinking and why is it important? *Review of Educational Research*, 82(3), 330–348. DOI: 10.3102/0034654312457429

Redecker, C., & Punie, Y. (2017). *European Framework for the Digital Competence of Educators: DigCompEdu*. Publications Office of the European Union.

Savery, J. R. (2015). Overview of problem-based learning: Definitions and distinctions. In Walker, A., Leary, H., Hmelo-Silver, C., & Ertmer, P. A. (Eds.), *Essential Readings in Problem-Based Learning* (pp. 5–15). Purdue University Press. DOI: 10.2307/j.ctt6wq6fh.6

Schuller, T., & Watson, D. (2009). *Learning Through Life: Inquiry into the Future for Lifelong Learning*. National Institute of Adult Continuing Education (NIACE).

Selwyn, N. (2011). *Education and Technology: Key Issues and Debates*. Bloomsbury Publishing.

Siemens, G. (2005). Connectivism: A learning theory for the digital age. *International Journal of Instructional Technology and Distance Learning*, 2(1).

Siemens, G., & Downes, S. (2005). *Connectivism: A learning theory for the digital age*. International Journal of Instructional Technology and Distance Learning.

Tyack, D. B. (1964). *The One Best System: A History of American Urban Education*. Harvard University Press.

Voogt, J., & Roblin, N. P. (2012). A comparative analysis of international frameworks for 21st century competences: Implications for national curriculum policies. *Journal of Curriculum Studies*, 44(3), 299–321. DOI: 10.1080/00220272.2012.668938

Vygotsky, L. S. (1962). *Thought and Language*. MIT Press. DOI: 10.1037/11193-000

Vygotsky, L. S. (1978). *Mind in Society: The Development of Higher Psychological Processes*. Harvard University Press.

Warschauer, M. (2004). *Technology and social inclusion: Rethinking the digital divide*. MIT Press.

Wood, D., Bruner, J. S., & Ross, G. (1976). The role of tutoring in problem-solving. *Journal of Child Psychology and Psychiatry, and Allied Disciplines*, 17(2), 89–100. DOI: 10.1111/j.1469-7610.1976.tb00381.x PMID: 932126

KEY TERMS AND DEFINITIONS

Blended Learning: An educational approach that combines online digital media with traditional face-to-face classroom methods.

Collaborative Learning: An educational approach where learners work together in groups and with faculty to accomplish a common goal in education.

Facilitative Teaching: A teaching approach where the instructor guides and supports students' learning processes rather than delivering information directly.

Mentorship: A professional relationship in which an experienced person provides guidance and support to a less experienced person to help them develop their skills and career.

Professional Development: Ongoing education and training for professionals (Educators) to enhance their skills and knowledge in their field

Student-Centered Learning: An approach to education that focuses on the needs, abilities, interests, and learning styles of students.

Student Engagement: The degree of participation, attention, interest, and passion that students show when they are learning or being taught.

Technology Integration: The use of technology tools and resources in educational settings to enhance teaching, learning, and assessment.

APPENDIX I

Questionnaire

Dear colleague, I humbly request for your valuable ten minutes to fill for me this questionnaire designed to gather insights on the evolving roles of faculty in modern lecture halls. Your feedback will be valuable in understanding the evolving roles of faculty and improving teaching and learning experiences in modern lecture halls. Thank you.

The Evolving Roles of Faculty in Modern Lecture halls.

Section 1: Demographics

1. **What is your age group?**

a) Under 25
b) 25-34
c) 35-44
d) 45-54
e) 55-64
f) 65 and above

2. **What is your gender?**

a) Male
b) Female
c) Non-binary/Third gender
d) Prefer not to say

3. **How many years of teaching experience do you have?**

a) Less than 1 year
b) 1-5 years
c) 6-10 years
d) 11-20 years
e) More than 20 years

Section 2: Teaching Methods

4. **How often do you incorporate interactive teaching methods (e.g., group discussions, problem-solving activities) in your classes?**

a) Always
b) Often
c) Sometimes
d) Rarely

e) Never

5. **To what extent do you agree with the following statement: "The role of a faculty member should primarily be that of a facilitator rather than a lecturer."**

a) Strongly agree
b) Agree
c) Neutral
d) Disagree
e) Strongly disagree

6. **Which of the following best describes your current teaching approach?**

a) Traditional lecture-based
b) Mostly lecture-based with some interactive elements
c) Balanced mix of lectures and interactive activities
d) Mostly interactive with some lectures
e) Fully interactive/facilitation-based

7. **What percentage of your classroom time is dedicated to direct lecturing?**

a) 0-20%
b) 21-40%
c) 41-60%
d) 61-80%
e) 81-100%

Section 3: Classroom Dynamics

8. **How effective do you find interactive teaching methods in enhancing student learning outcomes?**

a) Very effective
b) Effective
c) Neutral
d) Ineffective
e) Very ineffective

9. **What challenges do you face in implementing a more facilitative teaching approach? (Select all that apply)**

a) Lack of time for preparation
b) Large class sizes
c) Insufficient training/professional development
d) Resistance from students
e) Inadequate resources (technology, materials, etc.)
f) Other (Please specify)

10. **In your opinion, how do students respond to a facilitative teaching approach compared to traditional lecturing?**

a) Much more engaged
b) Slightly more engaged
c) No difference
d) Slightly less engaged
e) Much less engaged

11. **What skills do you believe are essential for faculty to effectively transition to a facilitator role? (Select all that apply)**

a) Communication skills
b) Classroom management

c) Technological proficiency
d) Collaborative planning
e) Adaptability and flexibility
f) Knowledge of student-centered teaching methods
g) Other (Please specify)

Section 4: Institutional Support

13. **How supportive is your institution in promoting faculty's shift from lecturers to facilitators?**

a) Very supportive
b) Supportive
c) Neutral
d) Unsupportive
e) Very unsupportive

14. **What type of institutional support would be most beneficial for faculty transitioning to a facilitator role? (Select all that apply)**

a) Professional development workshops
b) Access to teaching resources and technology
c) Smaller class sizes
d) Peer mentoring programs
e) Administrative support
f) Other (Please specify)

15. **Have you participated in any professional development programs focused on interactive or facilitative teaching methods?**

a) Yes
b) No

16. **If yes, how would you rate the effectiveness of these programs?**

a) Very effective
b) Effective
c) Neutral
d) Ineffective
e) Very ineffective

Section 5: Open-Ended Questions

17. In your experience, what are the most significant benefits of shifting from a lecturer to a facilitator in the classroom?

18. Can you share any specific strategies or techniques that have been successful for you in adopting a more facilitative role?

19. What advice would you give to other faculty members who are considering transitioning from a traditional lecturer role to a facilitator role?

20. Any additional comments or thoughts on the evolving roles of faculty in modern classrooms?

Thank you for your participation.

Chapter 10
A Model for Developing Multi-Competence in Graduates for a Supercomplex World

Charles Mottanya Nyandusi
Moi University, Kenya

ABSTRACT

The world today is characterized not only by fluidity in the creation, dissemination and decay of knowledge and meaning, but also by the proliferation of variegated frames of reference and understanding. It is a supercomplex world. It is this world that the 21st century university has to serve. To remain relevant in such supercomplexity necessitates that the university needs to sustain its traditional intrinsic function -- the advancement of knowledge and the search for truth, while at the same time espousing a newer, extrinsic function – the preparation of students for the world of work; that is, enhancing the employability of graduates. This Chapter posits that the two functions can and should be integrated, so that the university can develop a multicompetent graduate through the Holistic Graduate Identity Curriculum (HoGIC) model proposed here.

DOI: 10.4018/979-8-3693-6930-2.ch010

INTRODUCTION:

The Idea of a University

The question 'what is a university?' has exercised thinkers and practitioners over the centuries. Attempts at addressing this question invariably end up answering a corollary question: 'what is the function of a university'? In order to meaningfully discuss the functions of a university, it is necessary to go back in time and trace the arguments that have shaped the concept of a university. One of the earliest and most famous commentators on university education is Cardinal John Henry Newman who was the Rector of the Catholic University in Dublin in the 1850s. Newman conceived a university as:

The place to which a thousand schools make contributions; in which the intellect may safely range and speculate, sure to find its equal in some antagonist activity, and its judge in the tribunal of truth. It is a place where inquiry is pushed forward and discoveries verified and perfected, and rashness rendered innocuous and error exposed by the collision of mind with mind and knowledge with knowledge (cited in National Institute for Newman Studies, 2007, p.16)

Newman's ideas about the place and purpose of a university resonate with those of an earlier thinker, Wilhelm von Humboldt, founder of the University of Berlin, now renamed Humboldt University in Germany. Humboldt, who is actually credited as being the originator of 'the idea of a university', held that the function of a university was to advance knowledge by original and critical investigation rather than the mere transmission of culture and the teaching of skills. Humboldt vigorously advocated for the autonomy of the university so that its research and teaching functions would be based on an unbiased search for truth, free from ideological, cultural, economic, and political pressures. Both Newman and Humboldt therefore championed "a liberal education in its broadest sense, a focus on the person more than the skills, universities containing the broad range of human knowledge, and a general sense of anti-utilitarianism" (Lucey, 2014).

Over the years, but especially in the last decade of the 20th century and now in the 21st century, Humboldt's and Newman's ideas of a university have elicited criticism that they are elitist, focusing inwards to what McCowan (2015) has termed the intrinsic value of university education. The contention continues to be that an intrinsic focus is irrelevant to the new and emerging pressures that confront the 21st century university. These pressures are many and varied, but they are all about what Wedekind and Mutereko (2016) term responsiveness. Responsiveness of a university refers to a multi-dimensional accountability to students, faculty, employers, the wider economy, society as a whole, and the natural environment, with the ultimate aim being the "enhancement of the quality of life" (Gibbons, 1998, p.2).

It has been suggested that responsiveness in university education has four dimensions: *economic responsiveness* – which considers the expectations of employers and the needs of the wider economy; *cultural responsiveness* – which addresses ethnic, cultural, religious and other diversities; *disciplinary responsiveness* – which takes into account the needs and interests of the various discipline communities that generate new knowledge through research and practice; and *student responsiveness* – which serves the needs and interests of the student in the university (Moll, 2005). To this list may be added a fifth dimension: *environmental responsiveness* – which would be about how university education prepares for and responds to the vagaries of the natural environment. These five dimensions of responsiveness may well be viewed as the framework for defining the functions of a university. In sum then, the university has five functions: the economic function, the cultural function, the knowledge (disciplinary) function, the individual development function, and the environmental function.

The contention has been that, in the Humboldtian and Newman ideal, the university serves only the knowledge and individual development function, to the detriment of the other three functions. As has been pointed out, this is an intrinsic focus. There is increasing pressure for universities to have an extrinsic focus; that is, to adopt an instrumental value so as to be relevant. Yet there is a caution that 'instrumentalism' is narrow hence actually constrictive to university education (Harvey, 2000). The fear here is that if "the kinds of enquiry undertaken in universities ... are tied to specific, pre-defined forms of instrumental benefit (either in their motivations or in the parameters of their outcomes) then that enquiry is undermined and impoverished" (McCowan, 2015, p.277). There is therefore need for balance between the intrinsic and the instrumental when determining the worth of university education. To this end, the argument is that instrumentalization of university education should only be pursued as a corollary of the university's intrinsic value. Thus, "the instrumental value of universities should exist alongside and emerging from its intrinsic value, rather than replacing it" (McCowan, 2015, p.282).

However, the argument about maintaining the intrinsic while espousing the instrumental seems to be largely theoretical and confined to academia (Prewitt, 2016). The practical reality, however, is that the drivers of the discourse(s) on relevance in university education are occupants of spaces of power outside of the universities. Majorly, these are governments and employers. Their perspective of relevance in university education is not only overtly instrumental; it often narrows down to only the economic responsiveness of the university curriculum. Emanating from such discourse is a general consensus on the fact that relevance refers to the fit or the match between what higher education institutions do and what society expects of them (see for instance Baron & McCormack, 2024; Bennett, 2018; Frankham,

2017; ILO, 2021; Mohee, 2019; Nalami & Waswa, 2023; Republic of Kenya 2020; World Bank, 2019).

This conception of relevance is captured more concisely by Otunga (2010, p.13) when she defines curriculum relevance as "the learning in which students learn to apply knowledge, concepts, and/or skills to solve real-world problems." She goes further to say that this learning should be both contextual and interdisciplinary. This notion of curriculum relevance is indicative of the conceptual and structural shifts in the world of work. These shifts have occasioned glaring quantitative and qualitative mismatches between labour supply and demands. The essence of these shifts is in the fast and ever changing nature of knowledge and the move towards knowing (Barnett, 2000a).

This fluidity in the creation and dissemination of knowledge is symptomatic of the complexity of life in the 21st century and beyond. To appreciate this complexity, it is necessary to pay attention to the concept of supercomplexity.

Supercomplexity: Multiple Frames of Reference for the Individual

University education "is faced with not just preparing students for a complex world; it is faced with preparing students for a supercomplex world" (Barnett, 2000b, p.257), which is "a world subject to infinite interpretability" (Barnett, 2000a, p.6). A supercomplex world is characterized, initially, by a *situation of complexity*, then, aggregately and ultimately, by a *situation of supercomplexity*.

According to Barnett (2000a, p.6), "a situation of complexity exists where one is faced with a surfeit of data, knowledge or theoretical frames *within* one's immediate situation". He explains this by giving the example of a medical doctor who, in the course of his professional duties, has to deal with multiple new drugs appearing on the market, keep abreast with new forms of surgery or new equipment and instrumentation. At the same time, the doctor has to be accountable to the hospital management (or even *be* part of the management), deal with patients queries comments, and perform a myriad other tasks related to the job.

A situation of supercomplexity arises when the same doctor, apart from discharging his already complex professional duties, has to occupy and act in a variety of other equally important and necessary social, cultural, economic spaces, for instance as a parent, a role model, and a bread-winner. Supercomplexity is thus a multiplication of spaces, or, as Barnett calls them, frames of reference for the individual.

In short, professional life is increasingly becoming a matter not just of handling overwhelming data and theories *within* a given frame of reference (a situation of complexity) but also a matter of handling multiple frames of understanding, of action, and of self-identity. The fundamental frameworks by which we might understand the world are multiplying and are often in confict. Of the multiplication of frameworks, there shall be no end. It is this multiplication of frameworks that I term *supercomplexity*. (Barnett, 2000a, p.6).

In such a situation of supercomplexity, "pedagogies are required that provide capacities for coping with supercomplexity; which encourage the formation of human being that maintains a purposive equilibrium in the face of radical uncertainty and contestability" (Barnet 2000c, 419). Thus "education in a supercomplex world needs to address not just ways of knowing (disciplinary epistemology), but ways of being (ontologies) (Wilson & Morieson, 2022, p.3). in sum, therefore, for a university in a supercomplex world, "the educational task is primarily an ontological task" (Barnett, 2012, p.69), concerned essentially with developing holistic identity of a student and, concomitantly, a graduate.

Graduate Identity: the Concept of Multicompetence and the Construct of Employability

Graduate identity is an aspect of higher education that rarely receives due attention. Graduate identity is an amalgam of competences exhibited by an individual graduate. It is characterized by four components: 1) Values, which include personal ethics and shared (community) norms and values; 2) Intellect, which is the graduate's capacity for critical and lateral thinking, continuous learning, creativity, innovativeness, and problem solving; 3)Performance, which is the graduate's application of their knowledge and skills to successfully accomplish given tasks at the workplace and/or in the community, and their attitude or disposition to performing these tasks; 4) social engagement, which is characterized by social responsibility, awaereness of diversity and appreciation of inclusivity, and successful interpersonal interactions and transactions (Bennett, 2019; Hinchliffe and Jolly, 2010)

The identity of a graduate in a supercomplex world is of necessity a holistic one, espousing the reality of the multiple, even innumerable, frames of reference that characterize an individual's day to day life. These frames of reference, as we have seen, are "a multiplication of incompatible differences of interpretation" (Barnett 2012, p.67). In order for an individual to successfully interpret and navigate each of the different frames of reference in their daily endeavors, a particular competence or set of competences is required. At this point, the individual can be said to be *competent*. Due to the inevitable multiplication of frames of reference due to supercomplexity, the competences also multiply in tandem. This is when the individual is now said to be *multicompetent*. In short, a holistic graduate identity is characterized by multicompetence.

This concept of multicompetence forms a logical premise for the understanding of employability as a construct. Employability may be generically conceived as the entire corpus of a university graduate's attributes, which consist of the knowledge, skills, attitudes, competencies and dispositions that may qualify them for one or more positions of employment, including self-employment, and which would help them to remain progressively productive and valuable in all the personal, social, and economic spheres of their life. Globally, the mandate of enhancing employability seems to be vested mainly in universities and other related institutions of higher learning. Indeed, it has been argued that the responsibility for preparing and inducting graduates into professional life and into citizenship majorly lies with Higher Education institutions (Barnett, 2018; Frankham, 2017; McIlveen, 2018; Pukelis, Pileicikiene, Allan & Dailidiene, 2007).

The question is: "should employability be the primary basis that shapes the direction of universities?" Asked differently, "is a university's purpose to be defined solely by the expectations of the employers?" (UNESCO, 2012, p.3). This question, in various forms, dominates current employability discourse. Whatever its form, its essence is a trichotomy proposed by Catcheside (2012). Catcheside opines that in the employability debates there is a thesis (universities are not about markets, business and student employability), an anti-thesis (oh yes, they are!), and a synthesis that shall be discussed later on in this chapter. This trichotomy will shape the discussion for the rest of this section.

The employability debate is a political discourse. It is a discourse of who wields 'the power' of determining what constitutes employability and how *that* employability may be developed. This discourse is typically characterized by disputation between two entrenched protagonists: job market players, who hold the view that the university *is* a purveyor of employability as per the wishes employers, and academic purists in the universities, who eschew the 'anti-intellectual' narrative of employability and therefore the subordination of the university to wishes of employers. There is, in recent times, a growing 'voice of integration', that seeks to reconcile the positions of both protagonists and forge a commonality of purpose and process, a *praxis* as it were, in university education and its relevance to the universe.

Though this voice of integration is certainly being *heard*, at least in academic circles, it is still yet to be *listened* to, especially by the job market players. The significance of this is that reconciling the two positions remains mostly a theoretical enterprise. The current political reality is that it is the job market players; that is, employers, who wield the power in the employability debate, and they drive the employability agenda which, as pointed out earlier, is essentially a 'skills' agenda. As Hinchliffe (2005) points out, "in case anyone has doubts about the relevance of skills to graduate employability in the eyes of employers they need only to read any set of graduate job adverts" (p.6). Since university graduates wish to be employed, and the universities themselves wish to shore up their graduate-destinations ratings, academics find themselves, grudgingly most certainly, in the service of employers, perpetuating the employers' narrative of employability. It is this reality that has led to the suggestion among many employers and policy makers that universities "need to transform their curricula and pedagogies in the service of employability" (McGrath, 2009, p.6), or at the very least universities should "alter the curricula to close the gap and ensure that their products and the knowledge created benefits the individual, prospective employers and the broader economy" (Pheko and Molefhe, 2016, p.6). This school of thought focuses on the supply of 'job ready' individual graduates into the job market. This has been labeled 'supply side' thinking (McQuaid and Lindsay, 2005).

In such a scenario, it becomes necessary to reconceptualize Catcheside's trichotomy. In this reconceptualization, there is a thesis (universities are about producing graduates who have skills and competencies which fit into the employability definitions of employers), an anti-thesis (oh no, they are not! They are about developing an all-rounded human being), and a synthesis (producing employable graduates and developing all-rounded human beings is actually one and the same thing).

A useful starting point for the argument(s) against the 'skills agenda' would be the concise assertion by the United Nations Education, Scientific and Cultural Organization that university education "should not be directed only towards meeting the needs and requirements of employers; as 'industry ready' is not synonymous with 'society ready'" (UNESCO, 2012, p.28). In this assertion, producing a graduate who is 'society ready' is the goal towards which universities should aspire. To achieve this goal, universities should promote "comprehensive excellence" in their graduates (UNESCO, 2012)

Comprehensive excellence in a graduate is achieved when the definition and development of "employability goes well beyond the simplistic notion of key skills, and is evidenced in the application of a mix of personal qualities and beliefs, understandings, skillful practices and the ability to reflect productively on experience" (Yorke, 2006, p.13). It is noteworthy that in this perception of employability, 'understandings' and 'skillful practices' replace the more commonly used 'knowledge' and 'skills' because the former "signal the importance of a rich appreciation of the relevant field(s) and of the ability to operate in situations of complexity and ambiguity." The end result in this conception of employability is "a capable person", a 'society ready' individual, who "can work effectively on unfamiliar problems in unfamiliar contexts as well as on familiar problems in familiar contexts (which is really a matter of routine)" (Yorke, 2006, p.13). The accent here seems to be on what the graduate is able to do. Thus:

Employability is not just about getting a job. Conversely, just because a student is in a vocational course does not mean that somehow employability is automatic. Employability is more than about developing attributes, techniques or experiences just to enable a student to get a job, or progress within a current career. It is about learning and the emphasis is less on 'employ' and more on 'ability'. In essence, the emphasis is on developing critical, reflective abilities with a view to empowering and enhancing the learner (Harvey, 2003, p.3)

Such arguments that are antithetical of the skills agenda invariably refer to the thesis – employability is about graduates' skills in relation to the job market – in order to advance their counter-argument. What is instructive in the counter-arguments is that they do not dismiss the skills agenda; rather, they characterize it as narrow or hollow, focusing on the job-readiness of an individual graduate rather than on the situation of supercomplexity which defines that individual's milieu. There is a feeling that:

the concept of employability – particularly as applied within many supply-side labour market policies – has been 'hollowed out' in many current theoretical and policy discussions. In many cases, the interactivity supposedly at the center of the concept appears to have been replaced by a singular focus on the individual and what might be termed their 'employability skills'. The employability skills or individual assets possessed by job-seekers, and the extent to which they tie in with the immediate needs of employers, have come to define many policy-makers' identification of skills gaps and understanding of the concept of employability (McQuaid and Lindsay, 2005, p.205)

The interactivity referred to here is based on a broader and holistic conception of employability. In this broader conception, employability involves "an interaction between the individual and the other actors and conditions in the labour market" (McQuaid and Lindsay, 2005, p.202). Thus, as Pheko and Molefhe (2016) point out, employability is "a complex mosaic – involving the employed, the unemployed, current employees, future employees, governments, employers (both current and future), sponsors, and the general labour market" (p. 5). This seems to reflect a much earlier, but nonetheless still valid, assertion by Kleinman and West (1998) that employability is "the outcome of a complex of different factors, located in the labour market, in schools, in the recruitment procedures of businesses, and the economic policies implemented by the government" (p.174).

On the premise of broadening the understanding of employability, there have been attempts to conceptualize frameworks that take into consideration both individual factors and labour market conditions. This is evident in a broad perspective model developed by McQuaid and Lindsay (2005) which contains three interrelated components which influence employability: *Individual factors* which include attributes (e.g. basic social skills), competencies (e.g. motivation and confidence), transferable skills (e.g. literacy, numeracy, problem solving, communication, adaptability and team-working skills), qualifications and educational attainment; *Personal circumstances* that relate to the individual's social and household circumstances (e.g. family and caring responsibilities, access to resources); and *External factors* that cover labour demand conditions (e.g. macroeconomic factors, vacancy characteristics, recruitment factors) and enabling support factors (e.g. accessibility to public services and job matching technologies).

Similarly, Rothwell and Arnold (2007) as cited in Lowden, Hall, Elliot and Lewin (2011, p. 4) propose a broad contextual approach for understanding employability based on interrelated components: the student's academic performance and engagement in his/her studies; the student's confidence in his/her skills and abilities; the student's ambition; the student's perception of the strength of the university's brand; the reputation the student's university has within his/her field of study; the status and credibility of the student's field of study; the student's awareness of opportunities in the external labour market; the student's perception of the state of the external labour market; and the external labout market's demand for peoples in the student's subject field.

A critical analysis of most of these broader conceptions of employability reveals that, ultimately, the onus remains on the universities to enact the employability agenda. This scenario is aptly explained thus:

While a shared responsibility between the multiple stakeholders in the employability mix is acknowledged, institutions of higher learning are generally viewed as critical stakeholders since they are: (1) a direct bridge to the world of work; (2) fundamental for talent identification (e.g. through selecting students for appropriate programs and courses); and (3) instrumental for talent development (through the specific training and development programs) (Pheko and Molefhe, 2016, p.5).

This kind of thinking is self-contradicting. It advocates for that which it advocates against. In arguing against the skills agenda *while* asserting the centrality of the university as the developer or generator of employability, such discourse propagates instrumentalism in university education. Instrumentalism is usually manifested in instrumental learning, where the students are typically prepared for careers in appropriate industries or professions. Such instrumental learning is "extremely narrow and intended primarily to secure a qualification or a job rather than reflect an holistic [sic] learning experience" (Harvey, 2000, p.9). Evidently, in this case, the anti-thesis reverts to the thesis.

There is therefore need for a truly broad and holistic conception of employability which espouses all the arguments advanced above and goes further as it seeks to ensure the notion of comprehensive excellence as discussed in preceding paragraphs of this chapter. What is critical to note here is that in essence, in the aforementioned trichotomy, the thesis advances a narrow conception of employability; the anti-thesis advances a broad conception of employability; while the synthesis advances a holistic conception of employability. However, as the previous paragraph shows, the lines between such categorizations, while clearly distinct in definition, get blurred in actual disputation.

The assertion here therefore is that a broad conception of employability *is* a holistic conception. In other words, the anti-thesis and the synthesis merge, but not in contradistinction to the thesis. Rather, the thesis is sub-summed in the anti-thesis, and the resultant claim is the synthesis. The synthesized conception is *both* broad and holistic. In this conception, university education "should not only be measured in terms of the employment rate of graduates but should also be measured by the extent to which [it] has addressed all of its purposes" (UNESCO, 2012, p.28). This is critical because:

When higher education institutions are confined to meeting the demands of employers, this neglects the important role of universities in nurturing the characteristics that help graduates to function across all aspects of life after they graduate (the concept of "graduateness"). In other words, individuals must not only be geared towards serving the work sector, but must also develop the skills that allow them to benefit their family, community, and the nation (UNESCO, 2012, p.28).

In the supercomplexity that characterizes the world today, and even more so in the future, employability should of necessity be understood as a multi-dimensional construct whose definition and assessment should consider as many and as varied aspects of life as possible.

To repeat, employability is the entire corpus of a university graduate's attributes, which consist of the knowledge, skills, attitudes, competencies and dispositions that may qualify them for one or more positions of employment, including self-employment, and which, subject to the prevailing and/or emerging socio-cultural, political, economic, and physical/natural environments would help them to remain progressively productive and valuable in all the personal, social, and economic spheres of their life.

Such understanding of employability foregrounds the concept of graduate identity, which is a comprehensive composite of attributes that cover the personal, social, and vocational abilities, competencies and dispositions of an individual graduate. From extant literature, 19 graduate attributes were crystallized to flesh up the construct of employability. Each attribute is now discussed in the following paragraphs.

Specialized/professional/vocational Competence

This refers to the specific knowledge of concepts, principles, methods, procedures and techniques, or simply the expertise required to perform specific tasks in a particular occupation or profession. The basis of this competence is taken to be disciplinary knowledge. Hence the development of this competence – which is also commonly referred to as 'job-specific skills' or 'technical skills' – has been traditionally assumed to be the function of universities through the teaching of job-specific, or vocational, or, in the current vocabulary, 'market-relevant' courses (Barnett, 2000).

Oral Communication Competence

This denotes the ability and capacity of an individual to articulate ideas and opinions verbally to the extent that the message they intend to pass across will be understood by the recipients. This is a universal attribute which is vital in practically every sphere of a graduate's life. Oral communication can be either informal, such as real-time, face-to-face person to person or group conversations, or telephone and other online conversations; or formal, such as real-time formal presentations (with or without the aid of technology), formal video presentations, formal group conversations and interviews. Another component of this attribute is the ability to negotiate, which entails the quality of expressing one's own feelings and opinions while respecting the feelings and opinions of others in order to achieve a 'win-win' outcome (STEMNET, 2017).

Written Communication Competence

Closely related to oral communication competence is the ability and capacity of an individual to relay information in writing in a clear, concise and coherent manner so that the recipient can understand the message. Written communication competence is gauged through the ability to produce all or any of the following: memos, letters, technical reports, speeches, briefings, press releases, emails, newspaper articles, website content and other pieces of writing. Just like in oral communication competence, the ability to negotiate is an integral characteristic of written communication competence. The components of this competence include language (both linguistic and grammatical correctness), audience (who the message is intended for – culture is a concomitant here), conventions (for instance, what is the stipulated format of the particular piece of writing), and others. Just like oral communication, written communication is developed progressively throughout all levels of the education system culminating in the university (Clokie and Fourie, 2016).

Mathematical Competence

Sometimes referred to as ‘numerical competence’ or ‘numeracy’, mathematical competence is the ability and agility to use mathematical concepts, principles and procedures to obtain meaningful information, present and support evidence, or to demonstrate a point (STEMNET, 2017). Mathematical competence is manifested in various ways including: an understanding and application of the language and concepts of mathematics especially the basic mathematical operations: addition, subtraction, multiplication and division, the ability to use statistical software, data analysis and interpretation, calculating and interpreting percentages, decimals and fractions, working with ratios and proportions, understanding basic finance, and analytical thinking (Othman, Buntat, Sulaiman, Salleh & Herawan, 2010).

Digital Competence

Digital competence or ‘digital literacy’ is a new terminology in the literature. The older terminology refers to ‘computer literacy’ or ‘ICT competence’. Though the latter terminology is more commonly used especially in curriculum and instructional technology discourse, the former is adopted for this study because is deemed to be broader and more futuristic. Digital competence may be defined as the effective and efficient use of digital technology, communicative tools and/or networks to access, manage, integrate, evaluate, create, and disseminate information in order to function progressively and productively in a knowledge society (International ICT Literacy Panel, 2002). This competence entails ICT or computer literacy, information literacy, media literacy, and communication and collaboration using digital media (McLoughlin, 2011).

Critical Thinking and Problem-Solving Ability

The ability to think critically and solve problems is a vital characteristic of all successful individuals in both professional and personal life. In fact, it was predicted, and it came to pass, that by the year 2020, complex problem solving (with critical thinking as an implied concomitant) would be one of the core graduate attributes in the world of work (World Economic Forum, 2016). Critical thinking has been defined as “the intellectually disciplined process of actively and skillfully conceptualizing, applying, analyzing, synthesizing and/or evaluating information gathered from, or generated by, observation, experience, reflection, reasoning, or communication, as a guide to belief and action” (Scriven and Paul, 1987, para 1). From this definition, critical thinking is a cognitive process which culminates in the ‘action’ that is problem solving. It follows then that problem solving is the process of discovering or identifying or anticipating a problem and seeking its solution *through* critical thinking. Critical thinking and problem solving are thus integral components of a processes, whose ultimate goal is the formulation of appropriate and effective solutions to current and future problems that either an individual or a group may encounter. This process may be viewed as a continuum, with critical thinking initiating the process and problem solving concluding it.

Self-drive

Also referred to as autonomy, self-drive is an individual's quality of generating own ideas and personally processing the transformation of these ideas into reality. Self-drive is an intrinsic attribute which manifests an individual's internal locus of control. The internal locus of control is a composite of an individual's self-concept – how the individual views and appreciates oneself, especially the appreciation of one's strengths and weaknesses; self-confidence – an individual's feeling of trust in one's abilities, qualities and judgment including, and especially, trust in one's ability to endure and overcome challenges and setbacks; personal initiative – an individual's innovativeness and the quality of pioneering ideas and actions; self-efficacy – an individual's belief in one's capacity to accomplish certain tasks or play certain roles effectively and efficiently, and in one's ability to influence and even control the events that affect one's life; and self-management – an individual's personal discipline and regulating of one's emotions, passions, and motivations. This includes the ability to take responsibility for one's behavior and the ability to plan for and organize one's time and use of resources (Bandura, 1994; Glossary of Education Reform, 2013).

The Ability to Work in a Team

More commonly referred to as 'teamwork', this denotes an individual's disposition to and competence in working harmoniously with other individuals from diverse philosophical, disciplinary, cultural, geographic, social, and economic backgrounds to accomplish a common task or achieve a shared goal. This can be during conversations, projects, meetings, or any other collaborative activities (Indeed, 2019; STEMNET, 2017, Wagner, 2010). The ability to work in a team work is a generic competence and one of the most sought for essential employability attributes by employers. Yet the relevance and significance of this attribute transcends employment or the world of work. It is applicable and required in every aspect of an individual's life where working and indeed living with others is the norm.

Integrity

Integrity refers to an individual's quality of holding and exhibiting strong ethical and moral principles, and being honest and honorable at all times in all places irrespective of who is or is not watching, and regardless of the consequences. Integrity is a fundamental human virtue which is expected and required of every individual in virtually every culture. Thus integrity is an essential attribute in every sphere of an individual's life. An individual of integrity would typically exhibit most or all of the following attributes: honesty, trustworthiness, dependability, loyalty, fairness and justice, loyalty, respect, humility, generosity, graciousness, responsibility, diligence, patience, and kindness. Such an individual exhibits moral uprightness and high ethical values. These are attributes that define a holistically virtuous person in a family, in an institution of learning, in the workplace, among friends, and in the wider society (ICI, 2016; Indeed, 2019; Price-Mitchell, 2015).

Responsibility

Responsibility is the obligation of an individual to satisfactorily perform a role, duty, or task that is either assigned or ascribed to him or her, and to be answerable for the performance. Responsibility is thus the sum of an individual's choices and decisions concerning that which is expected of them, whether at home, or in school, or in the workplace, or in the wider community (Armstrong, 2016). A corollary of responsibility is accountability, which is a responsible person's willingness and readiness to accept the consequences of his or her actions. In other words, a person who assumes responsibility automatically becomes accountable for his or her performance. Responsibility is therefore an absolute individual attribute which cannot be delegated. Where an individual is assisted to perform his duties through delegation, the responsibility for the performance of that duty lies with that individual and never with those that assisted (Armstrong, 2016).

Adaptability

Adaptability, also referred to as 'flexibility', 'coping skills' or even 'cope-ability', is a core skill of the future. This reference to the future is deliberate and appropriate; adaptability is essentially a response to what happens a moment after the present. The future is as unpredictable, uncertain and unknowable as it is 'super-complex' and ever-changing (Barnett, 2000). Yet the individual is expected and has to anticipate, fit into, and thrive in this future. The most appropriate and essential tool for doing so is adaptability, which is the ability and willingness to respond quickly and positively to new information, changing conditions or circumstances, and unforeseen challenges at work and in life as a whole. Some of these challenges include new 'knowledges' and new ways of knowing, new technologies, new kinds of competition, new processes, new roles and responsibilities and new and more complex ways of relating and interacting (Conference Board of Canada, 2000; Duszynski, 2020).

The Willingness to Learn Continuously

Learning is the quality of understanding new knowledge and skills, and adjusting one's behavior in order to apply these knowledge and skills effectively in appropriate contexts. The willingness to learn continuously denotes an individual's disposition, tendency and commitment to learn so as to enhance or improve one's knowledge, skills and abilities frequently and continuously (Babos, Lubyova & Studena, 2015; Indeed, 2019). This has three aspects: willingness to learn, which has to do with an individual's attitude toward and motivation for learning – that is, liking and wanting to learn; ability to learn, which has to do with an individual's strategies, techniques, skills and methods of learning – that is, how an individual learns; and continuity of learning, which has to do with both the frequency and the scope of learning – that is, how often and how much does an individual deliberately set out to learn.

Creativity and Innovation

Creativity and innovation are employability buzz words that are commonly misunderstood. More often than not, they are used as synonyms, which they are not. They are closely related yet distinct concepts. Creativity is "the ability to produce novel and useful ideas that are not only original and make a unique contribution to the field, but also serve some purpose or fulfill a need" (Lai, Yarbro, DiCerrbo and De Geest, 2018, p.3), or the disposition to be original or inventive and to apply lateral thinking – which is the ability to perceive patterns that are not obvious. On the other hand, innovation is "the successful application of creativity within an organization. Innovation requires implementing a creative idea and bringing it to fruition" (Lai et al., 2018, p.6). Creativity is therefore "a precursor of innovation" (Rampersad and Patel, 2014, p.3). As Kingsley (2020) asserts, "it is creative thinking which assists a person to come up with new and brilliant ideas," while innovation "is the process of bringing those ideas to life" (para.2)..

Commitment to Work

Commitment to work, or having a strong work ethic, is 'a must-have' trait for any individual engaged in any kind of work (Cote, 2019). This is because an individual who is committed to work operates on the "principle that hard work is intrinsically virtuous or worthy of reward" (Jenkins, 2017, para.6). Such an individual approaches any work with a positive attitude of determination and dedication to work, and will therefore be dependable, productive and valuable in whatever he or she does. It is no wonder then that employers rank commitment to work very highly among their preferred employability attributes (Cote, 2019; ICI, 2016; Indeed 2020).

Interpersonal Intelligence

Sometimes referred to as social intelligence, social skills, interpersonal skills, people skills, being people-smart, or even the generic life skills or soft skills, interpersonal intelligence is one of Howard Gardner's 'multiple intelligences'. It refers to the ability and disposition of an individual to interact and relate meaningfully and effectively with other people in all avenues of life at all times (Gardner, 1983). Since inter-person interaction is inevitable and essential for virtually every individual, "it is no exaggeration to say that interpersonal skills are the foundation for success in life." This is because "people with strong interpersonal skills tend to be able to work well with other people, including in teams or groups, formally and informally." Moreover, such people "communicate effectively with others, whether family, friends, colleagues, customers, or clients." As a result, those with high interpersonal intelligence enjoy "better relationships at home and at work" (SkillsYouNeed, 2017, para.2).

Time Management

Time management is closely related to planning and organizational competence (which shall be discussed later on), but it is distinctly critical as a graduate attribute required in all facets of an individual's life. Time management is the ability of an individual to plan and utilize time effectively, efficiently and productively. Proper time management is highly valued by employers. Yet it is not only employers who value time management; whether at home, in school, or anywhere else, time management is a highly ranked and absolutely expected attribute. For the individual, good time management has the following benefits: greater productivity and efficiency, a better professional reputation, less stress, increased opportunities for both personal and professional advancement, a healthy life-work balance, and greater opportunities to achieve important life and career goals (Mindtools, 2020).

Leadership

Leadership is the ability and disposition to influence others to envision a common goal and the act of motivating them to work together to attain the goal. Leadership is a highly sought after attribute for all people, but more especially for university graduates, both in the workplace and in society as a whole (Indeed, 2020). Leadership as an act should be distinguished from leadership as a position. There are many individuals who occupy positions of leadership yet they are bereft of the qualities and traits of leadership. Leadership is not 'a skill' *per se*; rather, it is "a set of traits, skills and behaviors which relies on character, integrity, attitude and self-awareness" (Holmes, n.d.). Thus leadership is combination of competencies and traits working together (Allio, 2005; Harvey, 2003; Indeed, 2020; Wagner, 2010).

Appropriate Dressing and Personal Grooming

Appropriate dressing and personal grooming form the first impression about an individual and are therefore critical factors that determine how the individual will be viewed and treated by others. Appropriate dressing and personal grooming is "a way of expressing respect for the situation and the people in it" (Goman, 2012, para.7). There are three primary goals of appropriate dressing and personal grooming: one, to feel comfortable and good about oneself, hence enhancing self-confidence and esteem; two, to make others comfortable being around you, hence enhancing your dignity and respectability; and three, to be safe and secure when performing specific tasks which may require specific ways of dressing and grooming so as to avoid damage or injury (McKay, 2018).

Planning and Organizational Competence

These are two closely related graduate attributes that are essential for both individual and corporate success. Planning is the ability and disposition of an individual (or a team) to envision a desired future, set goals and targets to actualize that desire, and develop strategies to attain the goals and accomplish the targets while anticipating and putting in place ways of mitigating potential challenges that may complicate or even sabotage the realization turning of the vision. On the other hand, organizational competence, or simply organizing, refers to the capacity of an individual or organization to harness and use time, energy, mental capacity, physical space, people, and other relevant resources effectively and efficiently in order to achieve a desired outcome (Duszinsky, 2020). Planning precedes organization, and organization emanates from planning. Planning is the thinking, while organization is the action.

These 19 attributes balance the personal, intellectual, social and productive dimensions that compose a graduate identity. They are therefore holistic and universal. To realize a graduate identity that comprises these characteristics, there is need for a model of holistic graduate development. One such model is proposed here.

The Holistic Graduate Identity Curriculum (HoGIC) Model

The literature on employability exhibits a proliferation of models conceived as frameworks to explain or describe the construct of employability. Some of the more commonly cited of such models include: the USEM model (Knight & Yorke, 2002); the DOTS model (Law & Watts, 1977); the SOAR model (Kumar, 2015); CareerEDGE key to employability model (Dacre Pool & Sewel, 2007); the Educator-Employee-Employer-Employability (4E) framework (Pheko & Molefhe, 2016); the employABILITY thinking model (Bennet, 2018); the Graduate Employability 2.0 model (Bridgstock, 2020); and the Relational Graduate Employability paradigm (Lackovic, 2019). These models focus either on how individuals (should) develop skills for personal success, or on how the development of individual skills includes social and /or cultural aspects (Cook, 2022). What is missing here is a model that explicitly foregrounds the university curriculum as the arena for developing and/or enhancing the individual's employability through a holistic process of defining graduate identity and the relationship between the curriculum and the environment within which it is enacted. To fill this gap, a Holistic Graduate Identity Curriculum (HoGIC) model is hereby proposed.

The HoGIC model is essentially a framework with three integral components: the environment within which curriculum is enacted, the curriculum of a specific institution, and graduate identity. While these components may seemingly be considered in isolation, in the HoGIC model they are interdependent and interrelated. The HoGIC model is presented in graphic form in figure 1:

Figure 1. The Holistic Graduate Identity Curriculum model

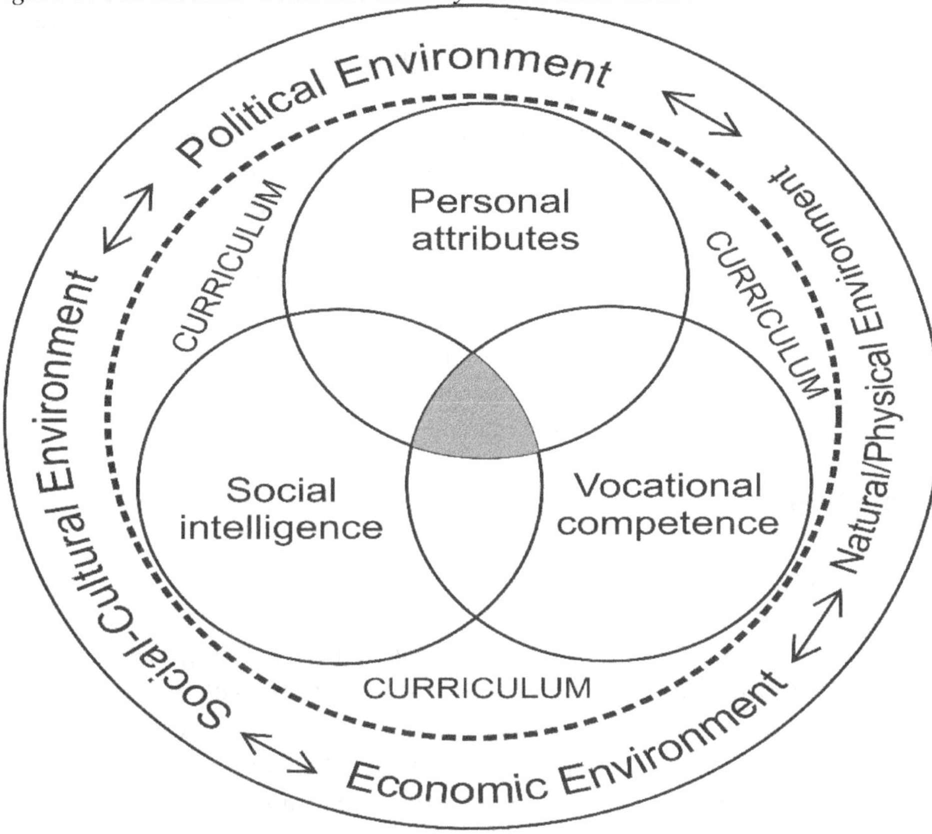

Note: conceptualized and designed by the author

Environment

The environment within which a curriculum is conceptualized and operationalized is crucial to the success or failure of that curriculum. Every curriculum developer needs to acknowledge and understand this environment. It is important to consider how the environment, or aspects of it, will influence the curriculum and also how the curriculum may influence it. The curriculum environment, or milieu, or context is the totality of the forces which influence and which may be influenced by curriculum. While such forces are numerous, the HoGIC model narrows them to four: political, socio-cultural, economic, and natural/physical environmental forces.

The political environment refers mostly to political decisions and actions that impact on the design and delivery of curriculum in the university. This includes laws and policies that have a direct or indirect bearing on university education. The sociocultural environment refers to the many and varied societal and cultural forces that influence what goes on in the university. The economic environment refers mainly to both the financial and material resources available to institutions and individuals (especially students) in the pursuit of curriculum outcomes, and the opportunities available to graduates to exploit their potential in the world of work. The natural/physical environment refers to both the physical elements such as topography and climate and unpredictable natural phenomena such as floods, famines, pandemics which may somehow influence the operations of a university.

As is evident in Fig.1, the environment encompasses the curriculum. Yet the boundary, if it may be referred to as such, between the environment and the curriculum is porous. This porosity signifies the constant symbiosis between the environment and the curriculum; the environment impacts on or influences the curriculum, while the curriculum in turn seeks to either manage or manipulate the environment.

Curriculum

Each university has its own unique curriculum. Irrespective of this uniqueness, it is important, for the purpose of this model, that a common conception of curriculum is adopted. Thus in the context of the HoGIC curriculum is conceptualized as "the intentions for learning; the actions, interactions, and processes elicited and directed by these intentions; and the actual learning that emanates from the prevailing context" (Nyandusi, 2017). This conceptualization denotes a holistic curriculum, one that evinces the relationships between the four fundamental components of a curriculum namely: the context, the inputs, the process(es), and the product(s).

Such a holistic curriculum is achieved through action in three key arenas: one, pedagogy and assessment, where the focus is on experiential and practical learning approaches such as exploration, experimentation, learning by doing and reflection in authentic contexts, and assessment methodologies that focus on evaluating understanding and knowledge transfer rather memory and knowledge recall. Two, work experience, which refers to authentic work-based, work-related, or work-integrated learning such as attachment, internship, fieldwork, or practicum, or at the very least, work-related learning such as case studies, employer/expert talks, role playing, workplace simulation, or work place tours and field trips. Three, an institutional culture that fosters and promotes employability. Such a culture includes a deliberate, diverse and vibrant co-curricular activities program, a compulsory careers education complement where learners develop, among others, job searching skills, CV construction skills, interview competencies, and career selection and planning skills (Cook, 2022; Lau et al., 2014; Lowden et al., 2011; Rowe & Zegwaard, 2017).

As far as employability curriculum is concerned, out of the proliferation of conceptions and models, there are three principal approaches to delivering employability through the university curriculum: total embedding, explicit embedding and integration, and parallel development. In total embedding, employability skills are implicitly taught but not explicitly assessed. Employability as a concept has low visibility and is often not taught in a real work context. Explicit embedding and integration is an approach where employability skills are explicitly taught and overtly assessed. Employability is therefore a highly visible concept that is always taught in a real work context. In parallel development, employability skills are taught in or as separate courses, often as 'bolt-on' courses with limited or little contextualization. While it is true, as Knight and Yorke (2004, p. 2) point out, that in the supercomplex world of employability, "no single, ideal prescription for the embedding of employability can be provided", the general consensus is that of the three approaches discussed here, explicit embedding and integration has the highest impact in developing employability in university students (Cook, 2022; Fraser et al., 2019; Rowe & Zegwaard, 2017; Yorke & Knight, 2004). As such, the explicit embedding and integration approach is the one advocated for in the HoGIC model.

In the HoGIC model, there are three integrated curriculum spaces across which leaning is intended to take place: academic curricular learning, co-curricular learning, and extra-curricular learning. these learning spaces, and the specific learning activities activities for each space, are presented in table 1.

Table 1. Learning Spaces in the HoGIC model

Academic Intra-curricular Learning	Co-curricular learning	Extra-curricular learning
• Discipline-specific coursework including assessment • Research • Cross/trans-disciplinary learning • General education • Work Integrated Learning i.e. internship, industrial or field attachment, practicums • Workplace tours and field trips	• Academic/profession-related clubs and societies • Conferences, workshops and seminars • Employment/career fairs • Career guidance and counseling • Careers education including help with CV writing, cover letter writing and interview skills • Personal Development Planning	• Voluntary community service • Games and sports • Non-academic/profession-related clubs and societies • Creative and performing arts • Hobbies • Part-time non-discipline-related jobs (including university work-study programs) • Student leadership

Graduate identity

The ultimate purpose of the curriculum is to produce a graduate who will either adapt to or manipulate the environment so as to remain productive and valuable to self and the community. To produce such a graduate, the curriculum, across its three spaces, should endeavor to develop in each of its graduates a holistic identity that is the confluence of personal attributes, social intelligence, and vocational competencies. This confluence is achieved in the shaded segment at the center of fig.1. At this confluence, a graduate may be said to have achieved multicompetence.

Personal attributes are qualities, characteristics or personality traits that define an individual's abilities, disposition and behavior. These include intellectual capacity, self-drive, emotional intelligence, resilience, creativity and innovativeness, critical thinking and problem solving skills, responsibility, integrity, willingness to learn continuously, adaptability, time management, and appropriate dressing and personal grooming.

Social intelligence is an individual's ability to successfully get into and maintain interpersonal relationships, to navigate diverse social contexts, and to be a valuable and productive member in a social setting. Social intelligence is manifested through: oral communication competence, effective listening skills, interpersonal intelligence, cross-cultural intelligence, the ability to work in a team, conflict management and resolution skills, empathy, leadership, and social networking and relationship management skills.

Vocational competence refers to both an individual's technical or specialized knowledge and skills which predispose them to occupy a given position in a given occupation and the individual's broad and transferable skills and aptitudes that are applicable across various positions in diverse occupations. Vocational competence is exhibited through: job-specific skills or professional/occupational expertise, digital competence, written communication skills, a positive work ethic, mathematical skills, planning and organizational competence, and career planning and development, including opportunity awareness and job searching skills.

CONCLUSION

This chapter has advanced the argument that university education is faced with and has to respond to the supercomplexity that defines life and living in the 21st century. To do this, university curricula have to transcend traditional and narrow conceptions of the function of a university and adopt wider frameworks for producing graduates who will fit into and manage the supercomplex world. One such wide framework that has been comprehensively discussed here is employability.

This chapter has taken the stance that employability is a composite construct that defines a graduate's holistic identity – characterized the nineteen elaborated attributes/competencies -- in relation to their total environment. This relationship is mediated by explicitly embedded and integrated university curricula enacted across three spaces: the intra-curricular or academic space, the co-curricular space, and the extra-curricular space. The end-result in such a curriculum enterprise is a multicompetent graduate who exhibits a high degree of personal attributes, social intelligence, and vocational competence.

FUTURE RESEARCH DIRECTION

While the university is charged with producing a multicompetent graduate for a supercomplex world, the initial levels of education form the foundation of learning for the graduate. It is therefore incumbent upon graduate identity and employability researchers to interrogate the nexus between the university curriculum and curricula in the earlier phases of education such as early childhood, primary, and secondary schools.

REFERENCES

Allio, R. J. (2005). Leadership development: Teaching versus learning. *Management Decision*, 43(7), 1071–1077. DOI: 10.1108/00251740510610071

Armstrong, J. (2016). *Responsibility in the workplace*. https://www.linkedin.com/pulse/responsibility-workplace-jason-armstrong

Babos, P., Lubyova, M., & Studena, I. (2015). *Lifelong learning is a growing factor in employability*. Policy Brief. LLLight in Europe Research Consortium.

Bandura, A. (1994). *Self-efficacy*. John Wiley & Sons.

Barnett, R. (2000a). *Realizing the university in an age of supercomplexity*. Open University Press.

Barnett, R. (2000b). Supercomplexity and the curriculum. *Studies in Higher Education*, 25(3), 255–265. DOI: 10.1080/713696156

Barnett, R. (2000c). University knowledge in an age of supercomplexity. *Higher Education*, 40(4), 409–422. http://www.jstor.or/stable/3448008. DOI: 10.1023/A:1004159513741

Barnett, R. (2012). Learning for an unknown future. *Higher Education Research & Development*, 31(1), 65–77. DOI: 10.1080/07294360.2012.642841

Baron, R., & Kenny, D. A. (1986). The moderator-mediator variable distinction in social psychological research: Conceptual, strategic and statistical considerations. *Journal of Personality and Social Psychology*, 51(6), 1173–1182. DOI: 10.1037/0022-3514.51.6.1173 PMID: 3806354

Bennett, D. (2018). Graduate employability and higher education: past, present and future. *HERDSA review of higher education*, 5, 31-61. https://www.herdsa.org.au/herdsa-review-higher-education-vol-5/31-61

Bridgstock, R. (2020). *Graduate employability 2.0: Enhancing the connectedness of learners, programs and higher education institutions* [Final report]. Australian Government Department of Education, Skills and Employment. https://ltr.edu/au/resources/FS15-0241_Bridgstock_report_2020.pdf

Catcheside, K. (2012, March 5). The benefits of a university education. *The Guardian*. https://www.theguardian.com/higher-education-network/blog/2012/mar/05/benefits-of-a-university-education

Clokie, T. L., & Fourie, E. (2016). Graduate employability and communication competence: Are undergraduates taught relevant skills? *Business and Professional Communication Quarterly*, 79(4), 442–463. DOI: 10.1177/2329490616657635

Conference Board of Canada (2000). *Employability skills 2000+*. www.conferenceboard.ca/education

Cook, E.J. (2022). A narrative review of graduate employability models: their paradigms, and relationships to teaching and curricula. *Journal of Teaching and Learning for Graduate Employability*. DOI:DOI: 10.21153/jtlge2022vol3no1art1483

Cote, A. (2019). The benefits of a strong work ethic, and howit can help you land and keep your dream job. https://medium.com/paymo/the-benefits-of-a-strong-work-ethic

Crosling, G., & Ward, I. (2002). Oral communication: The workplace needs and uses of business graduate employees. *English for Specific Purposes*, 21(1), 41–57. DOI: 10.1016/S0889-4906(00)00031-4

Dacre-Pool, L., & Sewell, P. (2007). The key to employability: Developing a practical model of graduate employability. *Education + Training*, 49(4), 277–289. DOI: 10.1108/00400910710754435

Duszynski, M. (2020). *Top 10 employability skills: definition and list of examples*. https://zety.com/blog/employability-skills

Frankham, J. (2017). Employability and Higher Education:The follies of the 'productivity challenge in the teaching excellence framework. *Journal of Education Policy*, 32(5), 628–641. DOI: 10.1080/02680939.2016.1268271

Fraser, C. J., Duignan, G., Stewart, D., & Rodrigues, A. (2019). Overt and covert: Strategies for building employability skills of vocational education graduates. *Journal of Teaching and Learning for Graduate Employability*, 10(1), 157–172. DOI: 10.21153/jtlge2019vol10no1art782

Gardner, H. (1983). *Frames of mind: a theory of multiple intelligence*. Basic Books.

Gibbons, M. (1998, October 5-9). *Higher education relevance in the 21st century*. [Paper presentation]. *UNESCO World Conference on Higher Education*, Paris, France.

Glossary of Education Reform. (2013). *Locus of control*. https://edglossary.org

Goman, C. K. (2012). *What it really means to dress for success*. https://www.forbes.com

Harvey, L. (2000). New realities: The relationship between higher education and employment. *Tertiary Education and Management*, 6(1), 3–17. DOI: 10.1080/13583883.2000.9967007

Harvey, L. (2003). *Transitions from higher education to work*. ESECT.

Hinchliffe, G. (2005, January 27-28). *Graduate employability: a need for realism?* [Paper presentation]. Ninth quality in higher education international seminar, Birmingham, UK.

Holmes, M. (n.d.). Can leadership be taught? https://www.academia.edu/can-leadership-be-taught

Indeed (2019). *Employability skills: definition and 10 examples*. https://www.indeed.com/career-advice/finding-a-job/employability-skills?from=careeradvive-US&subfrom=article#4

International Careers Institute (ICI). (2016). *The top 8 skills employers are looking for*. https://www.ici.net.au/blog/the-top-8-skills-employers-are-looking-for

International ICT Literacy Panel. (2002). *Digital transformation: a framework for ICT literacy*. https://www.ets.org/media/research/pdf/ICTREPORT.pdf

International Labour Organization (ILO). (2021). *Assessment of public employment and active labour market policies in Kenya*. ILO.

Jenkins, R. (2017). *1 useful way to instill a strong work ethic in millennials*. https://www.inc.com/ryan-jenkins

Kingsley, D. (2020). Can innovation be taught? http://channels.theinnovationenterprise.com/can-innovation-be-taught

Kleinman, M., & West, A. (1998). Employability and the new deals: Employability is what the government wants but what exactly is it? *New Economy*, 5(3), 174–179. Advance online publication. DOI: 10.1111/1468-0041.00038

Knight, P. T., & Yorke, M. (2002). Employability through the curriculum. *Tertiary Education and Management*, 8(4), 261–276. DOI: 10.1080/13583883.2002.9967084

Kumar, A. (2015). *Enabling all learners to SOAR for employability: an inclusive, integrative pedagogy*. Higher Education Academy Innovative Pedagogy Series.

Lackovic, N. (2019). Graduate employabilityparadigm shift: towards greater socio-emotional and eco-technological relationaties of graduates' futures. In Peters, M., Jandric, P., & Means, A. (Eds.), *Education and technological unemployment* (pp. 193–212). Springer., DOI: 10.1007/978-981-13-6225-5_13

Lai, E. R., Yarbo, J., Di Cerbo, K., & De Geest, E. (2018). *Skills for today: what we know about teaching and assessing creativity*. Pearson.

Law, B., & Watts, A. G. (2003). *The DOTS analysis: original version*. http://hihohiho.com/memory/Gafdots.pdf

Lowden, K., Hall, S., Eliot, D., & Lewin, J. (2011). *Employers' perceptions of the employability skills of new graduates*. University of Glasgow.

Lucey, B. M. (2014). *How far have we drifted from the Newman/Humboldt idea of a university?* http://brian.lucey.worldpress.com/2014/06/06/how-far-have-we-drifted-from-the-newman-humboldt-idea-of-a-university?

McCowan, T. (2015). Should universities promote employability? *Theory and Research in Education*, 13(3), 267–285. DOI: 10.1177/1477878515598060

McGrath, S. (2009). *What is employability? Learning to support employability* [Project paper]. University of Nottingham.

McIlveen, P. (2018). *Defining Employability for the new era of work*. Sydney: Select Committee on the future of work and workers.

McKay, D. R. (2018). *How to dress professionally*. https://www.thebalancecareers.com/how-to-dress-professionally-524789

McLoughlin, C. (2011). *What ICT related skills and capabilities should be considered central to the definition of digital literacy*? https://researchbank.acu.edu/cgi/viewcontent.cgi?article=2658&content=fea_pub

McQuaid, R. W., & Lindsay, C. (2005). The concept of employability. *Urban Studies (Edinburgh, Scotland)*, 42(2), 197–219. DOI: 10.1080/0042098042000316100

Mindtools (2020). *What is time management? Working smarter to enhance productivity*. https://www.mindtools.com/pages/article/newHTE_00.htm

Mohee, R. (2019). *A guide to integrating employability in higher education institutions: The Commonwealth of Learning's employability model*. Commonwealth of Learning.

Moll, I. (2005). Curriculum responsiveness: the anatomy of a concept. In Griesel, H. (Ed.), *Curriculum responsiveness: case studies in higher education* (pp. 1–9). South African Universities Vice Chancellors Association.

Nalami, J., & Waswa, S. (2023). FKE urges training institutions to tailor their programmes to bridge the skills divide. http://www.kenyanews.go.ke

National Institute for Newman Studies (2007). *Newman reader – works of John Henry Newman.*

Nawaz, N. (2013). Role of employability skills in management education: A review. *Zenith International Journal of Business Economics and Management Research*, 3(8), 34–45.

Nyandusi, C. (2017). Conceptualizing Curriculum. In A. Syomwene, C.M. Nyandusi, & A.M. Yungungu (Eds.) *Core Principles in Curriculum.* Pp. 3-13. Eldoret: Utafiti Foundation

Othman, H., Buntant, Y., Suleiman, A., Salleh, B. M., & Herawan, T. (2010). Applied mathematics can enhance employability skills through problem based learning (PBL). *Procedia: Social and Behavioral Sciences*, 8, 332–337. DOI: 10.1016/j.sbspro.2010.12.046

Otunga, R. N. (2010). *The dilemma of curriculum relevance in Kenya.* Moi University Press.

Prewitt, K. (2016). Higher education, society, and government: Changing dynamics. *Journal of Higher Education in Africa*, 2(1), 35–56. DOI: 10.57054/jhea.v2i1.1681

Price-Mitchell, M. (2015). Integrity in the classroom. *Psychology Today*. https://www.psychologytoday.com/blog/the-moment-youth/201509/integrity-in-the-classroom

Pukelis, K., Pileičikiene, N., Allan, A., & Dailidiene, E. (2007). European and National level strategies for competency-based curriculum development. HEGESCO. www.decowe.comstatic/uploaded/htmlarea/finalreporthegesco/European_National_and_Universities_Strategies_summary.pdf

Rampersad, G., & Patel, F. (2014). Creativity as a desirable graduate attribute: Implications for curriculum design and employability. *Asia Pacific Journal of Cooperative Education*, 15(1), 1–11.

Republic of Kenya. (1999). *Report of the Commission of Inquiry into the Education System of Kenya.* Government Printer.

Republic of Kenya. (2020). *National Skills Development policy.* Nairobi: Ministry of Education Rowe, A. D., & Zegwaard, K. E. (2017). Developing graduate employability skills and attributes: curriculum enhancement through work integrated learning. *Asia Pacific Journal of Cooperative Education*, 18(2), 87–99.

Scriven, M., & Paul, R. W. (1987). *Defining critical thinking.* [Paper presentation]. 8th Annual International Conference on Critical Thinking and Education Reform. https://www.criticalthinking/pages/defining-critical-thinking

SkillsYouNeed. (2017). *Interpersonal skills.* https://www.skillsyouneed.com/ips/interpersonal-skills.html

STEMNET. (2017). Top 10 employability skills. https://www.exeter.ac.uk/ambassadors/HESTEM/resources/General/STEMNET-employability-skills-guide.pdf

UNESCO (1998). *World declaration on education for all for the twenty first century: vision and action.*

UNESCO (2012). *Graduate employability in Asia*

Wagner, T. (2010). *The global achievement gap: why even our best schools don't teach the new survival skills our children need – and what we can do about it.* Basic Books.

Wedekind, V., & Mutereko, S. (2016). *Employability and curriculum responsiveness in post-school education and training*. Labour Market Intelligence Partnership.

Wilson, R., & Morieson, L. (2022). Belonging as a responsive strategy in times of supercomplexity and change. *Journal of University Teaching & Learning Practice*, 19(4). Advance online publication. https://ro.uow.edu.au/jutlp/vol19/iss4/03. DOI: 10.53761/1.19.4.3

World Bank. (2019). *Improving higher education performance in Kenya: A policy Report.* The World Bank.

World Economic Forum. (2016). *The future of jobs report.* http://www3.weforum.org/docs/WEF_future_of_jobs_.pdf

Yorke, M. (2006). *Employability in higher education: what it is – what it is not.* Higher Education Academy.

FURTHER READING

Abegglen, S., Burns, T., Maiers, S., & Sinfield, S. (2020). Supercomplexity: Acknowledging students' lives in the 21st century university. *Innovative Practice in Higher Education*, 4(1), 20–38.

Barnett, R. (2017). *The ecological university: a feasible utopia*. Routledge. DOI: 10.4324/9781315194899

Bengsten, S. S. E. (2017). Supercomplexity and the university: Ronald Barnett and the social philosophy of higher education. *Higher Education Quarterly*. Advance online publication. DOI: 10/1011/hequ/12153

Maxwell, R. and Armellini, A. (2019). *Identity, employability and entrepreneurship: the ChANGE framework of graduate attributes*. Higher education, skills and Work-based learning 9(1), 76-91 https://doi.org/DOI: 10/1108/HESWBL-02-2018-0016

Siivonen, P., Isopahkala-Bouret, U., Tomlinson, M., Korhonen, M., & Haltia, N. (Eds.). (2023). *Rethinking graduate employability in context*. Palgrave Macmillan., DOI: 10.1007/978-3-031-20653-5

DEFINITIONS OF KEY TERMS

Competencies: Competencies are the personal and professional attributes through which an employee lives up to the demands and expectations of his or her work. Competencies are the responsibilities, abilities, strengths and dispositions that characterize an employee in the course of discharging his/her duties in a given workplace.

Curriculum: Curriculum refers to all the programs and activities that shape or are meant to shape the intellectual, personal, social, and productive learning experiences of a student over the duration of their stay at the university.

Curriculum relevance: Curriculum relevance refers to the applicability and appropriateness of a given curriculum to the needs, interests, aspirations and expectations of learners and the society in general at a particular point in time, and the responsiveness of the curriculum to the continuously changing realities of everyday life and the world of work.

Employability Employability: is the entire corpus of a university graduate's attributes, which consist of the knowledge, skills, attitudes, competencies and dispositions that may qualify them for one or more positions of employment, including self-employment, and which would help them to remain progressively productive and valuable in all the personal, social, and economic spheres of their life.

Graduate identity: This is the composite of qualities, understandings, skills, capabilities and dispositions that are characteristic of an individual who has graduated from a university.

Supercomplexity: Supercomplexity is a situation characterized by multiple and contesting frames of reference in which an individual is obligated to make decisions

University: This is a formal institution of learning authorized to offer undergraduate courses across disciplines and specializations.

Chapter 11 Sustainability Competency Framework: A Practical Guide for Re-Orienting Higher Education Curricula

Peter Ngwa
The University of Yaounde I, Cameroon

Awono Mengada Gisèle Xaverie
The University of Yaounde II, Cameroon

ABSTRACT

It has become increasingly important worldwide, especially in the context of higher education, to support these skills in order to prepare students for employment in the 21st-century labor market that is focused on sustainability and alternative industries.A conceptual framework that describes the sustainability competencies that should be emphasized in higher education curricula to provide graduates with employability skills. Findings demonstrated take into account the needs of the labor market

INTRODUCTION

It is necessary to reorient higher education curricula to support competencies (disposition, ability and behaviour) in order to address sustainability competencies in the teaching and learning processes (Sinakou, Donche & Van Petegem, 2022). This review of the literature looks critically at concerns related to sustainability education and sustainability competences, examining several facets of the field. Additionally, it requires a critical analysis of the literature on global initiatives to enhance learners' sustainability competencies and to improve 21st century learners' knowledge and

DOI: 10.4018/979-8-3693-6930-2.ch011

employability in the knowledge economy, particularly in the context of Africa. In this context, this study presents the sustainability competence framework, a model for reorienting courses in higher education. Its goal is to help students develop their sustainability competencies. The study also looks at the inherent promise and challenges of such curriculum reorientation processes.

To attain the said aim this study examines the following questions:

1. What sustainability competencies should be fostered in higher education curricula to enable learners become change agents and better competitors for employability in the 21st century knowledge economy?
2. What are the challenges and opportunities inherent in re-orienting higher education curricula to foster learners' sustainability competencies and enable them gain employment in sustainability alternative industries?

BACKGROUND

The globe of the twenty-first century faces numerous sustainability concerns, to mention a few: poverty, consumerism, pollution, and climate change. Humanity must be able to find answers to the worldwide sustainability difficulties that are becoming more and more complicated in order to improve living conditions and make the world a more sustainable environment. In this regard, education is a crucial tool since it can be utilized to reorient students' ideas and attitudes toward sustainability, inspiring them to work toward changing both society and themselves and so encouraging sustainable actions (Chambers, 2009). Higher education must reorient its curricula to promote sustainability competencies in order to meet these goals. This will produce graduates who are more competitive in the labor market for sustainability-focused jobs and who have the knowledge, skills, and abilities to find novel and creative solutions to the global sustainability challenges (Sinakou, Donche & Van Petegem, 2024).

Higher education is still falling behind in these views, despite the growing need for sustainable alternatives to global issues. Research indicates that individuals with higher education degrees engage in more environmentally unfriendly behavior when making policy decisions and taking other actions. This can be partially explained by the fact that their higher education training has not adequately prepared them to handle sustainability issues.

It is now globally imperative to prepare graduates with the necessary sustainability competencies to become change agents in the knowledge economy, particularly in Africa's emerging economies, which are attempting to meet the challenges of African sociocultural, political, and economic development in addition to competing with the rest of the world in the labor market (Wu & Wang, 2024).

Wade (2012) makes the case that, in order to address some of the sustainability-related issues that mankind is currently facing, sustainability education is desperately needed. The "major challenges of climate change, environmental degradation, poverty and social inequality" that humanity faces, according to her explanation, "have made it clear that learning to live sustainably has never been more urgent" (p.147). Thus, in order to contribute both individually and collectively to the search for solutions to these sustainability-related issues, people everywhere must increase their knowledge, awareness, comprehension, and skill sets (Vargas-Merino, Rios-Lama & Panez-Bendezú, 2024). Thus, in order to contribute both individually and collectively to the search for solutions to these sustainability-related issues, people everywhere must increase their knowledge, awareness, comprehension, and skill sets (Vargas-Merino, Rios-Lama & Panez-Bendezú, 2024). In this sense, higher education has the capacity to play a significant role in the dissemination of knowledge and the development of sustainability competencies in students, which may lead to the generation of creative solutions and alternative ways of thinking in response to these societal and environmental issues.

The goal of this study is to modify higher education curricula to promote sustainability competencies. By doing this, we hope to give students the skills they need to become change agents for sustainability and to make them more employable in the technologically advanced and sustainability-focused labor market of the twenty-first century (Reimers, 2024).

Defining Sustainability Education

The concept of sustainability remains controversial with no universally acceptable definition. Generally, sustainability is conceived as the ability to maintain something for a long time at a specific rate or level (Das, Lekhya, Shreya, Shekinah, Babu & Boopathi, 2024). It is an undefined set of ideals which allow people and other living and non-living things to have dignity and satisfaction, and for human actions to be geared towards protecting the environment, fostering societal justice, economic prosperity and equity, and promoting cultural vitality and diversity (Vartiainen, Sormunen & Kangas, 2024). Many academics see the term "sustainable development," which is sometimes used synonymously with "sustainability," as an oxymoron because it is so ambiguous and loaded with meanings. It is still "fundamentally contradictory and irreconcilable" (Kates et al., 2005, p. 20). For instance, sustainability requires development to raise humankind's standard of living, yet development itself—whether sustainable or not—entails environmental damage and the disruption of some form of natural ecosystem, of which humans are a part.

The introduction of human civilization into the ecological system disrupts the homeostatic balance of the natural system, and when nature restores its equilibrium, it brings about catastrophic events for human cultures, including but not limited to earthquakes and tsunamis. What utility is a sawmill without a forest? posed this question in 1989 by ecological economist Herman Daly. This analogy illustrates the debates surrounding the idea of sustainable development quite well. While the goal of sustainable development is to minimize the impact of one subsystem's actions on the overall health of the primary ecosystem, development in one sector of the ecological system results in loss or degradation in the other sector.

Top-down methods of setting priorities and directing public policy are still crucial. This is demonstrated by the Sustainable Development Goals (SDGs), which take a comprehensive approach to identifying the evolving patterns of development. However, it is becoming more and more important to examine the small-scale, bottom-up projects that come from citizen engagement and civil society. These micro-level projects include intentional sustainable communities (ISCs), also referred to as ecovillages (Nogueira, Marques & Pinto, 2024).

Since the United Nations-sponsored World Commission on Environment and Development, Our Common Future published the Brundtland Report in 1987, which defined sustainable development as "development that meets the needs of the present without compromising the ability of future generations to meet their own needs" (UN, 1987), the term "sustainable development" has gained popularity worldwide and given rise to a wide range of definitions in the discourse (Mebratu, 1998). Sustainable development is defined as "improving the quality of life whilst living within the carrying capacity of the supporting ecosystems" (p. 2) by Huckle and Sterling (1996). Makrakis, Kostoulas-Makrakis, and Kanbar (2011) have expounded on sustainable development, stating that it involves "acting upon those decisions for advancing social, economic, and environmental wellbeing" (p. 6) and "making informed, contextual, and conscious decisions driven by the principles of solidarity, justice, accountability, equity, and transparency for the good of present and future generations, locally and globally."

Whether we view sustainable development as our greatest challenge or a subversive litany, every phase of our education system is being urged to declare its support for education for sustainable development (Vare & Scott, 2007, p.1 as cited in Makrakis, 2011b, p.6). In order to promote sustainability values and increase people's abilities to handle environmental and development concerns, education is essential. In order to achieve environmental ethics understanding, beliefs, and attitudes that support sustainable development, education is also essential (Huckle & Sterling, 1996). The process of learning how to make decisions that take into account the long-term health of the economy, the environment, and the fair development of all communities while fostering their cultures is known as education for sustainable development, or ESD. It makes it possible for people to acquire the values, information, abilities, and skills that support sustainable behavior, improve quality of life today, and protect the environment for coming generations. ESD equips people with the knowledge and skills to make decisions that lead to more environmentally friendly behavior. According to Shaeffer (2007), ESD is a collaboration that involves a variety of sectors and stakeholders, such as the media and the commercial sector, and employs a range of techniques to increase public awareness, educate the public, and provide training in order to advance sustainable development. It improves people's comprehension of the interconnections and complexity of the global sustainability issues that are tied to "their own values and those of the society in which they live" (p. 4).

Importance of Education for Sustainable Development

The relationship between ESD and life is highlighted in UNESCO's recently accepted framework for implementing ESD globally, called ESD for 2030. According to UNESCO (2020), ESD contributes "to the collective survival and prosperity of humanity." In light of the current environmental catastrophe, the framework emphasizes that all people have a duty. It states that we must "learn to live differently" (6) as well as "learn to live together sustainably on this planet" (iii). Thus, global ESD is presented in the framework as an inclusive endeavor involving all of humankind with the goal of enlightening individuals and groups to adopt new lifestyles. Nonetheless, considering how uneven the world is, the idea of implementing ESD globally on an equal footing with everyone appears problematic (Bylund, 2024).

ESD is vital for human development. UNESCO's vision of sustainability centres on developing a world where everyone can benefit from quality education and learn the values, behaviours and lifestyles required for a sustainable future and for positive societal transformation (UNESCO, 2005). ESD "informs people's values through an exploration of the fundamental principles of the way we live our lives now and the impact our lifestyles have on the environment and society" (Scottish Executive, 2006, p. IV). ESD "is a life-wide and lifelong endeavour which challenges individuals, institutions and societies to view tomorrow as a day that belongs to all of us, or it will not belong to anyone" (UNESCO, 2006, n.p.). Thus, Education for Sustainable Development is a process of learning how to make decisions that consider the long-term effects of human actions on the environment, promoting diversity in cultures, values and beliefs, equitable and green economic development as well as societal justice.

Figure 1. The Four Cornerstones of Sustainability

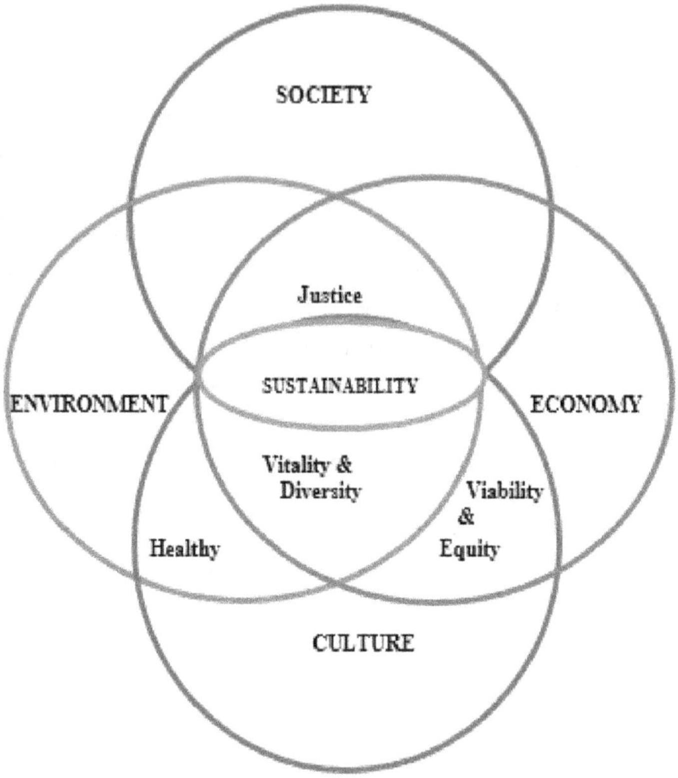

Source: (Besong, 2017)

ESD is synonymous with Education for Sustainability (EfS) and Sustainability Education (SE), and can be conceptualized as a holistic system with four interconnected and interdependent components, as shown in Figure 1. These components: economy, society, culture and the environment are important in attaining sustainability. Any actions in one area have positive and/or negative consequences on the other components. According to Yencken and Wilkinson (2001), the goal is to attain a positive balance on all the four components.

ESD assists learnrers in gaining information and honing skills necessary to lead sustainable lives and engage in civic engagement on Sustainable Development (SD) issues (Carban & Fisher, 2017). In order to assist learnrers comprehend the complexity of SD issues and acquire the skills required to address them, teachers play a critical role (Hungerford, 2010). Since they have a significant impact on students' development of SD-related action competence, the instructional strategies that teachers use while teaching SD concerns are extremely important Sinakou, Donche, Boeve-de Pauw & Van Petegem (2019a). However, the instructional beliefs and interests of teachers regarding instructional practice theory impact their actual practices in the classroom (Fang, 1996; Schiefele, Streblow Retelsdorf, 2013). These factors can also help or hinder teachers in implementing SD-related practices in their instruction (Schiefele, Streblow Retelsdorf, 2013).

These ESD teaching profiles serve to illustrate the practical application of ESD instruction. Investigating teachers' attitudes and behaviors in connection to their ESD instruction is one method of keeping an eye on ESD teaching methods in schools. To create new ESD programs for formal education settings, it is imperative to keep an eye on the way ESD is already being implemented and assess its practical application (UNESCO, 2014, 2020, UN, 2015; 2020, for example).

In the context of this study, the terms education for sustainable development (ESD), sustainability education (SE) sustainability is considered to mean one and the same thing, and are used interchangeably.

Instructional Practices in Education for Sustainable Development

According to a review of the research on in-class instructional strategies in ESD, action-oriented, pluralistic, and holistic teaching are crucial for developing students' action competence in relation to sustainable development concerns (Sinakou, et al. 2019a). All three approaches should be incorporated into the educational process, according to the literature, in order to provide students with a strong basis on which to build when addressing SD concerns as adults (Gericke, Höglund & Bergman, 2012, Sinakou et al., 2019a; 2019b). If one of these techniques is not applied, ESD instruction will not increase students' action competence in response to SD difficulties (Sinakou et al, 2019a). According to a recent definition provided by Sass, Boeve-de Pauw, Olsson, Gericke, De Maeyer & Van Petegem (2020), action competence is “the willingness, commitment, knowledge, skills and confidence to engage in finding solutions” to SD concerns (p. 6). Action competency enables learners to operate as (future) agents of change towards sustainability, hence facilitating their active participation in SD issues (UNESCO, 1977).

In holistic instructional practices, the environmental, economic, and social dimensions of sustainable development—as well as the ways in which they are interconnected—are all taken into account (Öhman, 2008; Sinakou, Boeve-de Pauw, Goossens & Van Petegem, 2018). It is also important to take into account the implications for the past, present, and future as well as for the local, regional, and global levels (Öhman, 2008; Summers & Childs, 2007). According to Berglund and Gericke (2016) and Sinakou et al. (2018), holistic teaching of ESD content highlights the consequences of SD concerns for each dimension and that SD issues should be explored across all dimensions at the same time. This is due to the fact that inconsistencies between the various dimensions would not be readily apparent if each dimension were addressed alone (Berglund & Gericke, 2016). However, in order to be able to make judgments, one must establish priorities when faced with the contradicting implications of the SD aspects (Berglund & Gericke, 2016). It is recommended that all three dimensions be analyzed in two ways: either as an integrated approach, as demonstrated by the works of Sinakou et al. (2018) and Berglund & Gericke (2016), or as independent considerations. Scholars that are ecocentric are skeptical about holism. As Kopnina (2014) notes, teaching ESD, which emphasizes all three aspects of SD, draws students' attention away from environmental problems. However, students' understanding of sustainability issues is enhanced by a teacher's comprehensive teaching methods, according to empirical research (Boeve-de Pauw, Gericke, Olsson & Berglund, 2015).

Pluralistic instructional practices enhance learners' ability to think critically, foster discussion, and push them to develop their own perspectives (Rudsberg & Öhman, 2010; Wals, 2007). When it comes to SD concerns, pluralistic teaching approaches acknowledge their complexity, uncertainty, and competing values (Ojala, 2013). Pupils are urged to discuss, consider, render decisions, and ultimately acknowledge the advantages of opposing viewpoints (Jickling, 1994). The educator permits the pupil to be exposed to a variety of viewpoints, presumptions, opinions, and values (Rudsberg & Öhman, 2010). Students will be able to comprehend the range of options when thinking about SD concerns in this way (Rudsberg & Öhman, 2010). This is especially crucial as, according to Van Poeck, Östman, and Öhman (2019), concerns related to SD are broadly political as well as moral and ethical (Van Poeck & Östman, 2019). According to Harness & Drossman (2011), Varela-Losada, Vega-Marcote, Pérez-Rodríguez, & Álvarez-Lires (2016), Hasslöf & Malmberg (2015), and other scholars, learners should be able to analyze, understand, and evaluate information and sources as well as question and challenge authorities in their capacity as "political subjects." It is important to motivate them to take an active part in their education, develop independent thought, accept accountability, and make well-informed choices (Hasslöf & Malmberg, 2015). A teacher should create learning environments with intentional connections between speaking and listening in order to prevent pushing students toward preset objectives (Birdsall, 2010). (Andersson & Öhman, 2016.). According to Ojala (2013), in class discussions, the majority of students will endorse or at the very least accept the views with the strongest evidence. However, as Sund (2008) contends, educators unavoidably communicate specific opinions, set an example for behavior, and send messages that are not explicitly stated.

By encouraging their learners to take action, teachers that use action-oriented educational approaches assist their pupils in being more action competent when it comes to SD issues (Chambers, 2009). Recent research indicates that educators ought to implement the subsequent action-oriented teaching strategies in their classrooms (Sinakou et al., 2019a; Sinakou, Donche, Van Petegem, 2022):

- ***Action-taking:*** learners adopt everyday lifestyle behavioural options. They can also recognize behavioural options at policy and business levels that may foster or at least not hinder sustainability. The students consciously participate in concrete actions in order to solve SD problems at personal, policy, and business levels. The actions may be direct, addressing the root of the problem, or indirect, aimed at making others aware of the problem and motivating them to take actions to solve it. The actions may be public or private, and taken at the individual or collective level.
- ***Leadership in learning and teaching:*** Students adopt an active role by taking responsibility and making decisions related to SD issues. They may shape their lessons regarding SD issues in collaboration with the teacher. The teacher should take the students' interests into account or the students themselves can indicate which themes they want to work on, instead of working with fixed themes chosen by the teacher alone.
- ***Peer interaction:*** While in class, the students should practice working individually, in small groups, and collectively.
- ***Community involvement:*** Students get out into the local community, or the local community comes into the school. The students seek knowledge about SD issues or looks for support in order to initiate actions about specific SDrelated problems. The community could be the students' parents, their neighbourhood, or other agents of the local region.
- ***Interdisciplinarity:*** Teachers should integrate multiple disciplines to help students obtain broad knowledge and adopt various methodologies which lead to informed actions. In relation to the above ESD action-oriented instructional practices, there may be some concern that (young) students may not be able to decide on appropriate actions, to initiate them, and successfully undertake them (Birdsall, 2010). However, it is through reflection on their lived experiences (Cincera & Krajhanzl, 2013; Padmanabha, 2018) that students (and thus future adults) can develop their willingness, commitment, knowledge, skills, and confidence to take part in actions to address SD issues (Sass et al, 2020). Moreover, action-oriented instructional practices give students the opportunity to become engaged in and for the community by going beyond the school boundaries and being confronted with, learning about, and addressing contextualized SD issues (Reid, Dillon, Ardoin & Ferreira, 2021).

Instructional Beliefs, Interests and Practices in ESD

There seems to be a correlation between instructors' beliefs and the methods they use in the classroom. As demonstrated above, in addition to beliefs, a teacher's interest is a major factor in determining the instructional strategies they will use when teaching ESD. The teacher's level of interest affects how ESD instructional beliefs are translated into instructional practices because interest acts as a mediator between instructional beliefs and practices (Reimers, 2024). Individuals are viewed as ordered wholes with interconnected components from a person-oriented perspective (Bergman & Lundh, 2015). As a result, we must investigate the instructional techniques, beliefs, and general interest in ESD among the teachers. As previously mentioned, ESD instructional approaches are influenced by the attitudes and interests of educators in the field (Anane, 2020). Empirical studies demonstrate the correlation between educators' opinions and areas of interest and how they approach teaching. According to (Reimers, 2024), teachers need more than just enthusiasm to be motivated. But it also strengthens other personal elements, such the drive for more in-depth understanding or interaction with the subjects of interest (Renninger & Hidi, 2011). Teachers' attitudes about education can be influenced by their interest (Reimers, 2024). The instructional behaviors of teachers are subsequently influenced by their instructional beliefs (Fang, 1996 & Fives & Buehl, 2012). Therefore, a teacher's interest could potentially directly affect the way they teach (Schiefele, Streblow Retelsdorf, 2013).

Sustainability in Higher Education

It is critical that higher education incorporate sustainable education practices and ideals. According to the DAAD/UNU-VIE report, integrating sustainability education into higher education institutions aids in their efforts to "promote social cohesion, enhance resource use efficiency, attain excellence in teaching and high-quality research, and project the status of such institutions as sustainable institutions" (2009). Therefore, it is imperative that institutions of higher learning adopt a sustainable education strategy.

Teaching the public about sustainability's tenets and practices helps promote education for sustainable development. The main engine for encouraging people to adopt sustainable behaviors is education for sustainable development. The goal of education for sustainable development, or ESD, is to provide citizens with the information, skills, and competencies necessary to build sustainable practices and procedures that will enable them to take action toward a sustainable future for all. In order to empower students to become real-world problem solvers and innovators and to give them a competitive edge when looking for jobs in the 21st-century sustainability-focused alternative industries, curricula in higher education must be reoriented to promote sustainability education competencies.

ROLE OF HIGHER EDUCATION IN FOSTERING THE DISSEMINATION OF SUSTAINABILITY

Education

Through awareness and education gained through formal, non-formal, and informal educational procedures, human behavior may change to embrace sustainability. Similar to other educational settings, higher education institutions have a significant role to play in disseminating knowledge and providing training on sustainability education (Besong, 2017). Universities and other higher education institutions are essential in promoting the principles of sustainability because they "train the coming generations of citizens" and possess the knowledge in all academic and scientific fields necessary to develop curricula and other solutions to issues related to unsustainable human behavior and development, as stated in the University Charter for Sustainable Development (Copernicus, 1994). The Talloires Declaration (2005), which was signed by twenty-nine university presidents, rectors, and vice chancellors from around the world, has further reinforced the urge for higher education to get involved in spreading the word about sustainability education. In order for their institutions to participate in offering sustainability education to their students and communities, university presidents were urged in the Talloires Declaration to "provide leadership and support to mobilize internal and external resources."

In relation to ESD, the goals of the UN Sustainable Development Agenda 2030 (UN, 2015), the Global Action Plan (2015), and the UN Decade of Education for Sustainable Development (DESD, 2005–2014) are to promote sustainable development values, activities, and principles in education to support a shift in learners' attitudes, behaviors, and values to ensure a more sustainable future for all. By 2030, all learners must have the knowledge and abilities necessary to advance sustainable development, including the promotion of competencies that allow learners to advance gender equality, human rights, sustainable living, peace and non-violence, global citizenship, and tolerance and appreciation of cultural diversity, according to Sustainable Development Goal 4.7.

It is the responsibility of higher education institutions and other educational environments to promote the exchange of knowledge and instruction regarding the methods of education for sustainable development. In order to provide learners, the skills they need to become change agents for sustainability and more employable in the information economy of the twenty-first century, one of the most important aspects of sustainability education is to integrate sustainability competencies into the teaching and learning process (Besong & Holland, 2015).

The Sustainability Curriculum

In higher education, addressing sustainability in programs and courses focuses on the processes of curriculum design, implementation, and evaluation. There are various ways to envision a curriculum. A curriculum is "the sum of all the formal and informal teaching and learning experiences" in educational courses or programs, according to UNESCO (2010). The curriculum with a focus on sustainability encompasses all of the learning opportunities that students have during the teaching and learning process. The curriculum with a focus on sustainability encompasses all of the learning opportunities that students have during the teaching and learning process (Besong, 2017). This covers the development, execution, and assessment procedures for creating a sustainable curriculum. The goal of this research is to better understand the competencies that should be cultivated in sustainability education in order to provide students with the skills they need to compete in the 21st-century sustainability alternative industries (Besong & Holland, 2015).

Sustainability Competencies

The idea of competence is complicated, difficult to define, and has diverse meanings in different situations and areas of practice (Stevenson 1996; FitzGerald, Walsh, and McCutcheon 2001; Watson, Stimpson, Topping, and Porock, 2002; Pedersen, 2007).

Competency is described (FitzGerald, Walsh, and McCutcheon 2001) as "a combination of skills, knowledge, characteristics and traits that contribute to outstanding performance in a particular job". According to Pedersen (2007), these are "individual abilities or characteristics that are key to effectiveness in work." Teamwork, "adaptability, commitment, creativity, motivation, foresight, leadership, independence, emotional stability, analytical [and critical] reasoning, and communication skills" are a few examples of abilities required for the workplace (Levett-Jones, Gersbach, Arthur and Roche, 2011).

Orr (1991) defines competencies as "human capabilities and work-related behaviours that provide a competitive advantage to an organization" (p.2). In the same light Wiek (2010, n.p.) defines a competence as "a functionally linked complex of knowledge, skills, and attitudes that enable successful task performance and problem solving". Ouane (2002) argues that "generally, competence is interpreted as the possession of actual capacity to use some skills in order to learn something, to do something or to reach an aim. This can be applied to individual dispositions or to the distribution of such dispositions within a social group or an institution" (p.135). The US department of the Interior (2013) argues that competencies provide a means for understanding performance. In the same vein, Abdulaal, Al-Bahi, Soliman & Iskanderani (2011) explain that competencies include aptitudes, attitudes (beliefs, values, traits and motives) skills and knowledge.

According to Orr (1991). competencies are "human capabilities and work-related behaviors that provide a competitive advantage to an organization." Accordingly, a competence is described as "a functionally linked complex of knowledge, skills, and attitudes that enable successful task performance and problem solving" by Wiek (2010). According to Ouane (2002), "competence is typically understood as the actual capacity to use some skills in order to learn something, to do something, or to achieve an aim." This can be used to describe a person's dispositions or how those dispositions are distributed throughout an organization or social group (p. 135). According to the US Department of the Interior (2013), competences offer a way to comprehend performance. Similarly, Abdulaal et al., (2011) states that competences comprise aptitudes, knowledge, skills, and attitudes (beliefs, values, qualities, and reasons).

According to Ouane (2002), "an inductive search for the same competence in a real situation may conflict with the normative, generic, and derivational definition of competence." Therefore, the question to be asked will be how competence is defined in specific contexts as well as how it is defined generally, i.e., how normative agreements are created. Performance, or the actual demonstration of skill, is what ultimately validates its existence (p. 135). In this context, Gonczi (2002) contends that performance determines competency rather than direct observation. Gonczi goes on to say that although an individual's actions are observable, the qualities that motivate them are assumed. According to him, competency is the result of combining knowledge, abilities, attitudes, and values. Therefore, in addition to specific knowledge and personal dispositions, people's ability to undertake tasks and activities "rests on more general capacities such as reasoning and making judgements" (2002, p. 120). Since the ability to carry out particular tasks will always require a combination of knowledge, abilities, and dispositions, understanding competence in this way eliminates the need to distinguish between specific and key competencies. The notion of sustainability competencies is consistent with this all-encompassing and integrated approach. People must learn how to integrate a variety of qualities, abilities, attitudes, and dispositions that support sustainable actions in a particular setting if they are to live sustainably.

Thus, sustainability competences are described as "complexes of knowledge, skills, and attitudes that enable successful task performance and problem-solving with respect to real-world sustainability problems, challenges, and opportunities" by Wiek (2010) (n.p.). According to Mochizuki and Fadeeva (2010), competency is defined as what students can accomplish by the completion of a learning task.

This research examines the notion of competence in connection to sustainable practice. Thus, it is proposed that learner sustainability skills be action-oriented and include performance. The Delors Report, Learning: the Treasure Within (UNESCO, 1996), which identifies four key competencies in education—learning to know, learning to do, learning to be, and learning to live together—aligns with the position with UNESCO's identified key competencies of education for the twenty-first century. These essential educational competencies have been accepted as crucial foundations for sustainability competencies. Furthermore, the Shaeffer UN Report (Shaeffer, 2007) has identified a fifth cluster of sustainability abilities, one of which is "learning to transform oneself and society." The five essential sustainability competences required for sustainability education are collectively represented by these five competency clusters.

Literature Review Appraisal

This review of the literature looked at definitions of sustainability education, sustainability competencies, and the sustainability curriculum; it also analyzed the literature on the subject, highlighting the significance of sustainability in higher education and its role in helping students develop sustainability competencies. Overall, the literature review indicates that even with growing interest in sustainability education, there is still more work to be done in integrating sustainability into higher education programs and courses, particularly in terms of defining the skills and learning outcomes that are essential to the process.

RESEARCH METHODOLOGY

In order to identify and conceptualize the kinds of sustainability competencies that should be promoted in higher education curricula to boost learners' sustainability related capabilities and make them more competitive and employable in the 21st-century labor market focused on alternative industries, this study combines the critical documentary research method with a qualitative exploratory design approach. The framework for sustainability competency was formulated using qualitative data that surfaced from a critical analysis of sustainability education literature and an assessment of sustainability practices in Irish higher education institutions. This included an analysis of the opportunities and difficulties associated with shifting higher education curricula to promote sustainability competencies among students during the teaching and learning process. Eventually, these research initiatives led to the formulation of the sustainability competencies that should be emphasized in curricula for postsecondary education.

The methodical collection, examination, and interpretation of study data by the researcher is known as documentary research technique (Payne and Payne 2004; Mogalakwe, 2006). The authenticity and dependability of the data gathered from websites, peer-reviewed journals, academic databases, books, government publications, magazines, and newspapers, as well as the rigorous examination of the documentary contents, have been established as the means of ensuring that the information used in this study is authentic and reliable.

At the National Seminar on the Use of ESD Formative Assessment Methods in Undergraduate Teacher Education Programmes, May 31, 2023, GMIT Galway, the Sustainability Competency Framework and the Dispositions, Abilities and Behaviours (DAB) assessment tool were presented as tools for identifying and profiling higher education learners' sustainability competencies from a seminar paper entitled "Assessing ESD competencies among higher education learners." The participants expressed great interest in the presentations of the DAB sustainability assessment tool and the sustainability Competency Framework. The response was overwhelmingly positive, with participants from higher education staff expressing interest in both tools as well as representatives from the Department of Education and Skills' educational curriculum service. These individuals subsequently sent an email to request further information about the framework and DAB tool and how they could be used in sustainability education assessments in Cameroonian schools and higher education institutions. The conference attendees' thoughts, criticisms, comments, and recommendations were helpful in improving the sustainability competency framework, which in turn informed and/or supported the inclusion of certain framework components.

This study employs a documentary research methodology to investigate and pinpoint the kinds of sustainability education competencies that ought to be nurtured in the sustainability learning and teaching processes. The goal is to improve learners' capacities to become more innovative, strategic, and practical thinkers and problem solvers who can find solutions to the sustainability issues confronting the world and who can compete more successfully for jobs in the technologically driven, globally integrated labor market. The purpose of this study is to offer baseline data that will guide policy decisions regarding the necessary steps to promote sustainability education competences among students pursuing higher education.

The documentary research approach is suitable for this study since it is affordable, offers readily usable material, and removes participant biases from the research findings as well as issues related to enticing participants to participate in the study. Nevertheless, this research methodology has its own drawbacks in that not all data on how to develop sustainability competences in students pursuing higher education may be accessible to the general public. Furthermore, as information is always changing in the technologically advanced day, certain information may change after the investigation has already been completed.

RESULTS

Notwithstanding, the goal of this study is not to offer a manual for reorienting curricula to develop sustainability competencies in higher education students, but rather to provide baseline data from which policymakers can infer the necessary steps to develop these competencies in higher education learning and teaching processes within the Cameroonian context. This leaves room for future research on the sustainability practices of Cameroonian higher education institutions, which will aid in identifying the particular needs of these institutions with regard to promoting sustainability and developing students' sustainability competencies to enable them to become competitive and secure employment in the 21st century labor market that is focused on sustainability.

Sustainability Competency Framework

One important instrument for sustainability education is the sustainability competence framework, which lists the many sustainability competencies that should be promoted in sustainability teaching and learning procedures. The tool directs educators toward the kinds of learning outcomes required for teaching and learning sustainability that provide students the behavioral shifts they need to become change agents for sustainability.

Features of the Sustainability Competency Framework

The sustainability competency framework's main objective is to define and elucidate the various sustainability competencies that should be promoted in the process of teaching and learning sustainability. These competencies can aid in modifying the attitudes, behaviors, and beliefs of students and help them develop into environmentally conscious citizens. Moreover, use these skills to generate creative concepts and solutions that promote sustainability and help you stand out in the globalized sustainability alternative industries.

Learners need to develop foresight—creative and imaginative thinking that could provide solutions for future anticipated problems that might result from the unsustainable actions of the present societies—in order to be prepared for the sustainability challenges facing the world and to become citizens who are minded about sustainability. Learners of sustainability must cultivate the traits, abilities, and capacities that allow them to anticipate and consider the future. In order to be change agents for a sustainable world, learners must thus acquire and develop the abilities and qualities of sustainability.

According to the framework for sustainability competencies, a person can cultivate a cluster of skills, traits, knowledge, attitudes, and dispositions that are relevant to sustainability and that they can use to advance sustainability (Besong, 2017). These sustainability-related abilities can be easily modified to fit unique learning environments and the particular sustainability actions that call for the specified sets of these competences.

The Sustainability Competencies diagram below illustrates the five clusters of sustainability competencies that should be fostered in a sustainability infused curriculum. These include: (1) Learning to Know (2) Learning to Do (3) Learning to be, (4) Learning to Live Together (5) Learning to Transform Oneself and Society (Besong, 2017).

Figure 2. The Four Cornerstones of Sustainability

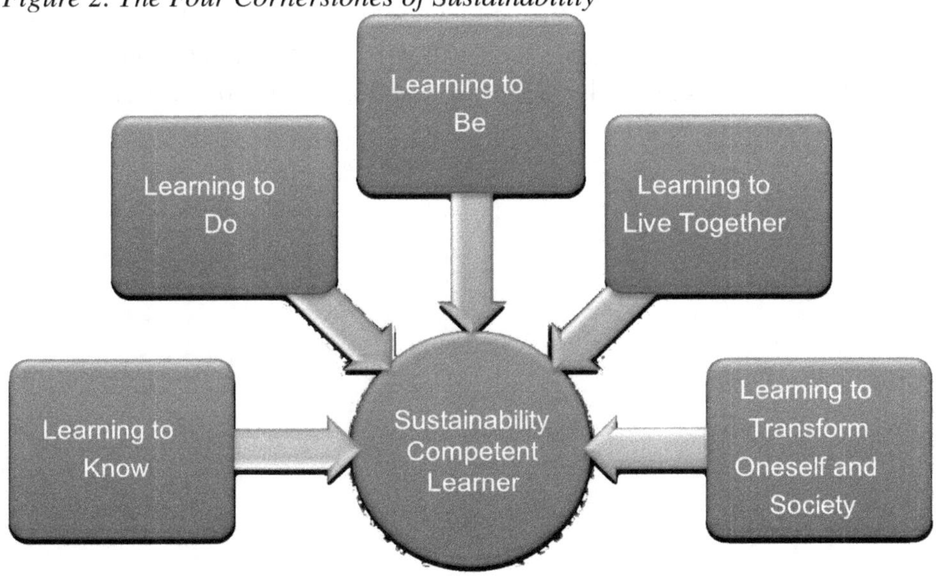

Source: (Besong, 2017)

Learning to know: involves "acquiring the instruments of understanding, or learning how to learn" (UN, 1996, p.21). It includes *Learning to Learn:* which is "the ability to assess how new tasks can be tackled; the capacity to transfer skills and capabilities to a new situation; internal acceptance of a given task, internationalization of motivation; autonomy and selfcontrol; the willingness and readiness to engage in tasks-oriented activity" (Etelalahti &Sahi, 2001 as cited in Rychen, 2002, p. 31).), *Learning to do*: relates to the application of "learned knowledge in daily life and act[ing] creatively and responsibly in one's environment" (UN, 1996, p.21).

Learning to be: encompasses the acquisition of "universally shared values; developing one's personality, self-identity, and self-knowledge; becoming immersed in one's own culture and its wisdom; being empowered to learn about oneself and become more fully human" (Besong, 2017).

Learning to live together: relates to "education for international and inter-cultural understanding; the social dimension of human development; the basis for cohesion and harmony, conflict avoidance, non-violence, and peaceful coexistence; the recognition that difference and diversity are opportunities rather than dangers and are a valuable resource to be used for the common good; the ability to tolerate, respect, welcome, and even celebrate difference and diversity in people and in their histories, traditions, beliefs, values, and cultures, and to use this diversity to enrich our lives and our classrooms" (Besong, 2017).

Learning to transform oneself and society: involves working towards "a gender-neutral, nondiscriminatory society; to act to achieve social solidarity and international understanding; above all, to live sustainably (Shaeffer, 2007, p17). The sustainability competencies on the table below presents the five sustainability competencies corresponding to the sustainability skills that should be fostered in a curriculum.

Table 1. Sustainability Competencies/ Skills Table

Sustainability Competencies	Sustainability Skills
Learning to Know	**Normative skills:** Ability to convey, apply, and negotiate sustainability values, goals, and targets. Ability to assess issues and develop more sustainable visions or solutions for them. Ability to evaluate sustainability issues taking into consideration issues of justice, equity, social-ecological integrity, and ethics of sustainable development (Wiek, Withycombe, & Redman, 2011).
Learning to Do	**Strategic Planning and Designing Skills:** Ability to get things done Ability for designing and implementing interventions and transformative strategies to promote sustainability. Ability to identify real-world sustainability challenges, political understanding of power structures and relationships; the Ability to explain technical issues in layman's terms, Ability to complete tasks within deadlines. Ability to take actions to enable transitions toward a sustainable future (Wiek, Withycombe, & Redman, 2011). **Anticipatory Skills** Ability for future visioning to articulate analyze, evaluate, and articulate the long-term future solutions to sustainability problems and build future sustainable communities
Learning to Be	**Intra Personal and Communication Skills** Ability to make critical reflections of one's values and beliefs in relation to sustainability
Learning to live Together	**Systemic thinking skills:** Ability to analyse complex systems across different fields (environment, society, economy and culture etc.). Ability to analyse issues in terms of scales and time (from local to global) while considering systemic features and problemsolving frameworks. Ability to understand the present status and underlying causes of complex sustainability problems, while considering the direct and indirect effects of different inputs or interventions on the system and on future sustainable development objectives. ***Interpersonal* Skills** Ability for collaborative and participatory engagements with others to seek solutions to sustainability problems. Ability to "understand, compare, and critically evaluate different positions, perspectives, and preferences across cultures, social groups, communities, and individuals" (Wiek, Withycombe, & Redman, 2011, p.31).
Learning to Transform Oneself and Society	**Transformative Skills** Ability to act as a change agent Ability to live sustainably

Source: (Besong, 2017)

Acquisition of Sustainability Competencies

One outcome of the sustainability learning and teaching process is the acquisition—or lack thereof—of sustainability competences. It involves the interactions between the teacher, students, and the learning environment in addition to the various components of the curriculum that are infused with sustainability. The lively animation of the learning process, which includes the use of transformative, learner-centered pedagogic approaches and the cocreation of knowledge through participative, collaborative, authentic situated and values-based pedagogies, will determine how effectively the emergent and/or anticipated sustainability competencies are gained or acquired in the learning process. The identification of the sustainability competency clusters that should be supported in curricula that include sustainability is the main topic of this article. More study needs to be done on the operationalization of the sustainability competences framework.

Opportunities and Challenges for Fostering Sustainability Competencies

within Higher Education Curricula

Governments and higher education institutions must take action to address these issues in order to ensure that sustainability competencies are promoted in higher education learning and teaching processes. There are numerous obstacles that could make it difficult to reorient higher education curricula to foster sustainability competencies.

ESD is an interdisciplinary field of study that is still in its infancy. However, some higher education personnel find the idea of co-developing courses objectionable because higher education fosters faculty and disciplinary silos (UNECE, 2007). It is especially challenging to integrate sustainability into the curriculum and to promote sustainability capabilities because disciplinary topic orientations are so common in higher education programs and courses (UNESCO, 2005a). UNESCO further identifies the difficulty of positioning education for sustainable development alongside many other competing interests either at faculty or departmental levels as well as the lack of educational leadership to support the infusion of sustainability in learning and teaching in higher education.

Huckle (2008) further contends that because ESD is cross-curriculum in nature, it is frequently marginalized in the curricula, which in turn reproduces and maintains the academic knowledge divides that exist between the humanities, social sciences, and natural sciences and ignores lay and tacit knowledge.

Furthermore, the environmental pillar of sustainable development has frequently received more attention than the other three pillars—social, cultural, and economic—even in situations where sustainability education is being taught (UNECE, 2007). Another major obstacle to addressing sustainability and cultivating sustainability capabilities in higher education is the absence of qualified experts to provide inspired ESD (Ibid).

The absence of ESD-related in-service training, according to UNESCO (2005a), is a barrier to addressing sustainability and advancing sustainability capabilities in higher education.

In addition, many national education ministries do not support the promotion of sustainability, which makes it difficult to incorporate sustainability issues and develop sustainability capabilities into curricula for higher education (UNESCO, 2005a). Makrakis and Kostoulas Makrakis (2012) draw attention to the reality that, in many instances, experts have revised curricula to address sustainability without taking end users' feedback into account. Another obstacle to the integration of sustainability in higher education, according to UNESCO (2005a), is that ESD programs are frequently developed without input from members of the local community and other stakeholders, ignoring the realities of the local context and rendering the programs irrelevant, particularly to the local communities and stakeholders.

One more obstacle to addressing sustainability in higher education, according to (UNESCO 2005a), is the lack of inter-ministerial coordination efforts between ministries such as education, health, agriculture, and environment, which are responsible for addressing and/or promoting sustainability. Moreover, UNESCO points out that one obstacle to tackling sustainability in higher education is the staff members' ignorance of the significance and idea of ESD. The fact that many academics in higher education complain that they have "too many disparate initiatives [and] too little time for thinking about new ideas" like ESD (p. 29) is another grievance expressed (UNESCO (2005a). Additionally, integrating sustainability and developing sustainability capabilities into the teaching and learning processes is hampered by institutional ethos that upholds strong power relations, particularly in the learning environment. Collegial relationships are necessary in the classroom to enable students to participate as co-authors of information during the teaching and learning process.

Opportunities for Deploying the Sustainability Competency Framework

There are many of resources available to support teachers in promoting sustainability competences in higher education curricula, despite the various obstacles that may stand in their way. There are sustainability champions in higher education institutions who work on sustainability-related research consortia projects alone or together. Transdisciplinary cooperation is necessary in these circumstances and could serve to spark interest in the field of sustainability education. Institutions of higher learning must shift their policies and procedures to be more sustainable. Policymakers must create institutional visions for sustainability education at the institutional level. By doing so, they may pique educators' interests in incorporating sustainability into their curricula and programs, thereby promoting sustainability competencies in the teaching and learning process (Mezirow, 2000).

According to Sterling (2009), in order to address sustainability, there has to be a shift in the political environment as well as the creation of favorable conditions for change. The academic community should feel like they own the change process through engagements, and higher education institutions should implement policies that set the stage for sustainability practice. Teachers should be provided with resources, information, and staff development through training workshops and conferences on addressing sustainability in programs and courses (Mezirow, 2000). These policy orientations should take a bottom-up approach that encourages collaboration.

People resist change if they feel it is externally imposed (Sterling 2009). "Innovation has a greater chance of success if it is perceived as helpful, plausible, possible, and likely to be fruitful" (p. 82). He goes on to say that administrators in higher education must have an open mind and be eager to learn about sustainability. Administrators in higher education should be open to embracing the necessity of unified policies in sectors such as commerce, environment, health, development, and sociocultural issues, alongside their counterparts in other commercial and public ministries. In order to further the institution's sustainability agenda, administrators in higher education should make use of the pool of current sustainability experts within the organization, support their work, and establish research and monitoring committees.

To effectively advance the institutional sustainability agenda, changes must be made. These changes must be democratic, inclusive, and give people the time and space to reflect and participate in the reform process. Resources and funding must also be set aside for the implementation of these changes (Sterling, 2009). Higher education staff members must respect the contributions made by their peers, work together and exchange ideas with colleagues in other departments to address sustainability, and support the inclusion of sustainability capabilities in curricula. Also, higher education staff with knowledge in sustainability education help policy makers and programme chairs and others on sustainability re-orienting schemes providing examples of addressing sustainability and promoting sustainability competencies in the curriculum process and networking with others to share ideas about fostering sustainability competencies in the learning and teaching process (Sterling, 2009).

There is the need to create an institutional culture in higher education that is dedicated to sustainability and which promotes interdepartmental collaboration, where champions of sustainability take the responsibility in collaboration with the administration in providing training on what measures to take in addressing sustainability competencies in the curriculum (Levey& Marans, 2012). There is also, the need for educators to change higher education culture to embrace systemic, connective, inclusive, transformative, ecological and values-based learning approaches in promoting sustainability competencies so that it engenders in learners' real-life changes that foster sustainability (Sterling, 2002; Burns, 2011).

In order to enable students to use technology and bring prior knowledge into the classroom and take ownership of their education, educators should also encourage students to use ICT to facilitate sustainable learning. This will help students become more proficient in both teaching and learning processes.

Prospects for Learners' Employability in the Sustainability Alternative

Focused Industries

There are many opportunities in the context of emerging Cameroon's economy that learners can easily gain self-employment in areas such as:

3R: (REDUCE, RE-USE, RE-CYCLE); ENERGY: Electricity, (Wind Energy, Solar Energy) Bio Fuels (Energy from animal/ waste- human- faeces/ Energy from farm waste (wood, crops etc.); Rain Water Harvesting/Water Purification and Carbon Sequestration.

Figure 3. Sustainability Alternative Industries

Source: (Besong, 2017)

Higher education graduates need to think outside the box and use their entrepreneurial skills to generate employment for themselves and others and take advantage of the different labour market opportunities provided by the state through subventions for new business start- ups, opportunities for professional training (eg through the National Employment Fund), and different financial opportunities provided by the state and other agencies (the World Bank, NGOs) for employability.

CONCLUSION

Higher education institutions are the citadels of learning through which changes in human behaviours could be promoted. Higher education thus has a key role to play as drivers of education, training and policy enhancement for sustainability. As advocated in the University Charter for Sustainable Development (Copernicus, 1994), the Talloires Declaration (2005), the UN Decade of Education for Sustainable development 2005-2014 (UNESCO, 2007), higher education institutions are called upon to play a critical role in mobilising and fostering learners' acquisition of sustainability competences. Higher education institutions have the expertise to foster the knowledge and skills necessary to enable students devise solutions to sustainability related challenges facing the world now and in the future. In this regard, the sustainability competency framework emergent from this study comes at a valuable time when higher education is required to prepare graduates who are vested with knowledge and competencies that enable them to better compete in the technology-oriented knowledge economy of the 21st century. The sustainability framework thus offers higher education institutions, educators and/or researchers with a tool to better understand the conceptualization and development of sustainability competencies within higher education curricula.

REFERENCES

Abdulaal, R. M., Al-Bahi, A. M., Soliman, A. Y., & Iskanderani, F. I. (2011). Design and implementation of a project-based active/cooperative engineering design course for freshmen. *European Journal of Engineering Education*, 36(4), 391–402. DOI: 10.1080/03043797.2011.598498

Allen-Gil, S., Walker, L., Thomas, G., Shevory, T., & Elan, S. (2005). Forming a community partnership to enhance education in sustainability. *International Journal of Sustainability in Higher Education*, 6(4), 392–402. DOI: 10.1108/14676370510623874

Alvarez, A., & Rogers, J. (2006). Going "out there": Learning about sustainability in place. *International Journal of Sustainability in Higher Education*, 7(2), 176–188. DOI: 10.1108/14676370610655940

Anane, E. (2020). A multiple mediation analysis of the effect of prior performance on academic achievement through student teachers' motivational orientations. *Higher Education Research*, 5(4), 118. DOI: 10.11648/j.her.20200504.12

Berglund, T., & Gericke, N. (2016). Separated and integrated perspectives on environmental, economic, and social dimensions–an investigation of student views on sustainable development. *Environmental Education Research*, 22(8), 1115–1138. DOI: 10.1080/13504622.2015.1063589

Bergman, L. R., & Lundh, L. G. (2015). Introduction: The person-oriented approach: Roots and roads to the future. *Journal for Person-Oriented Research*, 1(1-2), 1–6. DOI: 10.17505/jpor.2015.01

Birdsall, S. (2010). Empowering students to act: Learning about, through and from the nature of action. *Australian Journal of Environmental Education*, 26, 65–84. DOI: 10.1017/S0814062600000835

Boeve-de Pauw, J., Gericke, N., Olsson, D., & Berglund, T. (2015). The effectiveness of education for sustainable development. *Sustainability (Basel)*, 7(11), 15693–15717. DOI: 10.3390/su71115693

Borg, C., Gericke, N., Höglund, H. O., & Bergman, E. (2012). The barriers encountered by teachers implementing education for sustainable development: Discipline bound differences and teaching traditions. *Research in Science & Technological Education*, 30(2), 185–207. DOI: 10.1080/02635143.2012.699891

Burns, H. (2011). Teaching for transformation: (Re) Designing sustainability courses based on ecological principles. *Journal of Sustainability Education*.

Bylund, L. (2024). Education for sustainable development among rich and poor: Didactical responses to biopolitical differentiation. *Environmental Education Research*, 30(3), 419–431. DOI: 10.1080/13504622.2023.2172140

Calder, W., & Clugston, R. M. (2003). International efforts to promote higher education for sustainable development. *Planning for Higher Education*, 31(3), 30–44.

Caldwell, R. (2006). *Agency and change: Rethinking change agency in organizations*. Routledge. DOI: 10.4324/9780203087565

Carbach, E., & Fischer, D. (2017). Sustainability reporting at schools: Challenges and benefits. *Journal of Teacher Education for Sustainability*, 19(1), 69–81. DOI: 10.1515/jtes-2017-0005

Chambers, D. (2009). Assessing and planning for environmental sustainability—A framework for institutions of higher education. *Sustainability at universities: Opportunities, challenges and trends*, 287-298.

Cincera, J., & Krajhanzl, J. (2013). Eco-Schools: What factors influence pupils' action competence for pro-environmental behaviour? *Journal of Cleaner Production*, 61, 117–121. DOI: 10.1016/j.jclepro.2013.06.030

Copernicus, A. (1994). *The university charter for sustainable development.* Association of European Universities.

Council of the European Union (February, 2011). The role of education and training in the implementation of the 'Europe 2020' Strategy. Conclusions of the Council.

DAAD/UNU-VIE. (2009) The Role of Education for Sustainable Development in Higher Education. German Academic Exchange (DAAD)/ United nations University-Vice Rectorate in Europe (UNU-VIE) Report of the joint Workshop of the UNESCO World Conference on Education for Sustainable Development 31 March-2 April 2009.

Das, S., Lekhya, G., Shreya, K., Shekinah, K. L., Babu, K. K., & Boopathi, S. (2024). Fostering Sustainability Education Through Cross-Disciplinary Collaborations and Research Partnerships: Interdisciplinary Synergy. In *Facilitating Global Collaboration and Knowledge Sharing in Higher Education With Generative AI* (pp. 60-88). IGI Global.

Declaration, H. (1991). Creating a common future: University action for sustainable development. *Accessed May, 16*(2015), 209-227.

Declaration, T. (2005). Talloires Declaration on the civic roles and social responsibilities of higher education.

Fang, Z. (1996). A review of research on teacher beliefs and practices. *Educational Research*, 38(1), 47–65. DOI: 10.1080/0013188960380104

FitzGerald, M., Walsh, K., & McCutcheon, H. (2001). An integrative systematic review of indicators for competence for practice and protocol for validation of indicators of competence.

Goldberg, D. S. (2012). Social justice, health inequalities and methodological individualism in US health promotion. *Public Health Ethics*, 5(2), 104–115. DOI: 10.1093/phe/phs013

Gonczi, A. (2003). Teaching and learning of the key competencies. In *Contributions to the second DeSeCo symposium* (pp. 119-131). Swiss Federal Statistics Office.

Harness, H., & Drossman, H. (2013). The environmental education through filmmaking project. In *The Media, Animal Conservation and Environmental Education* (pp. 147-167). Routledge.

Hasslöf, H., & Malmberg, C. (2015). Critical Thinking as Room for Subjectification in Education for Sustainable Development. *Environmental Education Research*, 21(2), 239–255. DOI: 10.1080/13504622.2014.940854

Huckle, J. (2008). An analysis of New Labour's policy on education for sustainable development with particular reference to socially critical approaches. *Environmental Education Research*, 14(1), 65–75. DOI: 10.1080/13504620701843392

Hungerford, H. R. (2009). Environmental education (EE) for the 21st century: Where have we been? Where are we now? Where are we headed? *The Journal of Environmental Education*, 41(1), 1–6. DOI: 10.1080/00958960903206773

International Association of Universities. (1993). *Kyoto Declaration on Sustainable Development*. International Universities Bureau.

Jickling, B. (1994). Studying sustainable development: Problems and possibilities. *Canadian Journal of Education/Revue canadienne de l'éducation*, 231-240.

Knowles, M. S. (1970). *The Modern Practice of Adult Education*. Andragogy versus Pedagogy.

Kolb, D. A. (1984). *Experiential learning: Experience as the source of learning and development*. FT press.

Kopnina, H. (2014). Education for sustainable development (ESD): Exploring anthropocentric–ecocentric values in children through vignettes. *Studies in Educational Evaluation*, 41, 124–132. DOI: 10.1016/j.stueduc.2013.12.004

Levett-Jones, T., Gersbach, J., Arthur, C., & Roche, J. (2011). Implementing a clinical competency assessment model that promotes critical reflection and ensures nursing graduates' readiness for professional practice. *Nurse Education in Practice*, 11(1), 64–69. DOI: 10.1016/j.nepr.2010.07.004 PMID: 20727825

Makrakis, V., & Kostoulas-Makrakis, N. (2012). Course curricular design and development of the M. Sc. programme in the field of ICT in education for sustainable development. *Journal of Teacher Education for Sustainability*, 14(2), 5–40. DOI: 10.2478/v10099-012-0007-7

Mezirow, J. (2000). *Learning as Transformation: Critical Perspectives on a Theory in Progress. The Jossey-Bass Higher and Adult Education Series*. Jossey-Bass Publishers, 350 Sansome Way, San Francisco, CA 94104.

Mochizuki, Y., & Fadeeva, Z. (2010). Competences for sustainable development and sustainability: Significance and challenges for ESD. *International Journal of Sustainability in Higher Education*, 11(4), 391–403. DOI: 10.1108/14676371011077603

Mogalakwe, M. (2006). The use of documentary research methods in social research. *African Sociological Review/Revue Africaine De Sociologie, 10*(1), 221-230.

Nogueira, C., Marques, J. F., & Pinto, H. (2024). Intentional sustainable communities and sustainable development goals: From micro-scale implementation to scalability of innovative practices. *Journal of Environmental Planning and Management*, 67(1), 175–196. DOI: 10.1080/09640568.2022.2106553

Öhman, J. (2008). *Values and democracy in education for sustainable development: contributions from Swedish research*. Liber.

Ojala, M. (2013). Emotional awareness: On the importance of including emotional aspects in education for sustainable development (ESD). *Journal of Education for Sustainable Development*, 7(2), 167–182. DOI: 10.1177/0973408214526488

Orr, D. W. (1991). *Ecological literacy: Education and the transition to a postmodern world*. State University of New York Press.

Ouane, A. (2003). Defining and selecting key competencies in lifelong learning. In *Contributions to the Second DeSeCo Symposium* (p. 133).

Padmanabha, C. H. (2018). Critical Thinking: Conceptual Framework. *Journal of Educational Psychology*, 11(4), 45–53.

Payne, G., & Payne, J. (2004). Key concepts in social research.

Reid, A., Dillon, J., Ardoin, N., & Ferreira, J. A. (2021). Scientists' warnings and the need to reimagine, recreate, and restore environmental education. *Environmental Education Research*, 27(6), 783–795. DOI: 10.1080/13504622.2021.1937577

Reimers, F. M. (2024). The sustainable development goals and education, achievements and opportunities. *International Journal of Educational Development*, 104, 102965. DOI: 10.1016/j.ijedudev.2023.102965

Renninger, K. A., & Hidi, S. (2011). Revisiting the conceptualization, measurement, and generation of interest. *Educational Psychologist*, 46(3), 168–184. DOI: 10.1080/00461520.2011.587723

Rudsberg, K., & Öhman, J. (2018). Pluralism in practice–experiences from Swedish evaluation, school development and research. In *Environmental and Sustainability Education Policy* (pp. 193–209). Routledge. DOI: 10.4324/9780203732359-13

Rychen, D. S. (2002, February). A frame of reference for defining and selecting key competencies in an international context. In *DS Rychen, LH Salganik & ME McLaughlin (2002). Definition and selection of key competencies: Contributions to the Second DeSeCo Symposium, Geneva, Switzerland* (pp. 11-13).

Sass, W., Boeve-de Pauw, J., Olsson, D., Gericke, N., De Maeyer, S., & Van Petegem, P. (2020). Redefining action competence: The case of sustainable development. *The Journal of Environmental Education*, 51(4), 292–305. DOI: 10.1080/00958964.2020.1765132

Schein, E. H. (1995). Kurt Lewin's change theory in the field and in the classroom: Notes toward a model of managed learning. *Systems Practice*, 9(1), 27–47. DOI: 10.1007/BF02173417

Schiefele, U., Streblow, L., & Retelsdorf, J. (2013). Dimensions of teacher interest and their relations to occupational well-being and instructional practices. *Journal for Educational Research Online*, 5(1), 7–37.

Shaeffer, S. (2007). *Education for Sustainable Development: A Framework for Reform.* UNESCO Bangkok, Asia and Pacific Regional Bureau for Education.

Shriberg, M. (2002). Institutional assessment tools for sustainability in higher education: Strengths, weaknesses, and implications for practice and theory. *Higher Education Policy*, 15(2), 153–167. DOI: 10.1016/S0952-8733(02)00006-5

Sinakou, E., Boeve-de Pauw, J., Goossens, M., & Van Petegem, P. (2018). Academics in the field of Education for Sustainable Development: Their conceptions of sustainable development. *Journal of Cleaner Production*, 184, 321–332. DOI: 10.1016/j.jclepro.2018.02.279

Sinakou, E., Donche, V., Boeve-de Pauw, J., & Van Petegem, P. (2019). Designing powerful learning environments in education for sustainable development: A conceptual framework. *Sustainability (Basel)*, 11(21), 5994. DOI: 10.3390/su11215994

Sinakou, E., Donche, V., & Van Petegem, P. (2022). Action-orientation in education for sustainable development: Teachers' interests and instructional practices. *Journal of Cleaner Production*, 370, 133469. DOI: 10.1016/j.jclepro.2022.133469

Sinakou, E., Donche, V., & Van Petegem, P. (2024). Teachers' profiles in education for sustainable development: Interests, instructional beliefs, and instructional practices. *Environmental Education Research*, 30(3), 397–418. DOI: 10.1080/13504622.2023.2168622

Sterling, S. (2002, 2009). Towards sustainable education: re-visioning learning and change. In *Learning for a sustainable future: the role or communication, ethics, and social learning in environmetnal education. VIIIth Conference on Environmental Education in Europe. Gent: Provincie Oost-Vlaanderen.*

Stevenson, J. (1996). The metamorphosis of the construction of competence. *Studies in Continuing Education*, 18(1), 24–42. DOI: 10.1080/0158037960180102

Summers, M., & Childs, A. (2007). Student science teachers' conceptions of sustainable development: An empirical study of three postgraduate training cohorts. *Research in Science & Technological Education*, 25(3), 307–327. DOI: 10.1080/02635140701535067

Sund, P. (2008). Discerning the extras in ESD teaching-A democratic issue.

UNECE – UNESCO (United Nations Economic Commission for Europe – United Nations Educational, Scientific and Cultural Organisation). (2007). Good practices in education for sustainable development, Sweden Sustainable School Award.

UNESCO. (1996). Learning: The Treasure Within. Report to UNESCO of the International Commission on Education for the Twenty-first Century. Paris: UNESCO. UNESCO (1998). Higher Education in the Twenty-First Century: Vision and Action. World Conference on Higher education.

UNESCO (2005). United Nations Decade of Education for Sustainable Development (DESD) 2005-2014.

UNESCO (2005a). Guidelines and Recommendations for Reorienting Teacher Education to Address Sustainability. UNESCO Education for Sustainable Development in Action Technical PaperNo.2.

UNESCO. (2006). *UNESCO's Role, Vision and Challenges for the UN Decade of Education for Sustainable Development (2005-2014)*. UNESCO International Science, Technology & Environmental Education Newsletter.

UNESCO. (2014). *Roadmap for implementing the Global Action Programme in Education for Sustainable Development*. UNESCO.

United Nations -Assembly, U. G. (2015). Transforming Our World: the 2030 Agenda for Sustainable Devel¬ opment (UN General Assembly Resolution nº 70 [I] A). *New York*. USA department of the Interior University (2013). Career Development: Competencies.

United Nations Educational, Scientific and Cultural Organization (UNESCO). (2020). Education for sustainable development: A roadmap.

Van Poeck, K., & Östman, L. (2019). Political moves: How teachers can open up for and handle poignant experiences of the conflictual aspects of sustainability issues. In *Sustainable Development Teaching* (pp. 162–174). Routledge. DOI: 10.4324/9781351124348-14

Van Poeck, K., Östman, L., & Öhman, J. (2019). Ethical moves: how teachers can open up a space for articulating moral reactions and deliberating on ethical opinions regarding sustainability issues. In *Sustainable development teaching* (pp. 153–161). Routledge. DOI: 10.4324/9781351124348-13

Varela-Losada, M., Vega-Marcote, P., Pérez-Rodríguez, U., & Álvarez-Lires, M. (2016). Going to action? A literature review on educational proposals in formal Environmental Education. *Environmental Education Research*, 22(3), 390–421. DOI: 10.1080/13504622.2015.1101751

Vartiainen, J., Sormunen, K., & Kangas, J. (2024). Relationality of play and playfulness in early childhood sustainability education. *Learning and Instruction*, 93, 101963. DOI: 10.1016/j.learninstruc.2024.101963

Vela, J. (1994). *Learning to listen, learning to teach: The power of dialogue in educating adults*. Jossey-Bass.

Wade, R. (2012). Pedagogy, places and people. *Journal of teacher Education for Sustainability, 14*(2), 147-167.

Wals, A. E. (2007). Creating networks of conversations. In *Social learning towards a sustainable world* (pp. 497–506). Academic. DOI: 10.3920/9789086865949_032

Watson, R., Stimpson, A., Topping, A., & Porock, D. (2002). Clinical competence assessment in nursing: A systematic review of the literature. *Journal of Advanced Nursing*, 39(5), 421–431. DOI: 10.1046/j.1365-2648.2002.02307.x PMID: 12175351

Wiek, A. (2010, June). Sustainability science–what are the core competencies? In *Second International Conference on Sustainability Science,* Rome (Vol. 24).

Wiek, A., Withycombe, L., & Redman, C. L. (2011). Key competencies in sustainability: A reference framework for academic program development. *Sustainability Science*, 6(2), 203–218. DOI: 10.1007/s11625-011-0132-6

Wu, J. I., & Wang, C. H. (2024). The Importance of International Education at Various Educational Stages From the Perspective of Sustainable Development Education. *The Journal of Educational Research*, (361), 94–108.

Chapter 12
The Role of Institutional Research (IR) in Informing Higher Education Governance Practices in East Africa

Charles Eryenyu
https://orcid.org/0000-0003-3560-7454
Busitema University, Uganda

Dennis Zami Atibuni
Busitema University, Uganda

ABSTRACT

This chapter examines the role of institutional research (IR) in higher education governance in East Africa (EA). It aims to provide insights into data-driven practices for informed decision-making within academic institutions and national higher education systems. The chapter serves three distinct purposes: (a) to offer perspectives on the future paths and prospects for research-driven policies and practices in East African higher education space; (b) to suggest methods for reinforcing IR roles and improving governance practices within the EA higher education sector; and (c) to serve as a wakeup call to East African higher education institutions (HEIs) to embrace the concept of IR, adapt its practices, recognise it as a management strategy for good governance, and make provisions for practicing it. The discussions in the chapter comprehensively examine how institutional research can contribute to evidence-based policy and governance practices in higher education

DOI: 10.4018/979-8-3693-6930-2.ch012

in the East African context and recommend a framework for implementing IR in the East African region.

INTRODUCTION

This chapter discusses the role of institutional research (IR) in higher education (HE), particularly in the East African (EA) context. It contains a number of sections, including the introduction, which highlights the contents of the chapter. The background explores the concepts of institutional research and higher education governance, elaborating on the link between IR and management decision-making, institutional performance, strategic planning, program and institutional accreditation, regulatory compliance and accountability, and the promotion of continuous quality improvement. The section on the Historical Context of Higher Education Governance in East Africa discusses East Africa's post-independence reforms, which aim to strengthen governance education policy frameworks, promote regional higher education, and align higher education with national development agendas. The section on Manifestation of Institutional Research in East Africa traces the formal and informal versions of IR in East African higher education institutions (HEIs). It also examines the challenges and opportunities of implementing IR in higher education institutions globally, specifically focusing on the East African region. It further discusses the historical context of higher education governance in East Africa and the emergence of the East African Community Common Higher Education Area (EACHEA). The Case Studies section describes case studies of HEIs that formalised IR as a management function. The section on Implementing IR discusses the challenges and future directions of IR in the East African higher education context. It further explores the reasons behind the lack of a more prominent and deliberate implementation of IR in higher education institutions (HEIs) in East Africa. The chapter concludes by providing recommendations for establishing and enhancing institutional research in East African universities, emphasising the need for dedicated IR offices and support from regional organisations like the Inter-University Council for East Africa (IUCEA).

BACKGROUND

The concept and practice of institutional research started after World War II as a response to the growth and expansion of higher education in America (Sepahi et al., 2021; Yorke, 2004). The growth led to a need for institutional management to provide direction and justify support for the growing institutions. The emphasis was on resource accountability and demonstrating institutional performance, which led to the establishment of institutional research offices throughout the country.

The increasing complexity, size, and concern for quality standards in institutions led to the emergence of institutional self-studies focused on management and accountability (Saupe, 1990; Calderon & Mathies, 2013). Organizations, institutions, and associations initiated the formal development of institutional research by organizing seminars to establish methods for resource accounting and conducting research on faculty work and student characteristics. Over time, the expectations placed on institutional researchers evolved in relation to the external political environment. Consequently, the development of institutional research offices led to an increase in the number of institutional researchers and managers. The Institutional Research (IR) offices gather empirical data on academic, administrative, and support functions to assist in institutional planning, policy formulation, and decision-making processes. In the 1990s, the field of institutional research experienced global growth, primarily due to the influence of market models in higher education. People acknowledged institutional research for enhancing the quality of academic programs, planning, and administration procedures by providing precise information.

In Africa, north, west, and southern Africa formally practise IR, while the East African region treats it as an ad hoc phenomenon embedded within general management practices. At least by the start of the 21st century, the American Association of Institutional Research (AIR) did not include the East African region in its list of international affiliate organisations. The list, which includes various associations for institutional research, including AAIR, CIRPA, EAIR, MENA-AIR, PNAIRP, SEAAIR, SAAIR, and TW-AIR[1], does not feature the sub-Saharan African region.

CONCEPTUALIZING INSTITUTIONAL RESEARCH

Different writers have described institutional research in various ways, depending on the specific situation. According to Saupe (1990), IR is the process of conducting research within a higher education institution to gather knowledge that aids in institutional planning, policy creation, and decision-making. This term encompasses institutions at different tiers, including a solitary campus, a multi-campus system, or a bigger consortium of colleges and universities. Volkwein (2008) also agrees with this description, defining IR as activities that facilitate institutional planning, policy development, and decision-making. Terenzini (1993, 2013) expanded upon Cameron Fincher's (1978) characterisation of IR as organisational intelligence by providing further details on the three levels: technical and analytical intelligence, problem intelligence, and contextual intelligence. Technical and analytical intelligence refers to the process of gathering and analysing factual information about an institution, such as admissions, enrolment, and finances. The process employs tools such as spreadsheets, statistics, and survey research abilities. Problem intelligence encompasses information pertaining to unique challenges encountered by the institution, such as diversity, resource allocation, and program evaluation. Contextual intelligence involves understanding the institution internally and externally, including its history, culture, and external environment. The way Terenzini breaks down organisational intelligence fits with how Altbach (2014) and Saupe (1990) described institutional research: an activity that academic institutions do on purpose and in a planned way to gather and analyse data for management decisions, planning, and improvement.

It should be noted that institutional research in HEIs is distinct from higher education research in that the latter is an interdisciplinary academic field that aims to advance knowledge and practice in higher education (Teichler, 2005). Higher education research focuses on higher education as a hub for knowledge generation, innovation, and invention, as well as the dissemination of such academic outputs (Altbach, 2014). Conversely, institutional research concentrates on specific colleges, universities, or systems. While it may contribute to wider knowledge about how institutions and individuals function, its primary purpose is to provide information for specific planning, policy, or decision-making situations (Saupe, 1990). Often, institutional research applies itself to address specific questions about course offerings, tuition rates, attrition rates, faculty salaries, and program outcomes (Saupe, 1990).

Different titles such as analysis, information, reporting, or self-studies identify the institutional research function in higher education institutions (Volkvein et al., 2012). In some institutions, it falls under self-assessment, self-evaluation, or performance assessment (Volkvein et al., 2012). Volkvein et al. further assert that offices of strategic planning, enrolment management, budget analysis, or policy analysis can also engage in institutional research and its functions. In the American higher education landscape, strong connections or formal organisational arrangements unite people in three main analytical functions of IR: institutional reporting and administrative policy analysis; strategic planning, enrollment and financial management; and outcomes assessment (Volkvein., 2008). According to Volkvein, these three functions constitute the golden triangle of institutional research.

THE LINK BETWEEN IR AND HIGHER EDUCATION GOVERNANCE

For more than 50 years, the United States has recognized institutional research (IR) as a distinct profession in higher education. IR is now a global concept. Institutional research (IR) is the systematic collection, analysis, and dissemination of data within an institution to support decision-making, planning, and policy development.

On the other hand, university governance involves the structures, processes, and mechanisms through which universities are managed, directed, and controlled. Institutional research (IR) is therefore a good tool for data-driven decision-making in higher education institutions. The practice of IR entails collecting and analyzing data about an institution's characteristics and performance to support decision-making and policy formulation (Calderon & Mathies, 2013; Calderon & Webber, 2015; Webber, 2020). However, Eryenyu et al. (2020) observed inadequacy in incorporating IR practices into internal quality assurance (IQA) planning and other institutional decision-making processes, thereby highlighting the challenges of implementing IR practices.

Generally, Institutional Research (IR) offers factual information and understanding about many aspects of university operations, allowing for well-informed choices in strategic planning, academic programs, budgeting, and policy formulation. IR also promotes accountability and transparency. IR practices are aimed at empirically (statistically) describing a college or university's many functions including teaching and learning, administration, and support. In particular, institutional planning, policy development, and decision-making utilize data from IR activities. Webber (2020) views IR as a specialized administrative function, where its practitioners provide organizational intelligence for many managerial decisions. IR professionals are responsible for conducting institutional policy-related research, promoting research-led plans, and accelerating institutional transformation. While there is no simple way to characterize what an average IR office performs or what is required of it, there are some similar duties, roles, and functions that constitute institutional research in today's higher education (Volkwein, 2008; Webber, 2020). IR offices are typically involved in data collection, analysis, and reporting, as well as more general academic planning, strategy, and quality assurance. Effective IR managers engage in senior-level discussions about data and its interpretations within their institution. Some IR managers also take a visionary approach to establishing and evaluating plans for institutions and higher education systems at the state and national levels. The institutional research framework and its operational limitations determine the depth and breadth of IR and decision support. In many educational systems around the world, government legislation and funding mandate institutions to give evidence of their success, emphasizing the need for IR. Institutional decision-makers decide IR's unique purpose, functions, activities, services, roles, and mission. The functions of an IR unit differ depending on the institution's organizational structure and reporting lines (Volkwein 2008).

More specifically, IR guarantees accountability by presenting unbiased data and evidence to stakeholders, enabling them to evaluate the performance and efficacy of the institution's governance structures and actions. In order to develop and execute an effective plan, organizations need to do a strengths, weaknesses, opportunities, and threats (SWOT) analysis, which involves identifying the internal strengths and weaknesses of the institution, as well as the external opportunities and threats. This analysis should be based on data-driven institutional research (IR) information. Furthermore, it is currently understood that institutional research offers a more profound comprehension of how resources are used, the cost-effectiveness of different academic and administrative operations, and the return on investment (ROI) within the institution. IR inherently facilitates quality assurance processes and accreditation standards by systematically collecting and analyzing data pertaining to academic programs, student learning results, faculty qualifications, research productivity, and institutional performance.

THE CONTEXT OF HIGHER EDUCATION GOVERNANCE IN EAST AFRICA

Globally, the integration of IR and QA has become necessary for effective governance and data-driven decision-making in higher education institutions. In regions such as North America, Europe, Australia, and South Africa, IR has become a dominant practice, helping to shape institutional planning and quality management. However, in East Africa, while QA is relatively well-institutionalised, IR remains underdeveloped in spite of its potential to support governance and planning in universities (ADEA, 2011; Eryenyu et al., 2020; IUCEA, 2020; Webber et al., 2016).

The advent of higher education in East Africa can be traced back to its roots in the colonial period, following the establishment of institutions such as the Uganda Technical School in 1922 which marked the beginning of formal HE education in the region. After independence, colleges in Kenya, Uganda, and Tanzania formed the University of East Africa. However, its dissolution in 1970 paved the way for the establishment of independent national universities in the three founding countries of East Africa: Makerere University in Uganda, the University of Nairobi in Kenya, and the University of Dar es Salaam in Tanzania (Oanda & Matiangi, 2018).

In the post-independence era, educational planning and governance focused on expanding access to education, with an emphasis on nation-building and developing skilled human resources. However, the rapid expansion of higher education in East Africa during the 1980s and 1990s posed significant challenges. Most universities lacked the structured data collection and analysis mechanisms required for informed decision-making and planning, which led to inefficiencies in managing growth and ensuring quality (Boden & Corckett, 2017; Kasozi, 2003). This led to the adoption of other management practices, such as quality assurance practices, while implicitly implementing elements of data collection for planning purposes.

The influence of global trends such as university ranking, cross-border higher education, online learning, and for-profit HE in the 1980s and 1990s spurred reforms in higher education across East Africa. This period saw the introduction of quality assurance frameworks and a subtle adoption of IR principles. Universities began conducting self-assessments, audits, and tracer studies to gather data for institutional improvement. However, these practices were often ad hoc and lacked formalised structures; they were sometimes implemented through committees of inquiries. The integration of IR into university governance has been slow, leading to scattered practices across planning units, quality assurance offices, and special committees of inquiries (Sanga, 2011; Oanda, 2018).

In 2009, the push for a unified East African Community Higher Education Area (EACHEA) gained momentum, supported by the Inter-University Council for East Africa (IUCEA). Several publications (*e.g.*, IUCEA, 2017; IUCEA/DAAD, 2010; Oanda, 2018) indicate that the IUCEA implemented several quality assurance initiatives aimed at regional cooperation, including the development of a regional quality assurance framework and the East African Qualifications Framework for Higher Education (EAQFHE). Despite these advancements, the lack of systematic establishment of formal IR offices left universities without comprehensive, ready-to-use mechanisms for data-driven decision-making (IUCEA, 2020; Webber et al., 2016). The Planning departments and quality assurance offices often embed some IR practices. Unfortunately, university planning units prioritise long-term strategic goals, while IR units are expected to provide the necessary data and research to support these plans. For example, IR units use data to monitor institutional performance, allocate resources, and benchmark against institutional long-term plans and the external environment for continuous improvement (IUCEA, 2020). This means that the effectiveness of the planning units and QA offices is highly dependent on the availability of reliable data from the IR offices.

The absence of well-structured IR units in many East African higher education institutions hinders their ability to make evidence-based decisions. Without formalised IR practices, education institutions lack the tools to systematically collect, analyse, and apply data to their governance and planning processes. This gap is particularly noteworthy because of the increasing demand for accountability and transparency in higher education, as well as the need to meet international quality standards (Boden & Crockett, 2017).

The globalization of higher education has further highlighted the significance of IR in East African universities. As institutions seek to align with global standards, trends, and forces, they require reliable data to track performance and ensure compliance with international accreditation standards. According to Sanga (2019), there is a symbiotic relationship between institutional research and globalization. While IR provides the data-driven insights necessary to meet global education trends, adopting global practices enhances its effectiveness in supporting institutional governance. Universities in East Africa, such as the University of Dar es Salaam and the University of Nairobi, have implemented reforms aimed at improving competitiveness and aligning with global standards. For instance, during the 1980s economic crisis, the University of Dar es Salaam established the Bureau for Industrial Cooperation (BICO) to promote consulting work, which highlighted the role of IR in supporting institutional growth and sustainability (Sanga, 2019).

According to Sanga (2019), the University of Dar es Salaam, University of Nairobi, and Makerere University have been implementing strategic reforms to enhance entrepreneurship skills, optimise resource utilisation, upgrade ICT infrastructure, increase academic support, improve staff quality, promote innovative modes of delivery, create a conducive environment for research and development, develop effective leadership systems, strengthen partnerships, diversify income sources, invest in e-learning, engage in international partnerships, boost quality assurance, and expand capacity in Science Technology Engineering and Mathematics (STEM) education. Other universities in the East African region have quickly adopted the innovations from these pioneering universities. Perhaps if these universities had explicitly institutionalised the practice of institutional research, they could have influenced other higher education institutions to be more deliberate in the implementation of institutional research practices.

While there has been some progress in integrating IR into East African universities, several challenges persist. In the East African region, IR practice remains underdeveloped, with many institutions lacking dedicated IR units. Data systems are fragmented, and limited resources and infrastructure hinder the full potential of IR in supporting institutional governance. Universities need capacity building to effectively manage and analyse institutional data, which requires trained staff (Webber, Botha, & Muller, 2016). However, there are promising opportunities for enhancing IR practices in the region. The Demographics of African Faculty in the East African Community (DAF EAC) Phase II project (2023-2025) aims to establish harmonised guidelines for data collection and management within the East African Community (EAC). This initiative has the potential to promote the institutionalisation of IR across East African universities, providing a framework for better data-driven governance and planning (IUCEA, 2024). Additionally, the growing emphasis on quality assurance and accreditation processes offers an avenue for strengthening IR. As HEIs in the East African region strive to meet international standards, the integration of IR with QA will become increasingly important for improving institutional effectiveness and promoting sustainable educational plans (Braun, 2008).

In general, institutional research is a necessary practice for East African higher education governance. However, the formalisation of this practice has been slow, which has limited institutions' ability to make data-driven decisions. The section below analyses the costs of not integrating institutional research in institutional decision-making.

THE COST OF LACKING INSTITUTIONAL RESEARCH UNITS IN EAST AFRICAN HIGHER EDUCATION INSTITUTIONS

Compared to South Africa and the rest of the world, East African higher education institutions have less formalized IR practices and weaker integration with national educational policies. This gap in utilizing IR for strategic planning and policy alignment potentially hinders institutional improvement and responsiveness to regional educational needs. The Demographics of African Faculty in the East African Community (DAF EAC) Phase II report, funded by the Carnegie Corporation of New York, highlights significant data gaps at institutional, national, and regional levels, revealing fragmented and inconsistent faculty data in higher education institutions (HEIs). Countries such as Burundi, South Sudan, Uganda, Rwanda, and Tanzania, in particular, require additional faculty members to bridge these gaps (IUCEA, 2024). The East African Community (EAC) faces a persistent data deficit, including financial metrics, human capital, student admissions, research outputs, and academic programs, which hinders the region from realizing its full potential (Guchu, 2023).

The challenges of incorporating IR into internal quality assurance (IQA) and other institutional decision-making processes in East Africa include limited data integration, access issues, ensuring data quality, adapting to technological changes, and navigating legal and ethical data-use frameworks (Eryenyu et al., 2020). Internal stakeholders in institutions that have not fully adopted IR as part of their management and decision-making processes often display limited cooperation in data collection and use, thereby limiting the influence of IR on governance and policy setting. This highlights the need for East African universities to strengthen their IR capabilities, integrate data-driven decision-making, and better align with national and regional educational policies to enhance governance and academic outcomes.

A deficiency of dedicated institutional research officers further worsens the challenges in African HEIs, particularly in addressing student welfare and academic issues. Problems such as student strikes due to rising tuition fees, inadequate practical training, biased assessment procedures, and poor campus living conditions remain widespread (Kakada & Deshpande, 2018; Sanga, 2019). Sanga (2019) also notes that the lack of institutional reforms in East African higher education is largely due to insufficient self-studies to guide strategic decisions. Without data-driven reforms, institutions face difficulties in achieving their goals effectively.

To address these challenges, institutional leaders must embrace IR as a tool not only for planning and decision-making but also for fostering institutional change, innovation, and long-term development. The need for institutional effectiveness and accountability is more critical than ever, especially in the face of changes and innovations reshaping higher education delivery globally. By institutionalising IR practices, East African institutions can significantly improve their ability to respond to governance challenges and contribute more effectively to national and regional educational policies.

CASE STUDIES HIGHLIGHTING THE BENEFITS OF INSTITUTIONAL RESEARCH UNITS IN HIGHER EDUCATION INSTITUTIONS

CASE 1: Geyser, H., & Murdoch, N. (2016). Quality assurance and institutional research. In J. Botha & N. Muller (Eds.), *Institutional Research in South African Higher Education* (pp. 143-166). African Sun Media.

Geyser and Murdoch (2016) investigated the link between Quality Assurance (QA) and Institutional Research (IR) and how the two can support institutional governance in South Africa. They described how the expansion of education after World War II led to the establishment and development of institutional research (IR), and how the practice of IR evolved as reporting and accountability requirements increased. However, formal quality assurance (QA) systems in higher education are a new phenomenon, with widespread adoption occurring in the 1950s and 1960s. In 1995, South Africa established the first national unit for QA, identifying planning, funding, and quality assurance as mechanisms to steer the higher education system towards national goals. To promote quality assurance in higher education and accredit programs, they established the Council on Higher Education (CHE) and the Higher Education Quality Committee (HEQC). In South Africa, quality is defined as fitness for purpose, providing value for money, achieving effectiveness and efficiency, enabling transformation, and meeting social and economic requirements. Internationally, references to quality enhancement (QE) started to emerge after 2000, and South Africa launched the National Quality Enhancement Project (QEP) in 2014. Driving forces for the expansion of QA include the diversification of higher education systems, the emergence of a private higher education sector, increasing demand for higher education, and internationalization of higher education. During the first QA cycle in South Africa, institutions underwent comprehensive quality audits and established QA units. They explored the extent to which these QA activities have impacted lasting and sustainable QA practices in institutions and the links between QA and IR activities.

Geyser and Murdoch (2016) noted that in higher education institutions, integrating QA (Quality Assurance) and IR (Institutional Research) is important because the data provided by IR and other support units may not always be immediately usable or user-friendly. As a result, IR units must use analysis and interpretation to convert it into information and institutional knowledge. They recommend allocating responsibility for applying this data in the context of institutional goals. And advised that institutions should also disseminate such data in multiple formats to inform recommendations and planning.

In an integrated model, IR and QA units take on progressive leadership roles, educate staff, and advocate for evidence-based decision-making. The use of QA and IR provides expertise in trends that affect their institutions and inform goals, vision, and mission. Collaboration between the two offices can achieve integration in various ways, including an integrated governance approach or unique institution-specific mechanisms. *Therefore, (*Geyser & Murdoch, 2016) concluded that the integration and collaboration between QA and IR are coincidental and reactive. However, both QA and IR should inform decision-making processes, and their contributions differ in terms of data collection and the types of intelligence produced. Institutions need a comprehensive and structured approach to address staff competence in QA, national collaboration, and data integration to support institutional goals.

CASE 2: Nel, H. (2016). The role of institutional research in support of strategic planning. In J. Botha & N. J. Muller (Eds.), *Institutional Research in South African Higher Education: Intersecting Contexts and Practices* (pp. 99-116). African Sun Media.

In the book chapter: The Role of Institutional Research in Support of Strategic Planning, Heather (2016) discussed how institutional research (IR) plays an important role in facilitating strategic planning and organisational transformation at Nelson Mandela Metropolitan University (NMMU). Heather highlights the significance of IR in strategic planning, drawing on Volkwein's (1999) and Serban and Luan's (2002) perspectives on the different aspects of IR, Terenzini's (2013) levels of organisational intelligence, and Uh-Bien et al.'s (2007) complexity approach to organisational learning and revitalisation. The data collected from the institution's internal members indicated a link between institutional research and the successful implementation of the strategic plan. In the study, Heather (2016) emphasized the significance of openness, creativity, and creating an environment conducive to innovation and learning.

The findings of Heather's case study demonstrate that the practice of institutional research (IR) at NMMU has facilitated an ongoing organisational improvement and utilised the innovativeness arising from institutional research practices. Nel and Heather's findings align with the Association for Institutional Research's (AIR) publication. According to AIR, institutions must engage in data-driven strategic planning to showcase their performance and fulfil stakeholder expectations (AIR, 2019). By integrating data and prioritizing smart objectives and methods, institutions can benefit substantially. AIR affirms that the creation and utilization of institutional research offices are critical in obtaining and transforming data into practical information for strategic planning.

CASE 3: Botha, J., & Muller, N. J. (2016). Roles and functions, and titles. In J. Botha & N. J. Muller (Eds.), *Institutional Research in South African Higher Education: Intersecting Contexts and Practices*. African Sun Media.

Botha and Muller (2016) noted in their study on adopting the practice of institutional research (IR) in South African universities that the primary responsibilities of IR offices are to furnish dependable information and evidence that facilitate decision-making, institutional governance, and quality management. The survey conducted on IR offices revealed that the predicted workload of the officers is expanding due to the state and its agencies' demands for policy implementation. They noted that most IR offices primarily dedicate their time to reporting. The organizations of institutional IR offices had a variety of structural arrangements and functions, such as small adhocracies and professional bureaucracy. In South Africa, the most advanced qualifications for IR workers are PhD degrees, while some possess master's degrees and even bachelor's degrees.

Three tiers of organisational intelligence can classify the duties carried out by IR offices in South Africa: technical or analytical intelligence, problem intelligence, and contextual intelligence. The main purpose of South African IR offices is to provide analytical intelligence. In South Africa, the most common position held by IR specialists is information officer. The primary focus of IR offices in South African institutions is mostly internal analysis, with a secondary emphasis on external authority, policy analysis, spin doctor, and research work. The institutional units where the lower IR offices are located determine and shape their foci, with offices in faculties often focusing on academic matters and those in central management focusing on external reporting of institutional data.

While the needs and interests of the institution can influence the organisational structure of institutional research (IR) offices, the location of the IR office within the structure can influence its effectiveness and authority. The institution's commitment to the IR function increases with the office's placement in the structure. Therefore, to benefit from the position of power, the office of institutional research should be as close as possible to the office of the institution's head (Botha & Muller, 2016). A typical bureaucratic or hierarchical cascade structure should guide this process. In South African higher education institutions, IR offices can report to positions such as Vice Chancellor, Deputy Vice Chancellor, Senior Director, Chief Operating Officer, and Chief Information Officer (Botha & Muller, 2016). The can be adapted for the East African higher education area.

CASE 4: Botha, J. (2016). The Synergy between the SAAIR Conference Events and South African Higher Education Policy Initiatives during 1994-2015. In J. Botha & N. J. Muller (Eds.), *Institutional Research in South African Higher Education: Intersecting Contexts and Practices* (p. 43). African Sun Media.

Botha (2016), in his article, "The Synergy between the SAAIR Conference Events and South African Higher Education Policy Initiatives during 1994-2015," analysed the relationship between Institutional Research (IR) practitioners and departments in South Africa and higher education policy developments from 1994-2015. He explored whether policy developments determined IR practitioners' priorities or if IR practitioners' work provided evidence for these policies. The study used data from the annual SAAIR conference programs to compile a demographic profile of conference proceedings. The analysis covered 560 conference events presented by 485 individuals (researchers) during the period analysed. The analysis results revealed a synergy between national policy developments and the interests and activities of IR professionals in South African higher education institutions. He also found a decrease in conference events which focused on traditional IR functions such as planning and monitoring. However, there was an increased focus on teaching, learning, and curriculum development. This suggests a synergy between the work of IR practitioners and national policy priorities in higher education. Botha observes that while the SAAIR maintains a distance from formal operational involvement in government departments and agencies, there are links between the work of IR practitioners and IR offices at an institutional level. IR practitioners value the freedom offered by their professional associations to go beyond their employer's work and interests. Botha's (2016) work confirms the relevance of IR departments in South African universities, which have contributed to institutional and national higher education policies. In general, IR and education policy work together. Since the practices of IR in East African universities are less formalised, the institutions and education systems in the region must be missing this synergy between IR and education policies.

Integrated Insights from the Case Studies

The case studies underscore the critical role of institutional research (IR) and quality assurance (QA) in higher education institutions for effective governance and decision-making. This chapter analysed four case studies from higher education institutions in the South African region and highlighted the evolving role of IR in relation to QA, strategic planning, institutional governance, and policy development (Geyser & Murdoch, 2016; Nel & Heather, 2016; Botha & Muller, 2016; Botha, 2016). The results show how IR and QA have changed over time in South Africa. They also show how important it is to combine these two practices for good institutional governance and a structured way of enhancing institutional quality (Geyser & Murdoch, 2016).

The case studies further illustrate how IR facilitates organisational intelligence and innovation through data-driven strategic planning, aligning with the principles of the Association for Institutional Research (AIR) (Nel & Heather, 2016). Botha and Muller (2016) point out that IR offices play a central role in providing data for decision-making, governance, and quality management. However, they also note the increasing demands placed on IR offices due to evolving policy requirements.

From the analysis of these case studies, a key conclusion emerges: institutional research (IR) is necessary for supporting mechanisms for institutional governance, quality assurance, and strategic planning in South African higher education institutions. The integration of IR and QA is key for ensuring data-driven decision-making, and IR units must assume more prominent leadership roles in shaping institutional goals and visions. Moreover, careful placement of IR offices within institutional hierarchies is necessary for their effectiveness (Botha & Muller, 2016). The higher the IR office, the more effective in influencing institutional policies. Botha (2016) also explores the relationship between IR practitioners and South Africa's higher education policy developments, confirming a strong alignment between IR activities and national policy priorities. This synergy has contributed to well-established IR practices in South African universities, which, in turn, inform and shape national higher education policies.

In contrast, IR practices in East African universities appear to be less formalised, which may hinder the alignment between IR and educational policies in the region. As a result, East African universities need to strengthen their IR capabilities and align them more closely with national and regional educational policies to enhance governance and academic outcomes. By learning from the best practices observed in South Africa, East African higher education institutions can work toward establishing and reinforcing institutional IR units, which would support institutional governance, quality assurance, and strategic planning in the region.

INSTITUTIONAL RESEARCH AS AN AGENT OF ENHANCED EDUCATIONAL OUTCOMES AND INSTITUTIONAL EFFECTIVENESS

The East Africa region has the potential to expand by fostering regional partnerships and utilising existing frameworks such as the Inter-University Council of East Africa (IUCEA). The existence of the IUCEA provides an important organisational framework within the East African Community (EAC) that can mobilise HEIs to promote the establishment and implementation of IR practices. In 2006,

IUCEA collaborated with the German Academic Exchange Service (DAAD) and the Germany Rectors' Conference (HRK) to establish a regional quality assurance system in East Africa. The Harmonisation of Higher Education QA in East Africa framework includes four operational tools: Principles and Guidelines for Quality Assurance in Higher Education, regional quality assurance instruments, academic program benchmarks, the East African Higher Education Quality Assurance Network, and the East African Qualifications Framework for Higher Education. The system necessitates careful planning and resource allocation, backed up by thorough institutional research. The successful development and implementation of the East African quality assurance framework demonstrate the ability to open new boundaries in higher education and the adoption of beneficial practices such as IR. The relevant higher education institutions and the IUCEA secretariat should conduct institutional research to support the careful planning and resource allocation required for the integration of IR into the regional education framework.

Since IUCEA has already played a leading role in developing the quality assurance system for East Africa, it implies that it has the potential to do the same for the development and implementation of institutional research practices in member institutions. The IUCEA could advocate for the establishment of the East African Association of Institutional Research (EAAIR), which could serve as the umbrella organisation for the successful implementation of IR activities in the region. Universities in the East African region need to employ IR officers because implementing quality assurance processes and strategic plans requires data from the office of Institutional Research to facilitate efficient planning and plan implementation. The IR teams will be responsible for methodically gathering, examining, and interpreting data to support decision-making and policy development on student demographics, academic achievement, faculty research productivity, and financial management, discovering patterns and areas of improvement.

The complexity of modern higher education, which requires the development of institutional policies tailored to specific institutional challenges, requires applying institutional research. This is an opportunity for institutional researchers to use their understanding of IR and practical aspects to solve specific institutional problems. The East African higher education system can improve education policy studies by undertaking IR, which focuses on specific institutions. Currently, the Institutional research practice in Ugandan universities, and perhaps most universities in the East African region, remains a disjointed effort across different departments and offices (Eryenyu, 2021). Predominantly, the work related to institutional research activities is undertaken by the university planner's office or the quality assurance directorate. However, the planning units are often deeper in data usage than data collection and analysis. This makes the units less practical for managing institutional research.

Universities, where there is a department of institutional research planning, use organised data to facilitate the planning units.

The Quality Assurance offices and the Academic Affairs Office also participate in some institutional research activities, primarily to maintain the quality and standards of academic programs and operations. At the same time, the Information and Communication Technology (ICT) Directorate manages the data systems, infrastructure, and analytics tools used for institutional research. The Academic Registrar's Office, in particular, manages student records, enrolment data, and academic schedules, contributing data and insights related to student demographics, enrolment trends, and academic performance to institutional research efforts. Faculty members and research committees may engage in research activities that contribute to institutional research goals, such as teaching effectiveness, curriculum development, and student learning outcomes. The quality assurance directorate also conducts external peer evaluations. Unlike universities with IR units, these departments conduct such studies on specific occasions. The fact that these activities are similar to what takes place in the offices of IR in universities are taking place within universities provides an opportunity to organise them into a structured organisational arrangement called the Office of Institutional Research. In the following section, this chapter presents a framework for operationalizing the implementation of an institutional research unit in higher education institutions in East Africa.

AN INSTITUTIONAL RESEARCH IMPLEMENTATION FRAMEWORK

The framework described here is a proposal for establishing the Directorate of Institutional Research in East African Higher Education Institutions. That is, to implement institutional research in East African higher education Institutions, this chapter recommends the establishment of a centralized institutional research unit (office, department, or directorate) that serves as a coordinating point for all institutional research activities and provides data-driven information for decision-making (Chirikov, Igor, 2013; Haskell, Chester, 2017; AIR, 2020). Enhancing the training and development programs for institutional research personnel can support the process of establishing IR offices; enhancing the ability of IR officers to conduct research and apply the results to improve institutional performance (Tashtoush, 2021; Terenzini, 2013). Collaboration with external stakeholders, such as other institutions and the industry, is also important for knowledge exchange (Altbach, 2013; Hwang, 2018). It is recommended to have professional institutional researchers who understand research ethics, data integrity, research regulations, and the socio-political aspects of institutional planning.

An institutional research directorate's core staff includes a director providing leadership data specialists in data analysis, data managers responsible for data collection and storage, and an administrative assistant for administrative tasks. They work with various data enumerators and other departments to ensure effective governance and coordination. Once established, the operationalisation of an institutional research directorate involves a need assessment, policy drafting, and human resource capacity building. This includes training methodologies, data analysis techniques, hiring qualified personnel, and establishing partnerships with mature or well-established IR systems. Institutions should integrate the directorate of IR into mainstream institutional budgeting systems, incorporating emerging best practices and trends. The operation of IR units can be budgeted for as a project before integration, but securing sufficient funding from government grants, international donors, university budgets, and private-sector partnerships is important for the project's success.

Specific recommendations for East African universities include enhancing institutional research practices such as establishing dedicated institutional research offices, building capacity for research professionals, fostering collaboration and partnerships, advocating for the establishment of an East African Association of Institutional Research, utilising existing frameworks such as the Inter-University Council of East Africa, improving data utilisation, and organising institutional research activities. These measures can help universities collect, analyse, and interpret data to support decision-making and policy development, ultimately improving the quality of higher education in the region.

All higher education institutions (HEIs) in East Africa should develop and operate institutional research offices, departments, or directorates. Building capacity for institutional research personnel or professionals should be the next step. The region should join the rest of the world in relying on data-backed evidence as a pivot for university governance. The IUCEA should seek collaboration from SAAIR or any other IR association on the formation and management of the East African Association of Institutional Research (EAAIR). The inter-university council should promote institutional research practices, starting with formally creating the East African Association of Institutional Research to promote and provide leadership to institutions in developing and managing institutional research developments.

The formation of the East African Association of Institutional Research (EAA-IR) could support institutional research practice and facilitate knowledge exchange and collaboration among East African member universities (Sepahi et al., 2021; Tashtoush, 2021). This would allow universities to address common challenges and learn from each other's IR research findings and best practices. Additionally, IR offers data-driven perspectives for formulating policies, strategizing plans, and making decisions. It helps overcome obstacles such as resource limitations, expansion challenges, and quality assurance concerns; promotes transparency, accountability, and ongoing development; and attracts international students and faculty.

Several conceptual frameworks for implementing IR in universities do exist; this chapter adopts and recommends institutional research as a service provider (Randy & Leah, 2016), Figure 1. Randy and Leah's (2016) model adheres to the AIR's six-component framework for institutional research. According to AIR (2019), a framework for establishing and maintaining an institutional research function in higher education institutions consists of six components: leadership and direction, organisational structure and roles, data management and integration, analysis and reporting, dissemination and communication, and professional development and evaluation. The model aims to define the role of institutional research in supporting university goals, establish a clear vision and mission, identify key stakeholders, and establish reporting lines and relationships with other departments. It is a widely accepted model among IR practitioners

Figure 1. **Institutional research as service provider to different Institutional units: Adapted from, A New Vision for Institutional Research, Change (Randy & Leah, 2016)**

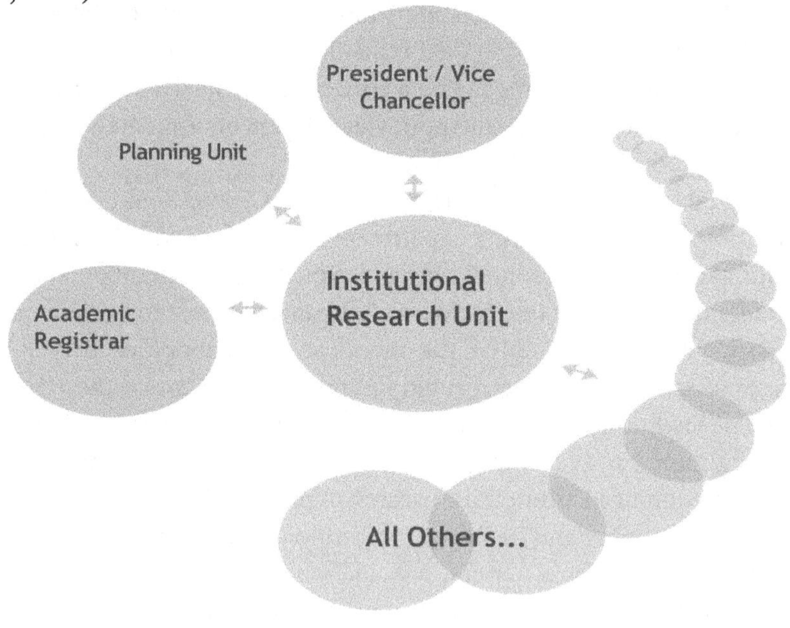

Whereas institutional research (IR) enhances universities' effectiveness, efficiency, and global strategic direction, East African universities seem to have lagged in explicitly applying IR practices in their governance landscapes. This chapter presents

a systematic proposal for establishing the Directorate of Institutional Research in a typical East African university. Universities that may be "small" can scale this proposal down to the Department of Institutional Research. If adopted, universities can significantly benefit from the systematic ways of guiding management decisions. The Directorate of Institutional Research can serve as a foundation for fostering excellence and innovation in higher education across East African universities, ensuring they remain responsive to the evolving needs of students, stakeholders, and society. By promoting a culture of evidence-based decision-making and continuous improvement, the Directorate will contribute to advancing higher education in East Africa and support broader socio-economic development goals. Therefore, each university should establish a directorate of institutional research.

The Scope and Objectives of Establishing the Directorate of Institutional Research

Based on the guidelines of (AIR, 2019), the Directorate of Institutional Research will be a centralized unit in the university to oversee and coordinate institutional research activities within universities, including developing standardised data collection methodologies, establishing a central repository, conducting student enrolment and retention analyses, monitoring progress towards strategic goals, providing regular reports, and facilitating staff professional development. Specifically, the direction will provide data to improve data-driven decision-making in East African higher education institutions, promote evidence-based policy formulation, support institutional effectiveness, foster research excellence, and facilitate knowledge sharing among universities and external stakeholders.

EXPECTED CHALLENGES FOR HIGHER EDUCATION INSTITUTIONS IN IMPLEMENTING INSTITUTIONAL RESEARCH

The case studies explored in this chapter indicate that implementing institutional research (IR) in educational institutions worldwide presents several common challenges that institutions often encounter. These challenges are more severe or prominent in regions or countries where IR is not formally recognised as an institutional management practice or where there are no associations of institutional research (IR) to promote its practices. The challenges facing IR globally include limited resources, lack of institutional culture, data quality, technical infrastructure, IR-skilled personnel, limited capacity building for IR, institutional politics, nontransparent governance practices, disengaged faculty, unethical use of internal data, and an inability to measure impact.

Although the COVID-19 pandemic has reactivated the necessity for universities to enhance their institutional data collection and analysis (Douglass & Chirikov, 2020), the majority of organisations continue to have inadequate formal policies and strategies for the recruitment of professional institutional researchers. Douglass and Chirikov(2020) observe that the use of institutional research (IR) in universities is primarily reactive, with an emphasis on meeting the increasing demand for data from ministries of education and other government agencies in order to comply with growing accountability schemes or participate in the global ranking competition of universities. The reactive nature of IR's application to institutional programs and the limited capacity for its implementation reduce its ability to address problems, foster innovation, or even support the enhancement of education quality assurance practices.

Eryenyu et al. (2020) point out that challenges to the use of IR include the underuse of collected data. But Douglass and Chirikov (2020) argue that short-term university leadership and a lack of organisational institutional research efforts (associations) are all prohibitive to the effective use of the principles of institutional research, not only in East Africa but globally. For practical implementation of institutional research in academic institutions, institutions need professional staff, an institutional research conceptual model, and collaborations with regional and national universities to build a comparative perspective of IR. These are all limiting factors, at least in terms of East African higher education.

People often explain that limited resources, particularly in developing regions, impede the development and maintenance of institutional research (IR). This belief among HEIs, however, ignores the fact that IR supports proper planning, and the application of IR saves resources. So, while it is argued that there are not enough resources to support the establishment and operationalisation of IR offices in institutions, this can also be seen as a lack of understanding of the power of data-driven planning or decision-making in saving resource wastage.

In the East African context, institutional research (IR) is relatively an emerging concept compared to regions like the USA, Canada, Australia, and Latin America, which have well-established IR practices and dedicated offices within universities. In East Africa, IR practices are more selective, implicit, less comprehensive, and ad hoc, largely tailored to quality assurance and regulatory compliance. Within institutions, the support for IR in East Africa is more sporadic, with funding, expertise, and institutional buy-in challenges. Within the East African HEIs, it is rare to find dedicated IR offices and professionals. There is no institutional research association to promote and advocate for the use of data-driven planning and decision-making.

Global challenges such as resource constraints, data quality concerns, technological infrastructure deficiencies, and the need for capacity building for IR professionals plague the implementation of institutional research (IR). We thus need a strategic approach that involves leadership commitment, stakeholder engagement, adequate resources, and continuous improvement to address some of these challenges. We dedicate the following section to proposing such strategies.

STRATEGIES FOR OVERCOMING THE INSTITUTIONAL RESEARCH IMPLEMENTATION CHALLENGES

Overcoming implementation challenges in institutional research requires a combination of strategic planning, effective communication, resilience, and adaptability. The following strategies, if properly employed in higher education institutions, can overcome common implementation challenges and ensure the successful integration of research initiatives into their operations.

1. Clear goals and objectives: According to Volkwein (2011, p. 12), "Establishing clear goals and objectives is essential for successful institutional research." Peterson and Corckett (2017, p. 25) assert that "clear goals and objectives help ensure that all stakeholders are working towards the same outcomes." This will help to avoid uncoordinated implementation and duplication of goals within the different units of the institution.
2. Stakeholder engagement: Before establishing an institutional research unit, "Stakeholder engagement is critical for building support and buy-in for institutional research initiatives" (Terenzini, 2013, p. 15). Stakeholder engagement ensures that researchers, administrators, and IT staff collaborate to ensure successful implementation of institutional research within the institution (Borden & Starobin, 2017).
3. Data management planning: A study by the National Science Foundation (2018, p. 5) posits that "a robust data management plan is essential for ensuring data quality, integrity, and compliance." Similarly, findings of a study by the Data Management Association (2019, p. 10) indicate that "effective data management planning can help mitigate risks and ensure the long-term sustainability of research data." Technical staff capable of handling data management effectively and efficiently must adequately staff the IR unit in this case.
4. Technical infrastructure: Inadequate infrastructure will undoubtedly challenge the establishment and implementation of an institutional research unit. The solution to this is the procurement of "adequate technical infrastructure... essential for supporting research data management and analysis" (National Institutes

of Health, 2019, p. 12). According to EDUCAUSE (2020, p. 15), "Investing in robust technical infrastructure can help ensure the success of institutional research initiatives.

5. Training and support: We highly recommend continuous training and support of the staff to sustain the effectiveness and efficiency of the institutional research unit's implementation. According to Börner et al. (2019, p. 18), "Providing training and ongoing support is essential for ensuring researcher proficiency with new tools and methods." Similarly, Cragin and Hansen (2017, p. 22) observe that "training and support can help build capacity and confidence among researchers and staff."
6. Change management: Institutional research will be a new initiative within higher education institutions. Therefore, reimagining the capacity of stakeholders for "Embracing a culture of adaptability [will be] essential for navigating the challenges of institutional research" (Kuh & Gonyea, 2019, p. 15). This will enable the institutions to be "prepared to pivot when faced with unexpected challenges or changes" (Boden & Corckett, 2017, p. 25).
7. Communication and feedback: To overcome the challenge of communication, Volkwein (2011, p. 18) asserts that "Regular communication and feedback are essential for building trust and ensuring the success of institutional research initiatives." This suggests that the institution must establish a culture of consistent communication and feedback to effectively implement the research initiatives. Peterson and McCockett (2017) note that "Soliciting feedback from stakeholders can help identify areas for improvement and ensure the implementation process is on track."
8. Risk management: The National Science Foundation (2018, p. 10) notes that "identifying and mitigating potential risks is essential for ensuring the success of institutional research initiatives." According to the Data Management Association (2019, p. 12), "Effective risk management can help minimise the impact of potential risks and ensure the long-term sustainability of research data." Therefore, institutions need to establish buffers for risk management in order to guarantee the sustainability of the institutional research units.
9. Scalability and flexibility: Research is always evolving. This implies that any initiative to institutionalize institutional research should consider the unit's growing needs. As noted by Börner et al. (2019, p. 20), "Designing implementation to be scalable and flexible can help ensure the long-term sustainability of institutional research initiatives." EDUCAUSE (2020, p. 18) similarly notes that "Scalability and flexibility are essential for accommodating evolving research needs and technological advancements."

10. Evaluation and continuous improvement: The success of any initiative is dependent on ongoing evaluation and improvement. Volkwein (2011, p. 20) observes that "Regular assessment and evaluation are essential for ensuring the success of institutional research initiatives." Also, Peterson and Corckett (2017, p. 30) note that "continuous improvement is critical for ensuring the implementation process is on track and making adjustments as needed." Therefore, institutions implementing institutional research as a unit must establish mechanisms to continuously evaluate the inputs, processes, and products for their suitability.

Future Research Directions for Institutional Research in East Africa

As the landscape of higher education in the East African region continues to evolve, institutional research is set for substantial growth that could transform the sector. Given that this field is still developing in the region, there are numerous research areas to explore for further advancement of the institutional research concept. These areas include, but are not limited to, the following:

1. Conducting a comparative analysis of IR practices across East African countries to understand the differences and similarities in IR practices. This analysis will help to understand how national policies, cultures, and governance structures impact the effectiveness of IR in informing higher education governance.
2. Assessing the human resource capacity required for optimal IR implementation in East African universities. This assessment will help determine the universities' readiness and capabilities to effectively implement IR.
3. Examining how institutional leaders perceive and utilize IR. This research will help in identifying the gaps between data collection and decision-making processes.
4. Assessing the ethical considerations in East African IR practices. Investigate the ethical dimensions of IR, including data privacy, the ethical use of student and staff information, and the maintenance of ethical standards in IR in East African institutions. This can boost the acceptability of IR practices.
5. A research on technology and data analytics in IR: To explore the potential of emerging technologies like big data, artificial intelligence, and machine learning in enhancing the effectiveness of IR in East African institutions.
6. Examining the role of IR in promoting equity and inclusion in East African higher education, focusing on gender, socioeconomic, and regional disparities
7. Investigating how Institutional Research influences Policy Implementation: The research problem here is to investigate the role of Institutional Research (IR) in translating research findings into actionable policies within East African higher

education systems, focusing on identifying the barriers to policy adoption based on IR findings and exploring strategies to mitigate these barriers.

8. A research to investigate the role of institutional research (IR) in enhancing funding allocation models in higher education. Specifically, it is important to explore how data-driven research can facilitate the equitable and efficient distribution of financial resources among departments, faculties, and universities.

Specific Recommendations for Higher Education Institutions

Based on the evidence from the reviewed cases and the historical record of institutional research (IR), this chapter suggests that East African higher education institutions should take certain steps to improve their IR practices and ensure that IR has a significant impact on governance and strategic decision-making. Specifically, institutions should:

1. Establish a dedicated institutional research office or directorate: Each East African University or institution should establish a centralised institutional research office or directorate to coordinate and oversee institutional research activities. These offices should be responsible for coordinating and overseeing data collection, analysis, and reporting. The established office or directorate should have a clear scope and objectives, and its staff should include a manager or director, data specialists, data managers, and the necessary administrative support.
2. Build capacity for institutional research personnel: Universities should invest in training and development programs for institutional research professionals. This will equip them to conduct research and apply the results appropriately and effectively.
3. Overcome implementation challenges, universities should set clear goals and objectives, engage stakeholders, develop data management plans, invest in technical infrastructure, provide training and support, implement change management strategies, and ensure effective communication and feedback.
4. Foster collaboration and partnerships: Universities should collaborate with other institutions and external stakeholders to share knowledge, exchange best practices, and promote research excellence. Establishing associations or networks dedicated to institutional research activities can accomplish this.
5. Advocate for the establishment of an East African Association of Institutional Research: The Inter-University Council of East Africa (IUCEA) should advocate for the creation of an association that focusses on promoting and supporting institutional research in the region. This association can provide leadership and

guidance, as well as mobilize resources for universities to develop and implement IR practices.

6. Improve data utilization: To support decision-making and policy development, universities should prioritize the collection, analysis, and interpretation of data. This includes data on student demographics, academic achievement, faculty research productivity, and financial management.
7. Organise institutional research activities: Universities should organise their institutional research activities by establishing clear goals and objectives, engaging stakeholders, developing data management plans, investing in technical infrastructure, providing training and support, and implementing change management strategies.

CONCLUSION

In conclusion, this chapter has demonstrated the vital role that institutional research (IR) plays in informing higher education governance practices. The findings from the case studies highlight the significance of IR in providing data-driven insights that enable informed decision-making, strategic planning, and policy development in higher education institutions. The effective use of IR has improved governance practices, leading to enhanced institutional performance, quality assurance, and student success in many countries and higher education institutions that have institutionalised IR. The chapter foregrounds the need for East African higher education institutions to prioritise the development and utilisation of IR capabilities to address the region's unique Educational challenges and opportunities. By leveraging IR, institutions can foster a culture of evidence-based decision-making, drive innovation, and ultimately contribute to the advancement of higher education in the region. If implemented, the proposed framework for implementing IR provides a roadmap for policymakers, institutional leaders, and researchers to harness IR's potential in transforming higher education governance in East Africa.

REFERENCES

Agasisti, T. & Bowers, A., (2018). Data Analytics and Decision-Making in Education: Towards the Educational Data Scientist as a Key Actor in Schools and Higher Education Institutions. .DOI: 10.4337/9781785369070.00014

Altbach, P. G. (2013). The internationalization of higher education: Motivations and realities. *Journal of Studies in International Education*, 17(3), 348–361.

Altbach, P. G. (2014). The emergence of a field: Research and training in higher education. *Studies in Higher Education*, 39(8), 1306–1320. DOI: 10.1080/03075079.2014.949541

Association for Institutional Research (AIR). (2019). Research and evaluation in East Africa. https://www.air.org/regions/east-africa

Association for the Development of Education in Africa (ADEA). (2011*). Creating an African Higher Education and Research Space*. https://sig.ias.edu/news/adea-creating-african-higher-education-and-research-space

Atchison, E. S. (2020). Enhancing institutional research capacity in the midst of a pandemic: A system approach. *New Directions for Institutional Research*, 2020(187–188), 55–63. DOI: 10.1002/ir.20347

Bai Gokarna, V., Mendon, S., Thonse Hawaldar, I., Spulbar, C., Birau, R., Nayak, S., & Manohar, M. (2021). Exploring the antecedents of institutional effectiveness: A case study of higher education universities in India. *Ekonomska Istrazivanja*, 35(1), 1162–1182. DOI: 10.1080/1331677X.2021.1959367

Bers, T. H. (2008). The role of institutional research in assessing student learning outcomes. *New Directions for Higher Education*, 141(141), 31–39. DOI: 10.1002/he.291

Bloom, D. E., Canning, D., Chan, K. J., & Luca, D. L. (2014). Higher education and economic growth in Africa. *International Journal of African Higher Education*, 1(1), 22–57. DOI: 10.6017/ijahe.v1i1.5643

Boden, D., & Corckett, J. (2017). Embracing change in research initiatives. *Sage (Atlanta, Ga.)*.

Borden, V., Massa, T., & Milam, J. (2001). Technology and tools for institutional research. In Howard, R. (Ed.), *IR: Decision support in higher education* (pp. 195–222). Association of Institutional Research.

Borden, V. M. H., & Starobin, S. S. (2017). *Collaborative approaches to research.* AERA.

Börner, A.. (2019). *Research support services.* Springer.

Bosch, A., & Taylor, J. (2011). A proposed framework for institutional research development phases. *Journal of Higher Education Policy and Management*, 33(5), 443–457. DOI: 10.1080/1360080X.2011.585742

Botha, J., & Muller, N. J. (Eds.). (2016). *Institutional research in South African higher education: Intersecting contexts and practices.* African Sun Media., DOI: 10.18820/9781928357186/01

Botha, J., Webber, K., Williams, J., & Woodfield, S. (2024). Building capacity in institutional research: Collaboration and complementarity? *Tertiary Education and Management*, 30(2), 129–145. Advance online publication. DOI: 10.1007/s11233-024-09139-0

Brown, J. (2008). Institutional research and external reporting: The major data seekers. *New Directions for Higher Education*, 141(141), 87–96. DOI: 10.1002/he.296

Calderon, A., & Mathies, C. (2013). Institutional research in the future: Challenges within higher education and the need for excellence in professional practice. *New Directions for Institutional Research*, 157(157), 77–90. DOI: 10.1002/ir.20040

Calderon, A. J., & Webber, K. L. (2015). Institutional research, planning, and decision support in higher education today. In Calderon, A. J., & Webber, K. L. (Eds.), *Institutional Research and Planning in Higher Education* (pp. 3–15). Routledge.

Chirikov, I. (2013). Research universities as knowledge networks: The role of institutional research. *Studies in Higher Education*, 38(3), 456–469. DOI: 10.1080/03075079.2013.773778

Chirikov, I. (2013). Research universities as knowledge networks: The role of institutional research. *Studies in Higher Education*, 38(10), 1716–1730. DOI: 10.1080/03075079.2013.773778

Cloete, N., Bailey, T., & Maassen, P. (2012). *Universities and economic development in Africa: Pact, academic core and coordination.* African Minds., DOI: 10.47622/9781920355807

Cragin, M. H., & Hansen, D. L. (2017). *Research data management training.* ARL.

Data Management Association. (2019). *Data management body of knowledge.* Retrieved from internet.

Douglass, J. A., & Chirikov, I. (2020). *Refocusing institutional research on university needs*.https://www.universityworldnews.com/post.php?story=20200518114757175

Eckles, J. E. (2009). Evaluating the efficiency of top liberal arts colleges. *Research in Higher Education*, 50(3), 266–293. DOI: 10.1007/s11162-009-9157-4

EDUCAUSE. (2020). *Research infrastructure for the future*. Retrieved from the internet.

El-Mahgary, S., Rönnholm, P., Hyyppä, H., Haggeén, H., & Koponen, J. (2014). Evaluating the performance of university course units using data envelopment analysis. *Cogent Economics & Finance*, 2(1), 1–19. DOI: 10.1080/23322039.2014.918856

Eryenyu, C., Holta, S., & Ssentamu, P. N. (2020). Towards a new model of internal quality assurance for Ugandan universities. *Journal of Research Innovation and Implications in Education*, 4(3), 75–87.

Haskell, C. (2017). Institutional research as a bridge: Aligning institutional internal data needs and external information requirements a strategic view. *Higher Education Evaluation and Development*, 11(1), 2–11. DOI: 10.1108/HEED-08-2017-001

Howard, R. D., McLaughlin, G. W., & Knight, W. E. (2012). *The handbook of institutional research*. Jossey-Bass. https://doi.org/ Prisacaru, V., & Litvin, A. (2017). Quality management in the higher education of the Republic of Moldova as a framework for university performance. *Scientific Annals of Economics and Business, 64*(4), 431–446. https://doi.org/DOI: 10.1080/09645292.2018.1471663

Hwang, Y. (2018). Current state of the institutional research office in higher education: Focus on the leader and staff. *Journal of Academic Administration in Higher Education*, 14(2), 27–34.

Inter-University Council for East Africa (IUCEA). (2010). *Quality assurance project on developing an East African higher education quality assurance framework: Project self-assessment report for impact assessment*. IUCEA Secretariat EADB Building.

Inter-University Council for East Africa (IUCEA). (2019). *East African higher education quality assurance framework*. Retrieved from https://www.iucea.org/wp-content/uploads/2019/07/East-African-Higher-Education-Quality-Assurance-Framework.pdf

Inter-University Council for East Africa (IUCEA). (2020). *Declaration by heads of state of the East African Community partner states on the transformation of the East African Community into a common higher education area*. Available at https://www.iucea.org/declaration-chea/

Inter-University Council for East Africa (IUCEA). (2024). *New phase of the demographics of African faculty project to enhance data management culture for faculty planning in the East African Community*. Available at https://www.iucea.org/new-phase-of-the-demographics-of-african-faculty-project-to-enhance-data-management-culture-for-faculty-planning-in-the-east-african-community/

Kakada, P., & Deshpande, Y. M. (2018). Relationship between institutional support and student satisfaction. *International Journal of Management and Business Research*, 8, 184–198.

Kangooni, H. E., & Zervopoulos, P. D. (2023). Efficiency measurement of the colleges at the University of Sharjah. In *Advances in Science and Technology* (Vol. 129, pp. 117–136). International Symposium on Engineering and Business Administration. Trans Tech Publications Ltd. https://doi.org/DOI: 10.4028/p-aGMOt9

Kasozi, A. B. (2003). *University education in Uganda: Challenges and opportunities for reform*. Retrieved from the internet.

Kearney, M.-L. (2013). Policy Imperatives in Research and Innovation Management. In A. Olssan, & L. Meek (Eds.), *Effectiveness of Research and Innovation Management at Policy and Institutional Levels: Cambodia, Malaysia, Thailand and Vietnam* (pp. 19-28). Kuala Lumpur: OCDE.https://www.oecd.org/sti/Effectiveness%20of%20research%20and%20 innovation% 20management%20at%20policy%20and%20institutional%20levels_Meek% 20and%20Olsson.pdf

Knapp, L., Glennie, E., & Charles, K. (2016). *Leveraging data for student success: Improving education through data-driven decisions*. RTI Press., DOI: 10.3768/rtipress.2016.bk.0018.1609

Knapp, M., Swinnerton, J., Copland, M., & Monpas-Huber, J. (2006). *Data-informed leadership in education*. Center for the Study of Teaching and Policy.

Kuh, G. D., & Gonyea, R. M. (2019). *Cultivating a culture of adaptability*. Wiley.

Lewin, T., & Mawoyo, M. (2014). *Student access and success: Issues and interventions in South African universities*. The South African Institute for Advancement
Makori, E. O., Njiraine, D., & Talam, P. (2015). Practical aspects of implementation of institutional repositories in Africa with reference to the University of Nairobi. *New Library World*, 116(9/10), 610–640. DOI: 10.1108/NLW-10-2014-0125

Lindsay, A. (1981). Assessing institutional performance in higher education: A managerial perspective. *Higher Education*, 10(6), 687–706. DOI: 10.1007/BF01676865

Lindsay, A. W. (1982). Institutional performance in higher education: The efficiency dimension. *Review of Educational Research*, 52(2), 175–199. DOI: 10.3102/00346543052002175

Masenya, M. (2023). Policies in higher education: The impact of global trends on the operation of the South African universities. *EDUCATIO Journal of Education*, 8, 201–215.

Matthias, G., & Wohlrabe, K. (2018). Super-efficiency of education institutions: An application to economics departments. *Education Economics*, 26(6), 610–623. DOI: 10.1080/09645292.2018.1471663

Molutsi, P. (2009). *The impact of institutional research (IR) on institutional effectiveness: are we closing the loop?* Paper presented as Keynote Speech to the Southern African Association of Institutional Research 2009 Forum, 21-23 September 2009, at Nelson Mandela Metropolitan University, Port Elizabeth, South Africa

Morgan (2024). *The role of institutional research in shaping higher education*. Retrieved from: https://www.marshall.edu/irp/2024/01/11/roleofirinhe/ on June 4, 2024.

Nabaho, L., Turyasingura, W., Kiiza, K. A., Andama, F., & Beinebyabo, A. (2020). Quality assurance of higher education governance and management: An exploration of the minimum imperative for the envisioned African common higher education space. *Higher Learning Research Communications*, 10(2), 38–52. DOI: 10.18870/hlrc.v10i2.1183

National Institutes of Health. (2019). *Research data management*. Retrieved from the internet.

National Science Foundation. (2018). *Dissemination and sharing of research results*. Retrieved from the internet.

Nel, H. (2016). The role of institutional research in support of strategic planning. In Botha, J., & Muller, N. J. (Eds.), *Institutional Research in South African Higher Education: Intersecting Contexts and Practices* (pp. 99–116). African Sun Media., DOI: 10.18820/9781928357186/06

Nguyen, N. T. (2017). A review on the interrelation between knowledge management and human resource management. *Finance and the Performance of Firms in Science, Education and Practice*. Retrieved from the internet.

Ogachi, I. O. (2018, December). The East African higher education area: A global or regional higher education space? *Forum for International Research in Education*, 4(3). Advance online publication. DOI: 10.32865/fire2018439

OSSREA. (2020). *Promoting social science research in Eastern and Southern Africa*. Retrieved from https://www.ossrea.net/about-us/

Parlier, T. R., IV. (2021). Perspectives of IR professionals regarding the impact of data analytic systems on institutional decision-making. (Publication No. 6512) [Doctoral dissertation, University of Tennessee]. TRACE. https://trace.tennessee.edu/utk_graddiss/6512

Peterson, G. T., & Corckett, J. (2017). *Building a culture of assessment*. Stylus Publishing.

Sanga, P. (2019). East African Higher Education and the limitations of institutional reforms: A case study of selected public universities. *African Journal of Teacher Education*, 8, 299–320. DOI: 10.21083/ajote.v8i0.5361

Saupe, J. L. (1990). *The functions of institutional research* (2nd ed.). The Association for Institutional Research.

Sepahi, V., Abbaspour, A., Khoshay, A., Rezaei, K., & Rezaei, M. (2021). Presenting a Conceptual Model of Institutional Research Office for the Medical Universities of Iran: A Case Study. *Educational Research in Medical Sciences*, 10(2). Advance online publication. DOI: 10.5812/erms.121865

Sepahi, V., Abbaspour, A., Khoshay, A., Rezaei, K., & Rezaei, M. (2021). Presenting a conceptual model of institutional research office for the medical universities of Iran: A case study. *Educational Research in Medical Sciences, 10*(2).

Sepahi, V., Abbaspour, A., Khoshay, A., Rezaei, K., & Rezaei, M. (2021). Presenting a conceptual model of institutional research office for the medical universities of Iran: A case study. *Education Research in Medical Sciences*, 10(2), e121865. DOI: 10.5812/erms.121865

Serban, A. M., & Luan, J. (Eds.). (2002). *Knowledge management: Building a competitive advantage in higher education*. Jossey-Bass.

Sheppard, R. S., & Kerrigan, M. R. (2018). Building institutional research knowledge and skills through communities of practice networks. *Mid-Western Educational Researcher*, 30(4), 6. https://scholarworks.bgsu.edu/mwer/vol30/iss4/6

Shiltz, M. (Ed.). (1992). *Ethics and standards and institutional research. New Directions for Institutional Research, 73*. Jossey-Bass.

Silaji, Turyamureeba & Muhammad, Tukur & Rahim, Abdul & Zikanga, Kiyundo & Extension, Kiu Publication. (2023). Organizational structure and Academic staff Performances in Private Universities in Uganda. *KIU Journal of Social Sciences, 5*(4), 249-258.

Society for Institutional Research. (2020). *What is institutional research?* Retrieved from https://www.airweb.org/what-is-institutional-research

Subbaye, R., Mlitwa, A., & Moyo, T. (2021). Institutional research utilisation and issues of legitimacy: Perspectives from practitioners at selected traditional universities. *Utilisation of South African Research on Higher Education*, 133, 133–161. Advance online publication. DOI: 10.52779/9781991201416/05

Swargiary, K. (2024, July 1). The impact of data analytics on educational decision-making: A mixed-methods study in Bengaluru higher education institutions. *SSRN*. https://ssrn.com/abstract=4897517

Swing, R. L., & Ross, L. E. (2016). A new vision for institutional research. *Change*, 48(2), 6–13. DOI: 10.1080/00091383.2016.1163132

Tashtoush, L. (2021). The Role of Information Systems Capabilities in Enhancing the Organizational Performance. *Journal of Information Systems and Informatics*, 3(2), 303–328. DOI: 10.33557/journalisi.v3i2.129

Teichler, U. (2005). Research on Higher Education in Europe. *European Journal of Education*, 40(4), 447–469. DOI: 10.1111/j.1465-3435.2005.00239.x

Terenzini, P. T. (1993). On the nature of institutional research and the knowledge and skills it requires. *Research in Higher Education*, 34(1), 1–10. DOI: 10.1007/BF00991859

Terenzini, P. T. (2013). "On the nature of institutional research" revisited: Plus ça change…? *Research in Higher Education*, 54(2), 137–148. DOI: 10.1007/s11162-012-9274-3

Terenzini, P. T. (2013). *Bringing the stakeholders to the table*. Routledge.

Tight, M. (2015). Research on higher education policy and institutional management. In *The Palgrave International Handbook of Higher Education Policy and Governance* (pp. 176–191). Palgrave Macmillan UK. https://doi.org/DOI: 10.1007/978-1-137-45617-5_10

Trinh, N. T. H. (2023). Higher education and its role for national development. A research agenda with bibliometric analysis. *Interchange*, 54(2), 125–143. DOI: 10.1007/s10780-023-09493-9 PMID: 37215230

Uhl-Bien, M., Marion, R., & McKelvey, B. (2007). Complexity leadership theory: Shifting leadership from the industrial age to the knowledge era. *The Leadership Quarterly*, 18(4), 298–318. DOI: 10.1016/j.leaqua.2007.04.002

Visser, H., & Skene, J. (2016). Institutional research and external reporting. In *Institutional research in South African higher education: Intersecting contexts and practices* (pp. 160–175). SUN MeDIA Bloemfontein. DOI: 10.18820/9781928357186/10

Volkwein, J. F. (1999). The four faces of institutional research. *New Directions for Institutional Research*, 1999(104), 9–19. DOI: 10.1002/ir.10401

Volkwein, J. F. (2008). The foundations and evolution of Institutional Research. [Wiley Periodicals, Inc.]. *New Directions for Higher Education*, 141(141), 5–20. DOI: 10.1002/he.289

Volkwein, V. F. (2011). *Enhancing institutional research.* Jossey-Bass.

Webber, K. L. (2019). Building Capacity in IR and Decision Support: Alliances for Higher Education Research (HER) and Institutional Research (IR). *Proceedings of the Austrian University Network.* Available at: https://ihe.uga.edu/rps/2020_001

Webber, K. L. (2020). Building capacity in IR and decision support: Alliances for higher education research (HER) and institutional research (IR). *IHE Research Projects Series, 2020*(001). https://ihe.uga.edu/rps/2020_001

Webber, K. L., & Calderon, A. J. (Eds.). (2015). *Institutional research and planning in higher education: Global contexts and themes.* Routledge. DOI: 10.4324/9781315777726

Yorke, M. (2004). Institutional research and its relevance to the performance of higher education institutions. *Journal of Higher Education Policy and Management*, 26(2), 141–152. DOI: 10.1080/1360080042000218221

Zheng, H. Y. (2015). Business intelligence as a data-based decision support system and its roles in support of institutional research and planning. In Webber, K. L., & Calderon, A. J. (Eds.), *Institutional research and planning in higher education: Global contexts and themes* (pp. 157–173). Routledge.

KEY TERMS AND DEFINITIONS

Accountability: Accountability in higher education governance is a process which involves institutions and leaders being transparent about their actions, decisions, and performance, particularly regarding academic outcomes, financial management, and policy effectiveness, often adhering to established national or international standards.

Data-Driven Decision-Making: Data-Driven Decision-Making in higher education means using quantitative and qualitative data to inform policies, allocate resources, and improve performance.

East Africa: East Africa, also referred to as Eastern Africa in this chapter, encompasses the countries within the East African Community. These countries include Burundi, Kenya, Rwanda, South Sudan, Tanzania, Uganda, the Democratic Republic of the Congo (DRC), and the Federal Republic of Somalia as of 24th November 2023 (EAC, 2023).

East African Community (EAC): refers to a regional intergovernmental organization comprising countries in East Africa, aimed at promoting economic, social, and cultural integration.

Governance: The structures, processes, and mechanisms through which higher education institutions are managed, directed, and controlled.

Higher Education (HE): This a stage of learning that occurs at universities, colleges, and other institutions that offer degrees or diplomas beyond secondary education.

Higher Education Governance: Higher Education Governance involves structures, policies, and processes guiding university and college management, influencing academic affairs, financial management, human resources, and strategic directions.

Institutional Effectiveness: The extent to which an institution achieves its mission and goals, often evaluated through performance metrics and stakeholder feedback.

Institutional Performance: means measure of how effectively an institution achieves its goals and objectives, often assessed through various metrics and evaluations tools.

Institutional Research (IR): This is the systematic process of collection, analysis, and interpretation of data within higher education institutions to support decision-making, strategic planning, and governance. It assists administrators and faculty in evaluating academic performance, student outcomes, resource allocation, and policy implementation to enhance institutional effectiveness.

Inter-University Council for East Africa (IUCEA): An organization that promotes cooperation and coordination among universities in East Africa, focusing on quality assurance and higher education standards.

Policy Development: Policy Development is the systematic process of developing and implementing rules, guidelines, and procedures in higher education institutions, ensuring they are aligned with the institution's goals and regulations.

Quality Assurance: Quality Assurance in higher education are mechanisms to ensure institutions meet teaching, learning, research, and administration standards through continuous assessment, evaluations and audits and improvement of programs, faculty qualifications, and performance.

Strategic Planning: Strategic planning in higher education involves defining long-term goals, strategies, academic priorities, resource optimization, and preparing for future challenges, with Institutional Research providing necessary data.

Endnote

1 Australasian Association for Institutional Research (AAIR)
Canadian Institutional Research and Planning Association (CIRPA)
European Association for Institutional Research (EAIR)
Middle East North Africa AIR (MENA-AIR) Pacific Northwest Association for Institutional Research and Planning (PNAIRP)Philippine Association of Institutions for Research South East Asia Association for Institutional Research (SEAAIR)
Southern African Association for Institutional Research (SAAIR)
Taiwan Association for Institutional Research (TW-AIR)

Chapter 13
Climate Change: Opportunities for Strengthening Research Capacity and Knowledge Dissemination

Billiah Nyamoita Gisore
https://orcid.org/0000-0002-5116-7615
Kisii University, Kenya

ABSTRACT

The IPCC Report indicates that by 2100, global temperatures will be 1.8-4 ° C higher than the current ones, causing many regions to experience severe and frequent droughts. This affects food security and causes health problems. The understanding climate change seems to be at a low levels in the community. This can be improved by strengthening research capacity to address the causes, impacts, mitigation and adaptation needs. It seems that the communication that has been occurring has not been effective, resulting in information deficit. More delay will cause the future impact be large and costly. From research, practical guidance on how to access, interpret and apply climate data and information should be availed to targeted users. There should be a strong research base with clear dissemination channels. Climate change adaptation and mitigation strategies should be context specific. Opportunities are available for strengthening research capacity and knowledge dissemination.

INTRODUCTION

Throughout Earth history, the climate has undergone many changes globally and locally caused by factors such as variations in the amount of solar radiation that comes in to Earth's system, the position of Earth relative to Sun, the position

DOI: 10.4018/979-8-3693-6930-2.ch013

of continents relative to the equator, and even whether the continents are together or apart. Additionally, human activities such as deforestation, urbanization, and air pollution have contributed to an increase in greenhouse gas levels in the atmosphere (Desonie, 2008). The author indicates that human activities remove carbon from reservoirs where it has long been sequestered and send it into the atmosphere. For instance, fossil fuel burning which is the most dominant among the activities, releases CO_2 that had been stored in the Earth for millions of years. Burning rain forests to create agricultural or ranch lands, a technique known as slash- and- burn agriculture that occurs in the tropics, releases the CO_2 stored in forests. Deforestation also decreases the amount of CO_2 that is absorbed from the atmosphere by plants. Other types of vegetation, such as crops and grassland, are much less efficient at removing CO_2 from the atmosphere.

The concentration of carbon dioxide (CO_2), as well as other gases in the atmosphere has increased dramatically since the second half of the nineteenth century (U.N.F.C.C.C. 2007), while other gases such as Methane (CH_4), Nitrous Oxide (N_2O), Hydrofluorocarbons (HFCs), Perfluorocarbons (P.F.C.s), Sulphur Hexafluoride (SF_6) and water vapor have led to a gradual increase in global warming. The Greenhouse gases have carried far more weight in determining modern climate than any other factor in the warming seen since 1950.

According to U.N.F.C.C.C. (1992), climate change means "a change of climate, attributed directly to human activities such as industrialization which leads to global warming due to the greenhouse effect and attendant anomalies in local temperature, humidity, wind speed, precipitation, soil moisture, and sea level. This has posed serious and potentially irreversible threats to the environment (Stein, 2008). This global change has clearly moved the planetary environment out of its 10,000-year-old Holocene state and into the new state of the Anthropocene (Steffen et al. 2007). This has enormous implications for the future of humanity, as societies and civilizations, and the ecosystems are tuned to the environmental envelope of the Holocene (Costanza et al. 2007).

Humans have never before been in the situation now confronting the planet (UNFCCC, 2010). Research indicates that people have diverse understandings and beliefs about climate change that vary depending on their location (i.e. where they live), cultural influences, wealth, gender and world views (Archer & Rahmstorf, 2010). The diverse understanding contributes to the challenges in developing an comprehension of anthropogenic climate change, which include invisible causes that generally do not directly impact human health or wellbeing; distant impacts, both geographically and temporally; delayed or absent gratification for taking action; powerful self-interests (Moser, 2009b). In sum, climate change is challenging to conceptualize and difficult to recognise from personal experience (Moser, 2010). There is need for climate change education to equip people with knowledge about how to face risk posed by climate change and the uncertainty that comes with the rapid change (Gisore &Njurai, 2023).

IMPACTS OF CLIMATE CHANGE

The most dramatic impacts being felt so far in the atmosphere and hydrosphere are the melting cyrosphere, rising seas, and the rise in extreme weather events. Wet regions are becoming wetter, and dry regions are becoming drier (Desonie, 2008). Warming ocean temperatures have resulted in rising sea level, increased erosion, and a change in deep ocean circulation. Warmer temperatures have increased extreme weather events in their frequency, severity, and longevity. There is evidence that the past few decades have seen an increase in extreme weather. According to Arche and Rahmstorf (2010), temperature patterns are changing continuously.

Temperatures are rising as atmospheric greenhouse gas levels increase, but temperature increases will lag behind greenhouse gas levels due to thermal inertia. Temperatures will not increase uniformly around the globe. Most lands will warm more than the oceans due to the thermal inertia of the seas, the Northern Hemisphere will warm more than the Southern because it is mostly land, and the Polar Regions will warm much more than the rest of the planet due to the transition of ice to liquid water (U.N.F.C.C.C, 1992).

In specific regions, climate models of the years 2080 to 2099 indicate that both Chicago and Paris will have more heat waves, 25% and 31%, respectively; and their length will increase 64% and 52%, respectively. Precipitation events will also increase, although in some regions summers will be a lot drier and droughts will become more common (Krasny & DuBois, 2016).

Not all changes have been detrimental. For some places, the temperature changes have improved production significantly as growing season has become longer, and some crops are now planted earlier in spring. In particular, the conditions for wine production have improved; for example in Alsace in France, the number of days favorable for grape growth - that is, with temperatures above 10 C - has increased from 170 to 210 days per year over the past 30 years. Productivity of forests has increased in some regions due to the longer growing season and the fertilizing effect of the carbon dioxide gas in the atmosphere (USGCRP, 2009). The authors add that on the other hand, the changing weather has created vulnerabilities in different parts of the world. Vulnerable populations are typically exposed to numerous stressors such as climate hazards, volatility in markets, unstable political regimes, all which compound the levels of risk and the potential impacts of any given climate event.

For instance, Africa is one of the most vulnerable continents, due to the extreme poverty, weak governance structures, frequent natural disasters, and a strong dependence on rain-fed agriculture which has led to agricultural production being "severely compromised." By the year 2020, about 250 million people had suffered from increased water stress due to climate change. But vulnerability is not restricted to the developing world: as hurricanes Sandy and Katrina have painfully demonstrated for the United States, even in contexts where governments are stable, infrastructure is engineered according to robust standards, and early warnings are relatively reliable and accessible, losses can be extensive and devastating. Crop yields in Asia have recently been declining, probably as a consequence of warming (Chen & Lackner, 2012). A wide variety of plants and animals have undergone recent range changes due to rising temperatures. Species are disappearing in the lower latitude portions of their ranges. In North America for example, the Edith's checker spot butterfly (Euphydryas editha) is almost extinct in Mexico but thriving in Canada. Adélie penguins are now thriving at their southernmost locations but have experienced large population declines where they are found farthest north on the Antarctic Peninsula.

At higher levels of warming, crop and livestock production have declined in all regions due to increased heat, pests and pathogens, water stress, and weather extremes. Some species are unable to adapt and thus decline in population, vanish from a particular region or even go extinct. On the other hand, pests are expanding their range, like the bark beetle in North America and the pine processionary moth in Europe (Rosenzweig et al., 2008).

Arid regions have tended to become warmer and drier, and wet regions have become even wetter. As a result, crop yields have grown in wet regions but shrunk in arid regions (Desonie, 2008). The author adds that the loss of crops due to a reduction in rainfall is intensified by the expansion of insect ranges and increased forest fires. Drier areas have also suffered from desertification, the process by which dry air evaporates moisture from the soil and the land turns to desert. Farmers in arid lands have had to increase the amount of irrigation, but where this is not possible, land that was once farmable has been lost. In the United Kingdom, drought has caused farmers to increase the percentage of crops they irrigate. In Europe, climate change impacts are split in a north - south direction: southern Europe will become (and is already becoming) drier, while northern Europe is getting wetter. Countries that are already straining to supply enough water for their people and crops may not succeed. As a result, famine may become more common in places such as sub-Saharan Africa and many other regions. The warmer temperatures are predicted to increase the range of plant diseases and parasites (Ogega, Lakey, Opisa, & Gyampoh, 2022).

People, and particularly farmers, care not only about the average amount of rain or snow that falls each year but also care about seasonality, about how much rain falls in winter, summer or spring. In some parts of the world, rainfall has gone down in summer but is on the rise in winter, causing little change in the annual total, but increased flood risk in winter and drought problems in summer. In other regions, where precipitation mostly falls in winter, a larger fraction is now falling as rain. This reduces the snow pack in the mountains, which is an important source of runoff in summer when water is most needed, as well as the basis of much winter tourism (NRC, 2010). As an example Mount Kilimanjaro is one of the most famous landmarks and tourist attractions of the African continent which is disappearing rapidly.

Additionally, Desonie (2008) indicates that Asia is suffering from rapid loss of glacier ice. Himalayan glaciers are the largest body of ice outside the big polar ice caps, and together with snow melt they contribute to the summer flow of major river systems such as the Indus, Ganges and Brahmaputra. These rivers form the lifeline for many millions of people; their flow initially increases during glacier melt, then is reduced, especially during the dry season, once the glaciers are gone. European mountain glaciers are lose between 30 and 70% of their mass by 2050. The loss of mountain glaciers is critical in Bolivia, Peru, Colombia, and Ecuador. Water supplies there are already affected, and the situation is expected to get worse as glaciers in the Andes disappear in coming decades. Water stress, weather extremes, sea level rise, and species extinctions are expected to affect Latin America (USGCRP, 2009). The Arctic will continue to melt. As ice is lost, animals such as polar bears and seals will become greatly reduced in number or will go extinct. By 2050, more than a billion people could be adversely affected by water stress arising from climate change.

According to USGCRP (2009), precipitation will decrease in drier areas, including in many mid-continental areas, and increase in wetter areas. Rainfall will decline in some locations in the summer, which will affect crop yields, increase forest fires and increase water stress. Currently, about 1.7 billion people live in countries that are water stressed: By 2025, that number will likely grow to 5 billion. Droughts will become longer and fiercer, making many marginal regions difficult or impossible to inhabit, including the western United States, northern China, and southern Africa. Deserts will become drier, and the Asian monsoon will be enhanced but will likely become more variable.

Another important observation is that heavy rainfall events are on the rise: in many parts of the world, the fraction of the total annual rainfall that comes down on just a few very wet days has increased (Archer & Rahmstorf, 2010). For instance, Latin America has been hit by a series of highly unusual weather extremes in recent years. In 2002 and 2006, Bolivia and Greater Buenos Aires area experienced Hail storms, intense rainfall in Venezuela (1999, 2005), flooding in the Argentine Pampas (2000–2) and drought in the Amazon (2005). Then there was the first ever hurricane in the South Atlantic (2004) and the record hurricane season of 2005 in the Caribbean The risk of flash floods has increased in many parts of the world.

In the Western United States, warmer temperatures and earlier springs have caused an increase in the number, duration, and destructiveness of wildfires. In Europe, the extreme heat wave of 2003 was an unexpected outlier at the time it occurred, but will be a normal summer by the 2040s. Majority of organisms and ecosystems are likely to have difficulty in adapting to climate change, and extensive species extinctions are expected. The increasing water stress in the Mediterranean region raises the fire risk there, as was illustrated by the dramatic fires in Greece in August 2007. It is also expected to reduce the hydropower potential by 20–50% by the 2070s (Zhang et al., 2007).

Forestry in many parts is expected to decline due to drought and fire problems, although initially some forest plantations in New Zealand may benefit from warming (Archer & Rahmstorf, 2010). In eastern Amazonia, savanna is expected to gradually replace the existing tropical forest, although a more dramatic collapse of rain forest cannot be ruled out.

The USGCRP (2009) indicates that the oceans_will experience large temperature rises, and ocean life will move pole ward where possible. A dramatic impact will be seen in coral reefs, which may die out almost completely in the next 50 years. A temperature rise of 1.8°F (1°C) is predicted to lead to extensive irreversible coral bleaching, particularly in years when other ocean warming events such as El Niño are superimposed. Between 2030 and 2050, the world's most magnificent coral reef, Australia's Great Barrier Reef, will experience annual bleaching due to warmer temperatures and other stresses such as higher sea level. Losing coral reefs does not only mean losing a unique and beautiful ecosystem and the food sources it contains. Coral reefs are nurseries for many types of fish. If reefs die, commercial fisheries, many of which are already currently being overfished, may collapse. For example, coastal Louisiana has already lost 1,900 square miles of wetlands in recent decades due to sea level rise and human alterations, weakening its capacity to absorb storm surges from hurricanes. Shoreline retreat has been observed along most U.S. exposed shores. Projected sea level rise could inundate portions of major cities such as Miami or New York during storm surges or even extreme high tides. Sea level rise can also lead to saltwater intrusion of freshwater aquifers in coastal areas that could reduce freshwater supplies (USGCRP, 2009). The IPCC Report (2007) indicates that by the year 2100 the acidity of ocean waters will very likely be greater than at any time during at least the past 20 million years.

Australia and New Zealand are already noticing the effects of warming temperatures and rising_sea levels, as well as an increase in the intensity of Australian droughts. As early as the year 2020, significant losses of biodiversity had been noted in some of the most beautiful and valuable ecosystems: the Great Barrier Reef, the Kakadu Wetlands, some sub Antarctic islands, and the mountain regions of both countries.

Drying and water shortages are the main future problems for people in large parts of Australia and New Zealand (Rosenzweig et. al., 2008).

Increases in extreme weather events has taken a toll on human health. Climate change directly affects human physical and mental health through changes in the frequency, intensity, and/or duration of extreme weather events. For example, an increase in heat waves has triggered a rise in heat related deaths (Kovats & Hajat, 2008). The authors add that by 2030, climate-related deaths by malnutrition and diarrhea will increase noticeably. Extremely dry conditions also contribute to the spread of disease. The 1999 outbreak of West Nile virus in New York corresponded with a severe drought, while African dust caused by climate change has been linked to respiratory disease in the Caribbean. The heat waves are expected to increase in quantity and severity in warm regions but will also be more common in cooler areas.

Data show that both malaria and the anopheles mosquito that carries the disease have recently spread into highland areas of Kenya that were free of them only 20 years ago. However, it has not been proven whether this is due to the temperature rise or perhaps some other factors. Another health issue is pollen allergies, where the climatic warming has caused the pollen season to start earlier in the year. Health effects can even occur an ocean away from their cause: a dramatic increase in respiratory diseases in the Caribbean has been attributed to increasing drought in Africa, leading to dust storms blowing dust across the Atlantic. Depending on the extent and effectiveness of adaptation measures, heat-related illnesses and deaths could increase over coming decades as heat waves increase in frequency, intensity, and duration (Kovats & Hajat, 2008)

MITIGATION

It has been easy to ignore the environmental effects of climate change, in part because no single incident can be attributed to global warming and because the most serious consequences will not occur until the future. It is easier to deny the contributions people are making to global warming than to recognize and deal with them and make the sacrifices that this will require. Climate will reach the tipping point when catastrophic change becomes inevitable, when it reaches the point where it is too late to act. Preparedness for current and potential consequences of climate change is essential individuals to take personal actions to mitigate climate change is necessary (IPCC, 2007b). Individual Contributions - individuals can make a difference by being conscious of what they do, what they buy, and what actions they take.

Mitigation refers to efforts to reduce the rate and magnitude of climate change by reducing the emissions of greenhouse gases (Lotz-Sisitka, 2010). To start dealing with the effects of climate change, it is recommended that society first work toward becoming more energy efficient, and then work toward converting entirely to energy sources that produce zero carbon emissions. It is also recommended that there are reductions in the emissions of other greenhouse gases. For example, changing farming practices to reduce methane emissions and stopping the production of man-made chemicals that contribute to greenhouse warming. Researching and developing more technologically advanced solutions, such as sequestering carbon and harnessing solar energy in space is also recommended (Solomon, Plattner, Knutti, & Friedlingstein, 2009).

Some climatologists say that the first tipping point will come in the next several decades if greenhouse gas emissions are not halved over the next 50 years (Desonie, 2008). This was proven to be wrong when hurricane Katrina hit North America in 2005 with a devastating aftermath. It clearly demonstrated that even highly advanced and wealthy nation are vulnerable to extreme events, and may be ill prepared despite repeated advance warnings. The people now in power and those who are now producing most of the greenhouse gas emissions are not the ones who will suffer most of the consequences. The ones who will be most affected by global warming are the young people of today and those yet to be born. It is especially important for young people to become educated in climate change science and to learn what to do to mitigate climate changes and adapt to them.

The Kyoto Protocol sought to stabilize greenhouse gas concentrations in the atmosphere at a level that would prevent dangerous anthropogenic interference with the climate system. The easiest and quickest way to reduce greenhouse gas emissions is to radically improve energy efficiency. Encouraging conservation, supporting the use of more energy-efficient technologies, and developing better technologies are some of the ways to reduce emissions of CO2 and other greenhouse gases (UNESCO & UNEP, 2011).

The technologies to reduce greenhouse gas emissions include use of Zero-carbon and lower carbon energy sources which could be improved and in some cases expanded. The dominant renewable forms of energy today are traditional biomass (wood-burning) for 9% of global energy production, and hydroelectric power, 6%. Other forms of renewable energy, such as wind, solar, and non-traditional biomass, are much smaller but growing quickly, with the potential for significant expansion in the future. There is enough sunlight hitting the Earth to cover our current energy demand 10,000 times over. There are two basic strategies for harvesting energy from sunlight. One is to heat water, either for local use or to generate electricity from steam. The other form of solar energy is photovoltaic (PV), using solar cells to generate electricity directly. The cost of solar PV energy currently exceeds that of wind energy, and for this reason, PV is only a small source of energy globally (Eakin, Lemos & Nelson, 2014).

The author adds that wind and solar power share the technical problem of intermittency. Traditional power plants can be used as backup energy sources, but this adds to the effective cost of wind or solar power, if one has to also build a traditional plant to go along with it. The solution would be to improve the electrical grid, such that power could be efficiently transported around the world or developing better means of storing power than are available at present, but this too adds to the cost and the technical challenge. Additionally, generating power by building new dams has been limited as most of the potential locations for new hydroelectric dams are in environmentally or culturally sensitive areas, such as the Yellow River in China.

An alternative to reducing greenhouse gas emissions is sequestering the emissions after they have been created. Carbon can be sequestered in natural systems, or technologies can be developed for carbon sequestration. Sequestering of carbon can also be done by increasing the content of organic matter in soils in order to increase the amount of carbon in that soil. Farming techniques that protect soil, such as no-till farming and crop rotation, can help sequester carbon. Artificial carbon sequestration is another possible approach. CO2 from power plants and other large sources can be captured and stored. Carbon is easily captured in gasification plants, where CO2 emissions can be reduced by 80% to 90%, and from natural gas and biofuel plants. Once the CO2 is captured, it is transported by pipelines or by ship to a storage site. CO2 can be stored in rock formations, the oceans, or carbonate minerals. The most promising idea is to inject CO2 into salt layers or coal seams where the gas cannot escape to the surface. Another approach to sequestration that has been researched is iron fertilization. In those parts of the ocean where the presence of nutrient iron is limited, scientists have discovered that adding iron dust to the ocean stimulates a plankton bloom. The plankton remove CO2 from the atmosphere, although for this to work as a means of sequestering carbon, the plankton must then sink out of the system into the deep sea or into seafloor sediment (Meehl et al., 2007).

Another way to address the problem by encouraging energy efficiency as money is often an effective motivator, and a good way to encourage energy conservation is with taxes. A carbon tax is a surcharge that is placed on the use of energy sources that release CO2 into the atmosphere. This tax can, for example, be added to the pump price of gasoline or onto the electrical bill for households and businesses that rely on coal-fired power plants. The more energy consumers use, the more tax they pay. The less energy they use, the less their tax bill. The tax gives people an economic incentive to be more energy efficient by driving less, purchasing fuel-efficient vehicles, buying energy-efficient appliances, and keeping the heat turned down. The money collected can be used for research on alternative fuels and to develop mass transit systems, among other things. Because a car- bon tax gives people and companies a financial incentive to conserve energy, industry has an incentive to produce more energy-efficient vehicles and appliances (Solomon, et al, 2009).

Another strategy could be to encourage people to drive smaller, lighter cars. Fuel efficiency is related largely to a vehicle's weight as the heavier the vehicle, the more energy is needed to propel it, and the more energy gets wasted. Estimates are that a car built of these materials could weigh 65% less than a modern passenger car, which would greatly improve fuel efficiency (Nelson, et al, 2007).

Offsetting carbon emissions can be another strategy whereby people can now pay to offset the carbon they produce. An average car produces about 10,000 pounds (4,535 kg) of CO2 per year. To offset that amount, a driver can donate $25 to $50 to a carbon-neutral organization. The money helps pay for the development of clean power by subsidizing the construction of new wind turbines or solar energy collectors, for example. Planting trees or buying forestland to preserve it is another way to offset carbon emissions. Organizations can counteract their carbon emissions, too (UNESCO & UNEP, 2011).

Mitigating the problem of climate change requires the political will to make the necessary changes to reduce emissions at all levels of human organization, from governments down to individuals (Eakin, Lemos & Nelson, 2014). People must take action on climate change and they must do it now.

ADAPTATION

Numerous myths exist about climate change, with a general lack of public knowledge of the problems it poses as well as a lack of understanding of how to adapt to it (Gisore & Njurai, 2023). Communities need to adapt to future impacts that are unlikely to be avoided as mitigation efforts, are not be enough to respond to climate change. Adaptation describes efforts to cope better with the consequences of a given climate change. It focuses on that which everyone can do for their own benefit. Adaptation is therefore altering human behaviors to adjust to those changes that are inevitable, and is contextual and local. It is predicted that if society delays action for 20 more years, emissions reductions will need to be 3 to 7 times more than if the reductions begin immediately. Adaptation is necessary to lower risk and vulnerability and build adaptive capacity and resilience. Adaptation is a dynamic social process that is place specific (Adger et al. 2003) and responds to modified circumstances. The growing recognition of the need to respond to climate change impacts has placed adaptation at the forefront of societal and governmental agendas around the world (Eakin, Lemos & Nelson, 2014).

Climate adaptations can fall into either of two categories: "no regrets" or "climate justified." No-regrets strategies are ones that can be justified without taking into account climate change but which also meet goals and objectives of adaptation to climate change. Examples of no-regrets adaptations include reforming insurance regulations to enable insurers to set rates that reflect risks. (Despite the label, "no-regrets" policies can entail winners and losers: they do not mean that all stakeholders are better off or satisfied.) Climate-justified adaptations, on the other hand, are those that are undertaken mainly because climate is changing or anticipated to change. For example, this might involve raising a flood barrier in anticipation of future increases in sea level or storm intensity (Reeder et al., 2009). Effective adaptation depends on an understanding of projected climatic changes at geographic and temporal scales appropriate for the needed response. Different regions can adapt to climate change by recognizing and preparing for their own potential problems (Adger et al. 2009).

All regions, regardless of development conditions, have varying levels and types of adaptive capacity, that is, the preconditions that enable any adaptation. The ability to prepare for and adapt to new conditions may be exceeded as the rate of climate change increases. Reducing our vulnerability to these impacts depends not only upon our ability to understand climate science and the implications of climate change, but also upon our ability to integrate and use that knowledge effectively (Krasny & DuBois 2016).

In agriculture, planting times and crop varieties can be adjusted, and land management can be improved to prevent soil erosion, e.g., by planting trees. In coastal zones, sea walls, dykes, and storm surge barriers can be built. Natural barriers against storm surges (e.g. marshlands and wetlands) can be protected. And in some cases a planned retreat from vulnerable coastal areas is advised before a storm surge disaster strikes. To adapt agricultural systems to a warmer world, agriculturalists may need to develop crop strains that require less water and less soil moisture. Farms may need to be moved to more climatically hospitable areas. Changing the timing of farming events, such as planting crops earlier, will need to continue (Lu, 2011).

In southern Africa, where droughts have become longer, farmers are making changes such as seeking out crops that are better adapted to the current climate, planting trees to protect the soil, and diversifying their livelihoods (UNESCO & UNEP, 2011). For instance in Punjab province of Pakistan, farmers adapt to climate-related risks at farm level using different strategies that can be grouped into four major categories: first, there is changing cropping practices, e.g. crop type and variety or planting date; secondly, changing farm management techniques such as fertilizer, pesticide, seed quality or irrigation; third, advanced land use management measures, i.e. changing farm management techniques such as sowing and harvesting, planting shade trees, stopping cutting trees, using less water, storing water and soil conservation; and fourth, there are livelihood options which include shifting from single to multiple crops, shifting from farming to livestock keeping, migration and renting more crop land (Ullah & Nihei, 2018).

For flood prone regions, having soft protection such as beach nourishment, increasing the capacity of rainwater storage systems to reduce the number of times flooding occurs, and having evacuation plans in place can be used among others (Nelson et al. 2007). Adaptation for water shortages can include water storage and conservation measures, rainwater harvesting, or sea water desalination plants, e.g., for small islands, as well as more efficient drip irrigation techniques (IPCC, 2007c).

CHARACTERISTICS OF ADAPTATION TO CLIMATE CHANGE

Because impacts of and vulnerabilities to climate change vary greatly across regions and sectors, adaptation decisions are fundamentally place-based, occurring at multiple scales, from that of the individual household or firm, to cities, regions, states, tribes, corporations, and economic sectors, to the level of the government and agencies within it that manage land and other resources. Adaptation therefore encompasses various characteristics which according to Lu (2011) include; first, it is multi-disciplinary as a vast amount of knowledge and information is required to assess the sensitivity of ecological systems and socioeconomic activities to key climate variables, and potential impacts of and vulnerability to projected climate change in the future; to identify and appraise possible adaptation options; and to evaluate the effectiveness of adaptation actions. Adaptation is a meeting place of scientists and experts from different disciplines to discuss key climate risks weighing up the pros and cons of different adaptation options, and learning from each other's experiences and good practices in managing risks. Adaptation efforts cannot be effective, efficient or sustainable if they are carried out as a single sector engagement. Rather, policy-relevant assessments and informed adaptation decisions depend on meaningful and long-term partnerships and collaboration among different stakeholder groups representing a diverse range of insights, expertise, and experiences.

Second, it should be multi-scale as climate risk assessment and adaptation planning entail the consideration of multiple scales, both in space and in time. Adaptation assessment and planning must address issues and systems at a wide range of spatial scales: (i) the global-scale climate system, (ii) regional-scale trans-boundary water basins, (iii) national-scale production and social wellbeing systems, (iv) local communities and (v) site-specific exposure units. Similarly, adaptation planning needs to consider a wide variety of time horizons: (i) seasons to several years for farm activities and provision of health services, (ii) decadal-scale tourism and protected area development, and (iii) infrastructure projects ranging from a few decades to over a century. Therefore, there is no one-size-fits-all answer to adaptation. The accumulation and application of information and knowledge to support adaptation are necessarily dependent on partnerships and collaboration among partners working at different scales.

Adaptation should be multi-dimensional in that for it to be effective and sustainable, adaptation to climate change needs to be integrated into ongoing planning processes, horizontally across different climate sensitive sectors (e.g. agriculture, energy, tourism, public health), and vertically across different administrative levels (e.g. local, national, global). Further, adaptation initiatives need to build on and exploit synergies with relevant ongoing processes and programmes in different sectors and at different administrative levels, for example, disaster risk reduction initiatives, national poverty reduction strategy papers, various national processes under the UNFCCC such as the National Communications and National Adaptation Programmes of Action (NAPAs). Existing institutions, expertise and experiences from these ongoing processes and relevant communities of practice can make significant contributions to enhancing the knowledge base as well as informing the decision-making for adaptation.

Thinking about adaptation, decisions are normally made under a cascade of uncertainties e.g. future trends in global economy, demography, technology and agricultural practices. The projections of global greenhouse gas emissions and their atmospheric concentrations therefore vary widely; this leads to a wider variation in projections of climate system responses at a global scale, which when compounded with an imperfect understanding of natural and socioeconomic systems, results in an even wider range of likely impacts and possible adaptive responses at regional and local scales. Given the fact that there is a certain degree of inherent unpredictability in natural and socioeconomic systems, uncertainty will be a standard feature in adaptation decision-making. Within this context, partnerships and collaboration can help determine the relative significance of different sources of uncertainty to ensure decisions are informed by the best available information and robust to a range of likely future conditions.

CHALLENGES TO ADAPTATION

Many challenges face adaptation efforts which include reluctance to invest in adaptation research and actions, partly due to the fact that climate change is a slow-onset, multigenerational problem while decision makers tend to focus on short-term concerns and benefits. Empirical evidence suggesting that when individuals and businesses plan for the future, they do not fully weigh the long-term benefits of investing in loss-reduction measures, especially if there is only a small likelihood of reaping financial returns. There is a tendency for people to focus on the short run and to ignore low-probability events below their threshold level of concern can have severe long-run consequences (Kunreuther & Michel-Kerjan, 2009). Because climate conditions by the later part of the 21st century will likely be outside the range of past human experiences, it is difficult to make decisions now about the full range of anticipated climate change impacts in 2050 or 2100. Policy makers will need to select options that are flexible enough not to inadvertently preclude other options that may be needed or become available in the future (Adger et al., 2009).

An additional challenge is that climate change impacts are rarely the key drivers of vulnerability. Other factors determining vulnerability include existing inequalities, demographics, land use and economic changes, dwindling nonrenewable resources, public health, and institutional and technological change (IPCC, 2007a). Developing proactive strategies and planning processes that consider multiple perspectives, multiple stressors, multiple time horizons related to intergenerational equity issues, and multiple competing interests is a complex challenge, calling for broad collaborations and partnerships.

Additionally, there have been political impediments whereby climate change adaptation has been neglected for several decades perhaps because it was perceived as secondary in importance to mitigation of greenhouse gas (GHG) emissions, or perhaps more importantly because it would actually take attention away from mitigation by implying that the country can simply adapt to future changes (Adger et al., 2009). Coupled with institutional and resource limitations, Identifying new financial resources that could be directed toward adaptation has been particularly because the world's economies struggle financially (NRC, 2009c)

OPPORTUNITIES FOR STRENGTHENING THE RESEARCH CAPACITY

Examination of the Climate Change Science has shown that investment in "human dimensions research," including but not mainly oriented toward adaptation, and non-research expenditures on decision support represent about 2 percent of the total climate change research effort (NRC, 2009c). Responding to climate change adaptively requires a continuing flow of information about impacts that are emerging and those that are being projected as well as a continuing flow of information about experiences with adaptation actions. It also requires effective mechanisms for ensuring that the information reaches adaptation decision makers in forms that are useful to them (NRC 2010).

Lu (2011) says that there is a range of opportunities that could facilitate the development and application of climate information in support of enhanced adaptation actions. They include understanding possible tipping points can help to inform adaptation choices to avoid reaching such points; it can help to design observational strategies and programs to monitor system changes to provide early warning of an impending threshold in time to consider adaptation options; and in some cases it can clarify limits of adaptation, perhaps pointing to the need for structural changes.

Research is of high priority as institutions shape climate change responses and institutional behavior affects adoption and implementation of adaptation strategies, as well as monitoring of the effectiveness of these adaptation strategies (NRC, 2009c).

Research over a longer term is needed to close a variety of gaps in the science of impact and vulnerability assessment which limit the ability to perform many kinds of adaptation assessments and option evaluations. Among the areas where research can expand adaptation opportunities is in developing new technologies and management approaches and improving information on climate change, particularly at the regional and local scales where adaptation decisions will be made. Needs for fundamental science and technology advances should include improved information about climate change impacts under different assumptions about multiple driving forces and stressors, improved information about costs of impacts and both costs and benefits of adaptation options, and improved capacities to assess and represent uncertainties (UNFCCC, 2010).

The Third and Fourth Assessment Intergovernmental Panel on Climate Change Reports indicate that historically, most of the attention to adaptation research has been focused on understanding differences in adaptation capacity, that is, determinants of the inclination and ability of a party to adapt. There is need for a high priority for science and technology advances is to create an adaptation database that offers the best available information about adaptation alternatives, their characteristics, and examples of best practices. The database should contain information about costs of impacts and both costs and benefits of adaptation options, as well as measures of effectiveness as they become available. As part of monitoring the implementation of adaptation options, information needs to be gathered about the decision and regional context and the socioeconomic considerations to enable the transferability of "lessons learned" about the adaptation options. In time, such a database should be interactive, ideally offering users the opportunity to go beyond simply surveying existing answers and to ask questions about database entries and consult experts about issues not covered by those entries (UNFCCC, 2010).

Research is urgently needed on the distribution of the climate change losses, the current modes of sharing (disaster relief, insurance, and government reimbursement), and new methods of sharing in the form of comprehensive or specialized climate insurance, catastrophe trust funds, and the like. The objective will be to determine the best balance between investments in local adaptations and investments in cost sharing in the event of low-probability, high-consequence events. This should involve (i) both avoiding inefficient redundancies in local self-insurance against low probability contingencies and realizing potentials for local adaptations to reduce the cost of insurance, and (ii) exploring the right balance between private- and public sector approaches to cost sharing (Dillon et al. 2016).

Science and technology advances observing systems need to deploy and use systems to monitor climate change impacts and to provide a continuing flow of information to decision makers. Developing an adaptive approach to adaptation and reassessing risk management as additional information about impacts and responses depend fundamentally on this kind of accurate and timely information. The development of risk analysis and management approaches is needed to provide tools and guidelines for adaptation decision makers such as the treatment of risks, the timing of adaptation actions, and benefits and costs of alternative actions, and for understanding of the likely winners and losers associated with any particular adaptation strategies and actions (Gisore & Njurai, 2023).

There is need to assess the outcomes of adaptation strategies and actions, asking such questions as what they have accomplished and whether they can be considered successes. The current state of the art and science for such assessments is very limited and is complicated by such factors as the need to define a baseline for comparison and the fact that multiple factors will influence the observed outcomes of any particular adaptation action. To build the knowledge base that allows the development of "best practices," the various factors that influence the choice and the outcome of the adaptation option need to be measured, archived, and analyzed. Ideally, a standard set of variable is monitored in every case to enable analyzing the link between option and geographic context. This is a significant cross-cutting adaptation research need in a field where, in at least some cases, practice is likely to proceed in parallel with knowledge enhancement, including needs to improve knowledge of the costs of adaptation (Kagawa & Selby, 2010).

It is also important to monitor the impacts of adaptation and mitigation actions as adaptation does not stop with adapting to direct changes in climate alone; it also faces challenges in adapting to what people do in responding to climate change. That includes actions to limit greenhouse gas (GHG) emissions as well as adaptation actions. Because these second-order adaptations have received very little attention, integrating them into adaptation planning and actions will be a challenge. For example, emissions-reduction strategies that raise the cost of some forms of energy, or geoengineering strategies that could have secondary consequences, may call for advances in adaptation research to support assessment, option identification, and option implementation (Krasny & DuBois, 2016).

In addition, there are many urgent research needs that cut across sectors that call for sector-specific action or plan, and the impacts and adaptation alternatives in one sector may have implications for others as well. This should be explored, at least in part, in a place-based context where interactions can be traced in detail. Improved understanding about when to implement adaptation actions is urgently needed. Timing issues are likely to differ among adaptation needs and options, but they include such considerations as whether adaptation now can be more participative and less expensive than emergency-based, reactive, and sudden problem solving; whether adaptation now is more likely to be placed in a broader sustainability context; and how important current uncertainties are in valuing investments in risk management. Furthermore, research is required to evaluate options for encouraging voluntary relocation from high-vulnerability areas such as retreat from vulnerable coastlines (United States Global Change Research Program, 2009).

BENEFITS OF CLIMATE CHANGE RESEARCH

For institutional research capacity strengthening to be effective and sustainable, the climate change activities need to be embedded within institution-wide systems and structures. Drawing from outcomes of the provision of best practice frameworks and resources, tailored consultations, training workshops, and train-the-trainer workshops, participating institutions are required to set and pursue their own capacity strengthening objectives. This can be done through institution-led needs assessments and the development of institutional action plans (Ogega, Lakey, Opisa, & Gyampoh, 2022).

Institutions need to action the development, strengthening, and formalization of academic mentoring schemes to provide support to early-career researchers as intergenerational mentoring within academia is a key enabler of research capacity strengthening (Schriever & Grainger, 2019).

According to Stevenson (2011), climate change education comprises two parts: climate and change. 'Climate' they explain involves the natural sciences, while 'change', or educating for change, involves engaging the sciences and humanities. For effective means of developing capacities for addressing the climate crisis, mainstreaming climate change education throughout formal education systems where research can be conducted is important. This is due to multiplier effects, where families and communities benefit when individuals share what they have learned especially in relation to adaptation and mitigation (Ullah & Nihei, 2018).

West et al (2009) indicate that the prospect of climate change is driving a renewed effort within the scientific community to develop a system of climate services to inform decision-makers about the potential impacts of climate change. These efforts are not altogether different from their predecessors, in which the scientific community attempted to harness its knowledge about climate to equip people with knowledge about climate variability to inform their decisions. At the heart of all of these efforts is the transmission of knowledge between two communities - scientists and decision-makers. This can take the form of simple web-based products to in-depth education to long-term collaboration. Underpinning all of these is a public that is capable of accessing and using the information provided by the scientific community.

Climate change research has faced many barriers both in the past and currently. For instance, scientists, and academics in general have the so-called cultural divide which is a barrier that needs to be overcome. Norms differ between researchers and practitioners, scientists and decision-makers. The scientific model of seeking objective truth may fall short within the problem-oriented, contextual, multidisciplinary, and normative realm of decision-making (Schriever & Grainger, 2019).

Cronbach and Suppes (1969) in one of their studies on the use of research identified procedural differences that introduced barriers to utilization. The traditional model of research is conclusion-oriented, aimed at finding some objective truth while policy needs are focused more on decision oriented inquiry, aimed at action. Webber (1992) noted that the policy environment relies upon subjective interpretation of data, not just objective analysis. This requires placing findings into the contextual environment in which decision-makers operate.

The curricula in academic institutions focus on scientific knowledge or the 'climate' in climate change education and ignore 'change', thereby paying little attention to the consequences of climate change or the need for adaptation to the impact on human settlement and activities (Stevenson, 2011). To deal with future challenges, research should yield transformative climate change mitigation and adaptation information that can harness creativity and empower action (Lotz-Sisitka, 2010).

DISSEMINATION OF CLIMATE CHANGE RESEARCH OUTPUT

Environmental communication has been defined by Cox (2012) as the pragmatic and constitutive vehicle for our understanding of the environment as well as our relationships to the natural world; it is a symbolic medium that is used in constructing environmental problems and negotiating society's different responses to them. Effective communication must embrace participation in order to promote inclusivity and fairness in climate change discussions and decision-making.

Climate information is fundamental to the understanding of climate risks and planning for adaptation. There is an urgent need to improve the provision and delivery of climate information (Lu, 2011).

The capacities which each player should provide are also diverse. Among them, various capacities have been identified at the national and regional levels including financial and human resources, scientific knowledge, access to scientific information, technological ability, social institutions, and infrastructure (Yohe & Tol, 2002). Scientists may not be able to control how information is used, but they can be more involved in how that information is initially presented. By being aware of how findings relate to societal issues, scientists can influence factors that will draw more positive attention to their work (Stern, 2007). The author says that climate literacy is part of a coordinated effort to make people aware of their natural environment and factors, both natural and anthropogenic that cause disruptions to that environment. It is geared toward making people more effective users of climate information that can cause changes in behavior. The societal value of climate information is dependent upon factors that include: (i) the strength and nature of linkages between climate, weather, and human activities; (ii) the nature of uncertainties associated with forecasts; (iii) the accessibility of credible and useful climate information by decision makers; (iv) the ability of users and providers to identify each other's needs and limitations; and (v) the ability of users to respond to useful information. As it is, there seems to a shortage of research on diffusion of knowledge and information making even the best research results not to be used. There is a need for mechanisms by which users select and adopt information.

Information must be provided in context, from the perspective of the historical record to guide understanding of natural variability and climate change. Evaluation, mutual information, and feedback are necessary to improve communication and accessibility of information. By working with individuals to increase their capacity to use information, it becomes more likely that they will use that information within their own, unique contexts (Shafer, 2008).

For a study to influence the decision-making process requires more than conducting it and letting the results "speak for themselves." Rather, results must be framed in the context of decision-maker needs for it to have an impact. It must be framed in a manner consistent with other information from which the decision maker is drawing as well as be constructed in way that makes sense to the decision-maker and others whom he or she must persuade (Lotz-Sisitka, 2010). The authors say that once a message is formulated, there are external factors that influence how it is received. These communication factors include content of the message, dissemination source, dissemination medium, and user characteristics. Methodology, credible outcomes, and cost-effectiveness are some objective factors of content that affect utilization. In addition, the information must both be understandable to users and relate to existing information. Whether the information is seen as useful may reflect whether the same information shows evidence of benefitting another individual in a similar circumstance. This is not unlike the cost-effectiveness measure that policy-makers seek; an individual producer would want to see evidence of benefits before accepting risks of changing practices.

For effective dissemination of climate change research output, there is need to consider interdisciplinary studies and capabilities as the recommendations reach different audiences. This can be done through: (i) development of regional enterprises designed to expand the nature and scope of climate services; (ii) increasing support for interdisciplinary climate studies, applications, and education; (iii) fostering climate policy education; and (iv) enhancing the understanding of climate through public education. Partnerships and education will enable the proposed National Climate Service to reach a broad user base with effective information - that is, information that is compatible with the values and decision-making styles in which users operate (Lie & Servaes, 2015).

There are many problems and many sources of information competing for the limited attention of decision-makers (Hilgartner & Bosk, 1988). By recognizing these limitations, a researcher may find niches where relevant climate information can be useful to decision-makers. For climate change information on mitigation and adaptation to be disseminated and be of use, the National Research Council report (2010) outlines the possible set of criteria which should be considered in the reports as that is what might be evaluated by the information consumers:

i. The focus should not only be on optimizing conditions for the current generation, but also look several generations ahead and consider ways to reduce risk over time.
ii. The reports should account for the impacts of adaptation decisions on natural and social systems as well as on individuals, firms, government institutions, and infrastructure.
iii. The reports should recognize that ecosystem structure and functioning are particularly vulnerable to climate change and need consideration in adaptation decisions.
iv. The reports should evaluate solutions from a perspective of sustainability so that social, economic, and environmental ramifications of proposed strategies and actions are explicitly recognized
v. They should acknowledge equity and justice in adaptation decisions; there is a need to prioritize the information to helping those with a higher degree of vulnerability to become more resilient.
vi. The reports should consider the expected costs and benefits from adaptation programs to those who are affected by them, including the potential for unintended consequence. This will give guidance on what to be planned for.
vii. They should include development of a portfolio for addressing adaptation problems, including a suite of technology and social-behavioral-economic options.
viii. They should develop methods of evaluation so that the risk of inactions can be compared with the risk of proposed actions.
ix. The reports should also recognize the international implications of a country's adaptation and emissions-reduction efforts, as well as the impacts on the country of decisions made by other countries.

The media can also provide a platform for engagement and empowerment as well as work as a watchdog, holding accountable the governments, policymakers and citizens at all levels of existence. The media evaluates, for example, the mitigation ambitions as proposed by different countries under the auspices of the United Nations Framework Convention on Climate Change (UNFCCC), comparing what is supposed to be done against what is actually happening. This role also involves making global political and business elites accountable to the electorates. The media is also instrumental in monitoring and exposing activities of industries that are responsible for carbon emissions, for example, oil companies and coal-based industries. Social media are useful vehicles for the sharing and exchange of information and to stimulate change at the global, regional, national, and local levels (Lie & Servaes, 2015).

WAY FORWARD

Without a well-integrated and coordinated effort, it will be difficult to deal efficiently and effectively with climate challenges. To provide a wider range of choices for the national climate adaptation program, sustained adaptation research effort will be needed. There is an urgent need to identify vulnerabilities, impacts, and adaptation options across the nation, at all levels of decision making. Gaps in the knowledge required to link anticipated impacts with appropriate adaptation strategies and actions need to be addressed as a high national research priority.

Uncertainty about the nature of future climate change impacts in specific locations is not a rationale for inaction but a call for better understanding and communication of the sources and nature of uncertainty in the context of decision making. As part of an integrated climate change research initiative, the federal government should undertake a significant climate change adaptation research effort designed to provide a reliable foundation for adapting to the impacts of climate change in a larger context of sustainability

CONCLUSION

Although human-caused climate change has been recognized as a distinct possibility for more than a century, and has been increasingly documented as a real and accelerating phenomenon in the last quarter century (IPCC, 2007a), surprisingly few climate change adaptation plans have been implemented anywhere in the world. Impacts and vulnerability are place-based and fundamentally driven by the scale at which the impact occurs. Many current and future climate change impacts require immediate actions to improve the ability of the nation to adapt. Adaptation has emerged as a pressing concern at all levels of government; but action is still hampered by a lack of directed research, poor understanding of vulnerability, and limited experience with the implementation of adaptation options. Adaptation options need to address current and projected changes in mean weather variables as well as increases in the frequency and intensity of many extreme events.

Adapting to climate change impacts will require doing our best to understand the factors that drive both the impacts and our ability to respond. Major uncertainties in determining future climate include the natural internal variability of the climate system, the trajectories of future emissions of GHGs and aerosols, and the response of the global climate system to any given set of future emissions (NRC, 2010).

Some of the challenge for decision makers when individuals and businesses plan for the future is that they do not fully weigh the long-term benefits of investing in loss-reduction measures, especially if there is only a small likelihood of reaping financial returns. There is a tendency for people to focus on the short run and to ignore low-probability events below their threshold level of concern can have severe long-run consequences (Kunreuther & Michel-Kerjan, 2009).

ACKNOWLEDGEMENT

I wish to acknowledge that this chapter is part of the earlier published work cited as:

Gisore, B. N., & Njurai, E. (2023). *Pedagogical Strategies to Enhance Climate Change Education.* US, IGI Global Publishers. Available at; https://www.igi-global.com/book/climate-change-education-sustainable-development/317416

REFERENCES

Adger, W. N., Huq, S., Brown, K., Conway, D., & Hulme, M. (2003). Adaptation to climate change in the developing world. *Progress in Development Studies*, 3(3), 179–195. DOI: 10.1191/1464993403ps060oa

Adger, W. N., Lorenzoni, I., & O'Brien, K. L. (Eds.). (2009). *Adapting to Climate Change: Thresholds, Values, Governance*. Cambridge University Press.

Archer, D., & Rahmstorf, S. (2010). *The Climate Crisis: An Introductory Guide to Climate Change*. Cambridge University Press.

Chen, W.-Y. W., & Lackner, T. S. (Eds) (2012). *Handbook of Climate Change Mitigation and Adaptation (2nd Ed)*. Switzerland: Springer International Publishing.

Costanza, R., Graumlich, L., Steffen, W., Crumley, C., Dearing, J., Hibbard, K., Leemans, R., Redman, C., & Schimel, D. (2007). Sustainability or collapse: What can we learn from integrating the history of humans and the rest of nature? *Ambio*, 36(7), 522–527. DOI: 10.1579/0044-7447(2007)36[522:SOCWCW]2.0.CO;2 PMID: 18074887

Cronbach, L. J., & Suppes, P. (Eds.). (1969). *Research for Tomorrow's Schools: Disciplined Inquiry of Education*. Macmillan.

Desonie, D. (2008). *Climate: Causes and Effects of Climate Change*. Chelsea House.

Dillon, J., Stevenson, R., & Wals, A. (2016). Introduction to special section: Moving from citizen to civic science to address wicked conservation problems. *Conservation Biology*, 30(3), 450–455. DOI: 10.1111/cobi.12689 PMID: 27153527

Eakin, H. C., Lemos, M. C., & Nelson, D. R. (2014). Differentiating Capacities as a Means to Sustainable Climate Change Adaptation. *Global Environmental Change*, 27, 1–8. DOI: 10.1016/j.gloenvcha.2014.04.013

Gisore, B. N., & Njurai, E. (2023). *Pedagogical Strategies to Enhance Climate Change Education*. IGI Global Publishers. DOI: 10.4018/978-1-6684-9099-0.ch010

Hilgartner, S., & Bosk, C. L. (1988). The rise and fall of social problems: A public arenas model. *American Journal of Sociology*, 94(1), 53–78. DOI: 10.1086/228951

IPCC. (2007). *Climate Change 2007: Impacts, Adaptation and Vulnerability.* Contribution of Working Group II to the Fourth Assessment Report of the Intergovernmental Panel on Climate Change, M. L. Parry, O. F. Canziani, J. P. Palutikof, P. J. van der Linden and C. E. Hanson (Eds.). UK and New York: Cambridge University Press.

IPCC. (2007a). *Climate Change: Impacts, Adaptation and Vulnerability.* Contribution of Working Group II to the Fourth Assessment Report of the Intergovernmental Panel on Climate Change, M. L. Parry, O. F. Canziani, J. P. Palutikof, P. J. van der Linden, and C. E. Hanson, eds. UK: Cambridge University Press.

IPCC. (2007b). *Climate Change: The Physical Science Basis. Contribution of Working Group to the Fourth Assessment Report of the Intergovernmental Panel on Climate Change* (Solomon, S., Qin, D., Manning, M., Chen, Z., Marquis, M., Averyt, K. B., Tignor, M., & Miller, H. L., Eds.). Cambridge University Press.

IPCC. (2007c). *Climate Change: Mitigation of Climate Change. Contribution of Working Group III to the Fourth Assessment Report of the Intergovernmental Panel on Climate Change* (Metz, B., Davidson, O. R., Bosch, P. R., Dave, R., & Meyer, L. A., Eds.). Cambridge University Press.

Kagawa, F., & Selby, D. (2010). Introduction. In Kagawa, F., & Selby, D. (Eds.), *Education and climate change: Living and learning in interesting times.* Taylor & Francis. DOI: 10.4324/9780203866399

Kovats, R. S., & Hajat, S. (2008). Heat stress and public health: A critical review. *Annual Review of Public Health*, 29(1), 41–55. DOI: 10.1146/annurev.publhealth.29.020907.090843 PMID: 18031221

Krasny, M. E., & DuBois, B. (2016). Climate adaptation education: Embracing reality or abandoning environmental values. *Environmental Education Research*, •••, 1–12.

Kunreuther, H., & Michel-Kerjan, E. (2009). From market to government failure in insuring U.S. natural catastrophes: How long term contracts help. In Brown, J. (Ed.), *Private Markets and Public Insurance Programs.* American Enterprise Institute.

Lie, R., & Servaes, J. (2015). Disciplines in the field of communication for development and social change. *Communication Theory*, 25(2), 244–258. DOI: 10.1111/comt.12065

Lotz-Sisitka, H. (2010). Climate injustice: How should education respond? In, F. Kagawa & D. Selby (Eds.), *Education and climate change: Learning and living in interesting times.* 71–88.

Lu, X. (2011). Provision of climate information for adaptation to climate change. *Climate Research*, 47(1), 83–94. DOI: 10.3354/cr00950

Meehl, G. A., Stocker, T. F., Collins, W. D., Friedlingstein, A. T., Gaye, A. T., Gregory, J. M., Kitoh, A., Knutti, R., Murphy, J. M., Noda, A., Raper, S., Watterson, I. G., Weaver, A. J., & Zhao, Z. (2007). Global climate projections. Pp. 747-845. In, *Climate Change: The Physical Science Basis.* Contribution of Working Group I to the Fourth Assessment Report of the Intergovernmental Panel on Climate Change. Cambridge: Cambridge University Press.

Moser, S. C. (2009b). Good Morning America! The Explosive US Awakening to the Need for Adaptation. Sacramento, CA: California Energy Commission; Charleston, SC: NOAA-Coastal Services Center.

Moser, S. C. (2010). Communicating climate change: History, challenges, process and future directions. *Wiley Interdisciplinary Reviews: Climate Change*, 1(1), 31–53. DOI: 10.1002/wcc.11

National Research Council. (2009c). *Restructuring Federal Climate Research to Meet the Challenges of Climate Change*. The National Academies Press.

National Research Council. (2010). *America's Climate Choices: Panel on Adapting to the Impacts of Climate Change*. The National Academies Press.

Nelson, D. R., Adger, W. N., & Brown, K. (2007). Adaptation to environmental change: Contributions of a resilience framework. *Annual Review of Environment and Resources*, 32(1), 395–419. DOI: 10.1146/annurev.energy.32.051807.090348

Ogega, O. M., Lakey, G., Opisa, R., & Gyampoh, B. A. (2022). Strengthening Climate Research Capacity in Africa: Lessons from the 'Climate Impact Research Capacity Leadership Enhancement' Project. *Regional Environmental Change*, 22(4), 135. DOI: 10.1007/s10113-022-01997-x

Recommended web link: www.ipcc.ch for The IPCC Reports.

Reeder, T., Wicks, J., Lovell, L., & Tarrant, O. (2009). Protecting London from tidal flooding: Limits to engineering adaptation. In Adger, W. N., Lorenzoni, I., & O'Brien, K. L. (Eds.), *Adapting to Climate Change: Thresholds, Values, Governance.* Cambridge University Press.

Rosenzweig, C., Karoly, M., Vicarelli, M., Neofotis, P., Wu, Q., Casassa, G., Menzel, A., Root, T. L., Estrella, N., Seguin, B., Tryjanowski, P., Liu, C., Rawlins, S., & Imeson, A. (2008). Attributing physical and biological impacts to anthropogenic climate change. *Nature*, 453(7193), 353–320. DOI: 10.1038/nature06937 PMID: 18480817

Schriever, V., & Grainger, P. (2019). Mentoring an early career researcher: Insider perspectives from the mentee and mentor. *Reflective Practice*, 20(6), 720–731. DOI: 10.1080/14623943.2019.1674272

Shafer, M. A. (2008). Climate Literacy and a National Climate Service. *Physical Geography*, 29(6), 561–574. DOI: 10.2747/0272-3646.29.6.561

Solomon, S., Plattner, G. K., Knutti, R., & Friedlingstein, P. (2009). Irreversible climate change due to carbon dioxide emissions. *Proceedings of the National Academy of Sciences of the United States of America*, 106(6), 1704–1709. DOI: 10.1073/pnas.0812721106 PMID: 19179281

Steffen, W., Crutzen, P. J., & Mcneil, L. J. R. (2007). The Anthropocene: Are humans now overwhelming the great forces of Nature? *Ambio*, 36(8), 614–621. DOI: 10.1579/0044-7447(2007)36[614:TAAHNO]2.0.CO;2 PMID: 18240674

Stein, J. V. (2008). The International Law and Politics of Climate Change Ratification of the United Nations Framework Convention and the Kyoto Protocol. *The Journal of Conflict Resolution*, 52(2), 243–268. DOI: 10.1177/0022002707313692

Stern, N. (2007). *The Economics of Climate Change: The Stern Review*. Cambridge University Press. DOI: 10.1017/CBO9780511817434

Stevenson, R. B. with Stirling, C. (2011). Environmental learning and agency in diverse educational and cultural contexts. In R. B. Stevenson & J. Dillon (Eds.) *Engaging environmental education: Learning, culture and agency (pp. 219–38).* Rotterdam: Sense Publishers.

Ullah, W., Nihei, T., Nafees, M., Zaman, R., & Ali, M. (2018). Understanding Climate Change Vulnerability, Adaptation and Risk Perceptions at Household Level in Khyber Pakhtunkhwa, Pakistan. *International Journal of Climate Change Strategies and Management*, 10(3), 359–378. DOI: 10.1108/IJCCSM-02-2017-0038

UN Framework Convention on Climate Change. (2007). *Investment and Financial Flows Relevant to the Development of an Effective and Appropriate International Response to Climate Change*. UNFCCC.

UNESCO & UNEP. (2011). *Climate change starters guide book*. UNESCO.

UNFCCC. (2010). *Report on the Technical Workshop on Advancing the Integration of Approaches to Adaptation Planning*. FCCC/SBSTA/2010/2. UNFCCC, Bonn. Available at: http://unfccc.int/resource/docs/2010/sbsta/eng/ 02.pdf (Accessed 5 September 2010).

U.S. Global Change Research Program. (2009). *Climate Literacy: The Essential Principles of Climate Science.*http://www.globalchange.go

USGCRP (United States Global Change Research Program). (2009). *Global Climate Change Impacts in the United States: A State of Knowledge Report from the U.S. Global Change Research Program, T. R. Karl, J. M. Melillo, and T. C. Peterson* (York, N., Ed.).

Webber, D. J. (1992). The distribution and use of policy knowledge in the policy process. In Dunn, W. N., & Kelly, R. M. (Eds.), *Advances in Policy Studies since 1950* (pp. 383–418). Transaction Books.

West, J. M., Julius, S. H., Kareiva, P., Enquist, C., Lawler, J. J., Petersen, B., Johnson, A. E., & Shaw, R. (2009). U.S. Natural Resources and Climate Change: Concepts and Approaches for Management Adaptation. *Environmental Management*, 44(6), 1–21. DOI: 10.1007/s00267-009-9345-1 PMID: 19636606

Yohe, G., & Tol, R. S. J. (2002). Indicators for social and economic coping capacity: Moving toward a working definition of adaptive capacity. *Global Environmental Change*, 12(1), 25–40. DOI: 10.1016/S0959-3780(01)00026-7

Zhang, X. B., Zwiers, F. W., Hegerl, G. C., Lambert, F. H., Gillett, N. P., Solomon, S., Stott, P. A., & Nozawa, T. (2007). Detection of human influence on twentieth-century precipitation trends. *Nature*, 448(7152), 461–464. DOI: 10.1038/nature06025 PMID: 17646832

ADDITIONAL READING

Feenstra, J. F., Burton, I., Joel, B., Smith, J. B., & Tol, R. S. J. (Eds.). (1998). *Handbook on Methods for Climate Change Impact Assessment and Adaptation Strategies.* UNEP: Institute for Environmental Studies.

Filho, W. L., Azul, E. M., & McGhie, U. M. A. (Eds.). (2018). *Handbook of Climate Change Communication.* Springer. DOI: 10.1007/978-3-319-70066-3

Romm, J. (2016). *Climate Change: What Everyone Needs to Know.* Oxford University Press.

Surampalli, R. Y., Zhang, T. C., Ojha, C. S., Gurjar, B., Tyagi, R. D., & Kao, C. M. (2013). *Climate Change Modeling, Mitigation, and Adaptation.* American Society of Civil Engineers. DOI: 10.1061/9780784412718

Vose, J. M., & Klepzig, K. D. (2014). *Climate Change adaptation and mitigation management options*. Taylor & Francis Group.

Woodward, J. (2008). *Climate Change*. Dorling Kindersley Limited.

KEY TERMS AND DEFINITIONS

Adaptation: A strategy that can be used to deal with climate change by changing behavior to deal with inevitable changes

Carbon Sequestration: Storage of carbon in one reservoir so that it is no longer part of the carbon cycle

Climate change: Long-term shifts in temperatures and weather patterns

Greenhouse Effect: The trapping of heat that is radiated from the Earth

Greenhouse Gases: Gases that absorb heat radiated from the earth

Knowledge Dissemination: Communicating information to target audiences so that it may be used to lead to change

Mitigation: Making changes that result in the reduction of greenhouse gas emissions

Research Capacity: The ability to define problems, conduct sound scientific research and identify solutions to climate problems

Compilation of References

A3ES (2018). *Guião para a autoavaliação. Ciclo de estudos em funcionamento (Ensino Universitário e Politécnico).* https://a3es.pt/sites/default/files/Gui%C3%A3o%20ACEF-PERA%202018-2023_PT_V1.0.pdf

Abdulaal, R. M., Al-Bahi, A. M., Soliman, A. Y., & Iskanderani, F. I. (2011). Design and implementation of a project-based active/cooperative engineering design course for freshmen. *European Journal of Engineering Education*, 36(4), 391–402. DOI: 10.1080/03043797.2011.598498

Adger, W. N., Huq, S., Brown, K., Conway, D., & Hulme, M. (2003). Adaptation to climate change in the developing world. *Progress in Development Studies*, 3(3), 179–195. DOI: 10.1191/1464993403ps060oa

Adger, W. N., Lorenzoni, I., & O'Brien, K. L. (Eds.). (2009). *Adapting to Climate Change: Thresholds, Values, Governance*. Cambridge University Press.

Aduol, F and Associates (2009). Financing University Education in Kenya: A Report to the Ministry of Higher Education, Science and Technology.

Agasisti, T. & Bowers, A., (2018). Data Analytics and Decision-Making in Education: Towards the Educational Data Scientist as a Key Actor in Schools and Higher Education Institutions. .DOI: 10.4337/9781785369070.00014

Aguilar, P. (2008). *Barriers to internationalization: Attitudes, resources, policy. Rapporteur: Martin Pantoja – Director.* International Relations, Universidad de Guanajuato.

Alanazi, A. (2016). A critical review of constructivist theory and the emergence of constructionism. *American Research Journal of Humanities and Social Sciences*, 2(1), 1–8.

Albanese, M. A., & Mitchell, S. (1993). Problem-based learning: A review of literature on its outcomes and implementation issues. *Academic Medicine*, 68(1), 52–81. DOI: 10.1097/00001888-199301000-00012 PMID: 8447896

Aldabbus, S. (2018). Project-based learning: Implementation & challenges. *International Journal of Education, Learning and Development*, 6(3), 71–79.

Aldrich, C. (2005). *Learning by doing: A comprehensive guide to simulations, computer games, and pedagogy in e-learning and other educational experiences*. John Wiley & Sons.

Alemu, S. K., Qu, M., & Sakhiya, Z. (2022). Voices of internationalization of higher education from Sub-Saharan Africa, China and Indonesia. *Learning and Teaching*, 15(3), 2–31. DOI: 10.3167/latiss.2022.150303

Aliftika, O., Astra, I., & Supriyati, Y. (2021). Project-based blended learning and independent learning on critical thinking skills. Journal of Physics: Conference Series, Asarta, C. J., & Schmidt, J. R. (2020). The effects of online and blended experience on outcomes in a blended learning environment. *The Internet and Higher Education*, 44, 100708.

Allan, O. (2020). *Economy hit hard as services slow down; Daily Nation April 29th 2020*. Nation Media Group.

Allen-Gil, S., Walker, L., Thomas, G., Shevory, T., & Elan, S. (2005). Forming a community partnership to enhance education in sustainability. *International Journal of Sustainability in Higher Education*, 6(4), 392–402. DOI: 10.1108/14676370510623874

Allen, I. E., & Seaman, J. (2017). *Digital learning compass: Distance education enrollment report 2017*. Babson Survey Research Group.

Allio, R. J. (2005). Leadership development: Teaching versus learning. *Management Decision*, 43(7), 1071–1077. DOI: 10.1108/00251740510610071

Alshaye, I. A., Tasir, Z., & Jumaat, N. F. (2023). The effectiveness of online problem-based learning tasks on Riyadh's secondary school students' problem-solving ability and programming skills. *Open Education Studies*, 5(1), 20220208. DOI: 10.1515/edu-2022-0208

Altbach, P. G., & Jalote, P. (2020). When will India Build World-Class Research Universities. World University News. Retrieved from: https://www.universityworldnews.com/post.php?story=20200921112203767

Altbach. J & Knight (2007)-The Internationalization of Higher Education: Motivations and Realities: Journal of Studies in International Education Fall/Win 11 -3-4, 290-305.

Altbach, P. G. (2013). The internationalization of higher education: Motivations and realities. *Journal of Studies in International Education*, 17(3), 348–361.

Altbach, P. G. (2014). The emergence of a field: Research and training in higher education. *Studies in Higher Education*, 39(8), 1306–1320. DOI: 10.1080/03075079.2014.949541

Altmann, S., Falk, A., Jäger, S., & Zimmermann, F. (2018). Learning about job search: A field experiment with job seekers in Germany. *Journal of Public Economics*, 164(C), 33–49. DOI: 10.1016/j.jpubeco.2018.05.003

Alvarez, A., & Rogers, J. (2006). Going "out there": Learning about sustainability in place. *International Journal of Sustainability in Higher Education*, 7(2), 176–188. DOI: 10.1108/14676370610655940

Anane, E. (2020). A multiple mediation analysis of the effect of prior performance on academic achievement through student teachers' motivational orientations. *Higher Education Research*, 5(4), 118. DOI: 10.11648/j.her.20200504.12

Anderson, J. R., Bothell, D., Byrne, M. D., Douglass, S., Lebiere, C., & Yang, Y. (2012). *An overview of the ACT-R 4.0 cognitive architecture*. Cambridge University Press.

Anderson, R. E., & Anderson, R. J. (2010). *Online professional development for teachers: Emerging models and methods*. Harvard Education Press.

Anderson, T., & Hira, A. (2020). The Impact of COVID-19 on Teaching and Learning: A Critical Perspective. *Journal of Educational Technology*, 51(4), 678–689.

Anderson, V., & Tomlinson, M. (2021). Signaling standout graduate employability: The employer perspective. *Human Resource Management Journal*, 31(3), 675–693. DOI: 10.1111/1748-8583.12334

Angelo, T. A., & Cross, K. P. (1993). *Classroom Assessment Techniques: A Handbook for College Teachers*. Jossey-Bass.

ANVUR. (2017). *Linee Guida AVA per l'accreditamento periodico delle Sedi e dei corsi di studio universitari*. https://www.anvur.it/attivita/ava/accreditamento-periodico/linee-guida-per-laccreditamento-periodico

Archer, D. (2016). Domestic tax and education. Background Paper for the Education Commission, available at: http://report. Education commission. org/resources/ (accessed November 1, 2019).

Archer, D., & Rahmstorf, S. (2010). *The Climate Crisis: An Introductory Guide to Climate Change*. Cambridge University Press.

Areba, G. N. (2020). COVID-19 pandemic impact on Kenyan education sector: Learner challenges and mitigations. *Journal of Research Innovation and Implications in Education*, 4(2), 128–139.

Armbrust, M., Fox, A., Griffith, R., Joseph, A. D., Katz, R., Konwinski, A., Lee, G., Patterson, D., Rabkin, A., Stoica, I., & Zaharia, M. (2010). A view of cloud computing. *Communications of the ACM*, 53(4), 50–58. DOI: 10.1145/1721654.1721672

Armstrong, J. (2016). *Responsibility in the workplace*. https://www.linkedin.com/pulse/responsibility-workplace-jason-armstrong

Association for Institutional Research (AIR). (2019). Research and evaluation in East Africa. https://www.air.org/regions/east-africa

Association for the Development of Education in Africa (ADEA). (2011*). Creating an African Higher Education and Research Space*. https://sig.ias.edu/news/adea-creating-african-higher-education-and-research-space

Atchison, E. S. (2020). Enhancing institutional research capacity in the midst of a pandemic: A system approach. *New Directions for Institutional Research*, 2020(187–188), 55–63. DOI: 10.1002/ir.20347

Australian Bureau of Statistics (2019) 5368.0.55.003 – International Trade: Supplementary Information, Financial Year, 2018-19.

Australian Bureau of Statistics (2020) – International Trade: Supplementary Information, Financial Year, 2019-20.

AVU. (2020). *Annual report*. African Virtual University.

Axtell, J. (1968). *The Educational Writings of John Locke: A Critical Edition with Introduction and Notes*. Cambridge University Press.

Aydin, O. T. (*2020) Local and International Students' Experiences at a Turkish University Social Interaction Between Students*. Available from: https://www.researchgate.net/publication/337185724_Local_and_International_Students'_Experiences_at_a_Turkish_University_Social_Interaction_Between_Students [accessed Jul 27 2024].

Babones, S. (2019). *The China Student Boom and the Risks It Poses to Australian Universities; Analysis paper 5*. The Centre for Independent. Sydney.

Babos, P., Lubyova, M., & Studena, I. (2015). *Lifelong learning is a growing factor in employability*. Policy Brief. LLLight in Europe Research Consortium.

Bai Gokarna, V., Mendon, S., Thonse Hawaldar, I., Spulbar, C., Birau, R., Nayak, S., & Manohar, M. (2021). Exploring the antecedents of institutional effectiveness: A case study of higher education universities in India. *Ekonomska Istrazivanja*, 35(1), 1162–1182. DOI: 10.1080/1331677X.2021.1959367

Baker, G., & Henson, D. (2010). Promoting employability skills development in a research-intensive university. *Education + Training*, 52(1), 62–75. DOI: 10.1108/00400911011017681

Baker, R. S., & Inventado, P. S. (2014). Educational data mining and learning analytics. In *Learning analytics* (pp. 61–75). Springer. DOI: 10.1007/978-1-4614-3305-7_4

Bakhshi, H., Downing, J., Osborne, M., & Schneider, P. (2017). The future of skills: Employment in 2030. Pearson and Nesta. https://futureskills.pearson.com/research/assets/pdfs/technical-report.pdf

Bamberger, A., Morris, P., & Yemini, M. (2019). Neoliberalism, internationalisation and higher education: Connections, contradictions and alternatives. *Discourse (Abingdon)*, 40(2), 203–216. DOI: 10.1080/01596306.2019.1569879

Bandura, A. (1994). *Self-efficacy*. John Wiley & Sons.

Banks, J., Carson, J. S., Nelson, B. L., & Nicol, D. M. (2014). *Discrete-event system simulation*. Pearson.

Barakabitze, A. A., William-Andey Lazaro, A., Ainea, N., Mkwizu, M. H., Maziku, H., Matofali, A. X., Iddi, A., & Sanga, C. (2019). Transforming African education systems in science, technology, engineering, and mathematics (STEM) using ICTs: Challenges and opportunities. *Education Research International*, 2019(1), 6946809. DOI: 10.1155/2019/6946809

Barnett, R. (2000a). *Realizing the university in an age of supercomplexity*. Open University Press.

Barnett, R. (2000b). Supercomplexity and the curriculum. *Studies in Higher Education*, 25(3), 255–265. DOI: 10.1080/713696156

Barnett, R. (2000c). University knowledge in an age of supercomplexity. *Higher Education*, 40(4), 409–422. http://www.jstor.or/stable/3448008. DOI: 10.1023/A:1004159513741

Barnett, R. (2012). Learning for an unknown future. *Higher Education Research & Development*, 31(1), 65–77. DOI: 10.1080/07294360.2012.642841

Baron, R., & Kenny, D. A. (1986). The moderator-mediator variable distinction in social psychological research: Conceptual, strategic and statistical considerations. *Journal of Personality and Social Psychology*, 51(6), 1173–1182. DOI: 10.1037/0022-3514.51.6.1173 PMID: 3806354

Barrows, H. S. (1996). Problem-based learning in medicine and beyond: A brief overview. *New Directions for Teaching and Learning*, 1996(68), 3–12. DOI: 10.1002/tl.37219966804

Barrows, H. S., & Neufeld, V. (1974). The "McMaster Philosophy": An approach to medical education. *Journal of Medical Education*, 49, 1040–1050. PMID: 4444006

Basheka, B. C., Muhenda, M. B., & Kittobe, J. (2009). *Programme Delivery, Quality Benchmarks and 143 Outcomes Based Education at Uganda Management Institute: A correlational approach*. NCHE.

Bastrikin, A. (2020). International Student Enrolment Statistics: educationdata.org. MI Bevis, T. B. (2002). At a glance: International students in the United States'. *International Educator*, 11(3), 12–17.

Bates, A. W. (2015). *Teaching in a Digital Age: Guidelines for designing teaching and learning*. BCcampus.

Bates, A. W. (2015). *Teaching in a digital age: Guidelines for designing teaching and learning*. Tony Bates Associates Ltd.

Becker, K., & Park, K. (2011). Effects of technology on student achievement: A meta-analysis of studies from 1990 to 2010. *Journal of Research on Technology in Education*, 43(2), 159–184.

Bennet, D., Knight, E., Divan, A., Kuchel, L., Horn, J., van Reyk, D., & Burke da Silva, K. (2017). How do research-intensive universities portray employability strategies? A review of their websites. *Australian Journal of Career Development*, 26(2), 52–61. DOI: 10.1177/1038416217714475

Bennett, D. (2018). Graduate employability and higher education: past, present and future. *HERDSA review of higher education*, 5, 31-61. https://www.herdsa.org.au/herdsa-review-higher-education-vol-5/31-61

Berglund, T., & Gericke, N. (2016). Separated and integrated perspectives on environmental, economic, and social dimensions–an investigation of student views on sustainable development. *Environmental Education Research*, 22(8), 1115–1138. DOI: 10.1080/13504622.2015.1063589

Bergman, L. R., & Lundh, L. G. (2015). Introduction: The person-oriented approach: Roots and roads to the future. *Journal for Person-Oriented Research*, 1(1-2), 1–6. DOI: 10.17505/jpor.2015.01

Bergmann, J., & Sams, A. (2012). *Flip Your Classroom: Reach Every Student in Every Class Every Day*. International Society for Technology in Education.

Bernacki, M. L., Greene, M. J., & Lobczowski, N. G. (2021). A systematic review of research on personalized learning: Personalized by whom, to what, how, and for what purpose (s)? *Educational Psychology Review*, 33(4), 1675–1715. DOI: 10.1007/s10648-021-09615-8

Bers, T. H. (2008). The role of institutional research in assessing student learning outcomes. *New Directions for Higher Education*, 141(141), 31–39. DOI: 10.1002/he.291

Betts, K. (2017). *The growth of online learning: How universities must adjust to the new norm*. Education Dive.

Bhalla, V. (2015). International students in Indian universities. *Industry and Higher Education*, 79(41), 24–31. DOI: 10.6017/ihe.2005.41.7500

Biggs, J. (2003). Aligning teaching and assessing to course objectives. *Teaching and Learning in Higher Education: New Trends and Innovations*, 2, 13–17.

Biggs, J. (2003). *Aligning teaching and assessment to curriculum objectives*. LTSN Generic Centre.

Biggs, J., & Tang, C. (2011). *Teaching for quality learning at university: What the student does*. McGraw-Hill Education.

Biggs, J., & Tang, C. (2011). *Teaching for Quality Learning at University: What the Student Does*. McGraw-Hill Education.

Birdsall, S. (2010). Empowering students to act: Learning about, through and from the nature of action. *Australian Journal of Environmental Education*, 26, 65–84. DOI: 10.1017/S0814062600000835

Bishop, J. L., & Verleger, M. A. (2013). The flipped classroom: A survey of the research. In *ASEE National Conference Proceedings,* Atlanta, GA (Vol. 30, No. 9, pp. 1-18). DOI: 10.18260/1-2--22585

Bista, K. (2019). Exploring the field: Understanding the international student experience. In K. Bista, K. (ed.), Global perspectives on international student experiences in higher education: Tensions and issues (pp. 1-16). Morgan State University: Routledge.

Black, S. (2020a).The problem with Stephen Grootes' views about online learning. Daily Maverick [online]. Available at https://www.dailymaverick.co.za/opinionista/2020-05-11-the-problem-with-stephen-grootes-views-ab out-online-learning/ [accessed 5th November 2020].

Black, S. (2020b). Conceptualizing school overcrowding: Exploring relations between (mal)distribution and (inadequate) provision at different scales. Unpublished working paper.

Blackmore, P., Bulaitis, Z. H., Jackman, A. H., & Tan, E. (2016). *Employability in Higher Education: A review of practice and strategies around the world.* Pearson Efficacy & Research. Pearson Education.

Bligh, D. A. (2000). *What's theon.* Cambridge university press.

Bloom, D. E., Canning, D., Chan, K. J., & Luca, D. L. (2014). Higher education and economic growth in Africa. *International Journal of African Higher Education*, 1(1), 22–57. DOI: 10.6017/ijahe.v1i1.5643

Blumenfeld, P. C., Soloway, E., Marx, R. W., Krajcik, J. S., Guzdial, M., & Palincsar, A. (1991). Motivating project-based learning: Sustaining the doing, supporting the learning. *Educational Psychologist*, 26(3-4), 369–398. DOI: 10.1080/00461520.1991.9653139

Boden, D., & Corckett, J. (2017). Embracing change in research initiatives. *Sage (Atlanta, Ga.).*

Boeve-de Pauw, J., Gericke, N., Olsson, D., & Berglund, T. (2015). The effectiveness of education for sustainable development. *Sustainability (Basel)*, 7(11), 15693–15717. DOI: 10.3390/su71115693

Bonabeau, E. (2002). Agent-based modeling: Methods and techniques for simulating human systems. *Proceedings of the National Academy of Sciences of the United States of America*, 99(Suppl 3), 7280–7287. DOI: 10.1073/pnas.082080899 PMID: 12011407

Boninger, F., Molnar, A., & Saldaña, C. M. (2019). *Personalized Learning and the Digital Privatization of Curriculum and Teaching*. National Education Policy Center.

Bonk, C. J., & Graham, C. R. (Eds.). (2006). *The Handbook of Blended Learning: Global Perspectives, Local Designs*. Pfeiffer.

Borden, V. M. H., & Starobin, S. S. (2017). *Collaborative approaches to research*. AERA.

Borden, V., Massa, T., & Milam, J. (2001). Technology and tools for institutional research. In Howard, R. (Ed.), *IR: Decision support in higher education* (pp. 195–222). Association of Institutional Research.

Borg, C., Gericke, N., Höglund, H. O., & Bergman, E. (2012). The barriers encountered by teachers implementing education for sustainable development: Discipline bound differences and teaching traditions. *Research in Science & Technological Education*, 30(2), 185–207. DOI: 10.1080/02635143.2012.699891

Borhan, M. T. (2014). Problem-based learning (PBL) in teacher education: A review of the effect of PBL on pre-service teachers' knowledge and skills. *European Journal of Educational Sciences*, 1(1), 10. DOI: 10.19044/ejes.v1no1a9

Börner, A.. (2019). *Research support services*. Springer.

Borrego, M., & Newswander, L. K. (2010). Definitions of interdisciplinary research: Toward graduate-level interdisciplinary learning outcomes. *Review of Higher Education*, 34(1), 61–84. DOI: 10.1353/rhe.2010.0006

Bosch, A., & Taylor, J. (2011). A proposed framework for institutional research development phases. *Journal of Higher Education Policy and Management*, 33(5), 443–457. DOI: 10.1080/1360080X.2011.585742

Boss, S., & Krauss, J. (2022). *Reinventing project-based learning: Your field guide to real-world projects in the digital age*. International Society for Technology in Education.

Botha, J., & Muller, N. J. (Eds.). (2016). *Institutional research in South African higher education: Intersecting contexts and practices*. African Sun Media., DOI: 10.18820/9781928357186/01

Botha, J., Webber, K., Williams, J., & Woodfield, S. (2024). Building capacity in institutional research: Collaboration and complementarity? *Tertiary Education and Management*, 30(2), 129–145. Advance online publication. DOI: 10.1007/s11233-024-09139-0

Boud, D., & Falchikov, N. (Eds.). (2007). *Rethinking assessment in higher education: Learning for the longer term*. Routledge. DOI: 10.4324/9780203964309

Boud, D., & Feletti, G. (1997). *The challenge of problem-based learning* (1st ed.). Routledge., DOI: 10.4324/9781315042039

Bowen, G. A. (2009). Document Analysis as a Qualitative Research Method. *Qualitative Research Journal*, 9(2), 27–40. DOI: 10.3316/QRJ0902027

Brandenburg, U., De Wit, H., Jones, E., & Leask, B. (2019). Internationalisation in higher education for society. *University World News*. Retrieved from https://www.universityworldnews.com/post.php?story=20190414195843914

Breaden, J., Do, T., dos Anjos-Santos, L. M., & Normand-Marconnet, N. (2023). Student empowerment for internationalisation at a distance: Enacting the students as partners approach in virtual mobility. *Higher Education Research & Development*, 42(5), 1182–1196. DOI: 10.1080/07294360.2023.2193728

Brickhouse, N. W., & Smith, J. P. (2000). The roles of ethnography and reflexivity in understanding teacher thinking, practice, and learning. *Educational Researcher*, 29(1), 4–13.

Bridgstock, R. (2020). *Graduate employability 2.0: Enhancing the connectedness of learners, programs and higher education institutions* [Final report]. Australian Government Department of Education, Skills and Employment. https://ltr.edu/au/resources/FS15-0241_Bridgstock_report_2020.pdf

Bridgstock, R., & Jackson, D. (2019). Strategic institutional approaches to graduate employability: Navigating meanings, measurements and what really matters. *Journal of Higher Education Policy and Management*, 41(5), 468–484. DOI: 10.1080/1360080X.2019.1646378

Brownell, S. E., & Tanner, K. D. (2012). Barriers to faculty pedagogical change: Lack of training, time, incentives, and...tensions with professional identity? *CBE Life Sciences Education*, 11(4), 339–346. DOI: 10.1187/cbe.12-09-0163 PMID: 23222828

Brown, J. (2008). Institutional research and external reporting: The major data seekers. *New Directions for Higher Education*, 141(141), 87–96. DOI: 10.1002/he.296

Brown, M., & McCormack, C. (2013). The Future of Open Universities in Australia. *Australian Educational Researcher*, 40(3), 263–279. DOI: 10.1007/s13384-013-0107-4

Bruner, J. S. (1961). *The act of discovery*. Harvard University Press.

Brunner, L. R. (2023). Settler nation-building through immigration as a rationale for higher education: A critical discourse analysis. *Higher Education Research & Development*, 42(5), 1086–1102. DOI: 10.1080/07294360.2023.2193732

Bryan, A., & Volchenkova, K. N. (2016). Blended learning: definition, models, implications for higher education. *Вестник Южно-Уральского государственного университета. Серия: Образование. Педагогические науки, 8*(2), 24-30.

Bryson, J. M. (2011). *Strategic planning for public and nonprofit organizations: A guide to strengthening and sustaining organizational achievement*. John Wiley & Sons.

Buchholz, B. A., DeHart, J., & Moorman, G. (2020). Digital citizenship during a global pandemic: Moving beyond digital literacy. *Journal of Adolescent & Adult Literacy*, 64(1), 11–17. DOI: 10.1002/jaal.1076 PMID: 32834710

Bunoti, S. (2011). The quality of higher education in developing countries needs professional support. Retrieved from http://www.intconfhighered.org/FINAL%20Sarah%20Bunoti.pdf on 6th August, 2020.

Burke, C., Scurry, T., Blenkinsopp, J., & Graley, K. (2017). Critical perspectives on graduate employability. In Tomlinson, M., & Holmes, L. (Eds.), *Graduate employability in context* (pp. 87–107). Palgrave Macmillan. DOI: 10.1057/978-1-137-57168-7_4

Burns, H. (2011). Teaching for transformation:(Re) Designing sustainability courses based on ecological principles. *Journal of Sustainability Education*.

Bylund, L. (2024). Education for sustainable development among rich and poor: Didactical responses to biopolitical differentiation. *Environmental Education Research*, 30(3), 419–431. DOI: 10.1080/13504622.2023.2172140

Calderon, A. J., & Webber, K. L. (2015). Institutional research, planning, and decision support in higher education today. In Calderon, A. J., & Webber, K. L. (Eds.), *Institutional Research and Planning in Higher Education* (pp. 3–15). Routledge.

Calderon, A., & Mathies, C. (2013). Institutional research in the future: Challenges within higher education and the need for excellence in professional practice. *New Directions for Institutional Research*, 157(157), 77–90. DOI: 10.1002/ir.20040

Calder, W., & Clugston, R. M. (2003). International efforts to promote higher education for sustainable development. *Planning for Higher Education*, 31(3), 30–44.

Caldwell, R. (2006). *Agency and change: Rethinking change agency in organizations*. Routledge. DOI: 10.4324/9780203087565

Cao, H. (2021). *MOOCs and Education Access: Evidence from New Zealand.* Open Access Te Herenga Waka-Victoria University of Wellington.

Capano, G. (2014). The re-regulation of the Italian university system through quality assurance. A mechanistic perspective. *Policy and Society*. 33, 199-213. DOI: . 001DOI: 10.1016/j.polsoc.2014.08

Capano, G., & Pritoni, A. (2020). What really happens in higher education governance? Trajectories of adopted policy instruments in higher education over time in 16 European countries. *Higher Education*, 80(5), 989–1010. DOI: 10.1007/s10734-020-00529-y

Carbach, E., & Fischer, D. (2017). Sustainability reporting at schools: Challenges and benefits. *Journal of Teacher Education for Sustainability*, 19(1), 69–81. DOI: 10.1515/jtes-2017-0005

Carbonell, K. B., Dailey-Hebert, A., & Gijselaers, W. (2013). Unleashing the creative potential of faculty to create blended learning. *The Internet and Higher Education*, 18, 29–37. DOI: 10.1016/j.iheduc.2012.10.004

Carroll, M., Goldman, S., Britos, L., Koh, J., Royalty, A., & Hornstein, M. (2010). Destination, imagination and the fires within: Design thinking in a middle school classroom. *International Journal of Art & Design Education*, 29(1), 37–53. DOI: 10.1111/j.1476-8070.2010.01632.x

Caruana, V., & Spurling, N. (2007). *The internationalisation of UK higher education-a review of selected material.* Higher Education Academy.

Castro, R. (2019). Blended learning in higher education: Trends and capabilities. *Education and Information Technologies*, 24(4), 2523–2546. DOI: 10.1007/s10639-019-09886-3

Catcheside, K. (2012, March 5). The benefits of a university education. *The Guardian.* https://www.theguardian.com/higher-education-network/blog/2012/mar/05/benefits-of-a-university-education

Celinšek, D., & Markič, M. (n.d.). Implementing a new approach in teaching and learning (problem-based learning) in a higher education learning organization. *In-Annual World International Congress for Effectiveness and Improvement,* Slovenia.

Centers for Disease Control and Prevention. (2018). Principles of epidemiology in public health practice. Retrieved from https://www.cdc.gov/csels/dsepd/ss1978/index.html

Centre for Innovation in Teaching and Learning. (n.d.). *Problem-based learning (PBL).*_https://citl.illinois.edu/citl-101/teaching-learning/resources/teaching-strategies/problem-based-learning-(pbl)

Chambers, D. (2009). Assessing and planning for environmental sustainability—A framework for institutions of higher education. *Sustainability at universities: Opportunities, challenges and trends*, 287-298.

Chege, M. (2015). Re-inventing Kenya's university: From a "Graduate-mill" to a development-oriented paradigm. *International Journal of Educational Development*, 44, 21–27. DOI: 10.1016/j.ijedudev.2015.07.002

Chen, W.-Y. W., & Lackner, T. S. (Eds) (2012). *Handbook of Climate Change Mitigation and Adaptation (2nd Ed)*. Switzerland: Springer International Publishing.

Chirikov, I. (2013). Research universities as knowledge networks: The role of institutional research. *Studies in Higher Education*, 38(3), 456–469. DOI: 10.1080/03075079.2013.773778

Cho, H., & Mosselson, J. (2018). Neoliberal Practices Amidst Social Justice Orientations: Global Citizenship Education in South Korea. *Compare: A Journal of Comparative Education*, 48(6), 861–878. DOI: 10.1080/03057925.2017.1364154

Chu, S. K. W., Reynolds, R. B., Tavares, N. J., Notari, M., Lee, C. W. Y., Chu, S. K. W., Reynolds, R. B., Tavares, N. J., Notari, M., & Lee, C. W. Y. (2017). Twenty-first-century skills and global education roadmaps. *21st century skills development through inquiry-based learning: From theory to practice*, 17-32.

Cincera, J., & Krajhanzl, J. (2013). Eco-Schools: What factors influence pupils' action competence for pro-environmental behaviour? *Journal of Cleaner Production*, 61, 117–121. DOI: 10.1016/j.jclepro.2013.06.030

Cloete, N., Bailey, T., & Maassen, P. (2012). *Universities and economic development in Africa: Pact, academic core and coordination.* African Minds., DOI: 10.47622/9781920355807

Clokie, T. L., & Fourie, E. (2016). Graduate employability and communication competence: Are undergraduates taught relevant skills? *Business and Professional Communication Quarterly*, 79(4), 442–463. DOI: 10.1177/2329490616657635

Colander, D. (2017). *Economics.* McGraw-Hill Education.

Conference Board of Canada (2000). *Employability skills 2000+.* www.conferenceboard.ca/education

Cook, E.J. (2022). A narrative review of graduate employability models: their paradigms, and relationships to teaching and curricula. *Journal of Teaching and Learning for Graduate Employability*. DOI:DOI: 10.21153/jtlge2022vol3no1art1483

Cook, E. J. (2022). A narrative review of graduate employability models: Their paradigms, and relationships to teaching and curricula. *Journal of Teaching and Learning for Graduate Employability*, 13(1), 37–64. DOI: 10.21153/jtlge2022vol-13no1art1483

Copernicus, A. (1994). *The university charter for sustainable development*. Association of European Universities.

Costanza, R., Graumlich, L., Steffen, W., Crumley, C., Dearing, J., Hibbard, K., Leemans, R., Redman, C., & Schimel, D. (2007). Sustainability or collapse: What can we learn from integrating the history of humans and the rest of nature? *Ambio*, 36(7), 522–527. DOI: 10.1579/0044-7447(2007)36[522:SOCWCW]2.0.CO;2 PMID: 18074887

Cote, A. (2019). The benefits of a strong work ethic, and howit can help you land and keep your dream job. https://medium.com/paymo/the-benefits-of-a-strong-work-ethic

Council of the European Union (February, 2011). The role of education and training in the implementation of the 'Europe 2020' Strategy. Conclusions of the Council.

Cragin, M. H., & Hansen, D. L. (2017). *Research data management training*. ARL.

Cremin, L. A. (1961). *The Transformation of the School: Progressivism in American Education, 1876-1957*. Knopf.

Creswell, J. W. (2014). *Research design: Qualitative, quantitative and mixed methods Approaches* (4th ed.). Sage.

Creswell, J. W., & Miller, D. L. (2000). Determining validity in qualitative inquiry: Theory into practice. *Theory into Practice*, 39(3), 124–130. DOI: 10.1207/s15430421tip3903_2

Cronbach, L. J., & Suppes, P. (Eds.). (1969). *Research for Tomorrow's Schools: Disciplined Inquiry of Education*. Macmillan.

Crosling, G., & Ward, I. (2002). Oral communication: The workplace needs and uses of business graduate employees. *English for Specific Purposes*, 21(1), 41–57. DOI: 10.1016/S0889-4906(00)00031-4

Cuban, L. (2013). *Inside the black box of classroom practice: Change without reform in American education*. Harvard Education Press.

Cunningham, M. (2015). Factors impacting on adoption of technology-enhanced learning techniques by universities in Nairobi, Kenya. *2015 IEEE International Symposium on Technology and Society (ISTAS), 12*, 1–7. DOI: 10.1109/ISTAS.2015.7439446

DAAD/UNU-VIE. (2009) The Role of Education for Sustainable Development in Higher Education. German Academic Exchange (DAAD)/ United nations University-Vice Rectorate in Europe (UNU-VIE) Report of the joint Workshop of the UNESCO World Conference on Education for Sustainable Development 31 March-2 April 2009.

Dacre-Pool, L., & Sewell, P. (2007). The key to employability: Developing a practical model of graduate employability. *Education + Training*, 49(4), 277–289. DOI: 10.1108/00400910710754435

Dai, C.-P., Ke, F., Pan, Y., Moon, J., & Liu, Z. (2024). Effects of artificial intelligence-powered virtual agents on learning outcomes in computer-based simulations: A meta-analysis. *Educational Psychology Review*, 36(1), 31. DOI: 10.1007/s10648-024-09855-4

Dakhi, O., Jama, J., & Irfan, D. (2020). Blended learning: A 21st-century learning model at college. *International Journal Of Multi-Science*, 1(08), 50–65.

Daniela, L. (2020b). *Pedagogies of digital learning in higher education*. Routledge 2 Park Square, Milton Park, Abingdon, Oxon OX14 4RN.

Daniela, L. (2020a). New perspectives on virtual and augmented reality. In *New Perspectives on Virtual and Augmented Reality*. Routledge. DOI: 10.4324/9781003001874

Daniel, J. (2012). Making Sense of Distance Education: A Critical Review. *Distance Education*, 33(1), 105–117. DOI: 10.1080/01587919.2012.667020

Daniels, J. D., Rodebaugh, L. H., & Sullivan, D. P. (2015). International Business Environments and Operations: Global Edition. 15 Edn. Pearson Education Limited. Edinburgh.

Darling-Hammond, L., Hyler, M. E., & Gardner, M. (2017). *Effective teacher professional development*. Learning Policy Institute. DOI: 10.54300/122.311

Das, P. P. (2023). Perspective Chapter: MOOCs in India–Evolution, Innovation, Impact, and Roadmap. In *Massive Open Online Courses-Current Practice and Future Trends*. IntechOpen.

Das, S., Lekhya, G., Shreya, K., Shekinah, K. L., Babu, K. K., & Boopathi, S. (2024). Fostering Sustainability Education Through Cross-Disciplinary Collaborations and Research Partnerships: Interdisciplinary Synergy. In *Facilitating Global Collaboration and Knowledge Sharing in Higher Education With Generative AI* (pp. 60-88). IGI Global.

Data Management Association. (2019). *Data management body of knowledge*. Retrieved from internet.

Daystar University. (2024). What's PBL? *Daystar University*. https://www.daystar.ac.ke/academic-affairs/problem-based-learning

De Wit, H., & Altbach, P. G. (2022). The impact of COVID-19 on the internationalisation of higher education, revolutionary or not? In Kumar, C. R., Mukherjee, M., Belousova, T., & Nair, N. (Eds.), *Global higher education during and beyond COVID-19: Perspectives and challenges*. DOI: 10.1007/978-981-16-9049-5_18

Declaration, H. (1991). Creating a common future: University action for sustainable development. *Accessed May, 16*(2015), 209-227.

Declaration, T. (2005). Talloires Declaration on the civic roles and social responsibilities of higher education.

Deming, D. J., & Noray, K. L. (2020). Earnings Dynamics, Changing job Skills and STEM Careers. *The Quarterly Journal of Economics*, 135(4), 1965–2005. DOI: 10.1093/qje/qjaa021

Denson, N., Loveday, T., & Dalton, H. (2010). Student evaluation of courses: What predicts satisfaction? *Higher Education Research & Development*, 29(4), 339–356. DOI: 10.1080/07294360903394466

Desonie, D. (2008). *Climate: Causes and Effects of Climate Change*. Chelsea House.

Deterding, S., Dixon, D., Khaled, R., & Nacke, L. (2011). From game design elements to gamefulness: Defining" gamification". In Proceedings of the 15th international academic MindTrek conference: Envisioning future media environments (pp. 9-15).

Dewey, J. (1938). *Experience and education*. Macmillan.

Dhanarajan, G. (1992). 'Dual Mode Institutions: The Off-Campus Centre of Universiti Sains Malaysia'. In Mudridge I. (ed), Distance Education in Single and Dual Mode Institutions, Vancouver, Commonwealth of Learning.

Dhawan, S. (2020). Online Learning: A Panacea in the Time of COVID-19 Crisis. *Journal of Educational Technology Systems*, 49(1), 5–22. DOI: 10.1177/0047239520934018

Di Pietro et al. (2020). *The Likely Impact of COVID-19 on Education Reflections Based on the Existing Literature and Recent International Datasets*. Publications Office of the European Union.

Dillon, J., Stevenson, R., & Wals, A. (2016). Introduction to special section: Moving from citizen to civic science to address wicked conservation problems. *Conservation Biology*, 30(3), 450–455. DOI: 10.1111/cobi.12689 PMID: 27153527

Dimitriadou, E., & Lanitis, A. (2023). A critical evaluation, challenges, and future perspectives of using artificial intelligence and emerging technologies in smart classrooms. *Smart Learning Environments*, 10(1), 12. DOI: 10.1186/s40561-023-00231-3

Divan, A., Knight, E., Bennett, D., & Bell, K. (2019). Marketing graduate employability: Understanding the tensions between institutional practice and external messaging. *Journal of Higher Education Policy and Management*, 41(5), 485–499. DOI: 10.1080/1360080X.2019.1652427

Douglass, J. A., & Chirikov, I. (2020). *Refocusing institutional research on university needs*. https://www.universityworldnews.com/post.php?story=20200518114757175

Downes, S. (2010). Learning networks and connective knowledge. In Yang, H., & Yuen, S. (Eds.), *Handbook of Research on Practices and Outcomes in E-Learning: Issues and Trends* (pp. 1–26). IGI Global.

Drummond, M. F., Sculpher, M. J., Torrance, G. W., O'Brien, B. J., & Stoddart, G. L. (2005). *Methods for the economic evaluation of health care programmes*. Oxford University Press. DOI: 10.1093/oso/9780198529446.001.0001

Duch, B. J., Groh, S. E., & Allen, D. E. (Eds.). (2001). *The power of problem-based learning*. Stylus Publishing.

Duszynski, M. (2020). *Top 10 employability skills: definition and list of examples*. https://zety.com/blog/employability-skills

Dwyer, M. M. (2004). More Is Better: The Impact of Study Abroad Program Duration. *Frontiers: The Interdisciplinary Journal of Study Abroad*, 10(1), 151–164. DOI: 10.36366/frontiers.v10i1.139

Dwyer, T. (2022). Conceptualizations of market orientation in the higher education literature. *Journal of Marketing for Higher Education*, •••, 1–23. DOI: 10.1080/08841241.2022.2089941

Eakin, H. C., Lemos, M. C., & Nelson, D. R. (2014). Differentiating Capacities as a Means to Sustainable Climate Change Adaptation. *Global Environmental Change*, 27, 1–8. DOI: 10.1016/j.gloenvcha.2014.04.013

East Africa, P. B. L. (n.d.). *PBL East Africa*. https://aaltoglobalimpact.org/pbl-east-africa/

Eckles, J. E. (2009). Evaluating the efficiency of top liberal arts colleges. *Research in Higher Education*, 50(3), 266–293. DOI: 10.1007/s11162-009-9157-4

EDUCAUSE. (2020). *Research infrastructure for the future.* Retrieved from the internet.

Efrat, K., Souchon, A. L., Wald, A., Hughes, P., & Cai, J. (2022). Mitigating coopetition tensions: The forgotten formation stage. *European Management Review*, 19(4), 527–548. DOI: 10.1111/emre.12498

Egron-Polak, E., & Hudson, R. (2014). *Internationalization of higher education: Growing expectations, fundamental values. IAU 4th Global Survey*. International Association of Universities.

Eisenhardt, K.M. (1989). Building Theories from Case Study Research. *Academy of Management Review*. 14(4), 532-550. DOI: . 4308385DOI: 10.5465/amr.1989

Elkin, G., Devjee, F., & Farnsworth, J. (2005). Visualising the "internationalisation of universities. *International Journal of Educational Development*, 19(4), 318–329.

Elkin, G., Farnsworth, J., & Templer, A. (2008). Strategy and the internationalisation of universities. *International Journal of Educational Management*, 22(3), 239–250. www.emeraldinsight.com. DOI: 10.1108/09513540810861874

El-Mahgary, S., Rönnholm, P., Hyyppä, H., Haggeén, H., & Koponen, J. (2014). Evaluating the performance of university course units using data envelopment analysis. *Cogent Economics & Finance*, 2(1), 1–19. DOI: 10.1080/23322039.2014.918856

Eryenyu, C., Holta, S., & Ssentamu, P. N. (2020). Towards a new model of internal quality assurance for Ugandan universities. *Journal of Research Innovation and Implications in Education*, 4(3), 75–87.

European Commission/EACEA/Eurydice (2014). *Modernisation of Higher Education in Europe: Access, Retention and Employability 2014*. Eurydice Report. Publications Office of the European Union. DOI: DOI: 10.2797/72146

European Commission/EACEA/Eurydice (2019). *Structural Indicators for Monitoring Education and Training Systems in Europe – 2019: Overview of major reforms since 2015*. Eurydice Report. Publications Office of the European Union. DOI:DOI: 10.2797/256641

European Union. (2015). Centre for Higher Education Internationalization (CHEI). Retrieved from https://www.europarl.europa.eu/studies/

Evans, C. (2020). *Measuring student success skills: A review of the literature on critical thinking*. National Center for the Improvement of Educational Assessment.

Evenddy, S. S., Gailea, N., & Syafrizal, S. (2023). Exploring the benefits and challenges of project-based learning in higher education. *PPSDP International Journal of Education*, 2(2), 458–469. DOI: 10.59175/pijed.v2i2.148

Facione, P. A. (1990). *Critical Thinking: A Statement of Expert Consensus for Purposes of Educational Assessment and Instruction*. The Delphi Report. American Philosophical Association.

Fakunle, O., & Higson, H. (2021). Interrogating theoretical and empirical approaches to em+ployability in different global regions. *Higher Education Quarterly*, 75(4), 525–534. DOI: 10.1111/hequ.12345

Fang, Z. (1996). A review of research on teacher beliefs and practices. *Educational Research*, 38(1), 47–65. DOI: 10.1080/0013188960380104

Farenga, S. A., & Quinlan, K. M. (2016). Classifying university employability strategies: Three case studies and implications for practice and research. *Journal of Education and Work*, 29(7), 767–787. DOI: 10.1080/13639080.2015.1064517

Felder, R. M., & Brent, R. (2005). Understanding student differences. *Journal of Engineering Education*, 94(1), 57–72. DOI: 10.1002/j.2168-9830.2005.tb00829.x

Ferguson, N. M., Laydon, D., Nedjati-Gilani, G., Imai, N., Ainslie, K., Baguelin, M., ... & Ghani, A. C. (2020). Impact of non-pharmaceutical interventions (NPIs) to reduce COVID-19 mortality and healthcare demand. *Imperial College COVID-19 Response Team*.

Fielden, J. (2008). *The Practice of Internationalisation: Managing International Activities in UK Universities*. The UK HE International Unit. Available at http:// www. Universitiesuk .ac.uk

Fink, L. D. (2013). *Creating Significant Learning Experiences: An Integrated Approach to Designing College Courses*. Jossey-Bass.

FitzGerald, M., Walsh, K., & McCutcheon, H. (2001). An integrative systematic review of indicators for competence for practice and protocol for validation of indicators of competence.

Fowler, C. (2013). Virtual reality and learning: Where is the pedagogy? *British Journal of Educational Technology*, 44(2), 174–185.

Frankham, J. (2017). Employability and Higher Education:The follies of the 'productivity challenge in the teaching excellence framework. *Journal of Education Policy*, 32(5), 628–641. DOI: 10.1080/02680939.2016.1268271

Fraser, C. J., Duignan, G., Stewart, D., & Rodrigues, A. (2019). Overt and covert: Strategies for building employability skills of vocational education graduates. *Journal of Teaching and Learning for Graduate Employability*, 10(1), 157–172. DOI: 10.21153/jtlge2019vol10no1art782

Freeman, S., Eddy, S. L., McDonough, M., Smith, M. K., Okoroafor, N., Jordt, H., & Wenderoth, M. P. (2014). Active learning increases student performance in science, engineering, and mathematics. *Proceedings of the National Academy of Sciences of the United States of America*, 111(23), 8410–8415. DOI: 10.1073/pnas.1319030111 PMID: 24821756

Freina, L., & Ott, M. (2015). A literature review on immersive virtual reality in education: State of the art and perspectives. In *The International Scientific Conference eLearning and Software for Education* (Vol. 1, p. 10). "Carol I" National Defence University. DOI: 10.12753/2066-026X-15-020

Frida, S. W., & Kising'u, T. M. (2024). Competency-based learning and entrepreneurial intention in university technical and vocational education and training institutions in Kenya. *Journal of Education and Practice*, 1(5), 93–116.

Frølich, N., Huisman, J., & Stensaker, B. (2017). Understanding strategy practices in universi-ties. In Bleiklie, I., Enders, J., & Lepori, B. (Eds.), *Managing universities: Policy and organizational change from a Western European comparative perspective* (pp. 167–188). Palgrave Macmillan. DOI: 10.1007/978-3-319-53865-5_7

Fullan, M. (2007). *The new meaning of educational change*. Routledge.

Galukande, M., Katamba, A., Kiguli, S., Kiguli-Malwadde, E., Kijjambu, S., & Sewankambo, N. (2015). Problem based learning: Tutors' views 5 years after implementation at a sub-Saharan university. *African Health Sciences*, 15(1), 261. DOI: 10.4314/ahs.v15i1.34 PMID: 25834557

Gardner, H. (1983). *Frames of mind: a theory of multiple intelligence*. Basic Books.

Gareis, E. (2012). Intercultural friendship: Effects of home and host region. *Journal of International and Intercultural Communication*, 5(4), 309–328. DOI: 10.1080/17513057.2012.691525

Garrison, D. R., & Kanuka, H. (2004). Blended learning: Uncovering its transformative potential in higher education. *The Internet and Higher Education*, 7(2), 95–105. DOI: 10.1016/j.iheduc.2004.02.001

Ghosh, S., & Krishnan, R. (2015). Integrating problem-based learning with simulation: A case study in an undergraduate business course. *Journal of Education for Business*, 90(5), 242–248.

Gibbons, M. (1998, October 5-9). *Higher education relevance in the 21st century.* [Paper presentation]. *UNESCO World Conference on Higher Education*, Paris, France.

Gibbs, G. R. (2007). Analyzing qualitative data. *Sage (Atlanta, Ga.).*

Gikandi, J. W., Morrow, D., & Davis, N. E. (2011). Online formative assessment in higher education: A review of the literature. *Computers & Education*, 57(4), 2333–2351. DOI: 10.1016/j.compedu.2011.06.004

Gilbert, N., & Troitzsch, K. G. (2005). *Simulation for the social scientist.* McGraw-Hill Education.

Gisore, B. N., & Njurai, E. (2023). *Pedagogical Strategies to Enhance Climate Change Education.* IGI Global Publishers. DOI: 10.4018/978-1-6684-9099-0.ch010

Gitonga, R., Onyango, G., & Rugar, T. (2017, November). Students' experiences in using Haiku learning platform to promote problem-based learning in a blended classroom in Kenya. In *Proceedings of the 2017 International Conference on Education and E-Learning* (pp. 30-33). DOI: 10.1145/3160908.3160919

Glasserman, P. (2013). *Monte Carlo methods in financial engineering.* Springer Science & Business Media.

Global Education Cluster. (2020). "Safe back to school: a practitioner's guide", 2020, *available at*https://educationcluster.app.box.com/v/Safeback2schoolGuide

Global Education Monitoring Report, "Policy Paper 41", available at https://unesdoc.unesco.org/ark:/48223/pf0000373844/PDF/373844eng.pdf.multi.

Glossary of Education Reform. (2013). *Locus of control.* https://edglossary.org

Goldberg, D. S. (2012). Social justice, health inequalities and methodological individualism in US health promotion. *Public Health Ethics*, 5(2), 104–115. DOI: 10.1093/phe/phs013

Goman, C. K. (2012). *What it really means to dress for success.* https://www.forbes.com

Gomez, M. (2019). Rural education in America: Challenges and solutions. *Rural Educator*, 40(2), 1–15.

Gonczi, A. (2003). Teaching and learning of the key competencies. In *Contributions to the second DeSeCo symposium* (pp. 119-131). Swiss Federal Statistics Office.

Gondwe, M.&Walenkamp, J. (2011). Alignment of higher professional education with the needs of the local labour market: the case of Ghana.

Gordon, E., McGee, M., & Hicks, J. (2016). *Simulations and games for teaching and learning*. Routledge.

Goren, H., & Yemini, M. (2017b). The Global Citizenship Education Gap: Teacher Perceptions of the Relationship between Global Citizenship Education and Students' Socio-Economic Status. *Teaching and Teacher Education*, 67, 9–22. DOI: 10.1016/j.tate.2017.05.009

Green, F., & Henseke, G. (2021). Europe's evolving graduate labour markets: Supply, demand, underemployment and pay. *Journal for Labour Market Research*, 55(2), 2. Advance online publication. DOI: 10.1186/s12651-021-00288-y

Grendler, P. F. (1989). *Schooling in Renaissance Italy: Literacy and Learning, 1300-1600*. Johns Hopkins University Press. DOI: 10.56021/9780801837258

Greville, R. (2008). Road Mapping: A Design of Implementation Plan for a Distance Teaching National University of Kenya.

Gufstafson, P., & Pollock, B. (2015). *District support strategies for a PBL launch*. https://www.edutopia.org/blog/district-support-strategies-pbl-launch-weyers-gustafson-pollock

Gumartifa, A., Syahri, I., Siroj, R. A., Nurrahmi, M., & Yusof, N. (2023). Perception of teachers regarding problem-based learning and traditional method in the classroom learning innovation process. [IJOLAE]. *Indonesian Journal on Learning and Advanced Education*, 5(2), 151–166. DOI: 10.23917/ijolae.v5i2.20714

Gündoğdu, B., & Merç, A. (2022). A systematic review of tech-supported collaborative creativity practices in the field of education. *Journal of Learning and Teaching in Digital Age*, 7(1), 76–89. DOI: 10.53850/joltida.953760

Guskey, T. R. (2002). Professional development and teacher change. *Teachers and Teaching*, 8(3), 381–391. DOI: 10.1080/135406002100000512

Halevi, G., Moed, H. F., & Bar-Ilan, J. (2016). Does research mobility have an effect on productivity and impact? *Industry and Higher Education*, 86(86), 5–6. DOI: 10.6017/ihe.2016.86.9360

Hamari, J., Koivisto, J., & Sarsa, H. (2014). Does gamification work?--a literature review of empirical studies on gamification. In *2014 47th Hawaii international conference on system sciences* (pp. 3025-3034). IEEE.

Hamari, J., Koivisto, J., & Sarsa, H. (2014). Does gamification work?--a literature review of empirical studies on gamification. In *2014 47th Hawaii International Conference on System Sciences* (pp. 3025-3034). IEEE.

Hammond, K. L., Webster, R., & Hammond, N. (2020). Antecedents of market orientation in higher education: Empirical results from four key informant perspectives. *Global Journal of Management and Marketing*, 4(1), 113–134. https://www.igbr.org/wp-content/uploads/2020/04/GJMM_Vol_4_No_1_2020.pdF.113

Harden, R. M., & Crosby, J. R. (2000). The good teacher is more than a lecturer—The twelve roles of the teacher. *Medical Teacher*, 22(4), 334–347. DOI: 10.1080/014215900409429

Harness, H., & Drossman, H. (2013). The environmental education through filmmaking project. In *The Media, Animal Conservation and Environmental Education* (pp. 147-167). Routledge.

Harvey, L. (2000). New realities: The relationship between higher education and employment. *Tertiary Education and Management*, 6(1), 3–17. DOI: 10.1080/13583883.2000.9967007

Harvey, L. (2003). *Transitions from higher education to work*. ESECT.

Haskell, C. (2017). Institutional research as a bridge: Aligning institutional internal data needs and external information requirements a strategic view. *Higher Education Evaluation and Development*, 11(1), 2–11. DOI: 10.1108/HEED-08-2017-001

Hasslöf, H., & Malmberg, C. (2015). Critical Thinking as Room for Subjectification in Education for Sustainable Development. *Environmental Education Research*, 21(2), 239–255. DOI: 10.1080/13504622.2014.940854

Hattie, J. (2009). *Visible Learning: A Synthesis of Over 800 Meta-Analyses Relating to Achievement*. Routledge.

Heacox, D. (2012). *Differentiating Instruction in the Regular Classroom: How to Reach and Teach All Learners*. Free Spirit Publishing.

Herreid, C. F., & Schiller, N. A. (2013). Case studies and the flipped classroom. *Journal of College Science Teaching*, 42(5), 62–66.

Hershkovitz, A., Margulies, A., & Dagan, Y. (2016). Cost-effective technology solutions for education: An exploration. *Journal of Educational Technology & Society*, 19(1), 77–89.

Hilgartner, S., & Bosk, C. L. (1988). The rise and fall of social problems: A public arenas model. *American Journal of Sociology*, 94(1), 53–78. DOI: 10.1086/228951

Hinchliffe, G. (2005, January 27-28). *Graduate employability: a need for realism?* [Paper presentation]. Ninth quality in higher education international seminar, Birmingham, UK.

Hofstede, G. (2001). *Culture's Consequences: Comparing Values, Behaviors, Institutions and Organizations Across Nations*. SAGE Publications.

Holland, J., & Holland, J. (2014). Implications of shifting technology in education. *TechTrends*, 58(3), 16–25. DOI: 10.1007/s11528-014-0748-3

Holmes, L. (2013). Competing perspectives on graduate employability: possession, position or process?. *Studies in Higher Education*. 38(4), 538-554. DOI: . 587140DOI: 10.1080/03075079.2011

Holmes, M. (n.d.). Can leadership be taught? https://www.academia.edu/can-leadership-be-taught

Holstein, J., Starkey, K., & Wright, M. (2018). Strategy and narrative in higher education. *Strategic Organization*, 16(1), 61–91. DOI: 10.1177/1476127016674877

Hooley, T. J., Bennett, D., & Knight, E. B. (2023). Rationalities that underpin employability provision in higher education across eight countries. *Higher Education*, 86(5), 1003–1023. Advance online publication. DOI: 10.1007/s10734-022-00957-y

Howard, R. D., McLaughlin, G. W., & Knight, W. E. (2012). *The handbook of institutional research*. Jossey-Bass. https://doi.org/ Prisacaru, V., & Litvin, A. (2017). Quality management in the higher education of the Republic of Moldova as a framework for university performance. *Scientific Annals of Economics and Business, 64*(4), 431–446. https://doi.org/DOI: 10.1080/09645292.2018.1471663

Huckle, J. (2008). An analysis of New Labour's policy on education for sustainable development with particular reference to socially critical approaches. *Environmental Education Research*, 14(1), 65–75. DOI: 10.1080/13504620701843392

Hudson, R. (2014). Why universities want to internationalise; what stops them? Hunter, F. (2015) What's in a name? Refocusing internationalisation of higher education. European Association for International Education. Retrieved from https://www.eaie.org/blog/whats-in-a-name-refocusing-internationalisation-of-higher-education.html

Hull, J. C. (2018). *Risk management and financial institutions*. Wiley.

Humburg, M., de Grip, A., & van der Velden, R. (2017). Which skills protect graduates against a slack labour market? *International Labour Review*, 156(1), 25–43. DOI: 10.1111/j.1564-913X.2015.00046.x

Hungerford, H. R. (2009). Environmental education (EE) for the 21st century: Where have we been? Where are we now? Where are we headed? *The Journal of Environmental Education*, 41(1), 1–6. DOI: 10.1080/00958960903206773

Hussein, S. (5 January 2021). Daystar introduces problem-based learning. *Involvement.* https://involvement.co.ke/daystar-introduces-problem-based-learning/

Hwang, Y. (2018). Current state of the institutional research office in higher education: Focus on the leader and staff. *Journal of Academic Administration in Higher Education*, 14(2), 27–34.

Idenburg, P. J. (1993). Four styles of strategy development. *Long Range Planning*, 26(6), 132–137. DOI: 10.1016/0024-6301(93)90215-2

IGNOU. (2022). *Indira Gandhi National Open University*. Retrieved from https://www.ignou.ac.in

IMF (International Monetary Fund). (2001a). *'Debt Relief under the Heavily Indebted Poor Countries (HIPC) Initiative'. A factsheet, April.* IMF.

IMF (International Monetary Fund). (2001b). *'100 Percent Debt Cancellation? A Response from the IMF and the World Bank'. A factsheet, July*. IMF.

Inamdar, N. (2019). Transcending Boundaries in Higher Education: Are We Really Ready? In Bhat, H. V., & Inamdar, N. (Eds.), *Internationalization of Higher Education: The Dynamics of Educational Ecology* (pp. 9–32). Manipal Universal Press.

Indeed (2019). *Employability skills: definition and 10 examples.* https://www.indeed.com/career-advice/finding-a-job/employability-skills?from=careeradvive-US&subfrom=article#4

International Association of Universities. (1993). *Kyoto Declaration on Sustainable Development.* International Universities Bureau.

International Careers Institute (ICI). (2016). *The top 8 skills employers are looking for.* https://www.ici.net.au/blog/the-top-8-skills-employers-are-looking-for

International ICT Literacy Panel. (2002). *Digital transformation: a framework for ICT literacy.* https://www.ets.org/media/research/pdf/ICTREPORT.pdf

International Labour Organization (ILO). (2021). *Assessment of public employment and active labour market policies in Kenya*. ILO.

International Monetary Fund (IMF). (2020). "World Economic Outlook: A Crisis Like No

Inter-University Council for East Africa (IUCEA). (2010). *Quality assurance project on developing an East African higher education quality assurance framework: Project self-assessment report for impact assessment*. IUCEA Secretariat EADB Building.

Inter-University Council for East Africa (IUCEA). (2019). *East African higher education quality assurance framework*. Retrieved from https://www.iucea.org/wp-content/uploads/2019/07/East-African-Higher-Education-Quality-Assurance-Framework.pdf

Inter-University Council for East Africa (IUCEA). (2020). *Declaration by heads of state of the East African Community partner states on the transformation of the East African Community into a common higher education area*. Available at https://www.iucea.org/declaration-chea/

Inter-University Council for East Africa (IUCEA). (2024). *New phase of the demographics of African faculty project to enhance data management culture for faculty planning in the East African Community*. Available at https://www.iucea.org/new-phase-of-the-demographics-of-african-faculty-project-to-enhance-data-management-culture-for-faculty-planning-in-the-east-african-community/

IPCC. (2007). *Climate Change 2007: Impacts, Adaptation and Vulnerability*. Contribution of Working Group II to the Fourth Assessment Report of the Intergovernmental Panel on Climate Change, M. L. Parry, O. F. Canziani, J. P. Palutikof, P. J. van der Linden and C. E. Hanson (Eds.). UK and New York: Cambridge University Press.

IPCC. (2007a). *Climate Change: Impacts, Adaptation and Vulnerability*. Contribution of Working Group II to the Fourth Assessment Report of the Intergovernmental Panel on Climate Change, M. L. Parry, O. F. Canziani, J. P. Palutikof, P. J. van der Linden, and C. E. Hanson, eds. UK: Cambridge University Press.

IPCC. (2007b). *Climate Change: The Physical Science Basis. Contribution of Working Group to the Fourth Assessment Report of the Intergovernmental Panel on Climate Change* (Solomon, S., Qin, D., Manning, M., Chen, Z., Marquis, M., Averyt, K. B., Tignor, M., & Miller, H. L., Eds.). Cambridge University Press.

IPCC. (2007c). *Climate Change: Mitigation of Climate Change. Contribution of Working Group III to the Fourth Assessment Report of the Intergovernmental Panel on Climate Change* (Metz, B., Davidson, O. R., Bosch, P. R., Dave, R., & Meyer, L. A., Eds.). Cambridge University Press.

Ishak, S., Che Omar, A. R., & Sum, MD, S. (2015). Implementation of problem-based learning: A review on the challenges. *International Journal of Education and Research*, 3(8), 381–394.

Islam, N., Beer, M., & Slack, F. (2015). E-learning challenges faced by academics in higher education. *Journal of Education and Training Studies*, 3(5), 102–112. DOI: 10.11114/jets.v3i5.947

Jabu, K. (2022). *Why it's time for Kenyan universities to adopt the problem-based learning approach*. [PBL-BioAfrica]. https://ruforum.wordpress.com/2022/06/01/pbl-bioafrica-why-its-time-for-kenyan-universities-to-adopt-the-problem-based-learning-approach/

Jacklin, H. (2020). Re-opening schools is an ill-considered move. *Daily Maverick [online]. Available at*https://www.dailymaverick.co.za/opinionista/2020-06-05-reopening-schools-is-an-ill-considered-move-ask-the-teachers-not-the-economists/ *[accessed 10 June 2020].*

Jackson, D., & Bridgstock, R. (2018). Evidencing student success in the contemporary world-of-work: Renewing our thinking. *Higher Education Research & Development*, 37(5), 984–998. DOI: 10.1080/07294360.2018.1469603

Jackson, D., & Bridgstock, R. (2021). What actually works to enhance graduate employabil-ity? The relative value of curricular, co-curricular, and extra-curricular learning and paid work. *Higher Education*, 81(4), 723–739. DOI: 10.1007/s10734-020-00570-x

Jackson, D., & Tomlinson, M. (2022). The relative importance of work experience, extra-curricular and university-based activities on student employability. *Higher Education Research & Development*, 41(4), 1119–1135. DOI: 10.1080/07294360.2021.1901663

Jenkins, R. (2017). *1 useful way to instill a strong work ethic in millennials*. https://www.inc.com/ryan-jenkins

Jibeen, T. (2015) Internationalization of Higher Education: Potential Benefits and Costs. International Journal of Evaluation and Research in Education. Retrieved from https://files.eric.ed.gov/fulltext/EJ1091722.pdf

Jickling, B. (1994). Studying sustainable development: Problems and possibilities. *Canadian Journal of Education/Revue canadienne de l'éducation*, 231-240.

Johnson, L., Adams Becker, S., Estrada, V., & Freeman, A. (2016). *NMC Horizon Report: 2016 Higher Education Edition*. The New Media Consortium.

Johnson, R. B., & Onwuegbuzie, A. J. (2004). Mixed methods research: A research paradigm whose time has come. *Educational Researcher*, 33(7), 14–26. DOI: 10.3102/0013189X033007014

Johnstone, D. B. (2005). Financing higher education: Who should pay? In *International handbook of educational policy* (pp. 637–655). Springer.

Johnstone, D. B. (2016). Financing higher education: Who pays and other issues. In Shin, J. C., & Teixeira, P. (Eds.), *Encyclopedia of international higher education systems and institutions* (pp. 1–4). Springer.

Jones, E. & Brown, S. (2007). Internationalizing higher education UK: Rutledge

Kabiru and Kinyanjui. (2006). *Public Universities Inspection Board, Peter Kinyanjui Report: Transformation of Higher Education and Training in Kenya.* Cited on.

Kagawa, F., & Selby, D. (2010). Introduction. In Kagawa, F., & Selby, D. (Eds.), *Education and climate change: Living and learning in interesting times.* Taylor & Francis. DOI: 10.4324/9780203866399

Kakada, P., & Deshpande, Y. M. (2018). Relationship between institutional support and student satisfaction. *International Journal of Management and Business Research*, 8, 184–198.

Kang'ethe, S., & Mutema, A. M. (n.d.). Innovative techniques in the training of health professionals: The case of Moi University, Faculty of Heath Sciences, Kenya.

Kangooni, H. E., & Zervopoulos, P. D. (2023). Efficiency measurement of the colleges at the University of Sharjah. In *Advances in Science and Technology* (Vol. 129, pp. 117–136). International Symposium on Engineering and Business Administration. Trans Tech Publications Ltd. https://doi.org/DOI: 10.4028/p-aGMOt9

Kapaale, R.S (1993). The Distance Education Programmes at the University of Zambia –Mimeograph.

Kapareliotis, I., Voutsina, K., & Patsiotis, A. (2019). Internship and employability prospects: Assessing student's work readiness, *Higher Education. Skills and Work-Based Learning*, 9(4), 538–549. DOI: 10.1108/HESWBL-08-2018-0086

Karanja, M. (2021). Employer Perceptions of Open University Graduates in Kenya. *Journal of Higher Education Policy and Management*, 43(2), 179–194. DOI: 10.1080/1360080X.2021.1924052

Karen Mundy & Susannah Hares. (2020). "Equity-Focused Approaches to Learning Loss during COVID-19", *Center for Global Development Blog, 16 April 2020, available at*https://www.cgdev.org/blog/equity-focused-approaches-learning-loss-during-covid-19

Kariippanon, K. E., Cliff, D. P., Lancaster, S. L., Okely, A. D., & Parrish, A.-M. (2018). Perceived interplay between flexible learning spaces and teaching, learning, and student wellbeing. *Learning Environments Research*, 21(3), 301–320. DOI: 10.1007/s10984-017-9254-9

Kasozi, A. B. (2003). *University education in Uganda: Challenges and opportunities for reform.* Retrieved from the internet.

Kaswan, K. S., Dhatterwal, J. S., & Ojha, R. P. (2024). AI in personalized learning. In *Advances in Technological Innovations in Higher Education* (pp. 103–117). CRC Press. DOI: 10.1201/9781003376699-9

Katwa, J. K., Obwoge, R. O., Baliddawa, J. B., Ayiro, L., & Kei, R. (2018). Knowledge and perception of lecturers regarding problem based learning as an educational approach in College of Health Sciences, Moi University. *IOSR Journal of Research & Method in Education (IOSR-JRME), 8(1),* 26-29.

Katwa, J. K., Ayiro, L., Kei, R., Obwoge, R. O., & Baliddawa, J. B. (2018). Successes and limitations of community-based education service at Moi University School of Medicine, Eldoret, Kenya. *World Journal of Medical Education and Research*, 16(1), 40–43.

Kavanagh, S. S., & Herrmann, Z. (2021). *How school leaders can support project-based learning.*https://www.gse.upenn.edu/news/how-school-leaders-can-support-project-based-learning

Kayalar, F. (2021). Importance of Enriched Virtual learning model in hybrid teaching application. *Proceedings of IAC in Budapest*, 23-27.

Kearney, M.-L. (2013). Policy Imperatives in Research and Innovation Management. In A. Olssan, & L. Meek (Eds.), *Effectiveness of Research and Innovation Management at Policy and Institutional Levels: Cambodia, Malaysia, Thailand and Vietnam* (pp. 19-28). Kuala Lumpur: OCDE.https://www.oecd.org/sti/Effectiveness%20of%20research%20and%20 innovation% 20management%20at%20policy%20and%20institutional%20levels_Meek% 20and%20Olsson.pdf

Kenya Institute of Curriculum Development. (n.d). *When did piloting of the new curriculum begin?*https://kicd.ac.ke/faqs/when-did-piloting-of-the-new-curriculum-begin/

Kezar, A. (2014). *How colleges change: Understanding, leading, and enacting change*. Routledge.

Kezar, A. (2014). *How Colleges Change: Understanding, Leading, and Enacting Change*. Routledge.

Kezar, A., & Gehrke, S. (2017). Sustaining daily peace: The student voice and leadership in creating sustained change. In *Handbook of student affairs administration* (pp. 419–438). John Wiley & Sons.

Khaiat, B. (2020). Key figures: Internationally mobile students around the world. Campus, France: campusfrance.org

Khorsandi, T. A. (2014). *A Critical Policy Analysis of Internationalization in Post-secondary Education: An Ontario Case Study*. Western University.

Kiguli-Malwadde, E., Kijjambu, S., Kiguli, S., Galukande, M., Mwanika, A., Luboga, S., & Sewankambo, N. (2006). Problem based learning, curriculum development and change process at Faculty of Medicine, Makerere University, Uganda. *African Health Sciences*, 6(2), 127–130. PMID: 16916306

Kinash, S., Crane, L., Judd, M., & Knight, C. (2016). Discrepant stakeholder perspectives on graduate employability strategies. *Higher Education Research & Development*, 35(5), 951–967. DOI: 10.1080/07294360.2016.1139555

King, A. (1993). From sage on the stage to guide on the side. *College Teaching*, 41(1), 30–35. DOI: 10.1080/87567555.1993.9926781

King, R. (1993). Neurath, Otto (1882–1945). In Audi, R. (Ed.), *The Cambridge Dictionary of Philosophy* (pp. 542–543). Cambridge University Press.

Kingsley, D. (2020). Can innovation be taught? http://channels.theinnovationenterprise.com/can-innovation-be-taught

Kinyanjui, P. (2007). *Public Universities Inspection Board, Peter Kinyanjui Report: Transformation of Higher education and Training in Kenya*. Government Press.

Kinyanjui, P. B. (2010). *The Republic of Kenya, A Proposal for the Establishment of the Open University of Kenya*. Government Press.

Kiptoo, A. K., Wambui, T. W., & David, G. (2015). Relevance of standardized class learning system on Y generation workforce, in Kenya. *International Journal of Academic Research in Business & Social Sciences*, 5(11). Advance online publication. DOI: 10.6007/IJARBSS/v5-i11/1901

Kirschner, P. A., Sweller, J., & Clark, R. E. (2006). Why minimal guidance during instruction does not work: An analysis of the failure of constructivist, discovery, problem-based, experiential, and inquiry-based teaching. *Educational Psychologist*, 41(2), 75–86. DOI: 10.1207/s15326985ep4102_1

Kirui, J. K. (2020). *Challenges in implementation of Problem-Based Learning (PBL) approach in Moi University School of Medicine Kenya: Perspectives of faculty members* [Unpublished doctoral dissertation], Moi University.

Kitainge, K. M. (2022). The status and challenges on the use of constructivist instructional methods in the implementation of in Higher Education in Kenya. *IOSR Journal of Research & Method in Education*, 12(2), 64–70.

Kleinman, M., & West, A. (1998). Employability and the new deals: Employability is what the government wants but what exactly is it? *New Economy*, 5(3), 174–179. Advance online publication. DOI: 10.1111/1468-0041.00038

Knapp, L., Glennie, E., & Charles, K. (2016). *Leveraging data for student success: Improving education through data-driven decisions*. RTI Press., DOI: 10.3768/rtipress.2016.bk.0018.1609

Knapp, M., Swinnerton, J., Copland, M., & Monpas-Huber, J. (2006). *Data-informed leadership in education*. Center for the Study of Teaching and Policy.

Knight, J. (2003). Updating the Definition of Internationalisation', The Journal of International Higher Education, 33 (Fall). Available at: https://www.bc.edu/bc

Knight, P. T., & Yorke, M. (2002). Employability through the curriculum. *Tertiary Education and Management*, 8(4), 261–276. DOI: 10.1080/13583883.2002.9967084

Knowles, M. S. (1970). *The Modern Practice of Adult Education*. Andragogy versus Pedagogy.

Kolb, D. A. (1984). *Experiential learning: Experience as the source of learning and development*. FT press.

Kolb, D. A. (1984). *Experiential learning: Experience as the source of learning and development*. Prentice Hall.

Kolstø, S. D. (2010). Scientific literacy for citizenship: Tools for dealing with the science dimension of controversial socioscientific issues. *Science Education*, 84(4), 291–310.

Kömür, İ. A., Kilinç, H., & Okur, M. R. (2023). The Rotation Model in Blended Learning. *Asian Journal of Distance Education*, 18(2), 63–74.

Kondakci, . (2008). Challenges of Internationalization from Foreign and Local Students' Perspectives: The Case of Management SchoolAsia Pacific. *Education Review*, 9(4), 448–463.

Kopnina, H. (2014). Education for sustainable development (ESD): Exploring anthropocentric–ecocentric values in children through vignettes. *Studies in Educational Evaluation*, 41, 124–132. DOI: 10.1016/j.stueduc.2013.12.004

Koreneva, I., Myroshnychenko, N., Mykhailenko, L., Matiash, O., & Kuzmenko, H. (2023). The Use of Innovative Technologies in Education: Analysis of effectiveness and implementation at different levels of education. *Cadernos de Educação Tecnologia e Sociedade*, 16(3), 625–638. DOI: 10.14571/brajets.v16.n3.625-638

Korucu-Kış, S. (2021). Preparing student teachers for *real* classrooms through *virtual vicarious* experiences of critical incidents during remote practicum: A meaningful-experiential learning perspective. *Education and Information Technologies*, 26(6), 6949–6971. DOI: 10.1007/s10639-021-10555-7 PMID: 33935573

Kotter, J. (1996). *The 8 steps for leading change.* https://www.kotterinc.com/methodology/8-steps/

Kovats, R. S., & Hajat, S. (2008). Heat stress and public health: A critical review. *Annual Review of Public Health*, 29(1), 41–55. DOI: 10.1146/annurev.publhealth.29.020907.090843 PMID: 18031221

Krajcik, J. S., & Blumenfeld, P. C. (2006). Project-based learning. In Sawyer, R. K. (Ed.), *The Cambridge Handbook of the Learning Sciences* (pp. 317–334). Cambridge University Press.

Krajcik, J. S., & Blumenfeld, P. C. (2006). Project-based learning. In *The Cambridge handbook of the learning sciences* (pp. 317–334). Cambridge University Press.

Krasny, M. E., & DuBois, B. (2016). Climate adaptation education: Embracing reality or abandoning environmental values. *Environmental Education Research*, •••, 1–12.

Kroese, D. P., Brereton, T., Taimre, T., & Botev, Z. I. (2014). Why the Monte Carlo method is so important today. *Wiley Interdisciplinary Reviews: Computational Statistics*, 6(6), 386–392. DOI: 10.1002/wics.1314

Kroher, M., Leuze, K., Thomsen, S. L., & Trunzer, J. (2021). Did the 'Bologna Process' Achieve Its Goals? 20 Years of Empirical Evidence on Student Enrolment, Study Success and Labour Market Outcomes. *IZA Discussion Paper*, No. 14757. IZA.

Kuh, G. D., & Gonyea, R. M. (2019). *Cultivating a culture of adaptability*. Wiley.

Kumar, A. (2015). *Enabling all learners to SOAR for employability: an inclusive, integrative pedagogy*. Higher Education Academy Innovative Pedagogy Series.

Kunreuther, H., & Michel-Kerjan, E. (2009). From market to government failure in insuring U.S. natural catastrophes: How long term contracts help. In Brown, J. (Ed.), *Private Markets and Public Insurance Programs*. American Enterprise Institute.

Lackovic, N. (2019). Graduate employabilityparadigm shift: towards greater socio-emotional and eco-technological relationaties of graduates' futures. In Peters, M., Jandric, P., & Means, A. (Eds.), *Education and technological unemployment* (pp. 193–212). Springer., DOI: 10.1007/978-981-13-6225-5_13

Lai, E. R., Yarbo, J., Di Cerbo, K., & De Geest, E. (2018). *Skills for today: what we know about teaching and assessing creativity*. Pearson.

Lamb, S., Maire, Q., & Doecke, E. (2017). Key skills for the 21st century: An evidence-based review.

Law, B., & Watts, A. G. (2003). *The DOTS analysis: original version*. http://hihohiho.com/memory/Gafdots.pdf

Lawlor, M. S. (2016). Mindfulness and social-emotional learning (SEL): A conceptual framework. *Handbook of mindfulness in education: Integrating theory and research into practice*, 65-80.

Lee, K., Fanguy, M., Bligh, B., & Lu, X. S. (2022). Adoption of online teaching during the COVID-19 Pandemic: A systematic analysis of changes in university teaching activity. *Educational Review*, 74(3), 460–483. DOI: 10.1080/00131911.2021.1978401

Levett-Jones, T., Gersbach, J., Arthur, C., & Roche, J. (2011). Implementing a clinical competency assessment model that promotes critical reflection and ensures nursing graduates' readiness for professional practice. *Nurse Education in Practice*, 11(1), 64–69. DOI: 10.1016/j.nepr.2010.07.004 PMID: 20727825

Lewin, T., & Mawoyo, M. (2014). *Student access and success: Issues and interventions in South African universities*. The South African Institute for Advancement
Makori, E. O., Njiraine, D., & Talam, P. (2015). Practical aspects of implementation of institutional repositories in Africa with reference to the University of Nairobi. *New Library World*, 116(9/10), 610–640. DOI: 10.1108/NLW-10-2014-0125

Lie, R., & Servaes, J. (2015). Disciplines in the field of communication for development and social change. *Communication Theory*, 25(2), 244–258. DOI: 10.1111/comt.12065

Lijphart, A. (1975). The Comparable-cases Strategy in Comparative Research. *Comparative Political Studies*, 8(2), 158–177. DOI: 10.1177/001041407500800203

Lim, L., & Choy, J. (2014). Preparing staff for problem-based learning: Outcomes of a comprehensive faculty development program. *International Journal of Research Studies in Education*, 4(3), 53–68. DOI: 10.5861/ijrse.2014.821

Lim, Z. Y., Yap, J. H., Lai, J. W., Mokhtar, I. A., Yeo, D. J., & Cheong, K. H. (2024). Advancing Lifelong Learning in the Digital Age: A Narrative Review of Singapore's SkillsFuture Programme. *Social Sciences (Basel, Switzerland)*, 13(2), 73. DOI: 10.3390/socsci13020073

Lindsay, A. (1981). Assessing institutional performance in higher education: A managerial perspective. *Higher Education*, 10(6), 687–706. DOI: 10.1007/BF01676865

Lindsay, A. W. (1982). Institutional performance in higher education: The efficiency dimension. *Review of Educational Research*, 52(2), 175–199. DOI: 10.3102/00346543052002175

Liu, G., & Liu, Y. (2021, December). Problem-based learning: Its advantages, current situations and future development. In *2021 4th International Conference on Humanities Education and Social Sciences (ICHESS 2021)* (pp. 347-352). Atlantis Press.

Lotz-Sisitka, H. (2010). Climate injustice: How should education respond? In, F. Kagawa & D. Selby (Eds.), *Education and climate change: Learning and living in interesting times.* 71–88.

Lowden, K., Hall, S., Eliot, D., & Lewin, J. (2011). *Employers' perceptions of the employability skills of new graduates*. University of Glasgow.

Lucey, B. M. (2014). *How far have we drifted from the Newman/Humboldt idea of a university?* http://brian.lucey.worldpress.com/2014/06/06/how-far-have-we-drifted-from-the-newman-humboldt-idea-of-a-university?

Lu, X. (2011). Provision of climate information for adaptation to climate change. *Climate Research*, 47(1), 83–94. DOI: 10.3354/cr00950

Lynch, G., Smyth, P., & Godfrey, A. (2020). AI and Machine Learning in Education. *EdTech Report*.

Maastricht University. (2024). *Problem-based learning.* https://www.maastrichtuniversity.nl/education/why-um/problem-based-learning#sevensteps

MacDonald, G.P. (2013). Theorizing university identity development: multiple perspectives and common goals. *High Education*. 65, 153.166. DOI: DOI: 10.1007/s10734-012-9526-3

Makrakis, V., & Kostoulas-Makrakis, N. (2012). Course curricular design and development of the M. Sc. programme in the field of ICT in education for sustainable development. *Journal of Teacher Education for Sustainability*, 14(2), 5–40. DOI: 10.2478/v10099-012-0007-7

Mallon, W. T. (2019). Does Strategic Planning Matter? *Academic Medicine*, 94(10), 1408–1411. DOI: 10.1097/ACM.0000000000002848 PMID: 31219813

Manyika, J., Chui, M., Brown, B., Bughin, J., Dobbs, R., Roxburgh, C., & Byers, A. H. (2011). *Big data: The next frontier for innovation, competition, and productivity*. McKinsey Global Institute.

Marangell, S. (2020). Investigating the student experience of internationalization at an Australian university [Doctoral dissertation, University of Melbourne]. http://hdl.handle.net/11343/242198

Marek, L. (2019). Why University of Illinois is insuring itself literally against a drop in Chinese students: Crain's Chicago Business. Chicago.

Marginson, S., & van der Wende, M. (2009a): "Europeanisation, International Rankings, and Faculty Mobility: Three Cases in Higher Education Globalisation" in Higher Education to 2030, Vol 2,Globalisation, (ed.), Organisation for Economic Cooperation and Development (Paris: OECD), 109-41. (2009b)

Marginson, S. (2016). *The dream is over: The crisis of Clark Kerr's California idea of higher education*. University of California Press.

Maringe, S. (2000). Strategies and challenges of internationalization in HE: An exploratory study of universities.

Marrou, H. I. (1956). *A History of Education in Antiquity* (Lamb, G., Trans.). Sheed and Ward.

Masenya, M. (2023). Policies in higher education: The impact of global trends on the operation of the South African universities. *EDUCATIO Journal of Education*, 8, 201–215.

Masinde, P., Arimi, J., Owiti, B., Maitethia, D., Nawiri, P., Wesonga, J., De Groote, B., Koomen, I., & Odhiambo, R. (2024). Innovative pedagogy of competence-based training in horticulture: Case study of TVET education in Kenya. *African Journal of Science. Technology and Social Sciences*, 2(2), 32–40.

Mavurah, R. (2020). The role of ICT in distance education at the University of South Africa. *Journal of Distance Education*, 35(1), 35–50.

Mbovane, T. (2020). Covid-19: SASSA runs out of food parcels in Uitenhage. GroundUp [online].*Available athttps://www.groundup.org.za/article/covid-19-sassa-runs-out-food-parcels-uitenhage/[accessed 20 October 2020].*

Mburu, P. (8 March 2024). AgriScale project redefining agriculture education in universities. *Daily Nation*. https://nation.africa/kenya/news/education/agriscale-project-redefining-agriculture-education-in-universities-4550004

McAfee, A., & Brynjolfsson, E. (2012). Big data: The management revolution. *Harvard Business Review*, 90(10), 60–68. PMID: 23074865

McCowan, T. (2015). Should universities promote employability? *Theory and Research in Education*, 13(3), 267–285. DOI: 10.1177/1477878515598060

McCulloch, A., & Little, S. (2017). Creating a comprehensive technology integration plan for higher education: A case study. *TechTrends*, 61(2), 149–158.

McGrath, S. (2009). *What is employability? Learning to support employability* [Project paper]. University of Nottingham.

McGraw Hill. (2023). *The 3 biggest challenges of problem-based learning and how to overcome them.* https://www.mheducation.es/blog/biggest-challenges-of-problem-based-learning#:~:text=Problem%2Dbased%20learning%20challenges%3A%20lack%20of%20time&text=Students%20will%20also%20have%20to,to%20find%20their%20own%20way

McGuinness, S., Pouliakas, K., & Redmond, P. (2021). Skills displacing technological change and its impact on jobs: Challenging technological alarmism? *Economics of Innovation and New Technology*. Advance online publication. DOI: 10.1080/10438599.2021.1919517

McIlveen, P. (2018). *Defining Employability for the new era of work.* Sydney: Select Committee on the future of work and workers.

McKay, D. R. (2018). *How to dress professionally.* https://www.thebalancecareers.com/how-to-dress-professionally-524789

McLeod, S. (2024). *Constructivism learning theory & philosophy of education.* https://www.simplypsychology.org/constructivism.html

McLoughlin, C. (2011). *What ICT related skills and capabilities should be considered central to the definition of digital literacy*? https://researchbank.acu.edu/cgi/viewcontent.cgi?article=2658&content=fea_pub

McQuaid, R. W., & Lindsay, C. (2005). The concept of employability. *Urban Studies (Edinburgh, Scotland)*, 42(2), 197–219. DOI: 10.1080/0042098042000316100

Meehl, G. A., Stocker, T. F., Collins, W. D., Friedlingstein, A. T., Gaye, A. T., Gregory, J. M., Kitoh, A., Knutti, R., Murphy, J. M., Noda, A., Raper, S., Watterson, I. G., Weaver, A. J., & Zhao, Z. (2007). Global climate projections. Pp. 747-845. In, *Climate Change: The Physical Science Basis.* Contribution of Working Group I to the Fourth Assessment Report of the Intergovernmental Panel on Climate Change. Cambridge: Cambridge University Press.

Meyer, V.Jr, Pascucci, L., & Mangolin, L. (2012). Gestão estratégica: Um exame de práticas em universidades privadas. *Revista de Administração Pública*, 46(1), 49–70. DOI: 10.1590/S0034-76122012000100004

Mezirow, J. (2000). *Learning as Transformation: Critical Perspectives on a Theory in Progress. The Jossey-Bass Higher and Adult Education Series.* Jossey-Bass Publishers, 350 Sansome Way, San Francisco, CA 94104.

Middlehurst, R., & Woodfield, S. (2007). Responding to the internationalisation agenda: Implications for institutional strategy. Higher Education Academy [Online]. Available at: http://www.escalate.ac.uk

Migiro, W. L. (2022). *The effect of selected teaching methods on acquisition of technical skills by mechanical engineering technician trainees: A case of national polytechnics in the western region of Kenya* [Unpublished doctoral dissertation]. University of Eldoret.

Miller, P. H. (2011). *Theories of Developmental Psychology* (5th ed.). Worth Publishers.

Mimang, D. (2017). The Role of Open Universities in South African Higher Education. *South African Journal of Higher Education*, 31(2), 56–71. DOI: 10.20853/31-2-860

Mindtools (2020). *What is time management? Working smarter to enhance productivity.* https://www.mindtools.com/pages/article/newHTE_00.htm

Ministry of Education. (2005). *Sessional Paper No. 1 of 2005, A Policy Framework for Education, Training and Research.* Government Press.

Ministry of Education. (2018). National Education Sector Strategic Plan for the Period 2018 –2022 Government Press: Nairobi.

Ministry of Education. (2024). Sessional Paper No. X of 2024.

Mintzberg, H. (1978). Patterns in Strategy Formation. *Management Science*, 24(9), 934–948. DOI: 10.1287/mnsc.24.9.934

Mintzberg, H., & Waters, J. A. (1985). Of Strategies, Deliberate and Emergent. *Strategic Management Journal*, 6(3), 257–272. DOI: 10.1002/smj.4250060306

Mirabeau, L., & Maguire, S. (2014). From Autonomous Strategic Behavior to Emergent Strategy. *Strategic Management Journal*, 35(8), 1202–1229. DOI: 10.1002/smj.2149

Mochizuki, Y., & Fadeeva, Z. (2010). Competences for sustainable development and sustainability: Significance and challenges for ESD. *International Journal of Sustainability in Higher Education*, 11(4), 391–403. DOI: 10.1108/14676371011077603

MoEST. (2012). *Sessional Paper No 2 of 2015.* Reforming the Education and Training Sector in Kenya Government Press.

Mogalakwe, M. (2006). The use of documentary research methods in social research. *African Sociological Review/Revue Africaine De Sociologie, 10*(1), 221-230.

Mohammed, A. B., Zegeye, R. T., Dawed, H. A., & Tessema, Y. M. (2024). Implementation of problem-based learning in undergraduate medical education in Ethiopia: An exploratory qualitative study. *Advances in Medical Education and Practice*, 15, 105–119. DOI: 10.2147/AMEP.S443384 PMID: 38404356

Mohee, R. (2019). *A guide to integrating employability in higher education institutions: The Commonwealth of Learning's employability model.* Commonwealth of Learning.

Mojapelo, N., & Mhlanga, M. (2020). Distance Learning and Its Impact on Traditional Universities in South Africa. *South African Journal of Education*, 40(1), 1–15. DOI: 10.15700/saje.v40n1a1864

Moll, I. (2005). Curriculum responsiveness: the anatomy of a concept. In Griesel, H. (Ed.), *Curriculum responsiveness: case studies in higher education* (pp. 1–9). South African Universities Vice Chancellors Association.

Molutsi, P. (2009). *The impact of institutional research (IR) on institutional effectiveness: are we closing the loop?* Paper presented as Keynote Speech to the Southern African Association of Institutional Research 2009 Forum, 21-23 September 2009, at Nelson Mandela Metropolitan University, Port Elizabeth, South Africa

Mondal, A. S., Zhu, Y., Bhagat, K. K., & Giacaman, N. (2024). Analyzing user reviews of interactive educational apps: A sentiment analysis approach. *Interactive Learning Environments*, 32(1), 355–372. DOI: 10.1080/10494820.2022.2086578

Morgan (2024). *The role of institutional research in shaping higher education.* Retrieved from: https://www.marshall.edu/irp/2024/01/11/roleofirinhe/ on June 4, 2024.

Moser, S. C. (2009b). Good Morning America! The Explosive US Awakening to the Need for Adaptation. Sacramento, CA: California Energy Commission; Charleston, SC: NOAA-Coastal Services Center.

Moser, S. C. (2010). Communicating climate change: History, challenges, process and future directions. *Wiley Interdisciplinary Reviews: Climate Change*, 1(1), 31–53. DOI: 10.1002/wcc.11

Mosham, D. (1982). Exogenous, endogenous and dialectical constructivism. *Developmental Review*, 2(4), 371–384. DOI: 10.1016/0273-2297(82)90019-3

Mpaata, A. K. (2010). *University Competiveness through Quality assurance*. The Challenging Battle for Intellectuals.

Mtebe, J. S., & Raisamo, R. (2014). Challenges and strategies in implementing e-learning in developing countries: A case of Tanzania. *International Review of Research in Open and Distributed Learning*, 15(2), 44–68.

Mulonda, K., Indeche, A., Chabala, L. M., Kaluba, P., Simfukwe, P., Siatwiinda, S. M., & Laitinen, E. (2022). Application of problem-based learning in higher education in soil and climate change studies in Sub-Saharan Africa. *HAMK Unlimited Professional*, 16(6), 2022.

Munene, I. I. (2021). *Universities and Labor Market Mismatch in Kenya. International*. Technology. Citizen Digital.

Munezero, M. D., & Bekuta, B. K. (2016). Benefits and challenges of introducing a blended project-based approach in higher education: Experiences from a Kenyan university. *International Journal of Education and Development Using Information and Communication Technology*, 12(2), 206–218.

Museus, S. D., Yi, V., & Saelua, N. (2017). The impact of culturally engaging campus environments on the sense of belonging. *Review of Higher Education*, 40(2), 187–215. DOI: 10.1353/rhe.2017.0001

Mutammimah, H., & Padli, P. (2023, June). Problem-based learning in English teaching: A systematic literature review. In *English Language and Literature International Conference (ELLiC). Proceedings*, 6, 487–503.

Nabaho, L., Turyasingura, W., Kiiza, K. A., Andama, F., & Beinebyabo, A. (2020). Quality assurance of higher education governance and management: An exploration of the minimum imperative for the envisioned African common higher education space. *Higher Learning Research Communications*, 10(2), 38–52. DOI: 10.18870/hlrc.v10i2.1183

Nalami, J., & Waswa, S. (2023). FKE urges training institutions to tailor their programmes to bridge the skills divide. http://www.kenyanews.go.ke

Narenthiran, O. P., Torero, J., & Woodrow, M. (2022). Inclusive design of workspaces: Mixed methods approach to understanding users. *Sustainability (Basel)*, 14(6), 3337. DOI: 10.3390/su14063337

National Academies of Sciences, Engineering, and Medicine. (2018). *The integration of the humanities and arts with sciences, engineering, and medicine in higher education: Branches from the same tree*. National Academies Press.

National Institute for Newman Studies (2007). *Newman reader – works of John Henry Newman.*

National Institutes of Health. (2019). *Research data management*. Retrieved from the internet.

National Open University of Nigeria. (2023). *National Open University of Nigeria*. Retrieved from https://www.nou.edu.ng

National Research Council. (2009c). *Restructuring Federal Climate Research to Meet the Challenges of Climate Change*. The National Academies Press.

National Research Council. (2010). *America's Climate Choices: Panel on Adapting to the Impacts of Climate Change*. The National Academies Press.

National Research Council. (2012). *Discipline-based education research: Understanding and improving learning in undergraduate science and engineering*. National Academies Press.

National Science Foundation. (2018). *Dissemination and sharing of research results*. Retrieved from the internet.

National University. (n.d). *Constructivism in education: What is constructivism?* https://www.nu.edu/blog/what-is-constructivism-in-education/#:~:text=Constructivism%20is%20an%20action%2Doriented,activities%20to%20help%20students%20learn

Nawaz, N. (2013). Role of employability skills in management education: A review. *Zenith International Journal of Business Economics and Management Research*, 3(8), 34–45.

Nel, H. (2016). The role of institutional research in support of strategic planning. In Botha, J., & Muller, N. J. (Eds.), *Institutional Research in South African Higher Education: Intersecting Contexts and Practices* (pp. 99–116). African Sun Media., DOI: 10.18820/9781928357186/06

Nelson, D. R., Adger, W. N., & Brown, K. (2007). Adaptation to environmental change: Contributions of a resilience framework. *Annual Review of Environment and Resources*, 32(1), 395–419. DOI: 10.1146/annurev.energy.32.051807.090348

Neufeld, V. R., & Barrows, H. S. (1974). The "McMaster philosophy": An approach to medical education. *Academic Medicine*, 49(11), 1040–1050. DOI: 10.1097/00001888-197411000-00004 PMID: 4444006

Neugebauer, F., Figge, F., & Hahn, T. (2016). Planned or Emergent Strategy Making? Exploring the Formation of Corporate Sustainability Strategies. *Business Strategy and the Environment*, 25(5), 323–336. DOI: 10.1002/bse.1875

Ng, P. M. L., Chan, J. K. Y., Wut, T. M., Lo, M. F., & Szeto, I. (2021). What makes better career opportunities for young graduates? Examining acquired employability skills in higher education institutions. *Education + Training*, 63(6), 852–871. DOI: 10.1108/ET-08-2020-0231

Nguyen, N. T. (2017). A review on the interrelation between knowledge management and human resource management. *Finance and the Performance of Firms in Science, Education and Practice*. Retrieved from the internet.

Nicol, D. J., & Macfarlane-Dick, D. (2006). Formative assessment and self-regulated learning: A model and seven principles of good feedback practice. *Studies in Higher Education*, 31(2), 199–218. DOI: 10.1080/03075070600572090

Nogueira, C., Marques, J. F., & Pinto, H. (2024). Intentional sustainable communities and sustainable development goals: From micro-scale implementation to scalability of innovative practices. *Journal of Environmental Planning and Management*, 67(1), 175–196. DOI: 10.1080/09640568.2022.2106553

Nyandusi, C. (2017). Conceptualizing Curriculum. In A. Syomwene, C.M. Nyandusi, & A.M. Yungungu (Eds.) *Core Principles in Curriculum*. Pp. 3-13. Eldoret: Utafiti Foundation

O'Brien, F. S., & Ryan, T. C. I. (1999). *'Aid and Reform in Africa: Kenya Case Study'. Aid and Reform in Africa Papers*. The World Bank Group.

O'Neil, C. (2016). *Weapons of math destruction: How big data increases inequality and threatens democracy*. Broadway Books.

O'Reilly, M. (2020). Social media and adolescent mental health: The good, the bad and the ugly. *Journal of Mental Health*, 29(2), 200–206.Organization for Economic Cooperation and Development (OECD).(2020). "A 'debt standstill' for the poorest countries: How much is at stake?", 27 May 2020, available at http://www.oecd.org/coronavirus/policy-responses/a-debt-standstill-for-the-poorest-countries-how-much-is-at-stake-462eabd8/#endnotea0z2

Odhiambo, G. (2018). The role of Kenyan universities in national development. *FIRE: Forum for International Research in Education, 4*(3).

OECD. (2021). *Education Policy Outlook 2021: Shaping Responsive and Resilient Education in a Changing World*. OECD Publishing.

Ogachi, I. O. (2018, December). The East African higher education area: A global or regional higher education space? *Forum for International Research in Education*, 4(3). Advance online publication. DOI: 10.32865/fire2018439

Ogega, O. M., Lakey, G., Opisa, R., & Gyampoh, B. A. (2022). Strengthening Climate Research Capacity in Africa: Lessons from the 'Climate Impact Research Capacity Leadership Enhancement' Project. *Regional Environmental Change*, 22(4), 135. DOI: 10.1007/s10113-022-01997-x

Ogunyemi, A. (2020). Impact of Open Universities on Nigerian Higher Education Policies. *Journal of African Higher Education*, 10(1), 22–34. DOI: 10.1080/23323256.2020.1750293

Öhman, J. (2008). *Values and democracy in education for sustainable development:contributions from Swedish research*. Liber.

Ojala, M. (2013). Emotional awareness: On the importance of including emotional aspects in education for sustainable development (ESD). *Journal of Education for Sustainable Development*, 7(2), 167–182. DOI: 10.1177/0973408214526488

Okay-Somerville, B., & Scholarios, D. (2017). Position, possession or process? Understanding objective and subjective employability during university-to-work transitions. *Studies in Higher Education*, 42(7), 1275–1291. DOI: 10.1080/03075079.2015.1091813

Okay-Somerville, B., & Scholarios, D. (2022). Focused for Some, Exploratory for Others: Job Search Strategies and Successful University-to-Work Transitions in the Context of Labor Market Ambiguity. *Journal of Career Development*, 49(1), 126–143. DOI: 10.1177/08948453211016058

Okpara, G. C., & Ezeador, C. N. (2024). Philosophy of Teaching: Exploring Various Teaching Methods for Improved Education in nigeria. *Nnadiebube Journal of Philosophy, 7*(3).

Oladele, J. I., Ndlovu, M., Spangenberg, E. D., Daramola, D. S., & Obimuyiwa, G. A. (2024). Transitioning to problem-based learning in higher education: Opportunities for producing 21st- century pre-service teachers in Sub-Saharan Africa. *Kurdish Studies*, 12(2), 609–626.

Oluoch, J., & Osida, J. (2014). Building strengths in information communication and technology in Kenyan universities: Way forward for the 21st century. *Wyno Academic Journal of Social Sciences*, 2(2), 10–16.

Ondieki, C., Kimani, G. N., & Tanui, E. K. (2018). Deficiencies of competency based education and training in higher education institutions in Kenya. *Scholars Journal of Arts. Humanities and Social Sciences*, 6(7), 1437–1447.

Ondigi, S. R. (2011). Globalization of university programs and community linkages: A case of two Kenyan universities. *International Journal of Humanities and Social Science*, 1(3), 96–105.

Open Universities Australia. (2023). *Open Universities Australia*. Retrieved from https://www.open.edu.au

Open University. (2022). *The Open University*. Retrieved from https://www.open.ac.uk

Oranga, J., Nyakundi E. & Obuba, E. (2020). Is internationalization of higher education the way to go? Journal of Research Innovation and Implications in Education, 4(3), 133-144.

Orr, D. W. (1991). *Ecological literacy: Education and the transition to a postmodern world*. State University of New York Press.

Ossiannilsson, E. (2019). Innovative Learning and Innovative Learning Spaces. *Asian Journal of Distance Education*, 14(1), 98–116.

OSSREA. (2020). *Promoting social science research in Eastern and Southern Africa*. Retrieved from https://www.ossrea.net/about-us/

Othman, H., Buntant, Y., Suleiman, A., Salleh, B. M., & Herawan, T. (2010). Applied mathematics can enhance employability skills through problem based learning (PBL). *Procedia: Social and Behavioral Sciences*, 8, 332–337. DOI: 10.1016/j.sbspro.2010.12.046

Otunga, R. N. (2010). *The dilemma of curriculum relevance in Kenya*. Moi University Press.

Ouane, A. (2003). Defining and selecting key competencies in lifelong learning. In *Contributions to the Second DeSeCo Symposium* (p. 133).

Owoc, M. L., Sawicka, A., & Weichbroth, P. (2019). Artificial intelligence technologies in education: benefits, challenges, and strategies of implementation. *IFIP International Workshop on Artificial Intelligence for Knowledge Management.*

Padmanabha, C. H. (2018). Critical Thinking: Conceptual Framework. *Journal of Educational Psychology*, 11(4), 45–53.

Pantelidis, V. S. (2010). Reasons to use virtual reality in education and training courses and a model to determine when to use virtual reality. *Themes in Science and Technology Education*, 2(1-2), 59–70.

Papert, S. (1980). *Mindstorms: Children, Computers, and Powerful Ideas.* Basic Books.

Parlier, T. R., IV. (2021). Perspectives of IR professionals regarding the impact of data analytic systems on institutional decision-making. (Publication No. 6512) [Doctoral dissertation, University of Tennessee]. TRACE. https://trace.tennessee.edu/utk_graddiss/6512

Partnership for 21st Century Skills. (2009). *Framework for 21st Century Learning.*

Paul, R., & Tait, A. (2019). Special Issue: Open Universities: Past, Present and Future. *International Review of Research in Open and Distributed Learning*, 20(4), i–viii. DOI: 10.19173/irrodl.v20i4.4575

Payne, G., & Payne, J. (2004). Key concepts in social research.

Peng, R. D. (2011). Reproducible research in computational science. *Science*, 334(6060), 1226–1227. DOI: 10.1126/science.1213847 PMID: 22144613

Perraton, H. (2016). *Open and distance learning in the developing world.* Routledge.

Peterson, G. T., & Corckett, J. (2017). *Building a culture of assessment.* Stylus Publishing.

Piaget, J. (1952). *The Origins of Intelligence in Children.* International Universities Press. DOI: 10.1037/11494-000

Piaget, J. (1973). *To Understand Is to Invent: The Future of Education.* Grossman Publishers.

Pogue, M. (2019). *Computer self-efficacy as an inherent characteristic of digital natives in online learning environments.* Northcentral University.

Pon, C., & Schendel, R. (2020). Exploring processes of teaching and learning in African university contexts: The case of education for critical thinking in Ghana, Kenya and Botswana. *International Journal of African Higher Education*, 7(1). Advance online publication. DOI: 10.6017/ijahe.v6i2.11355

Porter, L. (2000). *Student behaviour: Theory and practice for teachers*. Allen & Unwin.

Prawat, R. S. (1992). Teachers' beliefs about teaching and learning: A constructivist perspective. *American Journal of Education*, 100(3), 354–395. DOI: 10.1086/444021

Prewitt, K. (2016). Higher education, society, and government: Changing dynamics. *Journal of Higher Education in Africa*, 2(1), 35–56. DOI: 10.57054/jhea.v2i1.1681

Price-Mitchell, M. (2015). Integrity in the classroom. *Psychology Today*. https://www.psychologytoday.com/blog/the-moment-youth/201509/integrity-in-the-classroom

Prince, M. J., & Felder, R. M. (2006). Inductive teaching and learning methods: Definitions, comparisons, and research bases. *Journal of Engineering Education*, 95(2), 123–138. DOI: 10.1002/j.2168-9830.2006.tb00884.x

Priya, J. J., & Gowrishankar, M. (2022). Blended Learning Approach: Significance of Flex and Self-Blend Models. *Constructivism in Teaching and Learning*, 178.

Pukelis, K., Pileičikiene, N., Allan, A., & Dailidiene, E. (2007). European and National level strategies for competency-based curriculum development. HEGESCO. www.decowe.comstatic/uploaded/htmlarea/finalreporthegesco/European_National_and_Universities_Strategies_summary.pdf

Raes, A. (2022). Exploring student and teacher experiences in hybrid learning environments: Does presence matter? *Postdigital Science and Education*, 4(1), 138–159. DOI: 10.1007/s42438-021-00274-0

Ragg, M., & Piers, J. (2017). Competency-Based Blended Learning: Flipping Professional Practice Classes to Enhance Competence Development. *IAFOR Journal of Education*, 5(SI), 47–66. DOI: 10.22492/ije.5.si.02

Raj, R., & Sulaiman, T. (2018). The impact of MOOCs on open universities: A case study of IGNOU. *Journal of Educational Technology*, 21(4), 29–40.

Rampersad, G., & Patel, F. (2014). Creativity as a desirable graduate attribute: Implications for curriculum design and employability. *Asia Pacific Journal of Cooperative Education*, 15(1), 1–11.

Rane, N., Choudhary, S., & Rane, J. (2023). Education 4.0 and 5.0: Integrating artificial intelligence (AI) for personalized and adaptive learning. *Available atSSRN* 4638365. DOI: 10.2139/ssrn.4638365

Rawls, J. (1971). *A Theory of Justice.* Harvard University Press.

Razzouk, R., & Shute, V. (2012). What is design thinking and why is it important? *Review of Educational Research*, 82(3), 330–348. DOI: 10.3102/0034654312457429

Recommended web link: www.ipcc.ch for The IPCC Reports.

Reddy, Y. M., & Andrade, H. (2010). A review of rubric use in higher education. *Assessment & Evaluation in Higher Education*, 35(4), 435–448. DOI: 10.1080/02602930902862859

Redecker, C., & Punie, Y. (2017). *European Framework for the Digital Competence of Educators: DigCompEdu*. Publications Office of the European Union.

Region: External situation report 30 / 2020. *World Health Organization. Regional Office for Africa.*https://apps.who.int/iris/handle/

Reid, A., Dillon, J., Ardoin, N., & Ferreira, J. A. (2021). Scientists' warnings and the need to reimagine, recreate, and restore environmental education. *Environmental Education Research*, 27(6), 783–795. DOI: 10.1080/13504622.2021.1937577

Reimers, F. M. (2024). The sustainable development goals and education, achievements and opportunities. *International Journal of Educational Development*, 104, 102965. DOI: 10.1016/j.ijedudev.2023.102965

Renninger, K. A., & Hidi, S. (2011). Revisiting the conceptualization, measurement, and generation of interest. *Educational Psychologist*, 46(3), 168–184. DOI: 10.1080/00461520.2011.587723

Republic of Kenya. (1981). *Second University in Kenya: Report of the Presidential Working Party Republic of Kenya. (1964). Kenya Education Commission Report.* Government Printer. Nairobi.

Republic of Kenya. (1988). *Sessional Paper No. 06 of 1988 on Education and Manpower Training for the Next Decade and Beyond.* Government Press.

Republic of Kenya. (1999). *Report of the Commission of Inquiry into the Education System of Kenya.* Government Printer.

Republic of Kenya. (2005). *Sessional Paper No. 1 of 2005 A Policy Framework for Education, Training and Research Republic of Kenya. (2007). Report of the task force for the development of the National Strategy for University Education (The Wandiga Report).* Government Printer.

Republic of Kenya. (2005). Sessional Paper No.1 of 2005 on a policy framework for Education Training and Research. Nairobi: MoEST.

Republic of Kenya. (2007). *Government of Kenya, Vision 2030.* Nairobi: Government Press Public Universities Inspection Board (PUIB) Report (2006) Transformation of Higher Education and Training in Kenya Government Press: Nairobi.

Republic of Kenya. (2008). *Sessional Paper No. 1 of 2008 A Policy Framework for Education, Training and Research.* Government Press.

Republic of Kenya. (2008). *Sessional Paper No. 14 of 2012 A Policy Framework for Reforming Education and Training Sectors in Kenya.* Government Press.

Republic of Kenya. (2009). *Kenya Education Sector Support Programme (2005 - 2010).* Government Press.

Republic of Kenya. (2009). *Sessional paper No 1 of 2019 on Reforming Education, Training and Research for Sustainable Development.* Government Press.

Republic of Kenya. (2010). The Constitution of Kenya. Nairobi: Government Press: Nairobi.

Republic of Kenya. (2012). *Session Paper No. 14 (2012). Reforming Education and Training in Kenya.* Government Press.

Republic of Kenya. (2012). *Universities Act, 2012.* Government Press.

Republic of Kenya. (2020). *National Skills Development policy.* Nairobi: Ministry of Education Rowe, A. D., & Zegwaard, K. E. (2017). Developing graduate employability skills and attributes: curriculum enhancement through work integrated learning. *Asia Pacific Journal of Cooperative Education*, 18(2), 87–99.

Rieckmann, M. (2018). Learning to transform the world: Key competencies in Education for Sustainable Development. *Issues and trends in education for sustainable development, 39*(1), 39-59.

Rogers, E. M. (2003). *Diffusion of innovations* (5th ed.). Free Press.

Rosenzweig, C., Karoly, M., Vicarelli, M., Neofotis, P., Wu, Q., Casassa, G., Menzel, A., Root, T. L., Estrella, N., Seguin, B., Tryjanowski, P., Liu, C., Rawlins, S., & Imeson, A. (2008). Attributing physical and biological impacts to anthropogenic climate change. *Nature*, 453(7193), 353–320. DOI: 10.1038/nature06937 PMID: 18480817

Rubin, E. S., & Davidson, J. E. (2001). *Introduction to engineering and the environment*. McGraw-Hill Higher Education.

Rudsberg, K., & Öhman, J. (2018). Pluralism in practice–experiences from Swedish evaluation, school development and research. In *Environmental and Sustainability Education Policy* (pp. 193–209). Routledge. DOI: 10.4324/9780203732359-13

Rumble, R. (2008). *Republic of Kenya, Road Map for Open University*. Government Press.

Rychen, D. S. (2002, February). A frame of reference for defining and selecting key competencies in an international context. In *DS Rychen, LH Salganik & ME McLaughlin (2002). Definition and selection of key competencies: Contributions to the Second DeSeCo Symposium, Geneva, Switzerland* (pp. 11-13).

Sahni, J. (2019). Does blended learning enhance student engagement? Evidence from higher education. *The Journal of Learning in Higher Education*, 2019, 1–14. DOI: 10.5171/2019.121518

Saito, E., & Pham, T. (2021). A comparative institutional analysis on strategies deployed by Australian and Japanese universities to prepare students for employment. *Higher Education Research & Development*, 40(5), 1085–1099. DOI: 10.1080/07294360.2020.1800596

Sajja, R., Sermet, Y., Cikmaz, M., Cwiertny, D., & Demir, I. (2023). Artificial Intelligence-Enabled Intelligent Assistant for Personalized and Adaptive Learning in Higher Education. *arXiv preprint arXiv:2309.10892*.

Sanga, P. (2019). East African Higher Education and the limitations of institutional reforms: A case study of selected public universities. *African Journal of Teacher Education*, 8, 299–320. DOI: 10.21083/ajote.v8i0.5361

Sass, W., Boeve-de Pauw, J., Olsson, D., Gericke, N., De Maeyer, S., & Van Petegem, P. (2020). Redefining action competence: The case of sustainable development. *The Journal of Environmental Education*, 51(4), 292–305. DOI: 10.1080/00958964.2020.1765132

Saupe, J. L. (1990). *The functions of institutional research* (2nd ed.). The Association for Institutional Research.

Savery, J. R. (2015). Overview of problem-based learning: Definitions and distinctions. In Walker, A., Leary, H., Hmelo-Silver, C., & Ertmer, P. A. (Eds.), *Essential Readings in Problem-Based Learning* (pp. 5–15). Purdue University Press. DOI: 10.2307/j.ctt6wq6fh.6

Sawant, S. (2021). Online collaborative learning tools and types: Their key role in managing classrooms without walls. In *Human-computer interaction and technology integration in modern society* (pp. 12–41). IGI Global. DOI: 10.4018/978-1-7998-5849-2.ch002

Schartner, A., & Cho, Y. (2017). 'Empty signifiers' and 'dreamy ideals': Perceptions of the 'international university' among higher education students and staff at a British university. *Higher Education*, 74(3), 455–472. DOI: 10.1007/s10734-016-0057-1

Schein, E. H. (1995). Kurt Lewin's change theory in the field and in the classroom: Notes toward a model of managed learning. *Systems Practice*, 9(1), 27–47. DOI: 10.1007/BF02173417

Schiefele, U., Streblow, L., & Retelsdorf, J. (2013). Dimensions of teacher interest and their relations to occupational well-being and instructional practices. *Journal for Educational Research Online*, 5(1), 7–37.

Schmidt, H. G. (1993). Foundations of problem-based learning: Some explanatory notes. *Medical Education*, 27(5), 422–432. DOI: 10.1111/j.1365-2923.1993.tb00296.x PMID: 8208146

Schmidt, R. A., & Bjork, R. A. (1992). New conceptualizations of practice: Common principles in three paradigms suggest new concepts for training. *Psychological Science*, 3(4), 207–217. DOI: 10.1111/j.1467-9280.1992.tb00029.x

Schraw, G. (2010). Measuring self-regulation in computer-based learning environments. In *Handbook of research on educational communications and technology* (pp. 397–408). Routledge.

Schriever, V., & Grainger, P. (2019). Mentoring an early career researcher: Insider perspectives from the mentee and mentor. *Reflective Practice*, 20(6), 720–731. DOI: 10.1080/14623943.2019.1674272

Schuller, T., & Watson, D. (2009). *Learning Through Life: Inquiry into the Future for Lifelong Learning*. National Institute of Adult Continuing Education (NIACE).

Schwab, K., & Zahidi, S. (2020). World Economic Forum.(2020). *The Global Competitiveness Report–How countries are performing on the road to recovery.*

Scriven, M., & Paul, R. W. (1987). *Defining critical thinking*. [Paper presentation]. 8th Annual International Conference on Critical Thinking and Education Reform. https://www.criticalthinking/pages/defining-critical-thinking

Seaman, J., & Allen, I. E. (2018). *Grade level: Tracking online education in the United States*. Babson Survey Research Group.

Sebatana, M. J., & Dudu, W. T. (2022). Reality or mirage: Enhancing 21st-century skills through problem-based learning while teaching particulate nature of matter. *International Journal of Science and Mathematics Education*, 20(5), 963–980. DOI: 10.1007/s10763-021-10206-w

Selwyn, N. (2011). *Education and Technology: Key Issues and Debates*. Bloomsbury Publishing.

Sepahi, V., Abbaspour, A., Khoshay, A., Rezaei, K., & Rezaei, M. (2021). Presenting a conceptual model of institutional research office for the medical universities of Iran: A case study. *Educational Research in Medical Sciences, 10*(2).

Sepahi, V., Abbaspour, A., Khoshay, A., Rezaei, K., & Rezaei, M. (2021). Presenting a Conceptual Model of Institutional Research Office for the Medical Universities of Iran: A Case Study. *Educational Research in Medical Sciences*, 10(2). Advance online publication. DOI: 10.5812/erms.121865

Serban, A. M., & Luan, J. (Eds.). (2002). *Knowledge management: Building a competitive advantage in higher education*. Jossey-Bass.

Serrano, D. R., Dea-Ayuela, M. A., Gonzalez-Burgos, E., Serrano-Gil, A., & Lalatsa, A. (2019). Technology-enhanced learning in higher education: How to enhance student engagement through blended learning. *European Journal of Education*, 54(2), 273–286. DOI: 10.1111/ejed.12330

Sgobbi, F. (2023), How intentional are the employability strategies of Higher Education Institutions? *DINÂMIA'CET Working Papers*, 2023-02. Lisbon: DINÂMIA'CET-Iscte, DOI: DOI: 10.15847/dinamiacet-iul.wp.2023.02

Shaeffer, S. (2007). *Education for Sustainable Development: A Framework for Reform*. UNESCO Bangkok, Asia and Pacific Regional Bureau for Education.

Shafer, M. A. (2008). Climate Literacy and a National Climate Service. *Physical Geography*, 29(6), 561–574. DOI: 10.2747/0272-3646.29.6.561

Sheppard, R. S., & Kerrigan, M. R. (2018). Building institutional research knowledge and skills through communities of practice networks. *Mid-Western Educational Researcher*, 30(4), 6. https://scholarworks.bgsu.edu/mwer/vol30/iss4/6

Shikulo, Lukas and Mapheleba Lekhetho (2020). Exploring student support services of a distance learning centre at a Namibian university, Cogent Social Sciences. International Review of Research in Open and Distributed Learning.

Shiltz, M. (Ed.). (1992). *Ethics and standards and institutional research. New Directions for Institutional Research, 73*. Jossey-Bass.

Shriberg, M. (2002). Institutional assessment tools for sustainability in higher education: Strengths, weaknesses, and implications for practice and theory. *Higher Education Policy*, 15(2), 153–167. DOI: 10.1016/S0952-8733(02)00006-5

Shurygin, V., Saenko, N., Zekiy, A., Klochko, E., & Kulapov, M. (2021). Learning management systems in academic and corporate distance education. [iJET]. *International Journal of Emerging Technologies in Learning*, 16(11), 121–139. DOI: 10.3991/ijet.v16i11.20701

Siemens, G., & Downes, S. (2005). *Connectivism: A learning theory for the digital age*. International Journal of Instructional Technology and Distance Learning.

Siemens, G. (2005). Connectivism: A learning theory for the digital age. *International Journal of Instructional Technology and Distance Learning*, 2(1).

Sife, A., Lwoga, E., & Sanga, C. (2007). New technologies for teaching and learning: Challenges for higher learning institutions in developing countries. *International journal of education and development using ICT, 3*(2), 57-67.

Silaji, Turyamureeba & Muhammad, Tukur & Rahim, Abdul & Zikanga, Kiyundo & Extension, Kiu Publication. (2023). Organizational structure and Academic staff Performances in Private Universities in Uganda. *KIU Journal of Social Sciences, 5*(4), 249-258.

Simonson, M., Smaldino, S. E., Albright, M., & Zvacek, S. (2015). *Teaching and Learning at a Distance: Foundations of Distance Education*. Pearson.

Sinakou, E., Boeve-de Pauw, J., Goossens, M., & Van Petegem, P. (2018). Academics in the field of Education for Sustainable Development: Their conceptions of sustainable development. *Journal of Cleaner Production*, 184, 321–332. DOI: 10.1016/j.jclepro.2018.02.279

Sinakou, E., Donche, V., Boeve-de Pauw, J., & Van Petegem, P. (2019). Designing powerful learning environments in education for sustainable development: A conceptual framework. *Sustainability (Basel)*, 11(21), 5994. DOI: 10.3390/su11215994

Sinakou, E., Donche, V., & Van Petegem, P. (2022). Action-orientation in education for sustainable development: Teachers' interests and instructional practices. *Journal of Cleaner Production*, 370, 133469. DOI: 10.1016/j.jclepro.2022.133469

Sinakou, E., Donche, V., & Van Petegem, P. (2024). Teachers' profiles in education for sustainable development: Interests, instructional beliefs, and instructional practices. *Environmental Education Research*, 30(3), 397–418. DOI: 10.1080/13504622.2023.2168622

Sin, C., & Amaral, A. (2021). Academics' and employers' perceptions about responsibilities for employability and their initiatives towards its development. *Higher Education*, 73(1), 97–111. DOI: 10.1007/s10734-016-0007-y

Sin, C., Tavares, O., & Amaral, A. (2019). Accepting employability as a purpose of higher education? Academics' perceptions and practices. *Studies in Higher Education*, 44(6), 920–931. DOI: 10.1080/03075079.2017.1402174

Sisol Recruitment(March,1,2024).*Balancing academic knowledge with necessary skills for employment.* Sisol Recruitment (24) Balancing academic knowledge with necessary skills for employment. | LinkedIn.

SkillsYouNeed. (2017). *Interpersonal skills.* https://www.skillsyouneed.com/ips/interpersonal-skills.html

Slevin, D. P., & Covin, J. G. (1997). Strategy Formation Patterns, Performance, and the Significance of Context. *Journal of Management*, 23(2), 189–209. DOI: 10.1177/014920639702300205

Smith, I. M., & Griffiths, D. V. (2014). *Programming the finite element method.* John Wiley & Sons.

Society for Institutional Research. (2020). *What is institutional research?* Retrieved from https://www.airweb.org/what-is-institutional-research

Soliman, S., Anchor, J., & Taylor, D. (2019). The international strategies of universities: deliberate or emergent?. *Studies in Higher Education*. 44(8), 1413-1424. DOI: . 2018.1445985DOI: 10.1080/03075079

Solomon, S., Plattner, G. K., Knutti, R., & Friedlingstein, P. (2009). Irreversible climate change due to carbon dioxide emissions. *Proceedings of the National Academy of Sciences of the United States of America*, 106(6), 1704–1709. DOI: 10.1073/pnas.0812721106 PMID: 19179281

Spires, H. A., Paul, C. M., & Kerkhoff, S. N. (2019). Digital literacy for the 21st century. In *Advanced methodologies and technologies in library science, information management, and scholarly inquiry* (pp. 12–21). IGI Global.

State Department of Early Learning and Basic Education, Kenya (SDELBEK). (2020). *Kenya BasicEducation COVID-19 Emergency Response Plan* .

Steffen, W., Crutzen, P. J., & Mcneil, L. J. R. (2007). The Anthropocene: Are humans now overwhelming the great forces of Nature? *Ambio*, 36(8), 614–621. DOI: 10.1579/0044-7447(2007)36[614:TAAHNO]2.0.CO;2 PMID: 18240674

Stein, J. V. (2008). The International Law and Politics of Climate Change Ratification of the United Nations Framework Convention and the Kyoto Protocol. *The Journal of Conflict Resolution*, 52(2), 243–268. DOI: 10.1177/0022002707313692

STEMNET. (2017). Top 10 employability skills. https://www.exeter.ac.uk/ambassadors/HESTEM/resources/General/STEMNET-employability-skills-guide.pdf

Sterling, S. (2002, 2009). Towards sustainable education: re-visioning learning and change. In *Learning for a sustainable future: the role or communication, ethics, and social learning in environmetnal education. VIIIth Conference on Environmental Education in Europe. Gent: Provincie Oost-Vlaanderen.*

Stern, N. (2007). *The Economics of Climate Change: The Stern Review*. Cambridge University Press. DOI: 10.1017/CBO9780511817434

Stevenson, R. B. with Stirling, C. (2011). Environmental learning and agency in diverse educational and cultural contexts. In R. B. Stevenson & J. Dillon (Eds.) *Engaging environmental education: Learning, culture and agency (pp. 219–38).* Rotterdam: Sense Publishers.

Stevenson, J. (1996). The metamorphosis of the construction of competence. *Studies in Continuing Education*, 18(1), 24–42. DOI: 10.1080/0158037960180102

Strauss, A., & Corbin, J. (1990). Basics of qualitative research: Grounded theory procedures and techniques. *Sage (Atlanta, Ga.).*

Strobel, J., & Van Barneveld, A. (2009). When is PBL more effective? A meta-synthesis of meta-analyses comparing PBL to conventional classrooms. *The Interdisciplinary Journal of Problem-Based Learning*, 3(4). Advance online publication. DOI: 10.7771/1541-5015.1046

Subbaye, R., Mlitwa, A., & Moyo, T. (2021). Institutional research utilisation and issues of legitimacy: Perspectives from practitioners at selected traditional universities. *Utilisation of South African Research on Higher Education*, 133, 133–161. Advance online publication. DOI: 10.52779/9781991201416/05

Sultana, R. G. (2018). Precarity, austerity and the social contract in a liquid world: career guidance mediating the citizen and the state. In Hooley, T., Sultana, R. G., & Thomsen, R. (Eds.), *Career Guidance for Social Justice: Contesting Neoliberalism* (pp. 63–76). Routledge.

Summers, M., & Childs, A. (2007). Student science teachers' conceptions of sustainable development: An empirical study of three postgraduate training cohorts. *Research in Science & Technological Education*, 25(3), 307–327. DOI: 10.1080/02635140701535067

Sund, P. (2008). Discerning the extras in ESD teaching-A democratic issue.

Suri, H., & Weiner, L. (2011). The case for collaborative teaching in teacher education. In *Second international handbook of educational change* (pp. 579–598). Springer.

Suwastini, N. K. A., Puspawati, N. W. N., Adnyani, N. L. P. S., Dantes, G. R., & Rusnalasari, Z. D. (2021). Problem-based learning and 21st-century skills: Are they compatible? *EduLite: Journal of English Education. Literature and Culture*, 6(2), 326–340.

Swargiary, K. (2024, July 1). The impact of data analytics on educational decision-making: A mixed-methods study in Bengaluru higher education institutions. *SSRN*. https://ssrn.com/abstract=4897517

Swing, R. L., & Ross, L. E. (2016). A new vision for institutional research. *Change*, 48(2), 6–13. DOI: 10.1080/00091383.2016.1163132

Tadesse, S. G., Tadesse, D. G., & Dagnaw, E. H. (2022). Problem based learning approach increases the academic satisfaction of health science students in Ethiopian universities: A comparative cross-sectional study. *BMC Medical Education*, 22(1), 334. DOI: 10.1186/s12909-022-03397-5 PMID: 35501812

Tait, A. (2013). Open Education and the Development of Open Universities. *Open Learning*, 28(2), 102–115. DOI: 10.1080/02680513.2013.793829

Tashtoush, L. (2021). The Role of Information Systems Capabilities in Enhancing the Organizational Performance. *Journal of Information Systems and Informatics*, 3(2), 303–328. DOI: 10.33557/journalisi.v3i2.129

Tefera, A. S., Melaku, E. E., Urgie, B. M., Hassen, E. M., Tamene, T. D., & Gebeyaw, E. D. (2024). Barriers to implementing problem-based learning at the School of Medicine of Debre Berhan University, Ethiopia. *BMC Medical Education*, 24(1), 501. DOI: 10.1186/s12909-024-05252-1 PMID: 38711080

Teichler, U. (2005). Research on Higher Education in Europe. *European Journal of Education*, 40(4), 447–469. DOI: 10.1111/j.1465-3435.2005.00239.x

Terenzini, P. T. (1993). On the nature of institutional research and the knowledge and skills it requires. *Research in Higher Education*, 34(1), 1–10. DOI: 10.1007/BF00991859

Terenzini, P. T. (2013). "On the nature of institutional research" revisited: Plus ça change…? *Research in Higher Education*, 54(2), 137–148. DOI: 10.1007/s11162-012-9274-3

Terenzini, P. T. (2013). *Bringing the stakeholders to the table*. Routledge.

Thahir, M., Widiawati, W., & Baitillah, N. (2023). The post-pandemic education: A blended learning approach for teaching and learning in higher education in the new normal era. *International Journal of Ethno-Sciences and Education Research*, 3(3), 99–108. DOI: 10.46336/ijeer.v3i3.461

Tight, M. (2015). Research on higher education policy and institutional management. In *The Palgrave International Handbook of Higher Education Policy and Governance* (pp. 176–191). Palgrave Macmillan UK. https://doi.org/DOI: 10.1007/978-1-137-45617-5_10

Tight, M. (2022). Internationalisation of higher education beyond the West: Challenges and opportunities–the research evidence. *Educational Research and Evaluation*, 27(3–4), 239–259. DOI: 10.1080/13803611.2022.2041853

Tomlinson, M. (2007). Graduate employability and student attitudes and orientations to the la-bour market. *Journal of Education and Work*, 20(4), 285–304. DOI: 10.1080/13639080701650164

Tomlinson, M. (2012). Graduate Employability: A Review of Conceptual and Empirical Themes. *Higher Education Policy*, 25(4), 407–431. DOI: 10.1057/hep.2011.26

Torp, L., & Sage, S. (2002). *Problems as possibilities: Problem-based learning for K-16 education* (2nd ed.). Association for Supervision and Curriculum Development.

Trinh, N. T. H. (2023). Higher education and its role for national development. A research agenda with bibliometric analysis. *Interchange*, 54(2), 125–143. DOI: 10.1007/s10780-023-09493-9 PMID: 37215230

Trujillo Maza, E. M., Gómez Lozano, M. T., Cardozo Alarcón, A. C., Moreno Zuluaga, L., & Gamba Fadul, M. (2016). Blended learning supported by digital technology and competency-based medical education: A case study of the social medicine course at the Universidad de los Andes, Colombia. *International Journal of Educational Technology in Higher Education*, 13(1), 1–13. DOI: 10.1186/s41239-016-0027-9

Turnbull, D., Chugh, R., & Luck, J. (2021). Transitioning to E-Learning during the COVID-19 pandemic: How have Higher Education Institutions responded to the challenge? *Education and Information Technologies*, 26(5), 6401–6419. DOI: 10.1007/s10639-021-10633-w PMID: 34177349

Tyack, D. B. (1964). *The One Best System: A History of American Urban Education*. Harvard University Press.

U.S. Global Change Research Program. (2009). *Climate Literacy: The Essential Principles of Climate Science.* http://www.globalchange.go

Uchkun, E. (2023). Learning Strategies in Blended Learning. *Conferencea*, 18-23.

Uhl-Bien, M., Marion, R., & McKelvey, B. (2007). Complexity leadership theory: Shifting leadership from the industrial age to the knowledge era. *The Leadership Quarterly*, 18(4), 298–318. DOI: 10.1016/j.leaqua.2007.04.002

Ullah, W., Nihei, T., Nafees, M., Zaman, R., & Ali, M. (2018). Understanding Climate Change Vulnerability, Adaptation and Risk Perceptions at Household Level in Khyber Pakhtunkhwa, Pakistan. *International Journal of Climate Change Strategies and Management*, 10(3), 359–378. DOI: 10.1108/IJCCSM-02-2017-0038

UN Framework Convention on Climate Change. (2007). *Investment and Financial Flows Relevant to the Development of an Effective and Appropriate International Response to Climate Change*. UNFCCC.

UNECE – UNESCO (United Nations Economic Commission for Europe – United Nations Educational, Scientific and Cultural Organisation). (2007). Good practices in education for sustainable development, Sweden Sustainable School Award.

UNESCO & UNEP. (2011). *Climate change starters guide book.* UNESCO.

UNESCO (1998). *World declaration on education for all for the twenty first century: vision and action.*

UNESCO (2005). United Nations Decade of Education for Sustainable Development (DESD) 2005-2014.

UNESCO (2005a). Guidelines and Recommendations for Reorienting Teacher Education to Address Sustainability. UNESCO Education for Sustainable Development in Action Technical PaperNo.2.

UNESCO (2012). *Graduate employability in Asia*

UNESCO Institute for Statistics (UIS). (2017). "Out-of-School Children and Youth", *available at*http://uis.unesco.org/en/ topic/out-school-children-and-youth

UNESCO, UNICEF, WFP, World Bank. (2020a). Framework for reopening schools", available at https://unesdoc.unesco.org/ark:/48223/ pf0000373348 and "Reopening schools. UNESCO. (2020b).How to get education back on track after. https://www .iiep.unesco.org/en/reopening-schools-how-get-education-back-track-after-covid -19-13424

UNESCO. (1996). Learning: The Treasure Within. Report to UNESCO of the International Commission on Education for the Twenty-first Century. Paris: UNESCO. UNESCO (1998). Higher Education in the Twenty-First Century: Vision and Action. World Conference on Higher education.

UNESCO. (2006). *UNESCO's Role, Vision and Challenges for the UN Decade of Education for Sustainable Development (2005-2014).* UNESCO International Science, Technology & Environmental Education Newsletter.

UNESCO. (2014). *Roadmap for implementing the Global Action Programme in Education for Sustainable Development.* UNESCO.

UNESCO. (2020). *Education in Emergencies: A Focus on Equity and Inclusion.* UNESCO Publishing.

UNESCO. (2020c): "The impact of Covid-19 on the cost of achieving SDG 4", GEM Report Policy Paper 42. 6 Ibid.

UNESCO. (2020d). International Commission on the Futures of Education, "*Education in a post COVID-19 world: Nine ideas for action", 2020, available at*https://unesdoc.unesco.org/ark:/48223/pf0000373717/PDF/373717eng.pdf.multi

UNFCCC. (2010). *Report on the Technical Workshop on Advancing the Integration of Approaches to Adaptation Planning.* FCCC/SBSTA/2010/2. UNFCCC, Bonn. Available at: http://unfccc.int/resource/docs/2010/sbsta/eng/ 02.pdf (Accessed 5 September 2010).

UNICEF. (2021). *Building Resilient Education Systems: Lessons from the COVID-19 Pandemic.* UNICEF Publications.

United Nations -Assembly, U. G. (2015). Transforming Our World: the 2030 Agenda for Sustainable Devel¬ opment (UN General Assembly Resolution nº 70 [I] A). *New York*. USA department of the Interior University (2013). Career Development: Competencies.

United Nations Development Programme. (2020). COVID-19 and human development: *Assessing the crisis, envisioning the recovery. 2020 Human Development Perspectives, 2020, New York: UNDP, available at*https://hdr.undp.org/en/hdp-covid

United Nations Educational, Scientific and Cultural Organization (UNESCO). (2020). Education for sustainable development: A roadmap.

Universities, U. K. (2005). Universities UK's international strategy -London: Universities UK. Vernon, R. (1966). International Investment and International Trade in the Product Cycle -. *The Quarterly Journal of Economics*, 80(2), 190–207.

University of Buffalo. (2024). Constructivism: Creating experiences that facilitate the construction of knowledge. *Center for Educational Innovation, University at Buffalo*. https://www.buffalo.edu/catt/teach/develop/theory/constructivism.html

University of Nairobi (UON). (n.d). *UON among varsities to roll out PBL-Bio Africa project in Africa*.https://sciencetechnology.uonbi.ac.ke/latest-news/uon-among-varsities-roll-out-pbl-bio-africa-project-africa

University of Phoenix. (2023). *University of Phoenix*. Retrieved from https://www.phoenix.edu

University of South Africa. (2023). *University of South Africa*. Retrieved from https://www.unisa.ac.za

USGCRP (United States Global Change Research Program). (2009). *Global Climate Change Impacts in the United States: A State of Knowledge Report from the U.S. Global Change Research Program, T. R. Karl, J. M. Melillo, and T. C. Peterson* (York, N., Ed.).

UWEZO. (2020). *Are Our Children Learning? The Status of Remote-learning among School-going Children in Kenya during the COVID-19 crisis*.https://palnetwork.org/wp- content/uploads/2020/05/Usawa-Agenda-2020-Report.pdf

Van Poeck, K., & Östman, L. (2019). Political moves: How teachers can open up for and handle poignant experiences of the conflictual aspects of sustainability issues. In *Sustainable Development Teaching* (pp. 162–174). Routledge. DOI: 10.4324/9781351124348-14

Van Poeck, K., Östman, L., & Öhman, J. (2019). Ethical moves: how teachers can open up a space for articulating moral reactions and deliberating on ethical opinions regarding sustainability issues. In *Sustainable development teaching* (pp. 153–161). Routledge. DOI: 10.4324/9781351124348-13

Varela-Losada, M., Vega-Marcote, P., Pérez-Rodríguez, U., & Álvarez-Lires, M. (2016). Going to action? A literature review on educational proposals in formal Environmental Education. *Environmental Education Research*, 22(3), 390–421. DOI: 10.1080/13504622.2015.1101751

Vartiainen, J., Sormunen, K., & Kangas, J. (2024). Relationality of play and playfulness in early childhood sustainability education. *Learning and Instruction*, 93, 101963. DOI: 10.1016/j.learninstruc.2024.101963

Vault, T. (November 7,2023). Theory VS Practice(Knowledge and application). *Vivekanand Education Society*. Theoretical Knowledge Vs Practical Application (ves.ac.in)

Vela, J. (1994). *Learning to listen, learning to teach: The power of dialogue in educating adults*. Jossey-Bass.

Visser, H., & Skene, J. (2016). Institutional research and external reporting. In *Institutional research in South African higher education: Intersecting contexts and practices* (pp. 160–175). SUN MeDIA Bloemfontein. DOI: 10.18820/9781928357186/10

Volkwein, J. F. (1999). The four faces of institutional research. *New Directions for Institutional Research*, 1999(104), 9–19. DOI: 10.1002/ir.10401

Volkwein, J. F. (2008). The foundations and evolution of Institutional Research. [Wiley Periodicals, Inc.]. *New Directions for Higher Education*, 141(141), 5–20. DOI: 10.1002/he.289

Volkwein, V. F. (2011). *Enhancing institutional research*. Jossey-Bass.

Voogt, J., & Roblin, N. P. (2012). A comparative analysis of international frameworks for 21st century competences: Implications for national curriculum policies. *Journal of Curriculum Studies*, 44(3), 299–321. DOI: 10.1080/00220272.2012.668938

Vygotsky, L. S. (1962). *Thought and Language*. MIT Press. DOI: 10.1037/11193-000

Vygotsky, L. S. (1978). *Mind in Society: The Development of Higher Psychological Processes*. Harvard University Press.

Wade, R. (2012). Pedagogy, places and people. *Journal of teacher Education for Sustainability, 14*(2), 147-167.

Wagner, T. (2010). *The global achievement gap: why even our best schools don't teach the new survival skills our children need – and what we can do about it.* Basic Books.

Wallerstein, I. (1974). *The modern World System I: Capitalist Agriculture and the Origins of the European World-Economy in the Sixteenth Century.* Academic Press.

Wallerstein, I. (2004). *World-Systems Analysis: An Introduction.* Duke University Press.

Wals, A. E. (2007). Creating networks of conversations. In *Social learning towards a sustainable world* (pp. 497–506). Academic. DOI: 10.3920/9789086865949_032

Warschauer, M. (2004). *Technology and social inclusion: Rethinking the digital divide.* MIT Press.

Watson, R., Stimpson, A., Topping, A., & Porock, D. (2002). Clinical competence assessment in nursing: A systematic review of the literature. *Journal of Advanced Nursing*, 39(5), 421–431. DOI: 10.1046/j.1365-2648.2002.02307.x PMID: 12175351

Webber, K. L. (2019). Building Capacity in IR and Decision Support: Alliances for Higher Education Research (HER) and Institutional Research (IR). *Proceedings of the Austrian University Network.* Available at: https://ihe.uga.edu/rps/2020_001

Webber, K. L. (2020). Building capacity in IR and decision support: Alliances for higher education research (HER) and institutional research (IR). *IHE Research Projects Series, 2020*(001). https://ihe.uga.edu/rps/2020_001

Webber, D. J. (1992). The distribution and use of policy knowledge in the policy process. In Dunn, W. N., & Kelly, R. M. (Eds.), *Advances in Policy Studies since 1950* (pp. 383–418). Transaction Books.

Webber, K. L., & Calderon, A. J. (Eds.). (2015). *Institutional research and planning in higher education: Global contexts and themes.* Routledge. DOI: 10.4324/9781315777726

Wedekind, V., & Mutereko, S. (2016). *Employability and curriculum responsiveness in post-school education and training.* Labour Market Intelligence Partnership.

Wenger, E. (1998). Communities of practice: Learning, meaning, and identity. Cambridge University Press.Top of Form

Western Governor's University. (2020). *What is constructivism?* https://www.wgu.edu/blog/what-constructivism2005.html

Western Governors University. (2023). *Western Governors University*. Retrieved from https://www.wgu.edu

West, J. M., Julius, S. H., Kareiva, P., Enquist, C., Lawler, J. J., Petersen, B., Johnson, A. E., & Shaw, R. (2009). U.S. Natural Resources and Climate Change: Concepts and Approaches for Management Adaptation. *Environmental Management*, 44(6), 1–21. DOI: 10.1007/s00267-009-9345-1 PMID: 19636606

West, S. M. (2019). Data capitalism: Redefining the logics of surveillance and privacy. *Business & Society*, 58(1), 20–41. DOI: 10.1177/0007650317718185

Wiek, A. (2010, June). Sustainability science–what are the core competencies? In *Second International Conference on Sustainability Science,* Rome (Vol. 24).

Wiek, A., Withycombe, L., & Redman, C. L. (2011). Key competencies in sustainability: A reference framework for academic program development. *Sustainability Science*, 6(2), 203–218. DOI: 10.1007/s11625-011-0132-6

Wiggins, G., & McTighe, J. (2005). *Understanding by design.* ASCD.

Wihlborg, M., & Robson, S. (2018). Internationalisation of Higher Education: Drivers, Rationales, Priorities, Values and Impacts. *European Journal of Higher Education*, 8(1), 8–18. DOI: 10.1080/21568235.2017.1376696

Willcox, K. E., Sarma, S., & Lippel, P. H. (2016). *Online education: A catalyst for higher education reforms.* Massachusetts Institute of Technology.

Wilson, R., & Morieson, L. (2022). Belonging as a responsive strategy in times of supercomplexity and change. *Journal of University Teaching & Learning Practice*, 19(4). Advance online publication. https://ro.uow.edu.au/jutlp/vol19/iss4/03. DOI: 10.53761/1.19.4.3

Wood, D., Bruner, J. S., & Ross, G. (1976). The role of tutoring in problem-solving. *Journal of Child Psychology and Psychiatry, and Allied Disciplines*, 17(2), 89–100. DOI: 10.1111/j.1469-7610.1976.tb00381.x PMID: 932126

World Bank. (2019). *Improving Higher Education Performance in Kenya: A Policy Report. Report No: AUS0001105.* The World Bank.

World Bank. (2019). *Improving higher education performance in Kenya: A policy Report.* The World Bank.

World Bank. (2020). *Investing in Education for Long-Term Resilience. World Bank Publications World Bank. (2020a). The COVID-19 Pandemic: Shocks to Education and Policy responses.* World Bank.

World Bank. (2020b). Literacy rate, adult total (% of people ages 15 and above). https://data.worldbank.org/indicator/SE.ADT.LITR

World Economic Forum. (2016). *The future of jobs report.* http://www3.weforum.org/docs/WEF_future_of_jobs_.pdf

Wu, J. I., & Wang, C. H. (2024). The Importance of International Education at Various Educational Stages From the Perspective of Sustainable Development Education. *The Journal of Educational Research*, (361), 94–108.

Wurdinger, S., & Carlson, J. (2010). *Teaching for experiential learning: Five approaches that work.* R&L Education.

Yin, R. K. (2018). *Case Study Research and Applications: Design and Methods* (6th ed.). Sage.

Yohe, G., & Tol, R. S. J. (2002). Indicators for social and economic coping capacity: Moving toward a working definition of adaptive capacity. *Global Environmental Change*, 12(1), 25–40. DOI: 10.1016/S0959-3780(01)00026-7

Yorke, M. (2004). Institutional research and its relevance to the performance of higher education institutions. *Journal of Higher Education Policy and Management*, 26(2), 141–152. DOI: 10.1080/1360080042000218221

Yorke, M. (2006). *Employability in higher education: what it is – what it is not.* Higher Education Academy.

Zabotto, M. A. C., & Alves Filho, A. G. (2019). Formulation and monitoring of strategic plans in a public university: An analysis based on strategy as practice. *Gestão & Produção*, 26(2), e2546. DOI: 10.1590/0104-530x2546-19

Zain, F. M., & Sailin, S. N. (2020). *Students' experience with flipped learning approach in higher education.* Universal Journal of Educational Research. DOI: 10.13189/ujer.2020.081067

Zakaria, M. I., Noor Nasran, N. A., Ahmad Alhassora, N. S., & Pairan, R. (2024). Unleashing problem-based learning method among mathematics teachers. *International Journal of Academic Research in Progressive Education and Development*, 13(1). Advance online publication. DOI: 10.6007/IJARPED/v13-i1/20492

Zhang, X. B., Zwiers, F. W., Hegerl, G. C., Lambert, F. H., Gillett, N. P., Solomon, S., Stott, P. A., & Nozawa, T. (2007). Detection of human influence on twentieth-century precipitation trends. *Nature*, 448(7152), 461–464. DOI: 10.1038/nature06025 PMID: 17646832

Zhou, J., & Cole, D. (2017). Comparing international and American students: Involvement in college life and overall satisfaction. *Higher Education*, 73(5), 655–672. DOI: 10.1007/s10734-016-9982-2

About the Contributors

George Ngwacho Areba, Ph.D, (Kabarak University); MED (Kenyatta University) & BED Arts(Egerton University) is the immediate former Dean and Postgraduate Coordinator, at the School of Education & Human Resource Development (SEDHURED), Kisii University & Senior lecturer at the Department of Education Foundations, Educational Administration, Planning and Economics (EDFO/EAPE). He is an accomplished researcher, writer, supervisor, examiner, and reviewer with several institutions of higher learning. Before joining higher education as a lecturer, he served as a high school tutor teaching English Literature in several institutions. He is also an experienced thespian in Drama and music as a trainer, facilitator, and adjudicator at all levels. His research appears in a range of international peer-reviewed scholarly journals and books like Global IGI among others.

Billiah Gisore, PhD (The Catholic University of Eastern Africa, M.ED (University of Nairobi), B.ED (Kenyatta University), is a lecturer in the school of education at Kisii University, Kenya. Dr Billiah is the coordinator, Teacher Education in the Faculty of Education. She is an instructor, researcher, and examiner in the university and an external examiner in other universities. She is co-author of the books: Understanding Sustainability with Pedagogical Practice: A Contribution from Geography Education Toward Sustainability Competence Based Curriculum: A Handbook for Teachers, Handbook of Research on Innovative Digital Practices and Globalization in Higher Education, Pre-Service Teachers' Pedagogical Knowledge and Perceptions of Climate Change Education, Pedagogical Strategies to Enhance Climate Change Education Outcomes among others. Her professional background is in educational research and evaluation. Her interests are in Education Administration, Teacher Education, Classroom Assessments, Equity, Sustainability Education, and lately, Climate Change Education and virtual learning.

Evelyn Wanjiru Njurai, B.Ed. Sci (Hons), MSc (Pure Maths), PhD (Mathematics Education), is currently a lecturer of Curriculum Studies and Mathematics Education courses at Kisii University. She has wide experience in qualitative research in and out of academia. She is the author of Dictionary of Mathematics for Secondary Schools, Kenya (2019) and is a co-editor of and co-author of, Competence Based Curriculum: A Handbook for Teachers Education. She has co-authored book chapters on climate change and education. Evelyn has co-edited the book Artificial Intelligence, Digital Learning, and Leadership: Redefining Higher Education, published by IGI Global in 2024 accessible through https://www.igi-global.com/book/artificial-intelligence-digital-learning-leadership/358055. Her research interests include mathematics education, the use of technology for mathematics instruction, and STEM.

* * *

Daniel Robert Aswani holds a Ph.D. in corporate and government communication from Daystar University. He also holds MA (Ethics) and MA (Corporate Communication) degrees from The University of Nairobi and Daystar University respectively. Aswani's interest areas include political communication, government communication, corporate communication, African philosophy, philosophy for communication, and qualitative research. Aswani is a senior lecturer at Daystar University and heads the Strategic and Organizational Communication (STOC) department in the School of Communication. He has published papers in corporate and government communication, ethics, and general philosophy.

Dennis Zami Atibuni is a Research Fellow at Ali Mazrui Centre for Higher Education Studies (AMCHES) at University of Johannesburg – South Africa following his postdoctoral research fellowship (PDRF) under the mentorship of Professor Michael Cross (RIP) and Professor Emnet Tadesse Woldergiorgis at the same centre. An Associate Professor at the Department of Education, Faculty of Science and Education, Busitema University – Nagongera Campus, he has served as the chairperson of Faculty Higher Degrees Committee, Head of Education Department, Departmental Examinations Coordinator, Faculty Quality Assurance Focal Point, Faculty Representative on the Busitema University Ceremonies Committee, School Practice coordinator, member of Faculty Welfare Committee, and member of Academics and Disciplinary Committee. His research interests include student (research) engagement; educational assessment; pre-service and in-service teacher education; student and staff mentorship; diversity, equity, and inclusion; and psychological determinants of effective academic leadership at higher educational institutions. He has authored and co-authored several refereed articles, book chapters, and a book volume in addition to serving as a reviewer and board member for different international journals. He has undertaken several continuous professional development courses including Higher Education Leadership under Council for the Development of Social Science Research in Africa (CODESRIA); Working with Literature under African Doctoral Academy (ADA); and Gender Mainstreaming under FAWEU, among others. Outside academia he serves as a mentor, counsellor, and catechist of vulnerable learners, and facilitator of FAWEU programmes.

Anne Anjao Eboi (PhD) is a lecturer in Media and Communication Studies at Daystar University, School of Communication, Languages, and Performing Arts. She is currently coordinating the Technical and Professional Communication program at Daystar University. Anne holds a PhD in Media Management; a master's degree in Communication Studies and a Bachelor's degree in Education (English/ Literature). She has authored an Academic Writing book, chapter, short stories, and journal articles. She has also developed an Academic Writing module for university students, currently being used globally. Anne's research interests are in new/social media in health communication, gender and social justice, online content moderation, leadership, general education topics, and corporate communication.

Eryenyu Charles, a Ugandan academic and researcher, is currently the Deputy Director of Quality Assurance at Busitema University. With a PhD in Management and Administration from Uganda Management Institute, studied MARIHE at the University of Tampere, and a Master of Science in Education from Makerere University, he has held various academic positions, including lecturer at Busitema University and teacher at Katikamu Secondary School. Eryenyu has published scholarly papers on education topics, including organizational politics, teacher turnover, career development, teacher mentorship and school board roles. He has also served on the editorial board for the Namibia Journal of Technical and Vocational Training and the National Council for Higher Education Institutional Accreditation team.

Awono Mengada Gisèle Xaverie is a researcher at The University of Yaounde II, with expertise in public management and organizational behavior. Her research examines the role of technology in enhancing public value creation.

Laith Shlash Ismail, a Jordanian humanitarian worker, is recognized for his leadership in diverse humanitarian and development interventions, spanning WASH (Water, Sanitation, and Hygiene), SWM (Solid Waste Management), livelihoods, agriculture, MHPSS (Mental Health and Psychosocial Support), and operations management. He holds a degree in Logistics Sciences from the German Jordanian

University and a Master's in European Studies from the University of Düsseldorf. Laith has also conducted research in the circular economy, showing a keen interest in sustainable development and climate resilience. Currently, he serves as the Field Coordinator for ACTION AGAINST HUNGER in Jordan, overseeing interventions across various sectors in the country. He is set to advance his career as the Country Representative for ACTION AGAINST HUNGER in Libya. Laith is a senior member of the Arab Trainers Union, a dedicated organization working to advance the training profession.

Osama Ismail is a dedicated e-mobility engineer turned educator who is passionate about teaching engineering. Osama graduated from the University of Antwerp with a master's degree in Sustainable Automotive Engineering and then went on to work for various automotive companies. After many years in the automotive industry, Osama took the initiative for education. He wanted to share his love of engineering and technology with the next generation, so he decided to become an automotive engineering teacher alongside his research in the e-mobility sector.

Daniel Karanja holds a Bachelor of Education Arts (English and Literature) degree and a Masters of Education (Educational Planning and Economics) degree, both from Kenyatta University, a Doctor of Philosophy in Educational Management degree from Egerton University. Currently works with State Department for Higher Education and Research as Research Policy Actor. He has served in the Technical Committee that established the Open University of Kenya in 2023. He has also been involved in university teaching as an adjunct lecturer with Laikipia University from 2013 to 2016, Egerton University from 2016 to 2021, and Presbyterian University of Eastern Africa from 2012 to date. He has co-authored a university level book entitled 'Research Methods, Data Analysis & Defenses: Building Competences in Education & Social Sciences Research.', published in refereed journals as well as presented in international conferences.

Eliud Nyakundi, Ph.D, (Maseno University), is a senior Lecturer at the School of Education & Human Resource Development (SEDHURED), Department of Education Foundations, Educational Administration, Planning and Economics (EDFO/EAPE) Kisii University. He is an accomplished researcher, writer, supervisor, examiner, and reviewer with several institutions of higher learning. Before joining higher education as a lecturer, he served as a high school tutor in several institutions. His research appears in a range of international peer-reviewed scholarly journals and books.

Levi Obonyo holds a PhD in Mass Media and Communication from Temple University in Philadelphia. He is the Dean of the School of Communication at

Daystar University in Nairobi, Kenya. He is the co-author of Journalists and the Rule of Law. His study interests include the history of African media and media policy and regulation.

Rose Atieno Opiyo is a passionate behavioral scientist -practitioner, who skillfully divides her time between training, consulting, scholarly mentorship, writing, research, and teaching, spanning from fields of: Behavioral Science, Teacher Education and Implementation Research She is a Senior Lecturer in department of Educational Psychology School of Education at Masinde Muliro University of Science and Technology (MMUST), Kenya. She sits in various Academic, Scientific, Technical and Advisory Boards shaping education and behavioral research scholarship mentorship and Intervention in Kenya and beyond. Opiyo affiliates to professional bodies, is a recipient of several Fellowship award – among them, the German Exchange Services (DAAD) In country Scholarship Award. She is the current recipient of Carnegie African Diaspora Fellow, International Society for the Study of Behavioral Development (ISSBD) Post-Doctoral Research Fellowship. She has coauthored two books and over 35 articles in refereed journals and book Chapters.

James Ouda is a Senior Lecturer and Researcher at Masinde Muliro University of Science and Technology (MMUST). He holds a PhD in Educational Research and Evaluation and a Diploma in Project Management. His expertise includes project management, Monitoring and Evaluation (M&E), advance research methodology, research management and administration, development of ethical approvals, participatory action research and impact evaluation. He has conducted research extensively and published widely in education and other related social issues. As an M&E specialist, Bill has been a consultant in several educational projects and programs. He has a passion for community service. Bill is a member of various school boards of management as well as providing guidance and counseling to the youth, including in church, schools and tertiary institutions as well as at community level.

Lydia Ouma Radoli is a former journalist, social researcher, and media lecturer at Daystar University's School of Communication, where she heads the Media and Film Studies (MFS) Department. She holds a doctorate focused on Media, Migration and Development from the Brandenburg University of Technology- Cottbus, Seftenburg. A tripartite master's in human Rights Practice from Gothenburg, Roehampton, and Trömso Universities, as well as a bachelor's in communication and Sociology from the University of Nairobi (UoN). Dr. Radoli has been research fellow at the Leuphana Institute of Advanced Studies in Culture and Society (LIAS-CAS),

Leuphana University Lüneburg, Germany. Her current research work addresses the Visual Witnessing Trauma Phenomenon among Journalists in East Africa. Her research interests are around media, migration, development, journalism and trauma, global cultures, political economy, and human rights. She has published and presented papers chaired sessions at local and international conferences.

Francesca Sgobbi, PhD, is an Associate Professor at Università degli Studi di Brescia (Italy) and an Integrated PhD Researcher at DINAMIA'CET ISCTE-IUL (Portugal). She lectures on Organisation Design and on Business Administration. Her research interests include labour economics, education economics, and organisation studies.

Caroline Sabina Wekullo is a Ph.D. in Educational Administration, with emphasis in Higher Education Financing and policy and Leadership. Lecturer and Research Scientist and statistician, Department of Educational Planning and Management, Masinde Muliro University of Science and Technology, Kenya. Her research interests' centres on Policy issues in financing of education, students' access, enrolment, retention and completion, Resource development and mobilization in institutions of higher learning. Her research interest extends well beyond financing and policy to mental health and wellness among students and faculty in institutions of higher learning. Caroline is a consultant certified in monitoring and evaluation and learning and an expert in mentoring.

Index

Symbols

21st-Century Competencies 139, 144, 145, 150, 155, 161, 166

A

abilities 64, 117, 118, 143, 148, 149, 164, 176, 216, 222, 226, 237, 260, 278, 290, 291, 292, 295, 297, 304, 312, 314, 316, 317, 323, 324, 325, 326, 327, 329, 350
academic learning 113, 114, 116, 118, 119, 122, 129, 130, 132, 133, 134, 137
academic rigor 215, 216, 218, 222, 238, 241
Attributes 61, 63, 87, 136, 288, 290, 292, 294, 295, 296, 298, 299, 300, 304, 305, 310, 312

B

behaviours 59, 60, 65, 317, 324, 327, 336
benefits 32, 58, 89, 90, 91, 94, 96, 97, 98, 99, 106, 110, 116, 118, 133, 144, 163, 170, 202, 207, 210, 215, 218, 220, 221, 222, 225, 226, 230, 233, 234, 238, 239, 241, 253, 263, 265, 266, 272, 273, 281, 289, 298, 306, 307, 339, 356, 395, 397, 398, 399, 401, 402, 404
Blended Learning 12, 139, 140, 141, 142, 143, 144, 150, 153, 154, 155, 157, 158, 159, 160, 161, 162, 163, 165, 167, 168, 169, 170, 171, 172, 173, 245, 248, 262, 266, 274, 275, 277
brain drain 89, 102, 103, 112

C

Case studies 61, 66, 69, 77, 78, 79, 80, 83, 155, 193, 195, 202, 215, 217, 218, 221, 226, 230, 233, 246, 302, 309, 348, 356, 359, 360, 365, 371
challenges 1, 2, 5, 6, 8, 9, 11, 19, 20, 27, 32, 33, 36, 39, 40, 42, 46, 47, 52, 65, 67, 72, 77, 89, 90, 91, 93, 94, 98, 99, 100, 105, 106, 109, 110, 111, 116, 121, 136, 143, 144, 148, 155, 157, 158, 161, 162, 163, 165, 166, 167, 168, 170, 171, 172, 175, 176, 177, 178, 179, 181, 182, 185, 189, 190, 192, 195, 197, 198, 199, 200, 201, 203, 204, 206, 207, 208, 209, 210, 212, 215, 216, 217, 218, 219, 220, 221, 222, 225, 226, 230, 232, 234, 235, 238, 239, 241, 245, 249, 254, 255, 258, 262, 263, 264, 267, 271, 272, 273, 280, 295, 297, 299, 314, 315, 317, 325, 328, 331, 332, 336, 339, 341, 344, 348, 350, 351, 352, 354, 355, 356, 361, 363, 364, 365, 366, 367, 368, 370, 371, 373, 375, 381, 384, 395, 398, 400, 403, 407
Climate Change 210, 221, 224, 227, 228, 250, 314, 315, 383, 384, 385, 386, 387, 388, 389, 390, 392, 393, 394, 395, 396, 397, 398, 399, 400, 401, 402, 403, 404, 405, 406, 407, 408, 409, 410
Collaboration 17, 28, 30, 32, 33, 49, 71, 78, 81, 89, 90, 91, 94, 98, 99, 104, 106, 112, 116, 131, 133, 139, 140, 141, 142, 143, 144, 147, 149, 150, 153, 154, 155, 156, 161, 163, 165, 176, 187, 192, 193, 194, 197, 203, 204, 217, 221, 232, 237, 238, 239, 241, 242, 255, 256, 257, 258, 260, 261, 265, 266, 267, 268, 271, 294, 317, 321, 334, 335, 339, 357, 362, 363, 370, 373, 394, 395, 400
Collaborative Learning 16, 132, 133, 147, 158, 171, 191, 224, 232, 262, 265, 266, 271, 278
commercialization of education 92, 100, 112
Competencies 43, 46, 47, 115, 120, 122, 123, 125, 130, 131, 134, 139, 140, 141, 143, 144, 145, 148, 150, 153, 155, 158, 161, 165, 166, 170, 173, 204, 218, 222, 225, 260, 271, 288, 289, 290, 292, 299, 302, 304, 305, 312, 313, 314, 315, 322, 323, 324,

325, 326, 327, 328, 329, 330, 331, 332, 334, 335, 336, 337, 340, 341, 342, 344, 345
Constructivism 144, 145, 170, 183, 184, 189, 195, 205, 209, 210, 212, 258, 259
Critical Thinking 13, 116, 117, 118, 122, 123, 130, 132, 133, 134, 139, 140, 141, 142, 143, 144, 145, 146, 150, 153, 154, 155, 156, 158, 161, 164, 165, 167, 168, 173, 175, 176, 178, 180, 186, 188, 191, 193, 195, 196, 204, 211, 216, 220, 221, 222, 223, 224, 226, 227, 232, 238, 249, 254, 255, 256, 257, 260, 261, 262, 265, 266, 267, 271, 275, 294, 295, 304, 310, 340, 341
Curriculum 12, 13, 16, 30, 33, 38, 54, 77, 88, 89, 100, 102, 114, 116, 122, 129, 130, 131, 152, 159, 164, 167, 172, 176, 179, 181, 186, 187, 188, 189, 190, 193, 200, 203, 208, 212, 218, 219, 223, 235, 238, 241, 243, 249, 277, 283, 285, 286, 294, 300, 301, 302, 303, 304, 305, 306, 308, 309, 310, 311, 312, 314, 324, 326, 327, 329, 330, 332, 334, 335, 359, 362

D

Daystar University 175, 177, 183, 185, 186, 187, 189, 191, 192, 195, 196, 204, 206, 207, 212
dispositions 288, 292, 312, 324, 325, 327, 329

E

Education for Sustainable Development 54, 170, 316, 317, 319, 322, 323, 332, 336, 338, 339, 340, 341, 342, 343, 344
Emergent strategy 60, 65, 78, 85, 87
Employability 57, 58, 59, 60, 61, 62, 63, 64, 65, 66, 67, 68, 69, 70, 71, 72, 73, 74, 75, 76, 77, 78, 79, 80, 81, 82, 83, 84, 85, 86, 87, 88, 97, 99, 113, 114, 115, 116, 129, 131, 132, 135, 136, 137, 181, 283, 287, 288, 289, 290, 291, 292, 295, 297, 298, 300, 302, 303, 305, 306, 307, 308, 309, 310, 311, 312, 313, 314, 335, 336
employability skills 62, 79, 80, 113, 114, 115, 116, 135, 136, 137, 290, 303, 307, 308, 309, 310, 311, 313
Equity 12, 17, 21, 25, 26, 41, 55, 149, 163, 164, 166, 315, 316, 331, 369, 396, 402
Experiential learning 31, 33, 44, 113, 114, 116, 117, 118, 126, 128, 129, 130, 131, 132, 133, 134, 135, 136, 137, 144, 146, 217, 218, 229, 238, 239, 246, 257, 258, 340

F

Facilitative Teaching 253, 255, 259, 260, 270, 271, 272, 273, 278, 280, 281
faculty 30, 64, 68, 71, 95, 96, 97, 99, 111, 113, 114, 116, 119, 120, 121, 122, 125, 126, 127, 128, 130, 131, 132, 133, 137, 159, 167, 176, 177, 179, 181, 182, 185, 186, 187, 188, 189, 190, 191, 192, 194, 195, 197, 198, 200, 201, 202, 203, 204, 208, 209, 215, 218, 222, 225, 230, 231, 232, 233, 234, 237, 239, 240, 241, 244, 253, 254, 255, 256, 258, 259, 262, 263, 264, 265, 266, 267, 268, 269, 270, 271, 272, 273, 274, 278, 279, 280, 281, 284, 332, 349, 350, 352, 354, 355, 361, 362, 364, 366, 371, 375, 380, 381
faculty training 176, 190, 192, 195, 215, 218, 222, 225, 230, 231, 234, 239, 240, 241

G

globalization of education 112
Graduate Identity 63, 283, 287, 292, 300, 304, 305, 312

H

Higher education 1, 19, 23, 25, 26, 27, 28, 30, 35, 36, 37, 38, 39, 40, 41, 42, 43,

45, 46, 47, 48, 49, 51, 52, 53, 54, 55, 57, 58, 62, 63, 66, 67, 81, 82, 83, 84, 85, 86, 87, 89, 90, 91, 92, 93, 94, 95, 96, 97, 98, 99, 100, 101, 102, 103, 104, 106, 107, 108, 109, 110, 111, 112, 113, 114, 116, 117, 129, 131, 132, 133, 134, 135, 136, 137, 140, 142, 143, 150, 155, 156, 157, 158, 159, 163, 164, 165, 166, 167, 168, 169, 170, 171, 172, 173, 175, 177, 181, 206, 207, 209, 210, 211, 215, 216, 217, 218, 219, 220, 222, 226, 230, 234, 235, 238, 239, 241, 244, 245, 246, 247, 248, 249, 253, 254, 262, 263, 274, 276, 285, 287, 288, 292, 306, 307, 308, 309, 310, 311, 312, 313, 314, 315, 322, 323, 324, 326, 327, 328, 332, 333, 334, 335, 336, 337, 338, 339, 341, 342, 343, 347, 348, 349, 350, 351, 352, 353, 354, 355, 356, 357, 358, 359, 360, 361, 362, 363, 364, 365, 366, 367, 368, 369, 370, 371, 372, 373, 374, 375, 376, 377, 378, 379, 380, 381

Higher Education Governance 82, 347, 348, 350, 352, 354, 369, 371, 376, 380

Higher education institutions 47, 57, 58, 81, 85, 87, 91, 92, 95, 96, 98, 101, 102, 104, 113, 114, 116, 129, 132, 133, 136, 137, 140, 143, 155, 163, 171, 177, 211, 217, 239, 241, 285, 288, 292, 306, 309, 322, 323, 326, 327, 328, 332, 333, 334, 336, 337, 347, 348, 350, 351, 352, 353, 354, 355, 356, 357, 358, 359, 360, 361, 362, 363, 364, 365, 367, 368, 370, 371, 372, 378, 379, 380, 381

Holistic 54, 115, 118, 130, 133, 134, 187, 202, 221, 236, 239, 241, 267, 283, 287, 290, 291, 292, 300, 302, 304, 305, 318, 319

I

Implications 1, 20, 25, 28, 55, 83, 96, 107, 111, 114, 116, 129, 131, 165, 167, 168, 197, 217, 223, 227, 230, 236, 237, 239, 254, 264, 277, 310, 319, 320, 342, 374, 384, 393, 398, 402

Innovative Learning Spaces 139, 140, 141, 142, 143, 144, 145, 146, 147, 148, 149, 155, 158, 159, 160, 161, 162, 163, 165, 170, 172, 173

Institutional Research 347, 348, 349, 350, 351, 352, 353, 354, 355, 356, 357, 358, 359, 360, 361, 362, 363, 364, 365, 366, 367, 368, 369, 370, 371, 372, 373, 374, 376, 377, 378, 379, 380, 381, 399

Internationalization of higher education 89, 90, 91, 92, 93, 94, 95, 96, 97, 98, 99, 100, 102, 103, 106, 107, 109, 110, 111, 112, 356, 372

Italy 57, 59, 60, 66, 75, 79, 80, 183, 275

K

Kenya 1, 3, 4, 7, 8, 10, 17, 18, 21, 22, 25, 28, 29, 31, 32, 33, 34, 36, 37, 38, 40, 41, 42, 44, 45, 47, 48, 49, 51, 52, 53, 54, 55, 89, 113, 115, 116, 118, 119, 135, 136, 159, 175, 176, 177, 178, 180, 181, 182, 183, 186, 196, 204, 206, 207, 208, 209, 210, 211, 212, 215, 253, 269, 274, 283, 286, 308, 310, 311, 352, 380, 383, 389

Knowledge Dissemination 383, 410

L

Labour market outcomes 65, 72, 78, 84

Learners 2, 3, 4, 5, 6, 7, 8, 12, 17, 18, 19, 22, 27, 28, 30, 31, 32, 33, 35, 36, 37, 40, 41, 42, 43, 44, 48, 49, 55, 91, 94, 95, 96, 97, 98, 100, 101, 102, 113, 114, 116, 118, 120, 130, 131, 134, 137, 142, 143, 144, 148, 151, 152, 157, 160, 162, 163, 164, 180, 183, 187, 188, 189, 190, 192, 197, 200, 218, 219, 257, 258, 259, 260, 264, 269, 276, 278, 302, 306, 308, 312, 313, 314, 319, 320, 321, 323, 326, 327, 328, 329, 335, 336

M

Mentorship 187, 202, 264, 266, 269, 273, 278
Monitoring and Evaluation 185, 190, 191, 204

O

Open University 25, 26, 27, 28, 29, 31, 32, 33, 34, 35, 37, 38, 39, 40, 41, 42, 46, 47, 48, 51, 52, 53, 55, 157, 306
Opportunities 2, 7, 11, 26, 27, 28, 30, 37, 38, 39, 40, 44, 45, 48, 49, 55, 62, 64, 77, 91, 93, 94, 96, 97, 111, 114, 116, 117, 118, 126, 130, 132, 133, 134, 136, 142, 144, 147, 155, 157, 160, 163, 165, 166, 167, 172, 182, 200, 210, 216, 217, 235, 238, 240, 241, 255, 258, 262, 263, 264, 265, 267, 270, 271, 272, 291, 298, 302, 314, 324, 325, 326, 330, 332, 333, 335, 336, 339, 342, 348, 351, 352, 354, 371, 375, 383, 396, 397

P

Pandemic 1, 2, 3, 4, 5, 6, 7, 9, 11, 12, 13, 15, 16, 17, 18, 19, 20, 22, 23, 36, 91, 140, 142, 167, 169, 171, 219, 366, 372
pedagogical innovation 235
Policies 1, 8, 9, 10, 12, 13, 14, 15, 16, 18, 19, 37, 45, 46, 47, 48, 49, 50, 52, 64, 93, 100, 101, 116, 165, 181, 190, 219, 220, 226, 228, 266, 267, 277, 290, 301, 308, 334, 347, 355, 356, 359, 360, 361, 363, 366, 369, 376, 380, 393
Policy 1, 2, 4, 5, 6, 7, 8, 9, 11, 12, 14, 15, 16, 17, 18, 19, 20, 21, 22, 23, 25, 28, 29, 32, 36, 37, 38, 44, 46, 47, 48, 49, 51, 52, 53, 55, 82, 83, 86, 102, 105, 107, 110, 114, 136, 159, 165, 167, 180, 181, 185, 186, 203, 204, 219, 221, 239, 244, 246, 249, 289, 290, 306, 307, 310, 311, 314, 316, 321, 327, 334, 336, 340, 342, 347, 348, 349, 350, 351, 355, 358, 359, 360, 361, 363, 365, 369, 370, 371, 373, 375, 378, 379, 380, 381, 394, 396, 400, 401, 402, 409
Portugal 57, 60, 66, 75, 79, 80
practical skills 46, 47, 117, 118, 137, 150, 153, 180, 186, 215, 216, 217, 218, 222, 225, 226, 230, 238, 241
problem-based learning 117, 175, 176, 177, 179, 206, 207, 208, 209, 210, 211, 212, 222, 223, 225, 243, 245, 249, 277
Professional Development 13, 15, 30, 40, 159, 163, 165, 166, 190, 201, 222, 225, 231, 240, 243, 244, 253, 254, 257, 262, 263, 264, 265, 268, 269, 272, 273, 275, 278, 280, 281, 364, 365
project-based learning 15, 118, 141, 143, 151, 155, 161, 167, 180, 206, 207, 208, 215, 222, 223, 224, 225, 244, 246, 249, 254, 257, 261, 274, 276

Q

quality 2, 4, 5, 12, 14, 17, 18, 30, 31, 32, 39, 41, 48, 54, 57, 58, 59, 66, 67, 75, 82, 89, 90, 91, 92, 94, 95, 96, 97, 99, 100, 101, 103, 104, 105, 106, 108, 111, 112, 114, 142, 143, 148, 150, 157, 158, 159, 180, 181, 186, 187, 190, 191, 192, 216, 218, 224, 237, 238, 243, 254, 265, 272, 274, 284, 293, 295, 296, 297, 308, 316, 317, 322, 348, 349, 351, 352, 353, 354, 355, 356, 357, 358, 359, 360, 361, 362, 363, 364, 365, 366, 367, 371, 374, 376, 380, 381, 393
Quality assurance 30, 31, 32, 59, 67, 82, 90, 99, 100, 101, 111, 190, 191, 351, 352, 353, 354, 355, 356, 357, 359, 360, 361, 362, 364, 366, 371, 374, 376, 380, 381

R

Relevance 30, 54, 181, 188, 196, 209, 261, 267, 285, 286, 288, 295, 307, 310, 312, 359, 379
Research Capacity 372, 383, 396, 399,

407, 410
Resources 4, 5, 6, 11, 17, 18, 19, 20, 26, 27, 30, 33, 39, 40, 43, 47, 55, 57, 58, 61, 68, 71, 73, 76, 77, 79, 93, 96, 100, 103, 107, 141, 142, 143, 144, 145, 146, 149, 150, 153, 154, 157, 158, 160, 163, 173, 178, 179, 181, 182, 185, 195, 196, 200, 202, 203, 204, 206, 213, 218, 221, 225, 230, 231, 232, 236, 240, 254, 257, 262, 263, 264, 265, 266, 267, 268, 270, 271, 272, 273, 278, 280, 281, 291, 295, 299, 302, 306, 311, 323, 333, 334, 352, 353, 354, 365, 366, 367, 370, 371, 380, 394, 396, 399, 400, 407, 409
Restructuring 1, 5, 7, 9, 19, 23, 189, 198, 407
risks 13, 14, 80, 99, 100, 106, 107, 221, 233, 265, 367, 368, 393, 394, 398, 400, 401

S

Skills 2, 4, 13, 16, 18, 28, 31, 32, 33, 34, 38, 43, 44, 46, 47, 58, 61, 62, 63, 64, 68, 70, 74, 77, 79, 80, 82, 83, 84, 87, 88, 97, 98, 112, 113, 114, 115, 116, 117, 118, 120, 122, 123, 125, 129, 130, 131, 132, 133, 134, 135, 136, 137, 139, 140, 141, 143, 144, 145, 146, 148, 150, 152, 153, 154, 155, 157, 158, 160, 161, 162, 164, 167, 168, 169, 173, 175, 176, 177, 178, 179, 180, 181, 183, 186, 187, 188, 191, 192, 193, 194, 195, 196, 199, 202, 204, 205, 206, 210, 211, 215, 216, 217, 218, 220, 221, 222, 223, 224, 225, 226, 227, 230, 231, 232, 236, 237, 238, 239, 240, 241, 242, 249, 254, 255, 257, 260, 261, 262, 263, 264, 265, 266, 267, 271, 272, 276, 278, 280, 284, 286, 287, 288, 289, 290, 291, 292, 293, 296, 297, 298, 299, 300, 302, 303, 304, 306, 307, 308, 309, 310, 311, 312, 313, 314, 315, 317, 318, 319, 321, 322, 323, 324, 325, 326, 327, 328, 329, 330, 331, 336, 354, 377, 378
statistical simulation 215, 216, 217, 218, 219, 220, 221, 222, 223, 224, 225, 226, 230, 231, 235, 236, 237, 238, 240, 241, 242, 249
Strategy 3, 12, 30, 32, 37, 38, 41, 42, 53, 57, 58, 59, 60, 61, 62, 63, 64, 65, 66, 67, 68, 69, 76, 77, 78, 79, 80, 83, 84, 85, 86, 87, 92, 94, 109, 111, 173, 224, 226, 228, 229, 249, 262, 311, 322, 339, 347, 351, 392, 395, 410
Strategy formation 57, 60, 65, 66, 76, 77, 80, 84, 85
student-centered learning 142, 145, 179, 187, 222, 255, 260, 262, 265, 266, 268, 278
Student Engagement 6, 117, 119, 120, 133, 137, 139, 141, 143, 144, 145, 152, 155, 156, 158, 160, 164, 165, 166, 170, 171, 173, 193, 220, 225, 226, 230, 234, 241, 249, 254, 260, 261, 265, 266, 267, 270, 278
students' perspectives 110, 122, 126, 137
Supercomplexity 283, 286, 287, 290, 292, 304, 306, 311, 312
sustainability curriculum 324, 326
Sustainability Education 313, 315, 318, 319, 322, 323, 324, 326, 327, 328, 333, 334, 338, 339, 342, 344

T

Technology 6, 11, 15, 16, 17, 20, 28, 29, 30, 32, 33, 34, 35, 36, 38, 39, 40, 44, 49, 51, 52, 69, 81, 84, 106, 115, 120, 135, 140, 141, 144, 145, 146, 154, 155, 156, 157, 158, 159, 160, 162, 163, 164, 165, 166, 167, 168, 171, 172, 173, 176, 180, 181, 182, 183, 187, 195, 200, 202, 203, 207, 209, 210, 211, 215, 217, 222, 226, 231, 234, 237, 239, 240, 241, 243, 245, 246, 247, 248, 249, 254, 256, 257, 258, 259, 260, 261, 262, 264, 265, 266, 268, 271, 273, 274, 277, 278, 280, 281, 293, 294, 335, 336, 344, 354, 362, 369, 372, 375, 395, 397, 398, 402

Technology Integration 11, 144, 146, 156, 171, 173, 234, 237, 247, 278
Training 5, 11, 13, 15, 21, 28, 30, 33, 36, 37, 38, 42, 43, 51, 52, 53, 54, 70, 74, 75, 77, 79, 80, 83, 86, 114, 115, 131, 135, 136, 153, 158, 159, 163, 168, 176, 178, 180, 181, 182, 186, 187, 188, 189, 190, 191, 192, 193, 195, 196, 197, 198, 200, 201, 202, 203, 204, 207, 208, 209, 211, 215, 218, 222, 225, 230, 231, 234, 239, 240, 241, 244, 247, 248, 249, 263, 264, 265, 267, 268, 270, 272, 278, 280, 291, 307, 309, 311, 314, 317, 323, 333, 334, 335, 336, 339, 343, 355, 362, 363, 368, 370, 371, 372, 373, 399

U

University 1, 21, 25, 26, 27, 28, 29, 31, 32, 33, 34, 35, 36, 37, 38, 39, 40, 41, 42, 43, 44, 45, 46, 47, 48, 49, 51, 52, 53, 54, 55, 57, 69, 70, 71, 72, 73, 74, 75, 76, 82, 83, 84, 85, 86, 89, 91, 93, 97, 101, 102, 104, 107, 108, 110, 111, 112, 115, 119, 120, 135, 136, 139, 146, 148, 156, 157, 158, 159, 167, 169, 170, 172, 173, 175, 176, 177, 178, 179, 180, 181, 182, 183, 184, 185, 186, 187, 189, 191, 192, 195, 196, 197, 198, 200, 201, 202, 203, 204, 206, 207, 208, 209, 210, 211, 212, 215, 221, 223, 224, 243, 244, 245, 246, 247, 248, 253, 256, 265, 266, 268, 274, 275, 276, 277, 283, 284, 285, 286, 287, 288, 289, 291, 292, 293, 299, 300, 301, 302, 303, 304, 305, 306, 309, 310, 311, 312, 313, 323, 336, 339, 341, 344, 347, 348, 351, 352, 353, 354, 357, 360, 361, 363, 364, 365, 366, 370, 374, 375, 376, 377, 379, 380, 383, 405, 406, 407, 408, 409

www.ingramcontent.com/pod-product-compliance
Lightning Source LLC
LaVergne TN
LVHW080349011026
849161LV00009B/2237
9798369369302